JUSTICE RISING

JUSTICE RISING

ROBERT KENNEDY'S AMERICA IN BLACK AND WHITE

PATRICIA SULLIVAN

THE BELKNAP PRESS *of* HARVARD UNIVERSITY PRESS

Cambridge, Massachusetts & London, England   2021

Second printing

Library of Congress Cataloging-in-Publication Data

Names: Sullivan, Patricia, 1950– author.
Title: Justice rising : Robert Kennedy's America in black and white /
  Patricia Sullivan.
Description: Cambridge, Massachusetts : The Belknap Press of
  Harvard University Press, 2021. | Includes index.
Identifiers: LCCN 2020050236 | ISBN 9780674737457 (cloth)
Subjects: LCSH: Kennedy, Robert F., 1925–1968. | Civil rights
  movements—United States—History—20th century. | Racial
  justice—United States—History—20th century. | Blacks—Civil
  rights—United States—History—20th century. | United States—
  Race relations—History—20th century.
Classification: LCC E185.61 .S934 2021 | DDC 323.1196/0730904—dc23
LC record available at https://lccn.loc.gov/2020050236

For my mother,

Doris M. Sullivan,

and

in memory of my father,

Thomas J. Sullivan

CONTENTS

PREFACE

"The Best a White America Has to Offer"

IN MAY 1963, Birmingham, Alabama, was edging toward a race war. Images of the city's police using dogs and high-pressure fire hoses to assault hundreds of protesting Black youth were televised across the country, thrusting America's racial crisis to the forefront of public awareness. Near midnight on Saturday, May 11, a series of bombs exploded at the hotel where Martin Luther King Jr. had been staying. The bombings brought thousands into the streets, where they battled police into the early hours of the morning. The violence in Birmingham set off a wave of demonstrations in cities across the country. James Baldwin's prophetic warning in *The Fire Next Time*, published just a few months earlier, seemed on the verge of being realized.

After two years of equivocating on the problem of race, President John F. Kennedy faced the enormity of the nation's racial crisis. History, law, custom, and politics had buttressed a repressive society that now appeared to be bursting at the seams. By spring 1963, the volume and the demands of Black protest could no longer be ignored. Malcolm X observed that it was the specter of Black people demonstrating "their ability to defend themselves" that finally stirred the Kennedy administration to action. But the president was reacting in at least equal measure to states and localities using their power to enforce segregation at all costs.[1]

Robert F. Kennedy, the thirty-seven-year-old US attorney general, was the administration's chief official in the area of civil rights. Since he took office in January 1961, escalating protests and defiance of court orders in the South had tested the reach of federal power. The early efforts of the attorney general and his staff to enforce school desegregation and prosecute officials who refused to register Black voters had far surpassed the record of previous administrations, but Kennedy's actions seemed overly cautious and politically calculated to those facing the brunt of southern lawlessness and violence.

On May 17, Bobby Kennedy and a team of Justice Department lawyers began the intensive work of drafting legislation that would outlaw the segregation of restaurants, department stores, movie theaters, hotels, and other public accommodations throughout America. The attorney general worked with his brother and his team to devise a strategy capable of defeating a filibuster led by southern Democrats, a feat few thought possible. At the same time, Bobby embarked on endless rounds of meetings—in Birmingham, Washington, and New York—with business and labor leaders, civil rights advocates, and elected officials. In the wake of the riots, members of the administration realized that the agreement to desegregate Birmingham's department stores had to be maintained if the city was to keep from dissolving into chaos. The Kennedy brothers also lobbied national business leaders to voluntarily end segregation in their southern-based stores as plans for legislation moved forward.

During these turbulent days, Robert Kennedy acted on a suggestion that he meet with James Baldwin. The two men had spoken briefly a year earlier at a White House dinner and had promised to talk again. Kennedy had read the *New Yorker* essay that formed the basis for *The Fire Next Time,* a searing indictment of white America's indifference to the nation's racial history and its devastating human consequences. Baldwin had focused on the abysmal conditions in segregated urban neighborhoods, pointing out that racism was a national problem, not just a southern one. "The brutality with which Negroes are treated in this country simply cannot be overstated," he wrote, "however unwilling white men may be to hear it." Nothing less than a national reckoning would make it possible to end "our racial nightmare," he suggested, and achieve "our country." Featured on the cover of *Time* magazine on May 17, the thirty-eight-year-old Harlem-born writer had emerged as the literary voice of the civil rights movement.[2]

On the morning of Thursday, May 23, Baldwin flew to Washington for a breakfast meeting with Robert Kennedy at his home. The flight was delayed, leaving the two men barely thirty minutes to talk. They briefly discussed the Justice Department's efforts, Baldwin later recalled. Kennedy was planning to be in New York the next day, and he suggested that they continue the conversation then. Baldwin agreed and volunteered to bring others along. "I was really quite impressed with him," Baldwin said. "As a black citizen, it is really a cold day in August when one is overwhelmed by any politician. But he seemed earnest and truthful. I felt there was a way to talk to him, to reach him."[3]

The next day, an eclectic group including artists, civil rights activists, and a social scientist joined Baldwin for an unusual meeting; "people whom I trusted," Baldwin later explained. People "who would not feel themselves compelled to be spokesmen for any organization or responsible for espousing any specific point of view . . . people who had paid some dues."[4] Lorraine

Hansberry, the thirty-three-year-old playwright who had won national acclaim for *A Raisin in the Sun,* was invited. Her 1959 dramatization of the
struggles of a Black family on the South Side of Chicago was the first play
by a Black woman performed on Broadway. Another attendee was Lena
Horne. One of the most famous Black performers of the day, she was also
outspoken in challenging segregation. Harry Belafonte joined the group. At
the peak of his singing career, he was a prominent supporter of the civil rights
movement and friendly with Robert and his wife, Ethel.

Baldwin also invited Kenneth Clark, a professor at City College and the
founding director of Harlem Youth Opportunities Unlimited. Clark was best
known for the "doll test," an experiment in which Black children were presented with dolls of various colors and asked to identify their preference for
one or another of the dolls. Most of the children picked white dolls as their
favorite, a result that spoke to the psychic harm of school segregation on
Black children and served as pivotal evidence in *Brown v. Board of Education.* Barely notified of the meeting before it was underway, Clark worried
that he would not have enough time to prepare. "Just come and talk," Baldwin
told him. Others at the gathering included Edwin Berry, the executive secretary of the National Urban League branch in Chicago; Clarence Jones,
an attorney who advised Martin Luther King; Baldwin's brother, David; and
Rip Torn, a white actor and Texas native who was Baldwin's friend. Henry
Morgenthau III, a television producer who had a date to film Baldwin and
Clark following the meeting, was also there.[5]

Only one member of the group came from the front lines of the civil rights
struggle raging in the Deep South. Jerome Smith was twenty-four years old,
a Congress of Racial Equality (CORE) activist, a native of New Orleans,
and among the first wave of sit-in protesters in 1960. Badly beaten during
the Freedom Ride to McComb, Mississippi, he had led direct-action protests and voter registration efforts in that state and in Louisiana. After nearly
three years of organizing and agitating, he bore the physical and psychological trauma of a soldier in what seemed like an interminable war. He was
in New York being treated for a fractured jaw and battered head when David
Baldwin invited him to the meeting with Kennedy. Smith's presence would
set the course of the meeting.[6]

The group gathered at 24 Central Park South, the Kennedy family apartment, on Friday afternoon. Robert Kennedy was joined by Burke Marshall,
US assistant attorney general for civil rights; the two had just come from a
difficult meeting with department-store owners who resisted taking any
initiative to desegregate their southern operations. Now, in a large sitting
room with Baldwin and his guests, Kennedy opened with brief remarks about
the administration's work on behalf of civil rights and about legislative

efforts then underway. The implication, Clark thought, was "that we should be grateful." That is doubtful. Kennedy knew that racial conditions had reached a breaking point. He was concerned about the growing appeal of Malcolm X and worried that further militant protests might jeopardize the passage of the civil rights bill he was helping to craft and usher through Congress. At this fragile moment, just days after the police violence in Birmingham, what Kennedy sought from this group was some insight into how to navigate the treacherous path ahead.[7]

A few polite exchanges followed Kennedy's initial comments. Clark, who had come armed with reports, read off some statistics on racial discrimination. This was all too much for Jerome Smith. He stammered through his anger, telling Kennedy he felt "nauseous" hearing about what the administration had done and planned to do while an American citizen like himself courted death simply for trying to move freely and vote. Smith assailed Kennedy for doing nothing to protect him and others like him seeking to exercise rights that most Americans took for granted. He demanded to know why the federal government could not do more to end the horrific violence in Birmingham.

Visibly startled, Kennedy turned away from Smith and looked toward the others. As Baldwin recalled, Hansberry said, "You have a great many accomplished people in this room, Mr. Attorney General, but the only man you should be listening to is that man over there." Kennedy stared at her for a long moment before turning again to Smith.

Smith spoke passionately about the violence in Birmingham. Horne later confessed that Smith's raw personal testimony was her first up-close look at the terror stalking young civil rights activists. Smith said he did not know how much longer he could remain nonviolent in the face of the beatings. At one point, Baldwin asked him if he would fight to defend the country. "Never," he said, not for a country that was unable or unwilling to ensure his freedom.

"How can you say that?" Kennedy exclaimed.

"We were shocked that he was shocked," Clark later recalled of Kennedy. "He seemed genuinely unable to understand what Smith was trying to say."

"If you can't understand what this young man is saying then we are without hope," Hansberry lamented during the meeting. "You and your brother represent the best a white America has to offer. If you're insensitive, there's no alternative to the streets and chaos."

The tone of the meeting was set. Kennedy tried to shift the conversation to plans for civil rights legislation and practical political considerations, but the others pushed back, determined to get him to acknowledge the depth of the crisis and to take action that would command public attention. When

Clarence Jones suggested that President Kennedy personally escort Vivian Malone and James Hood, two students who would enter the University of Alabama in early June, Robert Kennedy dismissed the idea as senseless and phony, a stunt. "No, not phony," Clark recalled saying. "This was the abrasive clash here—our insisting that the crisis demanded extraordinary acts and Bobby retreating and saying no . . . implying that we were ungrateful, that we were insatiable." Belafonte sought to lighten the mood by talking about his personal connection with the Kennedys and mentioning social visits to Hickory Hill, Bobby's family home in McLean, Virginia. But nobody paid attention to that. "We came back to the issue," Clark recalled, "and it went on for hours."

Kennedy's effort at a kind of reassurance only magnified the gulf that divided him from the assembled Black activists and intellectuals. He pointed out that his brother was the great-grandson of Irish immigrants, a group who had faced stigma and discrimination, yet he had risen to become president of the United States—and Kennedy predicted that a Black person could become president in forty years. "This was the last thing to say to this group," Clark later remarked. Baldwin curtly responded, "Your grandfather came over here from Ireland just a generation or so ago. . . . My ancestors came over here a couple of hundred years ago on a slave trip . . . and you [are telling me] when I can participate in this government?"

At this point, Kennedy stopped trying to explain the challenges he faced and gave up on defending the administration. He remained silent in the face of wide-ranging testimonies, accusations, and questions. Passions rose with the cumulative accounting: the abysmal performance of the FBI in the South; the appointment of flagrantly segregationist judges; the Justice Department's failure to intervene in a housing desegregation fight in Deerfield, Illinois; the racial consequences of "urban renewal," which increasingly functioned as a policy of "Negro removal." Horne told Kennedy that if he was so proud of his record, he should go up to Harlem, into the churches, barber shops, and pool halls, and speak with the people there. There was talk of sending arms to the South.

The meeting circled back to where it had begun. Smith described, in Baldwin's words, "the perpetual demolition faced . . . by Black men who pay a price literally unspeakable for attempting to protect their women, their children, their homes, or their lives." Hansberry replied that she was not all that worried about Black men, who "had done splendidly, all things considered." Then, standing and looking at Kennedy, she said sternly, "I am worried about the state of a civilization which produced that photograph of a white cop standing on that Negro woman's neck in Birmingham." She extended her hand to Kennedy, said goodbye, and left the room. The others followed, save for Clarence Jones and Harry Belafonte, who spoke briefly with Kennedy, acknowledging the efforts of the Department of Justice in Birmingham.

Baldwin and Clark were running late for their taping with Morgenthau when the meeting finally ended. As they drove to the television studio in midtown Manhattan, Baldwin said all he wanted was a drink. Clark later described the meeting as "*the* most dramatic experience I had ever had." Commenting on the complete breakdown in communication, he wondered that "we might as well have been talking different languages." For Baldwin, the gathering was one more example of "that panic-stricken vacuum in which Black and white, for the most part, meet in this country."[8]

———

THE KENNEDY-BALDWIN SUMMIT has been widely portrayed as an iconic moment of the civil rights era, a stark illustration of the distance between Black and white America. Some have suggested that the meeting marked a turning point in the political education of Robert Kennedy, but this is unlikely. By May 1963, Robert Kennedy had grappled with the pervasive racial segregation and discrimination that structured American life. As attorney general, he transformed the Department of Justice, using all the tools at his disposal to enforce school desegregation orders and creating a field operation of attorneys in the Deep South to fight voter discrimination. State defiance thwarted many of these efforts. "They're at war with this country," he told his colleague John Doar after mobs, condoned by local and state officials, assaulted Freedom Riders in 1961.[9]

From the start of his tenure as attorney general, Bobby Kennedy acknowledged the national reach of racial discrimination, turning his attention to conditions in urban areas, where segregation had become even more deeply entrenched since World War II. He established a series of federally supported community-based programs designed to help youth living in slum conditions and visited each of the neighborhoods covered by the policy, seeing firsthand the dilapidated housing, substandard schools, lack of recreational facilities, joblessness, and criminal justice inequities that defined life for Black families crowded on the margins of urban life. In a speech marking the centennial of the Emancipation Proclamation in March 1963, Kennedy spoke of a racial crisis "one hundred years in the making," declaring: "the problems that remain are massive. The results of racial discrimination carry on for generation after generation. To face this openly and try to meet it squarely is the challenge of this decade."[10]

The heated encounter with Baldwin and the other guests occurred as racial tensions in the United States approached a breaking point. Birmingham had brought the southern movement and white defiance to a precipice, while racial conflict escalated across the country. "The crisis in the North is boiling," Gertrude Samuels reported in her investigation of "the forms the Negro Revolution is taking in the North." When the New York meeting occurred, Kennedy was grasping for advice, wondering what could be done to ease tensions in urban areas while the administration pushed to secure civil rights legislation in the face of indifference and opposition. Associates described him as disgusted in the immediate aftermath of the meeting, but Jerome Smith had reached him. Kennedy, an aide recalled, acknowledged that he would probably have felt the same way about the country if he had been in Smith's shoes. What is particularly notable is that Kennedy did not turn away from the anger, intensity, and impatience in that room. He sat there for three hours and listened. That alone, Clark later reflected, affirmed the truth of Hansberry's offhand comment. Robert Kennedy *was* the best a white America had to offer.[11]

Bobby Kennedy's public life converged with the civil rights movement at the moment when sit-ins disrupted the repressive Cold War politics that had dominated American life in the 1950s and ignited civic activism on a scale not seen since the era of the New Deal and World War II. As US attorney general and top presidential advisor, then a US senator, and finally a presidential candidate, Kennedy was uniquely positioned to lead the country in a new direction. As his own ideas and efforts evolved across the tumultuous 1960s, Kennedy opened the eyes of many Americans to fresh possibilities.

John and Robert Kennedy were notably responsive to the challenges and opportunities brought to the fore by the civil rights movement. Historians of that era have tended to measure the Kennedy administration by isolated actions, pointing to the appointment of several segregationist southern judges or the wiretapping of Martin Luther King by the FBI. The Kennedys have also been blamed for doing too little in specific instances. The trouble is that critics often discount the political and legal constraints the administration faced and pay insufficient attention to the change the Kennedys did achieve in less than three years. Both brothers confronted the racial realities of their time and took action to remedy them, potentially at political cost greatly outweighing the benefits of appealing to Northern Black voters. Thurgood Marshall, director of the NAACP Legal Defense Fund and mastermind of the legal strategy behind *Brown v. Board,* recalled meeting with presidential candidate John Kennedy for several hours in the spring of 1960. "He knew all the problems," Marshall said. "I had no doubt that he was committed to the general principles involving civil rights—the equality of all Americans. . . . It would be pretty hard to talk to him and not get that impression." Marshall left the meeting convinced that Kennedy would put those principles of equality "above the normal leanings of a candidate."[12]

On June 11, 1963, President Kennedy announced plans to introduce far-reaching civil rights legislation. The speech, jointly drafted with Bobby, reflected the brothers' broad exposure to racial conditions across the country and marked the public alignment of the Kennedy administration with the struggle of African Americans for full equality. "Now the time has come for the Nation to fulfill its promises," Kennedy said in his televised address. "The fires of frustration and discord are burning in every city, North and South, where legal remedies are not at hand." The protests and demonstrations were manifestations of a "moral crisis," he warned, which could not be met by "repressive police action," token moves, or deploring the facts. It was time for action at all levels of government and "above all in our daily lives." He asked all Americans—especially white Americans—to think hard about their choices and what kind of a society they wanted to bequeath to their children. "A great change is at hand," he said, "and our task, our obligation is to make this revolution, that change, peaceful and constructive for all. Those who do nothing are inviting shame as well as violence. Those who act boldly are recognizing right as well as reality."[13]

Kenneth Clark was stunned and somewhat reassured to hear phrases spoken during the contentious meeting woven through the speech. JFK's address, Clark said, "established him in the minds of people as an outstanding advocate of constructive civil rights." The *Chicago Defender* described the administration's "remarkable appeal" as "a plea to the innate patriotic instincts of the average American. . . . an appeal to his conscience and sense of fair play." The president had presented opposition to segregation as "a measure of genuine Americanism" and thereby invited the whole of the nation to equate civil rights activism with patriotism.[14]

During the weeks and months that followed the announcement, Robert Kennedy and his team at the Department of Justice helped craft a strong civil rights bill. They also secured the support of leading Republicans and non-southern Democrats, a bipartisan coalition critical to surviving a southern-led filibuster. The bill passed the House Judiciary Committee on November 20, 1963, all but ensuring that it would pass the House of Representatives and move on to a fateful vote in the Senate. Two days later, John F. Kennedy was assassinated.

President Kennedy's assassination was a "shattering" experience for his brother, as several of Bobby's close friends observed. It marked the abrupt end of a remarkable partnership, but not before that partnership had shaped legislative efforts which would culminate in the 1964 Civil Rights Act and the 1965 Voting Rights Act. Still, by the time these historic legislative victories were won, Bobby Kennedy was aware of the limits of federal law in ending racial injustice and uprooting the structures of racial inequality.

In August 1965, the arrest of a twenty-one-year-old Black man in the Watts section of Los Angeles triggered a strong community reaction, leading to an explosive uprising and four days of clashes with police. Thirty-four people were killed, and large areas of the city were reduced to rubble. Calls for more aggressive policing as the solution to urban unrest, a major demand of Barry Goldwater's 1964 presidential campaign, were amplified in the wake of Watts. Kennedy, now a senator from New York, pushed back. "How can you ask Negroes in Harlem and Bedford Stuyvesant to obey the laws," he asked, "when the law is used against them?"[15] The next three years would be among the most volatile in American history, as the war in Vietnam rapidly escalated, antiwar protests grew, and more and more American cities became racial battlegrounds.

After Watts, Robert Kennedy persisted as a powerful voice for a more socially and economically just nation. He continued to focus on the history that had brought the nation to this moment of racial reckoning, and he worked with others to define the debate and seek remedial action at all levels of society. As a senator he participated in hearings, influenced legislation, and continued to move around the country, listening to people's stories and observing the conditions of life in urban areas, in the Mississippi Delta, on Indian reservations, and in migrant labor camps. The depth of American poverty shocked him. It was most glaring in the cities, where racism had created and sustained intolerable circumstances over successive generations, offering no way out.

Yet, after he left the Justice Department, Kennedy faced enormous challenges in realizing his political vision. He had arguably been the second most powerful man in the country while his brother was in the White House, but now he served in a government headed by a man who despised him. It is well known that Lyndon Johnson and Robert Kennedy did not get along on a personal level. More importantly, though less often recognized, there were very real differences in how the two men responded to the challenges of the time. They joined forces to pass the Civil Rights and Voting Rights acts, and Kennedy was among the strongest supporters of Johnson's War on Poverty when it was launched. But in their responses to Watts and successive summers of urban uprisings and civil disturbances, Johnson and Kennedy could not have been further apart. Johnson's escalation of the Vietnam War divided the country and sapped resources for anti-poverty programs at a time of urgent need. Kennedy and Martin Luther King emerged as leading critics of cutbacks to poverty programs and as increasingly vocal opponents of the war.

King and Kennedy were also closely aligned in their concerns about urban conditions and the oppression of Black youth. Early in 1966, King moved into a Chicago tenement and joined community groups in organizing a campaign to end housing discrimination. For their part, Kennedy and his aides met with residents, community leaders, and activists in the impoverished Brooklyn neighborhood of Bedford Stuyvesant and, drawing on what they learned from the community, established a major redevelopment project. The goal was to bring government, foundation, and private funds to bear on shortages of decent housing, jobs, recreational facilities, and education—all under the direction of a community board. The Bedford Stuyvesant Redevelopment Corporation marked a shift toward community control of urban revitalization, and the project remained a major focus of Kennedy's until the end of his life.

When King testified on the last day of 1966 Senate hearings concerning the crisis in American cities, he pointed to the Bedford Stuyvesant project as a model. Here was a community-support program developed and directed by the people it was designed to help. In a remarkable exchange with Kennedy, who helped organize the hearings, King talked about the "invisible" poor in America's ghettos, describing their "thoughts unknown, words unheard, feelings unfelt." To King, the results were predictable: "riots, in the final analysis, turn out to be the language of the unheard." Kennedy agreed that many Americans failed to understand or take interest in "the very bitter conditions" facing Black urbanites and expressed deep concern about "where this combination of factors is going to lead the United States."[16]

As a member of the Senate Subcommittee on Employment, Manpower, and Poverty, Kennedy took part in a nationwide review of antipoverty programs' responsiveness to community needs. In 1967 he traveled with the subcommittee to field hearings in Mississippi, Los Angeles, and Appalachia. Visiting migrant camps and Indian reservations, he again noted widespread hunger and joblessness, in spite of federal policies that were supposed to help. King had observed that the war on poverty was "scarcely a skirmish," and Kennedy was bearing witness to the truth of those words. In response, he pressured the Agriculture Department to face the hunger crisis by making its new food stamp program more accessible and by expanding distribution of surplus foods. Alas, these efforts secured minimal changes in policy.

Kennedy described the racial crisis that peaked during the late 1960s as the nation's greatest predicament since the Civil War. What troubled him most were the harsh white reactions to urban uprisings. The media's sensationalized coverage of the call for Black Power—famously issued by Stokely Carmichael during the June 1966 March against Fear in Mississippi—

coupled with televised images of cities in flames, amplified white fears and prejudices, making it difficult, in King's words, for whites "to grasp the depths and dimensions of racial injustice." Kennedy recognized white recalcitrance as a critical challenge and expressed sympathy for the Black Power position, although he did not endorse its most strident variants. When queried about Black Power, he noted the multiplicity and nuances of the idea and explained that he was for any efforts dedicated to Black advancement, including "building self-sufficiency and self-determination within the Negro community." His "judgement for the future of the country" remained "that blacks and whites must work together," but integration in law could not be expected to solve the problem of racism. As for the March against Fear, Kennedy praised it for demonstrating that Black citizens would keep up their efforts "until they establish equality." Two months after Carmichael's appeal caused such a stir, Kennedy published an article in *Look* magazine titled "Suppose God is Black."[17]

Given his stature, Kennedy stood out as a national voice challenging the racially coded politics of law and order and countering the ignorance, fears, and prejudices that drove white backlash. He trusted that people were basically decent and that they did not want to see other people suffer, and he worked continually to compel white Americans to see the conditions that fostered urban rebellion. He urged white audiences to consider the situation of Black youth, heirs, as he put it, to the "scarred heritage of centuries of oppression" and "trapped in poverty and joblessness and deteriorating neighborhoods." His harshest criticism was saved for leaders who fueled a politics of white resistance. "It is wrong, shameful, immoral, and self-defeating," he said, for any politician to exploit white fears and resentment "for momentary advantage." In a speech to 15,000 students at the University of California, Berkeley, in October 1966, he praised their generation's political and civic engagement and told them that "no area of national life needs this leadership more than the challenge we have gathered to consider, the revolution within our gates, the struggle of the Negro American for full equality and for full freedom."[18]

Kennedy's decision to run for president in 1968 was as much a response to Johnson's refusal to address the causes of the racial crisis as it was a challenge to the policy in Vietnam. Kennedy's campaign represented an effort to bridge racial divisions and summon the collective will to move forward. When King was assassinated on April 4, three weeks into the campaign, Kennedy found himself in the heart of Indianapolis's Black community, speaking extemporaneously from the back of a flatbed truck. He was consumed by the anguish of the moment. "Martin Luther King dedicated his life to love and justice between fellow human beings. He died in the cause of that effort," Kennedy said. "In this difficult time for the United States, it's perhaps well to ask what kind of nation we are and what direction we want to move in."[19] That was the central question of Kennedy's presidential campaign, which ended tragically two months later.

———

JUSTICE RISING IS INFORMED by other histories, but it is not comparable to traditional biographies of Robert Kennedy. The questions this book asks span several subject areas, and, joining a recent scholarly trend, the book collapses sharp distinctions between the civil rights and Black Power movements. By centering Robert Kennedy's public life within the historical context of struggles for racial justice and reckoning, the book offers a fresh account of the ways in which history, race, power, and politics intertwined during the 1960s.

A wealth of primary source guides my research. I draw on a range of print media outlets, from the Black press to major national newspapers whose enterprising journalists provide an immersive portrait of Kennedy's life and work and the 1960s more generally. Journalists such as Simeon Booker of *Jet* magazine, who traveled with the Freedom Riders; Gertrude Samuels, whose field research in five cities informed her story on "the Negro Revolution" in the North; and Richard Harwood, who covered the 1968 presidential campaign for the *Washington Post,* offered a raw first take on critical historical moments. While coverage of Robert Kennedy is expansive, certain of his contemporaries stand out as keen observers and informed critics.

Among the great finds during my research were the "Dispatches" from *Time* magazine correspondents archived in the Houghton Library at Harvard University. During the early 1960s, young reporters roamed the South for *Time* and wrote about the sit-ins and all that followed in their wake. Their stories are voluminous. Most did not make it into the magazine, but they shaped how major events were covered and offered rare firsthand accounts of the movement from the ground level. Meanwhile, *Time* journalists stationed in Washington provided extensive accounts of the Kennedy administration's response to Black protests, school desegregation, voter-registration efforts, and the crafting and passage of civil rights legislation. *Time*'s Hugh Sidey shadowed JFK on June 11, 1963, the day the University of Alabama was finally desegregated, reporting from inside the White House on that remarkable moment and on the civil rights address, written with Bobby, that the president delivered that night.

Oral histories have been enormously helpful for capturing personalities and illuminating the texture and complexities of a dynamic and contentious era. While the ranks of individuals who were active during the 1960s have thinned, over the course of my research I have been fortunate to interview a number of Robert Kennedy's friends and associates, as well as civil rights activists and others engaged in the political and racial struggles of the era. Alongside other archival collections at the John F. Kennedy Presidential Library, the JFK and RFK oral history collections have been invaluable. They are a treasure for scholars studying America during the 1960s.

———

TODAY FEW WOULD DISPUTE THAT 1968 was a pivotal year in US history. Robert Kennedy launched his presidential bid, and Martin Luther King organized the Poor People's Campaign. The assassinations of both men elevated them to iconic stature. Their historical significance and contemporary relevance, however, lives in their actions and the evolution of their ideas. Their faith in the capacity of democracy to advance a just, equitable, and humane society, while severely tested, was not defeated.

My hope is that *Justice Rising* will challenge and upend some of the interpretations that have framed our understanding of the 1960s. In studying Robert Kennedy's public life in relation to the Black freedom movement, this book reconsiders how the struggle for civil rights secured historic and far-reaching changes, exposed deep structures of racial injustice and inequity, and triggered a major political realignment. The divisiveness of the current moment reflects that realignment, which was largely a response to the racial reckoning that dominated the 1960s. Kennedy dedicated himself to the broad struggle to bend American political culture in a new direction—a task that remains urgent and unfinished.

CHAPTER ONE

Misfit

||

ON THE MONDAY AFTER EASTER in 1951, a third-year law student introduced Ralph Bunche to an overflow crowd in Cabell Hall at the University
of Virginia. Bunche had won the Nobel Peace Prize in December—the first
African American to do so—and that spring evening, he looked out onto
an audience of more than a thousand people. This, as it turned out, was another first: an integrated meeting of this kind was unprecedented at the
University of Virginia (UVA), where state law prohibited the mixing of races
in public places.[1]

The law student who introduced the speaker was Robert Kennedy, and
this event was all his doing. As head of the Student Legal Forum, he had
invited Bunche, who had agreed to come on one condition: he would not
speak before a segregated audience. Kennedy was determined that Bunche's
requirement be met. After fellow law students refused to join him in peti-
tioning the university for an open meeting, Kennedy, undeterred, made his
case to Colgate Darden, the university's president, citing the recent Supreme
Court rulings in *Sweat v. Painter* and *McLaurin v. Oklahoma State Regents*.
Darden finally agreed to a nonsegregated meeting on educational grounds.
In 1951 Virginia, a place soon to emerge as a center of massive resistance to
school desegregation, this was a notable achievement.

At twenty-five, Bobby Kennedy was married with a baby on the way and
looking forward to beginning a life in government. Race, he later confided,
was not something he paid particular attention to. Yet his actions at UVA
revealed certain fundamental aspects of his character. He would act on what
he thought was right, regardless of what others thought. And he would not
stand down. In high school, friends described him as a "misfit."

Growing up in a large Irish Catholic family, Bobby was a loner with
an instinctive sympathy for people who were having a hard time. He was
the most devout of nine children and possessed a moralistic streak, but his

questioning spirit helped guard against the rigidity that might have accompanied that attribute. The smallest of the boys in an intensely competitive family, he was both brave and physically strong, and he took pride in these traits. His powerful and devoted father was a major force in Bobby's young life, but the son was also shaped by an intense engagement with his surroundings. This "experiencing nature" was a defining characteristic early on. When he became counsel to the Senate Permanent Subcommittee on Investigations, better known as the Rackets Committee, Bobby would earn a reputation as ruthless and hard-charging, but the tough exterior masked a range of qualities that informed his character and influenced his approach to public life.

Bobby's grandparents, children of Irish immigrants, had worked their way to prominence. His grandfather John Francis Fitzgerald, known as Honey Fitz, served as Boston's mayor and educated his daughter Rose in convent schools in the United States and Europe. Bobby's father, Joseph Patrick Kennedy, was the son of a saloon keeper and ward leader and had attended Boston Latin High School and Harvard University before embarking on a career in banking. Joe and Rose first met when they were children, began dating in high school, and married in 1914. The sting of anti-Irish bias was partly responsible for the family's move from Boston to Riverdale, a borough of New York City, when Bobby was two. Joe Kennedy's brilliant success in multiple endeavors, from banking and stock trading to the movie industry, soon enabled him to claim a place at the upper reaches of society. He was the first chairman of the US Securities and Exchange Commission under Franklin Roosevelt and served as Roosevelt's ambassador to the United Kingdom, the first Irish Catholic to hold that position. He resigned the ambassadorship under a cloud following disagreements with the administration over the emerging war in Europe.[2]

Murray Kempton once commented that the one thing Franklin Roosevelt could have learned from Joseph Kennedy "was how to be a father."[3] Joe was often away from home—in Hollywood, London, and Palm Beach—and he sent his kids to boarding school, but he cultivated an affectionate and close relationship with them all the same. Joe spared his children "the necessity of supporting themselves" and encouraged them to study hard and travel in preparation for a life of public service. While Bobby was young, his father's ambitions were centered on Joseph Jr., who also went by Joe, and John, who went by Jack. Rose was closest to Bobby, but his father's attention provided ballast and direction during an early life marked by disruption and uncertainty.[4]

"I was the seventh of nine children," Bobby said, "and when you come from that far down, you have to struggle to survive." As the third son—eight years separated him from Jack—Bobby had grown up in the shadow of his older brothers. "The first time I remember meeting Bobby," Jack once recalled, "was when he was three and a half one summer on Cape Cod." Referred to as "the runt of the litter," Bobby was smaller and less physically adept than his older brothers. A biographer described him as "the gentlest and shyest" of the Kennedy boys and "the least articulate orally." A childhood nurse remembered him as "the most thoughtful and considerate of all the children."[5]

"What I remember most vividly about growing up," Bobby Kennedy later remarked, "was going to a lot of different schools, always having to make new friends, and that I was very awkward. . . . I was pretty quiet most of the time. And I didn't mind being alone." Early friendships were disrupted by the family's move to London during his father's ambassadorship and by his parents' efforts to find a suitable school, for Bobby struggled academically. By the time he was sixteen, he had attended six different schools. In the autumn of that year, 1942, he transferred from Portsmouth Priory, a Catholic school in Rhode Island, and enrolled as a junior at Milton Academy, a prestigious private boarding school outside Boston.[6]

He had a shock of sandy hair and a "moon face" when he arrived at Milton, a fellow student recalled, with "no hint" of the angularity that would later emerge. Bobby took to wearing a checkered coat, loud ties, and white athletic socks, setting him apart from his more conservatively attired classmates. His Catholicism also marked him as different in the overwhelmingly Protestant school. A friend from those years described Bobby as "shy and whimsical and a little bit solitary." He exhibited "a wonderful wry sense of humor" and could be caustic at times. His teachers commented on his weaknesses in the "fundamentals," but an English teacher noted Bobby's "refreshing habit of asking 'how' and 'why'" and predicted that "he should have no difficulty if he makes consistent effort." "Nothing came easily," fellow student David Hackett recalled. Bobby was no more gifted socially and athletically than he was academically, but "he wanted to excel, and he had a great determination to do well in everything he tried." "Determination," Hackett said, "was his distinguishing characteristic in those days."[7]

Bobby's first deep experience of friendship was with Hackett, and it lasted for a lifetime. A natural athlete who excelled in hockey, football, and baseball, Hackett was the model for Phineas in *A Separate Peace,* John Knowles's novel set in a New England boarding school during World War II. Like Phineas, Hackett was energetic and adventurous, a bit irreverent and offbeat, and enormously good-natured. Hackett recognized a kindred spirit in Bobby. "We were both misfits," Hackett recalled. Hackett was a day student who did not identify with the high status of most of his classmates. He was more interested in athletics than academics. Bobby joined Hackett on the football team as a blocking back, and they roughhoused together and enjoyed practical jokes. Bobby reported in a letter to his parents that he and Hackett tried out for the glee club on a lark, singing a duet "that went over very big."[8]

Hackett was attracted to his friend's fearless and impulsive nature and his tendency to go against the grain. Hackett recalled attending a Sunday mass with Bobby; when it was apparent that an altar boy was missing, Bobby hopped over the altar rail and volunteered to assist the priest. Several people who knew Bobby at Milton commented on his compassion toward boys who were less fortunate or had problems. If he saw an upperclassman bullying a younger student, Bobby would step in. Hackett thought that Bobby's own challenges and insecurities helped explain why he was so "so sympathetic to other people who did not have it easy."[9]

While at Milton, Bobby was itching to follow his brothers and join the war effort. Both Joe Jr. and Jack had enlisted the summer before Pearl Harbor. Joe went on to become a navy pilot, and Jack commanded a patrol torpedo boat in the South Pacific. By late spring 1943, their sister Kathleen, known as Kick, was working as a Red Cross volunteer in London. Joe and Rose were anxious to keep their third son closer to home, so Joe began working to secure a place for Bobby in the V-12 Navy College Training Program. Jack thought this plan was a good compromise. "Bobby is too young to be out here," Jack wrote his father, advising that Bobby go into V-12 training "and stay there for a long while." Besides, Jack added, "the fun goes out of war in a fairly short time." Bobby spent a week visiting the naval air station in Norfolk that summer before Joe Jr. took off for England. Two weeks later, Jack's boat was attacked by a Japanese destroyer and went missing for nearly a week. Badly injured in the assault, Jack led a heroic effort to save the lives of most of his crew.[10]

In October 1943, shortly before his eighteenth birthday, Bobby enlisted in the naval reserve as an apprentice seaman. Following his father's intervention, Bobby was assigned to report to the V-12 program at Harvard.[11] The program provided bachelor's degrees for future Navy officers. "We haven't really had too much action here in Harvard Square," Bobby wrote to his brother Joe in the spring of 1944, "but we're on the alert in every moment for an attack and I'm sure when it comes we will conduct ourselves according to Navy standards." Bobby's father counseled him to concentrate on his studies. The most important thing, his father said, was "to do a good job now and every day. After all, you've got your whole life ahead of you and . . . it's going to require all the brains anyone has to work out a satisfactory existence, and the only way to do that is to be well prepared to stick in there and work as hard as you can."[12]

Disappointment and tragedy soon roiled the Kennedy family. In May 1944, Kick married William "Billy" Cavendish, the Marquess of Hartington, in a civil ceremony in London, after all efforts to find a satisfactory compromise between the demands of the Catholic and Anglican churches had failed. Her decision to marry outside of the Catholic Church distressed her father, at least initially. (Joe Jr., who was stationed in London, stood in for his father at the wedding.) Rose was "heartbroken," "sick," and inconsolable. Her daughter, she believed, had cut herself off from the church and set a bad example for other young Catholic women. Kick reassured her father that she would "always live according to Catholic teaching" and prayed that "time will heal all wounds." His support in this, "as in everything," meant so much, she wrote. She added, "Please beseech mother not to worry."[13]

Rose comforted herself with the thought that her eldest son, Joe Jr., would be back home at the end of May for an extended leave after flying a series of bombing missions out of a London airbase. But Joe Jr. persuaded his crew to continue another month and extended his stay through June. Near the end of June, he told his parents he had volunteered to take over another crew and relieve a fellow pilot who wasn't feeling well "and wanted to get home pretty badly." "Don't worry about me," he reassured them. "I don't think I am in as much danger now as I was (knock on wood) and with any luck I should be home the end of July or first of August." Then came another letter, at the end of July, explaining that he would stay three more weeks. "I am going to be doing something different," he wrote, "it is secret, and I am not allowed to say what it is, but it isn't dangerous so don't worry." Besides, by staying longer his leave time would be extended.[14] "I quite understand how you feel about staying there," his father wrote on August 9, "but don't force your luck too much." The letter closed: "we are all hoping and praying that you will come back soon."

On August 12, while flying a dangerous bombing mission, Joe Jr.'s plane exploded in midair over England. His body was never recovered. Joe Sr. and Rose were devastated. Rose found solace in her faith. Joe Sr., according to his biographer David Nasaw, "would never recover from the death of his oldest son." Joe wrote a friend that his son's death "shocked me beyond belief." While all of his children were equally dear to him, "there is something about the first born that sets him a little apart—he is for always a bit of a miracle."[15] Less than a month later, Billy Cavendish, Kick's husband, was killed in action in Belgium.

The losses did not dim Bobby's desire to see action before the war ended. If anything, his brothers' heroism made him all the more anxious to join the fight. In March 1945 he wrote to Hackett, who was then serving as an Army paratrooper, "I wish to hell there weren't so many problems and people would let me alone to do as I wished." Bobby added, "I guess the rest of this war is going to be won by you and your brothers for I think the Kennedys have all shot their bolt." He ribbed his friend with a bit of gallows humor: "Just remember if your parachute doesn't open I will always act at parties just as if you were there and be terrifically funny and so carry out your un-said wishes on the home front of: 'Carry on no matter what!'"[16]

Bobby was released from officers' training in the fall of 1945 and assigned as a seaman to a newly commissioned navy destroyer, joining the *Joseph P. Kennedy Jr.*, named for his brother, on its first voyage to Guantanamo Bay, Cuba. He chronicled the trip in letters to his parents. Most of the crew was from the South, he wrote, "and I am certainly meeting people with a dif-ferent outlook and interests in life than I ever had." Their days were filled with "scrubbing and polishing and scrubbing a great deal more . . . then scrubbing yourself." The crew tested various capacities of the ship, tracking down and targeting submarines and trying out the mounted guns on the deck. They were on the sea most nights, which entailed work shifts at least eighteen and sometimes twenty hours long: "It doesn't mean you're working all the time, but you've got to sit around waiting to work, which is almost as tough." Anyone preparing to become an officer, Bobby concluded, should be required to take such a cruise. The ship returned to New England in May, and Kennedy was honorably discharged from the Navy just in time to work on his brother Jack's campaign for Congress that summer before returning to Harvard.[17]

———

THE FAMILY DYNAMICS CHANGED after Joe Jr.'s death. Joe's "success was so assured and inevitable," Jack later wrote, "that his death seems to have cut into the natural order of things."[18] Jack soon replaced Joe Jr. as the heir to their father's ambition to see a Kennedy in the White House. Jack cut his political teeth on a run for Congress from Massachusetts's Eleventh Con-gressional District. At this point, Jack viewed his younger brother as a nui-sance. "It's damn nice Bobby wants to help," Jack told Navy buddy Paul Fay, "but I can't see that sober, silent face breathing new vigor into the ranks." Jack joked that after the requisite photograph of "the brothers," Fay should take Bobby to the movies.[19]

Bobby was assigned to the Italian wards in East Cambridge, the home area of one of Jack's toughest opponents, a former mayor of Cambridge. "My job," Bobby recalled, "was to meet as many people as possible, hoping to reduce the vote against us." When he wasn't knocking on doors and button-holing locals, he was in the park across from campaign headquarters getting up a softball game with the neighborhood boys, which helped to counter

the image of the Kennedys as remote and elitist. By primary day, the anticipated margin of defeat in East Cambridge had been cut in half. Jack beat his
closest opponent in the ten-man race by a two-to-one margin and won the
general election handily.[20]

Bobby returned to Harvard in fall 1946 as a junior. He majored in government, but football was his real focus. Long hours at practice and a tenacious spirit helped compensate for his slight build—he was just five feet ten
inches tall, weighing in at 155 pounds—and earned him a place on the var-
sity team. He broke his leg in practice as a senior but kept playing until
he collapsed. His best friends were football players, including Kenneth
O'Donnell, who shared his interest in politics and history. Most of the players
were veterans who were a few years older than him, with their education subsidized by the GI Bill of Rights—not typical Harvard students. They were
an "irreverent and disinterested group of fellows just out of the service,"
O'Donnell recalled. "They had been all over the world" and had no interest
in who Robert Kennedy was: "They thought he was a rich kid just hanging
around." But after a while, Bobby became one of the group. His sister Eunice recalled that Bobby "picked friends who were sort of different. They
weren't in the usual social stream at all; they were tough and rough . . . all
big and bulky and very unsophisticated. . . . My father was always very im-
maculate and well dressed. . . . Bobby thought it was rather amusing to bring
people home who were neither."[21]

Bobby did not attend classes regularly and barely maintained a C average.
Anthony Lewis, a Harvard classmate who went on to become a reporter and
columnist for the *New York Times,* recalled that Bobby was "a remote
figure . . . sort of a football player" type. But he had developed an interest
in politics, and he would argue a lot about politics as well as sports. It was
in college, Bobby recalled, that he began to think about contemporary
issues.[22]

Joe Kennedy Sr. thought experiencing the world would help broaden his
children's education, and after Bobby's graduation in March of 1948, Joe arranged for the *Boston Post* to take Bobby on as a correspondent. The job was
a defining experience. Bobby's travels took him from Tel Aviv, on the eve of
Israel's creation, to Istanbul, Athens, Rome, and other cities across Europe,
and finally to Berlin during one of the first major confrontations of the Cold
War. His letters and diary, and his articles for the *Post,* reveal a spirit of daring
adventure, a restless curiosity, and a strong power of observation.[23]

Bobby traveled with his college roommate, George Terrien. After several
days in Egypt, the pair arrived in Palestine some six weeks before British
forces withdrew. They rode in an armored car over battle-scarred terrain to
Tel Aviv, where Jews, "with their backs to the sea," as Bobby wrote, fought

for their homes and the future. At one point, the pair were picked up by the police, blindfolded, and taken to the local headquarters of the Haganah, the Jewish security force. Profuse apologies followed after Bobby produced his identification. "Your name," he wrote his father, "is still very well known here and saved your son and George from a great deal of trouble." Bobby roamed widely, visiting Jerusalem, and spoke extensively with both Jews and Arabs for the four articles he wrote for the *Boston Post*.[24]

Hatred of the British was the sole common denominator he could find in this deeply divided region. "It is an unfortunate fact," he reported, "that because there are such well-founded arguments on either side each grows more bitter toward the other." A long conversation with a twenty-three-year-old Jewish woman whose family had lived and fought for six generations in Palestine enabled him to begin "to really see the immense tragedy and horribleness of it all." Jews, he predicted, would "fight with unparalleled courage" for what was "their greatest and last chance" to establish a homeland. He was guardedly hopeful that the establishment of a Jewish state would ultimately serve as a stabilizing force in the region, but he wrote that it would fall to other nations, notably the United States working through the United Nations, to "take the lead in bringing peace to the Holy Land."[25]

From the Middle East, the pair traveled through Istanbul, Greece, Italy, Belgium, Germany, Austria, and Czechoslovakia, ending up in Berlin. Bobby's travels combined meetings with US diplomatic officials and military personnel, informal interviews, and continual recording of observations and impressions. The wreckage of the war yielded occasionally to the beauty of an unspoiled seaside or pastoral scene. Bobby described the vista from a drive along Italy's Amalfi coast between Sorrento and Salerno as "the most beautiful . . . I have ever seen."[26]

While in Italy, near the midpoint of the tour, he received the devastating news that his sister Kathleen had died in a plane crash over France. Kathleen and her lover, Peter Fitzwilliam, were on their way to meet Joe Kennedy in Paris, where she would introduce her father to the man she planned to marry. The couple intended to spend a few days in Cannes before the meeting. After refueling in Paris, Fitzwilliam insisted the pilot of his two-engine plane fly despite warnings of a thunderstorm over the Rhone Valley. The plane never made it to Cannes. Joe Kennedy was awakened in Paris with the news. He went to the crash site outside of Privas and brought his daughter's body back to England, where he was the only family member to attend her funeral mass. Grief consumed him. "He wore a crumpled blue suit and he was crumpled, just like the suit," recalled Debo Devonshire, Kathleen's sister-in-law. "I never saw anything like it." Kick was buried in her husband's family plot in Chatsworth.[27]

A bout of jaundice kept Bobby from attending his sister's funeral, but he went to England a few days later to mourn her and visit her grave. He would name his first child after her. From London, he went on to Belgium, where he visited Kick's husband's grave. "War has passed through many times," he wrote, and the people "take it all rather objectively which is hard for me to understand."[28]

The final weeks of Bobby's travels took him through Germany and Austria and into Czechoslovakia. The war-torn cities of Aachen, Düren, and Cologne, he wrote, "were unimaginable." Some blocks were completely destroyed, with shells of building protruding from piles of rubble. "The people walk around in dazed silence," he observed, without "giving you more than a fleeting glance and trudging on." Although he had a visa to enter Hungary, he was turned back at the border of the Communist-controlled country, the one place where his name and connections worked against him. But he did manage to make it into Soviet-controlled Czechoslovakia, after being detained for an hour and searched by officials.[29]

On June 24, 1948, the Soviet Union initiated a blockade of Berlin, cutting off supplies of food and coal to the western part of the city, which was under Allied jurisdiction. The Allies began a massive airlift program to get supplies to the people of West Berlin. Bobby flew from Frankfurt and reported on the chaos and uncertainty in those earliest days of what would be a yearlong standoff.[30]

In his travels and through many conversations with those he met, he had found that the United States was not viewed kindly in many quarters. "We are certainly not the little saints we imagine ourselves to be," he wrote. America's support of a Jewish state drew the ire of the Arabs, but the United States' waffling policy also convinced Jewish settlers that they were on their own. Germans accepted the Americans as "the lesser of two evils" in the emerging rivalry between the United States and the USSR. Many in Europe worried that America wanted a war with the Soviet Union, to take advantage of the US monopoly on the atom bomb. Others saw in the Marshall Plan—the US economic aid program—imperialistic designs and efforts to create export markets. Suspicions and rumors were compounded by the "loud-mouthed Americans" Bobby encountered. Military officials and civilians, he wrote, were "always shooting their mouths off that the U.S. is best in everything," while refusing to hear any criticism. "Of course, ideally," he concluded, "we should be just the opposite."[31]

Bobby's experiences abroad did more than four years at Harvard had to awaken his interest in public affairs. He applied to law school, a common stepping-stone to a position in government. Poor grades had put Harvard Law beyond reach, but he was accepted at the University of Virginia School of Law, with a warning that if his academic performance did not improve, he was unlikely to succeed. He graduated in the top half of his class. Mortimer Caplin, one of Bobby's professors, recalled, "He never volunteered in class, but did reasonably well if you called on him."[32]

By the time Bobby started law school, he was flying regularly to New York to see Ethel Skakel, a student at Manhattanville College who was living with his sister Jean. Bobby and Ethel had met in 1946, when Jean brought Ethel to work on Jack's campaign. Ethel was smitten, but Bobby was interested in her sister Patricia. Ethel was undeterred. Gregarious, an excellent athlete, and highly competitive, she soon won him over. They had much in common. Ethel had grown up in a large, wealthy family, the second-youngest of seven children. A devout Catholic, she had considered becoming a nun. Her outgoing personality contrasted with Bobby's moody shyness. They became engaged in 1949, the year Ethel graduated from college, and married the following spring, at the end of Bobby's second year of law school. Ethel's love and complete devotion provided him with a kind of emotional security he had never known. "When he married Ethel," his sister Eunice commented, "he blossomed."[33]

In his third year at UVA, as president of the Student Legal Forum, Bobby arranged for major leaders in law, business, and government to visit the university and deliver public lectures on key topics of the day. He tapped into his family's vast network of connections to secure such notable figures as Supreme Court Justice William O. Douglas, journalist Arthur Krock, antitrust lawyer Thurman Arnold, and Senator Joseph McCarthy. Bobby also convinced his father and brother to come speak on campus. Early in his final spring term, he extended an invitation to Ralph Bunche, the chief mediator of the armistice agreement that ended the Arab-Israeli War. Bunche's invitation raised the thorny issue of racial segregation. Bobby had grown up in a white world and had never given much thought to race. The Jim Crow South, with its active enforcement of racial separation and Black exclusion, was new to him. There is no evidence that Bobby questioned these arrangements during his first years at his Virginia law school, but now he challenged the policy head on.

In 1950, segregation was firmly established in Virginia, but cracks were appearing in the foundation. That fall, Gregory Swanson—the first Black student to attend the University of Virginia—had enrolled in the law school after National Association for the Advancement of Colored People (NAACP) attorneys Thurgood Marshall and Oliver Hill won a ruling from the US District Court for the Western District of Virginia ordering Swanson's admission. The court ruled that Swanson was qualified, and UVA was the only institution in the state where he could pursue a graduate degree in law. Swanson lived off campus and was socially isolated from his fellow students.[34]

Some members of the legal forum objected to the choice of Bunche as speaker, despite his Nobel Prize. Their opposition only became more pronounced when he accepted the invitation on the condition that his audience be racially integrated. Virginia law prohibited the mixing of races in public places. Bobby met with representatives of each of the law school classes to get a resolution supporting a no-segregation policy for the talk. Several of the southern students who supported the resolution refused to sign it, for fear of repercussions at home. "Bobby blew his stack," Endicott Peabody, a fellow student, recalled. "He had a lack of understanding of the problems these people faced; to him, it seemed illogical to support something but be unwilling to sign for it." The episode, Peabody commented, revealed Kennedy's "black and white view of things" and offered a demonstration of his hair-trigger temper.[35]

Kennedy sought the advice of law school professors Hardy Dillard and Charles Gregory. One of them suggested that a section of the hall be designated for Blacks, while in practice seating would be open. Kennedy rejected the idea; it did not meet Bunche's requirement. Dillard and Gregory then advised that the three of them draft a letter to Colgate Darden, the president of the university. The five-page letter signed by Kennedy requested that Bunche's "lecture be held in the normal way," with no segregation. Speaking for fellow law students and faculty, the letter registered Kennedy, Dillard, and Gregory's "strong conviction, reinforced by our belief in the issues presented in the last war in which most of us fought, and by our belief in the principles to which this country is committed in the Bill of Rights and the United Nations charter, that enforcement of a segregation policy . . . is indefensible." Citing the recent Supreme Court ruling *McLaurin v. Oklahoma State Regents,* the letter argued that the university could not require Black citizens attending a lecture to sit in a segregated area. Darden accepted the legal argument, deciding that Bunche's lecture could be considered an educational meeting, and agreed it would not be segregated.[36]

———

EARLY ON THE EVENING OF MARCH 26, 1951, Ralph Bunche found an overflow audience of fifteen hundred waiting to hear him speak. Nearly one third of the seats were taken by African Americans. Bobby Kennedy introduced Bunche to the audience, calling him the man who could say "I brought peace to Palestine." At forty-six, Bunche had already traveled a long road, from civil rights activism as a young Howard University professor in the 1930s; to field researcher and major contributor to a seminal study on race relations by Gunnar Myrdal, *An America Dilemma;* to his current role as an internationally acclaimed diplomat and peacemaker. Bunche spoke about the United Nations and its challenges and opportunities, and commented at length on the conflict in Korea. Then, visibly moved by the mix of Black and white faces crowding the auditorium, he turned his attention to the global consequences of America's failure to live up to its ideals. In order to win the battle for democracy abroad, he told his listeners, there must be a convincing demonstration of democracy at home. Americans could not expect the people of Asia and Africa to embrace democracy if it was qualified by color. He expressed confidence that the American people would solve this problem, but he anticipated a steep climb. He closed by "urging strength of determination so deep that it will be capable of raising an abnormal effort to correct these aberrations."[37]

Bunche's visit to Charlottesville marked the beginning of a long and warm association with Bobby and Ethel Kennedy. The young couple had gone out to meet him at the airport and given him a driving tour of the university town. With no adequate hotel available for Blacks in Charlottesville, the Kennedys had also invited Bunche to spend the night at their home. Bunche, notes his biographer, greatly enjoyed meeting them and was impressed by Bobby's willingness "to flout the law for a good cause."[38]

Bobby graduated that spring, and on July 4, 1951, Ethel gave birth to a baby girl, whom the couple named Kathleen Hartington. The young family settled in Washington, where Bobby took a position with the Internal Security Division of the Department of Justice. Before settling into his new job, however, he went to San Francisco to cover the Japanese peace treaty conference for the *Boston Post.* Shortly after his return, he accompanied his brother on a tour through the Middle East and Asia—a trip arranged by their father to expand Jack's understanding of foreign affairs in preparation for a Senate run the following year.[39]

Up until then, the brothers were "almost like distant relatives," in the words of JFK's biographer Robert Dallek. Bobby and Jack had spent little time together and had very different life experiences. The cool, urbane Jack, now in his fifth year in Congress, thought his often-combative little brother would be "a pain in the ass" on the trip. But Jack yielded to his father's wishes, and in October the two brothers and their sister Patricia set off on a seven-week trip that took them though Israel, Iran, Pakistan, India, Indochina, Singapore, Thailand, Malaya, Korea, and Japan. Bobby was 25, Patricia 27, and Jack 34.[40]

The Kennedys moved across a world experiencing nationalist uprisings and Cold War jockeying two years after the triumph of Mao Zedong and the Communist Party in China. Bobby's diary and letters home reveal an intense curiosity about conditions in each of the countries he visited. He was sympathetic to the wave of nationalism sweeping the Middle East and Asia, critical of the French colonial regime in Indochina, and concerned about communism tipping the "scales heavily in favor of chaos." Both brothers were struck by the rigid Cold War framework that dictated American policy. They found that many in the diplomatic corps showed no interest in the human misery driving the social unrest surrounding them. In his letters and diary, Bobby remarked extensively on the conditions that were fueling the nationalist uprisings.[41]

Since his previous visit to the Middle East three years earlier, the conflict between the new state of Israel and the Palestinians had created a major refugee crisis. Nearly one million people had been pushed from their land, he wrote to his father, spilling into neighboring countries. Bobby visited refugee camps, where he found people living in temporary structures with no adequate schooling for the children, as the Palestinians held out hope of returning to their homes. Many neighboring countries feared further Israeli expansion, beyond the borders agreed to by the United Nations in 1947. Such conditions, Kennedy observed, stoked a growing hatred of the United States, which was widely considered in the region to be Israel's strongest ally. The situation was made more difficult by State Department officials who spoke about Arabs "as a teacher does a young child," he wrote. Bobby agreed with those who suggested that the United States should join with the liberal elements in Asia and the Middle East and prepare for nationalist revolutions, an idea scoffed at by diplomats who suggested that the United States was "not that type of nation." "I feel it is the *only* thing we can do" he wrote with urgency. "At least it is something positive."[42]

The Kennedys had access to leading figures during this formative postwar period. They dined with Jawaharlal Nehru, India's first prime minister, who according to Bobby "kept looking at the ceiling" and was more interested in talking to Patricia than to her brothers. Jack asked Nehru for his thoughts on Vietnam, and Nehru's comments made an impression. He told the Kennedys that the French were fighting a losing battle and the Americans were pouring money and arms down a bottomless hole. Nationalism, Nehru cautioned, was not the same thing as communism. The danger was that in the power struggle between the United States and the Soviet Union, communism had become something worth dying for because the communists had allied with the local insurgents. Western democracies, by contrast, offered nothing but the status quo.[43]

Bobby, Jack, and Patricia arrived in Saigon in October and found a city in the midst of a war that had been raging for nearly five years. What had begun as a conflict between the French, seeking to reestablish their colonial

outpost after World War II, and Vietnamese nationalists fighting for independence had become the center of the Cold War contest in Asia, with the
United States aligned with the French and the Soviet Union and China on
the side of the Vietnamese. Jack sought out Associated Press reporter Sey-
mour Topping, who told him that the French were losing and the United
States, held in high esteem immediately after World War II, was now deeply
resented. A conversation with Edmund Gullion, a young consular officer
with the US Embassy in Saigon, confirmed Topping's analysis. General Jean
de Lattre de Tassigny, the French commissioner and military commander,
arranged for the Kennedys to tour military fortifications in Hanoi. An Army
colonel told Bobby over lunch that "he was optimistic about the successful
end of the war, though it might not occur during our lifetime!!"[44]

By the end of their four-day visit, Jack reflected in his diary that the United
States should realize the enemy was not just communism but "poverty and
want," "sickness and disease," and "injustice and inequality"—all of which
defined the daily lives of millions of Asians and Arabs. Bobby observed that
there were "too many streets with French names, too many French flags, too
many French in high places." The French, he concluded, were most concerned with material gain and maintaining their colonial empire and the
prestige it afforded. If an election were to be held, he wrote, it was generally
believed that Ho Chi Minh, longtime leader of the fight for independence,
would win at least 70 percent of the vote. The United States was closely
identified with France's disastrous policies. "Our mistake," Bobby wrote,
"has been not to insist on definite political reforms . . . as a prerequisite for
aid. As it stands, we are becoming more and more involved to a point where
we can't back out." America, he feared, had lost whatever bargaining position it might have had. "It doesn't seem to be a picture with a very bright
future," he concluded.[45]

In a speech to the Boston Chamber of Commerce on the Kennedys' return, Jack called for a complete reevaluation of American policy. "In Indochina we have allied ourselves with the desperate efforts of the French regime to hang on to the remnants of an empire," he said. He noted that at
this point, a free election would "go in favor of Ho and his Communists."
Bobby acknowledged in his diary that problems of the postwar world were
"being made more difficult by communism" and that "communism and nationalism are becoming intermixed"—after which he concluded: "Food for
thought."[46]

The journey was one of discovery for both brothers. Jack saw Bobby in a
new light and appreciated his efforts to make sense of the social and political
turmoil they were witnessing. During their seven weeks together, they forged
a bond that would deepen in the years ahead. They went their separate ways

on their return—Jack back to Congress and Bobby to the Justice Department, where he soon joined the Criminal Division. But in 1952, Bobby would take over the management of Jack Kennedy's flagging campaign for the US Senate, marking the beginning of their close political partnership.

At this early stage of his public life, Bobby demonstrated no obvious awareness or concern about racial conditions in the United States. The protests of the New Deal era had receded, and racial segregation remained the norm throughout the country, going largely unremarked upon in the mainstream media and intellectual circles. As Gunnar Myrdal observed, most white Americans outside of the South knew more about conditions in foreign countries than about Black life in America. During the 1950s, prosperity's abundance coexisted with the specter of communism and nuclear annihilation as defining features of American society and culture.

African Americans lived in a parallel world, segregated by law and custom, but the racial landscape was dynamic and ever-changing. The experience of World War II and the continuing waves of migration from the South to cities in the North and West had disrupted old patterns of thought and forms of existence. Begun in the mid-1930s, the NAACP's steady assault on the legal underpinnings of the southern caste system was moving toward its greatest victory, while a new generation of activists began to explore the contours of the racial divide and experiment with new strategies of resistance. Rosa Parks, Martin Luther King Jr., and others would soon launch a major mass protest in Montgomery, Alabama, that would command national and international attention. James Baldwin and Malcolm X would spotlight the cumulative toll of segregation in northern cities. The racial realities and civil rights struggles of this period were far removed from the concerns of Robert Kennedy and the ambitious postwar generation now claiming leadership positions in government and politics—but a change was coming.

CHAPTER TWO

Along the Color Line

THE 1950S

║|║

BY 1951, the year Bobby Kennedy began his career in government, southern segregationists had reasserted their dominance over a Democratic Party that had been transformed during the New Deal and the war. The dramatic walkout of southern delegates from the 1948 national convention after the party platform endorsed antidiscrimination policies, and a subsequent third-party challenge led by South Carolina governor Strom Thurmond, had not harmed the segregationists' standing in the national party. And even though Black votes had proven pivotal to Harry Truman's upset victory in the 1948 presidential election—following his executive orders ending discrimination in the Armed Forces and the civil service—neither the Truman administration nor the majority Democratic Congress actively pursued civil rights initiatives during his second term. "In the matter of federal action on civil rights," the *New York Times* editorialized, "we will still be ruled from Birmingham."[1]

At the beginning of the 1950s, racial segregation was mandated by law in the South and was the norm throughout most of the United States. The mass migration of African Americans to the North and the West had accelerated over the course of the war, and urban segregation became more deeply entrenched. Federal housing policy and lending policies of financial institutions discriminated against African Americans, and white neighborhood associations actively enforced the color line. As Khalil Muhammad has explained, a social-scientific discourse linking race and criminality forged early in the twentieth century helped justify and reinforce segregation and racist law enforcement practices in northern cities. In 1943, racial tensions exploded in New York, Detroit, and other cities. James Baldwin was nineteen and living in Harlem when a police shooting of a Black soldier unleashed Black rage. Reflecting on the widespread damage after a mob attacked and looted white-owned businesses, Baldwin understood that "Harlem had needed something to smash."[2]

As the American government promoted freedom and democracy in a global contest with the Soviet Union, the issue of racial justice at home was largely absent from public debates. Communism, nuclear fears, corporate culture, and postwar material abundance were major topics among white intellectuals and social observers. Arthur Schlesinger's *The Vital Center: The Politics of Freedom* (1949), the manifesto of Cold War liberalism, mentioned race only once in passing. C. Wright Mills's seminal work, *The Power Elite* (1956), and John Kenneth Galbraith's critique of consumer culture, *The Affluent Society* (1958), ignored the racial divide altogether.

Signs of the youth protest that would rock the South a decade later emerged in the rural community of Farmville in Prince Edward County, Virginia, not far from where Ralph Bunche cracked the color line at the University of Virginia. On April 23, 1951, the 450-member student body at Robert Moton High School, led by sixteen-year-old Barbara Johns, staged a mass walkout, initiating a boycott to protest intolerable conditions at the grossly overcrowded, segregated school. The students sought the advice of Oliver Hill, the NAACP's lead lawyer in Virginia, and soon joined a legal challenge that would culminate with the 1954 *Brown v. Board of Education* ruling that racial segregation in public schools was unconstitutional. In a legal insurgency initiated by NAACP chief legal strategist Charles Houston in the 1930s, the courtroom had become an arena where southern African Americans could lay claim to fundamental rights, chipping away at the legal and psychological underpinnings of segregation. By 1950, legal barriers to their access to voting, transportation, housing, and higher education had been struck down—but little had changed for Black southerners in practice.[3]

The NAACP's campaign was largely ignored by the mainstream press and by national political leadership. Racial segregation was not only tolerated by most Americans but was largely accepted as a way of life. Robert Kennedy was not unlike most other Americans in this respect. During the 1950s, he earned a reputation as a hard-charging attorney investigating corruption for a major Senate committee and emerged as John Kennedy's most valued and trusted political adviser. But he moved in a racial world that was continually evolving, and he developed an approach to public life that was independent of the consensus politics that defined liberal Democrats in the Cold War era. He would ultimately engage America's race problem on his own terms.

KENNEDY'S FIRST JOB WAS with the Criminal Division of the Justice Department. In the spring of 1952, he was in New York preparing a case against two former Truman administration officials who had been charged with corruption when he received a desperate call from Kenny O'Donnell, his former Harvard classmate. O'Donnell, then working as an aide on Jack Kennedy's campaign for the US Senate in Massachusetts, reported that the campaign was in dire straits. While Joseph Kennedy had ensured that the campaign would have all the money it needed, his domination of campaign operations was a disaster in the making. Joe and his old-time cronies had elbowed aside Mark Dalton, the campaign manager, pushing him to the edge of a nervous breakdown. There was no organizing work being done around the state, and Jack, serving as a congressman in Washington, faced an uphill battle against popular incumbent Senator Henry Cabot Lodge Jr. Bobby initially resisted O'Donnell's plea for help; Bobby loved his job and knew nothing about Massachusetts politics. "I'll screw it up," he told O'Donnell. After several more imploring phone calls, Bobby became convinced. His brother needed him, so he went to Massachusetts.[4]

Bobby joined the campaign at the end of May and took charge. "We couldn't win relying on the Democratic Party machine," he recalled, "so we had to build our own." At a time when the parties traditionally launched campaigns after Labor Day and Massachusetts Democrats orchestrated statewide campaigns from Boston, he immediately set about creating a statewide organization from the ground up. With Kenny O'Donnell and Larry O'Brien acting as advance men, Bobby began by touring the state and personally interviewing potential campaign managers in sizable communities. He signed up 286 Kennedy "secretaries" at the head of local organizations across Massachusetts. JFK later marveled about his brother that "he did the job in three weeks."[5]

"Organization, organization, and more organization" was Bobby Kennedy's philosophy. He and his team organized various kinds of groups—by profession, ethnicity, however people came together—with duplication and overlapping, all dedicated to getting lots of people involved, doing different jobs. Many of the volunteers had not been active in politics before. In communities where Democrats were scarce, the team found people who liked Jack Kennedy and were attracted by the spirit emanating from the campaign. Bobby's cousins Polly Fitzgerald and Helen Keyes organized women's tea parties, which were wildly popular, drawing upward of five thousand women to huge receptions featuring mother Rose or one of the Kennedy sisters. Bobby chided Keyes and Fitzgerald that the halls were packed with Irish Catholics and told them they had better get some women from Polish, French, and other backgrounds or else it would all be a waste of time. The team broadened their targets, and by the end of the campaign thirty-five "teas" had taken place, entertaining around seventy-five thousand women, with Bobby often stopping in and eyeballing name tags.[6]

Ruth Batson, a young Black community activist in Boston who would emerge as leader in the fight against segregated schools, hosted a tea party in the Orchard Park Housing Project in Roxbury. "The party was so jammed" in her small four-room apartment, she recalled, that she had to let people enter in separate groups, while kids gathered outside to watch the excitement. Women did most of the volunteer work on the campaign, and an estimated 80 percent of them had been recruited through the tea parties. They checked voter lists, stuffed envelopes, and carried out a telephone campaign that reportedly aimed to reach every registered Democratic and Independent voter in the state.[7]

"The main difference between our campaign and others is that we did work," Bobby observed, betraying his low opinion of the political class. "Politicians do nothing but hold meetings and decide what work should be done." If he saw old-timers hanging around the headquarters, he would ask them to address envelopes. When Bobby found the leader of the American Federation of Labor and Congress of Industrial Organizations (AFL-CIO) lounging in the campaign office, Kennedy snapped, "If you're not going to work, don't hang around here." Responding to criticism that Kennedy was abrasive and even ruthless, he would say, "I don't care if anybody around here likes me as long as they like Jack." No one worked harder than Bobby. "There was no job that he wouldn't do," Dave Powers recalled. When Bobby discovered that a huge "Kennedy for Senator" poster was waiting to be hung on the side of a building so it could be seen from the heavily traveled bridge connecting Charlestown to Boston's North End, he got the longest ladder he could find, climbed it, and hung the poster while Powers held the ladder. Bobby described the 1952 effort as "the toughest campaign I've ever been in. We spent a lot of hours. We started early in the morning and worked until late at night, seven days a week. I lost 10–12 pounds. We never took any time off."[8]

Henry Cabot Lodge Jr., the incumbent senator, evidenced little concern about John Kennedy, the young three-term congressman. A descendant of the famous Boston Cabots, Lodge had served as a Republican in the Senate since 1936; his father had held the seat previously. Little distinguished Jack Kennedy from Lodge on the issues. Up until the Republican convention that summer, Lodge had devoted his energy to helping Dwight D. Eisenhower secure the nomination for President. Eisenhower, favored by moderate and liberal Republicans, had been in a tight race with Ohio senator Robert A.

Taft, longtime leader of the conservative wing of the party. After Eisenhower's nomination in July, Lodge took a vacation.

By the time Lodge began campaigning, after Labor Day, he realized that
he had lost significant ground to his opponent. Lodge faced what has been
described as "the most methodical, the most scientific, the most thoroughly
detailed, the most intricate, the most disciplined and smoothly working campaign in Massachusetts history." Still, up until the end, major Boston newspapers predicted a Lodge victory. Bobby, having calculated the anticipated
voter turnout with his slide ruler, remained confident during the long night
of Election Day. In the end, Jack Kennedy won by 70,000 votes. He was the
only Democrat to win statewide election, with Eisenhower taking Massachusetts by a margin of 200,000 votes.[9]

After helping to elect his brother to the Senate, Bobby took a job on the
staff of the Senate Permanent Subcommittee on Investigations, which came
under the chairmanship of Senator Joseph McCarthy in January. There
are conflicting accounts of how Kennedy obtained this position. Arthur
Schlesinger, citing Roy Cohn, claimed that Joe Kennedy used his influence
and friendship with the senator to secure a position for Bobby, but Edwin
Guthman, an investigative journalist and longtime associate of Bobby,
wrote that James McInerney, under whom Kennedy had worked in Truman's Justice Department, had recommended Bobby to subcommittee
general counsel Francis Flanagan. Kennedy met with Flanagan and Joseph
McCarthy regarding a position. According to Ruth Young Watts, the subcommittee clerk, Flanagan claimed he and he alone was responsible for hiring
Bobby.[10]

McCarthy had been riding high for more than two years with his widely
publicized claims that "card-carrying members of the Communist Party"
had infiltrated the government and major institutions. Jack thought it unwise for his younger brother to be publicly associated with the contentious
and divisive McCarthy. But McCarthy had been a friend of the family for a
number of years. He visited the Kennedys at Hyannis Port and got along
famously with Joe Kennedy. For a time, McCarthy dated Bobby's sister
Patricia. He was fun and a good sport, Ethel Kennedy recalled, nothing like
the scowling, mean-spirited poster boy for anticommunism who gained
national notoriety. Joe Kennedy thought this was a good opportunity for
Bobby. At that time, Bobby believed that there was a serious internal security threat and that McCarthy was the one figure in government attempting
to do something about it.[11]

Kennedy had little to do with the hearings that had become a spectacle
in Washington. Working directly under Francis Flanagan, he investigated

trade between American allies and Communist China while American and other Allied soldiers were fighting Chinese troops in Korea—a subject that had piqued his interest during his travels in the Far East the previous year. Through an exhaustive review of commercial statistics and shipping records, he uncovered evidence of substantial trading in strategic materials, especially by the British and the Greeks. In his report prepared for the Senate, he advocated firm action on the part of the US government—a course that was not pursued. Kennedy's work earned the respect of key Democrats on the committee and positive notice from journalists. Arthur Krock, Washington correspondent of the *New York Times,* praised the report as "congressional investigation at its highest level with documentation given for each statement represented as a fact and with conclusions and opinions expressed dispassionately." Doris Fleeson of the *Washington Star* described Kennedy's report as "a documented and sober story" and claimed that it "received much more credence than anything else Senator McCarthy's name was attached to."[12]

As chairman, McCarthy established a second investigative team and hired Roy Cohn as its chief counsel. A hard-charging former prosecutor for the Justice Department, the twenty-five-year-old Cohn had gained notoriety for his role in the prosecution and execution of Ethel and Julius Rosenberg for espionage. Cohn and Kennedy, both twenty-seven years old, apparently took an instant dislike for one another. Cohn, who joined the committee's staff on the same day as Kennedy, later said that Kennedy resented that Cohn had been hired as a chief counsel. Kennedy believed that it was Cohn who fueled the increasingly reckless tactics used by McCarthy in the hunt for subversives in the government. That winter, Cohn and David Schine, whom Cohn had hired as a consultant, barnstormed through American embassies in Europe, ferreting out offensive books and interrogating employees. "No real research was ever done," Kennedy later remarked. "Cohn and Schine claimed they knew from the outset what was wrong and they were not going to let the facts interfere." In June 1953, when McCarthy transferred Flanagan to the Government Affairs Committee and placed Cohn in charge of the entire subcommittee staff, Kennedy resigned.[13]

With the help of his father, Bobby obtained a position on the Commission on the Organization of the Executive Branch, led by Herbert Hoover. There, his talents languished among the old men who dominated the circle of the eighty-year-old former president. In January, Bobby had the opportunity to return to the Permanent Subcommittee on Investigations in the position of minority counsel to the Democrats. He took his new position shortly before McCarthy embarked on his ill-fated investigation of the US Army.

As Bobby prepared to work across the table from Cohn, he sought to learn more about the American Communist Party and arranged to meet with Earl Browder. Browder, a native of Wichita, Kansas, had led the Communist Party of the United States (CPUSA) during the Popular Front era, from the early 1930s through World War II. During this period, the party was closely aligned with labor, progressive, and civil rights groups. Browder was expelled in 1945 after a hard-line faction took control. He remained a socialist. While he opposed the course of the communist movement after 1945, he was more critical of the American government's persecution of American citizens during the Cold War era for their associations and beliefs.[14]

By all accounts, Kennedy's meeting with Browder was cordial and useful. In a letter thanking Browder for his kindness and time, Kennedy wrote that it was "of tremendous interest to me to receive your ideas and thoughts on the history of the Communist Party in this country. It is only with an understanding of the past that we can proceed to map the future." Browder found Kennedy "pleasant and eager." A friend of Browder's, who associated Kennedy "with the Joe McCarthy era," concluded that he must have "brought out the best side of Bobby's character."[15]

It was not long before Kennedy went head-to-head with Cohn; Bobby's first run-in with J. Edgar Hoover, director of the Federal Bureau of Investigation (FBI), followed. Cohn's interrogation of Annie Lee Moss, a Black woman who served as a teletype operator in the Army Signal Corps, prompted Kennedy to question Cohn on a matter of factual evidence, which he dismissed. In an effort to clarify the information the committee had on Moss, Senator Stuart Symington sent Kennedy to obtain the FBI's file on Moss. Kennedy was surprised when an assistant to Hoover told him that "outsiders" could not see FBI files; Cohn had obviously had access to the FBI records. Kennedy requested a decision from Hoover. Annoyed by Kennedy's insistence, Hoover observed that "the attitude of Kennedy in this matter clearly shows need for absolute circumspection in any conversation with him." Recalling this encounter, Kennedy described it as "a rather major dispute because they [the FBI] lied to me about some documents that they had made available to the committee. . . . So I had to fight with them, and that was really my first."[16]

McCarthy's pursuit of high-ranking Army officials was beginning to spiral out of control. Cohn became furious when the Army failed to yield to his insistence on special favors and privileges for David Schine, who had been drafted. Army leaders finally retaliated, releasing evidence that Cohn had threatened to "wreck the Army" if his demands were not met and that McCarthy also demanded preferential treatment for Schine. McCarthy responded by accusing of the Army of bribing and blackmailing subcommittee staff. Senators on the subcommittee voted for a special investigation of the charges and countercharges.[17]

The infamous Army-McCarthy hearings began on April 22, in the chandeliered Senate Caucus Room. Playing out over thirty-five sessions and carried live by television into the homes of millions of Americans, the hearings have been described as "one of the most boisterous, disorderly, ludicrous spectacles in the history of Congress." In his first appearance on television, Kennedy, slight, with short hair and horn-rimmed glasses, sat sandwiched between Senators John L. McClellan and Stuart Symington. As captivated television viewers looked on, Joe McCarthy's recklessness and cruelty took center stage.

On June 11, Cohn and Kennedy nearly came to blows. After the hearings had adjoined for the week, Cohn told Bobby that they were going to "get" Democratic committee member Senator Henry "Scoop" Jackson on Monday. That day, Jackson had cross-examined McCarthy and poked fun at an anticommunist plan Schine had proposed. "Don't you make any warnings to me about Democratic Senators," Kennedy instructed Cohn. "I'll make any warning to you that I want to—anytime, anywhere," Cohn replied. "Do you want to fight right here?" Then Cohn took a swing at Kennedy. Two others quickly separated the two men. Speaking with reporters later, Cohn said that he had accused Kennedy of having a "personal hatred" for the McCarthy side, which the press saw as an apparent reference to himself. The feud between the two was long-standing and widely known. Kennedy had nevertheless remained on friendly terms with Senator McCarthy himself.[18]

At the conclusion of the hearings, the subcommittee issued a report, prepared by Kennedy, with separate findings and summaries by Republicans and Democrats. The Republicans charged Cohn with seeking special treatment for Schine but did not implicate McCarthy. The Democrats, in a report written by Kennedy, held that "Senator McCarthy and Mr. Cohn merit severe criticism" for "inexcusable actions." The report also held McCarthy accountable for charges against military officials "which impugned their patriotism and loyalty [and were] totally unsubstantiated and unfounded." After fifty-seven days of televised hearings, popular support for McCarthy plummeted. At the end of the year, the full Senate voted to condemn their colleague, a step short of censure, dealing a near-fatal blow to the career of the man who came to symbolize the fear and hysteria of the Cold War era.[19]

Kennedy attempted to maintain a relationship with McCarthy. He had been a family friend prior to his star turn as the public face of the drive to root communists out of American life. Now, publicly disgraced and an increasingly erratic alcoholic, he had become a tragic figure. When he died on May 2, 1957, at the age of 48, Bobby noted in his diary, "Joe McCarthy died at 6:02 last night. Very upsetting for me. I am only happy that I had a friendly conversation with him last week. I arranged to have the children go over to see him. Jean called shortly later and told them Joe had to go out and so therefore not to come."[20]

The *New York Daily News* carried a photograph of Bobby and Ethel Kennedy at a requiem mass for McCarthy at St. Matthew's Cathedral in Washington. Bobby went to Appleton, Wisconsin, and attended the final internment. Kennedy, thirty-one, had known Joe McCarthy for about ten years. His feelings toward McCarthy at the end of his life were undoubtedly complicated, bearing the emotional weight of an old family association and Joe Kennedy's enduring friendship with the senator.[21]

Many liberal critics never forgave Kennedy for working with McCarthy, and for others the association remained a stain on RFK's reputation. Those he worked with and befriended later on did not find the relationship to square with the man they came to know. The journalist Peter Maas recalled bringing the subject up during a dinner they had together. "How could you?" he asked. "I just cannot understand how you could ever have anything to do with Joe McCarthy." As Mass tells the story, Kennedy responded, "'Well, at the time, I thought there was a serious internal security threat in the United States; I felt that Joe McCarthy seemed to be the only one who was doing anything about it.' And he then said, 'I was wrong.'"[22]

———

IN MAY 1954, while the nation was immersed in the drama of the Army-McCarthy hearings, the Supreme Court announced its unanimous ruling in *Brown v. Board of Education* outlawing racial segregation in public schools. The Court struck at the legal foundation of the South's caste system by ruling that segregation in public education violated the equal protection clause of the Fourteenth Amendment. While *Brown* was headline news across the country, there was no shared understanding of what the ruling actually required in practice. The Court postponed ruling on the implementation of the law; southern states prepared to resist any changes; and whites outside the South remained largely indifferent to what most viewed as a regional problem. For many Black Americans, though, *Brown* heralded a new era in the struggle for freedom and civil rights across the United States.

Writing a day after the ruling, North Carolinian Pauli Murray strained to find the words to convey her emotion in the face of "one of the biggest moments in American history." She described "a feeling of relief that we are now on the right track . . . and the principles are clear and in harmony with our most time-honored traditions." The ruling was "the greatest step forward . . . since the Civil War," a man told the *Pittsburgh Courier*. S. H.

Giles of Atlanta called the moment "the dawn of a new day." A new generation would give voice to the hopes stirred by *Brown*. Within weeks of the
Court's ruling, the twenty-five-year-old Martin Luther King Jr. took up his
ministry at Dexter Avenue Baptist Church in Montgomery, Alabama.[23]

Brown resonated throughout Black America, as northern and westward
migrations continued to shift America's racial landscape. The South emerged
as the front line in the battle to dismantle segregation enforced by law. Outside the South, however, segregated schools were also the norm, produced
by zoning, the location of schools, and segregated housing patterns—and
this kind of school segregation was beyond the reach of the *Brown* ruling.
In June 1954, when Malcolm X arrived in New York as minister of Harlem's
Mosque No. 7, the twenty-nine-year-old minister of the Nation of Islam
found a fragmented community contained by tight racial boundaries. There
was a small though notable class of successful Black people, a growing political elite, and a thriving cultural scene. But vast numbers of African Americans were mired in poverty and trapped in ghetto conditions. Black leaders
worked to marshal the political clout of the growing numbers of Black Americans outside the South, none more effectively than the charismatic Reverend Adam Clayton Powell Jr. Malcolm X's contrasting message of Black
self-help and separatism, however, steadily gained adherents among those on
the crowded margins of urban life.[24]

For Black parents in the Jim Crow South, *Brown* had immediate, tangible meaning, promising relief from decades of substandard schools. In
Jacksonville, Florida, when Lula Mae Kirkland's young son Avon asked her
about *Brown,* she responded, "Boy, it means you have a chance." Following
the ruling, mothers and fathers across the South, often with the aid of local
NAACP officials, petitioned local school boards to initiate desegregation. A
large number of school districts concentrated in border state communities
complied with the Court's decision in *Brown*. But Georgia, Mississippi, and
South Carolina pledged defiance, and Virginia and other states soon followed
suit. A subsequent Supreme Court ruling in May 1955 instructed federal district courts to oversee compliance "with all deliberate speed." This open-
ended directive helped fuel white opposition to *Brown* and any other challenges to the region's racial order.[25]

A low-intensity race war was brewing across the South as Black women
and men who sought to register to vote or to enroll their children in previously all-white schools were met with economic reprisals and violence. In
Orangeburg, South Carolina, the local white newspaper published the names
and addresses of parents who had petitioned for desegregation, marking them
as targets for retribution. The White Citizens' Council, founded in Sunflower
County, Mississippi, in July 1954, organized a movement across the South.

By the summer of 1955, Mississippi had emerged as the bloodiest battleground in this conflict. The Reverend George Lee, a local NAACP leader in Belzoni, Mississippi, was ambushed and shot through the head. Three weeks later, a Mississippi state representative assassinated voting rights activist Lamar Smith on the Lincoln County courthouse lawn in broad daylight. At the end of August, two white men murdered and mutilated fourteen-year-old Emmett Till after he allegedly made a flirtatious comment to a white woman. The incident, and the ultimate acquittal of the murderers, attracted national and international attention.[26]

That summer, Alabama NAACP youth leader Rosa Parks attended a workshop on school desegregation at Highlander Folk School, a New Deal–era center for labor organizers and one of the very few interracial meeting places in the South. Haunted by the murder of Emmett Till, Parks found it liberating and inspiring to meet and work alongside white people on an equal basis. She returned to Montgomery, Alabama, determined to continue her work with young people, though she did not hold out much hope that conditions in the Deep South would change in the near future. Part of the problem, she believed, was that the Black community in Montgomery was divided and fragmented. Just four months later, Parks would refuse to give up her seat to a white man on a Montgomery city bus, unifying Black Montgomery in a bus boycott that elevated the young Reverend Martin Luther King Jr., leader of the Montgomery movement, to national prominence.[27]

———

KENNEDY, HIS ATTENTION CONSUMED by his work as chief counsel for the Senate Subcommittee on Investigations, demonstrated no awareness of the *Brown* ruling and its fallout. His world was centered on Capitol Hill where, following Democratic gains in the 1954 elections, he became the committee's chief counsel. He helped steer the work of the committee from communism back to the more mundane subjects of fraud and corruption in government, and his reputation as a tough, hard-driving investigator grew. Early in 1955, he teamed up with journalist Charles Bartlett to investigate Air Force Secretary Harold E. Talbott, who had allegedly used his office to solicit business for his management advisory firm. In a hearing before the committee, Talbott denied any wrongdoing. "There was not a Senator who supported what we were doing," Bartlett recalled. No member of the committee was willing to question the highly respected Air Force secretary. Bobby continued, alone, with a thoroughgoing cross-examination that exposed Talbott's compromised dealings, compelling President Eisenhower to request the secretary's resignation. Bartlett, who was awarded a Pulitzer Prize for his story on Talbott, said that the case would never have been resolved without the efforts of Kennedy, "who worked against the odds to dig out the facts."[28]

On July 28, 1955, just hours after the Talbott investigation ended, Bobby Kennedy was on a plane to the Soviet Union. He traveled with Supreme Court Justice William O. Douglas, a longtime friend of his father. The result of another of Joe Kennedy's ceaseless efforts to broaden his son's experience, the trip lasted six weeks, with most of that time spent touring Central Asia. While Kennedy's suspicion of Soviet leadership and aversion to communism remained largely unchanged, his exposure to the people and appreciation of their work and culture convinced him of the need for greater understanding between the two countries. He found widespread admiration for American technical ability. The most frequent criticism he heard, he told an interviewer, concerned "the Negroes" and how they were "mistreated and discriminated against, segregated and lynched." Kennedy apparently thought the charge was an exaggeration. At a time when the State Department sponsored tours by artists and cultural figures like jazz greats Louis Armstrong and Dizzy Gillespie to counter America's negative image abroad, Kennedy seemed to view the problem largely as one of public relations. Noting that basketball was wildly popular in the Soviet Union, he concluded that "it would be a wonderful thing" if the famously entertaining Harlem Globetrotters "would consider going to Russia and touring the country for a month or so."[29]

While Bobby was in the Soviet Union, William Faulkner was touring Japan under the auspices of the State Department. Government officials hoped that the Nobel Prize–winning native Mississippian would offer a more positive representation of the American South. But Faulkner spoke openly about the growing racial crisis in the United States as a liability for the country in the Cold War. To the chagrin of his State Department handlers, he warned that Americans had to practice freedom at home if they were going to talk about it in a world where the vast majority of people were not white. In Rome, on his way back to the United States, he heard news of Emmett Till, whose broken body had been retrieved from the Tallahatchie River. When a reporter questioned Faulkner about Till's brutal murder, the writer mused apocalyptically, "if we in America have reached the point in our desperate culture when we must murder children, no matter for what reason or what color, we don't deserve to survive and probably won't."[30]

———

VIOLENCE AND OBSTRUCTIONISM IN THE SOUTH during the two years after *Brown* failed to prick the national conscience. For America's political leadership, it was the Black vote in the North, more than anything else, that compelled both major parties to attend to the festering problems of racial segregation and discrimination. In the lead-up to the 1956 presidential campaign, political journalist Theodore White asked in a widely publicized article whether "the Negro Vote" could elect the next president. "In the past ten years," White wrote, "all American politics has buckled under one of the great movements of history—the mass migration of millions of American Negroes from the lands of humiliation in the South to the democracy of big cities in the North." By 1956, Black voters constituted a strong bloc of voters in the nation's five largest cities and could easily determine electoral outcomes in delegate-rich northern states.[31]

The human dramas and looming constitutional crisis unfolding in the South cast a spotlight on the violence and abusive treatment experienced by African Americans, making it increasingly difficult for aspirants to national political office to safely ignore these developments. Early in 1956, as the boycott in Montgomery was getting underway, Martin Luther King Jr.'s house was bombed. Soon afterward, in a futile effort to break the boycott, police arrested eighty-eight Black leaders in Montgomery for violating an antiboycott law. Nearby, in Tuscaloosa, a mob effectively blocked Autherine Lucy from attending the University of Alabama, after a federal judge had ruled that she had to be admitted. In March 1956, nearly every southern representative in the US Congress signed the "Southern Manifesto," which instructed southerners to defy the court's ruling in *Brown*. Black Americans and their allies countered southerners' harassment, violence, and defiance of the law with fortitude and nonviolent protest.[32]

The Democratic Party, dominated by a unified southern wing, risked losing the allegiance of Black voters that had been secured by Franklin Roosevelt two decades earlier. During his first term in office, President Dwight Eisenhower had established the President's Committee on Government Contracts, dedicated to eliminating discrimination in federally funded programs and projects. The committee had paid special attention to ending employment discrimination in the District of Columbia, and Eisenhower's attorney general, Herbert Brownell, had actively advanced the desegregation of DC schools and public accommodations. Late in 1955, Brownell proposed a major civil rights bill that would expand the power of the attorney general to initiate school desegregation suits and provide voter protection in federal elections. In February 1956, Congressman Adam Clayton Powell announced that he would support Eisenhower against the probable Democratic candidate, Adlai Stevenson, with the inflated claim that Eisenhower had "made the greatest contribution to civil rights in the history of the United States."[33]

When the Democrats convened in Chicago in August 1956, the bus boycott in Montgomery had just entered its eight month. Adlai Stevenson, the presumptive nominee, hoped the convention would find a way to reassure Black voters, but the shadow of the southern walkout of 1948 loomed larger. Leading liberal Democrats seemed most concerned with placating a potentially rebellious southern wing as they attempted to claim a middle ground. Eleanor Roosevelt, a close friend of Stevenson, commented, "I think understanding and sympathy for the white people in the South is as important as understanding and sympathy for the colored people." Hubert Humphrey, angling for a possible vice presidential slot on the ticket, said he thought more in terms of "observance" than "enforcement" with regard to the *Brown* ruling. As for the platform, Humphrey promised the impossible. "We're going to have a strong plank on civil rights," he said, but one that would be acceptable to the South. The party's platform briefly referred to "the recent decisions of the Supreme Court relating to segregation in publicly supported schools" and "rejected all proposals for the use of force to interfere with the orderly determination of these matters by the courts"—a weak platform that did not ruffle southern delegates.[34]

Robert Kennedy attended his first national Democratic convention in 1956 as manager of his brother's vice presidential bid. Jack had decided to throw his hat into the ring despite his father's strong objections. It seemed highly unlikely that Stevenson could beat Eisenhower, and Joe Kennedy thought Jack's presence on a losing ticket would diminish his chances for the presidency. But the young, charismatic war hero, a favorite of the press, charged ahead. When Stevenson decided to let the delegates select the vice presidential nominee, the race quickly came down to a contest between Jack Kennedy and Senator Estes Kefauver of Tennessee, who had made a strong showing in the Democratic primaries. Jack and Bobby worked round the clock to enlist delegates and shore up support, while backers distributed buttons, placards, and noisemakers. Bobby spent time working the convention floor with Kenny O'Donnell, who recalled: "Bobby and I ran around the floor like a couple of nuts. We didn't know two people in the place."[35]

The Kennedy-Kefauver contest reflected the racial twists that were reshuffling political alliances. Kefauver, a liberal southerner, was one of the few representatives who did not sign the Southern Manifesto, causing his star to rise among northern liberals while alienating most southern delegates. With eyes set on the vice presidential nomination, John Kennedy, like Hubert Humphrey, had begun to couch his support for *Brown* in gradualist terms, advising that school desegregation should be left to the courts and the localities to implement. Reading the Massachusetts senator as sympathetic to their position, southern delegates were JFK's strongest supporters, with the likes of Senator Strom Thurmond, Georgia governor Marvin Griffin, and Mississippi governor James P. Coleman lining up behind him. Kennedy took

105.5 of the delegate votes from the South to Kefauver's 20.5 and came within a hair of winning the nomination. JFK's failure to clinch it distressed Bobby. "We lost because we weren't properly organized," he remarked. In the end, the publicity and exposure as well as his strong showing only enhanced JFK's reputation and elevated him to the stature of a national political figure. "He was the one new face that actually shone," one journalist noted.[36]

Jack Kennedy cultivated his connections with major southern party leaders and representatives as he prepared for a presidential run. At the same time, he began developing strategies for reaching out to Black voters nationally and found important allies in Belford Lawson and Marjorie McKenzie Lawson, Washington-based Black attorneys. Belford had worked on several NAACP cases and was a member of the Washington, DC, delegation to the convention as the sole DC delegate pledged to Kennedy. He told Kennedy that he believed JFK would be the nation's first Catholic president. Not long after the convention, Kennedy and his aide Ted Sorenson invited Belford to the senator's office in Washington to talk about JFK's plans for the future and to ask for Belford's help in broadening contacts among Black leaders and organizations.[37]

Belford and his wife, Marjorie McKenzie Lawson, who had been a popular columnist for the *Pittsburgh Courier,* one of the largest circulating Black newspapers, would serve as advisers to Kennedy up through the 1960 campaign. Educating him about the concerns of African Americans and the problems of race, the Lawsons believed, was essential to their efforts to enlist Black support. Marjorie, who served as general counsel to the National Council of Negro Women, joined JFK's staff as a paid adviser and became his primary contact to the Black press, Black organizations, and civil rights leaders. She recalled that Kennedy listened and was receptive to criticism, although he rarely agreed with her suggested approach, at least initially. "Events," she later recalled, would "prove where his heart was."[38]

Bobby left the convention appreciating the importance of the South to his brother's presidential ambitions. "It was the Southern states that gave Jack the initial start that kept going," he wrote in gratitude to Georgia supporter Charles Bloch shortly after the convention.[39] But Robert Kennedy's education in the art of electoral politics would begin in earnest when Adlai Stevenson invited Bobby to join the candidate's campaign staff. During six weeks on the road, he worked hard and effectively. "He was always available and always helpful," Stevenson aide William Blair recalled. Others were struck by Kennedy's analytical ability. But the image that endured was of Bobby quietly huddled in the back of the bus or on a plane or sitting on the railroad tracks while Stevenson gave a speech from the rear of a train—constantly jotting down observations. Kennedy later recalled, "Nobody ever asked me to do anything, nobody wanted me to do anything, nobody consulted me. So, I had time to watch everything—I filled complete notebooks with notes on how a Presidential campaign should be run."[40]

In the end, the Stevenson campaign was a disappointment. Stevenson's lackluster speechmaking proved impervious to suggestions, a problem magnified through the new medium of television. More exasperating for Bobby was Stevenson's indecisiveness, his profound lack of organization, and his detachment. He "was just not a man of action at all," Kennedy later explained. It was "the most disastrous operation" he had ever seen, he confided to Kenny O'Donnell. While the campaign was a distressing experience, it was an extremely valuable one. "I had the feeling after the Stevenson campaign that Bobby knew every single thing there was to know about a campaign," Harrison Salisbury recalled. "He just squeezed all that absolutely dry."[41]

——

KENNEDY'S BRIEF FORAY into presidential politics interrupted a looming investigation of corruption and mob activity in the labor movement. Clark Mollenhoff, an investigative journalist for the *Des Moines Register,* had persuaded Senator John McClellan and Bobby that labor racketeering, especially in the Teamsters Union, the largest and most powerful union at the time, merited the attention of the Senate Subcommittee on Investigations. Kennedy initiated a nationwide review of the labor scene, sending investigators to cities in the East and Midwest. Within days of the November election, he and Carmine Bellino, an accountant and former FBI agent, traveled to the West Coast, where they pursued an intensive on-the-ground review of Teamster operations. The two men examined records and financial statements, met with union officials and reporters, and pursued other leads in Los Angeles, Portland, and Seattle, returning east through Chicago. Kennedy and Bellino uncovered evidence of embezzlement, extortion, corruption, and violence on a massive scale. In January 1957, largely as a result of Bobby's efforts, a special committee drawn from members of the Subcommittee on Investigations and the Senate Labor Committee was established. Senator McClellan served as chair of the Senate Select Committee on Improper Activities in the Labor or Management Field—which came to be known as the Rackets Committee—and Kennedy continued in his position as chief counsel.[42]

Joe Kennedy thought the investigation was a big mistake. During the family's Christmas gathering at Hyannis Port in 1956, Joe had a heated argument with Bobby, charging that his efforts would jeopardize Jack's labor support. But Bobby would not be dissuaded, and he recruited Jack, who served on the Labor Committee, to join the Rackets Committee. While mindful of the risks, both men were also aware of the potential political dividends. Bobby had come to view labor racketeering and organized crime as among the great challenges facing the country. The issue appealed to his exacting moral code, his sense of individual responsibility, and his appetite for action. As he learned more, he felt a deepening obligation to the union rank and file, who were being cheated and exploited by corrupt labor bosses. Bobby ultimately won the respect of mainline labor leaders like George Meany, head of the AFL-CIO, and Walter Reuther of the United Automobile Workers (UAW). In the end, the high-profile investigations and hearings greatly enhanced the Kennedy brothers' public standing. But there was no clear sense of where the investigation would lead.[43]

At the age of thirty, Robert Kennedy proceeded into the "jungle" of labor racketeering, organized crime, and political high jinks "without guides or experience," as journalist Murray Kempton put it.[44] By now, Bobby and Ethel were the parents of five children—Kathleen, Joseph, Robert, David, and Courtney. The US Junior Chamber of Commerce had made Bobby one of their top ten "men of the year," and his boyish good looks elevated him to the rank of teen idol. But it was as head of the Rackets Committee that he established himself as a serious national figure running one of the largest congressional inquiries of its kind up to that time.[45]

Once the committee had been established, complaints poured in—of bribery, criminal activity, violence, and thievery that robbed union coffers, corrupted labor-management relations, and infected politics and public life. During the early stages of his work on the committee, Kennedy sought out and attracted investigative journalists, many of whom had taken the lead in exposing labor racketeering and mob activity in their cities. He established connections with at least twenty journalists around the country and developed a close relationship with several of them. Pierre Salinger of the *San Francisco Chronicle* joined the staff of the Rackets Committee, and Ed Guthman of the *Seattle Times* and John Seigenthaler of the *Nashville Tennessean* worked closely with Kennedy then and in years ahead.[46]

The committee staff peaked at 105, and included upward of thirty-five field investigators, forty-five accountants, and twenty stenographers and clerks. The committee was flooded with applicants. One of the field investigators, Walter Sheridan, recalled that Kennedy "interviewed me for a job going up the stairs on his way home. . . . It was typical because most of my conversations with him since then were while walking up steps or riding in cars or up and down elevators . . . because he was always on the move." Bobby's ability to identify, recruit, and motivate men (and it was nearly all men) who shared his vision and drive was impressive. Journalist John Martin Barlow described the core group as "irreverent, unimpressed with power. They have the moral certitude, the fervor, the lust for a better world that goes with youth."[47]

Kennedy cultivated an esprit de corps while creating a finely tuned operation. The Washington-based staff, often joined by investigators from the field, were crowded into three rooms in the basement of the old Senate office building, "where there were three times as many people as there were desks for them." Ruth Watts, chief clerk of the committee, recalled coming into the office in the morning and finding investigators who had slept on the floor after working through the night to prepare for a hearing: "There was dedication there, total dedication." Kennedy frequently brought investigators together at his home outside Washington in the evenings or on weekend afternoons to discuss cases and procedures. One aide described how Kennedy joined several investigators on a trip to a farm in Illinois, in search of the body of a woman reporter who had disappeared, allegedly murdered and disposed of in retaliation for her investigative work. Kennedy, shovel in hand, "pitched right in," literally digging for clues.[48]

By the end of 1957, the committee had established offices in eight cities and had fifteen major investigations going on. It was grinding, time-consuming work, involving painstaking investigations of financial records, bank statements, and other documents, as well as a fair amount of sleuthing. One of Kennedy's first cases involved Dave Beck, the high-living, powerful head of the Teamsters Union, who, after being interrogated by the Rackets Committee, was ultimately indicted, convicted, and imprisoned for larceny and income tax evasion. The case was an auspicious beginning. James "Jimmy" Hoffa, Beck's successor, with his deep mob entanglements and agile legal representation, became Bobby's arch nemesis. The seething contempt these two men shared has dominated most accounts of the Rackets Committee, but more than fifteen hundred witnesses appeared before the committee over the course of two and a half years, representing cases from all parts of the country and revealing the breadth and scope of the effort.

During the Rackets Committee hearings, the term "ruthless" became associated with Robert Kennedy. His relentless investigation of Hoffa first contributed to this characterization. Bobby was a tough inquisitor. The primary function of the committee was to expose corrupt practices within the labor movement and to mobilize public opinion and secure effective government actions. Legal scholar Alexander Bickel felt Kennedy crossed the line and engaged in a punitive ritual of public shaming, reminiscent of tactics used by Joe McCarthy. Bobby was at pains to avoid comparisons to the McCarthy hearings and surely bristled at such charges. "My biggest problem," Bobby admitted, "is to keep my temper." He said that witnesses who came before a Senate committee "had an obligation to speak frankly and tell the truth. To see people, sit in front of us and lie and evade makes me boil inside." Crime journalist John Bartlow Martin, who wrote an eight-part series on the hearings, expressed a general feeling of discomfort with the moral zeal of Kennedy and his team, but concluded that Kennedy had treated Hoffa fairly. Clark Mollenhoff praised Kennedy for serving as "a beacon to hundreds of reporters and editors, thousands of politicians and labor leaders, and rank and file union members" as a force for "good government and clean labor." Contrasting Bobby with his "charmingly detached" brother, Murray Kempton saw glimmers of "a Catholic radical" in Bobby's aggressive pursuit of wrongdoing. He was one, Kempton mused, "who represents, in his way, the survival of the spirit."[49]

Bobby proved adept at navigating the political minefields of a committee dominated by antilabor sentiment—with two southern Democrats and four Republicans, including Senators Barry Goldwater and Karl Mundt. The Republicans angled to rein in the chief counsel, eager to shift attention away from Hoffa, who was a Republican, to Walter Reuther and the UAW, the bedrock of liberal unionism and a major force in the Democratic Party. For conservative, antiunion Republicans, the UAW was a prime target. Goldwater charged that Reuther was a greater menace to the United States than the Soviet Union. Kennedy yielded to loud demands that the committee investigate a long, bitter UAW strike against the Kohler plant in Sheboygan, Wisconsin. It was a politically risky move; alienating Reuther could doom JFK's presidential ambitions. But Bobby felt the need to counter charges, leaked by Republicans to the press, that he was covering for Reuther and the UAW. He assigned Jack McGovern, a staff member hired on Goldwater's recommendation, to investigate the Kohler-UAW case.[50]

Walter Reuther took the offensive and decided to educate Kennedy about the UAW and conditions around the strike. Reuther's aide Jack Conway, the UAW's representative in Washington, and several lawyers on the UAW staff gathered all the relevant information—filling several large binders. Conway met with Kennedy and dropped the pile of documents on his desk. Conway told Kennedy to let Conway know if there was something Bobby knew about that was not covered in the material. Conway made it clear that the UAW was going to be open and aboveboard, and if Kennedy was as well, there would be no trouble. Kennedy was taken aback and seemed suspicious. But he took the time to read through the financial records and staff reports and then followed up with Conway. Kennedy raised a series of questions, suggesting that the reports had exaggerated the conditions and demonized the company. He was incredulous: "It can't be that bad." "Well, if that's what you think," Conway responded, "why don't you go out and take a look your-self." Kennedy said he would. Conway thought Bobby would probably make the trip when it was convenient, but Kennedy got on a plane that night and flew to Wisconsin.[51]

He spent the next day in the plant. He "met with company officials, went into the foundry, talked with the guys, found that, in fact, they did have to eat their lunches while they were working, that the temperature was one hundred twenty to one hundred thirty degrees and that all of the things that we had charged were true," Conway recalled. Nothing had prepared Kennedy for his visit to Sheboygan, a squalid company town worn down by a nearly three-year-long stalemate. The hatred between the company and the workers reminded him of the raw feelings between Jews and Arabs in the Middle East: "Unless you can see and feel for yourself the agony that has shattered this Wisconsin community it is difficult to believe that such a concentration of hatred can exist in this country." Bobby had gone to Wisconsin with no strong convictions about the strike. His visit to the grim industrial site and his meetings with workers, union organizers, and company representatives changed that perspective.[52]

When Jack McGovern produced a blatantly slanted report for the Rackets Committee defending Kohler, Kennedy recommended that the committee hold hearings on the strike. In the testimonies that followed, he exposed the cruelty and greed of the Kohler officials, at one point grilling a Kohler executive who defended company policy of a lunch break of just two to five minutes for workers in the enamel shop. The National Labor Relations Board ultimately charged Kohler with unfair labor practices and failure to bargain in good faith.

———

WHILE THE RACKETS COMMITTEE was commanding headlines, the issue of civil rights found its way onto the legislative calendar. President Eisenhower, fresh from his landslide reelection, was desperate to find a way to keep the simmering crisis in the South from coming to a boil. On November 13, 1956, one week after the election, the Supreme Court dealt another major blow to the legal edifice of Jim Crow. Ruling on the NAACP's bus boycott case from Montgomery, Alabama, the Court upheld a lower court decision that declared state and local laws segregating buses unconstitutional. This was a sweet victory for Montgomery's Black community after a yearlong bus boycott and a hopeful moment for civil rights advocates across the country. President Eisenhower disliked the Court's action, fearing that the ruling would only add fuel to the fire of white resentment and lead to more violence and unrest.[53]

Jack Kennedy, gearing up for a 1960 presidential race, aimed to stake out a middle ground as Black protest grew and white defiance of the law pushed the region to the edge of chaos. In the months following the 1956 convention, Kennedy nurtured his newfound support in the South with a speaking tour through the region. He delivered commencement addresses at the University of South Carolina and the University of Georgia in spring 1957. For Black observers, the Massachusetts senator often teetered too close to the segregationist side. His remark in a speech to a national organization of educators that school policies should be left in the hands of local school boards rather than "Washington bureaucrats" was radioactive in post-*Brown* America. The *Chicago Defender,* a widely circulating Black newspaper, blasted Kennedy for what sounded like an appeal to white southern prejudices. Kennedy immediately made amends, meeting privately with *Defender* editor John Sengstacke to reassure him of JFK's support for *Brown,* telling Sengstacke that the senator's door in Washington was always open to the editor and other members of the Black press.[54]

The battle over the Civil Rights Act of 1957, the first major civil rights legislation in eighty years, drew sharp lines between supporters and opponents of meaningful federal action, challenging JFK's ability to straddle the growing divide and giving the Republican Party an advantage. Eisenhower had secured the votes of 39 percent of Black voters, the largest percentage of Blacks to vote Republican since 1932; Stevenson carried only seven states, all except for Missouri in the Deep South. Black voters in the upper South and border states helped tip the balance to Eisenhower, suggesting the potential for building a Republican base in the region as the Black vote expanded. Meanwhile, Black voters would remain pivotal in northern industrial states. These factors, along with the president's desire to broaden federal authority over civil rights and diminish the need for military intervention, encouraged him to forge ahead with the ambitious civil rights bill drafted by Attorney General Herbert Brownell Jr. and initially introduced in Congress in 1956.[55]

The legislation provided for the creation of a bipartisan Civil Rights Commission and the establishment of a Civil Rights Division in the Justice Department. The bill empowered the attorney general to bring suits to secure voting rights and enforce school desegregation, providing the legal mechanism to prosecute discriminating practices by voting registrars. The old conservative coalition of Republicans and southern Democrats seemed to be yielding to a new alignment of Republicans and liberally inclined Democrats, who found common cause around civil rights as a winning political issue. But a steep climb remained before the bill could become law.

Fresh from the triumph of the Montgomery bus boycott and now head of the newly organized Southern Christian Leadership Conference, Martin Luther King Jr. waded into the morass of legislative politicking. He joined other Black leaders in pressing for an antiterror provision to be added to the bill. As the bill slowly made its way through the Senate, he pleaded for Eisenhower to come south to see what Black people faced on a daily basis. "If you cannot come south to relieve our harassed people," he warned, "we shall have to lead our people to you in the capitol." More seasoned operatives, including Roy Wilkins and Clarence Mitchell, prevailed on the young minister to pursue a less confrontational approach. In May, King led a "Prayer Pilgrimage" rather than a protest, observing the third anniversary of the *Brown* decision. King's attempts to meet with Eisenhower were brushed aside with warnings that such a meeting would be "disastrous for the civil rights bill." A meeting with Vice President Richard Nixon took place instead, establishing a cordial relationship between the two men.[56]

As the bill made its way through the Senate, Democrats with national political ambitions, notably Lyndon B. Johnson and John F. Kennedy, trod a narrow path between placating the dominant southern wing of their party while not completely alienating African Americans. Senator James Eastland's Judiciary Committee was traditionally the graveyard of civil rights legislation. Jack Kennedy voted against a provision that would have allowed the bill to bypass Eastland's committee, drawing stiff protest from Black leadership in Massachusetts, including Ruth Batson, who had hosted a tea party for JFK during the 1952 senatorial campaign. Batson was now head of the New England Regional Conference of the NAACP. While Kennedy lamely attempted to justify his vote on "procedural grounds," a bipartisan alliance of Democrats and Republicans succeeded in shepherding the bill past Eastland's Judiciary Committee for consideration by the full Senate.[57]

The bill's most hotly contested provisions were contained in section 3, empowering the attorney general to intervene in school desegregation cases, and section 4, providing for civil contempt trials in the case of obstructionist voting registrars. In a winding speech attacking section 3, Senator Richard Russell of Georgia dredged up the maligned Reconstruction era, charging that the bill would authorize the attorney general "to destroy the separation of the races in the Southern States at the point of bayonet" and predicting "bitterness and bloodshed" if the bill became law. With specific reference to *Brown,* Russell warned that there was not enough jail space to hold white southerners "who oppose the raw use of federal power to commingle white and Negro children in the same school." Eisenhower, never a strong supporter of *Brown* and haunted by the prospect of having to send the Army to the South to maintain order, quickly caved on section 3, publicly expressing doubts about its constitutionality. With Republican supporters left out on a limb by the president, the Senate voted to strike section 3 from the bill.[58]

The showdown over the Civil Rights Act now revolved around section 4. Majority Leader Lyndon Johnson led the effort to defang the provision providing that registrars who violated the rights of prospective voters could be tried before a judge for contempt, a standard practice for civil cases. Providing for trial by a judge rather than a jury was significant, since all-white juries in the South could hardly be counted on to convict officials for barring Blacks from voting. Shading the facts, LBJ insisted that such a provision denied citizens their constitutional right to trial by jury and proposed what became known as "the jury trial amendment" to the bill. Eisenhower was not prepared to give an inch on this measure. The main purpose of the bill was to protect voting rights, and he insisted that the provision go forward as written. Jack Kennedy hemmed and hawed, knowing that Black voters in Massachusetts and throughout the country would view his vote as a clear signal of where he stood. He consulted three Harvard Law professors about the legal issues involved. All agreed that the law as written was constitutional, but each advised that if passage of the bill depended on amending the statute to include the jury trial amendment, it was better to have a weak bill than no bill at all. In the end, this was the rationale Kennedy used, and he voted with the majority LBJ had managed to patch together. On August 1, the Senate voted 51–42 to add the jury trial amendment to the legislation.[59]

White House aides had never seen Eisenhower angrier. The *New York Times* speculated that he would rather have no civil rights bill than a watered-down one. Requiring a jury trial to protect voting rights, Eisenhower insisted, undermined "the basic purpose of the bill—that of protecting promptly and effectively every American in his right to vote." Vice President Richard Nixon described the Senate action as "one of the saddest days in the history of the Senate because it was a vote against the right to vote." It was difficult to miss the political silver lining as attention turned to the alliance of liberal and southern Democrats who had put the bill at risk. Lyndon Johnson and liberal Democrats feared that Eisenhower might veto the bill, causing Black voters to blame the Democrats for derailing the legislation. JFK's vote in support of the jury trial amendment would plague him as he sought to shore up African American support.[60]

Black political and civic leaders were now divided. The NAACP supported the passage of the legislation in an effort to "get something," while others like Ralph Bunche and presidential aide E. Frederic Morrow urged the president to veto a "fake bill." In the end, the Department of Justice worked out

a proposal that allowed for a federal judge to try a defendant in cases relating to voting rights when projected punishment did not exceed a $300
fine or ninety days in prison. LBJ was able to keep most of the southern
Democrats in line and forestall a crippling filibuster. On August 29, after a
one-man, twenty-four-hour-long filibuster by Strom Thurmond, the Senate
passed the Civil Rights Act of 1957 by a vote of 60–15. Eisenhower's civil
rights coalition of thirty-seven Republicans and twenty-three Democrats prevailed, with fifteen southern Democrats joined in united opposition. Adam
Clayton Powell praised the president for having kept his word and declared
"after 80 years of political slavery, this is a second emancipation."[61]

The Civil Rights Act of 1957 did little to enhance the power of the federal government in the face of an escalating racial crisis in the South. Nevertheless, the provisions that survived provided for the creation of the US
Civil Rights Commission and the creation of a Civil Rights Division within
the Department of Justice. Together these two measures expanded the institutional apparatus available to expose injustices, command national attention, and seek remedies. Martin Luther King Jr., who was among those
who believed that the bill in its final form was better than no bill at all, was
sanguine regarding the law's ultimate significance. "The full effect of the civil
rights bill," he contended, "will depend in large degree on a program of sustained mass movement on the part of Negroes. History has demonstrated
that inadequate legislation supported by mass action can accomplish more
than adequate legislation which remains unenforced for the lack of a determined mass movement."[62]

In the fall of 1958, the US Civil Rights Commission held hearings in
Montgomery, Alabama, investigating voter discrimination in Macon County,
Alabama, a majority Black county. Professors who taught at Tuskegee Institute and farmers were among the twenty-three Black witnesses who testified
that day on how voting registrars routinely refused to register them to vote.
The hearings were broadcast on television—an early glimpse of television's
power to bring the unvarnished reality of southern-style racial repression to
a national audience.[63]

———

SHORTLY AFTER THE PASSAGE of the Civil Rights Act, while Robert Kennedy was embroiled with the labor investigation, James Baldwin made his
first trip south. He was thirty-three years old. Baldwin had lived for most of
the previous nine years in and around Paris, where he had gone to escape
the pressures, poverty, and brutality that increasingly intruded on the daily
rhythms of life in Harlem. Living there, he wrote, was "like trying to breathe
in a very small room with all of the windows shut."[64] In Europe, Baldwin

blossomed as a writer. He completed his first novel, began a second, and published *Notes of a Native Son,* a collection of essays written between 1948 and 1955. The largely autobiographical collection established Baldwin as a social observer and critic capable of crossing the color line and capturing the attention of liberal whites.[65]

As confrontations around school desegregation commanded attention abroad, Baldwin prepared to return to the United States. He could no longer sit in Paris cafés discussing the problems of Black Americans as the battle for civil rights escalated in the United States. An invitation by Philip Rahv, editor of *Partisan Review,* to write a long piece on the South hastened Baldwin's departure: "I took a boat home in the summer of 1957, intending to go south as soon as I could get the bread together." With an advance from *Partisan Review* and *Harper's Magazine* for stories he would write for each journal, he left New York on September 2.[66]

The son of southern migrants, Baldwin was now making his first trip to the "old country," as northern-born African Americans referred to the region. His impressions were shaped by stories he had heard growing up about a place of terror and violence that his stepfather had fled. At one point, as the plane flew over Georgia, Baldwin looked down at the red clay landscape and imagined it drenched in the blood of lynching victims. Poet Sterling Brown advised Baldwin that the lynchings belonged to another time; Black people were imagining and shaping a different future now in this strange yet familiar place. The images of young people who braved howling mobs to go to school captivated Baldwin. He wanted to see them and their parents, talk with them, and attempt to understand the fortitude that was cracking the veneer of the South's racial order—and the cost of that courage.[67]

Baldwin started in Charlotte, North Carolina. In a city of fifty thousand Black citizens, four students had been admitted to previously all-white high schools, one to each, sending the city into convulsions. By the time Baldwin arrived, the father of Dorothy Count, one of the four students, had taken her out of Harry Harding High School, fearing for her life. Baldwin met with one of the remaining three students, fourteen-year-old Gus Roberts, and his mother. The young man, tall, with "a face disquietingly passive, save for his very dark, very large eyes," had little to say about his experience. He concentrated on his homework while his mother described the daily indignities and harassment—the name-calling, other students' attempts to bar her son's entry with a human blockade, the phone calls threatening to cut him "to ribbons." Baldwin asked Mrs. Roberts what had prompted her to have her son reassigned to the previously all-white school, where he was isolated and subject to daily harassment. She talked about how her son had been losing interest at his segregated school. He was not learning anything, she said; he rarely had any homework. He was "out in the streets, getting into mischief. . . . I could just see what was going to happen to him." "My boy's a good boy," she said, "and I wanted to see him have a chance."[68]

After a few days in Charlotte, observing the conditions of the segregated schools, Baldwin understood her wrenching decision. The all-Black schools were overcrowded and rundown. Teachers, often poorly prepared, were working under difficult circumstances, and evidence of the human toll of failing schools could be found on the street corners. In the ten days before Baldwin's visit, eighteen boys from Gus's former high school had been sentenced to the chain gang. White people, Baldwin wrote, did not understand how parents could send their children to face the mob, "because they do not know, and do not want to know, that the alternative to this ordeal is nothing less than a lifelong ordeal." But Baldwin could not help but wonder about Gus and how he bore up, knowing what he faced when he woke up each morning. Baldwin suspected that Gus managed the extreme tension of the situation by "a nearly fanatical concentration on school work; by holding in the center of his mind the issue on which . . . others would be forced to judge him," and by using "pride and silence" as his weapons.[69]

Baldwin traveled on to Atlanta, Montgomery, Birmingham, Tuskegee, Little Rock, and Nashville, observing the varied strands of Black lives and experiences at this transitional and fragile moment. He met Martin Luther King Jr. for the first time and described how King's Dexter Avenue congregation, in the aftermath of the victorious bus boycott, exuded "the joy achieved by people who have ceased to delude themselves about an intolerable situation . . . and who know that they can change their situation if they will." Baldwin felt the sting of Jim Crow's cruel humiliation after he inadvertently used the "white entrance" of a restaurant and was forced to move to a caged-off area. He marveled at the patience of Black men who had endured the indignities for so long without losing control. "In the face of such strength," Baldwin mused, "whites had something to be frightened of." In Birmingham (a "doomed city") he visited with Fred Shuttlesworth, the intrepid leader of the movement there, who lived as "a marked man." More than the public personae of these young leaders, Baldwin was struck by their private lives and how "they went about their daily tasks in the teeth of Southern terror."[70]

The explosiveness of the situation was palpable. One incident, Baldwin cautioned, could spark violent confrontation on a mass scale—"a policeman may beat up one Negro too many, or some Negro or some white man simply go berserk." A race riot anywhere in the South, Baldwin predicted, "will spread to every metropolitan center in the nation which has a significant Negro population"—not merely "because the ties between Northern and

Southern Negroes are still very close," but primarily because "the nation, the entire nation, has spent a hundred years avoiding the question of the place of the black man in it." That question loomed in fall 1957, elevated in large part by the insistent and dignified claims of Black youth. Whether change would come peacefully, Baldwin concluded, would depend on white Americans' willingness to finally face this question.[71]

A major showdown over school desegregation unfolded in Little Rock, Arkansas, while Baldwin was traveling in the South. Governor Orval Faubus, his eye on a tight reelection campaign, deployed the National Guard to block the admission of nine Black students to Central High School, in violation of a federal court order and in opposition to the careful plans laid by the Little Rock school board to facilitate integration. After weeks of fruitless efforts to persuade the governor to abide by the court ruling, with conditions around the school reeling out of control, Eisenhower sent in the 101st Airborne Division to oversee the integration of Central High School. The televised spectacle of nine teenagers being escorted into school by armed soldiers flashed around the country, and the images were picked up by newspapers around the world. For Julian Bond, then a sixteen-year-old high school student living in Philadelphia, the sight of his contemporaries braving the mob called up a mixture of anger and pride—and a desire to be like them. The following year, Governor Faubus, who was reelected in a landslide, closed the public schools in Little Rock.[72]

In 1959, five years after *Brown,* schools were still segregated in Prince Edward County, Virginia. That spring, the state Supreme Court of Virginia struck down the state's massive resistance legislation designed to block desegregation in public schools. The Fourth Circuit Court of Appeals ordered Prince Edward County to enroll Black students in previously all-white schools that September. The county responded by closing the public schools and establishing private schools for white children. The schools were underwritten with public funds and aided by local churches and businesses. More than fifteen hundred Black students in Prince Edward County and their parents were left to fend for themselves in a place that now provided no schooling for them.[73]

———

BY SPRING 1959, Bobby Kennedy's work on the Rackets Committee was winding down, and preparations for his brother's presidential campaign were underway. After close to three years of intensive work by the committee staff and nearly three hundred days of Senate hearings, Kennedy was more convinced than ever that organized criminal activity was one of the greatest internal threats facing the country. "The gangsters of today," he wrote, "work in a highly organized fashion. . . . They control political figures and threaten whole communities. They have stretched their tentacles of corruption and fear into industries both large and small."[74]

Yet little had changed since the hearings had begun; if anything, Kennedy believed, conditions had become worse. He attributed the degenerating situation to public apathy and the failure of various institutions to act against unethical practices or criminal behavior within their ranks. The weak response of major government agencies concerned him. He was shocked to realize how little information the FBI had collected on major crime figures, evidence of the agency's reluctance to take the problem of organized crime seriously. The bureau, he concluded, shied away from difficult cases. Kennedy grew impatient with the Eisenhower Justice Department, which moved slowly in prosecuting cases exposed by the hearings. Only three convictions had been secured during the course of committee's work. Justice Department officials countered that promising cases often unraveled once they were referred to the FBI or the Internal Revenue Service (IRS) for further investigation.[75]

In late summer 1959, Kennedy resigned from the Rackets Committee. Before turning his attention to his brother's campaign, Bobby devoted two months to writing a book about the committee, with John Seigenthaler of the *Nashville Tennessean* serving as a sounding board and editor. *The Enemy Within* was an effort to raise public consciousness about a deeply corrosive problem to which RFK would continue to devote attention.

In the conclusion to his book, Kennedy offered a critique of 1950s America and appealed for a renewal of moral commitment, civic activism, and individual investment in the larger social good:

The paramount interest in self, in material wealth, in security must be replaced by actual, not just vocal, interest in our country, by a spirit of adventure, a will to fight what is evil, and a desire to serve. It is up to us as citizens to take the initiative as it has been taken before in our history, to reach out boldly but with honesty to do things that need to be done.[76]

The spirit Kennedy evoked was stirring on college campuses and in communities across the South. During the hotly contested presidential campaign of 1960, the civil rights movement and Bobby Kennedy's ambitions would converge.

CHAPTER THREE

Faith, Hope, and Politics

||

"THIS MAY BE A SIGNIFICANT STORY in the making," a stringer for *Time* reported on February 1, 1960, from Greensboro, North Carolina. Three days earlier, four freshmen from North Carolina Agricultural and Technical State University had ordered coffee and insisted on being served at the "whites only" lunch counter in Woolworth's. "It is to my knowledge the first time that Negroes have made a mass assault upon downtown segregation, upon privately owned facilities as opposed to schools, libraries, parks, or municipal transit," the young reporter, Simmons Fentress, noted. He advised his editor in New York, "I think you should gather a file on this affair and await developments." There had been sit-in protests in Kansas City, Baltimore, Tulsa, Miami, and other places; but Greensboro would be different.[1]

Like many of his contemporaries, seventeen-year-old Joseph McNeil was fed up with the daily indignities of segregation and the glacial pace of change. He remembered thinking, "I don't want my children exposed to it."[2] McNeil talked with fellow students David Richmond, Franklin McCain, and Ezell Blair, and they decided to stage a protest. On the afternoon of February 1, all four went to the Woolworth's in downtown Greensboro, sat at the lunch counter, and ordered a cup of coffee. When they were refused service, they remained at the counter until the store closed. The next day, they returned with more students and this time filled the seats at the lunch counter. On the third day, several hundred students had crowded around the lunch counter. Their action ignited demonstrations that spread through North Carolina and to towns and cities across the South, as young people opened up a new front in the movement to end the racial caste system.[3] Their determination and courage fostered a new sense of possibility. "We want our rights. We know what they are. We want them now," said Spelman College student Marian Wright.[4]

As the campaign season heated up, news of the sit-ins reverberated across the country. The president of Oberlin College said the protests had brought students together as never before.[5] But many whites sympathized with store owners and felt they had a right to serve, or refuse service to, whomever they pleased. Former president Harry Truman quipped that if he were a store owner, he would run the demonstrators out. While the sit-ins spread, Congress was working on a second civil rights bill, to supplement and strengthen enforcement of the voting rights provisions of the Civil Rights Act of 1957. The bill that passed in the spring allowed the Justice Department to inspect and photograph voting records, but Congress avoided the thorny issue of racial segregation, ignoring the crisis building across the South.[6]

African Americans in northern and midwestern cities, many of them first- and second-generation migrants, were captivated by the growing challenge to Jim Crow segregation. These voters emerged as a strong bloc in northern industrial states, which held a large number of electoral college votes. Blacks were "in the driver's seat," claimed New York's leading Black newspaper, the *New York Amsterdam News,* positioned as never before to decide the outcome of a close contest. Holding on to the support of key southern Democrats while halting the drift of Black voters to the Republican Party presented a monumental challenge for any Democratic presidential hopeful. A candidate's response to developments in the South would be critical. As director of his brother's campaign, Bobby Kennedy cared about one issue: winning. To that end, the highly organized and improvisational political operative carved a fresh path through America's changing racial landscape, with consequences well beyond the ballot box.

A shift of historic proportions had reshaped the nation. In 1910, fewer than 10 percent of Black Americans lived outside the South; by the end of the 1950s, that number was nearly 50 percent. As Black migrants concentrated in cities like Philadelphia, New York, Chicago, Milwaukee, and Detroit, a web of private agreements, bank loan restrictions, and federal lending policies confined these city residents to overcrowded, underserved neighborhoods. Black communities were plagued by high rates of unemployment, poverty, crime, and police harassment. Neighborhood patterns and school district policies meant that Black students were also restricted to inferior, segregated schools. In his famous chronicle of the 1960 presidential campaign, Theodore White described racial conditions in northern urban areas as "explosive," observing that the "violent frontier" of America's race problem had "moved north."[7]

During and immediately after World War II, many whites had abandoned cities for the suburbs. Thanks to federally assisted mortgages and a housing boom, single-family dwellings in homogeneous new communities had become the embodiment of the American dream for an expansive white middle class. The growth of the suburbs was a change "so vast, profound and all embracing," White offered, that the exploration of its political consequences had yet to begin. The dramatic growth of these suburban enclaves extended the separation of the races at a time when the movement to end legally enforced segregation in the South was gathering momentum.

On October 28, 1959, shortly after Bobby Kennedy agreed to lead his brother's campaign, the candidate and his core team met in Hyannis Port, in the living room of Bobby and Ethel's home. Most of the dozen or so who gathered there had been working toward this moment for up to four years, but this was the first time they had all come together in one place. Many were veterans of World War II. None, except the candidate and his brother, had participated in a presidential campaign before. Marjorie Lawson was the only woman in the room and the only African American. Jack Kennedy opened the meeting with a remarkable three-hour long survey of the country, identifying key people and factions in each state. The team then broke the campaign down state by state, assigning each team member to a specific region. It was agreed that detailed reports would be submitted to Bobby following every trip into the field, along with the names of people contacted, to be collected in a massive card file.[8]

The campaign moved aggressively on multiple fronts. At the time, fewer than a third of states held primaries; candidates often skipped primaries because the selection of the nominee was negotiated by powerful party members and settled at the national convention. But for the upstart Kennedy campaign, the primaries offered a critical chance to show that a Catholic candidate could appeal to a cross section of voters. Marjorie Lawson tracked potential Black delegates and advised the campaign on outreach to the Black press and key leaders in various states. Bobby went South, to tackle the region that had become the Achilles' heel of the Democratic Party.[9] He worked through a network of friends to identify likely supporters in each state and measure just how far his brother could push on civil rights. Bobby learned that the powerful Georgia senator Herman Talmadge, son of the notorious white supremacist Eugene Talmadge, was "more flexible than his father" and concluded that the senator would put up a fight but would not desert the party. Bobby found Ernest "Fritz" Hollings, the young governor of South Carolina, to be "extremely friendly." Hollings estimated that JFK could already count on the support of one-third of the delegates in his state but advised that having South Carolina on board too early in the campaign might be harmful. Hollings would be a critical supporter. Governor James Lindsay Almond of Virginia, Bobby reported, was a foe of Senator Harry Byrd's powerful machine and "more moderate on race." Almond was friendly but noncommittal. Steadily, the foundation was being laid for a fresh approach to civil rights.[10]

ON JANUARY 2, 1960, John F. Kennedy announced his candidacy in the Senate caucus room and immediately took to the campaign trail. While his team moved into high gear, with a tight focus on key primary states, his chief rival, Lyndon Johnson, seized the initiative on civil rights in an effort to broaden his national appeal. In mid-February Johnson, who had been Senate majority leader since 1955 and minority leader before that, revived civil rights legislation from the previous session, adding amendments to a Missouri education bill. *Time* magazine anticipated "one of the great debates in the U.S. Senate," one that might affect "the political future of this year's presidential hopefuls, none more so than Johnson himself." Musing on the arc of history, the reporter observed, "one hundred years after the election of Abraham Lincoln to the presidency, the U.S. Congress appears at long last ready to guarantee to the Negro that most powerful of political social weapons, the right to vote."[11]

Civil rights dominated congressional business for two months. Johnson promised meaningful legislation that would "not be punitive" to the South. A backdoor agreement ensured that provisions on school desegregation and job discrimination, included in an earlier version of the bill, would not be revived. The legislation would be limited to voting. Johnson held the Senate in session for thirty days, one of the longest stretches in Senate history. In the heat of a presidential election year, various factions on both sides angled for advantage during a filibuster that "broke all endurance records."[12]

While Senate efforts stalled, the House passed a civil rights bill. Johnson promptly "executed an intricate parliamentary gambit," forcing the House bill through Senator James Eastland's Judiciary Committee in less than a week and on to the full Senate for consideration. LBJ's mastery of the legislative process was on full display as he orchestrated the final shaping of the bill, finessing a stew of competing interests and deftly bypassing the obstruction of filibustering southerners. His close negotiations with Georgia senator Richard Russell produced a bill that southern Democrats would ultimately allow to come to a vote. JFK left the campaign trail long enough to cast his vote on an amended version of the bill on April 8 that passed the Senate 71–18. The changes were approved by the House, and President Eisenhower signed the bill into law on May 6.[13]

In the *New York Times,* Russell Baker described the two-month ordeal leading up to the enactment of the Civil Rights Act of 1960 as "a long process of legislative erosion."[14] The major feature of the final bill was a convoluted plan to establish voting referees in places where it was determined that local officials systematically barred Black citizens from voting. To trigger the referees, prospective voters would have to file a complaint with the Justice Department, which if so inclined could then bring suit under the 1957 Civil Rights Act to obtain an injunction. The US attorney general would then separately ask the federal district court to determine whether there had been a "pattern or practice" of discrimination. If the federal district judge found this to be the case, referees would be selected to determine whether the Black voters in question were qualified under state law. Finally, the judge would issue a certificate entitling them to vote in state and federal elections, with the referee overseeing the process at the polls. Commenting on the bill's main feature, Thurgood Marshall scoffed that "it would take two or three years for a good lawyer to get someone registered under this bill," placing emphasis on the word "good." The NAACP called the bill a "fraud."[15]

New York's Representative Emanuel Celler and other leading supporters of civil rights legislation rationalized that the bill that ultimately passed was "the best one attainable." But most agreed it was a victory for the South. While southern Democrats were becoming increasingly isolated in their uncompromising defense of segregation and states' rights, these politicians' concentrated power, singular focus, and "skillful technique in working with the scalpel" trumped the welter of political factions and interests loosely aligned in support of a more serious civil rights bill. Lyndon Johnson's role in securing passage of the Civil Rights Act did little to distinguish him from the southern bloc and reinforced liberal opposition to his presidential ambitions. But the politics surrounding the passage of the act illuminated the deeper challenges inhibiting meaningful federal action. "The fact is," noted *New York Times* journalist Anthony Lewis, "it would take federal armed force to enfranchise the Negro in the rural South overnight. No one in his right mind thinks such a revival of Reconstruction would constitute progress in race relations."[16]

The legislative dance reflected a general complacency among white Americans about racial conditions in the South. Meanwhile, student protests grew, as young activists showed a faith in civic engagement, despite the seemingly impenetrable barriers to racial change.

———

WITHIN TWO WEEKS of the standoff in Greensboro, Claude Sitton, a correspondent for the *New York Times*, wrote of "a mounting determination" on the part of Black southerners "to use every means at their disposal to bring a speedy end to segregation in all fields." By mid-March, demonstrations had taken place in forty-eight cities in eleven southern states, "setting off a great swell of mass arrests." Two hundred students from six Atlanta colleges staged the first mass sit-in in Georgia. Seventy-seven of them were arrested under a hastily enacted anti-trespassing law. Police gassed marching students in Orangeburg, South Carolina, where 350 protesters were arrested, and there were mass arrests in Rock Hill, South Carolina, where students sought to integrate the public library, the drug store, and the bus terminal. With every new arrest the protests grew. The week President Eisenhower signed the Civil Rights Act into law, *Time* magazine reported, "all over the South, students were on the march last week in a widespread, nonviolent protest, the likes of which the United States has never seen."[17]

The sit-ins broke through the stalemate that had settled over the South in the aftermath of *Brown v. Board of Education.* Five years after the Supreme Court had called for schools to be integrated with "all deliberate speed," fewer than 6 percent of Black children in the South attended desegregated schools. In the Deep South—Alabama, Georgia, Louisiana, Mississippi, and South Carolina—that percentage ranged from 0.1 to 1 percent. The battles would continue to be waged, district by district and state by state. The NAACP was forced into a rearguard action as southern states attempted to drive the organization's members from the region. Robert L. Carter, NAACP lead counsel, opened a new front of legal activism as he fought a bevy of state laws aiming to cripple the organization and harass its members. There was little will or political courage within the ranks of the federal government to confront the South's defiance of the courts.[18]

The protests spread and soon included picket lines, boycotts, marches, and mass meetings. White appeals to prominent Blacks to halt the demonstrations bore little fruit. Black professional and business leaders publicly supported the protests and, in many cases, provided financial assistance. Martin Luther King Jr. observed that it was "enormously unfashionable for a Southern Negro, regardless of his position, to oppose the sit-ins and what the younger members of the race have done these last few months." He credited the success of the movement to its reaffirmation of dignity and use of nonviolent direct action and passive resistance. While Congress dithered over a shrinking civil rights bill that avoided the issue of segregation, the demonstrations in the South offered African Americans a platform to damn segregation as intolerable.[19]

The mass demonstrations left journalists and reporters scrambling to understand what forces had been set loose and what they might mean. Ralph McGill, longtime editor of the *Atlanta Constitution,* described the new turn of events as "guerilla warfare amid the wreckage of that old status quo." Yet these guerilla forces were "orderly and polite," with men sporting shirts and ties, and women in dresses and saddle shoes. Younger reporters dug deeper, seeking to identify the "leaders" of this bewildering assault.[20]

Southern Black colleges seemed to be the epicenter of the movement— places that were almost completely foreign to young white male reporters. It is doubtful that any recognized what was unfolding as a fulfillment of W. E. B. Du Bois's prediction, thirty years earlier, that Black institutions would give the Black community the strength to challenge and ultimately dismantle the barriers to full and equal citizenship. In a special article on "Black College Youth," *Time* magazine noted the independence, lack of fear, and educational attainments of the "young college Negroes now leading" the movement. "Short of closing every Negro college, the South can't crush the challenge presented by young Negro college men and women," the reporter observed. Lonnie King Jr., a student at Morehouse College in Atlanta, commented, "I don't think the young Negro will stop. The movement has become an obsession with too many students. . . . They see equality in sight."[21]

In the spring of 1960, reporters for *Time* attempted to craft a profile of those on the front lines of the protests. They were mostly southern, from both rural and urban backgrounds, and women were well represented. The reporters found "high-achieving" young people who took "tough courses" and were "more mature" than white students their age. Among them were Marion Barry, a graduate student in chemistry at Fisk University; Diane Nash, who was majoring in English at Fisk; Bernard Lee, an Air Force veteran and twenty-four-year old economics major at Alabama State University; and Marian Wright, a social science major at Spelman College.

The twenty-one-year-old daughter of a Baptist minister from Bennettsville, South Carolina, Marian Wright was valedictorian of her class and a leader in the Atlanta student movement. "Without a speck of doubt," Dudley Doust of *Time* observed, she "was the most interesting and articulate student we ran up against." Her visceral account of the cruelties and injustices of segregation must have startled Doust, who was charmed by the attractive, self-confident young woman in the living room of Abby Aldrich Rockefeller Hall, her dormitory at Spelman. She described the Jim Crow South as "an insult" and recounted how she had fought physically with white boys and girls who'd harassed her. When she was ten, she had beaten a boy with a tree branch for calling her a nigger. Her parents, she recalled, worried that she "had too much pride and was riding for a fall." Wright was one of the first to enlist in Atlanta's sit-in movement. The protests absorbed her energies and intellect and elevated her hopes for the South and for the country. She immersed herself in the study of Mahatma Gandhi, whose doctrine of nonviolent resistance became the subject of her senior thesis, and saw the future in a new light: "We've got the struggle ahead, and it is visible for us, and isn't a struggle one of the great things in life?"[22]

The students viewed their protests as principled civic action. "We're filled with theoretical democracy," Marion Barry explained. And "this isn't democracy," he quipped. Bernard Lee recalled that he had been aware of the nation's founding principles ever since he was a child. Educated through text-books "in the foundations of democracy," he said, "we know what we can demand." He clarified that the movement was about much more "than a hot dog and a cup of coffee. We're now involved in the greatest test since the Civil War. Can the nation exist half free and half slave?" For Diane Nash, a transplant from Chicago, the stark realities of Jim Crow segregation had activated her sense of civic responsibility. "In a democracy, every person has a responsibility to make a social system," she said. Nash, described as "a born leader," established contacts with student activists around the South and said, "I'll probably be involved in this, in some way, for the rest of my life." Barry, who planned to spend the summer working on voter registration, expressed great "faith and pride" in the movement's collective strength.[23]

In mid-April, a week after the Senate passed the Civil Rights Act of 1960, Wright, Lee, Nash, and Barry joined three hundred student leaders from across the South at Shaw University in Raleigh, North Carolina. They were responding to an invitation from Martin Luther King Jr. and Ella Baker, a Shaw graduate who was then serving as acting executive director of the Southern Christian Leadership Conference (SCLC), to a conference sponsored by the SCLC. The meeting was Baker's idea. A seasoned activist and former field organizer for the NAACP, Baker believed in the power of community-based organizing to cultivate the power and leadership of ordinary people. Biographer Barbara Ransby explains, "Baker wanted to bring the sit-in participants together in a way that would sustain the momentum of their actions, provide them with much needed skills and resources, and create space for them to coalesce into a new, more militant, yet democratic force." Encouraged by Baker, the young people voted to establish their own organization to give focus and direction to the protests. This was the beginning of the Student Nonviolent Coordinating Committee (SNCC).[24]

Most southerners, Black and white, understood that change was inevitable. But what form would it take? The struggle around school desegregation revealed the lengths to which whites would go to maintain segregation. When a federal court moved to compel school desegregation in Orleans Parish, Louisiana, white parents said by a margin of six to one that they would rather abolish public schools than integrate. When the sit-in protests reached Birmingham in April, they sent "convulsive tremors" through the heavily policed community. Protesting youth were promptly arrested for trespassing. Writing from Birmingham, *New York Times* journalist Harrison Salisbury described a climate of "fear, force and terror, punctuated by striking acts of courage." Birmingham was a raw city where "every inch of middle ground has been fragmented by the emotional dynamite of racism, reinforced by the whip, the gun, the bomb, the torch, the club, the knife, the mob, the police, and many branches of the state's apparatus." A Black woman he interviewed expressed dismay. "I just don't understand the white people around here. They seem to act so crazy. . . . Don't they now there is a limit to what people will stand?"[25]

Longtime civil rights activist Virginia Durr observed developments with apprehension. In the years since *Brown v. Board of Education* and the Montgomery bus boycott, whites had demonstrated a desire to maintain segregation at all costs, while national leadership remained remote. President Eisenhower, who had never publicly endorsed the *Brown* ruling, suggested that Blacks and whites form biracial commissions to work out their differences. On April 7, 1960, two weeks after South African police massacred sixty-nine demonstrators in the Black township of Sharpeville, Durr wrote from Montgomery, Alabama, that "the feeling here is just almost as bad as South Africa." She could not "see any peaceful solution . . . anymore. The police and political powers are not going to give an inch and the Negroes are not going to back down, and I think it will finally have to come to fighting or some kind of violence."[26]

———

FIFTEEN STATES AND THE DISTRICT OF COLUMBIA held primaries in 1960, pitting Jack Kennedy against Hubert Humphrey while Lyndon Johnson, Adlai Stevenson, and Stuart Symington, leading contenders for the Democratic nomination, sat the primary season out. For the youthful Kennedy, the first Catholic to actively seek the presidency since Al Smith's crushing defeat in 1928, the primaries were essential to establish his appeal.[27] Humphrey, the popular liberal senator from Minnesota, wanted to prove his vote-getting ability beyond his home state. A win for Kennedy in Humphrey's neighboring state of Wisconsin on April 5, while devastating for Humphrey, did little to settle the issue of whether Kennedy's faith was a liability, since a large number of Catholic voters were in the six districts he carried. "Damn the religious thing," JFK complained. West Virginia, a state where less than 5 percent of the population was Catholic, would be the ultimate test—the place, in Robert Kennedy's words, where they would "meet the religion issue head on."[28]

The well-financed and carefully calibrated Kennedy campaign faced its greatest challenge in a mostly white, solidly Protestant, impoverished state. Kennedy's Catholicism, Bobby quickly learned, was the main issue on the minds of potential primary voters in a state where Kennedy lagged behind Humphrey by 30 percent points in the polls. For Jack, the fact that an aspect of his personal life over which he had no control could determine his political fate was sobering. Bobby did what he did best, orchestrating a massive on-the-ground effort, with volunteers going door-to-door to introduce wary voters to the young senator and war hero. Meanwhile, Jack barnstormed through the state, meeting with small and large groups. He was exposed to a level of poverty and destitution in the depressed mining towns and hollows that shook him to the core. "Kennedy's shock at the suffering he saw in West Virginia," wrote Theodore White, "was so fresh that it communicated itself with the emotion of original discovery." Seeing the raw face of poverty was, Marjorie Lawson recalled, "a tremendous experience for him." JFK's growing familiarity with West Virginia and its people prepared him to address the issue of his faith with a directness and candor that defused many of the doubts clouding the minds of potential voters.[29]

The issue of civil rights barely registered in the statewide primary races, which were concentrated in midwestern and northern states. In West Virginia, Black protesters picketed Humphrey for dining at the segregated Hotel West Virginia. Humphrey remained silent on the issue, as it promised few dividends in this majority white state, but Bobby made sure that Marjorie Lawson was given room to cultivate the small coterie of Black voters concentrated in the southern part of the state. She organized a campaign appearance at Bluefield State College, a historically Black college with 150 white students. Several hundred mostly Black students crowded into "the grim old gymnasium" to hear Jack Kennedy speak. When he was asked about the sit-in movement, he said that so long as people were able to move freely, "the sit-in seems to me to be in the great tradition of American peaceful protest." In response to a question on school desegregation, Kennedy said that if he were president, he "would make it clear that the 1954 Supreme Court decision is the law of the land and the law is going to be enforced—and not just the law, but the moral spirit of the decision." Lawson recalled that the audience "just loved him." Word of his appearance at Bluefield quickly spread through the state's Black communities.[30]

On May 10, primary day, JFK braced himself for a decisive loss. He returned to Washington to wait out the returns with friends at his Georgetown home, while Bobby was in Charleston. Jack won the primary in a landslide, taking 60.8 percent of the vote and sweeping every part of the state, with more than 95 percent of the vote in every Black precinct in the state. He flew back to West Virginia late that night to celebrate the win. Addressing an enthusiastic crowd in Charleston, JFK declared, with deep satisfaction, "The religious issue was buried here in the soil of West Virginia. I will not forget the people of West Virginia, nor will I forget what I have seen and learned here."[31]

It is striking to consider the circumstances that enabled Jack Kennedy to secure the unlikely victory that paved the way for his insurgent campaign.

Humphrey's failure to take Wisconsin ended his chances of being a serious contender. The most he could hope for by a win in West Virginia was to end Kennedy's quest for the presidency, keeping the door open for the party's favored candidates. In the end, Humphrey provided Kennedy with a chance to prove that his Catholicism was not an obstacle to victory. While there would be other hurdles to clear, Kennedy's success in the primaries gave him a shot at the nomination. Richard Goodwin, a top campaign aide, recalled that while Wisconsin and West Virginia were hardly "typical," "the whole country had watched Kennedy's arduous, thrilling struggle to victory." In the end, Goodwin concluded, the campaign had successfully "used the primaries—hitherto symbolic—to capture the Democratic Party, setting in motion an irreversible change in American politics."[32]

———

BY MAY, ATTENTION SHIFTED TO THE CONVENTION in Los Angeles and what promised to be a major long-term challenge: winning the Black vote. Political commentators predicted that Black voters would be more decisive in 1960 than they had been in 1948, when northern Black voters had helped secure Harry Truman's upset victory. For two decades, the Black vote had been strongly pro-Democratic. But in 1956, there had been a significant shift to Eisenhower. The *Brown* ruling had elevated racial equality over the economic issues that had drawn Black voters to the party of Roosevelt— where, as a key segment of the party's New Deal coalition, they coexisted with southern segregationists. In 1956, Adlai Stevenson, who had remained silent on the federal enforcement of *Brown,* had carried only 64 percent of the Black vote, the lowest percentage for a Democratic presidential candidate since 1928. Four years later, in Illinois, Pennsylvania, New York, and Michigan, with a total of 132 electoral votes—half the number needed to win the election—Black voters were in a position to decide the outcome.[33] A study commissioned by Bobby on the northern Black voter, completed in early May, underscored the critical importance of Black voters, concentrated in large metropolitan areas in delegate-rich northern states. The study concluded that "the current sit-ins plus the riots in South Africa will almost certainly increase the salience of the civil rights issue during the current months." As Murray Kempton wryly observed, the response to the sit-ins had finally managed "to make politicians understand that there are persons to whom this issue means something."[34]

"We're in trouble with the Negroes," Bobby told Harris Wofford, who joined the campaign staff that spring. "We really don't know much about this whole thing." For the previous three years, Marjorie Lawson had worked to introduce John Kennedy to Black leaders and members of the Black press.

She had represented him at major national meetings of Black religious, political, and women's organizations and found that he had "very little factual understanding" of racial realities but was interested in learning. Still, he had done little to distinguish himself on civil rights, and some had serious questions about his commitment.[35]

Kennedy's decision to vote for the jury amendment that had weakened the voting rights provision in the 1957 Civil Rights Act remained a "great stumbling block" to efforts to build Black support. Worse was JFK's association with Alabama governor John Patterson, one of the most notorious segregationists in the country. Shortly after his inauguration as governor in January 1959, Patterson had sought a meeting with Kennedy. The young senator then invited Patterson to an early breakfast meeting at JFK's home in Georgetown, which was how he normally began his day, and Patterson brought along Alabama state senator Sam Engelhardt, head of Alabama's White Citizens' Council. Kennedy thought nothing of meeting with a governor and did not know Engelhardt, and the meeting had escaped the attention of the mainline press. But the visit set off alarm bells among African Americans. When Patterson announced his support for Kennedy's presidential bid, one could easily infer that a deal had been made. Patterson's endorsement remained a burning issue in the spring of 1960. "It is very difficult for thoughtful Negro voters to feel ease over the endorsement of Senator Kennedy by Governor James Patterson of Alabama," said Roy Wilkins, head of the NAACP. Jackie Robinson predicted that Kennedy would get "fewer Negro votes than any Democrat ever."[36]

By 1960, evidence suggests that John Kennedy had studied the issues raised by the civil rights movement. That spring, at Kennedy's invitation, Thurgood Marshall, the nation's leading civil rights lawyer, met with him in his Senate office for lunch. They spent most of the afternoon together and had, in Marshall's words, "a frank discussion." Kennedy "knew all of the problems" concerning voting and registration, with "the figures to back it up," Marshall recalled. Kennedy had "a full grasp of the school situation," and he understood the issue "from both sides." By the end of the afternoon, Marshall said, "I had no doubt at all that he was committed to the general principles involving civil rights—the equality of all Americans. . . . It would be pretty hard to talk to him and not get that impression." Marshall left the meeting convinced that Kennedy "would put that above the normal political leanings of a candidate." And that commitment, along with JFK's Catholicism, was why "I was not too certain he would be elected." As director of the NAACP Legal Defense Fund, Marshall could not publicly endorse a candidate. But he talked with people privately and shared his feelings.[37]

As campaign strategist, Robert Kennedy was determined to win the trust and support of Black voters in the North and South, even at the risk of white defections. Harris Wofford would play a critical role in that effort. Wofford was a rare breed among white liberals, one whose politics, as Black journalist Louis Martin put it, "developed out of new, strongly held convictions rather than some vague liberal sentiment." Born in New York in 1926 to a wealthy southern family, Wofford embraced the "one world" philosophy championed by 1940 presidential candidate Wendell Willkie during the war. After graduating from the University of Chicago in 1948, Wofford spent eight months in India studying Gandhi's life and philosophy, after which he attended Howard University School of Law to study civil rights law. Wofford made several trips to the South during this time, visiting the Highlander Folk School in Tennessee and writing a thesis titled "The Status of the Negro in Dallas County, Alabama." Wofford sought out Martin Luther King Jr. during the Montgomery bus boycott and helped arrange King's first visit to India early in 1959. Two years earlier, Wofford had accepted a position on the US Commission on Civil Rights, and he edited its first report on the state of race relations across the country. Wofford was teaching law at the University of Notre Dame when he was asked to join the Kennedy campaign as a speechwriter.[38]

Bobby had enlisted Wofford to serve as the coordinator of what would become the "Civil Rights Section" of the campaign. But first and foremost, Kennedy urged Wofford to "tell us where we are in all this" and to do "everything you can to deliver every Negro delegate going to the convention." JFK's efforts to secure the support of two leading Black Americans, baseball hero Jackie Robinson and Congressman Adam Clayton Powell, had been a disappointment. Robinson favored Humphrey and was a vocal opponent of Kennedy's, and Powell slammed JFK's record on civil rights and indicated he was leaning toward Lyndon Johnson. Both Wofford and Harry Belafonte advised Kennedy that the person he should really be focused on was Martin Luther King Jr. Not yet well known among white Americans—the *New York Times* identified him as "the young Negro minister who led the bus boycott in Montgomery, Alabama"—King had emerged as the voice of the protest movement.[39]

Margaret Lawson had been trying to arrange a meeting between King and JFK since the fall of 1958, but her efforts had been frustrated by the pair's travel schedules. Now, a meeting with King became a priority, and Wofford succeeded in setting one up on June 23 in New York. King went in thinking that the young senator lacked depth, but after meeting with him alone for an hour and a half over breakfast, King's opinion changed considerably. He reported to his friend Chester Bowles, the congressman and former governor of Connecticut who had served as ambassador to India, that the two had had "a fruitful and rewarding conversation." They talked about the sit-in movement, King later recalled, and Kennedy explained how the protests "had caused him to re-evaluate his thinking" about the injustices and indignities Blacks faced all over the South. King was "impressed with his concern and his willingness to learn."[40]

Later that day, in a speech to ambassadors from African countries, Kennedy made his strongest endorsement of the sit-in movement to date, describing the protests as "a sign that the American spirit is coming alive again." He acknowledged that "unrest and turmoil and tension" were "part of the price of change" and said "the fact that people were peacefully protesting the denial of their rights was not something to be lamented." In a clear contrast to Truman, who claimed that communists were behind the sit-ins, Kennedy said it was in the American tradition to stand up for one's rights, "even if the new way to stand up for one's rights is to sit down." He embraced the broad goals of the movement, calling for "equal access to the voting booth, to the classroom, to jobs, to housing and to public facilities, including lunchrooms."[41]

Kennedy dropped a bombshell in a meeting with the Liberal Party of New York that evening, telling the group he hoped to win the Democratic nomination without a single southern vote. The convention was now in less than three weeks. Jack had said what Bobby knew to be true, but Bobby dashed off a memo advising him to clarify his statement and to say "that you feel that you will be nominated without Southern votes, not that you are not interested in having votes in the South." Pierre Salinger followed up, telling the press that Senator Kennedy had merely intended to describe the facts, as almost all of the delegates from the South were committed to Lyndon Johnson.[42]

———

MARION BARRY, head of what was still considered the "temporary" Student Nonviolent Coordinating Committee, arrived in Los Angeles by train several days before the start of the Democratic National Convention. The sit-ins had established civil rights as a dominant issue in the presidential campaign, but SNCC remained a fledgling group, operating with one paid staff member out of a corner of the Southern Christian Leadership Conference office in Atlanta, where Ella Baker was serving her final days as acting executive secretary. With Baker's encouragement, Barry went to Los Angeles to join the leaders of established civil rights organizations in demanding that the Democratic convention take a strong stand in support of civil rights. As Julian Bond recalled, "we wanted them to know that *we* were the people who were causing all of the trouble, that *we* were the ones sitting in and getting arrested, that *we* were the ones running the boycotts."[43]

The Black population of Los Angeles had increased more than fivefold since 1940 to number close to a half million people, partly as a result of the explosive growth of defense production during the war. Many residents were crowded into segregated neighborhoods in South Central Los Angeles and the Watts neighborhood and were confined to low-paying, physically demanding jobs. Their children attended poor, segregated schools, and law enforcement officers were often perceived as an occupying force. These conditions made for a potent brew. But racial conditions in Los Angeles remained largely invisible to the delegates, reporters, and spectators drawn to the downtown section of the sprawling city.

The big story going into the convention was John F. Kennedy, whose campaign had taken the party establishment by storm. Theodore White observed that a generational shift was on display in Los Angeles. Bobby Kennedy, at thirty-four, presided over an inner circle of supporters in their mid-thirties to early forties, most of whom were veterans. They made for a lean, coolly confident, tightly organized force. Riding on their sweep of primary victories, the tough, young, determined, and dynamic political campaign operation seemed to be ushering in a new era.[44]

In a sharp reversal from 1956, when southern Democrats had provided the strongest base of support for Kennedy's vice presidential bid, JFK was now angling to win the nomination without southern delegates. Bobby's personal relationship with key party leaders had convinced him that southern Democrats would not bolt if a strong civil rights plank were adopted. Looking to November, he had concluded that the northern Black vote would be critical to victory and that his brother would have to take an aggressive stand on civil rights if the slide of Black voters to the Republican Party were to be reversed. Kennedy was the only candidate to run what Anthony Lewis described as "a full scale civil rights operation" at the convention, which included informal breakfast meetings with "rights conscious" delegates and the "constant button holing" of delegates by civil rights advocates friendly to the senator. The party platform would be a test of how far the Democratic party would go in aligning itself with the cause of civil rights.[45]

It was Kennedy's good fortune that Chester Bowles had been appointed head of the platform committee the previous spring. Bowles was determined that the platform would break from the past and offer more than an exercise in vague generalities. He wanted to develop a document that would offer "a fresh statement of Franklin Roosevelt's Four Freedoms in the context of 1960" and hoped to make specific recommendations for how the country could move forward in key areas of domestic and foreign policy. Under

Bowles, the preparation of the party platform became a more public exercise than it had ever been before. The committee sponsored a series of regional hearings that spring, culminating with three days of public hearings in Los Angeles just before the start of the convention on July 11.[46]

Civil rights, by far the most contentious issue, was left to the third and final day of the hearings. A joint statement by Martin Luther King Jr. and Black union leader and activist A. Philip Randolph included ten specific recommendations for federal action "to meet the just and insistent demands of the Negro people for free and unconditional citizenship." Marion Barry appealed for support of the sit-ins and challenged critics who accused the students of being inspired by communism. "The ache of every man to touch his potential is the throb that beats out the truth of the American Declaration of Independence and the Constitution," he said, linking the protests to America's founding principles. Meanwhile, UAW leader Walter Reuther demanded a pledge of "unequivocal support" for the Supreme Court's desegregation decisions."[47]

Southerners on the committee warned that advocating "extreme" action on civil rights threatened to drive the South from the party. Florida senator Spessard Holland advised, "You can put in generalities, but don't be specific," sparking laughter from the audience and chants of "No! No!" In a message to the committee, Robert Kennedy confirmed that his brother would "insist" on "more precise" language. Appeals for moderation and party unity were as far as the southern representatives would go in this public forum, not wanting to jeopardize the candidacy of Lyndon Johnson. Mrs. Vel Phillips of Wisconsin, the first African American to sit on the Democratic platform committee, asked how the United States could command "the respect of the world if we adopt a weak civil rights plank." Speaking for white southerners, Holland responded that the Democrats could not expect to win in November if "you adopt a plank that flaunts the traditions and experiences of the fifty million people of the South." Phillips countered, "We aren't winning at all if we don't win right." The lines were drawn: the battle would continue behind closed doors.[48]

Bowles asked Harris Wofford to prepare a draft of the civil rights plank. Bowles suggested that Wofford go for a "maximum plank" that "says everything we can think of that we ought to do, and we'll negotiate as much of it as we can." Wofford included all the recommendations of the 1960 *Report of the US Commission on Civil Rights,* which he had edited, and more. He had spoken in general terms with Bobby Kennedy, who indicated that he wanted a strong civil rights plank, but Wofford did not expect Kennedy to approve such a bold agenda and was prepared to trim and revise. At breakfast the day before presenting the final draft to the platform committee,

Bowles insisted that Bobby read the civil rights plank. Bobby glanced at it but did not comment.[49]

The next morning, Wofford joined the campaign workers crowded into Suite 8315 of the Biltmore Hotel for their daily briefing from Bobby Kennedy. The campaign manager made an "electric impression" at these daily meetings, recalled Arthur Schlesinger—"a slight and boyish figure, jacket off, tie loose, climbing on a chair to call his troops to order, stating the tasks of the day with a singular combination of authority, incisiveness, humor and charm." On July 12 he began the day's instructions by telling his team to support "the full Bowles" draft of the platform. He described it as "the best civil rights plank the Democratic party has ever had" and instructed them to be clear that Jack Kennedy was "unequivocally" for it. When the group broke out into loud applause, Bobby repeated, "Remember, all the way with the Bowles platform." As Wofford later wrote, "the strongest new momentum for Kennedy among Black voters came from an uncoordinated combination of Chester Bowles and Bob Kennedy on the platform."[50]

Later that day, the committee ignored the doomsday warnings of the party's southern members and endorsed the civil rights plank, with only minor changes. The *New York Times* called it "astonishing," describing what had happened as a "major shift" for the Democratic Party. The civil rights section of the platform was four times as long as it had been in 1956—when it was "a pallid six paragraphs," as Anthony Lewis had then noted—and included specific recommendations in a pledge to use federal power to end all forms of discrimination. On the subject of school desegregation, the civil rights plank declared that a new Democratic administration would use its full powers to ensure "the beginning of good-faith compliance with the Constitutional requirement that racial segregation be ended in public education" and proposed that all school districts affected by the *Brown* ruling "submit a plan for providing for at least first-step compliance by 1963." The platform asserted that the attorney general would use the full powers of the Civil Rights Acts of 1957 and 1960 to secure the right to vote for all Americans and stipulated that if these proved inadequate, further powers would be sought. The civil rights plank also stated that a Democratic administration would support federal legislation to establish a Fair Employment Practices Committee, "the reddest of flags that could be waved in front of the South," wrote Lewis. "The time has come to assure equal access to all areas of community life," the platform concluded, "including voting booths, school rooms, jobs, housing and public facilities."[51]

In a notable departure, the platform observed that "in every city and state in greater or lesser degree there is discrimination based on color, race, religion or national origin." While "discrimination in voting, education, the administration of justice or segregated lunch counters" were issues in one part of the country, "discrimination in housing and employment may be pressing questions elsewhere." No one was in doubt about the challenge of realizing the ambitious goals outlined in the platform. Efforts to achieve these changes would require "executive orders, legal actions brought by the Attorney General, legislation and improved Congressional procedures to safeguard majority rule," the platform acknowledged, a veiled reference to the way southerners had relied on the filibuster to derail effective civil rights legislation.

Passed on the eve of the vote to nominate the Democratic candidate, the platform laid bare the party's divisions. Leading southern Democrats damned the civil rights plank as an effort to implement "government enforced social equality" and warned that it was "a calculated effort . . . by the radicals" to force the South to desert the Democratic Party. Senator Strom Thurmond called it "the most extreme, unconstitutional and anti-southern [measure] ever conceived by any major political party," saying that "even the NAACP, for all its fervor, has never proposed more drastic steps." The *New York Times* concluded that the plank marked an effort "to attract the largest possible Northern Negro vote in November." African American leaders and spokespersons, while recognizing the limited reach of a party platform, saw the civil rights plank as a major development. Roy Wilkins marveled, "they gave us all we asked." According to the *Chicago Defender,* the platform "apparently went beyond the expectations of Negro leaders." Journalist and political operative Louis Martin observed, "Even the most cynical . . . must admit that a forthright, strong civil rights plank is a giant step in the right direction."[52]

The final test of the Kennedy operation would come the following day, with the first roll call vote. A first-ballot win, Bobby contended, was essential in the face of a still active opposition. The coalition to stop Kennedy, led by party luminaries like Eleanor Roosevelt and Harry Truman, had disintegrated in the face of "an electronic age steamroller," as Russell Baker described it, "that crunched systematically against the old-fashioned, disordered opposition on the convention floor." But nothing had been left to chance. Dry runs had tested a floor operation dedicated to keeping tabs on delegates and coping with any unexpected turn of events. An elaborate system of phone banks and walkie-talkies allowed for instant communications, linking campaign workers assigned to state delegations with a floor general and with the communications center; from there, lines reached JFK in his private hideaway and at the presidential suite. Bobby served as a roving patrol. His careful tabulations had predicted a win on the first ballot. Wyoming put Kennedy over the top. In the end, he took 806 votes. The closest competitor was Lyndon Johnson, with 409.[53]

After winning the long-sought prize, the Kennedy campaign seemed to stumble in the face of its first major decision: the selection of a running mate. Much has been written about what transpired over the next twenty-four hours. What seems clear is that John Kennedy offered the number two spot to Lyndon Johnson in a pro forma manner, assuming that the Senate Majority leader would not accept. When he did, Jack and Bobby spent hours agonizing over what to do. It was, Bobby recalled, "the most indecisive time we ever had." During an uphill fight for the nomination, Johnson's contempt for Kennedy's youth and inexperience spilled out into a series of vicious personal attacks on Kennedy and his father, whom LBJ accused of being a Nazi sympathizer. And JFK's liberal base was staunchly united against LBJ. But Johnson offered an opportunity to hold onto key southern states. Acting as his brother's emissary, Bobby visited Johnson's suite twice: once to determine whether he really did want to be vice president and the second time to try to persuade Johnson to withdraw from consideration on political grounds. When an emotional Johnson insisted that he wanted to be vice president and would make a strong fight with JFK to win in November, Bobby realized that there was no turning back. Later that evening, Joe Kennedy consoled his sons. "Don't worry, Jack," he said. "Within two weeks they'll be saying it's the smartest thing you ever did."[54]

It did not take that long. Kennedy's selection was immediately hailed as a brilliant political move, viewed by seasoned reporters and opinion writers as one more example of the boldness and precision of the Kennedy campaign. William Nunn of the *Pittsburgh Courier*, one of the most widely read Black newspapers in the country, observed that after the Kennedy team had forced "a militant civil rights plank" down "the gagging throats of the South," they had to make peace with the southern Democrats immediately. The choice of Johnson, who represented southern solidarity at the convention, "swept away" doubts about the region's loyalty in November, according to *New York Times* reporter Claude Sitton. James Reston described Kennedy as "cool and tough in the face of anti-LBJ liberals," demonstrating good sense as well as good politics. Reston anticipated a revised and modernized version of Franklin Roosevelt's winning coalition.

Leading Black newspapers joined in praising the dexterity of the Kennedy team. A rejuvenated Democratic Party emerged from Los Angeles, noted the *Chicago Defender*, with "youth, vigor, brains and political savvy." Now that Kennedy had prevented a full-scale southern revolt, wrote Nunn in the *Pittsburgh Courier*, it would be up to him to sell the ticket to Black voters and the rest of the country in the months leading up to the election.[55]

CHAPTER FOUR

Black Votes

|||

RACE DOMINATED ONE OF THE most closely fought presidential elections in American history. Since the historic crossover of Black voters to the party of Franklin Roosevelt in the mid-1930s, the growing number of northern Black voters had shifted the balance of national politics. As the civil rights movement secured gains through the courts, the power of white southerners in the Democratic Party was on full display in the struggle around the *Brown v. Board of Education* ruling and the Civil Rights Acts of 1957 and 1960. In 1960, a year marked by shifting political alliances, both parties reckoned with two constituencies that crystallized America's racial divide: the white South, bulwark of racial segregation, and emboldened African Americans demanding racial equality and full citizenship rights.

By the time the Republican Party gathered in Chicago in July, it was left to Vice President Richard Nixon, who was running uncontested, to mediate between the conservative wing of the party, anxious to build on recent gains among white southern voters, and the eastern liberal wing, dominated by New York governor Nelson Rockefeller. Dedicated to curbing the power of the federal government, the Republican Party would appear to many a natural home for white southerners determined to preserve state sovereignty in the area of race relations. This in any case was how Barry Goldwater and his supporters saw it, insisting that securing southern votes was the surest road to victory.

Key liberal Republicans, proud of the fact that the party could claim credit for the first major civil rights legislation since Reconstruction, pushed for a different course. Following his own inclination and yielding to pressure from Rockefeller, Nixon endorsed a plank that matched the Democrats' in its call for federal enforcement of equal rights. As vice president, Nixon was closely associated with Eisenhower's relatively progressive record on civil rights and saw an opportunity to expand on Republican inroads among

northern Black voters. But as the campaign ground on, Nixon would equiv-
ocate, seeing greater promise south of the Mason-Dixon Line.[1]

Political calculations, strategic considerations, and a growing awareness
of racial conditions aligned as Bobby Kennedy immersed himself in the final
fifteen weeks of the campaign. As he presided over expanded efforts to build
support among Black voters, his impatience with the tight hold of southern
Democrats on the political and legislative process became more pronounced.
His political instincts and his orientation to the future enabled him to grasp
the power of Black demands for civil rights and racial justice at a crucial
juncture.

The Kennedy campaign's efforts to cultivate Black support intensified now
that the ticket was set. At the close of the convention, Jack Kennedy met
with more than one hundred Black delegates and political leaders and introduced Lyndon Johnson to the group. In a meeting covered by the press,
Johnson pledged his unconditional support for the bold civil rights plank in
the platform. Soon after the convention, the candidate announced the official establishment of a civil rights section of the campaign. This would not
be merely a "minorities" section, dedicated to turning out the Black vote.
Instead, "Negroes," the founding statement declared, would be "integrated
on a functional basis into all parts of the campaign."[2]

The Kennedy campaign reached out to Durham-based businessman John
Wheeler and civil rights attorney Earl Dickerson of Chicago to help with
fundraising efforts as well as appeals to Black voters. Harry Belafonte, one
of the most popular Black celebrities of the day, was featured in a "Citizens
for Kennedy" television ad. At the same time, the civil rights section would
"include people of all races" and focus on the broad range of problems involving race in America. Staff members and volunteers would help shape the
campaign's approach while promoting voter registration, enlisting leaders of
the Black community, and publicizing the positions of the candidate. The
civil rights section would focus attention not only on the South but also on
pivotal northern urban areas, recognizing that Black voters had a growing role
to play in shoring up support.[3]

Marjorie Lawson was named director of the civil rights section, although
it quickly became clear that Sargent Shriver and Harris Wofford were in
charge. Shriver, married to Bobby's sister Eunice, had been head of the Catholic Interracial Council in Chicago in the late 1950s. Frank Reeves, a Black
Washington attorney who had previously worked with Hubert Humphrey,
also joined the effort and traveled with John Kennedy on his campaign trips.
Early in August, in an effort to build on established contacts, Reeves accompanied Bobby Kennedy; Congressman Frank Thompson Jr., chief of the
Democratic Party's voter registration drive; and several other national party

officials. "Here for the first time," Marjorie Lawson commented, "a candidate had made a staff and funds available in recognition of Negro voters and had helped them organize and get out the vote." The Democratic Party under Kennedy, predicted Earl Brown of the *Amsterdam News,* would once again "give Negroes a feeling of belonging."[4]

The Kennedy campaign enlisted some of the most experienced Black political activists and civil rights advocates in its effort to reach Black voters. Oliver Hill, a World War II veteran and the NAACP's lead attorney in the Prince Edward County school case that was one of the five cases in *Brown v. Board of Education,* volunteered to help register and organize Black voters in the South. Franklin Williams, also a war veteran, who had been NAACP field director for the West Coast, took a leave from his position as California's assistant attorney general to work with Black churches to organize a major get-out-the-vote effort in hard-to-reach areas. But arguably the most important of the new recruits was Louis Martin, a seasoned Black journalist who joined the Civil Rights section as the campaign's liaison to the Black press.[5]

Born in Savannah in 1912, Martin attended Fisk University and the University of Michigan before working briefly as a journalist for the *Chicago Defender.* He then moved to Detroit to head up the *Michigan Chronicle,* serving as its first editor and publisher. In 1941, Martin played an important role in the successful effort to open the UAW to Black workers. His initiation to Democratic Party politics came under the tutelage of William Dawson, a longtime congressman and Black power broker from Chicago. As assistant publicity director for the Democratic National Committee (DNC), Martin helped support FDR's reelection. After the war, Martin went into business and served as president of National Newspaper Publishers Association, an organization of Black publishers. In 1960 he was working for the BBC in Nigeria and returned just in time to attend the Democratic National Convention. Early in August, Sargent Shriver invited him to a meeting in Washington, DC. Martin agreed to join the civil rights section on a part-time basis, commuting several days a week from Chicago to Washington. He quickly proved indispensable and joined the campaign staff full-time in DC.

Within the narrow window of time leading up to Election Day, Martin played a major role in building on the groundwork laid by Marjorie Lawson, whom he described as "very effective." His first words of advice were that the DNC pay its debt from the 1956 campaign of more than $45,000 in advertising bills from Black newspapers. He worked tirelessly to cultivate publishers, editors, and opinion writers, telling them about Kennedy's positions on civil rights issues, publicizing JFK's appearances, and ensuring full and

fair coverage for the candidate. In the process, Martin built a strong relationship between the campaign and Black news and media outlets. Wofford
and Shriver marveled at his political savvy and connections and his knowledge of the inner workings of Black politics and civic engagement. "He became our chief counselor, colleague, and co-conspirator," Wofford recalled.[6]

Martin was on the job for more than a month before he was introduced
to Robert Kennedy at a meeting of the civil rights section. He remembered
his first impression: "a wiry young man" who "looked like a college freshman"
and exuded a kind of "human electricity." Kennedy opened the meeting by
asking each person to report on exactly what he or she was doing. He grew
impatient as one after another recited vague generalities and briskly said these
efforts were not enough. Martin took exception. "Having been out of the
country," he later recalled, "I was not aware of the legend that surrounded
Bobby Kennedy." When Bobby turned to him, Martin spelled out exactly
what he was doing boldly—apparently a little too boldly. Shriver and Wofford interrupted, saying, "You know this man is from Chicago." Martin was
unfazed. He pointed out that there were critical things only a campaign manager could do, and Kennedy had failed to do them. For instance, RFK had
yet to meet William Dawson. The seventy-four-year old Dawson was the
longest-serving Black political leader in Congress, a powerful figure in Chicago, and a leader of Black Democrats since the 1940s.[7]

As the meeting came to an end, John Seigenthaler asked Martin to stay
behind, saying that Kennedy wanted to talk with him. In their private
meeting, Martin did not hold back. He wondered out loud if the campaign
really wanted the Black vote. "If you want it, you can get it, but you're going
to have to work for it," he said, "you're going to have to fight for it, and you're
going to have to spend money." Martin understood that the campaign was
focused on reaching out to the younger leadership, and the two men discussed the importance of getting as close to a commitment as possible from
Martin Luther King Jr. But he felt it was unwise to discount establishment
figures like Dawson. "We needed everybody," he said, the old guard as well
as the new. To his surprise, Kennedy "took it all in very good spirits," and
their relationship "was beautiful from that moment on." Soon after the
meeting, Kennedy asked Martin to arrange a meeting with Dawson. For the
remainder of the campaign, Bobby would call Martin directly. They talked
frequently and worked closely together. Kennedy later told Anthony Lewis,
"Louie Martin was the best, had the best judgment." No one else came close.[8]

While Bobby focused on ways to reach Black voters, Jack Kennedy and
Lyndon Johnson secured grudging support from several leading southern
Democrats. Alabama's Governor Patterson stood alone in claiming that the
JFK-LBJ ticket was "one of the strongest in the history of the Democratic

Party." Senator James Eastland made an appeal for party unity, arguing that southern control of major committee chairmanships was the best line of defense in the fight to preserve segregation. He warned that the South "would collapse like a house of cards" if these positions were lost. Such concerns, along with efforts by Kennedy and Johnson to mend fences with key southern representatives, bore fruit. Kennedy enlisted his old friend Senator George Smathers of Florida to serve as the campaign coordinator for the southern states. Smathers accepted, but not without blasting the civil rights plank as "obnoxious and unrepresentative." Still, Smathers believed the Democratic Party would serve the interests of Florida and the nation better than the Republican Party would. Lister Hill of Alabama promised to work for the ticket but publicly deplored its civil rights platform. Senator Olin Johnston and Governor Fritz Hollings of South Carolina and Senator Russell Long of Louisiana were among the high-profile endorsers. Senator Richard Russell of Georgia led the "hold-outs," which included Senator Harry Byrd and Representative Howard Worth Smith of Virginia and Senator Strom Thurmond of South Carolina.[9]

Bobby Kennedy was less accommodating. Appearing on a late-night talk show in New York City at the end of August, he let loose with a blunt attack on two of the most powerful figures in Congress: Senator Harry Byrd, chair of the Finance Committee, and Congressman Smith of Virginia, chair of the Rules Committee. His comments were prompted by a question from host Dave Barry about legislation Senator Kennedy had sponsored in a special session of Congress that summer, which would have provided medical care for the aged, increased the minimum wage, and offered federal aid for education. The bills were defeated by conservative Republicans and southern Democrats. RFK allowed that the Democratic Party had to take responsibility for those in its ranks who had voted against these progressive measures—policies that, he maintained, had the support of the great majority of the American people and of their representatives in Congress. He singled out Howard Smith of Virginia, who, by virtue of his position as head of the House Rules Committee, often blocked bills from coming to a vote. "It's just a deplorable situation," Bobby said, that one man could deny Congress the opportunity to vote on legislation that, in this case, would have benefited the entire country. When asked what JFK planned to do in response, Bobby said that Jack would take the issue to the American people and pledge to fight for change as president of the United States.[10]

In the localized media world of 1960, Bobby Kennedy might not have thought that comments made on a midnight radio show broadcast on a local New York station could find their way to Virginia. But he soon received notice that Representative Smith was deeply offended. Bobby promptly wrote the congressman that he was sorry his comments had "become a source of personal annoyance," assuring Smith that it was certainly not intended. But, Bobby went on to say, "I have very strong feelings for our own survival and the survival of our children that this country must have internal strength." Referring specifically to the legislation that would have provided federal aid to education, he noted that he had visited more than one hundred high schools and colleges over the previous year and realized how much help was needed in this area. "I feel the people acting through the government must assist in this area," he wrote, "and in this field as others I think members of Congress should at least have the right to vote one way or another. This is legislation that may well affect the destiny of our country and should be considered by our representatives. These are my convictions and I have no apologies to make for them." He concluded by saying that he very much regretted "having personally offended you and realize that you began your service to this country long before I was born."[11]

Smith was hardly placated. In his return letter he acknowledged Kennedy's "thoughtfulness" in writing but said that Kennedy had failed to refute widely circulated reports that he had "accused me of deliberately sabotaging legislation." Smith did not appreciate being put in "the role of whipping boy for all the disgruntled elements who are unhappy that the American people have not embraced more readily the ultraliberal platform adopted at Los Angeles." Such an attack, in a close presidential race, was "untimely" and not the best way of "winning friends and influencing people." Smith ultimately obtained a transcript of Kennedy's interview on the Dave Barry show and sent relevant excerpts from the interview along with copies of his correspondence with Kennedy to all southern representatives in Congress.

"We're with you all the way," wrote Harry Dent, assistant to Strom Thurmond. Future Supreme Court Justice Lewis Powell, then serving as chair of the school board of Richmond, Virginia, charged that Kennedy's attack seemed to go "far beyond the usual excesses of campaign oratory" and reported that Bobby's statements were being incorporated into the campaign literature of the "Democrats for Nixon / Lodge" group. In a weak effort at damage control, JFK apologized for his brother's statement when asked about it during a meeting with Florida and South Carolina Democrats, saying that Bobby was "young and very hot-headed."[12]

Constant travel for the campaign opened Robert Kennedy's eyes to aspects of American life that had been invisible to him previously, engaging his interest and curiosity. Scott Peek, assistant to Senator George Smathers, recalled a campaign trip to Savannah that fall. When they arrived at the airport, Bobby asked their advance man if the route to the hotel was through the predominantly Black section of the city. That was not the plan. At his insistence, and to Peek's great annoyance, the trip was rerouted. When they arrived at the De Soto Hotel, he asked Peek how many Black people would attend. "I knew we weren't going to have any because that hotel did not have Blacks back in those days," Peek recalled. None, he said. As Peek later recalled, Bobby said, "Well, we're not going to have the dinner unless you get some Blacks there, okay?" Peek spoke with the management, which agreed to make an exception, and several Black people attended the event. He added that Bobby "was very difficult to work with, very difficult."[13]

The protests across the South had opened new possibilities for mobilizing Black voters in the region, particularly in urban areas—and Bobby was obviously aware of these possibilities. Beyond the short-term need to mobilize votes to win in November, he was beginning to see how southern Black voters could play a key role in liberalizing the Democratic Party, with important consequences for leadership of Congress. Developments parallel to the presidential campaign were laying groundwork for the voting rights struggles that would soon gain critical momentum.

———

ON JULY 4, 1960, Robert P. Moses, a twenty-five-year-old high school math teacher in New York City, got off a bus in Atlanta, Georgia. He had come to Atlanta to "see the movement for myself," as he put it. Bob Moses may have seemed an unlikely recruit in the burgeoning southern struggle. A graduate of Hamilton College with a master's degree in philosophy from Harvard University, he had grown up in Harlem, where he was born two months before the 1935 Harlem riot, a conflict ignited by poor conditions, race discrimination, and abusive policing. His grandfather, William H. Moses, had come to New York from Virginia and was a prominent Garveyite minister. Bob's parents had instilled values of racial pride and social awareness in their son and emphasized the importance of education.

After attending a segregated public school in Harlem, Moses had been accepted at the highly competitive Stuyvesant High School in lower Manhattan. He then went to Hamilton College, a prestigious liberal arts college in upstate New York, on a scholarship, one of three African Americans in a student body of 750. Moses was interested in philosophy, particularly existentialism, and drawn to social justice, nonviolence, and pacifism. In 1956, he began his doctoral studies in philosophy at Harvard, but a few months after earning his master's degree, his forty-three-year-old mother died suddenly, and his father suffered a mental breakdown. Bob returned home to care for his father and took a job teaching math at Horace Mann School.[14]

The sit-in movement that had begun in Greensboro, North Carolina, in February 1960 galvanized young African Americans across the country, and Bob Moses was no exception. He later recalled his reaction to the photographs of students sitting in at lunch counters: "they looked how I felt." He was "struck by the determination on their faces. They weren't cowed or apathetic," he said. "I simply had to get involved." Over spring vacation, he visited his father's brother, William Moses, a professor at Hampton University in Virginia. When he saw people picketing at the local Woolworth's, he joined in. "From the first time a Negro gets involved in white society," he mused much later, "he [starts] repressing, repressing, repressing. My whole reaction through life to such humiliation was to avoid it, keep it down, hold it in, play it cool. . . . But when you do something personally to fight prejudice, there is a feeling of great relief." Moses returned to New York to finish out the school year. He volunteered at the Southern Christian Leadership Conference's New York office and, once school was out, took a bus to Atlanta hoping to work with Martin Luther King Jr.'s organization for the summer.[15]

In the space of two short months, Bob Moses's life was transformed. It was not long before he would become a formative figure of the civil rights movement. The summer began inauspiciously in the small three-room office that served as SCLC headquarters and accommodated the Student Nonviolent Coordination Committee's sole paid staff member, Jane Stembridge. This was hardly the center of activity Moses had imagined. He made himself useful stuffing envelopes and joined the occasional picket line. He soon developed a close relationship with Stembridge and found a kindred spirit in Ella Baker, whose approach to grassroots organizing and social activism resonated with him.

Early in August, Stembridge suggested that he travel through the Deep South to recruit participants for a SNCC conference later that fall. Moses jumped at the chance. Julian Bond and other young SNCC volunteers were awestruck at the courage of this stranger from New York, heading alone into the heart of the Jim Crow South. For three weeks, SNCC's first field representative went by bus through Alabama, Mississippi, and Louisiana, following up on contacts Ella Baker had made in the region.

Moses felt a deep affinity for the people he met, from urban rebels like Fred Shuttlesworth in Birmingham to the resisters dotting the poverty-stricken landscapes of the Mississippi Delta. Amzie Moore, a World War II veteran and seasoned political activist based in Cleveland, Mississippi, helped Moses understand the nature of the struggle in this desperately poor, majority Black region, where fewer than 5 percent of African Americans were registered to vote. Moses spent nearly a week with Moore, listening, touring neighboring towns, learning the history, and meeting locals. In the Delta, the integration of school and public facilities was not the primary concern. People wanted first and foremost to secure the right to vote.

The near total disfranchisement of Black Mississippians was a stunning revelation to Moses—especially in light of America's pointed Cold War propaganda about the suppression of democracy in Eastern Europe. Moses marveled at the patient struggles of those working their way through citizenship schools to prepare for the voter registration test and of those helping men and women to register in the face of terror and economic intimidation. Through Moore, Moses recalled, "we stumbled on the key." Moses left Moore with funds for a bus ticket to attend the October meeting in Atlanta and promised he would return to Mississippi the following summer. He brought more than two hundred contacts back to Atlanta along with the draft of a voter registration program for the SNCC conference. Moses then left for New York to complete his teaching contract at Horace Mann.[16]

As Bob Moses was crisscrossing the Mississippi Delta, John Doar arrived in Washington to take a position as first assistant in the Justice Department's Civil Rights Division. Luck and timing were at work here: several attorneys had turned down the position before it was offered to Doar. With just six months of the Eisenhower administration remaining, this was not an especially promising career move. For Doar, looking for an interesting experience, the position was a ticket out of New Richmond, Wisconsin. A graduate of Princeton University and the University of California, Berkeley School of Law, Doar had been practicing law with his father for ten years. Doar had a passing acquaintance with the racial issues roiling the South, thanks to his friendships with southern students at Princeton and his experience of having been stationed at an Air Force training base in West Helena, Arkansas, during World War II. When he read about the sit-ins, Doar remembered thinking that "nothing really had happened" since the *Brown* ruling "as far as solving the problem." As a midwestern Republican, he thought the inflated power of the southern segregationist bloc disadvantaged states like Wisconsin.[17]

Doar found a talented and dedicated group of lawyers working in the Civil Rights Division, but the Justice Department's prosecution of voting rights cases was almost entirely ineffectual. Nearly three years after the passage of the 1957 Civil Rights Act, only three cases had been filed, in Georgia, Alabama, and Louisiana. Attorney General William Rogers was moving cautiously in anticipation of a Supreme Court ruling that would decide the extent of federal power to interfere with what had long been considered a purview of the states. Another problem was that the FBI, the investigative arm of the Justice Department, proved largely ineffectual. The 1960 Civil

Rights Act had given the Justice Department authority to inspect and photograph voter registration records. Civil Rights Division lawyers worked with the FBI to secure and review voter registration records, but this was a time-consuming task.

Doar and his colleagues were closely following the situation in Haywood and Fayette Counties, Tennessee, where seven hundred sharecropper families had been evicted from their homes in the wake of a voter registration drive. The FBI reports from Tennessee were thin on the facts that would be essential for legal action. Doar took the matter up with two other lawyers in the division who were equally frustrated with the FBI's ineptitude. Having conducted his own investigations for personal injury cases back in Wisconsin, Doar decided to travel south and "see what it was all about."[18]

Armed with a $19 Brownie camera, he went to western Tennessee, where Blacks outnumbered whites by three to one but only a handful were registered. In 1941, when a group of local activists had tried to initiate a voter registration effort, a mob that included the local sheriff had lynched NAACP leader Elbert Williams and driven his fellow activists from town. During the spring of 1960, organizers in Haywood and Fayette Counties had added 2,200 Black voters to the rolls—still a small fraction of the total population, but an alarming number so far as local whites were concerned.[19]

The Fayette Civic and Welfare League, sponsor of the voter registration effort, arranged for Doar to meet with men and women who had registered to vote. Doar introduced himself as a representative from the Department of Justice and told the nearly one hundred people gathered in a small rural church that he was there to help. When he asked how many of them had been evicted from their farms, he said, "every single person in the room raised their hand." He learned about the hardships they had endured. Their names had been circulated around town. Merchants refused to sell them groceries or gasoline, local clinics refused medical treatment, banks refused to advance them credit. Doar was deeply moved by what he heard. After the meeting, he spent several days taking pictures of the families. "I wanted to do all I could to help them," he later recalled. "I resolved to work as hard as I could to enforce the 1957 Civil Rights Act." Back in Washington, Doar and several other attorneys prepared suits against the landowners, shopkeepers, and bankers responsible for obstructing the voting rights of Blacks in Haywood and Fayette Counties. The attorneys filed cases in federal court on September 13 and December 14. A new course had been set for the Justice Department and its Civil Rights Division.[20]

———

AS LABOR DAY APPROACHED, JFK's campaign strategists were concerned that Kennedy had not yet broken through to the great majority of Black voters. Harris Wofford arranged for Martin Luther King Jr. to meet with Kennedy and a small group of advisers at the candidate's Georgetown home in September. King told an interviewer in 1964 that he felt Kennedy had developed "a much greater comprehension" of the racial problem since their first meeting in June. While King assured the assembled group that he had confidence in Kennedy's commitment to civil rights, King acknowledged that questions persisted for many Black Americans, given Kennedy's vote on the 1957 Civil Rights Act and his support among southern Democrats. King suggested that JFK do "something dramatic" to convince Black voters of his commitment to civil rights. Discussions continued after the meeting, and there was talk of his sharing a platform with King at an SCLC meeting in a southern city. In the end, Miami, not part of the traditional Deep South, was as far "south" as the campaign was willing to go. As plans for a possible meeting began to solidify early in October, King allowed that since his group was nonpartisan, he would have to extend an invitation to Nixon as well. Kennedy felt that the possibility of a summit with King featuring both candidates would provide little help for his candidacy among Black voters, and perhaps erode his base in key southern states. The meeting never took place.[21]

Kennedy used the first televised presidential debate, on September 26, to address the consequences of racial injustice with a directness that distinguished him from his rival. In preparation for the debate, Harris Wofford had provided JFK with statistics that measured racial inequality—"the kinds of facts Kennedy liked to absorb," Wofford recalled. Drawing on this material, Kennedy provided a stark portrait of the injustices that defined the life chances and opportunities of Black and white children in the United States. "The Negro baby born in America today," he began, "has about one-half as much chance of completing high school as a white child born in the same place on the same day, one-third as much chance of completing college . . . twice as much chance of being unemployed . . . a life expectancy that is seven years shorter, and the prospects of earning only half as much." When moderator Howard K. Smith invited Nixon to respond, he said, "No comment."[22]

After two months on the campaign, Louis Martin came to believe that Kennedy "really could initiate a new era of race relations in this country." He worked with the campaign's Civil Rights Division to create opportunities for Kennedy to communicate more directly and forcefully about racial injustice at events that could be covered in the Black press. In late September, Martin arranged for Kennedy to meet with representatives of the National

Bar Association, the major organization of Black lawyers, and address concerns about the near total absence of Black representation in the federal judiciary. Kennedy pledged to remedy the situation and to use his power to ensure that the federal judiciary and federal service would be "a model of Americanism," with no traces of any form of discrimination. Two weeks later, in an interview on *Meet the Press,* JFK commented on the absence of African Americans in the federal government and said that greater efforts must be made "to bring Negroes into higher branches in government."[23]

On October 7, Kennedy addressed an enthusiastic audience at Howard University's Andrew Rankin Memorial Chapel, which was packed to capacity, with an overflow crowd outside the chapel. He was introduced by the law school dean, Spottswood Robinson III, a leading member of the small team of NAACP lawyers who had mounted the campaign that culminated with *Brown v. Board of Education.* In comments that ranged across domestic and foreign policy concerns, Kennedy spoke of freedom in a way that moved beyond the rigid paradigms of the era. Whites, he remarked, were a minority in a world being transformed by liberation struggles in Africa and Asia: "Man's desire to be free is the strongest force not only in this country, but around the world. We should associate ourselves with it."

Kennedy spoke again about the deep inequities defining the prospects for Black children and white children in the United States, noting that too many Americans were ignorant of or uninterested in these realities. The problems facing the United States in 1960, he said, were on a par with those the country had faced at the height of the Depression and in many ways comparable to the ones Lincoln had faced a century earlier. Presidential leadership now, as then, was critical. Kennedy vowed that, as president, he would strongly support the extension of constitutional rights to all Americans, work to ensure equal opportunity in employment and education, and press for vigorous enforcement of existing laws, including the Civil Rights Act provision empowering the attorney general to sue for voting rights. Acknowledging that he was in a tight contest for the presidency, Kennedy promised that, win or lose, the Democratic Party of the future would be identified with the pursuit of a better life for all Americans in all parts of the country, whatever their race or religion.[24]

Four days after the Howard University speech, the campaign sponsored a National Conference on Constitutional Rights and American Freedom in New York City. Promoted by the Civil Rights Division, the meeting was opposed by several key advisers, who saw it as a risk. Jack and Bobby supported the idea, however. At Lyndon Johnson's suggestion, the words "Constitutional Rights" were substituted for "Civil Rights" in the conference title. The two-day conference, promoted as nonpartisan, was a showcase for top Democratic figures, including Eleanor Roosevelt, Mayor Robert Wagner Jr. of New York, and Hubert Humphrey. Leading Republicans dismissed the gathering as a platform for attacking the Eisenhower administration's record on civil rights. Of course, the meeting did serve that purpose, but in scope and content it was a more ambitious undertaking.[25]

More than four hundred people, representing forty-two states, attended the conference, held at the Park Sheraton Hotel in midtown Manhattan. They included "the real pros in the civil rights field," observed the *New York Amsterdam News*. Martin Luther King Jr., who had a previous commitment in Shreveport, Louisiana, was one of the few major figures not present. Participants chose from a series of workshops in a variety of policy areas including education, voting, housing, administration of justice, employment, and public facilities. The conference culminated with a plenary session in which representatives from each workshop delivered reports providing facts and making recommendations. Kennedy, after listening to the various reports, delivered what many described as his strongest statement yet. He pledged, if elected, to employ executive action in support of civil rights and said he would host a series of conferences to create a climate of compliance with the *Brown* ruling. He also promised to introduce a comprehensive civil rights bill within the first hundred days, setting a high bar that he would ultimately fail to meet. Promises aside, looking back on the conference, Louis Martin was of the view that the "exposure of the Senator . . . to leaders who had never been active in a Democratic campaign in my view was one of the most hopeful and helpful things in the whole campaign."

A mass campaign rally in Harlem followed the end of the conference. Thanks to Martin's tireless efforts (and a hefty sum of money contributed for political work), Adam Clayton Powell was now fully on board. Sharing a platform with Eleanor Roosevelt, he introduced the candidate as "the kind of young, vigorous, imaginative leadership America needs in the challenging 60s." An estimated eight thousand people gathered outside the Hotel Theresa, the scene of an infamous meeting between Nikita Khrushchev and Fidel Castro several weeks earlier. Referencing that meeting, Kennedy said he was glad the two leaders had visited Harlem. "The world is coming to Harlem," Kennedy exclaimed, for "Harlem is a part of the world revolution." It was up to the United States, he said, "to prove our faith in the equality of all men by practicing it here at home." Then he said, "This is a fight we must finish."[26]

In an editorial endorsement on October 11, the *Chicago Defender* opined that Kennedy had a "superior capacity for leadership and for understanding the issues in the context of human equality." Gardner Taylor—head of Concord Baptist Church of Christ in Brooklyn, the second largest Black Baptist congregation in the United States, and a close friend of Martin Luther King Jr.—issued a strong endorsement of Kennedy and expressed faith in the Democratic Party he represented. "We need a president whose sights are set on the sixties and the huge thrust of history which this decade is seeing," Taylor said. "I am supporting John Kennedy because I believe in the Democratic Party, not blindly, but analytically. I believe the Democratic Party has a larger number of people who are part of the answer to the problems of caste, color and creed than it has people who are part of the problem."[27]

As promising as these endorsements were, they fell short of the kind of "dramatic event" that might mobilize active support among Black voters on Election Day.

—

ON OCTOBER 14, several hundred young women and men convened in Atlanta for the Student Nonviolent Coordinating Committee's first regional conference. Amzie Moore had come from Mississippi, but his proposal for a voter registration campaign had been overshadowed by plans for mass demonstrations. More than eight months after the Greensboro sit-ins, segregation of lunch counters in Atlanta remained, now reinforced by an antitrespassing law hastily passed by the Georgia legislature. Encouraged by activists from across the South, students in Atlanta made it clear they were prepared to fill the jails. Lonnie King and other student leaders appealed to Martin Luther King Jr., who had relocated to Atlanta earlier in the year, to join them.

King thought the plan was poorly timed. His frequent contacts with Harris Wofford left him sensitive to warnings that mass demonstrations and arrests, with the election just weeks away, might undermine Kennedy's fragile hold on Black voters. While King's father had recently joined other ministers in Atlanta in endorsing Richard Nixon—largely on account of Kennedy's Catholicism—King himself had come to believe that Kennedy would be responsive to the goals of the civil rights movement. King advised the students to postpone the protests until after the election. As far as SNCC activists were concerned, however, the looming election ensured that their protests would put pressure on the candidates and draw national attention to the situation in the South. SNCC would not wait.

On October 19, activists spread out to lunch counters and restaurants across the city. King joined the group of students seeking service at the Magnolia Room in Rich's Department Store, one of the largest department stores in the South. The activists were promptly arrested and jailed. After four days in prison, the protesters were released following an agreement negotiated by William Hartsfield, the progressive mayor of Atlanta, to end segregation in the city's public eating establishments. But King was not freed.

Judge Oscar Mitchell of DeKalb County, a Ku Klux Klan stronghold in the western part of Atlanta, charged that the thirty-one-year-old minister had violated the six-month parole attached to his arrest and conviction several months earlier for the absurd charge of driving with an Alabama license after having resided in Georgia for barely six weeks. King was transferred to the county jail and, at a packed hearing, Judge Mitchell revoked King's probation, sentenced him to four months of hard labor, and refused to set bail. Before dawn the next morning, county police took him from the prison in handcuffs and leg irons and drove him to the state prison in Reidsville, two hundred miles from Atlanta.[28]

There are varying accounts of what transpired over the next several days. What is clear is that the Kennedy campaign's edgy yet carefully orchestrated effort to secure Black votes while holding onto just enough southern white support faced its ultimate test. Recent polls had indicated that Kennedy might suffer the worst losses of any Democratic presidential candidate in the South. At the same time, the mass arrests of demonstrators and King's raw and punitive treatment reminded Black voters that the Democratic Party was the political home of the most vicious racists in the country. In the end, the improvisational style of the Kennedy campaign, personal relationships, and the power of the civil rights movement converged to create what may have been the most consequential moment of the campaign.[29]

Top Kennedy advisers remained wary of Wofford, Louis Martin, and the civil rights contingent of JFK's campaign and were determined to tread carefully through what all perceived to be a political minefield. Wofford called Coretta Scott King, who was then six months pregnant and in desperate fear for her husband's safety. Wofford also spoke with Morris Abram, an Atlanta-based lawyer, to express personal concern for King's welfare. This conversation was soon publicized, incorrectly, as an inquiry on behalf of Senator Kennedy, setting off alarms in the upper reaches of the Kennedy campaign. Wofford then contacted a sympathetic Sargent Shriver, who was with JFK in Chicago, and suggested that Kennedy phone Mrs. King. When Shriver found a quiet moment alone with the candidate at O'Hare Airport in Chicago, Shriver proposed that Kennedy call Mrs. King to express his sympathy. Kennedy liked the idea and promptly placed a call. He spoke warmly and reassuringly, expressing his concern and inviting her to call him directly if there was anything he could do. That same day, Kennedy also placed a confidential call to Ernest Vandiver, the governor of Georgia.[30]

Meanwhile, back in Washington, Louis Martin met with Bobby Kennedy at campaign headquarters to discuss the situation. Martin told Bobby that he had heard that Jackie Robinson and Richard Nixon were planning to call a press conference in which they would blame the Democrats for King's brutal treatment. Kennedy, Martin recalled, was most exercised by the fact that King could be jailed and sentenced to hard labor for having an out-of-state driver's license and, on top of that, be denied bail—a blunt introduction to the way the law worked in the Jim Crow South.

When Bobby learned of his brother's call to Mrs. King, he exploded, warning Wofford and Martin that the presidential contest was "razor close" and saying that if the incident were publicized, it could cost them the election. Bobby did not reveal then that he and JFK were working quietly behind the scenes to secure King's release.[31]

Governor Vandiver wanted to be rid of the problem, and he wanted to help John Kennedy get elected, but not at the price of his own political future. It would have been "political suicide," he recalled, for him to appear to be caving in to outside pressure on such a sensitive matter. After speaking with Kennedy, Vandiver conferred with a close circle of state Democratic Party officials and worked out an arrangement to secure King's release. All parties were careful to ensure that their efforts not become public. Through the intercession of a mutual friend, Vandiver was able to persuade Judge Mitchell to agree to set bond for King's release. Bobby phoned the judge from a pay phone to support the request. According to Bobby's account, he said he thought King was entitled to bond as a constitutional right and added that King's release would be helpful. They had a friendly conversation, and the judge set bail at $2,000. SCLC officials immediately chartered a plane and flew to Reidsville to post bail and bring King back to Atlanta.[32]

While the backroom negotiations remained secret, Bobby's call asking for King's release was publicized, but it did not become a major story partly because of initial confusion about the call. Kennedy's closest aides were incredulous when reporters asked them about a wire story reporting that "a brother of Senator Kennedy's" had placed such a call, knowing how Bobby Kennedy felt about any public association of the campaign with the King affair. Both John Seigenthaler and Harris Wofford categorically denied that Robert Kennedy had done any such thing. Their denials may well have been the reason that an inquiring David Brinkley did not use the story on the NBC evening news after speaking with Wofford. But both men soon learned from Bobby that he had in fact placed the call, and he sought their advice in drafting a statement explaining why. "Can't you just say I was inquiring about Dr. King's constitutional right to bail?" Wofford remembers Kennedy asking, "sounding uncharacteristically sheepish."[33]

Outside the state prison in Reidsville, King told a waiting group of reporters, "I am deeply indebted to Senator Kennedy, who served as a great force in making my release possible." In response to a question about possible political motives, he responded, "there are moments when the politically expedient can be the morally wise." Then he added, "I hold Senator Kennedy in very high esteem. I am convinced that he will seek to exercise the power of his office to fully implement the civil rights plank of his party's platform." King noted that he had not heard from Nixon and did not know whether the Republican Party had made any efforts on the civil rights leader's behalf. In a later interview, King recalled his surprise at Nixon's silence. King had known Nixon for several years, and Nixon had frequently called King to discuss certain issues. But "when this moment came," King commented in 1964, "it was like he had never heard of me."[34]

In the end, Nixon's silence, as he himself later acknowledged, may have cost him the election. During the course of the campaign, Nixon had angled to expand Republican Party inroads in the South, capitalizing on Kennedy's growing association with the cause of civil rights, a preview of the "southern strategy" that would become a hallmark of his political legacy. One of Nixon's final campaign appearances was on the steps of the statehouse in Columbia, South Carolina, where he was introduced by former Governor James Byrnes, former secretary of state under Truman and a leader in the resistance to school desegregation. Nixon said that there was no prouder moment for him than his introduction by Byrnes, "a great Democrat" and "a great American." During a time of change, it was no longer enough to vote as your father and grandfather had voted, Nixon told the crowd: "This time America must come first." Further underscoring this point, he charged that after adopting its platform in Los Angeles, the Democratic Party "forfeited their right to ask any Democrat to be loyal." Thurgood Marshall referred to this as Nixon's "The South Will Rise Again Speech."[35]

The political capital to be reaped from Kennedy's role in King's release was precarious. Most on his staff were anxious to avoid publicity, fearing that the mainstream press's mostly white readership would see the association as a negative. At Democratic headquarters back in Washington, dire predictions were made about how many votes and states the King affair might cost. Bobby firmly instructed the civil rights contingent not to issue any statements about the King affair.[36]

With ten days to go before Election Day, Harris Wofford, Louis Martin, and Sargent Shriver found a way to ensure that word of Kennedy's sympathetic response to King's arrest would reach deep into Black communities around the country, while staying off the radar of the white press. A pamphlet, *The Case of Martin Luther King,* was issued under the sponsorship of the hastily established "Freedom Crusade Committee," headed by two Black ministers in Philadelphia. Under the headline "No Comment Nixon versus a Candidate with a Heart, Senator Kennedy," the pamphlet told the story of Kennedy's call to Coretta Scott King through statements made by Mrs. King and Rev. Martin Luther King Sr., who had now officially transferred his support to JFK. Comments by Rev. Gardner Taylor and other Black leaders were also included. Within a week, more than two million of the blue-colored pamphlets had been printed and distributed through local contacts affiliated with Black institutions and organizations. Before dawn on Sunday, November 6, Wofford and Martin were at the bus station in Washington, DC, loading bundles of "the blue bomb," as they named it, onto Greyhound buses headed to Virginia and North and South Carolina, where the pamphlets were picked up and taken straight to churches—part of a final nationwide blast two days before the election.[37]

———

ON NOVEMBER 9, the day after one of the closest elections in American history, Robert Kennedy publicly stated that the Black vote was a major reason for his brother's victory. The popular vote was a squeaker: 49.7 percent for Kennedy, 49.6 percent for Nixon. The electoral college margin was more comfortable—303 to 219—with Kennedy carrying states that Adlai Stevenson had lost, like Illinois, Michigan, Minnesota, Missouri, and New Jersey, by close margins. While stories of voter fraud in Chicago have often been associated with the narrow win in Illinois, the Kennedy campaign's successful appeal to Black voters was a determining factor. Moreover, Kennedy would have won without Illinois. A large voter turnout among African Americans in northern urban areas, overwhelmingly in Kennedy's favor, contributed to his victories in New York, Pennsylvania, Michigan, and Illinois. Black voters were also a factor in his close wins in South Carolina, North Carolina, and Texas. According to one report, Kennedy carried the Black vote by eight to one in North Carolina, carrying him to victory in a state that he won with 52 percent of the vote.[38]

The fact that Robert Kennedy publicly acknowledged the pivotal role of Black voters was a hopeful sign, wrote *Amsterdam News* columnist Earl Brown. "His frankness and his courage in making this statement," Brown wrote, "may be a harbinger for an entirely new and honest approach to the Negro voter in American politics."[39]

One week after Kennedy's victory, on November 14, the Supreme Court in *Gomillion v. Lightfoot* unanimously overturned a plan to redraw the boundaries of Tuskegee, Alabama, to exclude Black voters. The *Gomillion* ruling marked a precedent-setting blow to state actions to disenfranchise Black voters. Three weeks later, deciding in favor of Howard University law student Bruce Boynton, the court struck down segregation in bus terminals serving interstate transportation. *Boynton v. Virginia* opened the way for a major assault on segregation during the first months of the new Kennedy administration and stoked an emboldened white resistance.

On December 16, 1960, president-elect John F. Kennedy named his thirty-four-year-old brother attorney general, a controversial appointment that Bobby accepted reluctantly at his brother's insistence. The former campaign manager, who had played a leading role in expanding the reach of the Democratic Party in the struggle for civil rights, assumed the position of chief law enforcer just as the movement to dismantle Jim Crow entered its peak period. Neither brother could have anticipated how quickly the escalating crisis in the South would test their ability to deliver on promises made in the heat of a hard-fought campaign. The legacy of America's racial past—not just in the South, but throughout the nation—would present Bobby Kennedy with his greatest challenge.

CHAPTER FIVE

Simple Justice

|||

ON HIS SECOND DAY AS ATTORNEY GENERAL, Bobby Kennedy turned up at John Doar's desk in the Civil Rights Division and asked him what he was working on. Doar told Kennedy about a case the division had filed several days earlier, on January 19, 1961, against the sheriff of East Carroll Parish, Louisiana, and ten businessmen for violating the provisions of the Civil Rights Act of 1957 prohibiting the intimidation or coercion of potential voters. The men had organized to cut off all supplies, services, and markets to Joseph Francis Atlas, a Black cotton farmer, after he testified before the US Commission on Civil Rights that he had been denied the right to vote. Louisiana was a segregationist stronghold. No African American had registered to vote in East Carroll Parish since 1922. "You picked a bad place to start," Kennedy said. "Well," Doar replied, "that's where Joseph Francis Atlas gins his cotton."[1]

Atlas, a fifty-six-year-old father of eight children, faced economic ruin. Kennedy took a personal interest in the case. He made several calls to businessmen and politicians he knew in Louisiana and within a week reported back to Doar that he'd received assurances Joseph Atlas's cotton would be ginned. That wasn't good enough, Doar said. A court injunction would be necessary to ensure that he would not continue to be a target of economic reprisal. With Kennedy's backing, the Civil Rights Division took the case to the federal district court in Monroe, Louisiana. On February 3, attorneys for the eleven defendants filed a pledge promising "no further intimidation," ensuring that Atlas could gin his cotton, purchase supplies, and market his crops. The new attorney general's prompt action struck Doar as "a good omen."[2]

As African Americans in some of the most retrogressive jurisdictions in the South challenged segregation, they were met with defiance, intimidation, and violence. Nearly seven years after the *Brown* ruling, schools remained completely segregated in Alabama, Mississippi, South Carolina, and Georgia. In November 1960, the color bar had been breached in Louisiana when Leona Tate, Tessie Prevost, Gaile Etienne, and Ruby Bridges were admitted to the first grade in two New Orleans schools under federal court order. The girls' attendance sparked four days of rioting, white boycotts of the two schools, and efforts by the state legislature to penalize the New Orleans school board and block any further school desegregation in the state. On January 9, Hamilton Holmes and Charlayne Hunter's arrival at the University of Georgia marked the first crack in Georgia's segregated public-school system. In response, a student-led "howling, cursing mob" (as the *New York Times* characterized it) of somewhere between five hundred and two thousand surrounded Charlayne Hunter's dormitory, igniting one of the largest riots in opposition to school desegregation.[3]

John Kennedy had promised to introduce a comprehensive civil rights bill "within the first 100 days," but his narrow victory, coupled with significant losses by northern Democrats—twenty-one seats in the House and two in the Senate went to Republicans—had amplified the power of southern Democrats, who now held most chairmanships in the House and the Senate. In light of these constraints, Harris Wofford suggested a strategy of "minimum legislation, maximum executive action," which appealed to the president and his brother. Making a virtue of necessity, Bobby Kennedy told Simeon Booker of *Jet* magazine that in the "sensitive area" of civil rights the previous administration provided neither White House leadership nor follow-up from the Justice Department. That, he said, would change.[4]

John Seigenthaler was the only other person in the room when the brothers met at Jack and Jackie Kennedy's Georgetown home on a snowy morning in December to discuss the position of attorney general. Seigenthaler recalled how Jack presented the matter. He said he needed someone he could trust, someone who would tell him the unvarnished truth, especially when there were problems. He immediately brought up civil rights. "You're from the South," he said, turning to Seigenthaler. "You know how difficult it is going to be." Turning back to Bobby, Jack went on to say, "I don't want somebody who is going to be fainthearted. I want somebody who is going to be strong, who will join with me in taking whatever risks or whatever downside exposure there was and who would deal with the problem honestly." He continued, "We're going to have to change the climate in this country. And if my administration does the things I want to do, I'm going to have to have someone as Attorney General to carry these things out on whom I can rely completely." He turned to Bobby and said, "You know that Bobby. You remember that." When Bobby, still not completely persuaded, interjected, "I've got some points I want to make," Jack cut his brother off. "There's no point to make," JFK said. "So that's it, general. Let's go." That afternoon, he an-nounced several cabinet appointments to the press, including his brother's appointment as attorney general.[5]

The choice of Robert Kennedy as attorney general was widely criticized. He was not qualified by any traditional standard. The *New York Times* charged that he lacked experience in the practice of law—either in the court-room or as a legal philosopher. Constitutional legal scholar Alexander Bickel found fault with Bobby's record as chief of staff of the Rackets Com-mittee, charging that he was self-righteous and overly ambitious in his pur-suit of suspected wrongdoers. JFK dismissed the charge that Bobby lacked courtroom experience as irrelevant. He was confident that his brother was eminently qualified to serve. The main requirement, Jack claimed, was "the ability to administer a great department." "In planning, getting the right people to work, and seeing that the job is done," he concluded, "he is the best person in the United States."[6]

Once Bobby was appointed, he began building what Bickel would come to describe as "the most brilliantly staffed department we have seen in a long, long time." RFK asked Byron White to consider serving as deputy attorney general. White, a legendary football hero, Rhodes Scholar, and Yale-trained attorney, had served as a Navy lieutenant in the Pacific, where he had forged a friendship with JFK. White was being considered for a cabinet appointment himself. When Bobby advised that White take a few days to think it over, he responded that he did not need to. "I imagine there will be some heat over where you are," he said, "and I'd rather be where there's some action."

White helped Kennedy identify people who could head up the various divisions of the Justice Department. Many had ties to Yale, including Nich-olas Katzenbach (Office of Legal Counsel), Louis Oberdorfer (Tax Division), and Burke Marshall (Civil Rights Division). Ramsey Clark, who was tapped to run the Lands Division, was also a key hire (he had dropped out of high school to join the Marines, later graduating from the University of Texas and the University of Chicago Law School). Some of those who were brought in had worked with Bobby during his years as a Senate staffer, like John Sei-genthaler and Pulitzer Prize–winning journalist Ed Guthman, who became press secretary. None of these men had yet reached the age of forty; most had served in World War II, and many were considered the most talented lawyers of their generation. Commenting on Kennedy's approach, Bickel noted: "One immediately had the sense of a fellow who wasn't afraid of having able people around him and . . . who had a vision of public service that would have done anyone proud."[7]

Kennedy's vision, youthful energy, and capacity to lead enabled him to tap remarkable talent and create a dynamic government enterprise, reminiscent of New Deal days. He brought an informality to the Justice Department, in a sharp break with tradition. A *Time* reporter noted that he was "supremely unselfconscious of appearance and willing to be photographed with his feet on the desk . . . not because it's a good picture, but because that's the way he works." He was an active presence throughout the department, dropping in to chat with an attorney, convening impromptu sessions with staff members across divisions to share information and talk through problems, and generally fostering a collaborative spirit. He listened, never lectured, and encouraged "free-flowing discussion and differing views." Bobby was determined, Nicholas Katzenbach recalled, that "we would work together as equals; no one was allowed to have a special claim on a particular turf based on a title." Kennedy saw the department "as a group of teammates working to carry out the responsibilities of public servants." He succeeded, many agreed, in communicating his own enthusiasm and energy to others, making them feel that they were members of a team, and that what they did mattered. During his tenure as attorney general, "morale in the Justice Department was in the stratosphere."[8]

In one of his first extended interviews as attorney general, with journalist Peter Maas for the popular *Look* magazine, RFK acknowledged that he did not have a great deal of experience in the field of civil rights—and quickly added, "therefore it is getting my immediate attention." He said his sympathies were with the sit-ins "morally," and his belief was that integration should "take place today everywhere." But he acknowledged that others had grown up "with totally different backgrounds and mores, which we cannot change overnight." While stating that his department would not tolerate "defiance of court orders," he indicated that adequate groundwork would need to accompany "sweeping changes." Some in the South wished to perpetuate "a vast disparity" for whites and Blacks, he noted, "and then use the same disparity to argue that the Negro isn't ready for full citizenship." He also pointed to people in the North "whose lives indicate that they would rather talk about integration than live it"—such as newspaper editors "who preach civil rights, but belong to restricted clubs and send their children to school where there are no Negroes."[9] Beyond that, Bobby acknowledged that it was time for the federal government to face the racial discrimination in its own ranks.

RFK expressed his feeling that the law, especially in criminal cases, favored the rich over the poor—in matters of bail, appeals, and the cost and quality of defense—and noted that he had established a study group to determine what could be done to make the law more equitable. Another area of "deep concern" was the problem of juvenile delinquency. He thought the federal government needed to develop more competency among all agencies to deal with this problem, which largely impacted poor youth. These concerns would result in a program dedicated to working with communities to focus on education, jobs, and other structural inequities that harmed the life chances of disadvantaged children. Kennedy, as one associate recalled, viewed the law as a tool to implement policy and "help people achieve a fairer and more just society." He "almost always tended to identify with the underdog, with the poor, the weak, the disenfranchised, and in a sense, he saw the law as the road to justice."[10]

On inauguration day, as the US Coast Guard marched by the viewing stand, President Kennedy noticed that "there was not a black face in the entire group." He immediately inquired and learned that there were no African Americans in the Coast Guard Academy. Later that day he spoke to his aide Richard Goodwin, calling this lack of representation "not acceptable." Kennedy instructed Goodwin to do something about it. Goodwin knew he was being told to act, not draft a statement or make a promise. He promptly placed a phone call from the White House to Treasury Secretary C. Douglas Dillon, who promised to get on the matter right away. By the summer, the first Black professor had been hired at the Coast Guard Academy, and in the fall four Black cadets joined the entering class.[11]

At thirty-five, Robert Kennedy was the youngest attorney general since Richard Rush had served under James Madison in 1814. Many felt his youthfulness, energy, and activist orientation embodied JFK's New Frontier. One observer commented that he "made his older brother seem a Tibetan contemplative by comparison."[12] At the start of his tenure, he toured the offices of the sprawling Department of Justice with John Seigenthaler, introducing himself and talking with employees. Seigenthaler, a former a reporter with the *Tennessean* (Nashville), was now Bobby's administrative assistant. When they had covered most of the building, Kennedy asked whether anything had struck Seigenthaler as strange. Seigenthaler said he was impressed to see everyone working so hard. "Yes," Bobby said, "but did you see any Negroes?" The response was no. Kennedy asked Seigenthaler to report back on how many Black lawyers were working in the Department of Justice.

Seigenthaler found a total of 10 Black lawyers out of more than 950 working at the Department of Justice in Washington, and 9 out of the 742 working in district attorneys' offices around the country. Further investigation revealed that relatively few African Americans had applied for positions as attorneys. Kennedy asked for steps to be taken immediately to open professional positions for Blacks in the Justice Department. He wrote personally to the dean of every law school in the country, asking that they provide the names "of qualified Negro attorneys of your acquaintance who might be interested in coming into the Department." RFK also asked them to encourage "promising law students to consider making a career here."[13]

At his first cabinet meeting, the new president discussed his impromptu order for the integration of the Coast Guard and instructed each cabinet member to examine the situation in his own agency and take "affirmative action" to recruit African Americans. Further investigation revealed that the lack of representation in the Department of Justice was mirrored throughout the federal government. While African Americans made up about 13 percent of the more than two million federal employees, most served on custodial staffs. A scant few were represented in the upper levels of employment. Early in March, Edward McVeigh, the personnel chief of the Labor Department, began an extensive tour of southern Black colleges to acquaint students with job opportunities in the federal government and encourage them to apply.[14]

On March 6, JFK issued Executive Order 10925 establishing the President's Committee on Equal Employment Opportunity, which had as its purpose to remove "permanently from government employment and work performed for the government every trace of discrimination because of race, color, creed and place of national origin." The new committee combined two existing committees, the President's Committee on Government Contracts, headed by former Vice President Richard Nixon, and the Committee on Government Employment Policy. Kennedy appointed Lyndon Johnson to chair the committee and named Labor Secretary Arthur Goldberg as vice chairman. The committee had a broad mandate, significant resources, and more sweeping powers than its predecessors, including the power to revoke contracts and use other sanctions to punish companies that failed to demonstrate compliance with the no-discrimination policy. Members of the committee included the attorney general and heads of major government agencies, including the secretary of defense, the secretary of commerce, the head of the National Aeronautics and Space Administration (NASA), and the chairman of the Civil Service and Atomic Energy Commission. Acknowledging the enormity of the challenge, the *Washington Post* noted that the evident determination of the Kennedy administration and the changing climate created by the sit-ins may well have advanced the day when equality of opportunity would become a reality.[15]

The Kennedy administration significantly increased Black representation at the upper levels of government. Robert Weaver, confirmed as federal housing chief in the face of strong southern opposition, filled the highest federal post held by an African American to date. Cecile Poole, nominated in the spring of 1961 as US attorney for the Northern District of California, became the first African American to hold that post outside the US Virgin Islands. By July, Louis Martin released the names of forty-seven African Americans who had been hired for high-level positions in the Kennedy administration. JFK kept pressing for more and would request factual evidence of gains in minority employment. By late 1961, the number of Black employees in the Labor Department at the GS-12 level and above had almost doubled, from 24 to 41. In the Department of Agriculture the number had tripled, from 15 to 46. Results in other departments were not as impressive, but there were small gains throughout the administration—a signal that "the doors of opportunity were opening." Former NAACP lawyer Franklin Williams, who took a position in the Washington office of the Peace Corps, commented in April 1961, "I've been tremendously surprised at the large number of colored people holding responsible positions in government that you never hear about in the press."[16]

In March, the National Civil War Centennial Commission planned to hold its annual meeting on the hundredth anniversary of the Confederate firing on Fort Sumter, the spark that ignited the Civil War. The commission, chaired by Major General Ulysses Grant III, grandson of the Union general, accepted an invitation from the state of South Carolina and arranged to hold the meeting at the Francis Marion Hotel in Charleston, a segregated establishment. This location became an issue when the New Jersey delegation protested the barring of Black attendees at the hotel. President Kennedy sent a letter to Major General Grant stating that the commission was obliged to see that all participants were accorded equal treatment. Grant, as reported on the front page of the *New York Times,* "rebuff[ed] Kennedy's Desegregation Plea," saying that the commission could not tell the hotel how to manage its property. Kennedy sent a stronger message in return, observing that the commission was a government body using federal funds and should thus hold its meetings at a place that was free of racial discrimination. He threatened the withdrawal of federal funds. The commission grudgingly moved its meeting to the Charleston Naval Base, where accommodations were open to all. Shortly thereafter, historian Allan Nevins replaced Grant as head of the commission.[17]

Early in April, a small group began to meet monthly at the White House to coordinate policy government-wide. Established by Fred Dutton and chaired by Harris Wofford, the Subcommittee on Civil Rights included a representative from every one of the departments and major federal agencies, most of whom were new Kennedy appointees personally committed to civil rights. Citing the president's mandate to the Equal Employment Opportunity Committee that "federal money should not be spent in any way that encourages discrimination," Dutton asked agency representatives to take action to bring their activities in line with this principle.[18]

Over the next several months Secretary of the Interior Stewart Udall issued regulations to end all segregation in national parks. Other agencies soon followed suit. Lunchroom and public facilities in federal buildings throughout the South were desegregated, and Robert McNamara, who was then secretary of defense, ordered that military police were never to be used to enforce segregation. Abraham Ribicoff, the secretary of health, education, and welfare, made his department's support of language, guidance, and counseling institutes under the National Defense Education Act conditional on a policy of nondiscrimination. Six southern institutions withdrew their requests for funding, but the great majority of language and counseling centers in the South accepted the new terms.[19]

Kennedy had expressed the commitment of his administration to "exercise affirmative leadership to discharge both its constitutional obligation and its moral duty to achieve opportunity for all" within the federal government. "All," in this case, included women. Kennedy established the President's Commission on the Status of Women to develop recommendations for "overcoming discrimination in . . . employment on the basis of sex" and (tellingly) for "services which will enable women to continue their roles as wives and mothers while making a maximum contribution to the world around them." Esther Peterson, assistant secretary of labor, was the major force behind the commission, and Eleanor Roosevelt served as chair. Acting on the findings of the committee, Kennedy ordered federal agencies to end sex discrimination in hiring in 1962 and the following year signed the Equal Pay Act, prohibiting gender-based wage discrimination.[20]

—

AFTER SOME INITIAL HESITATION, Bobby Kennedy tapped Burke Marshall, a thirty-eight-year-old partner at the law firm of Covington & Burling, to head the Civil Rights Division. Marshall, who had served in the army as a Japanese translator during World War II, came strongly recommended by Harris Wofford. The two had taught a corporate law course together at Howard University, and Wofford admired Marshall's quiet brilliance, fairness, and thoughtful manner. Like many of his generation, Marshall had been moved by President Kennedy's inaugural address and was eager to be part of what promised to be the most interesting and demanding lawyers' work in the country. His interview, however, was a bit of a bust. As a friend noted, "Burke thinks more than he talks." The meeting was notable for its long periods of silence. Marshall told his wife Violet, "I blew it." Bobby was unimpressed and doubted he could establish a relationship with Marshall but, in the end, chose him because of his reputation. "I asked a dozen people," Bobby said, "and they all said that Burke was the best young lawyer in Washington."[21]

The two men formed a partnership that would "mark the beginning of a sea change in the civil rights policies of the federal government," as legal scholar Owen Fiss has observed. Both were known for their capacity to listen, their willingness to question their own assumptions and judgment, and their decisiveness. While Marshall crafted finely tuned strategies and managed a growing team of lawyers, Kennedy remained action-oriented and keenly attuned to the political implications of their work. Both men, while beneficiaries of outstanding formal educations, recognized that they had only a limited understanding of the South. Three months into his work as assistant attorney general for civil rights, Marshall declined a request for a televised interview, explaining, "I am still learning . . . and probing the depths of my own ignorance." As for Bobby Kennedy, Marshall later recalled, "the more he saw, and this was true for me as well, the more he understood. The more you learned about how Negroes were treated in the South, the more you saw of that, the madder you became. You know, he was always talking about the hypocrisy. By the end of the year he was so mad about that kind of thing, it overrode everything else."[22]

Civil rights scholars have often overlooked the formative early months of the Kennedy administration, when Bobby Kennedy and Burke Marshall put the Justice Department firmly behind enforcement of the *Brown v. Board of Education* ruling and showed a new determination to use federal power to challenge voter discrimination. The Freedom Rides, which began in May, would change the dynamic of the Justice Department's relationship to the civil rights movement. But by the time Burke Marshall was confirmed by the Senate on March 28, he and Bobby had already set a fresh course, directly confronting the defiance of court orders. These were unchartered waters, testing the reach of federal power in a way that had not been attempted since Reconstruction. As Nicholas Katzenbach later confided, "None of us had taken courses on how to manage a peaceful revolution while preserving a government of laws."[23]

———

"ONE OF OUR NATIONAL PURPOSES is to achieve equal opportunity for all without respect to race, color, religion, national origin," Burke Marshall wrote to White House aide Richard Goodwin in February. "This includes achieving equal rights before the law, in the administration of justice, and equality of opportunity . . . in education, voting, holding office, participation in the community, and in the economic life of the country." He added, "the Federal Government has been remiss in finding out what it can do and should do toward fostering this national purpose." Starting with Louisiana, Marshall was dedicated to remedying this failure.[24]

After four first graders desegregated two elementary schools in New Orleans in November, the state legislature had engaged in a frenzy of lawmaking dedicated to overturning school integration in New Orleans and preventing integration from occurring anywhere else in the state. By the time the Kennedy administration took office, the legislature had abolished the compulsory school law and cut off state funding for New Orleans's schools. Early in February, Marshall spoke with state officials in an effort to negotiate a resolution. Robert Kennedy brought M. Hepburn Many, the US attorney in New Orleans, to Washington to confer about the situation and followed up with personal calls to several state officials, warning them that Kennedy would ask the federal court to hold them in contempt if they refused to restore funds to the New Orleans schools. State officials would not budge. On February 15, the Department of Justice filed charges against the state superintendent of education, Shelby Jackson, for his "open and flagrant efforts to interfere with court orders." The action served notice, the *Washington Post* reported, that the new administration intends to see "that court orders requiring desegregation in the public schools are obeyed." Facing the prospect of jail sentences, state officials ultimately yielded and restored funding. But other battles loomed.[25]

The Justice Department filed a motion to enter several pending school desegregation cases without awaiting the court's invitation; Kennedy told a reporter that one reason was that the department did not want to leave local school boards with the burden of securing compliance. On March 17, Judge Skelley Wright granted the motion, broadening the power of the Justice Department to intervene in school desegregation cases. The Justice Department immediately entered cases in Baton Rouge and St. Helena Parish, as well as two cases involving trade schools in six parishes. In each case the department sought and secured injunctions against state and local officials, preventing them from enforcing two statutes designed to block people from encouraging or assisting with school desegregation. In April, St. Helena Parish voted to authorize the school board to close schools rather than integrate, following the model of Prince Edward County, Virginia.[26]

At the end of February, while awaiting Judge Wright's ruling on the petition to intervene in Louisiana, Marshall talked to RFK about taking steps to enter school litigation in Prince Edward County. Home to one of the five cases in the *Brown* ruling, Prince Edward County was to many a symbol of diehard segregation. Its public schools had been closed since May 1959, when, in response to a school desegregation order, the Virginia legislature had repealed the state's compulsory school law and made the operation of public schools a local option. White officials quickly established the Prince Edward Academy, a private school for white students, supported by grants from the state and county tax credits. No schools were made available for the more than seventeen hundred Black school-aged children in the county.

Prince Edward County served as a model for St. Helena Parish in Louisiana and other southern communities considering school closure as an alternative to desegregation. Intervention by the Department of Justice, Marshall reasoned, would be in keeping with the statement President Kennedy had sent to a conference on school desegregation in Williamsburg, Virginia, at the end of February. "Our public-school system must be preserved and improved," the president had insisted, after paying tribute to the teachers and school administrators and praising the parents and children, Black and white, working to make that happen. "Our very survival as a nation depends on it. This is no time for schools to close for any reason, and certainly no time for schools to close in the name of racial discrimination."[27]

The Justice Department began by appealing to local and state officials to enforce court orders, listening to the officials' concerns while making it clear that the federal government would act if the law was defied. Immediately following Judge Wright's favorable ruling, Kennedy and Marshall invited Albertis Harrison, Virginia's attorney general, to Washington for a meeting. Kennedy advised Harrison that the Justice Department would intervene in Prince Edward County if the court's order continued to be undermined. Harrison denied that any court order had been violated. When Kennedy pressed for assurance that the public schools would be reopened, Harrison said the state had no authority over local schools. After a three-judge court upheld Judge Wright's ruling permitting federal intervention in Louisiana on April 19, Marshall filed a motion in federal district court seeking to intervene as a party plaintiff in Prince Edward County, joining a suit that had been brought by the NAACP. "We have tried to work this out to permit Negro children to go to school," Robert Kennedy said in announcing the action. "They are unable to. Court orders are being circumvented and nullified. Therefore, we have brought this action to protect the judicial integrity of the United States."[28]

As a party plaintiff, the Justice Department sought to expand the NAACP's complaint. NAACP lawyers had charged that the school closing frustrated a court order. The complaint challenged the use of public funds to operate segregated private schools and the use of public school property by a private corporation. In a bold move, the Justice Department attempted to do something that only the US government could do: sue the state. The attorney general petitioned the federal district court in Richmond to add the Commonwealth of Virginia, the comptroller of Virginia, and the Prince Edward School Foundation as defendants. The complaint required the defendants to desist from failing to maintain a free public school system, from issuing tuition grants to students through the Prince Edward School Foundation, and from permitting tax credits for donations to private schools so long as no public school was operating in the county. In a seemingly convoluted move, the complaint asked that the federal court order the state of Virginia to withhold state funds from all public schools in Virginia until Prince Edward County public schools reopened. The main contention of the petition was that the Black students of Prince Edward County were being denied their equal rights under the Fourteenth Amendment when public schools were closed to them and open elsewhere in the state.[29]

"I think President Kennedy is going to get our schools opened up," thirteen-year-old Michael Smith told a reporter for the *Washington Post* in April. "I saw him on television, and I can tell from the way he talks." Francis Griffin, the local leader of the NAACP, welcomed the attorney general's action "as the right and democratic procedure for the federal government." SCLC representative Walter Fauntroy observed that direct federal executive action of this sort would be "far more effective and speedy than the cumbersome process of getting a bill through both Houses." By bringing the federal government in as a "full-fledged participant in school desegregation cases," the *New York Times* editorialized on April 30, the Kennedy administration had demonstrated that it was "earnest in its avowed effort to enforce the Constitution as interpreted in the Supreme Court's 1954 *Brown* decision."[30]

Initial response on the part of state officials was predictably divided. Senator Harry Byrd, who had issued the call for massive resistance to school desegregation, blasted the Justice Department's "intemperate and ruthless" action, charging the department with attempting "to punish an entire state because the action of one county displeases the United States Attorney General." Governor Lindsay Almond initially urged "calm and restraint" and convened an emergency meeting of state officials to determine whether a compromise could be worked out. A plan being considered was to reopen public schools, which Black children could attend, while maintaining subsidized private schools for whites. Attorney General Harrison had no comment. Within a week, however, a united front of opposition to the Justice Department's action had congealed. A governor's race loomed, and Prince Edward County supervisors had dug in their heels. Governor Almond pledged to "fight for the preservation of our total education structure to which federal action poses a threat." Harrison, who was a candidate for governor, called the Justice Department's action "reckless" and "irrespon-sible." Segregationists throughout the South found a platform for attacking federal overreach. Senator Herman Talmadge of Georgia took to the floor of the Senate to warn that if successful, the Justice Department's efforts "would establish a precedent for federal control over any facet of life in which the Executive branch for any reason may choose to intervene."[31]

Federal District Judge Oren R. Lewis heard arguments in the Prince Ed-ward County school case on May 8 in Richmond. During the hearing the judge, a Republican from Arlington, Virginia, broke into the argument pre-sented by the assistant attorney general for Virginia and commented: "As a Virginian, I am proud of the way Virginia has acted in this complex situa-tion." In a ruling issued a month later, Judge Lewis denied the federal gov-ernment's motion to intervene in the Prince Edward County case, dooming efforts to get schools open by the fall of 1961. The judge ruled that there had been no defiance of the court's order by the state of Virginia or Prince Ed-ward County. Furthermore, he held that Congress had not authorized the Justice Department to intervene in school desegregation cases. The ruling marked a sharp setback for the Kennedy administration. Nevertheless, its efforts in Prince Edward County would continue, with Justice Department attorneys offering informal support as the NAACP's legal challenge made its way through the courts. In the meantime, Robert Kennedy tried to find a way to provide educational opportunities for Prince Edward County's Black students so long as the public schools remained closed. He would describe these young people as "lost children in an age of transition. They have been caught in a social revolution which, though not of their making, has made itself felt most directly on them."[32]

While battle lines were drawn in Louisiana and Virginia, Marshall and Kennedy worked with districts across the South to prepare for the imple-mentation of desegregation orders at the start of the next school year. Mar-shall developed connections with the Southern Regional Council and the Southern Education Reporting Service, while Kennedy reached out to southern attorneys who supported civil rights. He appointed thirty-two-year old Terrill Glenn, a white attorney deeply committed to the goals of the civil rights movement, to the position of district attorney in Columbia, South Carolina, and consulted with the network of civil rights lawyers who had grown up around the NAACP's campaign. Ernest Finney, a young African American attorney in Columbia, was among them. Finney declined feelers from the Justice Department to join the team in Washington. "My forte was South Carolina. That is where I saw the need." Finney, who met with Ken-nedy on several occasions, recalled, "he was so much a part of our history and the story" of the movement.[33]

During the late spring and early summer, Marshall and Seigenthaler visited twenty-three school districts that were scheduled to desegregate under court order in the fall. Often working through local contacts, the two met informally with local officials, offering assistance while making it clear that the government would act on its responsibility to enforce the court ruling. Atlanta, Dallas, and Memphis were of particular concern, and Marshall maintained close contact with members of the school boards, businessmen, Black leaders, and law enforcement. Desegregation proceeded in each place without any major problems.[34]

Working quietly and without fanfare, Marshall and Kennedy showed a strong commitment to school desegregation, pressing the limits of the federal government's power to challenge obstruction and defiance. That fall, court-ordered desegregation proceeded without major incidents in thirty school districts across the South, including four additional schools in New Orleans. In August, a three-judge panel ordered St. Helena Parish's schools to open. In most cases, noted *Time* reporter Calvin Trillin, desegregation involved "tremendous community effort." Many community leaders were anxious to avoid the violence and publicity that had marked the initial desegregation of schools in New Orleans. Pressure from the Justice Department undoubtedly bolstered the resolve of those inclined to accept the inevitable. In each case, a very small number of Black students were involved. In Atlanta, a total of nine Black students attended previously all-white schools that fall.[35]

While legal pressure for school desegregation mounted, the escalation of direct-action protests in the year since Greensboro brought a striking change in white southern attitudes. It was one thing, a reporter noted, for southerners to read about the legal and political machinations that were slowly yielding token school desegregation. It was "something else again on the Main Street of his own town to see hundreds of clean-cut, quiet, well-behaved college students sitting in and being hustled off to jail for having done no more than that." The myth that outsiders were pushing a radical agenda and that southern Blacks were content with the racial status quo could no longer be sustained. James J. Kilpatrick, the editor of the *Richmond News Leader,* who has been described as the South's "most dogged and articulate segregationist," wrote in March 1961 that "for the first time in their lives, thousands of Southerners are beginning to see the Negro in a way they never saw before. It is like getting new glasses . . . The Negro as citizen, as political being, possessed of equal rights . . . A sense of a Negro point of view, totally unrecognized before, stirs uneasily in the conscious mind and we resent the intruding sensation and we do not know exactly what to do about it."[36]

By the spring of 1961, the great majority of white southerners came to view desegregation as inevitable. Still, a March survey conducted by reporters for *Time* stationed across the South revealed deep resistance to meaningful integration. Most white Americans shared a set of assumptions about history that rationalized a society structured along racial lines, with its attendant injustice. Reporters from *Time*'s Atlanta and New Orleans bureaus noted that most who did not actively resist court-ordered desegregation supported only token integration, not out of respect for the law, but because the only alternative was violence and economic turmoil. Areas of resistance remained. Public schools were still segregated in Alabama, South Carolina, and Mississippi. Reporters in towns and cities across the South found a white population focused on local conditions and only grudgingly yielding to token integration, with many steeped in bitterness and resentment in the face of change. No "responsible civic leaders supported desegregation for the good of the community or because it was right," wrote Calvin Trillin from *Time*'s Atlanta bureau. All change was traced to direct pressure, mostly by African Americans—and in the spring of 1961, that was mounting.[37]

———

UPON TAKING OFFICE, PRESIDENT KENNEDY faced the reality that "hundreds and hundreds of thousands of individuals were barred from voting because they were Negro." Bobby soon came to decide that the enforcement of voting rights offered the most promising arena for advancing racial change in the South. John Doar, the holdover first assistant in the Civil Rights Division, was well prepared to carry this effort forward. As the case of Joseph Francis Atlas was being successfully resolved, RFK asked Doar to find a highly visible case that would demonstrate President Kennedy's commitment to help Black citizens in the South secure the right to vote. Within a couple of days, Doar received a call from Frank Johnson, a federal district judge in Montgomery, Alabama, who was setting a major voting case for February 21. *U.S. v. Alabama* was one of the first voting cases filed under the Civil Rights Act of 1957. After nearly two years of obstruction and delay on the part of Alabama officials, Judge Johnson wanted to know whether the new administration would be willing to work with the judicial branch to move this case forward. Doar assured the judge that the federal government would be ready for court on February 21.[38]

Doar and three other attorneys worked around the clock for eight days investigating records and conducting interviews in Macon County, Alabama. This was the exactly the kind of case the new administration was looking for. Macon County, a majority Black county in the heart of the Black Belt, was home to Tuskegee University and to the Tuskegee Civic

Association (TCA), which had led a vigorous voter registration effort since the 1940s. The TCA gave Doar full access to its files documenting discrimination; he also had access to records gathered by Justice Department officials the previous November, when they had tried unsuccessfully to pursue the case.

Doar interviewed Black professors, schoolteachers, and other professionals who had been turned away by registrars, while FBI agents spoke to whites who had successfully registered to vote and found that there was universal white suffrage in Macon County, regardless of literacy or intelligence. The pattern of discrimination was starkly evident. "There was romance in the records," Doar recalled. During the trial, the state of Alabama put up a weak defense. No registrar willingly testified. Determined to have some answers, Judge Johnson called on several registrars to testify as his witnesses.[39]

In a sweeping decree issued on March 17, Judge Johnson held that Macon County registrars "had deliberately engaged in acts and practices designed to discriminate against qualified Negroes," citing six ways the board had enforced a racial double standard. Johnson accepted the suggestion of the Civil Rights Division that all applicants who met the qualifications of the least qualified white voter immediately be registered. This stipulation, known as "freezing relief," meant that the only qualification for voting would be age and residence. The judge ordered that the board of registrars remain open certain hours, observe specific procedures, and submit a full report of the registrars' activities every month. Johnson denied "for the time being" the Justice Department's request that a federal referee be assigned to Macon County but said he would not hesitate to appoint one if the board did not follow his orders. *The New York Times* claimed that *U.S. v. Alabama* marked "the most complete victory ever won by the Federal government in a voting rights case." At the same time, the ruling hinged on a rare convergence of elements that would not easily be replicated.[40]

On March 19, two days after Johnson's ruling, Burke Marshall, John Doar, and several other attorneys from the Civil Rights Division met with Robert Kennedy and Courtney Evans of the FBI to outline a new strategy for enforcing the Civil Rights Acts. Doar brought along a detailed map of the South. Kennedy went directly to the point, as Doar recalled, and asked the attorneys what they were going to do about Louisiana, Mississippi, and Alabama. The attorneys explained that their strategy was to develop and file a case of voter discrimination against a registrar in one county in each of the seven judicial districts that made up the three states. "Too slow. It won't do," said Kennedy. "You've got to do more." He looked at the map, sizing up the number of counties in each state, and told them he wanted suits filed in every county where there was underregistration of Black people. And he wanted these suits filed, Doar wryly recalled, "the day before yesterday."

"Well, we're going to need more lawyers," Marshall told him. Kennedy asked, "How many?" Four, said Marshall. Five new positions were created without delay. Marshall also said that the division would need help from the FBI, to help investigate cases and ideally increase the division's capacity. This new role for FBI agents conflicted with their traditional relationship with local law enforcement agencies, most of whom, in the South, were dedicated to upholding segregation.[41]

Doar and the attorneys who had been with the division since the summer of 1960 had deeply investigated two cases. Now they would be totally immersed in a concentrated drive to challenge entrenched patterns of voter disfranchisement across the Deep South. Doar recalled, "Division lawyers had to master everything that goes into understanding the realities of a distant and unknown territory: the back roads; the operations of county registrars' offices; the states' registration laws; 100 years of history; the identity of the local leaders; the way the court in each judicial district functioned—the clerk, the judge's secretary, the marshals, the U.S. Attorney, the court reporter—you name it." The lawyers traveled the rural roads of Mississippi, Alabama, and Louisiana for weeks at a time and found, in Doar's words, "a complex legal and social network designed to protect and preserve the caste system" and a "rural white society . . . riddled throughout with bewildering patterns of suspicion and silence."[42]

Over the next three months, the Civil Rights Division requested, and the FBI completed, preliminary investigations in thirty-four southern counties. Preparing for litigation was labor intensive. Each case depended on painstaking investigations by division attorneys: analysis of voting rolls, compilation of demographic statistics, comparison of handwriting, interviews with registrars, and statistically significant samples of Black and white failed and successful registrants. The Justice Department filed its first voting rights suit in Dallas County, Alabama, on April 12. Blacks made up approximately half the voting age population, but only 156 out of approximately 15,000 were registered to vote. This suit was followed two weeks later by one in East Carroll Parish, Louisiana, home of Joseph Francis Atlas, in which the attorney general charged the state and the parish with preventing 4,183 Black citizens from registering to vote. Suits were filed in Ouachita and Madison Parishes in Louisiana; Forrest, Clark, Jefferson, Jefferson Davis, Walthall, Tallahatchie, and Panola Counties in Mississippi; and Bullock and Montgomery Counties in Alabama. Civil Rights Division attorneys met a nearly solid wall of resistance, obstruction, and defiance as they documented patterns of voter discrimination, filed legal challenges, and sought relief through the courts.[43]

EARLY IN MAY 1961, Robert Kennedy made his first trip to the Deep South as attorney general, to deliver the Law Day address at the University of Georgia. It had been four months since students had rioted on campus in a failed effort to drive out Charlayne Hunter and Hamilton Holmes. Kennedy's visit was prompted by an invitation from Jay Cox, president of the Law Student Advisory Council. John Seigenthaler cautioned Cox that if the attorney general accepted the invitation, he would speak on civil rights. That was the exact topic Cox had in mind. He responded that he knew that Kennedy had invited Ralph Bunche to speak at the University of Virginia a decade earlier and had admired RFK's action. Now, as a student leader himself, Cox hoped to provide a platform for an attorney general who was challenging the legal basis of segregation.[44]

When Kennedy arrived in Athens, Georgia, on Saturday, May 6, the Prince Edward County case, set for a hearing in federal court on Monday, loomed large. Just days earlier, Georgia senator Herman Talmadge had warned that if the Department of Justice's attempt to intervene in Virginia succeeded, it would establish a precedent that would allow the federal government to take over any facet of public life. Although more than 1,500 alumni, faculty and students crammed into the University of Georgia's Fine Arts Auditorium to hear Kennedy, major state political leaders were noticeably absent. Several leading government officials had publicly stated that they would boycott the speech. Others, like Governor Vandiver, claimed they had a previous commitment—to attend the Kentucky Derby. The only state official in attendance was Griffin Bell, the governor's chief of staff, who had managed JFK's campaign in Georgia. Bell was set to introduce Kennedy but then declined at the last minute. Jay Cox filled in. Charlayne Hunter, whose dormitory room had been the target of a student mob, was determined to be there that day. Like many young people at the time, she was "captivated" by the president and his brother and their "bold take-control style." She found the auditorium spilling over when she arrived but managed to find a seat. She was the only African American in the audience.[45]

A reporter from *Atlanta Constitution* described a tanned and athletic-looking Kennedy, sporting a blue suit and "jaunty red and blue striped tie," and observed that he could easily have been mistaken for one of the law students—until he rose and began to speak. Hunter "could feel the tension rising, including my own. I was still not sure about how much in control these people were of themselves." Kennedy began by allowing that this was his first formal speech since becoming attorney general. He said he'd heard that when speaking in Georgia, you should try and connect to Georgia and the South and, better yet, claim Georgia kinfolk. "As far as I can tell," he commented, "I have no relatives here and no direct ties to Georgia, except one. This state gave my brother the biggest percentage majority of any state in the union and in this last election that was even better than kinfolk." Laughter rose up from the audience, Hunter recalled, "but not the kind of raucous belly laughter that Georgians are prone to."[46]

A steely silence prevailed for the next forty minutes as Kennedy delivered a candid address. He conveyed a confidence in the audience's capacity to recognize the challenges and opportunities and the historic nature of the moment. "On this generation of Americans," Kennedy acknowledged, "falls the full burden of proving to the world that we really mean it when we say all men are created equal and are equal before the law." He noted that half of the countries represented in the United Nations had mostly nonwhite populations and that in Africa, Asia, and South America "people whose skins are a different color from ours are on the move to gain their measure of freedom and liberty." In the Cold War struggle between "Communist tyranny" and the "promise of Anglo-American liberty," he declared, "our deeds will speak for us." Placing the desegregation of the University of Georgia in this context, he contended that the graduation of Charlayne Hunter and Hamilton Holmes would "without question aid and assist" in the fight against communism.

Focusing on more immediate realities, Kennedy acknowledged the problems that arose "when the moral sense of a nation" produces a judicial decision like the 1954 *Brown* ruling, "which required difficult local adjustment." He was blunt in noting that so far as the *Brown* ruling was concerned, he believed the decision was right. But his belief did not matter. He acknowledged that many of his listeners might believe that the decision was wrong. That belief also did not matter, Kennedy said: "It is the law." The 1954 decision, Kennedy acknowledged, "required action of the most difficult, delicate and complex nature, going to the heart of Southern institutions." Pointing to the Prince Edward County case, Kennedy dismissed the charge that the Department of Justice was threatening local control or attempting to close all schools in the state of Virginia; the department was simply maintaining the order of the courts. "I cannot believe anyone can support a principle which prevents more than one thousand students in one county from attending public school," he added, "especially when this step is taken to circumvent orders of the court."

Kennedy explained that beyond the mandate of law, the issues involved went to the core of American beliefs: "If we are to be truly a great nation, then we must make sure nobody is denied opportunity because of race, creed or color." Integral to doing so, he noted, was "a total effort to guarantee the ballot to every American of voting age." In a statement that represented the expanded commitment of the Justice Department, he said that "the spirit of our democracy, the letter of our Constitution and our laws require that there be no further delay in the achievement of full freedom to vote for all. Our system depends upon the fullest participation of all its citizens." The ability of the federal government to protect and secure such basic rights would soon be severely tested as voter registration efforts increased in Mississippi, in Alabama, and across the South.

Kennedy acknowledged that the race problem impacted all sections of the country and that a great deal of hypocrisy surrounded the issue. He talked about how he had found that, in most departments of the federal government, "very few Negroes were employed above the custodial level" and noted that actions were being taken to remedy that lack. He spoke of "financial leaders" in the northeast who deplored discrimination in the South yet belonged to clubs where no Negroes or Jews were allowed and sent their children to all-white private schools. And he spoke of union officials who criticized southern leaders but tolerated discrimination in their unions.

The rule of law was a central theme. Those who "irresponsibly assail the court and defy its ruling" challenge "the foundations of our society," he noted early in the speech. Toward its end he underscored a point that was fully clear by then: "You may ask, Will we enforce the Civil Rights Statutes? The answer is: Yes, we will." The South, "perhaps more than any section of the country," he added, has been given both the opportunity and the challenge "of demonstrating America at its greatest—at its full potential of liberty under law."[47]

As Robert Kennedy returned to his seat, many in the audience were on their feet for a standing ovation, with some notable exceptions. "I tried to make up for those sitting on their hands," Hunter Gault recalled. "My hands were burning I was clapping so long and hard."[48]

While Kennedy spoke at the University of Georgia, an interracial group of thirteen men and women affiliated with the Congress of Racial Equality (CORE) were on the second day of their journey south to test the enforcement of *Boynton v. Virginia,* the 1960 Supreme Court ruling that barred segregation in bus terminals servicing interstate travel. *Jet* reporter Simeon Booker had mentioned the upcoming ride to Kennedy during an interview in April. Booker would cover the rides for *Jet.* The journalist was surprised to realize that Kennedy seemed to be unaware of the potential danger that awaited the group of travelers. In fact, Booker recalls Kennedy's "buoyant response—'I wish I could go with you!'" When Booker advised him that the riders may need federal protection at some point, Kennedy told him to call if trouble arose.[49]

The Freedom Rides, as they became known, focused a national spotlight on the young activists and revealed the extent to which local and state officials would tolerate and even encourage mob violence in defense of segregation and in defiance of a federal court order. The Freedom Rides sparked the first major civil rights crisis of the Kennedy administration, which would prove an international embarrassment to JFK at a time of heightened Cold War tensions. The crisis quickly became a test of whether the Justice Department could act swiftly in the face of a bold challenge to federal authority that put the lives of law-abiding citizens at risk.

The Freedom Riders left Washington on May 4, intending to arrive in New Orleans on May 17, the anniversary of the *Brown* ruling. The group planned to integrate bus station waiting rooms and other facilities along the way and expose places where the law was being violated. The travelers met some resistance in Virginia. In Rock Hill, South Carolina, young white men attacked John Lewis and a fellow rider who came to his aid, leaving Lewis cut up and with several bruised ribs. But during these early stops, the Freedom Riders mostly stirred curiosity. They made a brief stopover in Atlanta, where they transferred to two buses before heading farther south. Over dinner in Atlanta, Martin Luther King Jr. took Simeon Booker aside "and told me straight out," as Booker recalled, "I've gotten word you won't reach Birmingham. They're going to waylay you."[50]

Klan leaders in Alabama were prepared for the arrival of the Freedom Riders. In Anniston, Alabama, a mob of more than a hundred men wielding clubs and bats attacked the first bus on May 14, Mother's Day. A firebomb engulfed the bus in flames and the riders barely escaped alive. Riders on the second bus were also attacked, but that bus managed to continue to Birmingham, where some fifty white men were waiting, armed with bats, chains, and steel pipes. Birmingham's commissioner of public safety, Theophilus Eugene "Bull" Connor, made sure that police were not present, promising the Klan fifteen minutes with no interference. Years later, it was revealed that FBI Director J. Edgar Hoover knew of the attack in advance, based on reports from an informant within the Klan, but failed to notify the attorney general. The mob bludgeoned the riders as they entered the bus station and also attacked the newsmen. Several riders had to be hospitalized. The Mother's Day bombing and bus station riot dominated national news.[51]

Robert Kennedy learned about the violence in Alabama close to midnight on Sunday, when Byron White called him at home. He told White to instruct the FBI to monitor the situation in Birmingham and report back. With few connections on the ground in Alabama, RFK immediately started making phone calls Monday morning—the first to Simeon Booker, who had spoken earlier with John Seigenthaler. Booker described what happened, "the

beatings, the serious head wounds and body injuries . . . the lack of any police presence, and the uncertainty of what might happen next." There was
no bus willing to take them out of Birmingham. Kennedy spoke with Booker's host, the intrepid Birmingham civil rights leader Fred Shuttlesworth, and
gave him his personal phone number. RFK then called Bull Connor, who
told him that he would protect the bus station but not the bus once it left the
station. Kennedy tried unsuccessfully to reach Governor John Patterson to
get his assurance that the state police would enforce the law. He had known
Patterson since 1959, and the governor had been one of his brother's earliest
supporters. That relationship quickly soured.[52]

The attorney general spoke with several of the riders and learned that they
had decided to fly to New Orleans. He arranged to send Seigenthaler to
Birmingham to investigate the situation and fly with them to New Orleans.
Upon arriving at the air terminal in Birmingham, Seigenthaler found a
traumatized group, several with their heads bandaged. Three of the flights
to New Orleans were canceled because of bomb threats. Booker, Seigenthaler
recalled, was "very upset." He pointed to the people coming into the terminal and groups standing around and said, "I don't believe they'll let us
get out of Birmingham." Seigenthaler talked with the airline representative
and persuaded the airline to prepare for a quick boarding and takeoff. By
Monday evening, the battered band of riders were in the air, bound for New
Orleans.[53]

Mob action had halted Autherine Lucy's entry into the University of Alabama in 1955, thwarting a federal court ruling and setting school desegregation back in that state indefinitely. Marshall and Kennedy were mindful of
this setback and did not want the Freedom Rides to succumb to a similar
fate, but fast-moving developments tested their capacity to act. By the time
the CORE group arrived in New Orleans, a group affiliated with the Student Nonviolent Coordinating Committee was preparing to head to Birmingham from Nashville to continue the ride. Diane Nash, a leader of the
Nashville group, told an incredulous James Farmer, leader of the CORE
group, "We can't let them stop us with violence. If we do, the movement is
dead." For Farmer and his compatriots, the prospect of death had become
all too real. Marshall and Kennedy were troubled to learn from a concerned
member of the Nashville community that a new group planned to head to
Birmingham. At Marshall's urging, John Seigenthaler phoned Diane Nash
to warn her that some of her group might be killed. She said they realized
that was a possibility. If they were killed, more would come, she insisted,
and "sooner or later we'll get somebody through.[54]

Over the next five days, Robert Kennedy and his top advisers sought
to find ways to intervene in the unfolding crisis in Alabama. As Nicholas

Katzenbach recalled, options were limited because the men in Washington had no real knowledge of what local law enforcement might do. The Nashville group reached Birmingham on Wednesday, and Bull Connor had them confined to the bus, pasting newspapers over the windows as an angry crowd gathered outside the terminal. Governor Patterson, who continued to ignore Robert Kennedy's calls, told the press that no one "could guarantee the safety of fools." After a series of bomb threats, no bus driver was willing to take the group on to Montgomery. As evening approached, Connor had the riders taken into "protective custody" and removed to the city jail. With the governor seemingly refusing to take responsibility for the safety of the riders, it appeared that federal action would be necessary. Kennedy, Marshall, and several other Justice Department officials discussed how they might intervene. Lou Oberdorfer, a native of Birmingham, and Byron White proposed that federal marshals, including agents from various units—such as alcohol tax agents, Border Patrol agents, and prison guards—be dispatched to Alabama. RFK preferred the idea of a federal civilian force over the use of troops, which would further heighten tensions and bear the stigma of military occupation.[55]

The attorney general, Burke Marshall, and Byron White met alone with President Kennedy early Thursday morning over breakfast to brief him on developments and discuss how they might proceed. The president, still in his pajamas, was fresh off his first hundred days in office—a period punctuated by the Bay of Pigs fiasco a month earlier and preparations for his first meeting with Soviet Premier Nikita Khrushchev. Marshall was struck by the fact that Kennedy did not waste time complaining about the Freedom Riders or worrying about the political fallout within his own party. His focus was on the crisis and what could be done.[56]

Bobby and his aides described the gravity of the situation, explained what they were planning to do, and briefed the president on the actions he might need to take in the next two or three days. Burke Marshall outlined the president's powers "and what kind of legal action we could take that would most solidly give him a basis for doing whatever he had to do in the use of physical law enforcement capacity." Byron White described the preparations being made to use federal marshals. Discussions had also been initiated with the army about flying the marshals in and having army units on alert if necessary. Marshall informed the president that they intended to file a complaint with Judge Frank Johnson in Montgomery to enjoin the Ku Klux Klan from interfering with interstate movement and to censor the police for failing to protect interstate travelers. The men agreed that the president should try to reach Governor Patterson. Kennedy put a call through, and a receptionist answered that the governor was fishing.[57]

Robert Kennedy was determined to get the riders moving. In the twenty-four hours since the attorney general had met with the president, Bull Connor had attempted to remove "the problem" from the state. In the dead of night, he had the riders taken from jail, driven to the Tennessee border, and left stranded on the roadside. By noon on Friday, they had returned to Birmingham with a second group of riders. The interracial group of nineteen women and men arrived at the bus station to board the 3 p.m. bus to Montgomery. The driver walked off the bus, refusing to risk certain danger. Police sealed the riders off in the bus station as a mob gathered outside. Frustrated with Governor Patterson's failure to return phone calls, Robert Kennedy called the governor's office on Friday afternoon and told his assistant that the president was prepared to issue a public ultimatum as a prelude to federal intervention. Patterson grabbed the phone from his aide. Kennedy, who finally had the governor's ear, told him that the buses had to be protected and that it was his responsibility. Patterson responded with a political oration "against Negroes and the federal government and the Supreme Court" and dredged up the Civil War. Kennedy told his former ally that he did not need to make a speech; all he had to do was fulfill his responsibility to ensure that the riders could travel safely. Patterson instructed him to send a representative, and John Seigenthaler was promptly dispatched.

Arriving in Montgomery, Seigenthaler met with the governor on Friday night. Patterson was seated at a long table, with his entire cabinet assembled. After greeting Seigenthaler and directing him to his seat, Patterson launched into a long diatribe about Negroes and foreign troublemakers, excoriating the spineless people he had supported (namely, the Kennedys) for failing to stand up to the activists. He concluded with a warning that if federal marshals were sent into Alabama, there would be "blood in the streets." Seigenthaler politely acknowledged what the governor had said and turned his attention to the matter he had come to discuss: Would the state of Alabama meet its responsibility to protect travelers on its highways? Patterson made a formal pronouncement, stating that Alabama would provide safe travel for all who traveled the state's highways, including visitors. When Seigenthaler asked how, the governor said there would be no police escorts for the bus carrying the interracial group. He then added that Floyd Mann, head of the State Highway Patrol, would take care of the details. Mann immediately assured Seigenthaler, "I'll make sure they'll never be out of the sight of an Alabama highway patrol." With that statement, the governor allowed Seigenthaler to call the attorney general's office. Bobby called back from a pay phone at the Mayflower Hotel in Washington, where he was attending a reception. He repeated the governor's assurance that the state would provide safe passage for the riders, with Patterson standing there and others listening. Then Seigenthaler called a Greyhound bus official in Atlanta, who had provided his number for the late-night call, and repeated the governor's assurance. The bus official agreed to have a bus ready to go early the next morning. Burke Marshall arranged for the FBI to accompany the bus and report on developments. It seemed that all was in place for the riders to travel safely to Montgomery and at least complete that leg of the journey.[58]

A Greyhound bus carrying nineteen Freedom Riders left the Birmingham bus station early Saturday morning. Birmingham police cars led the bus to the city's edge, where state highway patrol cars took up the lead. A low-flying highway patrol plane tracked the bus along Highway 31, and several cars carrying plainclothes detectives, FBI observers, and reporters followed behind. Floyd Mann, who rode on the bus, received assurances from Montgomery police commissioner L. B. Sullivan that a large contingent of police would be waiting at the Montgomery bus station.

When the bus arrived in Montgomery at close to 10:30 a.m., there was not a police officer in sight. Instead, what awaited the riders was a mob of nearly two hundred men, women, and children, led by several of the Klansman who had organized the Birmingham riot and who had been assured by Sullivan that the police would not interfere. As the riders left the bus, a screaming mob seemed to emerge "out of nowhere" brandishing lead pipes, bricks, chains, tire irons, and a variety of gardening implements. They swarmed over the riders, beating and pummeling men and women alike. A few escaped over a low retaining wall next to the station. Newsmen were targets as well, as rioters beat and kicked reporters and smashed television cameras and equipment. Mann waded into the horrific scene and witnessed the brutal assault of William Barbee, one of the riders. The State Highway Patrol head pulled out his gun and fired two warning shots into the air, promising to shoot the next man who hit Barbee. Mann's intervention helped defuse the fever pitch of the mob.[59]

John Doar was on his way to the federal building in Montgomery to research a voting case when he saw violence engulf the bus station. He rushed upstairs to an office overlooking the station and called Burke Marshall. "They've mobbed them again," he exclaimed. Doar described a riotous scene—fists flying, people bleeding, shouts of "get 'em"—"There are no cops. It's terrible," he said. Seigenthaler, who had just had breakfast with Doar, was driving toward the bus station when he came upon the scene. He saw a young girl being assaulted by a woman and a boy around fifteen years old. He stopped the car; went to help the girl, who was now bleeding; and was trying to get her into his car when a white fellow asked, "Who the hell are you?" Seigenthaler responded, "Get back, I'm a federal man." In response, he was whacked over the head with a steel pipe and left lying in the road.

He lay there for twenty-five minutes before a police car picked him up and took him to the hospital, where a visibly shaken Floyd Mann visited Seigenthaler and apologized for the breakdown in Montgomery. The city's police commissioner, a notorious segregationist, had gone back on his agreement and let the mob run wild.[60]

In Washington, Marshall, White, Oberdorfer, Dave Hackett, and others gathered in the attorney general's office for an emergency meeting early Saturday afternoon. Kennedy made an unsuccessful attempt to reach Governor Patterson. After updating the president and securing his approval, Robert Kennedy and his team activated their plans to assemble the federal marshals in Montgomery and secure a federal court order injunction specifically prohibiting the Klan from interfering with interstate travel. Oberdorfer told Kennedy that they should be able to have 250 men by Sunday morning. Kennedy said crisply to send 500. White and Oberdorfer flew out later that afternoon to Maxwell Air Force base in Montgomery.

James McShane, a former New York homicide detective who had worked with Robert Kennedy on the Rackets Committee, headed the US Marshal Service. He and twenty deputies flew separately to Montgomery, and an assortment of Border Patrol agents, prison guards, and revenue agents from different parts of the country made their way to Montgomery. It was, as White recalled, "a hurry up collection of people" with varied backgrounds and experiences. Many had had riot training, but a large number had no actual law enforcement experience—and they had never worked together before. While the marshals were arriving in Montgomery, John Doar sought out Judge Frank Johnson to secure a court injunction, only to discover that he was spending the weekend at his summer home fifty miles outside of Montgomery. Doar reached the judge's summer home just after midnight, and Johnson signed a restraining order, which was limited to the suspected instigators of the riots at the Montgomery bus station.[61]

On Sunday morning, several marshals were sent out to patrol the streets of Montgomery and serve the injunction on the Klan leaders named in Judge Johnson's order. Fifty marshals met Martin Luther King Jr. at the airport and accompanied him to a private meeting with Diane Nash, John Lewis, and several of the riders. King had come for a mass meeting scheduled for 8 p.m. at the First Baptist Church. Tensions heightened over the course of the day as Governor Patterson seized the platform at the state capitol to protest the federal "invasion" of Alabama. At the governor's insistence, Byron White met with him in the glare of local media attention, with Patterson protesting the presence of federal marshals in his state and warning that they risked arrest if they challenged state sovereignty. News of the planned mass meeting of African Americans that evening was widely publicized on the radio. Justice

Department officials proceeded cautiously, hoping that the governor would acknowledge the need to prepare for certain trouble.

A dozen marshals were stationed outside the First Baptist Church as people started gathering several hours before the start of the meeting. Plans to transport reinforcements from Maxwell Air Force base hit a snag when local army officials refused to allow the use of army trucks. White hurriedly patched together alternative transportation, relying mostly on US Postal Service trucks and Air Force vehicles. By the time the meeting was scheduled to begin, close to 1,500 people had crowded into the church. The mob of angry whites outside of the church continued to swell, eventually numbering more than two thousand. Shortly after 8 p.m., as the program began, members of the mob overturned a car outside the church and set it on fire, causing the gas tank to explode and ratcheting up fears that the church would be attacked by the rock-throwing, volatile crowd. Shouts of "Let's clean the niggers out of here" and threats to burn the church down pierced the air. Confederate flags waved over the mob. There was no local or state police presence. The thin line of marshals protecting the church was on the verge of being completely overwhelmed.[62]

Bobby Kennedy and Burke Marshall kept vigil at the Justice Department, maintaining constant communication with Byron White. As the situation outside of First Baptist Church rapidly deteriorated, Kennedy called for the deployment of the marshals stationed at Maxwell. A convoy of more than four hundred marshals, headed by James McShane, was soon en route to the church. In the interim, King phoned the attorney general from the church basement, describing a dire situation and warning of impending disaster. Kennedy assured him that a large contingent of federal marshals would arrive shortly. In the course of the conversation, the attorney general asked King whether the Freedom Riders might agree to a cooling-off period, giving federal and state officials a chance to work out a solution. King allowed that he could not speak for the riders, but he said he would discuss the idea with them. Before the conversation ended, the marshals arrived, much to King's relief. But his ordeal was really only just beginning.

The marshals initially succeeded in pushing the mob back, clearing the area with a round of tear gas. But the protesters rallied and broke through, after which they tried to storm through the church door, hurling a brick through a large window of stained glass. Kennedy placed army forces at Fort Benning on high alert, and Governor Patterson, who had been listening in on conversations between Kennedy and White with the help of an operator at Maxwell Air Force base, finally decided to act. At 10 p.m. the governor declared "qualified martial rule." City police and Alabama National Guardsmen soon created a buffer in front of the church and dispersed the rioters from the immediate vicinity. When McShane offered to put the marshals under the command of the National Guard, the colonel in charge accepted and ordered the marshals to leave the scene. Adjunct General Henry Graham announced that the state of Alabama had everything under control and needed no help from federal authorities.[63]

A long night followed. With the mob subdued, the mass meeting in the church proceeded. Congregants celebrated the Freedom Riders, lifting their voices in song amid impassioned speeches by King, Shuttlesworth, and James Farmer. It was close to midnight when the meeting ended. As men and women attempted to leave the church, they found the exits blocked by National Guardsmen with drawn bayonets. Graham told King that the situation outside the church was still unstable and said it would likely be early morning before they could exit the church. Packed into the hot, crowded church since early in the evening, this form of "protective custody" bore the cruel and punitive mark of Alabama segregationists. An exasperated King called Kennedy. Still in his office monitoring the situation after a long and tense day, Kennedy had little sympathy for King's complaint. "If it hadn't been for the U.S. marshals," he said, "you'd be as dead as Kelsey's nuts." King and his compatriots inside the church settled into makeshift sleeping arrangements for the duration of the night.

Shortly after King's call, RFK heard from an angry governor. He blamed Kennedy for the crisis, saying that Alabama had things under control, "and you can get out and leave it alone." Kennedy ignored the governor's blast and asked whether he and the National Guard could guarantee the safety of the Freedom Riders and their associates once they left the church. Patterson responded that he could guarantee the safety of everyone except King. Shocked, Kennedy demanded that the head of the National Guard call him and tell him personally that he was not able to protect King. Patterson then backed down, explaining the political pressures he faced. "John," Kennedy responded, "it's more important that these people in the church survive physically than for us to survive politically." Meanwhile, Byron White and his team were working to persuade the National Guard to end the siege and allow people to leave the church. When William Orrick, a Justice Department representative, threatened to send the marshals back, Graham finally agreed to begin the evacuation. Near dawn, National Guard trucks and jeeps pulled up to the church, and the Freedom Riders and congregants finally left First Baptist.[64]

The reckless and defiant action of local and state officials was for Robert Kennedy a baptism by fire. "Those fellows are at war with this country" he told John Doar, "they're at war." "There was no fooling around about it," Doar said, recalling Kennedy's attitude. "He was very realistic and very accurate about what was actually taking place." In a situation that could easily have ended with the burning of the church and untold death and devastation, Robert Kennedy had seen the precarious nature of federal power when state officials flaunted constitutional mandates, tolerated mob violence, and refused to take responsibility for maintaining public safety. The FBI had proved mostly ineffectual. FBI agents had maintained their distance and refused, when asked, to provide logistical support, a complaint that President Kennedy personally forwarded to FBI Director Hoover. Hoover phoned the attorney general the next morning to assure him that his agents would henceforth cooperate with his efforts. He reported that four men affiliated with the Ku Klux Klan had in fact been arrested in connection with the bus bombing in Anniston. But when speaking to his staff, Hoover insisted that the major threat to the social order in the South were Martin Luther King Jr. and the civil rights protesters, whom Hoover viewed as radical provocateurs. At the beginning of 1962, the FBI director would embark on a dedicated effort to link Martin Luther King Jr. to the Communist Party as a way to discredit the movement.[65]

Dismissing Kennedy's public call for a "cooling-off" period, the Freedom Riders continued to Mississippi. The violation of the Supreme Court's ruling had been amply demonstrated so far as Kennedy was concerned, and he would have liked the rides to stop as he sought enforcement of the order through the Interstate Commerce Commission. Aware of the potential violence that awaited them, the Freedom Riders prepared for the journey with a workshop on nonviolence led by James Lawson. Former governor James Colman predicted that they would never reach Jackson, Mississippi, alive and warned that the Justice Department could not trust Governor Ross Barnett. Kennedy turned to Mississippi senator James Eastland and "probably had thirty or forty conversations with him" during this period about what would happen in Mississippi. Eastland assured Kennedy that the highway patrol would meet the buses at the state line and secure safe passage to Jackson and into the bus terminal, but Eastland predicted that any violation of the state's segregation laws would result in massive arrests. Kennedy accepted that he had no control over the fact that the riders would be arrested. His primary concern was their physical safety, and he sought assurances that they would not be mobbed and beaten.[66]

———

ON WEDNESDAY, MAY 24, a bus carrying twelve Freedom Riders left Montgomery for Jackson, Mississippi. A half dozen National Guardsmen and a dozen reporters rode with them. Alabama highway patrolmen escorted the bus as far as the state line, while three reconnaissance planes and two helicopters kept watch from above. Mississippi state highway patrol accompanied the bus into Jackson. Several hundred supporters greeted the riders at the bus terminal. When the riders attempted to enter the "whites-only" waiting room, police arrested them for trespassing and took them to the maximum security prison in Parchman, Mississippi. Two more buses came that week, bringing more Freedom Riders. All were arrested. Justice Department efforts to get federal court orders to enjoin these arrests were unsuccessful. In the weeks that followed, men and women from all over the country came south and participated in the protest. By summer's end, 324 had traveled by bus to Jackson, attempted to enter the white waiting area, and been arrested. The city of Jackson tried each case separately, despite the fact that the legal issues were the same. Each person had to hire a lawyer, put up bail, and return for trial in an endless procession.[67]

On May 29, Robert Kennedy petitioned the Interstate Commerce Commission (ICC) to end segregation in interstate travel. "The time has come," he stated, "for this commission to declare unequivocally by regulations that a Negro passenger is free to travel the length and breadth of this country in the same manner as any other passenger." Burke Marshall commented that "this was a much more imaginative and controversial step" than the commission, a "stuffy" quasi-legal body, was accustomed to taking. But Kennedy was determined to get a strong ruling. Marshall and Kennedy worked with William Tucker, a commission member from Massachusetts, to determine how best to approach particular commissioners. At Kennedy's request, Secretary of Defense McNamara and Secretary of State Dean Rusk wrote letters attesting to the negative effects of bus and train segregation on Black servicemen and on visiting diplomats. Still, Burke Marshall was stunned when the ICC unanimously adopted the rules proposed by Kennedy.

On September 22, the ICC issued orders mandating the desegregation of all buses and terminals servicing interstate transportation and requiring that rules be posted on carriers and in terminals specifically stating that discrimination based on race, color, or national origins was forbidden. Any drivers failing to report interference with the orders would be subject to fines of up to $500, as would all other violators of the order. All signs calling for separation by race had to be removed. The order became effective on November 1. During the next three months, the Justice Department actively monitored enforcement and filed six actions in federal court for violations. For the most part, communities and carriers across the nation complied with the new ruling. By early 1962, the Freedom Riders and Robert Kennedy's Justice Department had secured the desegregation of interstate travel.[68]

By the end of May, the struggle around race and civil rights had come to dominate Robert Kennedy's attention and concern. As his brother's closest adviser, Bobby was also deeply involved in foreign policy deliberations in the wake of the Bay of Pigs fiasco in Cuba. Having been burned by the inflated assessments and poor advice of military and intelligence officials, JFK became even more reliant on his brother's sharp mind, political acumen, and dedication. There was talk of Bobby taking over as head of the Central Intelligence Agency, but he was committed to the work of the Justice Department. He would not move to the CIA.

—

THE FREEDOM RIDES CONSTITUTED the first major domestic crisis Robert Kennedy faced as Attorney General. For more than a solid week of days that often stretched late into the night, Kennedy wrestled with "the amazing problem of how to get a small busload of U.S. citizens from one U.S. city to another U.S. city along U.S. highways," wrote a *Time* reporter who covered the crisis from the Justice Department. He observed that Kennedy immersed himself in the fast moving situation, and "carried on endless telephone conversations with college students, Negro ministers, southern governors, congressmen, senators, police chiefs, bus company officials, the FBI, Justice Department men on the scene, and his brother, the President." While RFK realized he could not control events, he could and did control the federal reaction to them. "There is a great deal of skepticism about Bobby Kennedy, kid brother to the president," the reporter observed, but "this week he proved himself. He was no brash kid recklessly making his weight felt, but a cool and determined public official maintaining a well-considered position in a hot-tempered time."[69]

Kennedy's crash course in the stark realities of the Jim Crow system and the movement dedicated to overturning that system crystalized his understanding of what was at stake. James Carroll, working as an intern at the FBI during the summer of the Freedom Rides, recalled a speech Kennedy delivered to the college interns late in the summer of 1961. Expecting to hear "a diatribe against communism or crime," Carroll was surprised when Kennedy spoke "feelingly" about civil rights. Carroll described the impact of the speech on him as "the source of a life changing epiphany." Kennedy, Carroll recalled, "identified the end of segregation as the most important challenge facing America, and the Justice Department."[70]

The Freedom Riders, through their well-publicized exposure of state-sanctioned defiance of federal law, hoped to raise national consciousness and awareness as well as secure enforcement of the law. Yet most Americans were unmoved by the brutality and lawlessness that met the riders. According to opinion polls, only one in four Americans supported the Freedom Rides. That summer, James Baldwin commented that even "well-meaning white people didn't realize that they didn't know anything about this at all." Speaking to a broader reality, he observed that "white people in New York talk about Alabama as though they had no Harlem. To ignore what is happening in their own back yard is a great device on the part of white people." In the face of a rising racial crisis, Baldwin contended that white Americans "won't be able to do anything about this until they're willing to face their own history. If you don't know what happened behind you, you have no idea of what's happening around you."[71]

CHAPTER SIX

The Challenge of a Decade

|||

ON MARCH 5, after an appearance on *CBS News* focused on international communism, Bobby Kennedy walked from CBS's headquarters on 65th Street to 103rd Street in East Harlem. He was scheduled to meet with youth worker Joseph Gomez and members of three street gangs: the Aces and Redwings, predominantly Puerto Rican and African American, and an Italian American gang. It was dusk when Bobby and his aide Ed Guthman arrived. Kennedy was early, so he sat for a while on the curb, observing.

The young men ranged in age from sixteen to nineteen. One had been in prison for murder, another for armed robbery; several had been arrested for selling narcotics. The meetings lasted close to three hours. "What are you doing here?" was the common question. The attorney general said he was interested in them. He asked where they lived, what they did with their time, where they worked. He found that none were in school and few had jobs. "There was much talk about violence and the need to protect their turf," Guthman later wrote. Kennedy asked members of each gang what they thought the federal government should do to help. They hesitated, thought about the question—and in the end, whether Black, white, or Hispanic, they offered the same answer: more jobs and more recreational facilities.[1]

Two days later, Kennedy announced plans to establish guidance centers to help juvenile defendants' transition from prison back to their communities. Too many young people go back to a life of crime, he said, when they return to the very conditions that got them in trouble in the first place. He would work with specialists in the Labor Department and the Department of Health, Education, and Welfare to provide intensive vocational training, academic training, and counseling—and help finding jobs. Moving away from the ever popular political sloganeering about being tough on crime, Kennedy was connecting with fresh thinking in the area of juvenile delinquency.[2]

In the early 1960s, there was considerable activity around this issue, challenging the traditional approach of social workers, who focused on individual maladjustment and dysfunctional families, and turning attention to social conditions in communities where poverty and substandard schooling shut adolescents out of most opportunities to contribute positively to society.[3] Even before JFK's inauguration, Robert Kennedy had been pondering the causes of juvenile delinquency and what could be done about it. After his brother became president, RFK appointed his high school friend David Hackett to investigate the issue, installing him in a small office that opened onto Bobby's own. At his first press conference, Kennedy commented on the "alarming increase" in the arrests of young people under eighteen—they had almost doubled since 1948. He said he recognized that this was not an isolated issue, and that juvenile crime was intimately connected to problems of poverty, substandard schools, and unemployment. The problem knew no racial boundaries, but it was amplified in hypersegregated urban areas.[4]

Hackett sought out influential sociologists Lloyd Ohlin and Richard Cloward at Columbia University, who published the pioneering study *Delinquency and Opportunity*. Hackett also reached out to community activists, including Kenneth Clark, an adviser on *Brown v. Board of Education* and now director of a Harlem-based youth project, and Richard Boone, who worked with Chicago youth and with community organizer Saul Alinsky, who emphasized that the poor and disadvantaged should play an integral role in shaping solutions to problems in their own communities. The team drilled into the structural underpinnings of youth criminality, which they identified as a lack of access to a decent education, rampant unemployment, racial discrimination, long-term poverty, poor health care, and poor recreational facilities. While social welfare agencies traditionally focused on treatment of the individual, Hackett and his team would play a key role in shifting attention to community-based solutions.[5]

Hackett's appointment showcased Kennedy's tendency to select people based on his own instincts rather than their resumes. Richard Boone thought Hackett's inexperience was probably an asset. "He had no ego problems," Boone reflected, and "this wonderful knack of understanding what he didn't know." Jule Sugarman felt that Hackett "had the kind of mind and the kind of interest that caused him to probe people rather deeply and to draw out their ideas."[6]

Hackett consulted with experts across different fields and came up with a plan that would bring together three major departments—Justice; Labor; and Health, Education, and Welfare (HEW). On May 11, a week after the start of the Freedom Rides, President Kennedy issued an executive order creating the President's Committee on Juvenile Delinquency and Youth

Crime. His brother would serve as chair, and David Hackett was named executive director. Arthur Goldberg, the labor secretary, and HEW secretary Abraham Ribicoff were also on the committee. The president accompanied his executive order with legislation asking for $50 million to fund a five-year program to help local and state governments develop community-based pilot projects directed at youth. In September, Congress passed the legislation, authorizing $30 million dollars for three years, and appropriated funds for new guidance centers on a one-year trial basis in four cities.[7]

The president's committee was really the attorney general's committee. It functioned out of his office and knitted together a group who became known as "the guerillas," initially drawn together around the problem of juvenile delinquency but in essence dedicated to tackling the twin ills of poverty and inequality. They met regularly to strategize and come up with ideas. Bobby Kennedy would find an hour here and there to join them—over breakfast, in the evening—pushing the group toward the goals he favored. His vision was for a program of federal assistance for community-based initiatives. Deep down, he believed that communities knew best what they needed.[8]

Cities across the country were invited to apply for funding to support pilot projects. Proposals were submitted from Cleveland; Charleston, West Virginia; Detroit; Los Angeles; Boston; and other cities. Projects were funded in sixteen cities and included employment programs, work-study programs, and teacher training programs—all involving a wide range of community organizations. Many served Black youth living in deeply impoverished and segregated urban conditions. One of these was the Harlem Youth Opportunity Unlimited, under the direction of Kenneth Clark. From late 1961 through 1962, Robert Kennedy visited every one of the pilot projects and took an active interest in several in Washington, DC. Hackett recalled that neither he nor Kennedy had ever been involved "up close" with poverty or race prior to this effort—and they were shocked as they began to see conditions around the country.[9]

———

WHILE THE CONSEQUENCES of racial discrimination in northern urban areas festered, in the early months of the Kennedy administration the nation's escalating racial crisis was centered in the South. The NAACP's string of Supreme Court victories had begun eroding the legal foundation of Jim Crow, but most of the voting population of the South was still dedicated to maintaining a segregated society. Supreme Court rulings could, it was felt, be ignored thanks to the power of southern Democrats who, by virtue of seniority, served as chairs of major House and Senate committees and proved capable of blocking or stripping down any legislation that threatened the region's racial order.

In 1961 and 1962, SNCC and CORE activists moved into communities across the Deep South, and in Mississippi, the heart of white resistance, Bob Moses and others mounted a bold insurgency to secure the right to vote. While local efforts of this sort drew a growing number of supporters, they received scant attention from the media and failed to sway national opinion. The one confrontation that did get attention took place in Albany, Georgia—where SNCC, the NAACP, and the SCLC all converged. Blacks made up more than a third of the population of Albany, a small city in southwest Georgia that was the home of Albany State College. A local branch of the NAACP and the Dougherty County Voters League had been active in the area for several decades, but local white leadership was determined to maintain the color line. City officials did not want a repeat of the violence that met the Freedom Rides or the negative publicity it might bring. Police chief Laurie Pritchett, who studied the tactics of Martin Luther King Jr., proved to be an effective enforcer of the city's policy.

In the fall of 1961, SNCC field secretary Charles Sherrod and fellow staffer Cordell Reagon went to Albany to work on voter registration. They found that segregation was being enforced at the railway terminal and bus station, in defiance of ICC rulings that mandated the desegregation of all bus and rail terminals servicing interstate travel. Later that fall, eight SNCC activists took a train to Albany and entered the white section of the train station. Police chief Pritchett forced them out and then arrested them for blocking the sidewalk. On December 6, the day of the activists' trial, more than 250 Black students marched on City Hall; Pritchett's police arrested them. More demonstrations followed, and by the end of the day, nearly five hundred people had been arrested. The protesters were charged with such things as parading without a permit, breach of peace, and failure to obey an officer. Arrests quickly exceeded the capacity of local jails, but Pritchett had made arrangements to use nearby prison facilities.[10]

SNCC's defiant action converged with efforts by local leadership to open negotiations with the city to end segregation in all public facilities. An uneasy alliance was established between the young activists and the more established NAACP leadership, local SCLC representatives, and other civic groups. Mayor Asa Kelley, recently elected with three-quarters of the Black vote, was inclined at least to talk with local Black leadership. Robert Kennedy and Burke Marshall, who had been monitoring the situation, each called the mayor and encouraged his efforts. The city commissioners, however, refused to meet or negotiate with Black leaders. The movement responded by mounting a boycott of white merchants, severely impacting many local businesses. The city refused to yield.[11]

"It is in the churches of the South that the script of the drama of desegregation is being written," wrote Robert Shelton, reporting on the Albany movement for the *New York Times*. Music infused packed rallies and mass meetings at Mt. Zion Baptist Church and Shiloh Baptist Church, with songs expressing the hope, suffering, and joy that had sustained generations of struggle. Lyrics of old spirituals were adjusted to reflect the moment. The words of "Go Down Moses" became "Go Down Kennedy, / Way down in Georgia land, / Tell old Pritchett, / To let my people go." When Martin Luther King Jr. visited Albany in late December, the freedom chants and musical expressions of faith and struggle that filled the churches reminded him of the early days of the Montgomery bus boycott. Responding to an appeal by Rev. William Anderson, the leader of the Albany movement, King became deeply involved in the struggle in Albany and would be jailed twice in connection with it.[12]

The boycott continued through the winter and spring, and demonstrations began again in July. Pritchett continued his policy of mass arrests, while maintaining order in the city. The affable former football tackle at the University of Georgia became a favorite of news reporters. The *New York Times* described him as "an outstanding example of the new breed of Southern policemen—tough, dedicated and intelligent." In July, frustrated Black onlookers threw rocks and bottles at the police as they arrested peaceful protesters outside a church. Pritchett was on the scene immediately and praised for his "bravery and judgement" in restoring order. An investigator for the Southern Regional Council saw it differently, reporting that he ran Albany "in the silent sure manner of an efficient police state."[13]

President Kennedy watched news reports of ministers being dragged off to jail in some degree of incredulity. "It was not only that they didn't give them any rights to any fair treatment," Burke Marshall remembered the president saying, "they wouldn't even let them complain about not having it." JFK was appalled by the refusal of the city leadership to meet with Black citizens. One weekend, Kennedy, who was in Hyannis Port, "somehow got it in his head that he was going to worry about Albany that weekend, and so he called me several times," Marshall recalled. Marshall explained the complexity of the situation—which involved local laws in part and federal laws in part—and said those matters were being dealt with in the courts.[14]

The two men talked about Albany in some detail shortly before the president was called to a press conference to discuss recent negotiations with the Soviet Union about nuclear testing. When a reporter asked Kennedy about Albany, he didn't hold back: "Let me say that I find it wholly inexplicable why the city council of Albany will not sit down with the citizens of Albany, who may be Negroes, and attempt to secure them, in a peaceful way, their rights," he said. "The United States government is involved in sitting down in Geneva with the Soviet Union. I can't understand why the government of Albany, the city council of Albany, cannot do the same for American citizens." Kennedy's statement drew a sharp rebuke from Georgia senator Richard Russell Jr. and Mayor Kelley.[15]

By midsummer, with no end in sight to the protests, the city of Albany secured an injunction from a federal district judge, J. Robert Elliott, barring mass demonstrations, picketing, boycotts, and other protest activities. Elliot had recently been appointed to the court by President Kennedy. In a press conference condemning the ruling as "unjust and unconstitutional," Martin Luther King Jr. suggested that recent events revealed that "there are some few federal judges in the South who are engaged in a conspiracy with state and local politicians to maintain the evil system of segregation." The movement immediately enlisted a coalition of lawyers to challenge the ruling. A small group of movement lawyers and leaders met with Robert Kennedy and Burke Marshall to discuss the situation.[16]

Five days later, the Justice Department filed an amicus brief opposing the city's request for an injunction. "The demonstrations in question were the direct product of the failure of Albany officials to take any steps to grant the Negro citizens of Albany their constitutional rights," the brief stated. "The city officials should not be permitted to use the situation thus created as a basis for a Federal injunction restraining demonstrations seeking to introduce constitutional right into Albany." Justice Department attorneys also argued that the court lacked jurisdiction in the case, since the city was seeking an injunction under Reconstruction-era statutes that were intended to govern the conduct of persons acting "under the color of law" (that is, passing themselves off as government officials). King praised the Justice Department's action, stating that it "vindicated" the position of the Albany movement and was "an expression on the part of the administration of their legal and moral support, of inestimable value for the ultimate solution of the problem."[17]

Over the course of eight months of boycotts and protests, more than one thousand people had been arrested, and segregation remained firmly intact. The numbers of people willing to join protest marches dwindled. In mid-August, Reverend Anderson announced that there would be no more protests; the movement would turn its attention to voter registration. The national press deemed the Albany movement a failure. But while there had been no tangible gains, the experience—the mass meetings, the protests, facing and surviving the experience of jail—had prepared Black people in Albany for the long haul. The movement would continue, and Martin Luther King Jr. left with lessons that would guide him in the future.[18]

King partially blamed the Kennedy administration for not doing more to pressure city officials. "The government enters the fray only at the periphery, filing an amicus curiae brief and a lawsuit," he later reflected. But there were other factors. The unyielding stance of the city commissioners and clever tactics of police chief Pritchett wore down a movement weakened by internal divisions. For Jack and Bobby Kennedy, Albany offered a lesson in how local and state power and a federal judge—in this case one JFK himself was responsible for appointing—could work in tandem to uphold segregation. The Kennedys' sympathies were with the movement and with the demands of the protesters. Marshall noted that Bobby "knew perfectly well that, if he were Black, that's exactly what he'd be doing." He was "really sympathetic to that cause and to everybody involved in it." At the same time, big demonstrations raised problems for the president. Awareness of those problems affected how Bobby looked at the situation.[19]

The Albany crisis convinced Bobby that voter registration should be a major focus of the fight to overturn the racial caste system in the South. He later recalled that he and King had several conversations about this topic during the Albany protests, and the two men "did not see eye to eye on some of these matters." But securing the vote was an area where the Justice Department had clear authority to act, and Kennedy believed that working on voting rights would be more helpful than anything else he could do. Voting rights were, he contended, the key to deeper changes.[20]

———

SOME OF THE OBSTACLES the civil rights movement faced in the South were a direct consequence of judicial appointments President Kennedy made during his first year in office. Early in his term, Congress created sixty new federal district judgeships, which Kennedy filled. The selection of federal judges, as Robert Kennedy explained in an interview, had "grown up as a senatorial appointment with the advice and consent of the President." The Justice Department was responsible for reviewing the background and record of candidates and, if no specific problem was flagged, the nomination would be made.[21]

For a Democratic president concerned with civil rights, judicial appointments presented a particular problem, as many of the southern Democratic Senators advising the president were committed segregationists. These senators had not been a problem for President Eisenhower, whose appointments to the federal bench included Elbert Tuttle, John Minor Wisdom, and Frank Johnson—outstanding jurists who went on to write sweeping decisions enforcing *Brown v. Board of Education* and voting rights laws. Eisenhower's attorney general invoked party affiliation in ignoring the preferences of southern Democratic senators, fulfilling Eisenhower's desire to appoint highly qualified, fair-minded judges. The Kennedys were aware of the problem they faced, and the Justice Department's vetting efforts were considerable. Nevertheless, President Kennedy ended up appointing several judges who were die-hard segregationists, including J. Robert Elliott of Georgia and Harold Cox of Mississippi.[22]

Senator Herman Talmadge had recommended Elliott for the US District Court for the Middle District of Georgia. Elliot had served in the Georgia state legislature as floor leader under both Talmadge and his father. Elliott's association with racist views and policies were of great concern to Robert Kennedy and his associates, but the highly respected appeals court judge Elbert Tuttle told Kennedy he thought Elliott would do his duty as a federal judge and uphold the constitution. Tuttle based his opinion on a conversation with William Bootle, the judge responsible for the desegregation of the University of Georgia. A. T. Walden, a prominent Black politician in Georgia, also supported Elliot's nomination. Marshall felt that Kennedy would have advised against the appointment if not for Tuttle's recommendation.[23]

Harold Cox was a different story. James Eastland, chair of the Senate Judiciary Committee, had recommended his former law partner for a position on the US District Court for the Southern District of Mississippi. Cox's close association with Eastland made Cox immediately suspect; this association was probably the reason the NAACP opposed his appointment. Kennedy asked Marshall to look for clues as to how Cox might function on the court. Marshall discovered that he was not a member of the White Citizens' Council, a favorable sign because the great majority of white Mississippi lawyers were members. In fact, Marshall found no instances of Cox's having taken a public position on racial issues. Marshall spoke with several African American contacts in Mississippi, who had no specific information on Cox. He was rated "exceptionally highly qualified" by the American Bar Association Committee. Still, there were concerns. Marshall, Kennedy, and Byron White discussed Cox at length. But in the end, as Marshall reluctantly confided, "we simply could not come up with anything against him."[24]

RFK invited Cox to the Justice Department and put the question to him directly. Sitting on the couch in his private office, Kennedy quickly got to the point: "I said that the great reservation I had," he recalled in a 1964 interview, "was the question of whether he'd enforce the law and whether he'd live up to the Constitution and the laws, and the interpretation of the Constitution by the Supreme Court; it's the law of the land." Cox said he would. "He was very gracious," Bobby recalled, "and he said there wouldn't be any problem about that, and that he felt he could accomplish a great deal, and that this would not be a problem to him." Based on Marshall's investigation and the interview, Robert Kennedy advised his brother to consent to the nomination of Harold Cox.[25]

Cox was John Kennedy's first judicial appointment. The judge took his seat on the US District Court on June 30, 1961, and proceeded to routinely rule against the Justice Department, blast federal overreach, and openly voice racist sentiments from the bench. In the growing struggle in Mississippi, Harold Cox would do everything within his power to obstruct and derail the voting rights cases painstakingly mounted and argued by the lawyers of the Justice Department's Civil Rights Division. Summing up the experience, Kennedy said, "I was convinced he was honest with me, and he wasn't."[26]

———

IN JULY 1961, Bob Moses sent a letter to the Justice Department informing it that SNCC was operating in Mississippi, encouraging Black citizens to register and vote. "What do you plan to do about Mississippi?" Bobby Kennedy asked Marshall after seeing the letter. Three months had passed since Justice Department attorneys had initiated a broad campaign to challenge voter discrimination in Louisiana, Alabama, and Mississippi. We "uncovered every scheme practiced by the resourceful Southern registrars who had spent five generations keeping Negro citizens from the vote," Doar recalled. The work of Bob Moses and SNCC volunteers changed the political dynamic in Mississippi overnight.[27]

In the wake of *Brown v. Board of Education,* the Mississippi legislature added an additional requirement to existing voter qualifications, mandating that prospective voters be able to interpret any section of the state constitution to the registrar's satisfaction. At the same time, members of the newly organized White Citizens' Council pressured African Americans who had registered to remove their names from the rolls. By the end of 1955, not a single Black person was registered in fourteen counties in rural Mississippi. That was the year when fourteen-year-old Emmett Till and two voting rights activists, George Lee and Lamar Smith, were murdered. The handful of local NAACP activists, like Amzie Moore, who had survived in Mississippi "were indispensable," Moses recalled. It was "inconceivable that we could have taken root without them." At the same time, the Freedom Rides "had permeated black consciousness in Mississippi," Moses observed, energizing young people and providing recruits for SNCC's effort.[28]

Mississippi emerged as ground zero in the struggle around voting rights. In a state where Black people constituted 43.3 percent of the population, fewer than 4 percent of those eligible were registered to vote. In more than half of the state's counties, fewer than 1 percent were registered. Activists moved into the most dangerous parts of the state, working with locals and with NAACP stalwarts, cultivating community-based leaders, and steadily building a state-wide voter registration drive in the face of unbridled terror. SNCC's campaign commanded the attention of Justice Department officials, who had been at work in the region since April, preparing to bring the first voting rights suits in the state. This was a painstaking process, involving an intensive review of voting records by division lawyers—after obtaining access from resistant local officials—who then contacted and interviewed Black citizens, documented evidence of voter discrimination, and identified witnesses willing to testify. By late summer, Moses and his fellow activists were conducting voting classes and accompanying men and women to the courthouse to register. The relationship forged between Bob Moses and the Civil Rights Division of the Justice Department would play a formative role in the interface between the federal government and the movement, testing and ultimately exposing the limited reach of federal support.[29]

In early August, Bob Moses and his fellow SNCC activists John Hardy and Reginald Robinson began to work in McComb, a small town in southwest Mississippi, at the invitation of C.C. Bryant, a World War II veteran and local NAACP leader. The activists canvassed the community, encouraging people to go to the courthouse to take a voting test. Moses led a voter education class at the end of the week, reviewing the form and likely questions. He accompanied a handful of people to the courthouse and helped them apply. Soon word spread to Walthall and Amite Counties, poverty-stricken neighboring areas with a reputation for violence. There were no Black voters registered in Walthall County, where the Justice Department had recently filed a suit, and only one in Amite County. Several Black farmers from both counties came over, eager to register, Moses recalled. He felt they couldn't turn down the tough areas, "or people would lose confidence in you." He and SNCC worker John Hardy set up registration schools in both counties.[30]

In Amite County, Moses worked with E. W. Steptoe, a fifty-three-year old dairy and cotton farmer who had set up a local branch of the NAACP. After taking two elderly women and one man to register at the courthouse in Liberty, Moses was stopped by the police and arrested on trumped-up charges. "Like any black person living in America, I knew racism," he recalled. "What I hadn't encountered before Mississippi was the use of law as an instrument of outright oppression." Awaiting trial that night, he requested his one phone call and used it to call John Doar. Speaking in a loud voice, he cited the violations of the 1957 and 1960 Civil Rights Acts and demanded an investigation—signaling to local officials that their actions were being exposed to federal scrutiny. Moses was found guilty but was given a 90-day suspended sentence and a small fine.

A week later, he was accompanying two men to the courthouse to register when Jack Caston, a cousin of the sheriff, beat him over the head with a knife handle. Moses continued onto the courthouse with the two men, his head bleeding profusely, and filed charges. When the case came to court, Caston testified that Moses had attacked him first and was acquitted by an all-white jury. Moses's cool courage in the face of these terror tactics reinforced his standing in the Black community and its receptiveness to his message. The Justice Department sent the FBI to investigate, but agents failed to interview key witnesses and did not report Moses's injuries.[31]

The voter registration drive in Mississippi slowed after the attack but did not end completely. John Hardy started a voting project in Walthall County on August 18. Civil Rights Division attorney John Kirby, who was working on a case in Walthall, contacted Hardy and obtained a set of forms he was using in his voter education class. Hardy conducted a few classes at the Mount Moriah Baptist Church and accompanied several small groups to the courthouse in Tylertown, the county seat, to register. On September 7, he took Edith Simmons Peters, 63, and Lucius Williams, 62, to the courthouse, where the registrar, John Wood, beat him on the head with a pistol. As Hardy staggered out of the courthouse, the sheriff arrested him on a charge of disorderly conduct. As soon as John Doar learned about the assault in the registrar's office, he sent two young lawyers, Bud Sather and Gerald Stern, to investigate. They gathered enough evidence for the Justice Department to sue to enjoin state criminal prosecution of Hardy.[32]

Doar made his first trip to Mississippi in mid-September. Arriving in southwest Mississippi, he commented, was like "going back into the nineteenth century." On September 20, two days before Hardy was scheduled to be tried, Doar filed a suit in federal district court charging that Black applicants for voter registration had been intimidated and requesting a temporary injunction against the prosecution of John Hardy. When the court refused the injunction, the government immediately appealed to the federal appellate court. Doar and the assistant attorney general of Mississippi flew to Montgomery for an evening hearing before Judge Richard Rives of the US Court of Appeals for the Fifth Circuit, who issued an order expediting the hearing and setting the date for October 3.[33]

On the evening of Sunday September 24, John Doar sought out Bob Moses at E. W. Steptoe's farm. Meeting for the first time, Doar was struck by the extent of Moses's injuries, which the FBI had failed to disclose. Steptoe said that he and Herbert Lee, a successful farmer and member of the Amite NAACP branch, had been threatened several times. A forty-two-year-old father of nine, Lee had attended voter registration classes and driven Moses around the county to meet with prospective voters. At one point, he reported that whites had been taking down license plate numbers of cars parked outside the church where voter registration classes were being held, which Moses, in turn, reported to the FBI and Justice Department. Moses and Steptoe took Doar to Lee's farm for a talk, but Lee wasn't home. Doar returned to Washington that night.[34]

The following morning, Herbert Lee drove several bales of cotton to the cotton gin near Liberty. E. H. Hurst, a member of the Mississippi legislature, drove up behind him and the two men began to argue—allegedly about money that Lee owed Hurst. Hurst had a gun in his hand. Bystanders heard a shot and saw Herbert Lee lying on the ground. Hurst said that Lee had had a tire iron in his hand and claimed to have acted in self-defense. Louis Allen, a Black man who was near the scene, corroborated Hurst's account at a coroner's hearing the next day. Devastated by Lee's murder, Bob Moses conducted his own investigation, interviewing Black people from the area, several of whom had been at the cotton gin that morning. He learned from one source that Hurst had been paid $1,000 to kill Herbert Lee. The murder of Herbert Lee, in broad daylight by a Mississippi state representative, had a chilling effect on the voter registration campaign in southwest Mississippi. But the murder deepened Moses's own commitment and that of his small band of activists.[35]

A month later, the Justice Department prevailed in the Hardy case. The legal victory was significant but had no direct impact on the day-to-day struggle of Black citizens in southwest Mississippi. In his argument before the Fifth Circuit Court of Appeals, Burke Marshall stated that the continued prosecution of John Hardy "was designed to and would intimidate qualified Negroes from attempting to register to vote in Walthall County." The case was less about Hardy's rights, Marshall said, than the impact of his prosecution. The 1957 Civil Rights Act provided that "no person shall intimidate, threaten or coerce any person for the purpose of interfering with the right of a person to vote." The act authorized the attorney general to institute a civil action for preventive relief. On October 27, a panel of the Fifth Circuit ruled 2–1 in favor of the government. Marshall noted the historic nature of the ruling: "this was the only time a federal court issued an injunction to prevent unadorned abuse of police power . . . turning on the special statutory interests of the United States in preventing intimidation of citizens seeking to vote in federal elections."[36]

Herbert Lee's murder clearly showed the dangers facing civil rights activists and Black citizens seeking to vote in a place where public officials would countenance any means to stop them. Over the following months, the witness Louis Allen told Moses that his testimony before the coroner's hearing had been coerced and that Hurst had killed Lee in cold blood. Allen was willing to testify to this effect before a grand jury if he could be guaranteed protection. Moses informed John Doar, who advised him that there was no way the Justice Department could provide protection for Allen—and in any case, whether he testified or not, Hurst would undoubtedly be found not guilty by an all-white jury. With no protection, Allen stuck with his original story, but when two local white men posing as FBI agents interviewed him he told the truth, leaving him a marked man. Allen suffered economic harassment, was jailed on false charges, and had his jaw broken by a deputy sheriff. Burke Marshall instructed the FBI to interview Allen and others, listing specific questions that might produce evidence to bring a federal lawsuit. But nothing came of it. Allen was preparing to leave the state, fearing for his life, when he was shot and killed outside of his home.[37]

———

THE JUSTICE DEPARTMENT'S EFFORTS to use the powers it had been granted by the Civil Rights Acts opened up a "crawl space," as Bob Moses put it, for SNCC activists in Mississippi. Early in 1962, SNCC joined with CORE and NAACP representatives to establish the Council of Federated Organizations (COFO), and secured a grant from the newly created voter registration project supported by the Taconic Foundation and the Field Foundation and informally endorsed by the president and attorney general. SNCC field secretaries fanned out across the Delta and set up operations in six communities. The young organizers energized local youth and worked slowly and methodically to engage all sectors of these poor communities in voter registration and political organizing. Women emerged as a major force in the Delta projects. Fannie Lou Hamer, a sharecropper from Sunflower County, became a powerful leader and organizer. For the mostly college-educated SNCC activists, exposure to the desperate poverty of the Delta was a radicalizing experience. They began to understand that ending segregation and securing the vote would not make up for generations of racial repression. In the short term, however, holding on to incremental gains in the face of unyielding white repression remained the greatest challenge, one that increasingly depended on the intervention of the federal government.

Civil Rights Division attorneys settled in for the long haul, spending weeks at a time in the field, working county by county in Mississippi, Alabama, and Louisiana. Their numbers grew from five to twenty-two over the course of two years and included the first Black attorney to work in the South for the Justice Department. Thelton Henderson, a recent graduate of UC-Berkeley Law School recruited by John Doar as part of the department's effort to hire Black attorneys, was initially assigned to work on voting cases in Shreveport, Louisiana. Years later he recalled both the excitement and fear that accompanied him as he made his first foray into the Deep South since his family left Louisiana when he was three. He had several encounters with police, including an arrest "for driving while black" in Mississippi, but his identification as a federal employee eased his way. What he remembered most vividly fifty years later were the people he met while interviewing citizens whose voter applications had been rejected. "They sometimes broke my heart," he remembered. "They would study, they would read. They really believed in the system. They didn't have a chance of passing." But after being turned away, they would study and go again. Seeing these people "work so hard to get a basic right to which they were entitled . . . stiffened my spine" and commitment to helping them, he said.[38]

The voting cases filed in the spring and early summer of 1961 were labor intensive and largely disappointing. Dallas County, Alabama, presented a typical example. From the registrar to the courts, the entire process was geared to stall and obstruct voter registration. The Justice Department filed *United States v. Atkins* in April 1961, but thirteen months would pass before Judge Daniel H. Thomas, a Truman appointee, called up the case. In the interim the registrars had resigned, and, after a hiatus, new registrars had been appointed. Under the new board some 114 Black voters had been added to the rolls, boosting Black registration to 242 out of 15,000 eligible voters. The judge ultimately ruled against the Justice Department—delivering his verdict six months after the trial—triggering an appeal to the Fifth Circuit. Marshall and Doar came to understand that Black voting in the Deep South was much more than a legal problem. They faced a vast entrenched legal, political, and cultural apparatus that, since the turn of the century, had been structured to sustain a caste system. Nevertheless, Marshall and Doar saw that the courage and determination of Black citizens seeking to exercise their rights was steadily driving change.[39]

By December of 1961, Marshall and his colleagues in the Civil Rights Division were challenging as unconstitutional legislation in Louisiana and Mississippi requiring literacy tests and other voter qualifications. The litigation, which would culminate with a major court victory, took four years and went all the way to the Supreme Court. In Haywood and Fayette Counties, Tennessee, sharecroppers who tried to register and vote were subject to mass evictions. The Justice Department ultimately prevailed against the local farmers and businessmen who had masterminded the economic retaliation, but the case took more than two years to resolve and had little impact on the broader struggle. In the aftermath of these legal victories, Black voter registration increased from 0 to 2,000 in Haywood County and from 38 to more than 3,000 in Fayette County.[40]

After a year of difficult and frustratingly limited litigation, Bobby Kennedy came to the conclusion that "the voting problem was so deep rooted and so manifestly unfair that . . . it demands a solution which cannot be provided by lengthy litigation and on a piecemeal basis." He decided to target the literacy test, the tool most often used to deny African Americans the right to vote. The Justice Department had collected reams of evidence that Black men and women who were clearly literate—including college graduates and professors—had "failed" the literacy test. The Civil Rights Division proposed new legislation holding that anyone who had completed six years of schooling should be considered literate for the purposes of registration. Multiple studies had concluded as much. The bill would not deny states the right to use literacy tests but instead would standardize practices to block racially discriminatory applications. President Kennedy agreed to let his brother champion the legislation, but Marshall thought the president didn't have much confidence it would go through.[41]

Senator Mike Mansfield introduced the bill in March 1962, and Robert Kennedy's testimony before the House Judiciary Subcommittee on March 15 sparked weeks of political skirmishes. The literacy bill was taken up by Congress at the same time as a constitutional amendment to abolish the poll tax, leading to extensive debate on voting rights, states' rights, and constitutional guarantees. Republicans, angling for an edge, complained that the literacy bill was not broad enough. Representative William McCulloch, the ranking Republican on the Judiciary Committee, pointed out that more than eight million Americans of voting age had less than a sixth-grade education. Emphasizing the need for bipartisan support, RFK urged members from both parties to get behind the literacy bill, claiming it had the best chance for success. He said it was "all well and good to make speeches, beat one's breast, and put out press releases. But the important thing is to get something done." To those who complained that the bill did not go far enough, the *New York Times* editorialized, "it would be the rankest politics to block a significant forward step on the grounds that it does not meet ultimate goals."[42]

The Senate Subcommittee on Constitutional Rights, chaired by Senator Sam Ervin of North Carolina, became the forum for a showdown between the attorney general and southern segregationists. The sixty-five-year-old Ervin, who would achieve celebrity status a decade later as chair of the Senate Watergate Committee, cultivated the image of a country lawyer, but the former associate justice of the North Carolina Supreme Court, with his Harvard Law degree, was a keen student of history and the Constitution. His blend of folksy humor and legal acuity was often disarming. Still, he met his match in the thirty-six-year-old attorney general. Bobby Kennedy began by observing that literacy tests were now the principal device used to keep Black people from voting. During his testimony, he emphasized that the purpose of the literacy bill was to eliminate "subjective" tests of voter qualifications, not to fix these qualifications. He observed that registrars exerted "wide discretion" in administering the tests, which were frequently used to disqualify Black voters. He urged the Senate to act promptly to curb these abuses.[43]

In a three-hour session, Ervin insisted that the bill was unconstitutional and invaded the rights of states to set voter qualifications. Kennedy suggested that the Fourteenth and Fifteenth Amendments prohibiting racial discrimination gave Congress ample authority to legislate on the issue. He went on to cite numerous examples of how the tests were "used to keep hundreds of thousands of our fellow citizens from voting." He noted how one would-be voter had failed to prove his "literacy" by incorrectly interpreting provisions from the state constitution involving debt liquidity. In another case, a schoolteacher was rejected because she pronounced the word "equity" as "eequity." He pointed to applicants who were denied because they had inserted "since birth" or "all my life" in the box asking for length of residence. Kennedy said he had many more examples, if Senator Ervin was interested, but that based on Kennedy's review of reams of evidence, "virtually no one with that amount of education [six years] has been turned down as a voter for other than racial reasons. Congressional action adopted to end this evil is not a question of innovation. It is long overdue."[44]

"If someone completes six grades and cannot read or write," Ervin opined, conveniently sidestepping Kennedy's examples, "I say he shouldn't be allowed to vote."

"Is this what happens in North Carolina schools?" Kennedy shot back. Ervin responded that it was "a question of fact."

"I just can't believe, Senator," Kennedy said, "in this day and age that you are arguing that someone who's passed the sixth grade is illiterate. . . . Doesn't it disturb you when you read of Negroes being denied the right to vote on these grounds. Doesn't it disturb you?"

"It does disturb me," Ervin said. "But it doesn't disturb me as much as nullifying the Constitution."[45]

Ervin suggested that instead of seeking new laws, the Justice Department should use existing statutes to bring lawsuits on behalf of those who were being denied the right to vote—exactly what Justice Department lawyers had been doing for a year, meeting a wall of obstruction. Kennedy explained that individual suits were time-consuming and difficult. The solution to the Negro voting problem could not be provided "by lengthy litigation on a piecemeal, county-by-county basis." He appealed to Ervin to reconsider his position: "I'd like to have you join with us in speeding this up," Kennedy said. "I would hope you would join with us in sponsoring this legislation, Senator." Ervin replied: "I love the Constitution too much to do so." "I love the Constitution too," Kennedy countered, "but this does not violate it." He returned to the widespread abuses that the bill was designed to meet, emphasizing that it did not interfere with the rights of states to set voter qualifications and was merely intended to ensure their fair application. The committee invited several witnesses to bolster the claim that a sixth-grade education was not an accurate measure of literacy. Alabama attorney general MacDonald Gallion testified that in the Black Belt counties of his state, "not one in fifty Negroes with a sixth-grade education are literate in the sense of knowledge or judgement relative to the voting process."[46]

Senator Richard Russell of Georgia had prepared his ranks for battle by the time the bill came for a vote in the Senate. Divided into four teams, nineteen southern Democrats launched a filibuster to block the bill from coming to a vote. During their "talkathon," the southerners hammered away at a central phrase coined by Sam Ervin, saying again and again that the bill was "unconstitutional and wholly unnecessary." Senators Richard Russell and John Stennis charged that the Justice Department had enough authority under the Civil Rights Acts of 1957 and 1960 and needed to do its job. Senator William Fulbright of Arkansas complained that the literacy bill was yet another example "of the long line of punitive measures directed against the South." Senate Majority Leader Mike Mansfield and Senate Minority Leader Everett Dirksen, both strong supporters of the legislation, worked to round up votes in both parties and bring the bill to a vote. Senator Russell lobbied to corral every possible vote against cloture, the only process by which it was possible to end a filibuster, requiring the vote of two-thirds of the senators present and voting. The Senate rarely invoked cloture and never had done so for a civil rights bill. Republican Senators, mostly from largely rural states with few Black voters, routinely joined southern Democrats in opposing cloture in such cases.

While the filibuster was grinding on, Kennedy told a group in New York, "regardless of the outcome, we will continue to press for legislation." In the spring of 1962, the prospects were not promising. Burke Marshall put his finger on the main problem: "There was no public pressure for the bill. We couldn't create any. We could hardly create any interest in the bill." Some senators "went through the motions," as Marshall recalled, but nobody cared about a bill "that should not have been controversial at all. They cared I guess more about keeping friends with Southern Senators or something else." Marshall went to see Senator Mansfield after the first vote and asked him whether there was any chance of bringing the filibuster to an end. Mansfield said no. They would need at least twenty-five Republicans to vote in favor of cloture. Marshall asked what he should tell people who were interested in civil rights legislation. As Marshall told the story, Mansfield said, "Tell them the truth." "What is the truth?" Marshall asked. Mansfield replied, "That you'll never get a civil rights bill with a Democratic president."[47]

After more than two weeks of droning oratory, Mansfield put cloture to a vote. The effort lost, 53–43, twenty-one votes short of the two-thirds needed. A strong majority voted not to table the bill. A second attempt was made several days later, with almost identical results. The bill was set aside, and the Senate moved on to business that had been backed up for three weeks. If the literacy bill had come to vote, all observers agreed, it would have passed comfortably. The bill "was filibustered to death by Southerners with such ease," one reporter noted, "that it was humiliating to the administration." And, the reported added, "it was clear the Southerners would fight until Christmas."[48]

———

ON MAY 3, Bobby Kennedy "ripped through southwest Virginia" like he was running for office, a *Washington Post* reporter observed, to promote the administration's civil rights efforts. He delivered the Law Day speech for the nonsegregated Virginia State Bar in Roanoke, fielded questions from two thousand people, held a press conference, and appeared on two half-hour television shows. Kennedy praised the Supreme Court's recent rulings in *Brown v. Board of Education* and *Baker v. Carr*, a landmark 1962 ruling that allowed federal courts to hear redistricting cases in which plaintiffs sought proportional representation based on changes in a state's population. The injustices the decisions aimed to remedy would, he said, ultimately be resolved by people acting locally. If states would act within the framework of these rulings and the Constitution, "states' rights" would take on a new meaning.[49]

Asked by a television interviewer about Prince Edward County, where 1,700 Black children were still without public schooling, Kennedy said the county was "a blight on Virginia and a reflection of our country." Then he added, "the Kennedy administration won't be satisfied until the schools are open and desegregated." Three days later, in New York, Kennedy insisted that ending voter discrimination was vital to American democracy. The civil rights struggle, he argued, was as critical as the arms race and the space race to the country's future.[50]

Five days after the literacy bill was shelved, Kennedy took religious leaders to task for failing to assume a more active role in the fight to end racial discrimination. Addressing six hundred delegates attending a conference of community leaders on equal employment opportunity, he said "it is difficult to understand how a preacher can get up on Sunday and talk about the love of God and the Ten Commandments, and then not speak up on civil rights." He appealed directly to clergy members in the audience, predicting that with the cooperation of the nation's clergy and private groups, the government could make great progress on the civil rights front. Just weeks earlier, Martin Luther King Jr. had told a meeting of 150 ministers that if the church failed to exert leadership in civil rights, "the church will go down in history as a solid bulwark of segregation in the United States."[51]

The Justice Department continued to use the tools at its disposal to engage in slow, tedious, labor-intensive efforts to chip away at a deeply entrenched system of discrimination. The department filed its first "contempt of court" case after a registrar in Forrest County, Mississippi, violated a previous court ruling forbidding him from discriminating against African Americans. The registrar had refused to register nineteen Black applicants—three college graduates and a National Science Foundation fellow among them. The district court rejected the case. Justice Department lawyers filed an appeal with the US Court of Appeals for the Fifth Circuit asking for the registrar to be found guilty of criminal and civil contempt. Later that month, the Justice Department widened the scope of its battle against voter discrimination in a suit against officials in Bibb County, Georgia. For the first time, the federal government challenged the actual conduct of elections, seeking an injunction against segregated voting booths and the separate counting of Black and white votes. Ruling early in June, federal judge William Bootle ordered all voting places in Bibb County to desegregate.[52]

Stunned by a *New York Times* story in July describing how Sheriff Zeke Matthews had burst into a voter registration meeting at Mount Olive Baptist Church in Terrell County, Georgia, announcing that he was "fed up with this registration business" and warning of reprisals, Robert Kennedy called for prompt action. Justice Department attorneys and FBI agents were immediately dispatched, and within two weeks a suit was filed against the sheriff. Less than a month later, Mount Olive Baptist Church and three other churches used for voter registration were burned to the ground. An FBI investigation resulted in the arrest of six men, four of whom were convicted in state court and sentenced to prison; two others faced federal charges.[53]

After nearly two years of investigation and litigation, Civil Rights Division lawyers had gained little traction. Local and state officials refused to recognize the rights of Black citizens and acted as if it was legitimate and right not to begin to do so until forced—and even then these officials cooperated only grudgingly. In Mississippi, Georgia, and Alabama, Black people who were active in voter registration continued to face economic retaliation and extreme physical danger.

———

IN FALL 1962, the contending forces of state and federal power nearly broke into open warfare in Mississippi when James Meredith, a twenty-nine-year-old Air Force veteran, became the first African American to enroll at the University of Mississippi. The crisis was several weeks in the making, the culmination of Meredith's sixteen-month-long effort to secure admission. On September 10, after a series of coordinated actions by state officials, Supreme Court Justice Hugo Black insisted that there be no further interference with the order of the Fifth Circuit Court of Appeals. The Kennedy Administration prepared to enforce the court's ruling in the face of a militantly segregationist governor. Sixty-four-year-old Ross Barnett, the son of a Confederate veteran and a member of the White Citizens' Council, dusted off the doctrine of "interposition," made famous by John C. Calhoun and first used in defense of slavery. On September 14, Governor Barnett delivered a public address pledging to "interpose" state authority to block the federal order mandating Meredith's admission. "It was a question from that moment," Burke Marshall recalled, "of trying to turn the state of Mississippi away from the course of actual insurrection."

The attorney general instructed the chief US marshal, James McShane, a veteran of the Freedom Riders crisis, to send federal marshals to enforce the law. McShane pulled together a contingent of nearly four hundred, who made their way to Memphis, eighty-five miles from the University of Mississippi. Bobby Kennedy and Burke Marshall enlisted various administration officials to work their contacts with twenty-five important companies doing business in Mississippi, asking them to "open up lines of persuasion" with individual members of the university's board of trustees. Meanwhile, the Justice Department took legal action to overcome Barnett's defiance. Burke Marshall flew to New Orleans and obtained a contempt of court citation from the Fifth Circuit against the chancellor, dean, and registrar of the university. The circuit court also held the thirteen members of the board of trustees in contempt for refusing Meredith's application. On September 24, the Court of Appeals found that the board members had willfully refused to comply with the court's order. With that, the board members unanimously agreed to admit Meredith. Barnett dug in his heels, saying that he would go to jail if necessary to prevent desegregation. He ordered any federal official who sought to arrest or fine a Mississippi official for defying desegregation orders to be imprisoned. In the two days that followed, Barnett and Lieutenant Governor Paul Johnson separately blocked two attempts by Meredith, accompanied by federal marshals, to register.[54]

"There was never any doubt or question about what had to be accomplished," Robert Kennedy recalled. The question was how and at what cost. During the highly publicized developments, caravans of agitators from outside Mississippi poured into Oxford to defend a citadel of segregation from a federal "invasion." Another attempt to enroll Meredith on September 27 was aborted as too dangerous; the campus was surrounded by two hundred state policemen armed with clubs, backed up by a crowd of 2,500 students and outsider agitators who had amassed on the campus. Striving to avoid a bloody battle, the administration worked to coax and pressure Barnett into accepting the inevitable. On Friday, September 28, Marshall secured a contempt order against Governor Barnett with an October 2 deadline. Refusal to enforce the court order would bring fines of $10,000 per day and likely jail time. At this point, it appeared that Barnett intended to put state patrols and a civilian army on campus, and the federal government would have to send troops to fight their way through.

President Kennedy called Governor Barnett on Saturday afternoon in one final attempt to resolve the standoff. This time, Barnett agreed that Meredith could be registered secretly in Jackson on Monday. He would then announce to the people of Mississippi that it was done and say that they must respect law and order. By Saturday night, the governor had changed his mind. That afternoon, he had been greeted like a conquering hero when he addressed a packed football stadium proclaiming, "I love Mississippi, I love the people of Mississippi. I love and respect our heritage." Afterward, calling Robert Kennedy at home, Barnett said he could not go through with the agreement.

For the Kennedys, time had run out. At midnight, President Kennedy issued a proclamation stating that the government was preparing to use military force to enable Meredith to register, putting the Mississippi National Guard in federal service and troops in Memphis on alert. The president planned to make an address on Sunday night in advance of action to secure James Meredith's enrollment at the university.[55]

Developments moved swiftly the following day. Late Sunday morning Bobby Kennedy and Burke Marshall made one last effort to persuade Barnett to cooperate. The governor angled for a face-saving arrangement whereby Meredith would be accompanied by gun-toting federal marshals who would force Barnett to concede after he had read a proclamation denying Meredith admission. RFK dismissed the idea as silly and dangerous, saying that the time for politics and theater was over. He told Barnett that President Kennedy would go on television that night and tell the country what he now had to do, and in the course of his televised speech, he would relay that Governor Barnett had made an agreement to secretly register Meredith and then broke his word. According to Burke Marshall, who was on the call, this threat was the only thing that made an impression on the governor, who "pleaded in a childish, whining sort of way that the President not do that." RFK had found the pressure point. "Let's get busy on it," Bobby said, as he made clear what had to be done. Barnett finally agreed that Meredith could arrive on campus that day. The governor said the state police would cooperate and maintain law and order, and he would urge the people of Mississippi to remain peaceful. Barnett was hardly trustworthy, but the prospect of a direct conflict between federal and state officials had seemingly been defused. After the call, Kennedy recruited a team of Justice Department officials who happened to be in the office on Sunday afternoon and dispatched them to Mississippi. Nicholas Katzenbach, who was one of them, would take charge of the marshals on campus. Meanwhile, plans were hashed out for the transfer of James Meredith with four hundred federal marshals from Memphis to Oxford.[56]

At 7 p.m., President Kennedy delivered a speech that was carried over radio and on television. Crafted with the help of his brother, the speech differed in tone and emphasis from the one the president had originally planned and was primarily an appeal to the students at the University of Mississippi. By the time the president spoke, Meredith had been quietly escorted by John Doar and several marshals onto campus and into his dormitory room. The president began by noting that James Meredith was now in residence on campus at the University of Mississippi. Kennedy offered a brief background to what had begun as a private suit by a young citizen challenging those who had excluded him from the university. The president explained that a series of federal courts, including the Supreme Court, had repeatedly ordered that Meredith be admitted to the university. When these orders were defied, the US Court of Appeals (the president named each of the eight judges on this court and the state each hailed from—including Mississippi, Alabama, Louisiana, Georgia, Florida, and Texas) made enforcement of the order the obligation of the federal government. If others had fulfilled their responsibility, he pointed out, the issue would have been resolved there, without the intercession of the federal government.

The president described "the observation of law" as "the eternal safeguard of liberty." Americans were free to disagree with a law but not to disobey it.

He praised those southerners who had contributed "to the progress of our democratic development in the entrance of students regardless of race" to the state-supported universities of Virginia, Georgia, North Carolina, Florida, Texas, Louisiana, Tennessee, Arkansas, and Kentucky. Kennedy granted that this period of transition was difficult for many people in the South and acknowledged the full reach of racial injustice. "Neither Mississippi nor any other Southern state deserves to be charged with all the accumulated wrongs of the last hundred years of race relations," he said calmly. "To the extent there has been failure, the responsibility for that failure must be shared by us all, every state, by every citizen." He ended his talk with a direct appeal to the students at the university. The most effective means of upholding law and order rested not with the state police or with the National Guard, he said, but with each and every one of the students.[57]

Rather than calm the waters, Kennedy's speech inflamed the hard-core segregationists who had rallied behind Barnett over the preceding weeks. The governor never publicly acknowledged his agreement with Robert Kennedy. While Meredith settled into his dorm room under the protection of a small contingent of federal marshals, a large convoy of marshals drove on campus in army trucks. There were roughly two hundred state police stationed there when they arrived. Katzenbach tried to downplay the presence of the marshals by having them temporarily housed in the gymnasium, but Mississippi State Senator George Yarborough, representing the governor, refused. The governor remained intent on Meredith's entrance remaining a federal operation, akin to an "invasion." The white-helmeted marshals stationed themselves around the Lyceum, the white-columned mansion that served as the university's administration headquarters. Assuming Meredith must be inside, protesters started gathering around the Lyceum. Before the president had finished his address, the crowd began attacking the marshals with stones, bricks, metal pipes, and flaming Molotov cocktails. The marshals launched tear gas grenades in an attempt to drive the crowd back. Instead it grew larger and more boisterous, waving Confederate flags and chanting "No, No Never." State police did nothing to interfere and left campus around 8 p.m. as the situation was reeling out of control. Shortly after the state police withdrew, Claude Sitton reported, "automobiles loaded with roughly dressed whites, some of whom were from Alabama, began pulling into the campus."[58]

The crowd ballooned from several hundred to around three thousand. Some students commandeered a bulldozer from a nearby construction site and attempted to ram the driverless vehicle into the front steps of the Lyceum. Another group set an army truck on fire. The marshals were armed but under orders not to fire—unless in direct defense of James Meredith. The rioting intensified. Protesters shot out or broke street lights, leaving the campus in darkness. "Shadowy forms raced back and forth behind Confederate battle flags" in a fog of tear gas, Sitton reported in the *New York Times.* Burning cars lit the night and gunfire pierced the air. The mob targeted journalists as well as the marshals, beating reporters and stomping on cameras. A sniper fired three shots at Karl Fleming of *Newsweek;* the bullets lodged into the door of the Lyceum. Paul Gielhard, a thirty-year-old journalist with Agence France-Presse, was shot in the back at close range. While his murder was never solved, he was attacked after snapping a picture of men unloading guns from a truck near a dormitory. Twenty-three-year-old Ray Gunter, a jukebox repairman whose curiosity had drawn him to campus, was also shot and killed by rioters that night.[59]

The president, attorney general, and Burke Marshall waited for news at the White House, receiving a steady stream of reports from Katzenbach from a pay phone on the university campus. By 10 p.m., they concluded that it was time to send in the army, and the order was given. A local contingent of the National Guard arrived soon after and provided welcome reinforcements. But a series of miscommunications and other complications slowed the movement of troops from Memphis. President Kennedy called Cyrus Vance, secretary of the army, several times to inquire about the delay, and Vance kept giving him misleading information, saying the troops had arrived when they had not.

Bobby Kennedy later spoke of the fear and frustration that gripped him as he monitored the situation from Washington. "Our marshals were being overwhelmed," he said, "two people were killed at the beginning, so we had visions of them getting in and killing Meredith." He would not lift the order barring the marshals from using live ammunition except to protect Meredith. He felt that if they fired into the crowd, they could easily spark an all-out shooting war. An overwhelming show of force would be needed to restore order. But as time passed and no troops arrived, they "could just visualize another disaster," Bobby recalled, on the scale of the Bay of Pigs. It was after 1 a.m. when twenty-five thousand troops rolled into Oxford. The soldiers covered the campus, searching out and rounding up snipers and dispersing the remnants of the mob. President Kennedy left the small group at 5 a.m. and went to bed, finally satisfied that order had been restored. Several hours later, John Doar and Jim McShane accompanied James Meredith to the administration building to register at a university that had become an armed camp.[60]

Claude Sitton, a native of Georgia, described the battle surrounding the desegregation of the University of Mississippi as "the most serious federal-state conflict since the Civil War." The cost in terms of dead and wounded, and the bitterness aroused, was, he wrote in the *Times,* the greatest thus far of any dispute over desegregation. In addition to the deaths of Paul Gielhard and Ray Gunter, one marshal was shot in the throat, and twenty-eight suffered gunshot wounds. In all, 166 marshals were injured. Military police armed with bayonet tipped rifles patrolled the campus and town for several weeks after the riots, reaching a peak strength of fifteen thousand. James Meredith attended classes in a sea of hostility. A handful of students befriended him, but many continued to taunt and harass him. Most completely ignored him.[61]

Governor Barnett remained defiant. He proclaimed that "placing Meredith in the University of Mississippi by armed might positively does not integrate the university—it only means that he is illegally at the University and that the campus and the city of Oxford are occupied by federal troops." While temporarily shaken by the deaths, injuries, and destruction left in the wake of the riots, most white Mississippians closed ranks behind the governor. Leading state newspapers and radio and television news outlets placed the blame for the riot on the marshals. Senator James Eastland called for an investigation of the marshals, claiming that "of course, the unfortunate firing of the gas shells provoked the students and others, which apparently detonated the activities that followed." Writing in the Jackson *Clarion Ledger,* Mississippi's main newspaper, Judge M. M. McMahon declared that "the courageous stand of Governor Barnett for the rights of the state and liberty and freedom of the people has electrified the South and in fact the entire nation."[62]

Robert Kennedy described that night as the worst of his life. The violent showdown at the University of Mississippi was a sobering experience for both brothers. Jack Kennedy told Bobby that "he never would believe a book about Reconstruction again." He had come to see that the dominant historical narrative about the Reconstruction era—one that portrayed a South victimized by vengeful federal officials, northern carpetbaggers, and ignorant Black voters, until white southerners "redeemed" the South and restored order—was false. If leading public officials and reporters in Mississippi "can say these things about what the marshals did and what we were doing at this period of time—and believe it," he reasoned, "they must have been doing the same thing a hundred years ago."[63]

Not one lawyer in Mississippi spoke out publicly in support of the rule of law during the crisis at Ole Miss, Bobby Kennedy observed. "I wouldn't have believed it could happen in this country," he said. The silence of the national bar was equally sobering. Regarding the enforcement of *Brown v. Board of Education,* Kennedy noted that "there have been no pronouncements in this matter by the American Bar Association." By fall 1962, both brothers recognized the magnitude of a challenge that had been a century in the making.

University of Virginia law student Bobby Kennedy and his fiancé Ethel Skakel at a picnic in Charlottesville, April 1950. Courtesy of Tyler Brandon

March 1951, Robert Kennedy
ranged for Ralph Bunche, who
d recently won the Nobel Peace
ize, to address a nonsegregated
blic audience on campus, a first
r the University of Virginia.
nnedy and Bunche are joined
re by Dean F. D. G. Ribble.
BY image courtesy of University of
ginia Law Library

With very best wishes,
Ralph J. Bunche
26 March 1957

Chief Counsel Robert Kennedy and Senator John F. Kennedy during the Rackets Committee hearings in 1957. Courtesy of the John F. Kennedy Presidential Library

On Thanksgiving weekend 1960, Bobby, his wife Ethel, and their children Joe, Kathleen, and Robe Jr. visited the Georgetown home Jack and Jackie Kennedy. Three weeks later, Jack would announce his brother's appointment as attorney general. Bettmann Archives Getty Images

The Kennedy administration faced its first major domestic crisis when an interracial group tested the enforcement of Supreme Court rulings outlawing segregation in interstate travel. Seven Freedom Riders escaped their bus when a mob set it on fire in Anniston, Alabama, on May 14, 1961.
Bettmann Archives/Getty Images

...rney General Robert Kennedy, ...is office at two o'clock in the ...ning on May 22, 1961. He is on ...phone with his deputy Byron ...ite in Montgomery, Alabama, ...r a raging mob attacked the First ...tist Church, where Martin Luther ...g Jr. and other supporters of the ...dom Riders had gathered. AP Photo

Bob Moses, who started working on voter registration efforts in Mississippi in 1961, in the field with Martha Prescod and Mike Miller in 1963. © Danny Lyon/Magnum Photos

A police dog attacks fifteen-year-o
Walter Gadsden in Birmingham c
May 3, 1963. Images like this
sparked mass protests across the
country. AP Photo/Bill Hudson

Burke Marshall and Robert
Kennedy on June 11, 1963, during
the desegregation crisis at the
University of Alabama. A map of
Tuscaloosa is on Kennedy's desk.
Walter Bennett/The LIFE Picture Collection
Getty Images

On June 14, 1963, Bobby Kennedy
addressed protesters gathered outside
the Justice Department, who called
for federal action to end segregation
in the South. By this point, Justice
Department lawyers were hard at
work drafting a strong civil rights
bill. Library of Congress

SNCC Chairman John Lewis and Robert Kennedy during an emergency eight-hour-long meeting in July 1963 to resolve an explosive racial conflict that broke out in Cambridge, Maryland, following nonviolent demonstrations to desegregate local businesses. Office of Congressman John Lewis

Movement leader Gloria Richardson and RFK announce an agreement with the city of Cambridge. "Robert Kennedy was very good for Cambridge," Richardson said, "though he was very hard-nosed." Afro American Newspapers/ Gado/Getty Images

The Kennedy administration initially opposed the March on Washington, for fear it would derail civil rights legislation, but RFK eventually put the resources of the federal government behind preparations for the historic event. More than 250,000 gathered in front of the Lincoln Memorial, where Martin Luther King Jr. delivered his iconic "I Have a Dream" speech. CBS Photo Archive/Getty Images

President Kennedy and civil rights leaders Whitney Young, Martin Luther King Jr., John Lewis, A. Philip Randolph, and Roy Wilkins met at the White House following the March on Washington. JFK's civil rights bill passed the House Judiciary Committee on November 20, 1963, two days before his assassination. Library of Congress, Prints and Photographs Division, LC-DIG-ds-04413

Ethel and Bobby visit the Prince Edward Free School in Farmville, Virginia, on May 11, 1964. The integrated school, established the previous fall with Kennedy's leadership, welcomed Black children while public schools remained closed for a fifth consecutive year. The county chose to close its public schools rather than desegregate. Courtesy of Michael Sullivan

Myrlie Evers, widow of Medgar Evers, and her children, Reena and Darrell, with the attorney general outside the Justice Department in June 1964.
Bettmann Archives/Getty Images

President Lyndon Johnson belatedly offers Robert Kennedy a handful of pens during the July 2, 1964, signing ceremony for the Civil Rights Act, a law that Bobby did more than anyone to champion and shape. Bettmann Archives/Getty Images

Bobby and Ethel with their children at the Bronx Zoo on November 3, 1964. That evening, Bobby would be elected senator from New York. AP Photo

While Meredith's admission had opened a crack in the rigid façade of segregation, Mississippi remained a reactionary stronghold.[64]

—

BARELY TWO WEEKS AFTER THE SHOWDOWN at Ole Miss, the Kennedy administration faced its gravest crisis. Surveillance photographs revealed that the Soviet Union had begun installing medium range missiles in Cuba, in part a response to the administration's belligerent policy toward Cuba, raising the specter of nuclear war. Robert Kennedy's role during the Cuban Missile crisis has been a matter of debate. The evidence is persuasive, however, that RFK's distinctive skills and approach—the prodding, questioning, getting the facts, exploring all options—and the nature of his partnership with his brother were critical to its resolution. Bobby presided over a committee of leading officials from defense, diplomatic, and intelligence agencies established to advise President Kennedy on the crisis—a group divided between those urging an immediate military strike and others advocating a blockade. Based on an extensive review of tapes of the daily meetings, biographer Evan Thomas described how Kennedy "tested and quarreled with assumptions. . . . He did not hesitate to reverse field or rethink an answer, in part to stimulate discussion, but also because he was working his own way through an extraordinarily complex set of problems." At the same time, he leveraged his close relationship with the president to move the discussion forward toward a conclusion that reflected the president's interests. Bobby succeeded in fashioning a consensus around a blockade of Russian ships, with the prospect of an invasion left on the table if the Soviets did not halt the development of missile capabilities. "Few others," wrote historian Matthew Hayes, "were able to bridge the dove / hawk divide in this way, and to do so in a way that had a pivotal impact on the president, his advisors, and the resolution of the crisis."[65]

War seemed imminent. Cubans shot down a U-2 spy plane that had crossed into Cuban air space, and Americans braced themselves for the unthinkable. JFK, resisting military pressure to invade Cuba, dispatched Bobby to meet the Soviet ambassador, Anatoly Dobrynin, for back-channel negotiations with Soviet Premier Nikita Khrushchev. On October 28, Khrushchev agreed to remove the missiles in return for a pledge that the United States would not invade Cuba and would remove US missiles from Turkey and Greece, ending the thirteen-day standoff. While several factors converged to pull the world back from the nuclear brink, Robert Kennedy, acting in concert with his brother, played an essential role. The evening of the day the crisis ended, JFK said to his friend Dave Powers, "Thank God for Bobby."[66]

———

LATER THAT FALL, the president fulfilled his long-awaited campaign promise and issued an executive order banning racial discrimination in federally assisted housing. The long and circuitous route to this moment revealed his narrow "operating margin in the field of civil rights," as *Time* aptly put it. Racial discrimination in housing, promoted by government and private policy, was largely responsible for reinforcing segregation, overcrowding, and poverty in urban communities, and it was an issue that most white northern politicians sought to avoid.

As a candidate, Kennedy had pledged that if elected he would end discrimination in housing "by a stroke of the pen." He intended to issue an executive order, but his first priority was to establish a cabinet-level Department of Urban Affairs. This effort, he thought, would be more difficult if he issued a housing order first. Meanwhile civil rights groups, pressing him to remember his promise, organized a mailing campaign, inundating the White House with pens. Burke Marshall recalled how Kennedy would mutter under his breath, to no one in particular, "a stroke of the pen . . . who put those words in my mouth?" Kennedy promoted a bill to establish a new Department of Urban Affairs early in 1962 and planned to elevate economist Robert Weaver to cabinet secretary. Kennedy would introduce the housing order after the midterm election.[67]

Kennedy had appointed Weaver to head the Housing and Home Finance Agency (HHFA) in the first weeks of the administration, the highest executive administrative post an African American had ever been named to. Weaver was one of the administration's most controversial appointments and one of the most highly qualified. At fifty-three, his record of government service was unimpeachable. The Washington, DC, native was one of two African American students in his class at Harvard College and the first African American to receive a doctorate in Economics from Harvard. He had just completed his PhD when he joined the Roosevelt administration's Interior Department in 1934 as race relations adviser to Harold Ickes. Over the next decade, he served as special assistant in the housing division of several government agencies, including the Works Progress Administration, the National Defense Advisory Commission, and the War Manpower Commission, and he assumed a leading position in FDR's informal Black Cabinet. In 1948 Weaver published a seminal book, *The Negro Ghetto,* an account of residential segregation in the North and the social and economic factors that structured and sustained it. Prior to joining the Kennedy administration, Weaver had served as Rent Commissioner for New York State. He was also vice chairman of the New York City Housing and Redevelopment Board.

In 1960, when he was national chairman of the NAACP, then-senator Kennedy sought Weaver's advice on civil rights issues.[68]

Weaver's confirmation hearings were highly contentious. Senate Banking and Finance Committee chair, Senator A. Willis Robertson of Virginia, began by refusing to start the proceedings until he received a letter documenting that the FBI had evaluated and attested to Weaver's loyalty. President Kennedy provided such a letter, which Robertson read to the packed hearing room. Southern members of the committee went on to interrogate Weaver about his "radical" affiliations in what one journalist called "bush league McCarthyism." Weaver acknowledged that he had been associated with three organizations that had later been branded as subversive by the Justice Department: the National Negro Congress, the Council on African Affairs, and the Washington Cooperative Book Shop. Senator William Blakely of Texas asked him to comment on the fact that a review of *The Negro Ghetto* had appeared in the *Daily Worker,* the Communist Party newspaper. Weaver asked the Senator whose byline was on the review. When Blakely replied that it was signed "J. Crow, Realtor" the committee room erupted in laughter. A puzzled Blakely asked Weaver if he knew J. Crow. "Yes, I've known Jim Crow," Weaver replied, "and he didn't write any book reviews."

When asked about his views on race and federal policy, Weaver said he believed "everyone should have equal access to housing that enjoys federal benefits." Jay Creswell, a retired businessman from Florida and former employee of the federal Small Business Advisory Committee, popped up from his front-row seat and moved to testify as a private citizen. "There was rejoicing in colored families and churches through the land," Creswell declared, when Weaver's appointment was announced. Creswell added that his own efforts to help African Americans buy houses had taught him that the door was blocked to those seeking federal guaranteed loans. At the conclusion of the hearings, the committee voted 11–4 to recommend Weaver to the full Senate, where he was promptly confirmed by voice vote.[69]

When Kennedy sought congressional approval for the creation of a new Department of Urban Affairs in January 1962, he felt quite confident that he could secure the necessary votes. Once it became known that Robert Weaver would likely be head of the new department, thus becoming the first Black cabinet member, the bill became a "civil rights issue." Southerners succeeded in pigeonholing the legislation in the Rules Committee. Kennedy immediately found an alternative path: he sent the bill directly to the House and Senate as part of a reorganization plan, making it clear that Weaver would be his choice to lead the department. The bill suffered a stinging defeat. Most Republicans voted against it, joined by southern and border state Democrats. Commentators speculated on the convergence of factors that contributed to the bill's failure. Opposition to the "creation of another mammoth organization to interfere with the states" was part of the problem, but so was concern about the elevation of an African American to such a powerful position at a time of broadening challenges to racial discrimination. This resistance, combined with Republicans' interest in dealing the president a defeat on civil rights, was enough to sink the bill.[70]

On November 20, 1962, the president issued an executive order banning discrimination based on race, religion, or national origin in the sale or rental of housing financed by federal aid. The order had gone through six drafts and had been informed by an extensive review of the existing laws against housing discrimination in several states. "The stroke of the pen sounded so easy," Burke Marshall recalled, but in reality, it was "a very, very difficult problem for the President in terms of the reaction of the country, and the acceptance of the need to better the position of the Negro." Discussions among Justice Department lawyers had gone on for a week. Kennedy was committed to using federal power to challenge racial discrimination, but his desire to unify the country around the issue also made him cautious. The president's order, effective immediately, applied to new housing, including single homes insured by the Federal Housing Administration or Veterans Administration, low-rent public housing subsidized by the federal government, and housing in urban renewal programs and on college campuses. Kennedy knew southerners would be unhappy and expected that the order would meet resistance in all parts of the country. So he decided to hold it until after the midterm elections.[71]

"Our national policy is equal opportunity for all," Kennedy said at a press conference on the afternoon of November 21 announcing the executive order, "and the Federal Government will continue to take such legal and proper steps as it may to achieve the realization of this goal." The response from southern Democrats was swift and fierce. Senator A. Willis Robertson of Virginia called the order "absolutely unconstitutional," Georgia's Senator Talmadge said it was "a grave disservice to the welfare of the United States," and Senator Stennis of Mississippi described it as "an audacious usurpation of power by the Executive Branch" and an attempt "to destroy the right of every American to choose his own associates." While many working to end housing discrimination had hoped the order would reach further, there was widespread support among Black leaders for the president's action. The NAACP's Roy Wilkins was "gratified," saying that the president's order placed "the national policy of no-discrimination squarely on the housing field." Martin Luther King Jr. claimed that the order "strikes at the very heart of the segregation system," for "integrated housing is the primary means by which we will have a truly integrate this society." The National Urban

League's Chicago director, Edwin Berry, called the order "a very significant step forward."[72]

By the end of 1962, racial segregation remained largely intact. The escalating conflict in the South had scant impact on the attitudes or concerns of most white Americans, who tended to view segregation, in Calvin Trillin's words, "as a regrettable regional peculiarity." Trillin, who covered the Freedom Rides for *Time,* recalled that when he returned to the magazine's Atlanta office in early 1963, after being gone for a year, a fellow reporter told him that "as far as he could tell, the civil rights story had pretty much petered out."[73] Martin Luther King Jr. described 1962 as "the year civil rights was displaced as the dominant issue in domestic politics." He noted that some gains had been made and acknowledged that the Kennedy administration "has outstripped all previous ones in the breadth of its civil rights activities." But he criticized the administration's "cautious tactics" and tendency to act primarily as a mediator when strong moral leadership was essential. King feared that concerned Americans were satisfied with token advances, which left "the disease and its ravages unaffected." As a consequence, he wrote, "the movement, instead of breaking out into the open plains of progress, remains constricted and confined. A sweeping revolutionary force is pressed into a narrow tunnel." King said he thought the Kennedy Administration was "at a historic crossroad." If it seized the moral high ground, "1963 can be a year of achievement."[74]

———

ON FEBRUARY 28, 1963, JFK sent his first civil rights message to Congress. He offered a stark picture of the wide gap in the life chances of a Black and white child born in any part of the United States. Racial discrimination was "a cruel disease," he said, that knew "no sectional or state boundary." He proposed a broad program of action on the part of Congress and the executive branch, in partnership with local and state government. His agenda was divided into four sections: voting, education, employment, and public accommodations. Voting was the main focus of his proposal for legislative action. Kennedy described the experience of Justice Department lawyers over the previous two years and pointed to defects in the existing civil rights legislation. He noted that registrars could still arbitrarily discriminate against Black applicants in the long time it took from filing a case to its conclusion. He said he hoped to introduce new legislation to expedite suits in federal court and provide for the appointment of temporary registrars to register Black voters while the suits were pending. "The legal maxim 'Justice delayed is Justice denied' is dramatically applicable in these cases," he observed. The new provision would ensure that the same standards were being applied to all citizens seeking to vote and would establish that a sixth-grade education could be considered proof of literacy.[75]

Coming in the wake of the disastrous defeat of the literacy bill, prospects for new civil rights legislation were nearly nil. Whether the president would push for such a bill in 1963 or 1964 remained an open question. In the early spring of 1963, as Nicholas Katzenbach recalled, the votes were not there. A series of Republican bills introduced in January were not taken seriously. The president felt the need to focus national attention on the problem and to pave the way for meaningful civil rights legislation.[76]

As Kennedy announced his civil rights initiative, the voting campaign in Mississippi was entering a new phase. Economic reprisals and targeted acts of violence increased in the wake of the Ole Miss crisis. In Leflore County, where African Americans made up 64 percent of the population, officials cut off the distribution of federal food surpluses to more than twenty thousand sharecroppers and tenant farmers who depended on the aid to make it through the winter months. The punitive action enraged local Black people and drew a swift response from SNCC. Activists organized a new voter registration drive and drew national attention to conditions in the county with a special focus on Greenwood, the county seat. "Friends of SNCC" groups in San Francisco, Chicago, Ann Arbor, and other cities participated in a food drive, and provisions were soon trucked in from various parts of the country. A local distribution system linked food aid to voter registration in a county where fewer than 2 percent of Black citizens were registered to vote. The program reached hundreds who had previously had no contact with the movement. At the makeshift distribution centers, sharecroppers and tenant farmers completed a form with personal information to determine their need and then were given a voter registration form and asked to fill it out. Project workers were standing by, ready to help. The numbers of Blacks going to the courthouse to register increased dramatically. Local officials responded with police action and terror. Key organizers were arrested and several buildings in the Black business area set on fire.[77]

On the evening of February 28, hours after President Kennedy delivered his message on voting rights, a white assailant ambushed a car carrying Bob Moses, Jimmy Travis, and Randolph Blackwell of the Voter Education Project, shooting and seriously injuring Travis. This brazen attack stiffened the determination of many to claim their rights. Over a two-day period, more than 150 people turned up at the courthouse to register, the largest single effort to enroll Black voters since Reconstruction. Voter Education Project director Wiley Branton summoned activists from other organizations to come to Greenwood and help and wired Robert Kennedy "so that you can provide . . . the necessary federal protection." SNCC brought its thirty-two in-state field organizers to Greenwood to keep up the food drive, support voter registration efforts, and lead demonstrations on the courthouse. The police chief bulked up his thirty-man force, recruiting twenty-four auxiliary police from adjoining counties. On March 28, a dozen police with a German shepherd waded into a group of forty men and women walking away from the courthouse after having applied to register. The dog attacked two people while bystanders shouted, "Turn him loose!" The group who had applied to register retreated to Wesley Chapel, and the police followed, arresting Bob Moses, James Forman, and eight other SNCC organizers on charges of disorderly conduct.[78]

Bobby Kennedy phoned John Doar and told him to file a case right away if there had been a violation of the Civil Rights Acts. Doar had already sent an attorney to Greenwood. Now he pulled together some papers in Washington and flew to Mississippi to file a case. Early on the morning of Saturday, March 30, Doar received a call from President Kennedy asking him what was being done about Greenwood. Doar told him about the case he was about to file. The Justice Department appealed for the release of the eight imprisoned activists and sought a restraining order against the police, blocking them from interfering with people attempting either to vote or to register. This suit marked the first confrontation over voting rights that went beyond the slow process of suing individual registrars. SNCC activists were euphoric. Chuck McDew exclaimed that finally they had "concrete proof . . . that the government is on their side."[79]

The backlash was swift and pointed. Mississippi's Senators John Stennis and James Eastland took to the Senate floor and attacked the "professional troublemakers" and their "mob marches," describing SNCC activists as purveyors of hate, strife, and discord. Senator Eastland denounced the Justice Department's suit and demanded that it be dropped. In Greenwood, Gray Evans, the city prosecutor, warned of the consequences, saying that "if the police power of the city, the county, and the state is suspended, then we cannot be responsible for anything that happens."

Within days of announcing the suit the Justice Department withdrew the case, and the hearing, which had been scheduled for April 3, was canceled. Burke Marshall had negotiated a settlement with the city, which provided for the release of eight imprisoned SNCC organizers and assurances that there would be no further obstruction of efforts to register. The city of Greenwood stipulated that the police would not interfere with individuals or small groups but would continue to break up large groups. For Black citizens in Greenwood and SNCC activists, this was a bitter conclusion to an intense struggle. "We got sold out in Greenwood," Bob Moses lamented. His relationship with John Doar cooled after that. The realization that the federal government could not be a true partner would dictate future strategies.[80]

There is no record of the considerations that led the Justice Department to withdraw its suit and reach a compromise that left voting rights in the hands of local officials. John Dittmer, a leading historian of the movement in Mississippi, suggests a number of factors may have been at play, including the Kennedy brothers' desire not to totally alienate Senators Eastland and Stennis. Dittmer believes the threat that law enforcement would stand aside if the injunction were to go forward factored high in the calculus. The "Kennedys feared a race war in Greenwood," Dittmer writes, "and that the injunction, if approved, would put the U.S. Army in the city's streets. It would be Ole Miss all over again, with local police withdrawing and a federal occupying force responsible for maintaining law and order." By withdrawing the suit, the city government and law enforcement, dominated by the White Citizens' Council, would be left to maintain control in Greenwood "and keep the even more reactionary Klan-types on the sidelines."[81]

By the spring of 1963, Bobby Kennedy was painfully aware of the limits of his efforts. After two years, the Justice Department's slow-moving suits against obstructionist registrars had not cracked the hard-core segregationists, particularly in Black Belt counties in the Deep South. In a speech delivered three weeks after the showdown in Greenwood, Kennedy warned that "the Negroes in this country cannot be expected indefinitely to tolerate the injustices which flow from official and private discrimination in the United States."[82]

On April 2, in a seemingly desperate and largely ineffectual effort to respond to the lawlessness and repression, RFK sent the draft of a civil rights bill to Congress. The legislation would expedite voting suits; provide for temporary voting referees to decide on the qualifications of prospective voters while voting suits were making their way through court; require uniform standards, practices, and procedures; and establish that a sixth-grade education could be considered a measure of literacy. In the accompanying letter, Kennedy emphasized the urgent need for Congress to act. He described the time lapse, often measured in years, between the filing of a suit and its conclusion.

Later that day, Kennedy held a rare press conference, his third since becoming attorney general. He handled questions "with ease and a relaxed manner," one reporter noted, from the office where his children's drawings hung on the wall. A battered marshal's helmet could be seen on the table. Kennedy outlined the provisions of the bill and the injustices it would remedy. If it passed, he predicted that hundreds of thousands of Black citizens would be added to the voting rolls in a matter of months. He expressed confidence that the bill reflected the desires of the great majority of Americans. But there was little evidence of public interest strong enough to surmount obstruction.[83]

In two short years, the Justice Department could point to notable gains: ending segregation in interstate transportation, advances in school desegregation, and inroads into voter registration. The department won a significant victory in East Carroll, Louisiana, home to Joseph Francis Atlas, where, on July 28, 1962, Black people voted for the first time since the 1920s—a significant if incremental victory. Exposure to conditions in poor and segregated Black ghettos in the North deepened Kennedy's understanding of America's racial divide and its corrosive human and social consequences. Speaking in South Carolina that spring, he said with feeling, "Time is fast running out for this country."[84]

On March 18, 1963, in a speech commemorating the centennial of the Emancipation Proclamation, Bobby Kennedy considered Lincoln's courage and vision. Lincoln, he said, had tied emancipation to "the essence of our national purpose, 'in giving freedom to the slave we assure freedom to the free.'" Yet after a brief period of progress, the doctrine of "separate but equal" had become enshrined in law only to "lay like a dead hand on the springs of progress." Now, he said, "we can see the toll exacted by discrimination— whether overt segregation or covert bigotry." He acknowledged the recent gains but cautioned that all who "have devoted their energies to the cause of racial justice" should recognize that meeting these challenges would take an outpouring of effort and energy unlike any to date. "The problems that remain are massive," he said. "The results of racial discrimination carry on for generation after generation. To face this openly and try to meet it squarely, is the challenge of this decade of change."[85]

CHAPTER SEVEN

Freedom Now

|||

IN JANUARY 1963, Alabama's new governor, George Wallace, emerged as segregation's defiant standard-bearer, famously declaring in his inaugural address, "Segregation now, segregation tomorrow, segregation forever." Wallace's pledge to personally block school integration would immediately be tested when a federal court ordered the University of Alabama to admit two Black students. Wallace, who held power over the university and state law enforcement and enjoyed a close alliance with the Klan, was determined to enhance his stature through a showdown with the federal government. Bobby Kennedy was hardly reassured when members of the university's board of trustees, following a special executive meeting convened by the governor in March, described Wallace as "scared," "crazy," and acting "like a raving maniac." At the same time, Martin Luther King Jr. and the Southern Christian Leadership Conference embarked on an audacious campaign to challenge segregation in Birmingham, one of the most segregated cities in the country.[1]

After their failure in Albany, King and the SCLC had set their sights on Birmingham as the place for a confrontation that could force the hand of the federal government. Birmingham had a reputation as a violent bastion of segregation—fifty bombs had been set off during the preceding year. Police commissioner Bull Connor, known as a symbol of police brutality, stood in sharp contrast to Albany's Laurie Pritchett. Applying the lessons of Albany, SCLC would orchestrate a more carefully focused campaign in Birmingham. "There had been no real dramatization to the nation of what segregation was like," Wyatt Tee Walker observed. "Birmingham would provide that kind of a platform."[2]

On April 3, the same day that the Justice Department withdrew its suit in Greenwood, Mississippi, the SCLC launched Project Confrontation. The beginning of the campaign, known as Project C, had been delayed nearly a month awaiting the resolution of the mayoral contest, which pitted the moderate Albert Boutwell against Commissioner of Public Safety Bull Connor. When Connor lost in the run-off, he challenged the legality of the election. The sitting mayor, Arthur Hanes, and the city commissioners refused to relinquish their offices. Local Black ministers and businesspeople privately urged King to wait for a resolution before activating the new plan, but he would wait no longer. Project C, a bold, risky, carefully orchestrated campaign, would go forward.[3]

The goal of the campaign was relatively modest: the desegregation of downtown department stores. But the likely response of Bull Connor, whose police force had ruled through violence and terror for more than twenty-five years, had the Justice Department on edge. Seasoned activists participated in both the planning and execution of the campaign. Fred Shuttlesworth had sustained Black protest in the city after the state shut down the NAACP in 1956, withstanding arrests, beatings, and bombings. James Lawson and James Bevel, veterans of the Nashville movement, had run nonviolence workshops, and the SCLC's Wyatt Tee Walker served as field commander, mapping out targets and establishing a new strategy. The campaign got off to a slow start. Several hundred men and women participated in sit-ins and demonstrations. Within a week, some 150 people had been arrested. On April 10, Connor secured a temporary injunction barring all marches and protests. King would not let this move defuse the momentum. Two days later, on Good Friday, dressed in blue denim overalls, he led forty protesters from 16th Street Baptist Church to City Hall and was promptly arrested and placed in solitary confinement in the city jail.[4]

King's imprisonment immediately drew the attention of the Kennedy brothers. His jailers initially barred even his attorney from unsupervised contact and allowed no other contact from the outside. Wyatt Walker phoned Burke Marshall at home close to midnight on Friday to seek federal help. Marshall said he would make inquiries. The next morning, President Kennedy called to find out what was going on. Marshall explained that there was no ground for federal action. Still unable to reach King, Walker telegrammed the president and finally persuaded Coretta Scott King to call the White House. She left a message with press secretary Pierre Salinger. In less than an hour, Robert Kennedy had called her back, expressing the administration's concern and assuring her that the Department of Justice would make inquiries regarding the conditions of her husband's imprisonment.

The next day, President Kennedy called Mrs. King and told her that FBI agents had reported that her husband was safe. Kennedy also said that arrangements had been made for him to phone her. Thirty minutes later, King called his wife from the jail. In a conversation that he knew was being taped, he asked her for details of the conversation with the president. "He assured me of his concern. He asked if we had any complaints and said if we did to be sure to let them know. He's very sympathetic," she said, "and kept saying 'How are you? I understand you have a little baby.'" King was elated at President Kennedy's gesture, and wanted to be sure it was well publicized. He would remain in prison for eight days. During this time he responded to white clergy who criticized the Birmingham protest as ill-timed with his powerful treatise on civil disobedience, "Letter from a Birmingham Jail."[5]

RFK had already planned a trip south to check in with federal district attorneys. He decided to take advantage of this opportunity to seek a face-to-face meeting with the governor. Wallace agreed to meet at the state capitol on the morning of April 25. Kennedy had been to Alabama once before, in 1958, when the "rackets buster" had been feted by the Birmingham Chamber of Commerce and praised by Governor Jim Folsom. But after the Freedom Rides, the Alabama Democratic Party had condemned Kennedy for "actions contrary to our Southern traditions." Bobby reached Montgomery on the afternoon of April 24 and gave an interview with a local television station, followed by a short press conference in which he voiced the hope that Alabama's race problems could "be resolved peacefully in the courts." He disputed a question that implied that the administration's civil rights actions were politically motivated. Politics, he said, "wouldn't change what I have done at the University of Mississippi or what I might do in the future. . . . We would have done the same thing even if it meant losing fifty states." A reporter asked, "Mr. Kennedy, are you a communist?" "No," he said, "and I am glad to clarify that."[6]

RFK spent the night at Andrews Air Force base, avoiding segregated accommodations. The next morning, Judge Frank Johnson joined the attorney general for an early breakfast. Few knew Wallace as well as Johnson. They had been classmates at the University of Alabama and had gone head-to-head several years earlier when Wallace, then a circuit court judge, had refused Johnson's order to open voting records to inspection by the Civil Rights Commission. In a bizarre late-night meeting at Johnson's home, Wallace had finally given in when he had been told he would go to jail if he did not comply. Johnson's briefing confirmed Kennedy's apprehensions. Little, however, prepared him for the scene that would greet him at the state capitol later that morning.

More than one hundred state police surrounded the capitol building, each with a Confederate flag emblazoned on his helmet. Governor Wallace had had the Confederate flag hoisted over the capitol the day before the visit— where it would remain for thirty years. At the front entrance of the capitol,

Kennedy and Marshall made their way around a wreath of red and white carnations and a Confederate flag marking the place where Jefferson Davis was inaugurated as president of the Confederacy. The women who had covered the marker stood close by. "We didn't want the enemy stepping on sacred ground," one told a reporter. As Robert Kennedy strode through the corridors of the capitol and made his way to Wallace's office, he was greeted by office workers and janitorial staff and paused briefly to shake hands with white and Black workers.[7]

Wallace began by announcing that he was going to tape the whole proceeding. That meant, Kennedy recalled, that they had to say things on the basis "that it was going to be played on the local radio station." He could not let anything Wallace say "go by as if it had been unanswered. It made it difficult." Wallace insisted his responsibility was to the people of Alabama. He charged that the central government was attempting to "rewrite all law" and preparing to force integration on the state with "troops and bayonets" as they had done in Mississippi, and he pledged never to submit voluntarily. He lashed out at Martin Luther King Jr., and asked Kennedy about crime in Washington, DC, and other northern cities, in a clear effort to link Black protest with criminality. Kennedy challenged every one of Wallace's misstatements. Kennedy said integration was a simple question of following court orders, and he rebutted the governor's claim that the federal government was poised to send troops. The two men traded charges and countercharges for ninety minutes.[8]

Wallace was determined to stand as a bulwark against integration and federal intervention. The defiant governor was at odds with the university's board of trustees, alumni council, and student legislature as well as local newspapers, all advocating that the university abide by the ruling of the court. Kennedy emerged from the meeting "slightly shaken," in the words of one reporter, but with a better understanding of Alabama's feisty governor. Later, at Maxwell Field before leaving for South Carolina, Kennedy said, "It's like a foreign country. There's no communication. What do you do? I've never been asked if I'm a communist before."[9]

———

WHEN BOBBY KENNEDY MET with George Wallace at the end of April 1963, the Birmingham campaign had reached a low point. Attendance at evening meetings had dwindled, and the flagging protest was no longer a focus of the national media. The situation changed almost instantly when King approved James Bevel's plan to enlist high school students to revive the demonstrations. On May 2, hundreds of young people converged at the 16th Street Baptist church and marched toward downtown. More than five hundred were jailed. That night, more than two thousand people packed the mass meeting.[10]

The youth protests infuriated Bull Connor. On the second day of protests, his police unleashed German shepherds on the young demonstrators, who generally ranged in age from seven to eighteen. The city fire department blasted them with high-power water hoses. The arrests and assault electrified the city's Black community and seized headlines across the nation. A widely reproduced image showed a Birmingham police officer holding a Black teenager with one hand and a dog by a leash in the other with the dog poised to sink his teeth into the young man's stomach. President Kennedy told several aides that the images from Birmingham made him sick. He understood that Birmingham marked a fundamental shift—stirring the feelings "of every Negro in the country" and many whites as well. Robert Kennedy and Burke Marshall agreed that Marshall should go immediately to Birmingham and "do something." But what?[11]

Every day the demonstrations grew. Police used dogs and fire hoses to physically contain protesters and arrested more than one thousand people. Marshall met with King, who remained focused on the goal of desegregating the downtown stores, and set about opening lines of communication between Black and white leaders. He persuaded David Vann, a young, sympathetic attorney who represented several department stores, to speak to his clients about taking the initiative on their own. Vann's initial response was that it was "hopeless—anything that King wanted was poison to them." Marshall employed his improvised brand of shuttle diplomacy. He met with store owners, then with Black leaders, and then arranged for a small group of local African Americans to come together with a very small group of local whites. "And then," he recalled, "I'd go meet with King in the middle of the night." The pattern would be repeated the next day as they tried to get issues clarified "and see if any agreement or consensus could be reached." Joe Dolan, who accompanied Marshall to Birmingham, was astounded by "the fear, ignorance and triviality" on the part of white store owners and their lack of communication among themselves. One warned that there would be riots if he desegregated store fitting rooms, while another said he had done so several months earlier with no problem. It became clear to Marshall that the store and lunch counter owners would do nothing without the backing of the power structure in Birmingham, often referred to as "the big mules"—US Steel, the banks, and other major financial institutions.[12]

Marshall turned his attention to Birmingham's power brokers, the large employers—some seventy men—known as the city's "Senior Citizens." This group was allied with Albert Boutwell, whose disputed election as mayor was in the process of being decided in court. Marshall took note of individuals who seemed open to discussion, passing their names along to the attorney general. Robert Kennedy and JFK arranged for members of the cabinet and others to call them. Secretary of Treasury Douglas Dillon and Defense Secretary Robert McNamara, the former chair of General Motors, phoned bankers and friends in industry. Eugene Rostow, the dean of Yale Law School, offered to contact US Steel chairman Roger Blough, a Yale graduate who was heading the school's capital campaign drive. Blough then phoned his associates at Tennessee Coal and Iron in Birmingham on behalf of the administration. Each one would discuss the situation in Birmingham, their responsibility as leaders in their community, and the fact that there was no way out of the crisis short of beginning to voluntarily desegregate stores. President Kennedy, Marshall recalled, phoned three or four people himself and was of great assistance in persuading them. Bobby also called several people. While "he wasn't well loved at the time by whites, he was very effective in explaining things," Marshall noted.[13]

The culminating meeting with the "Senior Citizens" was held at the Chamber of Commerce in Birmingham on Tuesday, May 7. Rioting broke out when close to three thousand demonstrators rampaged through the main business district and police turned fire hoses on the protesters, pushing them back, according to the *New York Times*, with "pressure so high that it skinned the bark off the trees in the parks and along the street." Bull Connor's armored truck resembled a tank as it roared back and forth on Sixteenth Street. Demonstrators threw rocks, bottles, and brickbats at the police. "For almost an hour a seesaw struggle was waged around the park and in side streets and alleys," Claude Sitton reported. Downed by a fire hose, Fred Shuttlesworth was taken to the hospital for chest injuries. Bull Connor commented, "I wish they'd carried him away in a hearse." That day in Montgomery, George Wallace addressed the opening session of the state legislature and promised "to take whatever action I am called upon to take." He added, "I am beginning to tire of agitators, integrationists, and others who seek to destroy law and order in Alabama."[14]

"There were fire engines going by all the time [and] sirens screaming," Marshall recalled, as he met with Birmingham's leading business and civic leaders. The police chief and sheriff said they "didn't think they could handle the situation for more than a few hours." When one member of the group called for the governor to declare martial law, send in troops, and suppress the demonstrations, Marshall feared the situation was headed downhill. But slowly the men the administration had contacted began to speak up. Sidney Smyer, chair of the meeting, said that some adjustment would have to be made in Birmingham and asked Marshall to explain the situation. Marshall emphasized that the solution was in the hands of those at the meeting:

namely to endorse steps by downtown merchants to begin desegregating lunch counters and hiring Black employees.

The meeting showcased the ignorance, bigotry, and denial that permeated the upper reaches of Birmingham society—but also showed that minds could be changed. In the end, voices of reason and self-interest prevailed. Marshall surmised that Birmingham's leading citizens "wanted Birmingham to look like Atlanta," able to resolve its problems on its own. They would "rather make concessions than have a great deal of racial disturbances." A consensus emerged that changes had to be made and the group—with two or three dissenters—approved the establishment of a committee to negotiate a settlement with Black leaders that would include the desegregation of downtown. At the end of the meeting, the editor of the *Birmingham News* told Marshall, "Now you can go back to Washington and tell the president to call off the demonstrations," a statement that appeared to echo the sentiment of many in the group. Marshall was struck by the narrow mindset of Birmingham's leading citizens. "It's a different mind and a different world and a different civilization," he told Kennedy. "They think Negroes are animals, so inferior that they can't do anything without being directed by someone else."[15]

Later that evening, four negotiators met with SCLC's Andrew Young, attorney Arthur Shores, and L. H. Pitts, president of Miles College. Marshall also attended the meeting, which was kept secret from Bull Connor. The white representatives maintained close contact with Albert Boutwell, the mayor-elect, whose installation would soon be resolved by the courts. For the Black leadership, the face-to-face meetings with whites over the previous days were a breakthrough—testimony to the power of protest. Still, the process of making concessions and negotiating a final agreement acceptable to both sides tested the group. The release of jailed protesters remained a sticking point. Robert Kennedy contacted UAW president Walter Reuther and Washington attorney Joe Rauh, who secured $160,000 to supplement the amount advanced by Birmingham businessman A. G. Gaston for the protesters' release on bail. After a final meeting on Friday, May 10, King, Shuttlesworth, Wyatt Tee Walker, and Ralph Abernathy gave a press conference at the Gaston Motel. Shuttlesworth read a statement outlining the terms of the agreement, which included a specific time frame for the desegregation of downtown stores and the promotion of Black employees to sales positions. While it fell short of the movement's initial demands, King characterized the agreement as a "great victory." Later that afternoon, Sidney Smyer released a statement acknowledging that white business leaders had endorsed the settlement in the interest of civic peace.[16]

—

ON SATURDAY NIGHT, a bomb tore off the front of the home of Rev. A. D. King, Martin Luther King Jr.'s younger brother. Less than an hour later, just before midnight, an explosion rocked the Gaston Motel, from which King had checked out earlier that day, injuring several people. African Americans streamed into the street outside the hotel from nearby bars and music joints. They met the arrival of police at the scene with rocks and bottles. A full-scale riot was soon underway, with the crowd swelling to an estimated 2,500 people. Some broke store windows; others overturned cars and pelted police and firemen with rocks and other objects. The police focused on containing the disturbance as Rev. Wyatt Walker and others worked to calm and disperse the crowd.

By 2 a.m., the police had things pretty well under control when 250 state troopers arrived, led by the Al Lingo, director of the Alabama Highway Patrol. Lingo, known as "hell on niggers," was a man who relished confrontations, a quality that appealed to George Wallace. Lingo brought along several deputy sheriffs and a posse under the command of Dallas County sheriff Jim Clark. The group was armed with a variety of weapons, including automatic firearms and double-barreled shotguns. Chief Moore of the Birmingham police tried to persuade Lingo to withdraw, telling him "we don't need your guns down here. You all might get somebody killed." "You're damn right it'll kill somebody," Lingo replied, brandishing a shotgun. He took charge, moving in on the crowd as troopers and Clark's men clubbed "anyone within reach." Black men fought back. Marshall saw the state police action as an effort by Governor Wallace and Bull Connor to blow up the desegregation agreement. Street battles carried on through the night, and several buildings were burned to the ground. Finally, by 5 a.m., white police working with Black civil defense workers aided by Wyatt Walker, Rev. A. D. King, and other local leaders succeeded in restoring order.[17]

Marshall was awakened in the middle of the night by a phone call telling him about the bombing and riots. The calls came quickly after that. "It sounded like all hell had broken loose down there," said a Justice Department aide. Later that morning, a helicopter transported Marshall from his farm in Berkeley Springs, West Virginia, to Bobby and Ethel Kennedy's home in McLean. Marshall and RFK began calling contacts to get the facts and try to calm things down. They spoke with King, who had returned to Atlanta for church services on Sunday; Wyatt Tee Walker, whose wife had been injured; Sidney Smyer; former state public safety commissioner Floyd Mann, an ally during the Freedom Rides; and Claude Sitton, among others.

Kennedy and Marshall drove to the Justice Department together that afternoon for a full-dress meeting with about a dozen attorneys and staffers on hand. President Kennedy, who was at Camp David with his family, learned about the situation when he woke up. He maintained telephone contact with his brother as he made his way back to Washington for an emergency meeting at the White House.[18]

Birmingham presented Kennedy with his greatest domestic crisis. The immediate concern was to salvage the desegregation agreement. But the nature of the challenge had fundamentally changed. "The president wanted to know what we should do," Marshall told Anthony Lewis, "not to deal with Birmingham, but to deal with what was clearly an explosion in the racial problem that could not, would not go away—that he had not only to face this himself, but somehow bring the country to face up to and resolve."[19]

The meeting went on for three hours. Kennedy and Marshall were joined by Nicholas Katzenbach; presidential press secretary Pierre Salinger; Secretary of Defense Robert McNamara; Secretary of the Army Cyrus Vance; and General Earle Wheeler, army chief of staff. This crisis was different from the Freedom Rides and desegregation of Ole Miss in several respects, including the fact that African Americans had fought back and met violence with violence. At the start of the meeting, JFK wondered whether Black Muslims were involved. "I doubt it," his brother replied. Then Bobby asked, "Have you got what happened last night? Do you want to hear a few things?" He provided the group with a description of events and said the bombings and aftermath threatened to unhinge the hard-won desegregation agreement. There was a consensus that the local police had behaved "reasonably well" in response to the riots, but angry complaints had been voiced about the force sent in by Governor Wallace. Wyatt Walker observed the bitter feelings in the wake of the violent assault on African Americans that night—and warned that some were threatening to target police. If violence broke out again, all agreed the situation would be "uncontrollable."[20]

Robert Kennedy led the discussion on possible action by the federal government. Since Governor Wallace had publicly proclaimed that he would maintain law and order, the DOJ did not have a strong basis for sending in troops. Yet the argument for forceful action was supported by likely developments. Wallace "had virtually taken over the city," he noted, and there was a strong possibility that "you're going to have his people sticking bayonets in people and hitting people with clubs and guns." Based on reports coming into the DOJ, he believed that further police brutality in Birmingham would trigger a violent reaction in Black communities across the country. "Negroes are saying we've been abused for all these years," he said, and their patience is running out. He predicted that increasing numbers of

African Americans would be attracted to the ideas of the Black Muslim movement, who preached that no whites could be trusted and that Black people had to rely completely on themselves. If, on the other hand, Black people felt that "the federal government is their friend and is intervening for them, this could head some of that off." The strongest argument for doing something, he said, was the high likelihood otherwise of more difficulties ahead.

The shadow of Ole Miss loomed. There was much talk of troops, logistics, and how they might be stationed so as not be provocative but close enough to be quickly deployed. President Kennedy wanted to know what Martin Luther King Jr., who had called on the president to make a statement, was hoping to hear. Marshall left the meeting briefly to phone King, who had returned to Birmingham earlier that day. Marshall reported back that King said he wasn't sure—he suggested that the president call on everyone to be decent and to respect law and order but also that he emphasize that people must be granted their rights. Marshall said King planned to address a mass meeting that evening and hoped to organize others to go around the community, talk with people, and defuse tensions. Kennedy concluded the meeting by turning attention to the statement he would make on television that evening.

Speaking to a national television audience, President Kennedy began by expressing "deep concern" about the bombings of Rev. A. D. King's home and the Gaston Motel and the violence that followed. Kennedy said the government would do what was needed to preserve order, protect lives, and uphold the law. He described the Birmingham desegregation agreement as "just and fair," one that recognized "the fundamental right of all citizens to be accorded equal treatment and equal opportunity." He declared that the federal government would not permit the agreement to be sabotaged and appealed to all citizens in the city to live up to the standards set by responsible leaders in reaching the agreement and to realize that violence only breeds violence and that good will and good faith would be critical.[21]

Robert Kennedy took three steps that day to ensure that the government was prepared to carry out its obligations: he asked Marshall to return to Birmingham to help facilitate a compromise; asked McNamara to dispatch select units trained in riot control to bases in the vicinity; and took preliminary steps to call the Alabama National Guard into federal service so that units would be promptly available should they be needed.

Over the next several days, a fragile peace was maintained in Birmingham, thanks to Black leaders including King and the active involvement of the Kennedy administration. Marshall met with businessmen, police, and movement leaders and was able to strengthen support for the desegregation agreement, though there were publicized disputes between white business leaders and SCLC regarding exactly what the agreement covered. Mayor Arthur Hanes, whose hold on the office was still being contested in court, blasted "Washington rabble-rousers" and pledged to maintain segregation.

In Washington, President Kennedy and Robert Kennedy met separately with twenty-six newspaper editors from Alabama and told them one by one that failure of the nonviolent movement would open the way to more militant leadership. Many reporters appeared sympathetic to these appeals. Robert Kennedy praised King's leadership and his commitment to nonviolence and suggested that southern officials allow protest rather than seek to repress it. In a separate briefing with reporters from national newspapers, he explained that troops would be activated under an 1871 Reconstruction statute and were prepared to intervene if state police attacked or terrorized the Black citizenry.[22]

On returning to Washington, Marshall told reporters that the agreement was holding. He described this as "pretty close to a miracle" in light of "the years of history in Birmingham [and] given the distrust of police." King said Marshall was "invaluable." Andrew Young later commented that "Bobby Kennedy, Burke Marshall, and Joe Dolan . . . did some phenomenal things. . . . You began to get the kind of unofficial personal reconciliation with both whites and blacks which was very new." The following week, the Alabama Supreme Court ruled in favor of Albert Boutwell and ordered Arthur Hanes, Bull Connor, and the rest of the commissioners to vacate their offices immediately, ushering in a new administration aligned with the business leaders who had participated in the desegregation agreement.[23]

Birmingham marked a seismic shift in the trajectory of the civil rights struggle. The widely reported youth demonstrations, police assaults, bombings, and rioting amplified protests in cities and towns across the country. The direct action movement that had begun with the sit-ins, reported *Time* magazine, "now burst into a feverish, fragmented, spasmodic, almost uncontrollable revolution." In the ten weeks following the bombing there were 758 demonstrations and 13,786 arrests in seventy-five cities across the South— targeting "whites only" restaurants, libraries, parks, beaches, theaters, pools, playgrounds, and hotels. The uprisings were more widespread and involved larger numbers than the sit-in demonstrations three years earlier, and by midsummer these activities would result in four times more arrests than the earlier wave. In northern cities, African Americans protested housing and job discrimination and segregated, substandard schools. "Is the Dam Breaking in Dixie North?" queried a headline in the *Chicago Defender*. On May 18, citing "explosive conditions," NAACP general counsel Robert Carter announced a major campaign targeting school segregation in the North and West.[24]

———

BOBBY KENNEDY FELT THAT Birmingham had changed the stakes just enough that it was now possible to move forward with a strong civil rights bill. "For the first time, people were concerned enough about it—and there was enough demand about it—that we could get to the heart of the problem and have some chance of success," he recalled in a 1964 interview. On Friday, May 17, Marshall, Ed Guthman, and Lou Oberdorfer accompanied Bobby on a flight to Asheville, North Carolina, where he was scheduled to give a speech. The hour-long flight each way, Marshall recalled, provided uninterrupted time "away from . . . meetings . . . the telephone, the demonstrations and whatnot to discuss legislation." Kennedy wanted to know the most pressing demand in the Black community. Marshall had concluded that the most urgent issue was ending segregation in public accommodations. The men spoke about every aspect of the problem that could be dealt with by law and legislation. Oberdorfer expressed concern that a law could not be passed in time to have an immediate effect. He recommended appealing to southerners to begin desegregating voluntarily.[25]

The next day, a Saturday, Kennedy convened a meeting in his office to discuss not whether there should be legislation, but what should be in it. Around fifteen people attended, including Marshall, Nicholas Katzenbach (deputy attorney general), Norbert Schlei (assistant attorney general), Ramsey Clark (Office of Legal Counsel), Louis Martin (then with the Democratic National Committee), and White House legal counsel Lee White. During a heated discussion, Schlei recalled that Kennedy asked, "Can we draft a public accommodations bill that would be constitutional?" Schlei said he thought the commerce clause would provide a strong foundation—an approach Marshall had suggested on the flight the previous day. Education was also a major focus, along with voting and employment. At the end of nearly five hours, Kennedy and Katzenbach turned to Schlei and told him to form a team and draft a bill by Monday.[26]

With a draft bill ready two days later, a tense period of concentrated activism followed. The nearest parallel, a key Kennedy aide confided to *New York Time* reporter Cabell Phillips, was the Cuban missile crisis the previous October. An informal task force, including Justice Department lawyers, a handful of White House aides, and top administrators and technicians from elsewhere in the government, came together and worked with the president and attorney general to shape the bill. "Suddenly we found ourselves in a race, trying not to be overcome by events—violent events that threatened to spread beyond Birmingham and Jackson and get out of hand," one participant recalled. "We were like a bunch of firemen trying to put out a big fire at the same time we were trying to set up a permanent code of safety regulations to abolish fires." President Kennedy was the "captain of the team . . . in the sense of a deep and continuous involvement in details as well as main policies," and his brother served in a chief of staff role. "Everybody around the place was involved to some extent."[27]

The likelihood of enacting a strong civil rights bill was not high. Twenty-five Republican senators would be needed to invoke cloture to end a filibuster and allow the bill to be voted on by the Senate—a hurdle that no civil rights bill had ever cleared. A head-on clash in Congress, observers warned, would threaten the president's other legislative initiatives—tax reduction, medical care for the elderly, and federal support of mass transit among them. And with the election looming, the president would risk losing southern states, while likely not fully satisfying African Americans. In light of such considerations, most of JFK's top advisers opposed the introduction of a major civil rights bill. Vice President Johnson advised against it, warning that the bill being proposed would not pass and would just cause trouble. "The conclusive voice within the government at that time," Marshall confided, "there's no question about it at all, that Robert Kennedy was the one. He urged it, he felt it, he understood it, and he prevailed. I don't think anyone in the Cabinet—except the President himself—felt that way on the issues, and he got that from his brother."[28]

In an off-the-record meeting, the attorney general acknowledged that passage of a strong civil rights bill would be tough, allowing that it was "doubtful that we can get it." But "we've got to make the fight," he insisted. There was greater demand for this legislation than at any time before. The federal government needed the tools to secure an end to segregation in public accommodations, the focus of many of the protests. Most important, RFK felt it was critical that the government demonstrate its commitment to ending racial discrimination. "Anybody who thinks the passage of legislation will make this problem go away is out of his mind," he told the journalists. He discussed the consequences of racial discrimination around the country— poor housing, high unemployment for African Americans, few job opportunities. As Anthony Lewis noted in the *New York Times,* Kennedy had long been saying that the United States was in for a long period of racial turmoil. He told the group, "We are paying for the sins of the past."[29]

Journalists in Washington picked up on what *Time* reporter Hugh Sidey described as a "formless sense of urgent struggle" emanating from the White House. There was a realization "that most Americans do not understand the civil rights problem or grasp the seriousness of the situation," as *Washington Post* reporter James Clayton reflected. While legislation was being drafted, the brothers moved on various fronts to elevate public awareness, speed up voluntary desegregation, and build maximum support for the bill. The attorney general worked largely behind the scenes, while the president used the power of his office to persuade business leaders and public officials to act, enlist the support of congressional leaders, and appeal to the American people to face the racial realities that threatened to tear the country apart.[30]

During this intense period, the questionable performance of the President's Committee on Equal Employment Opportunity (PCEEO), chaired by Lyndon Johnson, brought Robert Kennedy into conflict with Johnson—a singular but notable point of confrontation. Early in 1963, a Southern Regional Council report concluded that there had been only limited gains in Black employment in southern industries through the Plans for Progress program, despite pledges by business leaders to shift to nondiscriminatory hiring practices. The *New York Times* put its story on the front page, noting that only seven out of twenty-seven Atlanta-based companies involved in the program had produced any evidence of compliance and only three had vigorously complied. Johnson "was very upset and concerned" over the report, according to the *New York Times,* and "is known to regard his position on the committee as a political asset." In a memo to Johnson, President Kennedy allowed that the report may have been "less than objective," as statistics he had seen about the employment practices of participating companies had been "most encouraging," but the report did "point to the need to keep after these companies." He added, "unless there is constant review and pressure by the staff of the EEC I would expect there would be a tendency by many of the companies to believe they had done their part by simply entering an agreement."[31]

Robert Kennedy went "out of his way to avoid stepping on Johnson's toes," as one colleague remarked, but the critical importance of good faith efforts at this particular moment, and concern for how a scandal over inflated claims might impact his brother politically, prompted RFK to follow up. He had Secretary of Labor Willard Wirtz survey all companies with government contracts—roughly thirty-five thousand—and ask how many Black people the companies employed. More than two-thirds reported this number as zero. During the crisis in Birmingham, Robert Kennedy had asked John Macy, who represented the Civil Service Commission on the PCEEO, how many African Americans were employed in federal offices in Birmingham. The answer was 1 percent, in a city where Blacks made up 37 percent of the population. On May 22, Robert Kennedy met with Johnson to discuss what these investigations had revealed. The next day, Johnson sent Kennedy a memo saying that Hobart Taylor, executive director of the committee, would telephone twenty-six corporations in twenty-eight cities about improving their employment practices. Johnson wrote that commitments were being received from officials in charge of personnel "to give special emphasis to the hiring of minority personnel over the next few months." Bobby Kennedy, at this point, was looking for results.[32]

On May 29, with the racial crisis at a fever pitch, Bobby Kennedy attended a meeting of the PCEEO chaired by Lyndon Johnson. Kennedy sat quietly for a few minutes while James Webb, the head of NASA, addressed his agency's progress in meeting the new mandate. Then Kennedy began asking for facts and figures about Black employment for the companies NASA contracted with. He quickly established that NASA, which handled billions of dollars annually in contracts, had one person on staff, in addition to Webb, whose job it was to make sure that these companies did not discriminate. "I don't think this gentleman over here that spent a year and a half on this program—if he has, evidently other responsibilities, I don't think he is going to get the job done. He has got $3.9 billion dollars' worth of contracts." Webb tried to defend himself, but there was little of substance he could offer. "I am trying to ask some questions," Kennedy insisted; "I don't think I am able to get the answers." Johnson intervened to defend Webb: "Do you have any other questions?" he asked. "That's it for me," the attorney general replied.

"It brought tensions between Johnson and Kennedy right out on the table," Jack Conway, who was representing the Housing and Home Finance Agency at the meeting, recalled, "everybody was sweating under the armpits. . . . After completely humiliating Webb, and making the vice-president look like a fraud, and shutting Hobart Taylor up completely, he got up and left."[33]

Many of the committee members shared Bobby Kennedy's dissatisfaction with how the committee had been run, with meetings put on more for show than to tackle substance. In a letter following the meeting, Ralph Horton, undersecretary of defense and the Defense Department's representative on the committee, provided the statistics the attorney general had requested regarding defense agency contracts. Many government contractors were aware of the no-discrimination clause, Horton said, "but do not know what is expected of them." Johnson, Horton concluded, "sees the program as an opportunity to build his image as a liberal. Hobart Taylor . . . is interested in either becoming a federal judge, a representative to Congress, or [establishing] a lucrative law practice through business contacts made in the program." Horton added, "The Negro today wants jobs and speeches will not do the trick."[34]

Lyndon Johnson's relationship to the civil rights movement was ambiguous and evolving. While he played a key role in the passage of the Civil Rights Acts of 1957 and 1960, he also oversaw the process of paring both bills down to the bone to garner enough southern support to overcome a filibuster.

In January 1963, in an address at Wayne State University in Detroit commemorating the centennial of the Emancipation Proclamation, Johnson spoke out forcefully on the issue of racial justice and civil rights. Conservative Republicans had made inroads in the South in the 1962 midterm elections, and Black voters had become an important component of the Democratic Party's national coalition. In a Memorial Day speech at Gettysburg, Pennsylvania, on May 30, Johnson gave one of his most eloquent calls for racial justice. "One of the great men of the South has spoken out at last in the South's best tradition," the *Washington Post* opined. Johnson would continue to play an active role as the Kennedy administration accelerated efforts to mobilize public support behind civil rights legislation. Johnson did not participate in the crafting of the legislation and counseled against it, on the assumption that it could not pass, but he also offered valued advice and helped lay the groundwork with Congress.[35]

"Action" was the operative word from May into the summer. While Justice Department lawyers crafted the legislation, Bobby Kennedy and Burke Marshall sought to persuade owners of department stores, restaurants, movie theaters, and other public facilities in the South to voluntarily desegregate. These appeals were assisted by a Supreme Court ruling on May 20 barring cities and towns from prosecuting African Americans for seeking service in privately owned stores. Kennedy and Marshall met with businessmen and store owners on almost a daily basis. The meetings, organized by Lou Oberdorfer, were private and not publicized. Most were held in the attorney general's dining room, but Kennedy and Marshall sometimes went to New York. Marshall would describe what he had witnessed in Birmingham, and Kennedy would explain that unrest would continue and desegregation was inevitable. It could be done voluntarily and peacefully or resentfully and violently, and it would ultimately be accomplished by legislation. Businessmen, Marshall recalled, were very nervous; a number of them agreed to do what they could. Oberdorfer set up an information system at the Justice Department to help coordinate voluntary desegregation efforts. In addition to these meetings, upper-level officials and some White House staff members were enlisted to make hundreds of personal calls to businessmen and officials around the South.[36]

———

ON MAY 24, Kennedy and Marshall were in New York meeting store owners when RFK had his fateful encounter with a group invited by James Baldwin. The unusual gathering had its origins when, during the Birmingham crisis, Dick Gregory suggested to Burke Marshall that Bobby meet with Baldwin. Kennedy was receptive. He had met Baldwin at a White House function a year earlier and had been moved by the *New Yorker* article that became the basis for *The Fire Next Time*. Kennedy was beginning to understand that cities would be at the center of the country's intensifying racial struggle. He invited Baldwin to meet over breakfast at Hickory Hill on May 23. Baldwin's flight was delayed, leaving the men little time to talk. Kennedy was planning to be in New York the next day, and he suggested they continue the conversation there. Baldwin agreed, and said he would convene a few friends and associates to meet that afternoon.[37]

By the following day, a small group of Baldwin's friends representing the creative arts, law, social science, and the southern civil rights struggle had responded to his invitation, extended on Kennedy's behalf, for a private discussion. Such a forthright, unscripted meeting between Black Americans and two top representatives of the federal government, let alone the US attorney general, was without precedent. Kennedy and Baldwin approached the meeting with different expectations. Burke Marshall recalled that the idea was that Baldwin would bring together "some people who understood the problems of urban centers in the North and would have some suggestions as to the role the federal government could play. As I understood it, it was rather a clear topic of conversation." However, after speaking briefly with Kennedy over breakfast the previous day, Baldwin had concluded that Kennedy did not understand the depth of the problem and saw this as an opportunity to enlighten him. The quickly assembled group had no particular agenda. "Just come and talk," Baldwin told Kenneth Clark, one of the participants.[38]

As noted earlier, in addition to Clark, the participants included prize-winning playwright Lorraine Hansberry; Lena Horne, celebrated recording artist and nightclub performer who had battled the color line in Hollywood early in her career; Harry Belafonte, singer and performer at the peak of his fame; Edwin Berry of the Chicago Urban League; sociologist Kenneth Clark; and Clarence Jones, an attorney who had been with King in Birmingham. Jerome Smith, the most powerful voice to emerge at the impromptu meeting, was unknown to all but Baldwin and his brother David, who was also in attendance. From Louisiana, Smith had joined the first waves of sit-ins as a student at Southern University in Baton Rouge and had left college to work full time with CORE. He was in New York for treatment of a broken jaw and head injuries.

The meeting was held at the Kennedy family apartment at 24 Central Park South. Kennedy and Marshall had just come from a frustrating and largely unproductive meeting with storeowners regarding the desegregation of lunch counters in their southern establishments. After briefly greeting everyone, Bobby began by commenting on the seriousness of the racial crisis and telling them about what the administration had done and was planning to do. He noted that his brother did not engage in grandstanding gestures; he was focused on passing strong civil rights legislation which required building and holding onto political support, a challenging task. Kennedy said he was concerned that rising Black militancy in urban areas might undermine efforts to secure the votes needed to pass the legislation. His opening remarks were intended to set the framework for their meeting.

For twenty four year old Jerome Smith, the setting, the strained politeness, and the tone defied the hellish reality he had lived for more than three years. He had been beaten and jailed many times and had concluded that "integration" was meaningless in the absence of radical transformation. Impatient with the formalities, Smith spoke out, abruptly transforming the dynamics of the meeting and setting its course.[39]

"I don't know why I'm here," he said, looking at Kennedy. Then he confessed he was nauseated by the necessity of being in that room. Kennedy was startled. He turned toward the others, but Baldwin reported that Hansberry gestured toward Smith and said, "Mr. Attorney General, . . . the only man you should be listening to is that man over there." Smith assailed Kennedy for the government's failure to protect Black demonstrators in the South. "I am a citizen seeking rights everyone else has and I get beaten," he said. Kennedy tried to answer Smith several times. Smith cut him off, "Okay, but this time, say something that means something." Asked by Baldwin if he would fight for his country, Smith answered, "Never." Kennedy, visibly shaken, said, "How can you say that?" The rest of them, Clark recalled, "were shocked that he was shocked." When Kennedy seemed to accuse Smith of treason, "we all moved in to protect Jerome," Clark recalled, "and confirm his feelings and it really became an attack." No one was interested in hearing about what the administration was trying to do. The old approach would not work; the days of accommodating the Black struggle "to the white community's political necessities" were over. "What was wrong," Baldwin observed, "was very deep and could not be solved in the usual way."[40]

It was "a very beautiful and very ugly experience," Jerome Smith reflected several months later. "The beauty lies with the fact that for the first time the leadership of this country was able to hear what we black people of this country term as 'kitchen talk.' We told the truth about our situation." At one point early on, several suggested that President Kennedy make a dramatic gesture, such as personally escorting the two Black students who would integrate the University of Alabama in June. Bobby said no, that would be senseless and phony. "No, not phony," they insisted. "It was impossible to make contact with anyone," Kennedy recounted.

The explosion of outrage and urgency released in the wake of Birmingham fueled the impatience and tension in the room. The attorney general finally just sat there, silent, and listened to a collective accounting of what Black people faced on a daily basis throughout the United States. The participants' litany of accusations recited how the federal government had long been complicit in fostering discrimination, how the FBI routinely failed to vigorously investigate civil rights cases, and how citizens were still being beaten and murdered in the South for attempting to exert their rights. There was talk of sending arms to the South. When he heard that, Kennedy later said, "I almost screamed." Kenneth Clark described the three-hour ordeal "as one of the most violent, emotional verbal assaults and attacks that I have ever witnessed, before or since."[41]

After the meeting, Harry Belafonte phoned Martin Luther King Jr., who was anxious to hear all the details of the meeting. It was "a disaster," Belafonte began. As King listened to Belafonte's account, he responded that maybe this was just what Bobby needed to hear. Birmingham had changed everything. Jim Crow would end, King was now confident of that. The question was by what means: violence or nonviolence. King mentioned A. Phillip Randolph's idea for a march on Washington and said maybe it's time.[42]

James Baldwin and Kenneth Clark both spoke to the press about what had happened, leading to a flurry of news stories in the *New York Times,* the *New York Post,* and elsewhere. "They gave their version of the meeting and how I didn't understand the problems that the Negroes were facing throughout the country," Kennedy said in a 1964 interview. "There was nothing I could do or say about that. It was a mistake."[43]

According to close aides, Kennedy's initial response was anger and frustration. He was annoyed that Clarence Jones and Harry Belafonte failed to acknowledge the administration's role in the Birmingham crisis. After a day or two, an aide recalled, his feelings about the meeting began to shift. Smith had reached him. He had never heard any American say they would not defend the country. "I guess if I were in his shoes," he told an aide, "if I had gone through what he's gone through, I might feel differently about the country." During testimony before the Senate Judiciary Committee several months later he asked, "How long can we say to a Negro in Jackson, 'When war comes you will be an American citizen, but in the meantime you're a citizen of Mississippi—and we can't help you.'"[44]

After an off-the-record discussion with reporters early in June, one journalist observed that Kennedy "still displays signs of shock from that skull session with James Baldwin and his strange assortment in New York." Asked whether he was considering future meetings with Negro groups, Kennedy said yes before adding, "but the main problem lies with the whites—they're the ones who are denying Negro rights."[45]

———

THE SHOWDOWN AT THE UNIVERSITY OF Alabama was very much on Kennedy's mind when he met with Baldwin and his group. Three days earlier, on May 21, federal district judge Harlan Grooms had ordered the university to admit Vivian Malone and James Hood by June 10. Born and raised in Mobile and elected to the National Honor Society, Malone had received a BA from Alabama A&M University. When the school lost its accreditation, she had applied to the University of Alabama's School of Commerce and Business Administration and was admitted as a junior. James Hood had attended Clark College in Atlanta, part of the historically Black Atlanta University Center. He transferred to the University of Alabama to study clinical psychology, which was not available at Clark.[46]

In response to the judge's ruling, Governor Wallace repeated his pledge to personally bar the entrance of any Negro who attempted to enroll in the University of Alabama. On May 24, a complaint signed by Kennedy asked the federal court to enjoin Wallace from interfering with the students. In a sweeping injunction issued on June 5, Judge Seybourn Lynne forbade Wallace from "physically interposing his person" to block the entrance of the students. Violation of the judge's order would immediately result in civil contempt of court proceedings, leading to possible fines and jail time. Burke Marshall, who had gone to Birmingham for the hearing, said that Judge Lynne made it clear to the governor's lawyers that if Wallace violated the order in a substantial way, the punishment would be significant jail time, upward of six months. Afterward, Wallace publicly stated that he would not let the people of Alabama down. He would go to campus to raise "constitutional issues" against the "omnipotent march of the central government." To those with an ear to hear, a slight change could be detected: Wallace appealed to his fellow Alabamians to maintain law and order and to stay away from the campus. The injunction clamped a tight rein on the governor. Whether he would recognize the authority of the court remained a matter of speculation until the students' arrival on campus in June.[47]

While Justice Department lawyers managed the mechanics of the legislation and Bobby worked behind the scenes on various fronts, the president put the full force of his office behind the effort to bring all Americans to face the deep racial injustices manifest in every part of the nation. He focused on the short-term need to build political support for the civil rights bill, but he knew legislation alone could not remedy a problem with such deep roots. Action was needed in all sectors, now. Kennedy reached out to local and state officials; businessmen; store, hotel, and theater owners; and, increasingly, to the public at large, conveying a sense of urgency and appealing to a shared commitment to fairness, justice, and civic responsibility.

On May 29, during a previously scheduled luncheon meeting with nine governors, the president turned the conversation to civil rights, a topic that had not been on the agenda. Governor Otto Kerner Jr. of Illinois later commented that there was little reference to region or particular states. The consensus was that "we should all be more forward in all our areas to overcome inequities as they still exist." The governors responded favorably to the discussion, and several followed up with letters to the president. Several days later, on June 4, the president, vice president, and attorney general met with around one hundred businessmen who owned chains of hotels, theaters, restaurants, and variety stores in the South. In his telegram inviting them to the White House, Kennedy had suggested that he wanted "to discuss the difficulties experienced by minority groups in many of our cities in securing employment and equal access to facilities and services generally available to the public." Participants reported that most everyone welcomed the president's initiative and appreciated a forum for discussing the challenges they faced. C. O. Fulghum of Oklahoma City, chairman of the board of Video Theaters, who had met with Robert Kennedy the previous week, reported that since then movie theaters had been desegregated in twenty-five to thirty towns across the South. But not everyone was on board. Paul Troast, the chairman of S. H. Kress & Co., a variety store with lunch counters, asked for more time and told reporters afterward that few at the meeting supported a public accommodations law mandating desegregation. The president told the group that a new bill banning segregation in facilities serving the public would be sent to Congress the following week.[48]

The next day, JFK left for a four-day tour of military installations in New Mexico, Texas, Colorado, and California. Senator Richard Russell of Georgia, chairman of the Senate Armed Services Committee, was among those traveling with him—providing a chance for the president to discuss the pending civil rights bill with the leader of the southern pro-segregation bloc. While touring naval bases in southern California, Kennedy visited San Diego State College to receive an honorary degree and deliver the commencement address. The twenty thousand people jammed into the outdoor stadium heard the president talk about the consequences of educational disparities and racial segregation.

"We must recognize that segregation in education—and I mean *de facto* segregation of the North as well as proclaimed segregation of the South— brings with it serious handicaps to a large portion of our population," he said. The president noted that one-third of fifth graders would not finish high school, and only two out of ten would graduate from college. He identified two main barriers to equal education—one economic, the other racial. The nation, he insisted, must move ahead quickly to meet conditions that were "damaging the American school system and endangering the nation's future." During the trip, Kennedy's press secretary announced a last-minute addition to the tour, made at the urging of the attorney general; from California, the president flew to Hawaii to address the United States Conference of Mayors.[49]

The president seized a timely opportunity to deliver his first major speech on the racial crisis. Standing before more than four hundred mayors, he began by making it clear that racial discrimination was "not northern or southern, eastern or western, but a national problem, a national challenge, a problem and challenge, and responsibility and opportunity." During the previous week, mass arrests and violence in Jackson, Mississippi, had threatened to dissolve into a Birmingham-like crisis, with police behaving like "storm troopers," in the words of NAACP leader Medgar Evers. Chicago was described as a "tinder box" of racial tension. Demonstrations at a construction site in Philadelphia and protests against school segregation in Boston also captured national attention. The president's speech, delivered in "plain and blunt language," reflected Robert Kennedy's influence and the brothers' shared understanding of the nature of the problem, the centrality of cities, and the need for action on multiple fronts. Kennedy provided a broad outline of the legislation he planned to submit and the kind of assistance it would offer. But "the final responsibility now and after such legislation is enacted," he said, "will rest with you, as mayors at the local level." In communicating the urgent nature of the crisis, the president sometimes used language "with the bark off of it," as one reporter noted. The time for token moves was over, Kennedy told the group. "These rights are going to be won, and . . . it is our responsibility, yours and mine, to see that they are won in a peaceful and constructive manner."[50]

Kennedy outlined areas where the mayors could initiate action. He began by debunking a common notion that trouble was caused by outsiders. "Well," he said, "this is one country, people can move from one city to another, especially those with strong convictions about the best way to meet the problem." If that disturbs you, then "establish communications within the community . . . and make sure [there is] understanding among all groups, what they want, what it is they need, what they feel they're entitled to." He urged the mayors to follow nondiscriminatory practices in the employment and promotion of municipal workers: "No city government can expect to understand the views of its Negro citizens and no Negro community can be expected to look favorably on the city government unless men and women of all races are employed at all levels, in all parts of the government."

Every local government should spell out the rights of those who live in the community, including equal employment opportunity, fair housing, and equal access to public accommodations. Some communities in the South, he pointed out, had done this over the past twelve months "with astonishingly successful results." According to a story in that day's *New York Times,* the mayor of Greensboro, North Carolina, had told businessmen in his community, "I say to you who own and operate places of public accommodation in the city, the hotels, motels and restaurants that now is the time to throw aside the shackles of past customs." That, Kennedy added, "I think is good advice for all of us." Finally, he asked every mayor to commit personally to undertaking a campaign that summer to lessen unemployment among unskilled youth of both races by tackling the problem of school dropouts. "There is nothing more wasteful than to lose the opportunity to educate a boy or girl," he said. The consequences, he made clear, were far-reaching.[51]

In the course of the speech, Kennedy addressed the mayors as "my fellow chief executives," deliberately emphasizing their shared concerns and responsibilities. The president noted that over the previous two and a half years the federal government had actively worked to hire more African Americans in upper-level positions—and acknowledged that the numbers were still far too low. Experience had shown that passing a law was not enough. What was required was a concentrated effort by employers, unions, governors, and the states. He realized that the mayors' responsibilities were more localized but noted that "we also in the District of Columbia are responsible for a city." While formal racial barriers had come down, the federal government was actively intervening to open jobs in the building trades, and the Commissioners of the District of Columbia were prepared to enact a fair housing ordinance if Congress failed to act. The Kennedy administration had urged Congress to provide home rule for the District, "so that all of our citizens can participate more effectively and responsibly in the burdens of government."

A reporter covering the event observed that Kennedy not only said that Negroes had a just cause but also "tried to persuade the mayors to see it that way." In closing, the president underscored the need for action: "Justice cannot wait for too many meetings. It can't wait for the action of Congress and the courts. We face a moment of moral and constitutional crisis and men of generosity and vision must make themselves heard in every section of the country."[52]

Kennedy left Hawaii late Sunday afternoon for the long flight back to Washington. He reached the White House just after 9 a.m. Monday and was scheduled to be at American University at 10:30 a.m. to deliver the commencement address. After bathing and getting dressed, he spoke briefly with Bobby by phone. "Good speech in Hawaii," Bobby told his brother. The attorney general was on his way to Capitol Hill that morning to brief congressional leaders about the pending civil rights legislation. The brothers agreed to meet at the White House later in the afternoon to discuss developments in Alabama. Vivian Malone and James Hood were scheduled to enter the university the next day, and Wallace had not retreated from his pledge to block them.[53]

That morning at American University, John Kennedy delivered one of the most important speeches of his presidency. In his address to the graduating class of 1963, he called for a fundamental change in America's approach to foreign affairs and US-Soviet relations. Elevating the goal of peace over Cold War rivalries and brinkmanship, he announced negotiations with the Soviet Union for a nuclear test ban treaty. The speech reflected the evolution of his thinking in the wake of the Cuban missile crisis and months of personal backdoor diplomacy with Nikita Khrushchev. At a time when the US-Soviet arms race left the world perched on the brink of nuclear devastation, Kennedy asked his fellow citizens to "reexamine our own attitudes as individuals and as a nation." He spoke of the deep interests of both societies in seeking a just and genuine peace and called for a halt to the nuclear arms buildup.

While not minimizing the challenges involved and acknowledging the need for a continuing defense of vital interests, Kennedy sought a total reorientation of a nation steeped in anti-Soviet propaganda. Peace was a process, a frame of mind, and it would depend on the collaboration of many nations, he said. But the world's future course depended in large measure on a better understanding between the United States and the Soviet Union, increased contact, and increased communication. "Let us not be blind to our differences," he said, "but let us direct our attention to our common interests. If we cannot end our differences now, at least we can help make the world safe for diversity. For in the final analysis, our most basic common link is that we all inhabit this small planet. We all breathe the same air. We all cherish our children's future. And we are all mortal."

"Peace and freedom walk together," Kennedy said toward the end of the twenty-seven-minute-long speech, as he segued into a brief discussion of the quality and spirit of American society. "In too many of our cities today, the peace is not secure because freedom is incomplete." Echoing his challenge to the mayors the previous day, he now said that it was "the responsibility of the executive branch at all levels of government to provide and protect the freedom of all our citizens by all the means within our authority." He added that whenever that authority was inadequate, it was "the responsibility of the legislative branch at all levels . . . to make it adequate," and it was the responsibility of all citizens in all sections to "respect the rights of others and respect the law of the land."

The audience responded with applause. Kennedy added that these matters were not unrelated to world peace—for "is not peace in the last analysis, basically a matter of human rights—the right to live our lives without fear of devastation . . . the right of future generations to a healthy existence."[54]

———

DURING THIS PIVOTAL THREE-DAY PERIOD, the *New York Times* carried a front-page story on June 10 reporting "Dr. King Denounces the President on Rights." In an interview with David Susskind that had aired on television the previous day, King issued his broadest attack to date on Kennedy, charging him with a failure of leadership. Comparing JFK's record to Eisenhower's, King said that Kennedy had "substituted an inadequate approach for a miserable one." King urged the president to talk about integration in moral terms, rather than purely as a political issue, and suggested that he revive FDR's "fireside chats" to explain civil rights to the American people. Within two days, King would completely revise his assessment of John Kennedy's leadership.[55]

By late afternoon on Monday, June 10, the inspired ideals of the president's speech yielded to the raw realties of yet another major battle in the slow and violent demise of Jim Crow. JFK met in the Oval Office with his brother and Burke Marshall to discuss the pending showdown in Tuscaloosa at the University of Alabama. Over the next forty-eight hours, a series of events would mark a turning point in the country's racial history.

The court-ordered desegregation of the University of Alabama had finally reached its day of reckoning. Bobby Kennedy and his team were as ready as they could be. In addition to securing a federal injunction setting legal limits on Governor Wallace's actions, RFK and Marshall had cultivated a broad network of support and intelligence in Alabama. Floyd Mann, the former head of the Alabama Highway Patrol, offered confidential information to Marshall and John Doar about preparations for possible violence. Frank Rose, president of the university, had known Bobby Kennedy for ten years, and the two had spoken many times about the unfolding events. "He was on our side," Kennedy recalled. Rose wanted the students enrolled and quietly did all he could to cooperate. Meanwhile, over the preceding weeks, RFK, Marshall, and others in the administration had reached out to businessmen and civic leaders in Alabama, enlisting their support and appealing to their interest in seeing that the inevitable desegregation of the university did not dissolve into violence. The riots at Ole Miss had been followed by the exodus of the provost, several department heads, and distinguished faculty, as well as a dramatic drop in student enrollment from outside the state. The Kennedys could be confident that leading citizens of the state had made their concerns known to the governor. Still, Wallace remained the wild card. "What made it so difficult," Bobby recalled, "was not really knowing exactly what the governor was going to do. If it collapsed into violence—you could never explain why you didn't do more."[56]

Bobby and Marshall went to the White House Monday afternoon to meet with the president. The brothers, who had not seen each other for six days, spoke briefly together in the Oval Office before joining others in the adjoining meeting room. Presidential aides Theodore Sorenson, Kenny O'Donnell, and Larry O'Brien were present at various points. Nicholas Katzenbach was in Tuscaloosa, reviewing the logistics and plans for the next day. Kennedy and Marshall reported on the preparations and various scenarios that might unfold. No one had been in direct communication with Wallace since Bobby had met with the governor at the end of April. It was clear that Wallace would at least initially block the students' entry. Would he get out of the way? Would he resist in such a way as to compel the federal government to arrest him for contempt? A university official warned that if Wallace was arrested, "all hell would break loose." While Wallace had publicly committed himself to ensuring there was no violence, could he maintain order if violence erupted? Two nights earlier, 1,500 had participated in a Ku Klux Klan rally just outside Tuscaloosa, where a fifty-foot cross had been burned. Katzenbach and Robert Kennedy were both in close contact with General Creighton Abrams, ensuring that there would be no confusion about the role of the military. If troops were ultimately needed, it was agreed they could be mobilized quickly and with less fanfare by the National Guard. There was some concern as to whether Alabamians in the Guard would perform their duties under such circumstances. President Kennedy was interested in all the details and intimately involved in discussions and strategizing. The Justice Department would not settle on a final course of action until Tuesday morning.[57]

At some point during the meeting, the timing of the introduction of the civil rights bill was discussed along with the idea of having President Kennedy address the nation. Sorensen, O'Donnell, and O'Brien opposed an address. They thought it would involve the president personally in a way that would be politically disadvantageous. Bobby had a different view. He thought it was important for the president to go on television and address the nation during this time—not only to discuss legislation but also to talk about the problems the country faced and to demonstrate that he was concerned and directly involved. JFK listened to both positions, but he had already made up his mind. He told them all to "help us get ready, because we may want to do it tomorrow." Bobby said he had a draft speech that included "some pretty good sentences and paragraphs." Whether the president would give the speech on Tuesday night would depend on what happened on the University of Alabama campus that day.[58]

Bobby was on the phone with Katzenbach late into the night and early the next morning. It was hard for Kennedy "to deal . . . with all of the uncertainties" from a distance, Katzenbach recalled. "The mess in Mississippi had to be on his mind all the time. His concern came through with every call." The two men knew that Wallace wanted a platform to publicly stand up to the federal government. The governor had marked out the place where he would stand in front of the admissions building in order to ensure the best angle for the television cameras. Kennedy and Katzenbach agreed that it was best to let Wallace have his show, so long as he retreated and allowed the students to enter. Wallace had indicated that he might back down in the face of troops. Kennedy made sure that the National Guard could be federalized in time to arrive on campus by the afternoon.

By early Tuesday morning, RFK, Marshall, and Katzenbach had finally settled on a strategy dedicated to achieving three primary ends—gaining the admission of the students to the university, avoiding having to arrest the governor, and managing to do so peacefully. The team in Tuscaloosa and Washington knew that the best-laid plans could unravel at any moment. In the aftermath, some charged that there had been coordination between Wallace and the administration officials; that was not true. "We didn't know what Wallace was going to do, and he didn't know what we were going to do," Marshall confided to a reporter several days later. "We guessed right."[59]

The desegregation of the University of Alabama occurred in "a circus like atmosphere," Claude Sitton reported in the *New York Times*. Entrances to the campus were sealed off by yellow barriers, and newsmen and state troopers dominated the campus. Governor Wallace arrived shortly before 10 a.m. at Foster Auditorium. The colonnaded three-story building housed the gym and served as the site for student registration. More than three hundred reporters, photographers, cameramen, and soundmen were clustered close by. The governor joked with newsmen as he was fitted out with a microphone attached to a public address system. The two cars carrying Katzenbach, John Doar, Vivian Malone, James Hood and several others arrived close to 10:30 a.m.

As was planned, Katzenbach left the students in the car and approached the governor, walking along a path lined by state troopers. A television cameraman asked Katzenbach to wear a microphone; he refused. Wallace, who was perched behind a wooden lectern in front of the entrance to the auditorium, held up his hand to signal for him to stop. Unwilling to be bossed, Katzenbach came several steps closer. With the temperature nearing 100 degrees, he stood under the blazing sun and handed the governor a proclamation from the president, directing the governor to admit the students in accordance with the law. Wallace interrupted Katzenbach and read a long statement, refusing to "willingly submit to the illegal usurpation of power by the federal government." Katzenbach told Wallace he was not interested in a "show." When the governor once again refused to step aside, Katzenbach told the governor that the orders of the court would be enforced. "These students will remain on this campus. They will register today. They will go to school tomorrow." Wallace stood defiantly in the door, head thrown back, lips tightly compressed, and Katzenbach left. As had been previously arranged, Vivian Malone and James Hood remained on campus and were taken to their dormitory rooms.[60]

Bobby Kennedy monitored developments from his office, now a command post, with Marshall and several other aides. They had four maps of Tuscaloosa, a television set and radio, and a radio-telephone hookup linking them to Katzenbach and other members of the administration on the ground. Bobby reported the standoff with Wallace to the president, who issued the order to federalize the Alabama National Guard.[61]

Three National Guard troop carriers, led by General Henry Graham, arrived on campus shortly after 3 p.m. and took up position outside Foster Auditorium. Wallace had gotten word to Graham, a Birmingham real estate developer and friend, that Wallace was prepared to leave quietly but wanted to say a few words first. While Katzenbach greeted the news with a large measure of relief, he resented the fact that Wallace would be given a chance to take an encore. Once again, the governor stood at the entrance to the auditorium. General Graham, dressed in combat fatigues with the Confederate flag of the 31st (Dixie) Division stitched on his breast pocket, saluted the governor and began in a grim voice, "it is my sad duty to ask you to step aside on the order of the President of the United States." Katzenbach was appalled by Graham's apologetic appeal to the rogue governor. Wallace acknowledged Graham's difficult position, and then issued one final blast at what he called "the trend toward military dictatorship." He pledged that he "would continue the constitutional fight in Montgomery" and then abruptly departed.

Within minutes, James Hood entered the auditorium, followed by Vivian Malone, to register for the summer term. Their enrollment marked the first crack in Alabama's segregated education system. Although he lost the battle, Governor Wallace had become the standard bearer of white defiance, couched as resistance to an intrusive and overreaching federal government.[62]

—

PRESIDENT KENNEDY HAD A FULL DAY of appointments at the White House on June 11. He began his morning, as always, by reading through a batch of newspapers. He was "one of the great news junkies," commented his friend Ben Bradlee, then the Washington bureau chief of *Newsweek*. Alongside front-page coverage of the president's speech at American University in the *Washington Post*, JFK read about a major clash in Danville, Virginia, where police turned fire hoses on 150 antisegregation demonstrators and the mayor threatened to fill every jail cell in the city with protesters. The president also learned that talks had broken down in Cambridge, Maryland, previously a scene of violent confrontations between police and protesters, and demonstrations would resume. A call, the first of the day, came in from Bobby reporting on news from Alabama. While the brothers were speaking, Kennedy's eyes caught the front page of the *Washington Examiner* and the photograph of a Buddhist monk on fire in Saigon, a public suicide in protest of the repressive Diem regime. "Jesus Christ," the president exclaimed as he stared at the image of the sixty-six-year-old Thich Quang Duc in flames. While developments at home would dominate his attention on this day and in the days ahead, Kennedy realized that strained relations with South Vietnamese president Ngo Dinh Diem were fast moving to a breaking point.[63]

A weekly legislative breakfast with Democratic congressional leaders was the first event on the president's calendar. *Time* reporter Hugh Sidey shadowed the president that day, providing a rare glimpse of his routine on what turned out to be one of the most consequential days of his presidency. As congressional leaders and presidential aides waited for Kennedy to arrive, Sidey heard grumblings about the anticipated civil rights bill. Few thought it had any chance of passing. Some worried the process would derail other legislation and that they would watch the Democratic majority "being blown all to hell." The mood brightened when Kennedy arrived, and the congressmen joined the president for breakfast in the family dining room. After some good-humored talk about his trip, Kennedy quickly turned to the matter of civil rights and outlined his plans for the legislation. They would touch "every single base possible," he said, and no legislation would go to the Hill without the most careful briefing preceding it. There would be a continual series of meetings over the coming week—with members of Congress, labor leaders, and others—starting with Republican leaders later that morning. Senate Majority Leader Mike Mansfield reported that he had already begun to set up a meeting for Robert Kennedy and his "experts" to explain the details of the civil rights legislation and begin cultivating support.

The rest of the president's morning was full of meetings and events, but his mind was at work on civil rights. He and Bobby snatched a few conversations and communicated through intermediaries throughout the day. At 10:30 a.m., JFK drafted a presidential proclamation that was transmitted by phone to Katzenbach for him to deliver to Wallace. At 12:45 p.m., the president, joined by Vice President Lyndon Johnson, met with the four leading Republicans in Congress: Senator Everett Dirksen of Illinois, the minority leader; Senator Thomas Kuchel of California, the minority whip; Representative Charles Halleck of Indiana, the House minority leader; and Representative Leslie Arends of Illinois. The atmosphere was cool, Sidey reported, and greetings were wary. "I asked you to come here to inform you on our plans for civil rights legislation," Kennedy told the group, wasting no time. He tested the waters regarding major provisions of the bill as he embarked on the critical effort of cultivating key Republican support. The president said the civil rights crisis was "our major problem now" and talked about how things had changed in the wake of events in Birmingham. Dirksen and Halleck told Kennedy they could not say anything until they knew more details and had a chance to talk to their members. Kennedy reassured them that legislation would not go up that week. There would be technical briefings over the next few days and another meeting of congressional leadership.[64]

JFK left the meeting briefly to take a call from Bobby, who told the president at this point that Wallace had turned Katzenbach away. As soon as the Republican leaders left, JFK signed the order federalizing the National Guard. In the midafternoon, he slipped into the office of his secretary, Evelyn Lincoln, to watch a rebroadcast of Wallace's last stand. When Bobby called later with news that Wallace had stepped aside, the president said he would go on television that evening. Kennedy instructed Ted Sorenson to prepare a speech, and Sorenson set to work against a very tight deadline. It was by then just after 5:30 p.m. The three major networks were notified to reserve airtime for a major speech by the president at 8 p.m. that night. JFK had two more brief meetings in his office and then headed to the White House pool for the swim he had missed at lunchtime.[65]

It was after 7 p.m. when Bobby and Burke Marshall arrived at the White House. Bobby found his brother at the pool, and the two talked while the president dressed. They joined Sorenson and Marshall in the Cabinet room. Sorenson presented a draft of the speech—which Bobby described as "unsatisfactory." He and Marshall gave their views, and Sorenson took notes and went back to his office. JFK and Bobby talked for twenty minutes. The president was beginning to realize that he might have to talk without a prepared text, so they discussed what he might say, and he took notes on the back of an envelope. At one point, he teased Marshall, "Come on. Come on, now Burke, you must have some ideas."[66]

Sorenson returned to the room with a revised draft of the speech just minutes before the president was scheduled to go on air. JFK looked the draft over during the next three minutes, while Bobby encouraged the president to do some of his talking extemporaneously. Marshall recalled that the president didn't seem fazed by the last-minute preparations. "He knew what he was going to say, and I guess it didn't make much difference whether it was typed or not." But Bobby, who was not usually bothered by things, "was shaken a bit by the president not having a prepared text." Bobby would quickly realize that there was no need for concern.[67]

CHAPTER EIGHT

"A Great Change Is at Hand"

||\

AT 8 P.M. ON JUNE 11, 1963, seated at his desk in the Oval Office, John F. Kennedy spoke to his fellow citizens. They listened on the radio and gathered around the family television set. Running just under fourteen minutes, his comments were a distillation of what he and his brother had learned and experienced over the past two and a half years. His words reflected a deep understanding of America's racial divide and a recognition of the urgency of the moment. "Never before," reported the *Chicago Defender,* "has a president of the United States addressed the nation on the subject of race relations so frankly and forthrightly."[1]

Kennedy began by noting the widely reported drama of the day in Tuscaloosa, which had concluded with the peaceful admission of "two clearly qualified young Alabama residents, who happened to have been born Negro" to the University of Alabama. The president then shifted to the central focus of his speech, expressing the hope that "every American, regardless of where he lives, will stop and examine their conscience about this and other related incidents." He quickly sketched out the contradictions that had been captured in images and news stories over the past few years—of mobs harassing students, consumers "forced to resort to demonstrations in the street" to secure equal access to restaurants and public facilities, citizens threatened and assaulted for exercising their right to vote. Stating what he said he trusted were shared sentiments, he suggested, "it ought to be possible for every American to enjoy the privileges of being American without regard to his race or his color . . . to be treated as he would wish to be treated, or one would wish his children to be treated." Unfortunately, as his short recitation of recent events showed, "this is not the case."[2]

Racial discrimination was not "a sectional issue," Kennedy said, but a condition that existed "in every city, every State of the Union." He described the human toll of racial discrimination by comparing the life chances "of a

Negro baby born in America today," regardless of what part of the country or state, with the chances of a white child. A wide racial gap marked key areas of life: education, employment, income, life expectancy. He pointed out that Black unemployment rates were two to three times higher than rates for whites; that African Americans, moving to cities to seek opportunity, were often unable to find work; that many young people out of work and without hope were denied routine rights. While new laws and legislation were needed, they would not be sufficient to redress the reality of segregation and injustice. "Law alone cannot make men see right," the president observed. "We are confronted primarily with a moral issue. It is as old as the Scriptures and is as clear as the American Constitution."

The meaning of freedom was a thread running through the speech, at odds with the boastful rhetoric of Cold War America. The challenge Americans faced in 1963 had been in the making for generations, Kennedy explained, reaching back to the Civil War. "One hundred years of delay have passed," he observed, "since President Lincoln freed the slaves, yet their heirs . . . are not fully free. They are not yet freed from the bonds of injustice. They are not yet freed from social and economic oppression." Kennedy instructed his fellow citizens that "this Nation, for all its hopes and all its boasts, will not be fully free until all its citizens are free."

"We preach freedom around the world, and we mean it," he said, "and cherish our freedom here at home." But "are we to say to the world, and much more importantly to each other that this is the land of the free except for the Negroes; that we have no class or caste system, no ghettos, no master race, except with respect to Negroes?" Kennedy praised those who had been working in their communities to end racial discrimination and division: "Like our soldiers and sailors in all parts of the world, they are meeting freedom's challenge on the firing line, and I salute them for their honor and their courage."

"Now the time has come for the Nation to fulfill its promise," he insisted. Echoing a sentiment expressed frequently by his brother, the president warned that time was running out: "The fires of frustration and discord are burning in every city, North and South, where legal remedies are not at hand." If Americans did not act now, he warned, redress would be sought in the streets, through demonstrations, parades, and protests. Many had already experienced protests and confrontations in their own communities, and all had been exposed to explosive racial conflicts through the news media. These were, the president emphasized, manifestations of a moral crisis that could not be resolved by repressive police action, by tokenism, or by deploring the facts. This was a time for action—in Congress, in state and local government, and "above all, in all of our daily lives." He continued, "A great change is at hand, and our task, our obligation is to make that revolution, that change, peaceful and constructive for all. Those who do nothing are inviting shame as well as violence. Those who act boldly are recognizing right as well as reality."

Kennedy then outlined what he intended to do. "Next week I shall ask the Congress of the United States to act, to make a commitment it has not fully made in this century to the proposition that race has no place in American life or law," he said. He noted that the federal judiciary, through a series of rulings, and the executive branch had acted already on this proposition. Critical aspects of the problem required congressional action, and toward that end he would ask Congress to enact new legislation. He highlighted a few important parts of the bill, starting with a provision affirming that all Americans had the right to be served in facilities open to the public— hotels, restaurants, theaters, stores. This was "an elementary right," he said. "Its denial is an arbitrary indignity that no American in 1963 should have to endure, but many do." He said he would ask Congress to authorize the federal government to participate more fully in lawsuits to end segregation in public education. While he acknowledged that many communities had committed themselves to the work necessary to desegregate their schools, he pointed out that in the nine years since the *Brown* ruling too many Black children continued to be confined to segregated, poorly resourced schools and would be entering segregated schools in the fall—suffering "a loss which can never be restored." The proposed legislation would also seek greater protection of the right to vote.

At the end of his speech, Kennedy spoke extemporaneously. Looking into the camera, he appealed directly to all who were watching and listening. "My fellow Americans," he said, "these are matters that concern us all, not merely Presidents or Congressmen or Governors, but every citizen of the United States." Speaking specifically to white Americans, he asked for their help "in making it easier for us to move ahead and provide the kind of equality of treatment we would want for ourselves" and for our children. In a reference to the rising militancy that marked protests and demonstrations, he expressed the expectation that Black communities would be responsible and "uphold the law," adding "but they have a right to expect that the law will be fair, that the Constitution will be color blind, as Justice Harlan said at the turn of the century." He concluded, "this is a matter which concerns this country and what it stands for and in meeting it I ask the support of all our citizens."

With this speech, John F. Kennedy aligned himself firmly with the civil rights movement, fully embracing its vision for America's future. Martin Luther King Jr. telegrammed the president immediately: "Your speech to the nation was one of the most eloquent, profound and unequivocal pleas for justice and freedom of all men ever made by a President." Kennedy's passionate acknowledgement of "the moral issue involved in the integration struggle" and his encouraging words, King wrote, "will bring a new sense of hope to the millions of disinherited people in our country." The legislation that he proposed, if enacted, would "move our nation considerably closer" to the American ideal.

Kenneth Clark was deeply moved by Kennedy's words. Clark was stunned and somewhat reassured to hear phrases expressed during the contentious meeting with Robert Kennedy woven through the speech. The *Chicago Defender* described Kennedy's "remarkable appeal" as "a milestone in racial history." The speech represented "a plea to the innate patriotic instincts of the average American," the editorial mused, "an appeal to his conscience and sense of fair play." The president set the tone and the climate, the *Defender* concluded, for a national campaign that would see public expression of opposition to segregation as "a measure of genuine Americanism."[3]

The guarded hopefulness inspired by the president's speech was violently punctured several hours later. Shortly past midnight, Medgar Evers, a World War II veteran and NAACP field secretary in Mississippi, was gunned down in the driveway of his home in Jackson by Byron De La Beckwith, a Klansman from Greenwood. Evers had been leading a mass protest challenging segregated public facilities in Jackson. King eulogized his compatriot in a commencement address at the City College of New York later that day. "In the death of Medgar Evers, America lost one of those rare patriots," he reflected. Evers had "died in the trenches on the front line in the last ditch stand of segregationists prepared to precipitate a blood bath rather than change the decadent status quo."[4]

On the morning of Wednesday, June 12, just hours after Medgar Evers's assassination, four men representing a spectrum of views and experiences gathered in a television studio in New York for a prescheduled taping of "Race Relations in Crisis." Wyatt Tee Walker, fresh from the front lines in Birmingham; James Farmer, the national director of CORE and a veteran of the Freedom Rides; Malcolm X, the nationally renowned Nation of Islam minister and Black Muslim leader; and Allan Morrison, New York editor of *Ebony* magazine, joined Richard Heffner, the host of *The Open Mind*, for a ninety-minute discussion. Their exchange conveyed the fragile nature of the moment. Malcolm X differed from the others on what he thought was ultimately possible or desirable in Black Americans' struggle for freedom. But all shared Malcolm's assessment that, "We have as much segregation practiced in the North as in the South," Racism was just as bad, even if the laws were less restrictive. The four men spoke about the deep structural inequities that had arisen from a history of racial discrimination, exclusion, and repression. "Token integration" would not be enough to address the problems. African Americans had reached what Farmer called the "climactic stage of the struggle."

Malcolm X had taken a clear lesson from Birmingham. "As soon as the spirit of rebellion, or of revolution, begins to spread among the masses of black people in this country and they begin to take an active part," he said, "and they showed that they weren't confined to this non-violent approach, then the government, or the power structure, began to sit up and take notice." The sense of urgency was palpable. "Negroes are saying, 'Not tomorrow. Not next week. But now,'" Farmer asserted. While all but Malcolm X expressed faith that President Kennedy would push ahead with meaningful legislation, they felt they could not wait for that process to unfold. There had to be some strong executive action now, Walker insisted. "It may be that we'll have to see martial law declared in several Southern states," he speculated. "You mean a military dictatorship?" Malcolm countered. "It'll take a military dictatorship to bring black and white people together in the same house. . . . If all of the token integration you've seen in the South has caused so much bloodshed, what do you think white people . . . both North and South will do on the basis of real integration?"[5]

———

KENNEDY MAINTAINED FAITH in America's capacity to meet the challenge, however daunting, and stand down the forces of reaction and resistance. In handwritten notes, prior to going on air he had jotted down that the "country must go far beyond symbolic breaking down of barriers." The speech won wide praise for elevating the discussion of the nation's festering racial crisis and proposing action on all levels. Southern senators, predictably, were the most strident critics. Georgia senator Richard Russell said he was "shocked to hear the president justify, if not encourage, the current wave of mass demonstrations" and described the proposal to outlaw segregation in restaurants, hotels, movie theaters, and stores as a step toward communism.[6]

The Kennedy brothers' approach to leadership—open, collaborative, activist, and improvisational—suited the moment. That approach was balanced by a sober understanding that much was beyond their control. During a meeting with Democratic senators on June 10, Robert Kennedy described the race issue as "a boiling kettle" that kept him up at night. He was more "worried" about racial tensions in the North, which, he warned, were approaching the point of explosion. He noted that there had been sixty "riots" over the previous week. Less than two weeks later, at a meeting of lawyers convened at the White House, he described racial tensions and militant protests in cities across the country as surface eruptions of an "internal disease," a malignancy that had been allowed to grow within the tissues of the nation. The disease could not be treated with bandages but had to be attacked at the source.[7]

"The crisis in the North is boiling," the *New York Times* Sunday magazine announced at the end of June. Described as "a report on the forms the Negro revolution is taking in the North," freelance journalist Gertrude Samuels's lengthy story drew on field research in New York, Chicago, Philadelphia, Detroit, and Los Angeles. Samuels captured the stark landscape of Black communities in America's biggest cities, where families were crowded into poorly served segregated neighborhoods in a sea of white hostility. Unemployment rates were two to three times higher for urban Blacks than whites. In Philadelphia, a protest against employment discrimination at a construction site had descended into a pitched battle with police. The city "has all the ingredients for an explosion and any number of forces could light the fuse," a community leader told Samuels. Residents in Los Angeles spoke about a "seething unrest" that left civic leaders scrambling "to avert public outbursts." That June, more than one hundred thousand African Americans in Detroit marched in a massive "Walk to Freedom," commemorating the 1943 race riot that had taken thirty-four lives and showing support for Birmingham's Black community. The murder of Medgar Evers just a few days earlier, Samuels observed, had affected the mood of African Americans in Chicago and Harlem as deeply as in the South. As they pushed up against punishing racial barriers in their own communities, they identified "militantly with the aspirations of Negroes everywhere."[8]

ROBERT KENNEDY WAS IN CHARGE of the strategy for the passage of the civil rights bill. At Bobby's urging, JFK broadened the reach of the White House civil rights conferences. The president "wanted to meet with leaders from all segments of our society about this," Burke Marshall recalled, including lawyers, business leaders, church groups, women's groups, labor leaders, and educators. Between 1,600 and 1,700 people participated in these meetings, held over a three-week period from June to early July. Each meeting was organized to ensure that all parts of the country would be represented, with at least one person from every state. Participants were invited to discuss their understanding of the racial crisis and its challenges and to facilitate discussions not just of the legislation but also of long-term issues such as employment, education, and the welfare of youth. The president, Robert Kennedy, and Vice President Johnson routinely met with these groups, and other cabinet members and aides joined sessions as appropriate. A major focus was to encourage businessmen and owners of hotels, theaters, and restaurants to desegregate their establishments, but the gatherings also sought to enlist clergy, lawyers, educators, and others to cooperate in fostering interracial communication in their communities. The goal, as one participant put it, was "to explore the basis of racial tensions and eliminate their causes."

The 208 labor leaders who met with Kennedy on June 13 included very few African Americans, reflecting the long history of racial discrimination in organized labor. Many in the group pledged to support the president in ending discrimination wherever it existed. In a pointed comment, President Kennedy said that one area where he hoped progress could be made was that of the "executive leadership" of labor unions. Later, a gathering of three hundred religious leaders tapped a growing commitment to racial justice among clergy and lay church leaders. Many said they were prepared to play a major lobbying role for passage of the civil rights bill. A religious advisory committee grew from the meeting, headed by J. Irwin Miller, chairman of the National Council of Churches.[9]

Rosa Slade Gregg, president of the National Association of Colored Women's Clubs (NAACW), told the president that he should "mobilize and utilize" the nation's womanpower to carry forward his civil rights program. Her suggestion led to a White House conference with three hundred women representing more than one hundred women's organizations. Assistant Secretary of Labor Esther Peterson, who helped facilitate the meeting, observed that this was the first time women from so many different groups, occupations, and walks of life had been called together to sit down and talk with the president of the United States on any issue. Organizations as varied as the NAACW, the Daughters of the American Revolution (DAR), SNCC, the Young Women's Christian Association (YWCA), the American Nurses Association, the Ladies Auxiliary to the Brotherhood of Railroad Trainmen, and Women Strike for Peace were among those represented.

Diane Nash, former leader of the Nashville movement, was the first to speak up. Most of the suggestions that had been put forward, she said, would not work in Mississippi. Kennedy acknowledged the difficulties that Mississippi presented and asked her what she wanted the administration to do. She responded, "Make arrests for breach of civil rights laws and give us the right to vote." Noting what it had taken to desegregate the University of Mississippi and reminding the group that four hundred troops were still stationed in Oxford, Kennedy conceded, "we have a long way to go in Mississippi." A National Women's Committee on Civil Rights was formed in the aftermath of the meeting, dedicated to carrying forward elements of the program they had discussed, including establishing local biracial leadership training courses for women, opening up club membership to all races, organizing programs to help keep students in school, and actively supporting local desegregation efforts.[10]

Apart from the NAACP, the National Bar Association, and the National Lawyers Guild, lawyers and the legal profession—including, notably, the American Bar Association—remained largely silent in the face of obstruction and violent resistance to court rulings. RFK's oft-repeated question "Where are all the lawyers?" had become an office refrain. A conversation with Bernard Segal, a Philadelphia lawyer shocked into action by Birmingham, prompted Kennedy to organize a White House conference for lawyers on June 21. Two hundred forty-four lawyers attended. Sixty were from the South. There were twenty-seven African American attorneys, including two women, Sadie Alexander and the NAACP's Constance Baker Motley. Robert Carter, legal director of the NAACP and a key architect of the *Brown* decision, was there, along with NAACP lawyers from cities across the country. John Satterfield, a Citizens' Council member from Mississippi who had been president of the American Bar Association the previous year, also attended. There were representatives of several state bar associations, three former US attorney generals, and the deans of three law schools: Howard, Yale, and Columbia. The meeting was closed to reporters, and no transcript was created. Several participants spoke with journalists afterward, however, and Philadelphia attorney Jerome Shestack offered an extended account of the gathering.[11]

"It was the first time a group of the nation's leading lawyers had come together to focus on civil rights," Shestack noted. The president, vice president, and attorney general each addressed the group. All emphasized that recent events were symptoms of a deeper crisis. They spoke of lawyers' unique role in effectively interpreting the Constitution and buttressing the rule of law, as well as lawyers' skills as negotiators and conciliators. Robert Kennedy spoke the longest. He talked about racism in America as a disease. He challenged the lawyers to address the problems of discrimination and segregation in their own communities and to confront segregation in the North, Midwest, and West, as well as the South. Emphasizing the national reach of racial segregation and inequality, he urged his listeners to dedicate their talents and efforts to ending de facto discrimination. Each of the speakers emphasized the need for attorneys to mobilize the legal profession in support of the struggle that African Americans had been engaged in, practically alone, for so long.[12]

A good portion of the two-hour meeting was open to questions and discussion. At one point, a white southern lawyer indicated that he believed the Kennedy administration was encouraging the demonstrations that were leading to violence. Several people disputed the charge and began to defend

the administration, but President Kennedy cut them off. He wanted participants to speak freely. Other white southern lawyers said that they couldn't
support the president's civil rights program. The main focus of the meeting,
as one participant noted, "was on peaceful solutions by cooperation." Toward
the end, President Kennedy invited the leaders of the bar to work together for
the public welfare. When attorneys Bernard Segal and Harrison Tweed offered their services going forward, Kennedy responded enthusiastically and
asked them to cochair a lawyers' committee to "help open up the lines of communication between the races." Segal and Harrison asked all interested to see
them following the meeting, and so was founded the Lawyers Committee for
Civil Rights, bringing together lawyers from different backgrounds and regions to work on behalf of the president's bold agenda for social justice.[13]

———

THE INTRODUCTION OF THE CIVIL RIGHTS BILL was delayed until
June 19. On Lyndon Johnson's advice, Bobby Kennedy and his team met
again with congressional leaders, soliciting their input and fine-tuning
provisions without compromising the bill's fundamental goals. As Burke
Marshall recalled, "the decision to ask for legislation and bring this problem
in a comprehensive and serious way to Congress was a very, very, important
decision." The president knew it was going to be tough to pass the civil
rights bill he was proposing and that the effort would tie up Congress for
the rest of the year. He also understood how much was at stake for him politically and for the country. Senate Majority Leader Mike Mansfield
commented several times that there was no chance at all of a Democratic
president passing a civil rights bill. Kennedy viewed passage of a strong civil
rights bill as central to the national interest and felt, like war, that it should
be above partisanship. But his party was fatefully divided.[14]

On June 19, John F. Kennedy introduced the civil rights bill to Congress,
declaring racial inequality "an explosive national problem" that required the
federal government to provide "both the nation's standards and a national
solution." The federal government had the responsibility to ensure "that race
has no place in American life or law." The president outlined the sections of
a bill decidedly focused on the southern dimensions of the problem, crafted
to secure significant change while tilting the odds in favor of mobilizing the
necessary Republican support. The bill provided for equal access to public
facilities, federal enforcement of full and fair employment, and the enforcement of the constitutional right to vote through various measures, including
the appointment of temporary registrars. The bill empowered the attorney
general to intervene in school desegregation suits and made it possible to
cut off federal funds to any program practicing racial discrimination. The

outlawing of segregation in privately owned public accommodations was the most controversial part of the bill, and the most essential. Many Republicans and some Democrats from outside the South were wary if not openly hostile to that section and questioned the administration's reliance on the commerce clause. Federal action on this front was consistent, Kennedy insisted, "with our concept of both property rights and human rights." In a society that was increasingly mobile and economically interdependent, he claimed that the federal government had the power to act under the Constitution's commerce clause. He also insisted Congress was specifically empowered under the Fourteenth Amendment to ensure that "no state law permits or sanctions unequal protection or treatment of any of its citizens." While an 1883 Supreme Court ruling had limited the application of the Fourteenth Amendment in relation to private parties, few believed the Supreme Court would uphold such a ruling now.[15]

On June 22, thirty Black and white leaders representing civil rights organizations came to the White House to meet with the president. John Lewis, who had just been elected chairman of SNCC, was among them, as were Roy Wilkins, Martin Luther King Jr., James Farmer, A. Philip Randolph, Walter Reuther, and James McBride Dabbs of the Southern Regional Council. Kennedy sought to outline the challenges and enlist their support. Plans for a march on Washington had been announced the previous week, and the president was deeply concerned that the protests would make his job harder. The march—originally proposed by A. Philip Randolph to focus attention on the issue of jobs, poverty, and the "social dynamite" in America's cities—would now also urge the passage of the civil rights bill.[16]

Over the course of the two-hour discussion, participants promised to offer active support. When the conversation shifted to the March on Washington, Kennedy said that demonstrations could give fence-sitters in Congress a reason to vote against the bill. King and others saw things differently. Demonstrations would continue over the course of the summer; there was no stopping them, he argued. He felt that a nonviolent mass march, organized by civil rights leaders, would actually help defuse racial tensions and mobilize public support for the president's civil rights bill. Kennedy remained unconvinced that the possible benefits would outweigh the risks, but he did not ask the leaders to call off the march. The meeting fostered a spirit of a shared enterprise and some acknowledgement of the different pressures and political realities each had to navigate. "Well, we all have our problems," Kennedy told the group.[17]

The meeting gave Bobby Kennedy an opportunity to speak to Martin Luther King Jr. about a concern that had taken on greater significance since the administration had aligned itself fully with the movement. Since early 1962, the FBI had been investigating King to prove that he was under the influence, if not control, of the Communist Party. The investigation began when J. Edgar Hoover discovered that Stanley Levison, a lawyer based in New York, was King's close friend and adviser. Levison had been a financial adviser to the Communist Party during the 1940s and early 1950s. His relationship with the party had ended in 1955, and the FBI had tried unsuccessfully to recruit him as an informant late in 1959. Levison's association with King became the entry point for a new obsession for Hoover, which would grow into a campaign to destroy King.

Starting in January 1962, Hoover flooded Robert Kennedy with memos describing King's association with subversive forces. Bobby asked Harris Wofford to speak with King and ask about Levison. Wofford reported back that King had said he trusted Levison, certainly more than he did the FBI. Hoover persisted, and RFK finally agreed to a wiretap on Levison's phones. The wiretap reports made it clear that Levison worked closely with King, as an adviser and speechwriter. One piece of information, however, seemed to give some credence to Hoover's charges. Levison had recommended Jack O'Dell to be King's executive assistant. O'Dell, who was working in New York's SCLC office, had been a labor activist and a member of the Communist Party. Late in October, the FBI planted stories in five newspapers linking O'Dell, the Communist Party, and the SCLC. Each one attributed the story to "a highly authoritative source," helping to spin a web of suspicion at a time when many white Americans, steeped in Cold War propaganda, viewed the civil rights movement as disruptive and perhaps subversive.[18]

The Kennedys did not believe King was under the influence of the Communist Party, but the brothers also knew that if King could be tainted with communist connections, a campaign of innuendo and misinformation could be used to defeat the civil rights bill. As the effort to organize enough support to surmount a southern filibuster got underway, concerns about King's connections to Levison and O'Dell became more pressing. Hoover would not let up. On the morning of June 22, Burke Marshall and Robert Kennedy spoke separately with King, urging him to sever all ties with Levison and O'Dell. Where was the evidence, King asked, of his friends' communist ties and subversive activities? Later that afternoon, the president took King into the Rose Garden. He spoke about friendship and loyalty and urged King to balance those values with what he would be risking if he continued to associate with Levison and O'Dell, who, the president reportedly said, were communists. King had to cut his ties with them, the president urged. He told King of reports that southern Senators were going to attack the civil rights bill and the whole movement as communist-inspired. "If they shoot you down, they'll shoot us down too—so we're asking you to be careful," he said. King listened and finally said, "I know Stanley, and I can't believe this." He made no commitments.

Afterward, Levison told King he agreed with Kennedy. With the civil rights bill in the balance, there was too much at stake. King ultimately dismissed O'Dell and told the president that he would end formal ties with Levison. In an interview twelve years later, Levison was sympathetic to Kennedy's position. "We weren't far away from the McCarthy period. They were so committed to our movement, their public support was so vast, they couldn't possibly risk what would have been a terrible political scandal. When I realize how hard Hoover was pressing them and how simultaneously they were giving Martin such essential support, I don't feel any enmity about their attitude towards me."[19]

———

HEARINGS ON THE BILL OPENED before the House Judiciary Committee a week later, with Robert Kennedy as the lead witness. The attorney general, accompanied by Marshall, arrived promptly at 10:30 a.m. at the Old House Office Building. The committee room was jammed with spectators three to four people deep lining the walls. In his opening statement, the attorney general summarized each section of the bill and concluded by underscoring the necessity for action. Racial discrimination, he observed, "has been with us long before the United States became a nation and we cannot expect it to vanish by laws alone." But "we must launch as broad an attack on the problem as possible, in order to achieve a solution as soon as possible." The demonstrations of the past months, he said, had only "served to point up what thinking Americans have known for years; that this country can no longer abide the moral outrage of racial discrimination."[20]

"Opening gun" was how the *Washington Post* characterized Kennedy's testimony, a presentation "infused with a feeling of urgency and a strong sense of history." The *Post* described it as the start of "a great national debate, a great national self-evaluation." During the four-and-a-half-hour session, Kennedy fielded a broad range of questions, challenges, and concerns. His commentary was "replete with references to the practical politics of how to win enough Democratic and Republican votes to get the bill through Congress." Seasoned Washington journalist Chalmers Roberts described Kennedy's manner as "carefully courteous to the Congressmen," while leavened with humor and a touch of annoyance. This was especially notable when the attorney general sparred with John Lindsay, the young Republican congressman from New York. Lindsay had introduced his own bill earlier in the year, which included a public accommodations section that relied on the Fourteenth Amendment, explaining that Republicans thought the commerce clause approach gave too much power to the federal government. The congressman became indignant when Kennedy said he had not read Lindsay's bill, and Lindsay needled him about rumors that the administration planned to bargain away the public accommodations section to placate southern Democrats. Summing up the session, Roberts wrote, "both the critical questions and the political sparring yesterday showed that it is going to be very tough to win Congressional approval." Kennedy's political acumen and agility were on full display. "No one can doubt that the Attorney General wants to eliminate every vestige of racial discrimination," Roberts noted. "But he clearly is prepared to sacrifice a little to get a lot, rather than to stand on a demand for everything now." The ensuing battle, which stretched into the autumn, would bear out the accuracy of this observation.[21]

HR 7152 began its journey in the House Judiciary Committee, with parallel hearings in the Senate Judiciary Committee and Senate Commerce Committee. Multiple hearings were part of an effort "to maintain a sense of urgency," recalled Marshall, "and give Negroes some reason not to despair." This "three ring show," as one reporter called it, captivated media and public attention for most of July. Southern Democrats, predictably, stood as a united front of opposition, with North Carolina senator Sam Ervin spearheading the attack on the bill as "a drastic assault on the principle of constitutional government and the rights of the individual." South Carolina's Strom Thurmond said the civil rights proposals reminded him of Reconstruction days and called them "unconstitutional, unnecessary, unwise and beyond the realm of reason." George Wallace claimed the front page with two days of testimony that lambasted the bill as an assault on private property rights and a concession to the pressures of a minority flouting law and order. The fiery governor warned that if the bill were passed, the government should prepare "to withdraw all of our troops from Berlin and the rest of the world because they will be needed to police America." Amplifying claims made by Governor Ross Barnett of Mississippi a few days earlier, Wallace charged that Martin Luther King was associated with "pro-Communist" individuals. At the end of July, Robert Kennedy sent a letter to senators who had voiced concern over these charges, stating that no civil rights leaders, including King in particular, "were Communist or communist-controlled."[22]

The hearings showcased the broad support the legislation enjoyed with testimony from civil rights leaders, religious groups, labor officials, and others. But President Kennedy's popularity rating had dropped from record high of 75 percent in the fall, following the Cuban missile crisis, to 59 percent, reflecting the full impact of the civil rights crisis. In the South, his popularity rating had dropped to 48 percent, while Robert Kennedy's sank to 25 percent in the region, damaged by targeted attacks from southern members of Congress. For example, Senator Stennis warned that if the bill passed, "Bobby Kennedy could ultimately have federal marshals and troops at every crossroads." The president's popularity among Black voters had meanwhile soared to 83 percent. The fate of his civil rights bill was precarious. Most watchers of Congress agreed with Anthony Lewis's observation that it would be "a miracle" if Republicans and northern Democrats could effectively unite behind the legislation, particularly the provision barring segregation in privately owned public facilities such as hotels, restaurants, and stores, which was the heart of the president's bill. Justice Department officials prepared to meet this challenge.[23]

The Kennedy brothers understood that the key to a meaningful civil rights bill was Republican support, critical to defeating a southern filibuster. From the moment the bill was introduced, Nicholas Katzenbach and Burke Marshall focused their energies on cultivating the Republican leadership in the House, specifically Congressman William McCulloch, the senior Republican on the House Judiciary Committee. McCulloch was a moderate from Ohio, well respected by his colleagues, and someone who could potentially unite the liberal and conservative wings of the Republican Party behind the legislation. Over the July 4 weekend, Marshall paid a visit to McCulloch's home office in Piqua, Ohio, to discuss the bill and seek his support. McCulloch had himself introduced a civil rights bill the previous January. He was receptive to Marshall's appeal and offer to meet privately with Justice Department officials to work out a compromise that he could accept. The congressman had two conditions: that the president not allow the Senate to gut the bill to buy off southern Senators and that the president publicly give the Republicans credit for passing the bill. There could be no changes in the bill after it went to the Senate without McCulloch's explicit approval. This became the basis for a joint strategy going forward. Emanuel Celler, the seventy-five-year-old chair of the Judiciary Committee, understood the need for Republican support and worked closely with McCulloch. The Ohio congressman secured the support of Minority Leader Charles Halleck. Together, they unified Republican ranks on the Judiciary Committee behind the legislation.[24]

During the summer months, a team of five Justice Department officials led by Marshall and Katzenbach and including Joe Dolan, William Geoghegan, and David Filvaroff, a young attorney hired to work full-time on the legislation, embarked on a major lobbying campaign. They met with every congressman (other than southern Democrats and liberal supporters of civil rights) to explain the legislation, answer questions, and enlist support. The public accommodations section was a major area of discussion. Republican congressman Odin Langen of Minnesota questioned the application of the law to privately owned establishments that served the public, such as restaurants, hotels, and movie theaters, arguing that "to create a new right for one man by destroying the right of another is no right at all." Wayne Hays, Democrat of Ohio, said his mail ran almost 100 percent against the civil rights bill. Further inquiry, Geoghegan noted, revealed that constituents who lived in areas with high unemployment or where job tenure was precarious had the impression that the bill would create more job opportunities for Blacks at the expense of whites, which was not the case. Hays also opposed the public accommodations section, even though Ohio's existing state public accommodations law was stronger than the president's bill. While gaining Hays's support would take more effort, Geoghegan reported that the administration could count on as many as fourteen to fifteen votes from Ohio's eighteen-person delegation. Most of the congressmen the team spoke with voiced concerns that the impending March on Washington would make it more difficult for the lawmakers to support the bill. They viewed it as an effort to pressure them into voting for the bill that would not be viewed positively by their constituents. Throughout the summer, Robert Kennedy met with congressional representatives identified by the Justice Department team for further discussion and explanation. He frequently took groups out on one of the White House yachts, a relaxed and confined social setting. Justice Department officials pitched in to cover the cost of the booze.[25]

———

THE SLOW PACE of the legislative process defied the urgency of the moment, with protests erupting around the country. "The big question loomed larger than ever," a *New York Times* story noted: "Could a racial explosion be headed off?"[26] Bobby Kennedy followed developments closely and pressed his aides, lawyers, and associates to make visible progress on voting and desegregation. In her investigation for the *New York Times*, Gertrude Samuels had found that "the greatest outrage" felt by the men she spoke with was the segregation of their children into poor, crowded, crumbling schools. Kennedy felt the urgency of what had become, for many, a struggle for the future.

During July, a standoff in Cambridge, Maryland, captured national attention. Race relations in the Eastern Shore town, less than two hours from Washington, were as bad as in the Deep South. Schools remained segregated, as did nearly all stores and restaurants. Housing conditions in the all-Black Second Ward were abysmal—only 18.8 percent of homes had sound plumbing. Unemployment was over 20 percent. Apart from the small number who owned their own businesses, most African Americans who were fortunate enough to have work were confined to low-wage, unskilled jobs. The few African Americans employed on the police force could not arrest whites. The mayor, city council, and local businesses refused to advance meaningful change. By the summer of 1963, growing demands and demonstrations were meeting violent white resistance. There were incidents of whites driving through the Second Ward and shooting into Black homes. Many Black residents prepared for armed self-defense. Efforts by Burke Marshall to negotiate a settlement earlier in the month had failed, and martial law was declared. On July 21, Gloria Richardson, leader of the Cambridge Nonviolent Action Committee (CNAC) warned that "unless something is done soon, then no one is going to be able to control these people who have been provoked by generations of segregation—by countless indignities—and now by uncontrollable white mobs in the street."[27]

The next day, Robert Kennedy convened an emergency meeting at the Justice Department with Cambridge mayor Calvin Mowbray and several state officials, including Maryland's attorney general and a top aide to the governor. Kennedy had also invited Gloria Richardson and Reginald Robinson of CNAC, John Lewis of SNCC, and a representative of the NAACP. The meeting, led by Burke Marshall, began at 3 p.m. and went on until nearly midnight. Richardson was leery of the Kennedy administration and its motives. John Lewis recalled that at one point, Bobby Kennedy attempted to break the ice, gently teasing, "Mrs. Richardson, do you know how to smile?"

Richardson had provided the attorney general with a copy of a report she had prepared, based on a door-to-door survey of the Second Ward, documenting the needs and desires of the community. The report highlighted the abject poverty, poor housing conditions, and lack of jobs that plagued the area, priorities well ahead of desegregation for most of the community. It soon became clear that Kennedy had read her report and that it had informed his approach to the meeting and the negotiations. Time had been set aside for Richardson and the other Black leaders to meet with Robert Weaver, the Housing and Home Finance Agency administrator. During a break in the grueling eight-hour session, Kennedy invited those gathered to join him in another room, where the Floyd Patterson–Sonny Liston heavyweight fight was being broadcast, to see how the match was going. As they stood watching the television, Kennedy took Lewis aside and said, as Lewis later recalled, "John, the people, the young people of SNCC have educated me. You changed me. Now I understand."[28]

At noon the following day, Kennedy, joined by Richardson and Mayor Mowbray, announced the agreement. Spokesmen for the protest movement agreed to cancel all demonstrations indefinitely and accept the mayor's pledge that most of their demands would be met. The city pledged to desegregate the remaining grades in the public schools by fall; file an application to the Federal Housing Administration for a low-rent housing project for the Black community (which Weaver assured would be quickly processed); appoint a biracial Human Relations Commission; and hire a Black interviewer for the Employment Security office no later than August 1. The agreement included a pledge to set up a federally funded manpower job training program, to be administered by Morgan State College, a historically Black institution in Baltimore. Kennedy arranged for the release of Dinez White and Dwight Cromwell, two high school students serving indefinite terms at the Maryland State Reform School for their movement activities.

Calm returned to Cambridge for a period after that. But white hostility and ill will would unravel the fragile peace the next summer. Still, Gloria Richardson later wrote, "when all was said and done, in the long run Robert Kennedy was very good for Cambridge, though he was very hard-nosed."[29]

———

BOBBY KENNEDY was gaining a reputation for getting things done. Again and again, when confronted with a standoff, setback, or roadblock, he would find a way to patch together a solution. In Black communities, word of his actions and his abilities began to circulate. People started to feel that they had an ally in Washington. This feeling made it possible to believe that real change was possible. That summer, Mildred Loving wrote to Robert Kennedy, asking for his help after she and her white husband were barred from returning to their home in Virginia because their marriage violated Virginia law. While the Justice Department could not help directly, Kennedy advised her to contact the American Civil Liberties Union, whose lawyers would represent the Lovings in a case that ultimately overturned Virginia's ban on interracial marriage.

Kennedy thought of the race problem in terms of young people. He focused on the idea that Black children should not experience the same disadvantages as their parents and insisted that Black youth would play an essential part in changing the nation. In particular, he took an active interest in conditions in Washington, DC, the first Black majority city in the United States, which mirrored major urban areas around the nation with large Black populations—characterized by poverty, inadequate resources, de facto segregated schools, lack of recreational facilities, and high unemployment. To make matters worse, the budget for the District of Columbia was appropriated by Congress and overseen by men who had little interest in the well-being of district residents and were politically unaccountable to them. Kennedy used his high profile in the administration, his position as chair of the

President's Committee on Juvenile Delinquency and Youth Crime, and his connections with various organizations and individuals in the city to facilitate several major projects that impacted youth and their communities in ways that would resonate beyond the summer of 1963.[30]

Largely through Kennedy's efforts, more than 725 government jobs were made available for Black students that summer through the Summer Jobs Program, and close to 300 in private business. High school students between sixteen and eighteen were eligible. For most, this would be their first job experience. Selection was based on financial need, parental consent, desire to work, and an ability to relate to an adult. Job placement was handled by the US Employment Service, with staff members located at the high school and working with school counselors to place students in available jobs. Prior to placement, students were counseled on their appearance, taught how to fill out an application, and told what to expect. For those who were given jobs, arrangements were made for weekly counseling sessions, and a contact was established between the employer and counselor.

Robert Kennedy sent a personal note to each of the more than one thousand young workers who were hired through the program, encouraging them to do well on the job and go back to school in the fall. On August 1, E. Barrett Prettyman, the Justice Department attorney and former law school classmate of Bobby's who managed the Summer Jobs Program, told Kennedy that whatever attitudes business leaders might have had about hiring Negroes or teenagers, the program had demonstrated that employers could expect responsible work. And, he added, "the community now has the right to expect hiring will be carried on without regard to race."[31]

Locally, Bobby Kennedy visited Washington's Dunbar High School in early spring and learned from the principal, Charles S. Lofton, that the school's swimming pool had been closed since 1954 as a result of lack of funding for necessary repairs and renovation. Swimming had been a required part of Dunbar's physical education program, and the school had had an award-winning swim team. The pool had also served as a major recreation center for the community during the summer and after-school hours. Its closing, Lofton said, had been "traumatic," with long-term consequences. Kennedy wrote to Walter Tobriner, president of the DC Board of Commissioners, to inquire about funding to restore the pool. Kennedy was told no funds were available. Tobriner explained that the city had "suffered cumulative fiscal neglect at the hands of the Congress over the years," forcing it to "choose between the absolute essential items and those only slightly less essential."

Kennedy immediately contacted religious organizations to raise the necessary $30,000. The Council of Churches of Greater Washington and the

Jewish Community Council each contributed $15,000, and the Catholic Interracial Council contributed $1,000. By the time classes started that fall, the pool was ready to open. "It took Attorney General Robert Kennedy and community religious groups only three months to do what the District and Congressional officials failed to do for nine years for the young people of Washington's Seventh District," the *Washington Post* reported.[32]

A cheering group of high school students greeted Kennedy early in September when he visited Dunbar to officially reopen the pool. He addressed an assembly of 1,200 students, urging them to buckle down and work hard. "The kind of effort you make here will make a major difference in what you do later on," he said. He encouraged them to seek to deepen their knowledge and do a little extra. "Everybody has enough problems without the extra burden of not being educated," he said. His message was positive and energizing: "What is going to happen in this city depends a great deal on you."

After his remarks, he went down to the pool, where one hundred boys and girls waited for the signal. "Go!" the attorney general exclaimed, and the students plunged in. *Washington Post* reporter Dorothy Gilliam spoke with some of the students. Maxine Petersen, an eleventh grader, summed up the sentiments of most when she said, "He's not like most important people. He seems to really care about young people."[33]

———

BY SUMMER 1963, nearly 1,700 African American children had been without access to public schooling in Prince Edward County for four years, a tragic disgrace that Bobby Kennedy described as "years that can never be regained."[34] A fifth year loomed. While the case was bogged down in the courts, the Kennedy brothers were determined to act. In February, President Kennedy told Burke Marshall to find a way for the federal government to help the children "so long as it is remotely legal or possible." That spring, the Justice Department and the Office of Education funded a study by Michigan State University looking into possible remedial programs. Not surprisingly, the study would reveal a 23 percent illiteracy rate among Black school-age children in Prince Edward County, 92 percent of which was concentrated among children who had come of school age over the past four years. In May, Robert Kennedy dispatched one of his assistants, William vanden Heuvel, to Virginia to investigate conditions on the ground and help determine what might be done. "All I want you to do is keep me posted," he said. "Talk to me every day—a minute is fine." Vanden Heuvel, a thirty-three-year-old attorney from New York City, met with a range of people from the community and with local and state officials, including Virginia governor Albertis

Harrison. As litigation stalled and Black protest became more insistent, vanden Heuvel found the governor open to finding a way out.[35]

Early in June, as it was becoming clear that schools would not open in September, vanden Heuvel suggested that they create a free private school system for the 1963–1964 school year. Bobby Kennedy was taken with the idea. "Let's see if we can do it," he said. Within weeks, with the active involvement of the president, the two men had forged a partnership between local, state, and federal officials and foundations to create a nonprofit corporation that would provide free education in Prince Edward County to any student who applied. Colgate Darden, a former Virginia governor who had been president of the University of Virginia while Bobby was a law student, agreed to serve as head of the school's board of trustees if Governor Harrison would issue a formal invitation, which he did. Harrison appointed an interracial board that included three white educators and three Black educators, chaired by Darden. The Prince Edward County school board agreed to lease public school buildings to the group. At a press conference on August 14, Governor Harrison announced the formation of the Prince Edward Free School Association, whose purpose was "to educate the children of Prince Edward without regard to race, creed or color." Flanking the governor as he made the announcement were vanden Heuvel; Rev L. Francis Griffin, president of the NAACP branch in Farmville; NAACP attorney Henry Marsh; and J. Segar Gravatt, the attorney for the Prince Edward County board of supervisors. The image of the governor of the state of Virginia seated with NAACP leaders, widely carried on the front page of Virginia newspapers, was a first.[36]

The next month, the board of trustees of the Prince Edward Free School Association raised more than one million dollars, with Bobby Kennedy's active assistance, mostly from foundations. Four school buildings that had been sitting vacant had to be refurbished and supplied. Bus transportation had to be arranged, and one hundred teachers hired. With help from Francis Keppel, US commissioner of education, vanden Heuvel identified the ideal candidate to serve as superintendent of schools: Neil Sullivan, an innovative public educator who had established one of the first nongraded school systems in the country while serving as superintendent of schools in a suburban Long Island district where children were grouped by learning ability rather than by age. After an initial inquiry by vanden Heuvel in mid-August, Sullivan met with Robert Kennedy at the Justice Department and then with Colgate Darden in New York, then visited Farmville. He accepted the position and began his term on August 27, less than three weeks before school was scheduled to open. Sullivan, with vanden Heuvel's help, promptly launched a nationwide search for one hundred teachers to staff the schools.

The two reached out to teacher training colleges and sought the assistance of the National Education Association, the US Office of Education, and the Peace Corps. School was set to open on September 16.[37]

———

THROUGHOUT THE SUMMER OF 1963, the March on Washington, scheduled for August 28, loomed large. *Washington Post* reporter Chalmers Roberts wrote that it "was rapidly becoming a focal point . . . in this centennial year of Emancipation." The march, initially proposed to protest "the outrage of joblessness among Negroes," had evolved, broadening its focus to include support for passage of the civil rights legislation. Roberts noted that this form of protest was as old as the Republic and just as honorable. Thirty years earlier, the Bonus Army of fifteen thousand World War I veterans had come to Washington to protest their unemployment and demand a redress of grievances. But that demonstration had ended in rioting, and federal troops had been called in to evict the men. Fear of similar violence accounted for some of the trepidation many felt that summer, a fear fanned by racial clashes around the nation. "People on the Hill," Burke Marshall recalled, "thought it would be terrible." Supporters of the bill worried that if violence broke out, the media would be ready to snap up images, providing grist for the segregationists and potentially dooming the civil rights bill.[38]

Unable to stop the march, the Kennedy brothers accepted it as a fact and set about doing all they could to make it a success. The first step was to ensure that the city would be prepared to manage a crowd that civil rights leaders predicted would number more than one hundred thousand. Early in July, Robert Kennedy asked John Douglas, who had joined Justice as assistant attorney general for the Civil Division earlier that year, to coordinate the efforts of all government agencies and work with the leaders of the march as they finalized plans.[39]

A major goal of the march was to bring Blacks and whites from across the country together to demonstrate their support for the bill and for the demands of the movement. There were divisions and disagreements among the leadership regarding the tone and direction, but A. Philip Randolph had a strong influence on the planning. "We are in a revolution, a human rights revolution, but it must be with peace and courage," he said. Randolph praised President Kennedy's civil rights program, calling it "noble and splendid."[40]

Douglas worked around the clock over the five weeks leading up to the march. He began by organizing a meeting between Bayard Rustin, the director of the national March on Washington (MOW) movement; representatives of several other civil rights groups; and DC police chief Robert Murray. That first meeting, Douglas recalled, was stiff and formal, with the movement leaders and police and government officials sitting on opposite sides, and people making formal statements. But the formality broke down and discussions flowed more freely in subsequent meetings, as all began to feel they were working toward a common goal. Douglas worked closely with Bayard Rustin and Walter Fauntroy, the MOW representative in Washington, on the schedule and logistics. Initial plans were to march on the Capitol and continue to the White House. Douglas and his team persuaded the organizers that this was "too much to bite off" and would make it difficult to control the day's events. The organizers finally settled on a more focused march from the Washington Monument to the Lincoln Memorial. Together, organizers and officials worked out the details of timing and the route. Once those matters were settled, Douglas recalled somewhat wryly, "other things fell into place."[41]

Douglas had been tasked with preparing the city for a gathering of indeterminate size; some were now predicting several hundred thousand people would attend. His team included his assistant Alan Raywid; John R. Reilly, the head of the Executive Office for US Attorneys; and US Chief Marshal Jim McShane. The four men met twice a day, morning and evening, and often consulted with other agencies over the course of the day—police, National Park, Pentagon planners, members of the DC government, and the Justice Department. At first a few of the agencies pulled in different directions, Douglas recalled, but very quickly that situation changed as an understanding developed that RFK's Justice Department "was thought quite properly to speak for the president." There was elaborate planning regarding traffic and transportation—routing through the city, arranging for parking, and working with officials in Virginia and Maryland. Government Services Support, Inc. (GSI) was tasked with having people on hand to dispense water, and the DC government would arrange to have sprinklers attached to hydrants. The National Council of Churches agreed to set up stations with food and water. Douglas's team also oversaw arrangements for toilets and trash cans and ensured that ambulances would be in proximity. He persuaded the UAW to provide funds for a first-rate sound system to ensure that the speeches would be heard.[42]

The goal was to "foster a feeling of safety and organization." Jim McShane, a former New York City policeman, helped organize five hundred Black policemen from New York who volunteered their time to serve as specially trained marshals, unarmed and in civilian clothes. Bobby Kennedy kept an eye on the planning from a distance, delegating responsibilities as was his style with people in whom he had complete confidence. His intervention during the weeks of preparation was rarely needed. One exception was when the DC police insisted that dog units be available. When the police would not accept Douglas's pushback, Kennedy contacted the police chief directly and settled the matter. There would be no dogs.[43]

At last, all were reasonably confident that they were ready for the momentous event. Rustin had coordinated a nationwide appeal, reaching out to Blacks and whites through organizations and churches, encouraging people to travel to DC by bus and train. Speakers and arrangements for the day were in good order. Douglas and his team, trying to anticipate every detail imaginable, had created an elaborate communications system, with police units around the city hooked up to police headquarters and linked to the Department of Justice, the White House, and the Pentagon. At the last minute, rumors that Black Muslims might try to disrupt the proceedings led Douglas to install a switch that could turn off the sound system. "By the time of the march . . . we wondered if it might come unstuck," he recalled.

On the eve of the march, the advance release of a copy of John Lewis's speech by SNCC communications director Julian Bond caused a minor crisis. Lewis had faced the full brunt of southern resistance and national indifference. The speech was meant to be militant and disruptive. It spoke of revolution, indicted the nation's political leadership, and described the civil rights bill as "too little too late." Archbishop Patrick O'Boyle, who was scheduled to give the opening invocation, said he would not participate if this speech was given. Lewis and his fellow activists dug in. After a tense standoff, Lewis finally yielded to the appeals of A. Philip Randolph and agreed to modify the speech. Administration officials assured the archbishop that the speech would be changed—and Lewis, James Forman, and Courtland Cox, seated in a small room beneath the Lincoln Memorial, were still working out the details when the program began.[44]

An eerie calm settled over Washington on the morning of Wednesday, August 28, 1963. The city was free of the commuters and workers who normally crowded the streets. Government offices, most businesses and retail stores, and all liquor stores and bars were closed for the day. The police were on alert, with an additional one thousand troops prepared to provide backup. An estimated five hundred television and radio reporters waited as buses began rolling in at dawn carrying men and women from all parts of the country. By late morning, more than a quarter of a million people had filled the mall area between the Washington Monument and the Lincoln Memorial. The marchers represented all segments of American society—battle-weary movement veterans, clergy, labor groups, sharecroppers, housewives, students, government workers, film and theater stars. It was estimated that 25 percent of the demonstrators were white. Nothing of this size and scale had ever taken place before in Washington, and no one knew what to expect. As the day unfolded, the city was enveloped in song, marching feet, and a sea of placards: "March to Freedom," "End Segregation," "We Demand Decent Housing," "We March for Jobs." It was, a seasoned Washington journalist wrote, "part camp meeting, part joyful picnic, and part a determined almost fierce political rally uniting people of so many kinds and conditions."[45]

The formal program began early in the afternoon, with the Lincoln Memorial serving as the platform. There were speeches by A. Philip Randolph, John Lewis, and other movement leaders, interwoven with music. Gospel queen Mahalia Jackson lifted the crowd with "How I Got Over" and "I've Been 'Buked and I've Been Scorned." Bob Dylan played his new song on the murder of Medgar Evers, "Only a Pawn in Their Game." Peter, Paul and Mary sang Dylan's "Blowin' in the Wind." The proceedings were punctuated by chants of "Pass this bill!" sweeping across a crowd that stretched as far as the eye could see.

Martin Luther King Jr. was among the last to take the podium. Standing before Lincoln's massive statue, King delivered an iconic speech known for its famous "I Have a Dream" refrain. He spoke of the manacles of segregation, police brutality, and the shameful conditions of so many living on a lonely island of poverty in a vast ocean of material prosperity. He closed with an appeal to our common humanity and then described his dream, fostering a collective sense of hope and possibility, transformed by the vision before him. Reflecting on the day, one reporter commented: "the magnitude, the spirited but serious tone of the demonstration left everybody in awe and wondering about the future." Those who came to Washington, King told reporters, "will go back to their communities and work with bold and grim determination."[46]

Savoring the moment, James Baldwin commented to a reporter, "The day was important in itself." Then he added: "What we do with this day is even more important." Journalists covering the capital reported that despite its power and urgency, the march "left much of Congress untouched—physically, emotionally and politically." Whether the march won votes "will probably depend on the overall effect of the day's events on the television audience," James Reston wrote in the *New York Times*. Representatives who were key to the fate of the bill were most concerned about the response of whites in northern and western suburbs, who, according to recent polls, "tended to feel the civil rights revolution is moving too fast."[47]

For African Americans from rural towns and cities in all corners of the nation, the gathering brought the powerful realization that they were not alone. Bob Moses had traveled with several busloads of sharecroppers and movement activists from Mississippi, including the widow of Herbert Lee. Moses saw how a media-oriented event like the March could be used to pressure the administration. In the wake of Medgar Evers's assassination, racial tensions in Mississippi were running high. The grinding, violent struggle for voting rights had yet to attract sustained national attention. Plans for a project in Mississippi the following summer began to take shape.[48]

———

BY FALL 1963, nearly a decade after *Brown v. Board of Education,* only 8 percent of Black children in seventeen southern and border states attended school with white students. During the weeks following the March on Washington, token desegregation of public elementary and high schools began in a number of southern cities, including Savannah, Charleston, Danville, Tuskegee, Mobile, Huntsville, and Birmingham—leaving Mississippi the only state without any school desegregation below the college level. On September 16, the Prince Edward Free School opened its doors. For the first time in four years, Black youth in the county would be attending school again. Four white students attended. The schools were staffed by one hundred teachers, many from across the United States. More than half were from Virginia, and a quarter of the teachers were white, making the Prince Edward Free School the first school in Virginia with an integrated faculty.[49]

Alabama remained a flash point of white defiance, with Governor Wallace floating feelers for a 1964 presidential run. On September 5, white supremacists bombed the home of longtime civil rights attorney Arthur Shores in Birmingham, injuring his wife and bringing more than a thousand people into the streets. The arrival of an armored police car triggered a street battle between the police and protesters, and a twenty-year-old Black man was killed by gunfire. School desegregation was scheduled to begin in Birmingham, Mobile, and Tuskegee two days later. Citing "riot conditions" and arguing that the entrance of Blacks would be "disruptive" and would compromise the rights of white students, Governor Wallace ordered state troopers to block Black students from entering the schools in all three cities. The governor was angling to force the Kennedy administration into another showdown, to dramatize Wallace's resistance to integration and what he described as the slide "toward military dictatorship." When the Justice Department obtained a court order prohibiting the governor and the state troopers from interfering with the desegregation of the schools, Wallace withdrew the troopers and replaced them with bayoneted National Guardsmen.

Before dawn the next day, President Kennedy federalized the National Guard and ordered the troops to return to their armories. The administration's actions cleared the way for local officials to open the schools. A total of twenty Black students were to attend five formerly all-white elementary and high schools. Local police were present at each school to maintain order. Several hundred students at West End High School in Birmingham protested the entry of two Black students, waving Confederate flags and urging a boycott of the school. Only 100 students out of a student body of 1,400 attended school that day. Ten white students were arrested for disorderly conduct. The entry of Black students at the other four schools proceeded without major incident. Wallace complained that he could not "fight bayonets with my bare hands." He pledged that the battle would continue and charged the federal government with employing "the most potent instrument of force in the world directed by the ruthless hand of the Attorney General against the people of Alabama."[50]

On Sunday, September 15, less than a week after the color bar was breached for the first time in Birmingham's public schools, a bomb exploded in the 16th Street Baptist Church. Denise McNair (age eleven) and Addie Mae Collins, Cynthia Wesley, and Carole Robertson (all fourteen years old), were killed in the blast, and twenty more people were injured. Black rage exploded in the streets. In the melee that followed, sixteen-year-old Johnny Robinson was shot in the back by a police officer and killed. In a separate incident, two white teenagers shot and killed thirteen-year-old Virgil Ware while he was riding on the handlebars of his brother's bicycle.

President Kennedy expressed "outrage and grief" and, in a clear reference to Governor Wallace, decried the "public disparagement of law and order that encouraged such violence." Martin Luther King Jr. was more direct, telling George Wallace in a telegram that "the blood of our little children is on your hands." King also implicated "the seeds of apathy and compromise planted all over the nation" as responsible for this "tragic harvest." Pressure on the Kennedy administration for prompt and strong federal action accelerated. "I'm convinced," King wrote the president, "that unless some immediate steps are taken by the federal government to restore a sense of confidence in the protection of life, limb, and property, my pleas will fall on deaf ears and we shall see in Birmingham and Alabama the worst holocaust the nation has ever seen."[51]

The bombing was an extreme expression of the racist and corrupt civic and political culture festering in Alabama. While George Wallace was most clearly to blame for fomenting lawlessness, Robert Kennedy felt some portion of responsibility also fell on business leaders and newspaper publishers who made no effort to counter the climate that made such horrific acts possible. Justice Department officials considered developing "an intelligence program separate and apart from the FBI" to secure better information on antigovernment extremists. Burke Marshall returned to Birmingham in the wake of the bombings to meet with King in a zone controlled and monitored by a Black civil defense unit. Two FBI agents drove Marshall to a parking lot where he was met by several armed African Americans, each wearing civil defense helmets. They drove him to the house where King was staying and gave Marshall a helmet to shield his face. The car was stopped at several checkpoints by other armed Black men, connected by radio to one another and to a central headquarters. The substance of his meeting with King was not recorded, but Marshall had a firsthand look at a community prepared to protect and defend itself.[52]

The killings in Birmingham resonated in ways that Emmett Till's murder had one generation earlier, but in a very different climate. Sixteen-year-old Lew Alcindor, a rising high school basketball star in New York City who would later take the Arabic name Kareem Abdul-Jabbar, was paying close attention. Abdul-Jabbar recalled his feelings: "As I watched the ineffectual moral outrage of the Black southern preachers, the cold coverage of the white media and the posturing of the John F. Kennedy White House, my whole view of the world fell into place. My faith was exploded like church rubble, my anger was shrapnel. I would gladly have killed whoever killed those girls by myself." Singer and musician Nina Simone recalled her reaction: "All the truths that I had denied to myself for so long rose up and slapped me in the face. . . . It came in a rush of fury, hatred and determination. In church language, the Truth entered me and I came through. . . . I had it in my mind to go out and kill someone." James Baldwin, addressing a Memorial gathering at New York City's Town Hall, charged that American society was engaged in a "conspiracy of silence" in the face of atrocities accumulated over years. The Birmingham bombing and its aftermath, he claimed, stood as chilling proof.[53]

In a book review published barely a week after the murders in Birmingham, *Washington Star* journalist Mary McGrory reflected a growing strain of white liberal thought, which identified perceived deficiencies in Black culture and community life as the root of the racial problem. In her enthusiastic discussion of *Beyond the Melting Pot* by Nathan Glazer and Daniel Patrick Moynihan, McGrory wrote approvingly about the thesis of the chapter entitled "Negroes," concluding that "a little more self-help and a little less self-pity may be the answer for their troubled existence." Daniel Patrick Moynihan would elaborate on this perspective in his "Report on the Negro Family," issued two years later. Where Kennedy had asked whites to look into their souls and act, many now began to exonerate themselves by shifting the focus of blame on to the "failure" of the Black family.[54]

———

IN THE WAKE OF THE MARCH on Washington, FBI Director J. Edgar Hoover's campaign to destroy Martin Luther King Jr. intensified. Shortly before the march, the FBI's domestic intelligence division had completed a sixty-eight-page report documenting the Communist Party's efforts to influence the civil rights movement and concluding that it had been a total failure. Hoover refused to accept the report's conclusions or its implications for the ongoing investigation of King. He reminded his agents that time had proven the division's initial assessment that Fidel Castro and his cohorts were not influenced by communists to be completely misguided. Stung by Hoover's harsh reaction, the domestic intelligence division reversed its position. A memo submitted by Assistant Director William C. Sullivan two days after the March on Washington stated, "the Director is correct" and discussed the nature of the communist influence, citing King's culminating oration as a "powerful demagogic speech." In what was surely pleasing to Hoover, Sullivan insisted, "we must mark [him] now, if we have not done before, as the most dangerous Negro to the future in this Nation from the standpoint of communism, the Negro, and national security."[55]

In the weeks that followed, the FBI reported to Robert Kennedy that wiretaps had revealed King was still in contact with Stanley Levison. Hoover claimed that the wiretaps conclusively demonstrated Levison's influence on King and on the civil rights movement more generally. On October 7, the Bureau submitted a formal request to tap King's phones, based on his association with Levison and Levison's alleged status as a secret member of the Communist Party. At RFK's request, Courtney Evans, the FBI's liaison to the Justice Department, met with Kennedy in his office on October 10. After some discussion, Kennedy approved taps on King's New York office and Atlanta residence on a trial basis, to be continued if results warranted.

During this time, the research section of the FBI's domestic intelligence office prepared a new report, "Communism and the Negro Movement," focused on the King-Levison relationship. Without offering any specific evidence, the report charged that Levison remained "a dedicated Communist" and King was "knowingly, willingly, and regularly taking guidance from communists." Signaling the future course of the Bureau's efforts to smear and discredit King, the report described him as "an unprincipled man" both in his political dealings and his private life. King's growing stature as "the leader among leaders of the Negro movement" made the situation particularly alarming. Following his review of the report, Hoover wrote to Sullivan, who had prepared it, "We must do our duty. I am glad you recognize at last that there exists such influence." On October 16, without the knowledge of the attorney general, the FBI forwarded copies not only to his office, but also to the White House, the secretaries of state and defense, the CIA, and all divisions of the military.

The FBI sent a second request to Kennedy on October 21, this time for a wiretap on King's Atlanta office. Courtney Evans reported that the attorney general was still uncertain about coverage of King and the SCLC. Kennedy signed the order with the proviso that coverage of King's residence and office be evaluated after thirty days. Kennedy's motives for agreeing to the wiretaps are not clear. He was confident that King was not under communist influence and had no doubt about his loyalty or integrity. Associates have speculated, and scholars concluded, that several factors were at play. Hoover consolidated his power through the implied threat of blackmail based on FBI surveillance, and had sent RFK reports of JFK's sexual indiscretions, most recently of the president's long-term relationship with Judith Campbell, the girlfriend of top mobster Sam Giancana. Evan Thomas speculates this may have been a factor in pushing RFK to go ahead with the wiretap. Kennedy aide Peter Edelman concludes that this was a probably a factor. At the core, however, was J. Edgar Hoover's relentless insistence and pressure, inundating RFK with "evidence" that King and Levison remained in contact after King had agreed to cut off the relationship. A leak by Hoover to the press implying King's association with communists could easily doom the civil rights bill. By authorizing a tap with a thirty-day limit, Kennedy may have hoped to satisfy Hoover in the short term—long enough to get to the other side of the civil rights bill's first hurdle—while providing a clear end point to the surveillance.[56]

On October 25, Bobby Kennedy was shocked to learn that the explosive and highly sensationalized report "Communism and the Negro Movement" was being widely discussed in the Pentagon and that it had been distributed to multiple federal agencies. Hoover's reckless action would have been troublesome under any circumstances, but such charges by the FBI, if leaked and widely disseminated, would have disastrous consequences for the administration's civil rights bill. Kennedy spoke to Courtney Evans and went directly to Hoover's office. As Kennedy recalled, he told Hoover he considered the report "very, very, unfair to King" and said it presented only one side of the story. He expressed concern that wide circulation of the document, with its unfounded accusations, could be fatal to the passage of the civil rights bill. Hoover finally conceded that the report should be recalled, and Kennedy agreed. Agents who served as liaisons with the various departments were sent to retrieve copies of the report, explaining that revisions needed to be made. Kennedy could only wonder about the damage that had already been done—and the motives of the FBI director.[57]

During this period, the president and attorney general worked furiously to salvage the civil rights bill. At this fragile moment, the legislation stood as a singular measure of the nation's willingness to acknowledge the racial

inequities that defined American life and the federal government's commitment to ending discrimination and securing justice. The skill and dexterity
of the Kennedy brothers, working in tandem, were on full display during
the final weeks of October as they navigated the minefield on Capitol Hill.[58]

When Congress returned from its Labor Day recess, the bill came before
the subcommittee of the Judiciary Committee for markup prior to going
to the full committee for a vote. By then, the original bill had been trimmed
to meet concerns and objections expressed in wide-ranging discussions with
members of Congress and one-on-one sessions between Katzenbach and
McCulloch. Emanuel "Manny" Celler, the seasoned chair of the Judiciary
Committee, was the man in the middle—caught between a Department of
Justice hoping to bring on board just enough Republicans to pass the bill,
on the one hand, and liberal Democrats pushing for a stronger bill, on the
other. Celler ignored a memo sent by Nick Katzenbach on August 23 outlining tactics RFK wanted Celler to follow. He had his own ideas, based on
the strategies that had worked in 1957 and 1960—namely, to craft a strong
bill for trading purposes. During the subcommittee markup, members inserted several amendments, putting more muscle into the bill and strength-
ening Title II on public accommodations—the most controversial section,
on which McCulloch and the Justice Department had agreed to compromise. Celler assured his colleagues that these additions were temporary, but
the full weight of the civil rights lobby had come down hard when word got
out about the backdoor meetings between McCulloch and Justice Department officials. On October 1, the veneer of bipartisanship was gone. Celler
called for a voice vote and declared that the revised version of the bill would
be reported favorably to the full committee.[59]

The Kennedy administration's carefully laid plans had collapsed. Mc-
Culloch called the bill "a pail of garbage," and the thirteen Republicans on
the Judiciary Committee were incensed. They refused to work with southerners on the committee to scale back the bill—which meant that it would
likely die in the Rules Committee or go down to defeat when it came before
the full House. In 1957 and 1960, with a Republican president, it had been
in the interest of Republican congressmen to help salvage the bills; that incentive was gone. Indeed, many of them would welcome a setback for a president they hoped to defeat the following year. "Can Clarence Mitchell deliver three Republicans?" an exasperated JFK asked, referring to the lead
lobbyist of the Leadership Conference on Civil Rights. "McCulloch can deliver 60. Without him, it cannot be done."[60]

The scheduled presentation before the Judiciary Committee on October 8
was postponed while the Kennedy brothers set up a round of emergency
meetings to salvage the bill. Robert Kennedy promptly summoned Emanuel

Celler. He blasted the powerful committee chair, telling him that the sub-committee bill did not have bipartisan support, was indefensible on policy grounds, and would be torn up if it made it to the House floor. On RFK's instruction, an angry but chastened Celler convened a meeting with Mc-Culloch, Katzenbach, and Marshall. McCulloch was prepared to reengage but required an ironclad guarantee that the Democrats would support any changes made to the subcommittee bill. In a separate meeting with House Speaker John McCormack and Katzenbach, House Minority Leader Charles Halleck insisted that Democrats on the Judiciary Committee—and not southern Democrats—join Republicans in offering half the amendments to the bill. Republicans on the Judiciary Committee, still fearful that they would be blamed for modifying the subcommittee bill, devised a plan to ensure that Republicans would not lead in amending the bill. They persuaded Celler to invite Robert Kennedy to appear before the full committee to comment on the administration's thoughts about the revised version of the president's bill and to suggest what changes should be made. The Kennedy brothers understood the calculation here; Bobby accepted the invitation.[61]

On October 15 at 10 a.m., Robert Kennedy arrived at the Cannon House Office Building, flanked by Burke Marshall and Nicholas Katzenbach. They made their way to the elegant caucus room on the third floor, where the Judiciary Committee sat in executive session, closed to all except committee members and staff. Chairman Celler opened the session by emphasizing the bipartisan nature of the civil rights bill, and then introduced the attorney general. Kennedy read a prepared statement, saying that he was there "to support the legislation which the President has submitted." He said he was pleased that the subcommittee had recommended "a print of HR 7152" that in many respects followed the bill as introduced. But, he added, the version of the bill he had come to discuss included several changes and additions that he felt were ill-advised. Kennedy then went over the subcommittee bill title by title, recommending changes that had already been agreed to by Mc-Culloch, Celler, and the Justice Department. When he had finished his presentation, the attorney general was met with a barrage of questions from committee members. When time ran out, Kennedy agreed to return the following day. He spent the following morning and part of that afternoon before the committee. Kennedy emphasized that modifications were necessary because "the vote on this bill is going to be very close."[62]

James Bromwell, Republican from Iowa, later described Kennedy's two-day appearance: "He used no notes. He had stacks of books in front of him and Katzenbach and Marshall behind him. He referred to neither. He had a complete grasp of the bill. Also, I was impressed with his forthrightness. There was no equivocation. He took full responsibility for the proposed cutbacks." After the meeting, surrounded by reporters who had been waiting outside the hearing room, Kennedy said with faint smile, "What I want is a bill, not an issue."[63]

Clarence Mitchell called Kennedy's testimony "a sellout." Arnold Aronson, executive secretary of the Leadership Conference on Civil Rights (LCCR), warned that weakening the bill would "encourage civil unrest and heighten racial tension." He urged all of the LCCR's member organizations to flood the White House with messages, telegrams, and phone calls. The Kennedys anticipated such a reaction—in principal, they favored most of the amendments that had been offered—but as Katzenbach recalled, "we were guided throughout by seeking the maximum we thought possible on the theory that success was vital." In 1957 and 1960, the strategy pursued by LCCR lobbyists and others was to load up the bill with provisions that they could then trade away to buy off southern opposition in the Senate and avoid a filibuster. The strategy had worked, but, as Katzenbach noted, it ended up delivering "a mouse when now what was needed was a lion." With Republican support—and only with Republican support—the legislation had a chance of defeating a southern-led filibuster. In the heat of the battle, Robert Kennedy bitterly observed that some of the liberals "would rather lose the legislation than make the effort we wished. A lot of them . . . were in love with death."[64]

There was more drama ahead. Celler stalled the Judiciary Committee while he and McCulloch worked through the details of a compromise. When Celler convened the committee on October 22, all seemed to be in place to push the revised version through. But Roland Libonati, one of the Democrats who had agreed to propose a key amendment concerning the voting section, withdrew it at the last minute. Once again, the Justice Department's carefully crafted strategy unraveled. Arch Moore, a Republican from West Virginia, then moved that the bill be reported to the House—a proposal that liberal Democrats and southerners could easily agree on, for different reasons, and one that would send the bill to almost certain defeat. Celler "was literally saved by the bell." The noon bell signaling the opening of the House's daily floor meeting allowed him to postpone the vote on Moore's motion.[65]

John F. Kennedy's political skills were on full display as he summoned the key figures to an early evening meeting in the Cabinet Room on Wednesday, October 23: Lyndon Johnson, House Speaker John McCormack, Majority Leader Carl Albert, Minority Leader Charles Halleck, Minority Whip Les Arends, William McCulloch, and Emanuel Celler. Marshall, Katzenbach, and RFK were hovering close by in case they were needed. During the two-hour meeting, the president emphasized the importance of the legislation, and the need for a bill that would not run the risk of being defeated in the House or derailed by a southern filibuster. "Let's get this bill, agree on what we can agree on, and get it to the House floor," he said. Halleck recalled that the president did not grovel, threaten, or try to intimidate. It was obvious that he was very bothered by the situation and anxious to do what he could to save the bill. There was some discussion back and forth about how the bill might be trimmed. McCulloch, in his "slow and deliberate midwestern tones," quieted the room and suggested that the Republicans were prepared to offer some compromises. The president suggested they run through the bill to see how far apart they were. "I don't think we are too far apart," McCulloch offered, to Kennedy's evident relief.

A lengthy discussion followed. In a gesture to liberal Democrats, McCulloch agreed to reinstate a fair employment provision, which had been removed during earlier negotiations. He also revised his position on Title II, supporting a broader application of the public accommodations section. The meeting concluded with an agreement that Katzenbach, Celler, and McCulloch would meet and work out a final draft of the compromise bill. Celler scheduled the Judiciary Committee meeting for the following Tuesday, October 29.[66]

JFK and Halleck would work in tandem to secure just enough votes to defeat Moore's motion and open the way for committee approval of the compromise bill—a steep climb, with no room for error. After hammering out the new language with Katzenbach, McCulloch turned to shoring up Republican support. He spent Sunday afternoon reviewing the compromise bill with New York congressman John Lindsay, a leader of the liberal wing of the Republican Party. Lindsay did not trust the Kennedy administration, but he respected McCulloch. He was pleased to see how far McCulloch had gone in supporting a strong public accommodation section and was ultimately persuaded to work with him in forging support for the revised bill. McCulloch and Katzenbach had a final meeting on Monday morning. That afternoon, stenographers in the Department of Justice typed up the fifty-six-page text of the bill. Late that evening, copies of the document were packaged up, and a fleet of limousines delivered a copy to the homes of the thirty-five Judiciary Committee members.[67]

McCulloch and Halleck began the day on October 29 at the White House for a brief meeting with the president, Celler, Katzenbach, and Marshall. Kennedy and Halleck tallied their votes. They appeared to be one short of the sixteen votes needed to overrule Moore's motion; Halleck was confident he could secure another. Celler gave a step-by-step outline of how he planned to move things through. "Like a locker room before the big game, the air was filled with gratuitous advice, occasional expletives, overlapping talk and bursts of laughter," as two congressional observers described it. "I think we got a pretty good bill here," the president exclaimed as the meeting concluded.[68]

Celler called the Judiciary Committee to order at 10:45 a.m. "No Broadway show was more carefully choreographed," as a former congressman described the scene. Moore's motion went down to defeat, with one vote to spare. A curious combination of representatives had voted for the motion that would have sent the subcommittee bill forward to certain defeat: seven southerners (five Democrats, two Republicans), five northern Democrats, and three northern Republicans. The fifty-six-page compromise bill was then read in full. Celler and McCulloch each offered brief explanations of the final version of HR7152. No questions would be entertained, nor would any amendments be considered. The compromise bill was put to a vote and passed, 20–14. William McCulloch had predicted that if the bill passed the House Judiciary Committee, its passage in the House was basically assured. An elated JFK phoned Halleck that afternoon and thanked him. "You did a great job," the president said. "You really did what you said." Robert Kennedy later acknowledged in an interview that without McCulloch and Halleck, "the possibility of civil rights legislation in this Congress would have been remote." He described the bill as better than the administration's original bill "in dealing with the problems of this nation."[69]

The final bill included most of the president's original language plus a few additions modified to meet Republican objections. The additions included a national prohibition of job discrimination and the establishment of a Fair Employment Practices Committee. Racial discrimination was outlawed in unions and in businesses engaged in interstate commerce. The bill allowed for the attorney general to intervene in civil rights suits initiated by private individuals. The reach of Title II, barring discrimination in public accommodations, was expanded. The voting section was scaled back to apply only to federal elections and the provision for registrars was eliminated, a concession to northern Republicans. RFK had hoped for more, but not at the risk of jeopardizing the whole bill. Finally, the amended bill made the Civil Rights Commission permanent.

It is a "miracle," a *New York Times* editorial declared, "that this bill is emerging from the committee in such good shape." Having cleared this first hurdle, and secured a foundation of bipartisan support, Robert Kennedy was optimistic that a strong civil rights bill would ultimately be enacted. He knew this would only be a beginning: "In the final analysis, only better education, more employment opportunities, better housing, and more enlightened social attitudes will enable Negroes to attain the full citizenship they have deserved for so long."[70]

On November 20, the House Judiciary Committee reported the bill to the House Rules Committee, the final step before the legislation would be considered by the full House. It was too late for the bill to make it to the House floor before the end of the year. The Rules Committee chair, Virginia Democrat Howard Smith, was "a master of delaying tactics" and an ardent opponent of the legislation. Mocking the ruling in *Brown v. Board of Education* eight years earlier, Smith had quipped: "The Supreme Court laid down a law that things should be done with all deliberate speed and I'm a law-abiding citizen."[71] But McCulloch had assured the Justice Department that Republicans on the Rules Committee would move the bill forward. He would not let Smith control its fate.[72]

——

ROBERT KENNEDY TURNED thirty-eight on November 20. Over the previous six months, he, his brother, and the team they had assembled had set the nation on a course of racial reckoning and change. Neither underestimated the challenges ahead. Political pressures and shifting alignments would be amplified by the 1964 presidential election, an effort Bobby assumed would soon consume his energy and attention. At a surprise office birthday party that afternoon, John Douglas and Ramsey Clark noted that RFK seemed depressed and melancholy. In a short sardonic speech, he conveyed the feeling that he had become a political liability for his brother.[73]

After the office party, Bobby and his entourage went to the White House to attend the annual reception for the judiciary. In addition to the attorneys on his staff, he invited long-term Justice Department employees to the gathering—clerks, secretaries, elevator operators. "There were an awful lot of people there," Bobby recalled. "But it was a terrific thrill for people who'd . . . been in Government for long periods of time and never been to the White House." He left the reception to go upstairs to the living quarters and talk with Jackie Kennedy. The president soon joined them and the three talked about JFK and Jackie's upcoming trip to Texas—to patch up divisions within the state Democratic Party and shore up shaky support in a state that the Kennedy-Johnson ticket had won by a slim margin in 1960. The two would leave the next morning.

Bobby and Ethel returned home. Family and friends had gathered for another birthday celebration that went on late into the night. It was a "large, loud, happy affair," one participant recalled. Instead of her usual humorous toast to her husband, Ethel asked the guests to drink to the president of the United States.[74]

CHAPTER NINE

On His Own

||||

NOVEMBER 22, 1963, was a sunny, unseasonably warm day in Washington. Robert Kennedy spent the morning at the Justice Department, presiding over a meeting on organized crime with attorneys from across the nation. During the lunch break, be brought his friend Robert Morgenthau, US attorney for the southern district of New York, and the chief of Morganthau's criminal division, Silvio Mollo, home to Hickory Hill for a swim and sandwiches. The three were sitting with Ethel by the pool preparing to return to the Justice Department when a nearby telephone extension rang. Ethel answered. On the line was J. Edgar Hoover.

The FBI director had never called Kennedy at home. Bobby instantly knew something unusual had happened. "I have news for you. The President has been shot,'" Hoover reported. "What?" Kennedy responded in disbelief. "The President's been shot," Hoover repeated. Later Bobby couldn't recall whether he asked about his brother's condition or whether Hoover immediately continued, but Kennedy remembered Hoover saying, "I think it's serious . . . I'll call you back when I find out more." By the time Hoover phoned again, Kennedy had heard from Clint Hill, the Secret Service agent who had been with the president, that JFK had died. Although Bobby didn't remember exactly what Hoover said when he called the second time to tell Kennedy his brother was dead, he could not forget the tone. The FBI director was not a bit upset, Kennedy recalled, adding wryly that Hoover was "not quite as excited as if he was reporting the fact that he found a communist on the faculty of Howard University."

"Shattered" was how friends described Bobby in the aftermath of the assassination. The two brothers had shared a rare intimacy forged by close collaboration at the cutting edge of public life and nurtured through almost daily contact. JFK, to Bobby, was "his hero, closest friend, sharer of the spirit," as Anthony Lewis wrote in the *New York Times*. In an instant his brother was gone. The loss at the pinnacle of their shared journey was hardly bearable. To those closest to him, Bobby exhibited an intense physical pain. "It was almost as if he was on the rack or he had a tooth ache or had had a heart attack. It was pain. It showed itself as pain," said John Seigenthaler. Decades later, William vanden Heuvel's memory of Bobby on the day after the assassination was crystal clear: "I have never seen anyone as grief stricken." For months, he seemed numbed by sorrow and depression.[1]

Some who knew him and others taking the measure of Robert Kennedy's life have concluded that the assassination changed him. But those who were close to him, like David Hackett and John Seigenthaler, disagree. While allowing that "he was certainly different" in the immediate aftermath of the tragedy, Burke Marshall insisted "he was basically the same person." Robert Kennedy's capacity for growth was a defining feature of his personality. Walter Sheridan, who had worked with Kennedy since the 1950s, recalled that his manner had been "much more reflexive and outgoing," and after the assassination "he was more soul-searching, and inward." But "he always had the basic compassion and feelings" and "was always what he was." Mortimer Caplin, who had known Bobby since law school and worked in the administration, put it this way: "He was like the blocking back for his brother. . . . But I think you got to know him much better after his brother's death. He was more and more himself."[2]

While there were isolated instances of gaiety in some segregationist strongholds, shock and sorrow pulsed through the country in the wake of the assassination. For many Black Americans, the murder of the president resonated in a deeply personal way. Reactions recorded in the Black press drew connections to the assassination of Medgar Evers, the murder of four girls in the Birmingham church bombing two months earlier, and the terror that had long met Black efforts to live as free and equal citizens. "The President's assassination," Edwin Griffin told the *Chicago Defender*, "shows just what type of people Negroes have been trying to protect themselves from for a hundred years."

Yvette Stigler, owner of a barbershop on the Southside of Chicago, told a reporter, "You can believe one thing. No Negro did this terrible thing." "I've heard the news," said Betty Carr. "I prayed and walked the floor. He was white, honey, but I know he did all he could." And then she sobbed "as if her heart would break." An elderly man turned away from an overflow crowd gathered for a memorial in Harlem and went home. "He was our man," he said. "And now he's dead." The *Pittsburgh Courier* editorialized, "Hatred Bears Bitter Fruit."[3]

John Kennedy was remembered for what he did, what he said, and what he had come to represent to many Black people. He kept his promises, wrote

George Barbour, a reporter for the *Pittsburgh Courier* who had covered the 1960 presidential campaign. While African Americans were irked by slow progress at times, Barbour observed that JFK did not waver in his appointments, his speeches, or his application of political power. He had gotten the civil rights bill through the Judiciary Committee and on its way just days before his death. Now the bill was that much nearer to becoming law.[4]

Thurgood Marshall was one of many to say that Black Americans had made more progress toward obtaining basic rights under Kennedy than at any time in the past. Civil rights activists had vastly accelerated the pace of change, and Kennedy's support had contributed to the growing strength of the movement as a moral force. "No president before him," wrote *Chicago Defender* editor John Sengstacke, "had labored so hard . . . to bridge the chasm that separated the races." JFK did more than any other president, editorialized the *Pittsburgh Courier,* "to humanize the American Negro in the eyes of his fellow American citizens." Morehouse College president Benjamin Mays qualified the frequent comparisons being made in the days after the assassination between John Kennedy and Abraham Lincoln. "Lincoln was not convinced the slaves should be freed at any price," Mays observed. Lincoln's primary concern was saving the union and winning the war. "No American President up to this time has dealt so forthrightly and so courageously with civil rights as the late John F. Kennedy," Mays went on. He had "real convictions, pushed with vigor civil rights legislation and expounded equality eloquently before the American people."[5]

In his first major address as president, Lyndon Johnson singled out the enactment of the civil rights bill as one of his highest priorities. "No memorial oration or eulogy," Johnson told a joint session of Congress, "could more eloquently honor President Kennedy's memory." Johnson's words were greeted with a storm of applause, notably not joined by southern members of Congress. Johnson evoked a sense of urgency and action as he pledged to carry forward the programs initiated by his predecessor in education, jobs, and tax reform, along with other progressive measures. Toward the end of his twenty-seven-minute speech, Johnson circled back to the major issue and cause "for which [President Kennedy] fought so long": "We meet in grief but let us also meet in renewed dedication and renewed vigor. Let us meet in action, in tolerance and in mutual understanding. . . . The time has come for Americans of all races and creeds and political beliefs to understand and respect one another." In a curious phrasing that reflected LBJ's approach, he added, "Let us turn away from the fanatics of the far left and the far right, from apostles of bitterness and bigotry, from the defiance of the law and those who pour venom into the Nation's blood stream."[6]

In the months following the assassination, Robert Kennedy and Lyndon Johnson would establish a new relationship dedicated to the passage of the civil rights bill—a fragile link in an association fraught with difficulties that went well beyond the personal animosity so famously associated with these two men. Their tense and often hostile relationship has invited much commentary and speculation, driving press coverage at the time and captivating historians and biographers since. But fundamental differences concerning policy, politics, and civic culture have often been overshadowed and discounted. In no other area were their disparate temperaments, values, and political sensibilities more consequential than in how each of them understood and navigated the dominant domestic issue of their time.

Presenting a study in contrasts, the personalities of Robert Kennedy and Lyndon Johnson, in the words of Nicholas Katzenbach, "were absolutely inconsistent." The two represented different generations and came from different regions of the country—one a southerner from the Texas hill country, the other an urban and urbane New Englander. Robert Kennedy's family and education had given him a sense of security and expectation, while Lyndon Johnson had a hardscrabble upbringing in central Texas. After graduating from Southwest Texas State Teachers College, Johnson had risen in politics through dint of his intelligence, hard work, and raw ambition. Bobby Kennedy proved to be a brilliant political tactician, but commitment to public service, reflecting his faith and class and the values of his family, was a defining aspect of Kennedy's political life. In contrast, power was Lyndon Johnson's lifeline. At a physically imposing six feet four inches, he was masterful in his drive to secure, hold, and wield power. After three years in the shadows as vice president, he was ready now to be in charge.[7]

As RFK made his way to meet the plane bringing his brother's body back to Washington, Kennedy commented to Ed Guthman, "People just don't know how conservative Lyndon really is. There are going to be a lot of changes." Beyond the deep personal loss RFK experienced, all that the administration had created and cultivated across the previous three years seemed to implode in an afternoon. As the days and weeks passed, Kennedy began to think "a lot, continuously in fact" about how to continue what he and his brother had begun together. "You see," he told an interviewer months later, "not the President alone, but we were all involved in certain tasks and certain dreams we wanted to translate into reality. . . . I understood it was up to me to carry them forward." Talking with Arthur Schlesinger and Richard Goodwin in December, Kennedy said, "There are a hundred men scattered through the government who are devoted to the purposes for which we came to Washington. We must all stay in close touch and not let them pick us off one by one. I haven't the answer in detail yet, but I am sure that the fundamental principle now is collective action."[8]

Kennedy considered several possibilities going forward, including the vice presidency, but his focus for the next stretch of months would be to finish the work he and his brother had begun on the civil rights bill. The ongoing effort that would culminate with passage of the Civil Rights Act of 1964 marked RFK's reentry into the public arena. Lyndon Johnson left it to Bobby and his team to determine strategy and move the bill forward through a Senate filibuster, which few thought possible. As Katzenbach recalled, Johnson told Bobby that the Justice Department "should call the shots, and [Johnson] would do what he asked." Kennedy fully understood what he was up to. As he later put it, "Putting the Justice Department out front in terms of the fight for the bill was a very good idea so far as Johnson was concerned." Johnson did not see how Kennedy and his team could get the votes for cloture, necessary to get the bill voted on by the Senate. If the bill failed, Johnson wanted to make sure "that the blame fell as far away from the Oval office as possible," observed Clay Risen in his history of the 1964 Civil Rights Act.[9]

——

ON FEBRUARY 10, 1964, the civil rights bill passed the House after ten days of debate by an overwhelming vote, 290 to 130. Praised by the as the *Washington Post* as the "most comprehensive civil rights bill in history," it included all the major provisions hammered out the previous October. The legislation strengthened voting guarantees for African Americans, banned discrimination in privately owned accommodations and publicly owned facilities, empowered the attorney general to sue for school desegregation and seek to bar discrimination in federally assisted programs, and prohibited discrimination by employers and unions. Title VII, the equal employment provision, was broadened to include sex, as well as race, religion and national origins, a powerful boost to the modern women's movement. "The bill was a triumph for Republican as well as Democratic leadership," the *Post* editorialized, "the best sort of bipartisanship."[10]

The four-month-long battle to win over the Senate began on February 17. From as far back as 1921, when they torpedoed an antilynching bill, southerners had succeeded in wearing down their opponents by stalling the work of the Senate with a filibuster.[11] Burke Marshall and Nick Katzenbach worked in tandem with a strong leadership team in the Senate, consisting of Majority Leader Mike Mansfield, a Democrat from Montana; Democrat Hubert Humphrey; and Republican Thomas Kuchel of California, with the vocal support of President Johnson. When the bill was first introduced in the summer of 1963, Bobby Kennedy's Justice Department had relied on education and persuasion to secure the necessary votes. Now his team embarked on an intensive lobbying campaign, targeting congressional officials and reaching out to churches, lawyers, women's groups, educators, and others in an effort to inform and enlist public support and pressure. Over the previous eight months Kennedy and his team had carved a fresh path to victory in the House. Now they were ready to push on to the Senate. But could they overcome determined resistance? Southerners began their filibuster on March 9. While the endurance of the Senate leadership would flag at times as the standoff dragged on, all ultimately stood firm on the goal of breaking the southern talkathon and bringing a strong bill to a vote.[12]

Justice Department attorney David Filvaroff had compiled two large loose-leaf binders with detailed answers to questions for House leaders. Now he provided a set of updated binders for each of the floor leaders in the Senate. Katzenbach and Marshall started meeting with individual senators early in the summer to hear their concerns, address them when possible, and begin cultivating senators' support. During his first visit with the staff of Illinois's powerful Republican senator Everett Dirksen, Marshall was stunned to learn that they had no conception of the "massive caste system" the bill was designed to end. Dirksen's staffers thought in terms of individual complaints and settlements, as under northern fair employment laws. Starting in February, a team of up to ten Justice Department lawyers began meeting with Senate legislative assistants to answer questions and chart where each senator stood. Aides clipped newspaper articles and tracked public opinion in key midwestern states. There was an ongoing effort to ensure that senators were fully informed about the bill, its provisions, and the injustices it was designed to redress, defusing the ignorance and misinformation that clouded the legislation. Through it all, Robert Kennedy, Katzenbach, and Marshall kept their sights set on Everett Dirksen, the wily and unpredictable Senate minority leader, whose support was essential.[13]

Starting in late February, the Coordinating Committee for Fundamental American Freedoms, a movement to organize white northerners in opposition to the legislation, launched a publicity attack on the civil rights bill. John Satterfield of Yazoo City, Mississippi, a member of the White Citizens' Council and former president of the American Bar Association, was the committee's mastermind, and William Loeb, conservative editor of the *Manchester Union Leader* in New Hampshire, served as chairman. Satterfield focused largely on midwestern states. He worked through trade and professional groups and small newspapers to mobilize opposition to the bill and bought mailing lists of tens of thousands of addresses to orchestrate a letter-writing campaign to senators. The committee charged that the provision for fair employment practices would result "in reverse discrimination through preferential hiring." In mid-March, the committee took out a full-page advertisement in two hundred newspapers outside the South headlined "BILLION DOLLAR BLACKJACK—THE CIVIL RIGHTS BILL." The ad claimed that the bill was unconstitutional and a major step toward socialism.[14]

On March 17, George Wallace launched his presidential campaign in Wisconsin. The defeat of the civil rights bill was a major plank of his candidacy. Wallace attacked the bill as a power grab by the "central government" that would undermine local and state control. He described it as an assault on property rights and freedom of association and played into white fears that the legislation would outlaw discrimination in the sale or rental of housing. Wallace distributed leaflets publicizing the points compiled by Satterfield, highlighting his credentials as a leading lawyer. Wallace won 260,000 votes in Wisconsin's April 7 crossover primary, in which both Democrats and Republicans could vote. Wallace carried 34 percent of the Democratic vote. He interpreted his strong showing as a move by the people of Wisconsin "to break the trend toward centralized government." Commenting on Wallace's showing, William F. Buckley Jr. wrote in the *National Review:* "What the white North is awakening to is the danger to individual liberty of the new radical plans breaking up traditional American patterns of racial assimilation and conciliation. For reasons that seem less and less coincidental the proposals tend to be backed by a segment of the community which is far gone in a commitment to state socialism, which despises the American way of life and civilization."[15]

Satterfield's campaign was reflected in a spike in the number of letters to members of Congress against the bill, which outnumbered the mail in support in some cases by 4–1 and as much as 10–1. Hubert Humphrey took to the floor of the Senate to denounce the ad run by the committee as a "reprehensible lie." "Who is a Socialist?" he asked. "Was it the minority leader of the House of Representatives"—Congressman Charles Halleck from Indiana—"who voted for it? Was it the distinguished representative from the state of Ohio who voted for it?" Taking on the role of a rapid response team, the Justice Department began issuing a daily bipartisan civil rights newsletter, promptly debunking misinformation while keeping senators and their staffs informed of developments. When asked about Wallace's strong showing in the primaries, Robert Kennedy said he did not believe it would seriously threaten the passage of the bill, but he added, "it's not helpful." Wallace, Kennedy said, "doesn't permit the truth or facts to interfere with what he has to say about the civil rights bill."[16]

Rising racial tensions in northern urban areas, stoked by expanding civil rights protests and growing white resentment and fears concerning housing, schools, and jobs, raised a different kind of challenge that spring—one that could not be explained away or easily resolved. Young Black activists and their allies, cynical about the meager results of more traditional tactics, were now engaging in massive civil disobedience in cities across the country. More than two hundred people were arrested in San Francisco for staging a "lie-down" in an auto showroom in protest of General Motor's "blatant violation" of federally mandated nondiscrimination provisions. In Rochester, New York, fifteen theology students chained themselves together and lay in the street, blocking traffic to protest housing discrimination. When protesters in Cleveland attempted to physically block the construction of a school as a protest against school segregation in the city, a young minister was accidentally crushed to death by a tractor. The Brooklyn chapter of CORE set New York City's Mayor Robert Wagner on edge when they threatened a "stall-in" on the city's major highways on April 22, the opening day of the World's Fair, to dramatize dissatisfaction with the pace of civil rights progress. Plans went forward after city officials failed to meet with the group to discuss a timetable for the integration of schools and action against job and housing discrimination and police brutality. The story was front-page news in the *New York Times* for three consecutive days. To the relief of officials in New York and Washington, the two thousand cars needed to mount the protest failed to materialize. A reporter chalked the failure up to "new leaders on the civil rights scene who promised much and delivered nothing."[17]

Writing on April 18, Anthony Lewis commented that the "simultaneous heightening of militancy among Negroes and of racial fears among Northern whites" revealed a "new tension in the racial struggle." President Johnson, Hubert Humphrey, and others warned that militant protests would jeopardize the passage of the civil rights bill. Robert Kennedy cautioned against "irresponsible activities" but added that the white community would have to do something to relieve Black frustration. Many participating in the protests understood that civil rights legislation would have its greatest impact in the South and worried it would do little to alleviate the more subtle yet equally harmful legacy of discrimination and exclusion in northern communities. Wallace's strong showing in key primary states fueled racial tensions. In New York City that April, white workers walked off a city housing project to protest the hiring of one African American and three Puerto Rican plumbers. Senator Richard Russell, leader of the southern opposition, was confident that if the vote could be stalled until summer, when many assumed tensions would explode into violence, opponents could sink the bill.[18]

———

ROBERT KENNEDY RESUMED AN ACTIVE schedule of speaking and travel during the spring months of 1964. While he remained closely involved in strategizing on the civil rights bill, his attention turned to the challenges and opportunities ahead. His speeches reveal an evolving understanding of the racial crisis gripping the country, with a strong focus on the interrelated issues of poverty and criminal justice. Young people continued to be central to his interest—from those who bore the toll of segregation and discrimination to college students, who were among the society's most privileged. He sought to raise their awareness of social ills and injustices and prod them to act. In an address in Toronto in April, Kennedy observed that young people in many parts of the world were in "a revolution against the status quo," turning their anger "on the systems which have allowed poverty, illiteracy and oppression to flourish." "Our future," he advised, "is tied up with what they think." He spoke similarly about the "revolution going on in the United States" to an audience at the University of Chicago, saying he sensed there was an opening at this moment in history, a time of genuine concern about social justice. Time, he said, is an "irreplaceable commodity."[19]

On April 16, Kennedy participated in a panel discussion in Washington entitled "After the Civil Rights Bill, What?" He addressed the misinformation being spread through ads and other media channels and clarified what the bill contained—and what it did not. The "mere passage of legislation," he explained, will not make racial difficulties disappear: "We are going to have to pay for what has gone on in the past." For Kennedy, one of the most important reasons to pass the bill was to "reestablish confidence that the Negro people and the white people can work together to solve our problems." Failure would confirm a growing feeling among African Americans, particularly young people, "that there is no future in this system." Legislation and federal action were essential but not enough. There must be "action by newspapers, local citizens, local political leaders," possibly starting with schools. "We can talk about it, we can make all the patriotic speeches we want to, but all these speeches are made by white people." It was time to act.[20]

———

ROBERT KENNEDY WAS A BIG supporter of Lyndon Johnson's ambitious antipoverty program, introduced to Congress in March as the Economic Opportunity Act. Johnson's legislative package built on the initiatives of the Kennedy administration but bore LBJ's own stamp. Johnson's understanding of poverty reflected his experiences growing up in Texas in the 1920s, his work for Roosevelt's New Deal in the 1930s during the depths of the Depression, and his brilliant political instincts. While the Johnson administration's antipoverty drive would incorporate the community action initiatives developed by Robert Kennedy and his team at the Justice Department, Johnson himself had little exposure to urban poverty and only a limited understanding of this particular challenge.[21]

In the early 1960s, a period of prosperity and abundance for many, an estimated 25 percent of Americans lived in poverty. Millions were unemployed or stuck in low-wage jobs, with minimal access to health care, stable housing, food, and education. Robert Kennedy's team of "guerillas," led by David Hackett and Richard Boone, shifted from a narrow focus on juvenile delinquency to more ambitious plans to tackle the problems of poor communities in general. This concept had tremendous appeal to Walter Heller, chair of the Council of Economic Advisers, whose interagency task force had been working on a series of proposals for President Kennedy. One member of Heller's task force, William Capron, recalled how Hackett and Boone spoke about the "tremendous energy and potential" of communities that "looked from the outside like they were desolate, dead and disorganized. With a little federal seed money there was a possibility for local groups to really come together and do something to help themselves." The key was to give them a sense of agency and ownership. "The fact is," Capron explained, if "people thought they were going to have some control over what happened to them . . . a lot could happen." A series of pilot projects were carefully tailored to the needs, culture and desires of each community: "there was tremendous variety . . . from one part of the country to another, from ghettos to smaller cities."[22]

"Community action," the term given to the program developed by RFK's group, was the centerpiece of the proposals Heller had presented to President Kennedy in a meeting two days before his assassination. JFK had given Heller the go-ahead, told him to devote additional staff and resources to the effort, and instructed him to make the poverty program a priority for the coming year. Heller met with Johnson the day after Kennedy's assassination and briefed him on the preliminary plans. Johnson did not hesitate. "That's my kind of program," he declared. "I'll find the money one way or another." He instructed Heller to speed up the planning.[23]

By famously declaring "an unconditional War on Poverty" in his first State of the Union address in January 1964, Lyndon Johnson branded the centerpiece of his domestic program. The Economic Opportunity Act of 1964 was a bold and eclectic package of programs that yoked together programs developed by Bobby Kennedy's team at the Justice Department with an array of training, educational, and social programs developed by the Johnson administration. VISTA (Volunteers in Service to America), which recruited volunteer antipoverty workers, and Head Start, for preschool children, bore the stamp of David Hackett and Richard Boone. Johnson and his advisors created programs for adult education, job training for unemployed fathers, job training for youth (Job Corps), aid to migrant workers and dependent children, and more. A new agency, the Office of Economic Opportunity, was set up to oversee the War on Poverty, headed by Sargent Shriver. The one component that was missing, from Robert Kennedy's perspective, was the direct creation of jobs for the poor. Johnson dismissed Walter Heller's proposal for a jobs program as too costly.[24]

Community action remained a cornerstone of the early War on Poverty. The legislation (thanks largely to Richard Boone) mandated the "maximum feasible participation of the residents of the areas and groups served by the programs"—mainly to ensure African Americans would not be excluded. As Johnson saw it, community action meant working through existing government agencies at the local level, in much the same way New Deal programs had worked. This distinction, between locally directed and government-led programs, would turn out to be essential, leading to conflicts that dramatically reduced the ambitiousness of the Community Action Program.[25]

Getting the Economic Opportunity Act through Congress at the same time as the Civil Rights Act was a major political challenge, one that commanded all of Lyndon Johnson's legendary skills. On April 8, Robert Kennedy delivered a presentation in support of the legislation. In a three-hour testimony before the House Committee on Education and Labor, he defended the program against its critics, puncturing the myths and misinformation floated by conservative opponents. In response to Republican charges that only Black people would benefit, he countered that of the nation's poor, approximately 20 percent were Black. Representative David Martin, Republican of Nebraska, warned that the program would stifle individual initiative and "ruin the pioneer spirit of many of our people." "Have you ever told a coal miner in West Virginia or Kentucky," Kennedy shot back, "that what he needs is individual initiative to go out and get a job where there isn't any?" He said he personally would favor including a minimum wage for migrant workers but deferred to the secretary of labor "on whether this should be done."[26]

As he championed the new initiatives, Kennedy became more outspoken about the interface between poverty and criminal justice. This had been an important focus of his efforts since 1961, when he'd established the Committee on Poverty and the Administration of Federal Criminal Justice, leading to the introduction of a criminal justice bill the following year. "The fact is," Kennedy said during a television interview in May, "there is no equal justice under law in the United States at this time." When it came to legal representation or access to bail, poor people were not on equal footing, and their rights were routinely compromised. Kennedy took an interest in the highly successful Manhattan bail project, developed by the Vera Institute of Justice, which had shown that people with strong ties to their community who were too poor to afford bail could be released and expected to show up for trial. That spring, the Justice Department and the Vera Institute partnered in sponsoring a national conference on Bail and Criminal Justice, attended by 450 judges, lawyers, prosecutors, and other law enforcement officials, and would go on to cosponsor a series of regional conferences to help state and local courts establish no-bail programs[27]

"I am deeply concerned over whether as professionals dedicated to the rule of law, we are meeting—or even seeing—the challenge which the peculiar character of our urban society is daily making," Kennedy told newly minted graduates of the University of Chicago Law School on May 1. Poverty, he said, is a condition not just of want but also of helplessness—namely, "an inability to assert real rights" with landlords, banks, employers, credit agencies, or the welfare bureaucracy. "The poor man looks on the law as the enemy," he said; it "is always taking something away."[28]

"No single set of experiences brought home" the need for a fresh approach to law enforcement in poor, underserved communities, he recalled, more than "the contacts I have had with juvenile delinquency." He spoke about the issue often, emphasizing that traditional understandings of law enforcement had to be reevaluated, shifting emphasis from the violators to the cause and seeing youth offenses as a symptom of deep social problems. One did not need to be a sociologist or social worker, he told the students at the University of Chicago, to see this connection. One "simply needs to walk the slums of Washington or New York or Chicago or through communities in Appalachia and talk with young people." You could not avoid sensing "the despair, the frustration, the futility and the alienation they feel." Breaking the law becomes a way of life when all conventional routes to success are blocked.[29]

Just two days earlier, Kennedy had returned to West Virginia for the first time since his brother's presidential campaign to look over plans for Action for Appalachian Youth, a multimillion-dollar project designed to train young people for jobs and to clean up poverty-stricken neighborhoods. The poverty and desperation he saw in Appalachia, he said, matched "any ghetto fenced by prejudice." In one community he visited, out of forty families only three fathers worked. Ninety-five percent of the children did not attend school, and the school he visited lacked indoor plumbing and had out-of-date books. The program for Appalachia was funded by a grant from the President's Committee on Juvenile Delinquency and Youth Crime, which RFK had set up in 1961, and would become a part of LBJ's antipoverty program.[30]

On May 7, the *New York Times* announced that the Justice Department had approved funding for a youth program developed by Harlem Youth Opportunities Unlimited, one of the original "pilot projects" of the President's Committee on Juvenile Delinquency and Youth Crime. One hundred and fifty young people had helped research and develop the program, which had multiple prongs focusing on education, recreation, and job training. The community was set to receive $110 million over a three-year period for the program's implementation.[31]

Later that week, Bobby and Ethel Kennedy helicoptered in to Farmville, Virginia, their first trip to Prince Edward County since the free school system had been established. The visit was deeply moving and showed what could be achieved through a dedicated commitment of resources, talent, and organizational effort: 1,574 children had enrolled in the four schools sponsored by the Prince Edward Free School Association. The students' response to the visit was "polite, smiling, and tremendously touching," observed a reporter, including gifts totaling $99.64 in pennies for the John F. Kennedy Library. At the Mary E. Branch School, "seven-year-old Susan Saunders stood as stiff as her starched turquoise dress" as she presented RFK with a bag of 1,800 pennies, tied with a red, white, and blue ribbon. Robert Kennedy spoke briefly at each of the schools, telling the students that President Kennedy had spoken about them frequently and had been deeply concerned about the closing of their schools. RFK was gratified to see the progress the students had made in reading and arithmetic over the past eight months, after having been out of school for four years. When superintendent Neil Sullivan asked the students at Wortham School for a show of hands from those who wanted to attend summer school, nearly all hands went up. That summer, the Supreme Court would rule that the school closings were unconstitutional. The county's public schools would reopen on a nonsegregated basis in September.[32]

Kennedy was "plainly surprised and moved" by the warm reception he received from white citizens in this stronghold of massive resistance. In Farmville, Virginia, as his car drove past Longwood College, a segregated women's school, the car was stopped by "hundreds of beaming, shrieking young women." When he paused in front of the courthouse on Main Street to let a local official out of the car, people clustered in and offered friendly greetings. Kennedy got out and shook hands all around. Later that afternoon, he spoke to students at Hampden-Sydney College, a conservative Pres-

byterian school for men founded in 1775. The assembly clapped loudly to
signal its repudiation of the civil rights bill. "I don't understand your opposition," Kennedy said, and he spoke briefly about his school visit earlier
in the day. He went on to deliver a passionate speech on the urgency of
passing the Civil Rights Act. The students listened and applauded. They were
impressed, noted a reporter, and many said so.[33]

Kennedy delivered half a dozen addresses to students in May and early
June. He believed that young people who had the advantage of a good education had a responsibility to participate in public life, to help meet the needs
and challenges of their society. "I cannot believe that all the sacrifices which
you and your parents and teachers have made so that you could obtain an
education," he had told the graduating class of Manhattan College two years
earlier, "were made solely to give you an economic advantage over less fortunate citizens in the years ahead." Now there was an even greater urgency
to his appeal.[34]

There was never a time in history, he told the graduating class at Marquette University, when "the need for active involvement by young people
has been stronger and the opportunity for them to do things of significance
has been greater." While scientific and technological advances were being
showcased at the World's Fair, people lived in nineteenth-century conditions
in major American cities and in remote, poverty-stricken towns. Labeling a
generation was risky, he said. But he was encouraged by this generation's "un-
usually genuine and intense concern with social justice and intellectual
freedom." His question for the class of 1964 was whether they would continue to act on these concerns. College had expanded their horizons, but it
had also prepared them for "a place in society far removed from these problems." He insisted that sympathetic concern was not enough: "it won't be
enough to lend your talents to your job, to raising a family, to leading a self-
sufficient life." Given their advantages, they must "participate wholeheartedly
in politics, government and community affairs."[35]

Kennedy's addresses gave him a platform to talk about the civil rights
bill, which was much in the news that spring. In one speech marking the
dedication of an interfaith chapel named for John F. Kennedy at the University of West Georgia, RFK segued from a reflection on religious tolerance to a broader discussion keyed to the moment. Those preaching intol-
erance, he noted, do not rely on persuasion to advance their ideas. They
spread false fears, seeking "to escape reality and responsibility by a slogan
or a scapegoat."[36]

A student asked him how the public accommodations section of the civil
rights bill would impact property rights, giving Kennedy a chance to address one of George Wallace's most damaging fabrications. "If it did what

Gov. George Wallace describes, I would be against the bill," he said. But what the section really meant was that "if a place is open to the general public it has to treat all of the public equally." He went on to report that a Black American soldier recently killed in Vietnam had been buried in Arlington National Cemetery. As his widow returned south after the burial, she had difficulty finding a motel or a restaurant where she was welcome. "This is a continuous insult," he said, before concluding that the end of segregation in public accommodations was long overdue. The fact that states like Alabama and Mississippi would never end segregation voluntarily meant "that the Negroes are entitled to have the Federal Government do it." The audience of several hundred white students at the small southern college broke into thunderous applause.[37]

———

AS THE CIVIL RIGHTS ACT confronted its final hurdles in Washington, a bold campaign was underway in Mississippi, where Bob Moses and a battle-weary group of activists had organized a series of mock election campaigns to sustain and broaden Black civic engagement and attempt to break through state repression. Starting in the summer of 1963, COFO, the SNCC-dominated coalition of civil rights groups, brought in college student volunteers from out of state to help set up a parallel gubernatorial campaign to support the candidacy of Aaron Henry and Edwin King on an interracial ticket. More than eighty thousand African Americans throughout Mississippi participated in the "Freedom Vote," as these mock elections were called. The effort gave COFO a statewide reach, in the face of intensifying violence. Moses and his compatriots began planning for a summer project designed to compel national attention and government action. They would bring hundreds of volunteers to Mississippi and would set up Freedom Schools and community centers to help with voter registration. COFO's ultimate goal was to build an alternative statewide party to challenge the all-white Democratic Party of Mississippi at the 1964 Democratic National Convention.[38]

By the early months of 1964, a siege mentality had taken over the state of Mississippi. In February, the White Knights of the Ku Klux Klan, a new group consisting entirely of Mississippians, was formed. Demonstrating exceptional courage, several hundred Black men and women turned out to register to vote in Hattiesburg and Canton during successive Freedom Days in late February and early March. Volunteers from the National Council of Churches came to observe, and media attention followed. Defiant registrars and heavily policed polling stations kept voter registration numbers low. A leading citizen of Canton boasted that there would be no marked increase in Negro participation "until Bobby Kennedy comes down here with some federal marshals."[39]

Still, segregation's stronghold was beginning to crack. In March, the federal court ordered Jackson, Biloxi, and Leake County to submit plans to desegregate their schools by the fall. As the civil rights bill made its way through Congress, Mississippi officials braced themselves for "the coming invasion" of close to one thousand volunteers as part of COFO's Freedom Summer program. That spring, the state legislature and the city of Jackson undertook what Claude Sitton of the *Times* described as "para-military" preparations. The legislature nearly doubled the strength of the state police force and passed laws barring demonstrations outside public buildings, expanding the coverage of statutes against breach of the peace, and mandating hefty fines and prison time for violators. In an escalating reign of terror, Klan activists bombed Black-owned businesses, burned churches, fired into homes, assaulted known civil rights activists and sympathizers, and were suspected in at least six murders, including that of Louis Allen. A witness to the murder of Herbert Lee, Allen was shot outside his home. On April 24, crosses burned in sixty-one locations across the state.[40]

———

THE FILIBUSTER OF THE CIVIL RIGHTS BILL dragged on through April and into May. While southern senators held the line, journalists mapped the conflicting pressures of white backlash and growing Black militancy and warned of a "long hot summer" ahead. Wallace's predictions of dire consequences attracted national attention and helped secure him votes throughout the spring primary season, as he moved from Wisconsin to Indiana and Maryland. Wallace took 29 percent of the vote in Indiana on May 5 and 42 percent of the vote in Maryland two weeks later. The *New York Times* reported that he had introduced a new concept of "winning without winning." Senator Barry Goldwater, a prime contender for the Republican Party nomination, amplified his opposition to the civil rights bill during the primary season, looking to mine southern disaffection and northern white backlash. People "don't want their property rights tampered with," Goldwater insisted, tapping white opposition to housing desegregation, which was not addressed by the bill. Expanding on Wallace's misinformation campaign, Goldwater declared, "I don't want to see a Federal police state."[41]

Religious groups, cultivated early on by President Kennedy, steadily emerged as an important force in mobilizing public pressure in support of the bill. The Senate galleries were filled by young men and women from churches and universities. On April 19, students from seventy-five seminaries

representing Catholic, Jewish, and Protestant denominations orchestrated a
round-the-clock vigil at the Lincoln Memorial. Theological students came
to pray in shifts, pledging to continue the vigil until the bill had passed. The
active presence of clergy in the Capitol gave the debate a moral tone that
placed the anti–civil rights forces somewhat on the defensive. Senator Richard
Russell, leader of the southern bloc, resented this, grumbling that "there has
never been as effective [a] lobby maintained in the city of Washington as
there is today," with so many clergy and "well-meaning people" assembled
in support of the civil rights bill.[42]

Sixty-seven votes—the votes of two-thirds of the Senate—were needed
to break the filibuster. Senate watchers counted sixty votes against the filibuster. The ground finally began to shift in mid-April when Senate Minority
Leader Everett Dirksen offered a series of amendments conceding to the
concerns of northern and midwestern states. Many of these states already
had fair employment and public accommodation laws, with local and state
mechanisms for enforcement, and were resistant to federal oversight in
these areas. McCulloch made a call on Dirksen, informing him that his proposed amendments would have to pass inspection and letting him know
that two were not acceptable. The discussions had begun.

Several sessions followed, culminating with a meeting on May 13, attended
by Robert Kennedy, Senator Hubert Humphrey, Senator Joe Clark of Pennsylvania, White House aide Larry O'Brien, and Majority Secretary Frank
Valeo. The group had met in advance to work out how to accommodate
Dirksen without making substantial changes. They were like a tag team, with
Kennedy "acting as McCulloch's lawyer," as Burke Marshall recalled. The
primary issue boiled down to who would enforce no-discrimination laws
when state laws already existed. The Justice Department agreed that individual employment discrimination claims could be referred to state agencies, but the department would not give up its ability to initiate suits when
a pattern of discrimination existed. Delicate rewording of the bill would
make it possible for Dirksen to persuade senators who were on the fence while
retaining the substance of the original bill. At the end of the daylong session, Dirksen told the press, "We have a good agreement." A grinning Bobby
Kennedy declared, "The bill is perfectly satisfactory to me."[43]

In the end, Dirksen was able to convince just enough Republicans to join
him in supporting the civil rights bill. The final tally in the vote to end the
filibuster was boosted by Lyndon Johnson's personal appeal to Senator
Howard Cannon of Nevada and intense lobbying efforts on the part of the
archbishop of Dubuque, who persuaded Iowa's Republican Senator Jack
Miller to change his vote.

On June 10, seventy-one Senators voted for cloture—four more votes than were needed to end the seventy-five-day filibuster, the longest in Senate history. Nine days later, the Senate voted 73–27 to pass the Civil Rights Act of 1964. Exactly a year had passed since President Kennedy had sent the legislation to Capitol Hill. The amended bill went back to the House for approval. McCulloch and Cellar succeeded in streamlining the process, blocking Howard Smith from stalling the bill in the House Rules Committee. At the start of July, the Civil Rights Act would be sent to the White House for Lyndon Johnson's signature.[44]

———

ROBERT KENNEDY WROTE TO PRESIDENT Johnson on May 21, noting "at least forty instances of Klan type police brutality" in Mississippi and warning, "I have no doubt that this will increase." Kennedy's power to respond had been dramatically curtailed after the death of his brother. For one thing, RFK no longer had any authority over the FBI. After November 22, 1963, J. Edgar Hoover ignored him and reported directly to Lyndon Johnson, a relationship that suited Johnson. The president shared Hoover's intense dislike of Robert Kennedy. As one scholar observed, LBJ seemed more concerned about the attorney general as a potential rival than about the activities of the Klan. On June 2, Kennedy sent Burke Marshall to southwest Mississippi, the Klan's stronghold, where he interviewed locals and civil rights veterans to find out what was going on. On his return, Kennedy sent a second memo to Johnson reporting on the close association between the Klan and Mississippi law enforcement agencies, recommending that the FBI consider how best to address this. Aware of Hoover's territorial nature, Kennedy suggested that the president persuade the FBI director to approach the Klan and its subversive activities much as it had the Communist Party—by infiltrating its ranks.[45]

While Johnson and Hoover hesitated, Kennedy dispatched Walter Sheridan, head of the Justice Department's organized crime unit, and his team of nine lawyers to investigate terrorist activity in Mississippi. They were deputized as federal marshals, with the right to carry guns. "The whole idea," Sheridan later recalled, "was just to be a presence there, a federal presence." The Criminal Division lawyers were told to investigate reported acts of terrorism, determine what weapons had been used, ascertain the extent of Klan involvement, and evaluate the Klan's infiltration of local and state law enforcement. When Hoover learned of this effort, he fired off a series of memos reminding Marshall that the FBI was *the* investigative arm of the Justice Department. This perceived affront helped prompt Hoover to ultimately take responsibility for investigating and infiltrating the Klan in Mississippi—but not until after the Freedom Summer campaign experienced its first casualties.[46]

———

ON JUNE 19, the day the Senate voted to pass the civil rights bill, the first group of summer volunteers was completing a week of training at Western College for Women in Oxford, Ohio. It included roughly three hundred college students, mostly white and many from elite institutions such as Harvard, Smith, and Stanford. Seasoned activists prepared the volunteers as best they could, warning them in explicit terms of the dangers that awaited. James Forman was particularly blunt. "I may be killed, and you may be killed," he said. "If you recognize that, the question of whether we're put in jail will become very, very minute." John Doar told the volunteers that there would be no federal police force to protect them. "Guide your conduct accordingly," he advised—a statement that was greeted by boos. "We don't do that," Moses interjected, silencing the group before reminding listeners that "we are all—the whole nation—deeply involved in the crimes of Mississippi."[47]

The next day, Andrew Goodman, a nineteen-year-old white student from Queens College, accompanied COFO workers Mickey Schwerner and James Chaney to Mississippi. Schwerner, twenty-four, was a white New Yorker, and James Chaney, twenty-one, was a Black Mississippian. They were leading a voter registration drive in Neshoba County and had spoken to members of Mount Zion Baptist Church about setting up a Freedom School. On Sunday, June 21, they went to investigate the burning of Mount Zion United Methodist Church outside Philadelphia, Mississippi, which Schwerner and Chaney had visited the previous week. The three young men never returned.[48]

Bob Moses was told of their disappearance while he was addressing the second group of volunteers. "They were dead," he thought; "I knew that in my bones." This shared recognition, he later recalled, "took the project in a different emotional space and level of commitment." It would be six weeks before the young men's bodies were found. Investigations later revealed that they had been stopped by Deputy Sheriff Cecil Price on Sunday on a speeding charge. James Chaney was charged, as the driver, and Schwerner and Goodman were taken to jail "for observation." Price released them later that night, after contacting Edgar Ray Killen, a leader of the White Knights of the Ku Klux Klan. Price stopped the men again outside Philadelphia and waited for Killen and his men to arrive. The White Knights took the young men to a remote area and executed them. Schwerner and Goodman were each shot once. James Chaney was brutally beaten and then shot three times. The bodies were buried in a dam that was under construction.[49]

When Robert Kennedy learned that the men were missing, he ordered a full-scale FBI investigation, instructing Hoover to treat the disappearance a kidnapping. Kennedy's brother Ted had just been seriously injured in a plane crash in Massachusetts. Bobby had been weighing a Senate race in New York. On June 23, he announced that he was removing himself as a potential candidate. His brother's injuries were a contributing factor, but more important, associates said, were the mounting civil rights problems which, it was now clear, would demand RFK's full attention. Kennedy spent most of the day on June 23 focused on the disappearance of the three men. Before the day was over, he had canceled plans to travel to Europe for a trip with Ethel and his three oldest children so he could personally ensure a federal response to the disappearance. He had been scheduled to be in Berlin for the first anniversary of John F. Kennedy's "Ich bin ein Berliner" speech.[50]

The Mississippi case, involving as it did two young white men from middle-class families, was front-page news across the nation. Following a meeting with Kennedy, Marshall, and Nicholas Katzenbach, President Johnson dispatched former CIA director Allen Dulles to Mississippi to confer with state and local leaders about the Klan and the law enforcement situation. Dulles recommended a substantial increase in FBI agents. Hoover established an FBI office in Jackson in July. A new influx of FBI agents would infiltrate the Klan, and, through informants, ultimately discover the bodies. Robert Kennedy learned about the new FBI office in Jackson from the newspapers. When he asked Hoover about the news, the FBI director told him to "direct his inquiries to President Johnson."[51]

Bobby Kennedy was now the primary contact for concerned parents begging the federal government to protect their children. He would tell anyone who listened that the Justice Department could not provide protection for the hundreds of young people working and traveling through Mississippi as part of the Freedom Summer project, but he assured them that the department was exploring every possible way of making its presence felt. Walter Sheridan and his team remained in the state for most of the summer, coordinating closely with John Doar and other Justice Department lawyers, who were in touch with Moses. Roy Wilkins and Myrlie Evers, the widow of Medgar Evers, met with Kennedy at the end of June to talk about Mississippi. When the attorney general emerged from the Justice Department with Mrs. Evers and two of her children, a crowd outside the building erupted into applause.[52]

ON THE EVENING OF JULY 2, as investigators searched for bodies in Mississippi and more than six hundred volunteers joined COFO organizers and Black Mississippians engaged in the Freedom Summer campaign, senators, congressmen, government officials, civil rights leaders, and reporters crowded into the East Room of the White House to witness Lyndon Johnson's historic signing of the Civil Rights Act of 1964. When the president entered the room, Robert Kennedy was the first to rise and lead the applause. Seated behind his desk, Johnson delivered a brief speech on the historic nature of the occasion and the significance of the Civil Rights Act for all Americans. He then grabbed for "the forest of pens" in front of him, "using each to draw a fraction of an inch of his signature" before handing it off to one of the men who had crowded around him. J. Edgar Hoover was quick to secure a pen. At some point, the brothers of UAW president Walter Reuther noticed Kennedy standing at the back of the room. "Surely no one contributed more to the moment than he," Victor Reuther remembered thinking. His brother Roy went over to Bobby, took him by the arm, and brought him over to the desk, telling the president that he knew he had reserved a pen for the attorney general. Johnson grabbed a handful and gave them to Kennedy, instructing him to give one to John Doar and one to Burke Marshall. Johnson's brusque treatment did not go unnoticed. "Our enthusiasm—that of Dr. King and myself—was sort of dampened by the sadness we saw in Bobby's eyes and the coldness with which the President obviously treated him," Walter Fauntroy recalled.[53]

The Civil Rights Act of 1964 was a historic achievement, directly addressing the racial caste system that had structured life in the South since the turn of the century and empowering the federal government to enforce school desegregation orders and eliminate discrimination in employment and other areas of life. However, the limits of legislation in remedying deep racial inequities quickly became evident, along with the potent force of white resentment and resistance to racial change. Northern union leaders and Democratic officials reported that white fears of housing integration and job competition from Black workers were fueling a backlash to civil rights policies.

In mid-July, Arizona Senator Barry Goldwater, a leading opponent of the Civil Rights Act, easily won the Republican party nomination over New York's Nelson Rockefeller and Pennsylvania Governor William Scranton. Goldwater spoke out against "forced" school integration, attacked the intrusive reach of the federal government, and stood on a platform of law and order. The convention, which met from July 13 to 17 in San Francisco, revealed the extent to which more moderate leaders were willing to cultivate white fears as a political strategy. In his address to the convention, former

President Dwight Eisenhower criticized what he described as "the maudlin sympathy for the criminal . . . roaming the streets with a switchblade knife." With the elevation of Goldwater, a major political realignment accelerated, as the Republican Party worked to make inroads among segregationists in the South as well as second and third generation ethnic groups in northern urban areas—traditional bedrocks of the Democratic Party.[54]

As Robert Kennedy entered the next phase of his public life, the fusion of race and politics on a national scale would challenge the opportunities opened by the Civil Rights Movement to face America's racial past and create an inclusive democracy. The struggles of the early 1960s had exposed deep structures of racial inequality and division. Kennedy understood that the difficult and necessary work of racial reckoning was just beginning, in an environment ripe for the politics of white grievance and backlash. His faith in the capacities of democracy and civic activism, forged on the front lines of racial change, would distinguish him as a public figure during one of the country's most tumultuous periods.

CHAPTER TEN

Transitions

|||

ON JULY 16, the day Barry Goldwater delivered his acceptance speech at the Republican National Convention, Thomas Gilligan, an off-duty New York police officer, shot and killed James Powell, a fifteen-year-old African American high school student, in a dispute outside an apartment building on the East Side of Manhattan. Several CORE chapters had planned a rally in Harlem focusing on the three missing civil rights workers in Mississippi; on the night of Powell's funeral, the planned rally was quickly transformed into a protest of police brutality. Judith Howell, a seventeen-year-old high school student "dressed in a button-down shirt, skirt and loafers without socks," called out sarcastically, "We got a civil rights bill . . . [and] we got Barry Goldwater and a dead black boy."

The several hundred who gathered that night marched on the police precinct in Harlem demanding that Gilligan be arrested. A confrontation between protesters and the helmeted and heavily armed police force sparked six nights of street battles, leaving one person dead, more than one hundred injured, and two hundred arrested. Protests also emerged in the Bedford Stuyvesant community in Brooklyn, where rioting and looting lasted three days. In the weeks that followed, racial conflicts erupted in Philadelphia, Rochester, Chicago and Jersey City, capturing headlines as the summer wore on.[1]

"I think the Communists are in charge of it," President Johnson said about the urban uprisings that exploded that summer. His most immediate concern was that the disorder gave Republicans an issue to use against him in the election. Johnson received floods of telegrams from frightened whites. By his account, a typical example was this message: "I am a working girl. . . . I am afraid to leave my house. I fear the Negro revolution will come to Queens." In a telephone conversation on July 21, Robert Kennedy and Johnson spoke frankly about the options facing the president in his campaign against Goldwater. Kennedy told Johnson it would be "a major mistake" to let Goldwater choose the battleground "and have the struggle in this election over the question of civil rights." Johnson agreed, describing the civil rights issue as "something around our neck." But the two men had different views of how Democrats should position themselves in the presidential contest.[2]

Tapes of conversations in the Oval Office reveal that Kennedy suggested a forward-looking approach, urging Johnson to face the challenges in urban areas and frame them in a constructive way—underscoring the critical role the federal government could play by setting up programs that would redress economic insecurities and by addressing the challenges poor and working people confronted. A "good deal of thought has to go into . . . these northern communities and these industrial areas," Kennedy said. He thought Johnson should speak about what he would do and what it would mean for struggling families when people got sick or could not make the rent—"basic lunch pail issues." "The best minds we have in this field should now be working on what's going on," Bobby said. He encouraged Johnson to focus on Chicago, Philadelphia, New York, Buffalo, and Los Angeles and to begin planning television spots around these issues.[3]

Johnson listened but wasn't convinced. "What we need to get on is his impetuousness and his impulsiveness," he offered, wanting to focus on Goldwater's personal weaknesses and his openness to the use of nuclear weapons. Kennedy acknowledged that this approach might scare people and could be helpful, but he brought the conversation back to what he thought would be the most effective and constructive approach—a positive emphasis on what Johnson's programs would do for people and how his policies would impact urban industrial areas.[4]

Johnson would make Goldwater's extremism and his willingness to embark on a path to nuclear war a major focus of the campaign, pursuing what he described as a "frontlash" strategy. This approach was designed in part to appeal to moderate white suburban Republicans, who were concerned about Goldwater's stand on nuclear war and uncomfortable with his views on civil rights. In the end, it would prove to be a winning strategy.

On August 6, Kennedy sent Johnson a memo, following up on a conversation two weeks earlier, outlining how he might set "into motion steps within various communities to cut down as much as possible the chances of continued racial violence." Kennedy recognized that the basic problems of providing access to jobs, training, and housing might take more than a generation to resolve but insisted that the success of the delinquency program and his own work in DC had convinced him that "community-based action directed at short-range difficulties existing among young Negroes" could

be helpful while demonstrating that "their government cares about their problems." Such immediate, specific action could be taken in cities across the
country if city leaders recognized the need and understood that something
could be done to address it. To this end, Kennedy suggested that Johnson
convene a conference of mayors of cities with populations of two hundred
thousand or more, attaching a list. Kennedy advised that such a conference
would require a good deal of work and would need to be held quickly if it was
to have any effect in quieting down the explosive unrest that summer. Whether
Johnson responded to this memo is not documented. Throughout the summer,
the president's approach to racial violence in urban areas was limited to
sending the FBI in to investigate, hoping to identify subversive influences.[5]

Johnson was focused on winning the presidency in his own right, and he
suspected Robert Kennedy of trying to force his way onto the ticket as vice
president. Kennedy was open about his desire to serve as vice president,
telling Ben Bradlee of *Newsweek* in an interview late in June that he saw
himself harnessing "all the energy and effort and incentive and imagination
that was attracted to government by President Kennedy"—hardly what
Johnson wanted to hear. There was considerable support for Kennedy within
the party, but Johnson was reluctant to tether himself to a man he could
not control and personally despised. "The President oughtn't to be required
to get in bed and sleep with a woman he doesn't like," he complained in an
unguarded moment. Seeking a more acceptable rationale for eliminating
Kennedy from consideration, he consulted with Chicago's Mayor Richard
Daley and Democratic Party "wise man" Clark Clifford. Both agreed that
Goldwater was likely to pluck off voters from the South and border states
and said that RFK would not help the ticket. When the president met with
Kennedy on July 29, Johnson explained that he needed a running mate who
could neutralize Goldwater's strength in key areas of the country. Kennedy
did not dispute this explanation, and Johnson was pleased by the even tone
of the meeting. But Kennedy would not agree to withdraw from consideration. Determined to make a public statement, yet not wanting to single out
Kennedy, Johnson decided to publicly rule out all members of the cabinet
from consideration—a broad brush that included several others who had had
their eye on the vice presidential slot. With that avenue closed, Kennedy reversed his earlier decision and decided to run for the US Senate from New
York. He would declare his candidacy three weeks later.[6]

Beyond the personal insecurities animating Johnson's relationship with
Robert Kennedy, LBJ's administration marked a sharp departure from the
confident, collaborative, and open engagement of his predecessor. This shift
was particularly notable when it came to the civil rights movement and the
racial turmoil increasingly dominating the news. LBJ worried about the po-

litical consequences of escalating racial tensions, as is clear from taped recordings of his conversations that summer. Beyond these calculations, the recordings are notable for what they reveal about his personal views of Martin Luther King Jr. and the president's reaction to the widely publicized Freedom Summer campaign in Mississippi, which would culminate with a challenge to the all-white Mississippi delegation at the Democratic National Convention in August.

Johnson's personal antipathy toward King was significant. He had no problem with J. Edgar Hoover's aggressive campaign to discredit the civil rights leader. Within two days of signing the Civil Rights Act, Johnson chided his press secretary, George Reedy, for saying that "the President has been in *continual* touch with Dr. King." "I haven't been in touch with him at all and don't want to be," Johnson sniped. "You know his record." Reedy responded that he had corrected the transcript to read "from time to time he has seen Martin Luther King." Johnson countered, "Well, *why* do you say that?" Reedy pointed out that reporters had seen the president with King at the signing ceremony of the civil rights bill two days earlier. "I'm sorry he was there," Johnson shot back. "It was very unfortunate he was there. And don't you get hung up on it."[7]

In several conversations over the following weeks, each reference to King was accompanied by charges and insinuations. Johnson told Hubert Humphrey, "the Communists have gotten ahold of him and they're managing and correcting him every day." In another conversation with Humphrey, LBJ said knowingly, "King is completely owned and directed by them." Johnson saw communists everywhere. "Every riot," he told labor leader Walter Reuther, "is led by members of the Communist Party."[8]

Johnson's feelings about King were undoubtedly influenced by the reports he was receiving from the FBI director. Hoover fed LBJ a steady stream of misinformation about King's alleged communist connections, much as he had Robert Kennedy. But unlike the Kennedys, Johnson was inclined to believe the worst. Starting in January 1964, when King was staying at the Willard Hotel in Washington, Hoover's agents began bugging King's hotel rooms; unlike wiretaps, these devices did not require the authorization of the attorney general. The tape recordings of King's extramarital affairs armed the FBI director with material he would use in an effort to destroy the civil rights leader. Hoover gave transcripts to Lyndon Johnson, and the material was leaked to reporters.[9]

In fall 1964, Ben Bradlee told Nicholas Katzenbach that Cartha DeLoach, an assistant director of the FBI, was playing tape recordings of King's sexual activities for the edification of the press. Katzenbach thought this conduct was "awful and dangerous" and, during a meeting with Johnson, told him about it. "He listened," Katzenbach recalled, "asked a few questions, and then moved on to other matters." Afterward, Johnson told his aide Bill Moyers to warn the FBI that Bradlee was unreliable.[10]

As Lyndon Johnson focused on winning the presidency, the planned challenge by the Mississippi Freedom Democratic Party (MFDP) to Mississippi's all-white delegation at the national convention loomed as a personal affront to the president's ambitions. Johnson speculated that Robert Kennedy was behind the effort in a plot to derail his clear shot to victory. In a state long dominated by Democrats committed to white supremacy, the MFDP was in many ways a sign of faith in the national Democratic Party. The prospect of two delegations from Mississippi vying for recognition at the convention confronted the party with a significant political challenge. But it was also, some would argue, an opportunity. Johnson's frantic response sheds some light on the nature of his relationship to the civil rights movement and the challenges it brought to the fore.

Johnson saw only disaster waiting if the MFPD succeeded in challenging the seating of the Mississippi delegates. He was convinced the entire South would go Republican. But if the all-white delegation prevailed following a floor fight, Black voters might not go to the polls in November, possibly costing the president key northern states. Beyond that, he feared that white Americans outside the South would recoil from the specter of a Black-dominated delegation prevailing at the convention. Johnson assured his southern allies that his sympathies were with the "Regulars." "I want to be for them. I want to help them," he told Florida senator George Smathers. "I just don't think [the southern states] can take this Nigra stuff, just keep pouring it in," Johnson confided to Governor John Connally of Texas.[11]

"There's just no justification for messing with the Freedom Democrats in Mississippi," Johnson told Hubert Humphrey, now a strong contender for the vice presidential slot. Johnson described the MFDP as a group of Negroes "that were elected to nothing," daring to ask that we "throw out the governor and the elected officials of the state." Acknowledging Johnson's concerns, Humphrey commented, "We're just not dealing with emotionally stable people on this." In the end, LBJ could not understand what more "they" wanted. "They got their president; they got their vice-president. They got their Congress. . . . They got every damn thing. They got their law and if they would just go and let us get an election . . . then we could have some good programs." Johnson looked for conspiracies, citing reports that the MFDP leadership was dominated by communists. Until the very end, he could not let go of the suspicion that Robert Kennedy was behind the MFDP challenge. "I rather think this Freedom Party," Johnson told his close aide Walter Jenkins, "was born in the Justice Department."[12]

BOB MOSES AND MARTIN LUTHER KING JR. BOTH APPEALED to Robert Kennedy to support the MFDP challenge. Moses, who had heard rumors that Kennedy wanted to organize against Johnson at the convention, asked Burke Marshall to intercede on behalf of the MFDP. King telegraphed Kennedy that "your experience as Attorney General has made you the man who is most aware of the plight which white and Negro citizens of Mississippi face when they work to establish a truly Democratic process in that closed society." King urged Kennedy to voice his support of the MFDP as the only delegation from Mississippi "which intends to work for all the people of Mississippi and for the candidate's platform and for the national Democratic Party." King concluded by saying that Kennedy's support would "carry great moral and political weight in favor of a just decision."[13]

There is no record of what Kennedy thought about the challenge. Burke Marshall told King that the attorney general "has, as you know, exerted every resource available to him to free the ballot for the Negro citizens of Mississippi, and has great sympathy for the efforts of others working on this most difficult problem." But, Marshall noted, Kennedy was not a delegate to the convention and the Justice Department had no official role.[14]

On August 21, the MFDP delegation arrived in Atlantic City with more than enough support to bring its challenge to the convention floor. Sympathetic delegates from northern states, such as Oregon congresswoman Edith Green, were willing to work toward a mutually satisfactory compromise. Johnson, determined to control the outcome, would have none of it. Thirty FBI agents monitored the MFPD delegation and their supporters at the convention, resorting to surveillance and infiltrating the group. Walter Reuther, an ally of the president, used his power as the employer of Joe Rauh, the MFDP's lawyer, to persuade him to side with the administration's plan. Meanwhile, Johnson saw to it that sympathetic members of the credentials committee were threatened with political reprisals, which succeeded in bringing the requisite number in line.

In the end, the credentials committee voted to accept the party leadership's offer to seat Aaron Henry and Ed King, two members of the MFDP, as "at large" delegates—not even representatives of Mississippi. The fact that the delegation was not invited to select the two token delegates was revealing. Johnson wanted to ensure that Fannie Lou Hamer, who had captured national attention with her powerful televised testimony before the credentials committee, would not be one of them. Humphrey, who oversaw the negotiations, insisted, "the President will not allow that illiterate woman to speak from the floor of the convention." As it turned out, all but four members of

Mississippi's regular delegation walked out, refusing to sign a pledge to remain loyal to the Democratic Party.[15]

Most MFDP delegates rejected the offer. Hamer expressed the view of many when she declared, "We didn't come all this way for no two seats." The regular Mississippi delegation ended up endorsing Barry Goldwater, and the MFDP supported the Democratic Party ticket in the fall election. As a result of the challenge, the national Democratic Party passed a resolution barring discrimination in future delegations—a significant rule change that would alter the face of the national convention in 1968. But that was four long years away. The cynical and high-handed way in which the MFDP challenge had been dismissed was a harsh lesson for those who had risked violence, economic reprisals, and even death simply for the right to participate in the electoral process. The impact of the experience on activists like Bob Moses, Stokely Carmichael, James Forman, and others is difficult to fully measure. Moses described the convention as "a watershed in the movement." Until then, "the idea had been that you were working more or less within the Democratic Party," he said. "We were working with them on voting, things like that. With Atlantic City a lot of movement people became disillusioned." Cleveland Sellers reflected, "afterwards, things could never be the same."[16]

Robert Kennedy arrived at the convention hall on the last day of the proceedings. R. W. "Johnny" Apple of the *New York Times* commented that when Robert Kennedy introduced the memorial film on his brother that evening, Bobby stood before a convention that was "almost completely dominated by Lyndon Johnson." Nevertheless, Johnson remained in "mortal fear" that somehow Kennedy, who had already declared his candidacy for the Senate, would disrupt the proceedings. Johnson arranged for FBI agents posing as NBC reporters to track Kennedy's activities. On Johnson's orders, the screening of the memorial film was moved to the last night of the convention and tied to remembrances of other prominent Democrats who had died since the 1960 convention, including Eleanor Roosevelt and Sam Rayburn, former speaker of the House of Representatives.[17]

John Seigenthaler, who accompanied Kennedy that day, thought he should seize the moment. RFK outpolled all other contenders for the vice presidency, and Seigenthaler had a feeling "he could make a real run." But Kennedy said no. "He knew Lyndon did not want him and could club it down and would." He wanted to use his time at the convention "to say thanks to a hell of a lot of people" who had helped his brother win the nomination in 1960. They visited several state delegations, including Wisconsin and West Virginia, that had set JFK on course for the nomination. Seigenthaler recalled that when they walked into the West Virginia suite, the applause was like thunder. When he visited the New York suite, Kennedy joked that his brief speech was the first of his senatorial campaign. That afternoon, before the screening of the film, Jacqueline Kennedy had hosted a reception for delegates at the Deauville Hotel.[18]

When Bobby Kennedy entered the hall later that evening, the sixty-odd party functionaries on the platform ignored him. He was, Seigenthaler recalled, treated like "the bastard at a family reunion." Dressed in a black suit and the black tie he had worn since his brother's assassination, he sat on the steps and read over his speech, penciling in edits. Shortly before 9 p.m., Senator Henry "Scoop" Jackson introduced Kennedy to a packed audience in the cavernous Boardwalk Hall in Atlantic City. As he stood up and walked slowly toward the podium, Seigenthaler recalled, "it hit . . . I mean it really hit." The estimated twenty thousand delegates and guests were on their feet, applauding. There was no shouting, no music, no parading. Just thunderous applause, which went on and on. When there was a slight lull, Kennedy would raise his hand and attempt to speak, but then the applause would grow loud again. "Why don't you just let them do it, Bob," Jackson told him— "let them get it out of their system." Kennedy watched impassively, his face bearing "only the slightest suggestion of a smile." The ovation went on for sixteen minutes—as spontaneous a demonstration as there ever was at a convention, according to Johnny Apple.[19]

Kennedy expressed his appreciation to all who had supported his brother four years earlier and thanked them for the encouragement and strength they had given JFK as president. Bobby spoke about how his brother had built on the best traditions of the Democratic Party and urged all to devote the same efforts and energy to President Johnson and Hubert Humphrey, for the benefit not just of the party but of the country. Kennedy closed by saying that Mrs. John F. Kennedy had asked that the film be dedicated to them and all those throughout the country who had helped make her husband president.[20]

Mary McGrory, whose columns for the *Washington Star* were a must-read in political circles, described Kennedy's appearance as "the most intense emotional communication in four days of heavy-handed rhetorical proceedings." As Kennedy left the platform, the "phonies" who had ignored him "were literally all over him," Seigenthaler reported. Johnson invited Bobby and Ethel to join him and Lady Bird in the presidential booth for the viewing of the film. Kennedy left right afterward and flew back to Washington that night. He asked Seigenthaler, who had been planning to return to Tennessee, to fly with him. David Hackett and a few other close friends accompanied Bobby and Ethel. Seigenthaler recalled "the veil coming down over his eyes," as it would occasionally in the months following JFK's death. "It was important to be there," Seigenthaler said, "for no other reason except that we wanted to be and he wanted us to be."[21]

———

ON THE EVENING OF SEPTEMBER 1, Robert Kennedy stood in front of the delegates to the state Democratic convention, sweltering in New York City's 71st Regiment Amory, and accepted the Senate nomination. When he publicly declared his candidacy five days earlier, Kennedy said that New York had a special role to play as "the supreme testing ground for the most acute national problems of our time—the problems of racial harmony, of employment, of youth, of education and of the quality of urban and sub-urban life." He based his candidacy "on the conviction that my experience equips me to understand New York's problems and do something about them." Many resented his "invasion" of the state but, as the *New York Times* quipped, "the barrenness of alternative talent in New York's Democratic Party created an opportunity that he had every right to avail himself of." No Democrat had been elected US senator from New York in fourteen years, and Kennedy had a chance to deliver a rare victory to the fractured party. Few underestimated the tough race ahead. He was up against a popular, moderate Republican incumbent, Kenneth Keating.[22]

The next morning, Kennedy rose at 5:15 a.m. and opened his campaign at dawn at the Fulton Fish Market. "Hundreds of fishmongers turned from their boxes of cod and mackerel to call out to him, shake his hand, and wish him well," Johnny Apple reported in the *Times*. He greeted them as "my fellow fishermen and New Yorkers," and spent forty minutes in "his immac-ulate gray suit and black tie," shaking hands with the hip-booted fish han-dlers. Kennedy remarked that he and Ethel had eight children, they all ate fish on Friday, and "from now on, we'll eat it twice a week." From there he went to the Manhattan terminal of the Staten Island Ferry, where he received an "uproarious reception." He stood atop a car to greet people as they poured off the boats. In a series of short speeches, he said, again and again, "I think what we started three and a half years ago can be continued. . . . I want to have a role in that. I want to be a good Senator for all New Yorkers." After each speech, he climbed down from the car and shook as many hands as he could. A reporter covering him that day observed that he did not need to approach perspective voters and ask for their vote. "As soon as he appeared, he was engulfed by excited people." He went on to a conference of the state AFL-CIO and then four more campaign stops after that. That night he and Ethel flew back to Washington, where he would spend his final day as at-torney general.[23]

At 10:30 the next morning, Bobby began "his big kind day," as Phil Casey of the *Washington Post* called it, at the stadium behind Cardozo High School. An audience of 3,500 high school students from throughout the city greeted the attorney general with a five-minute standing ovation. He walked the stadium track, waving to the cheering children before taking his chair on the platform. A parade of students took turns addressing him, blessing him "over and over." They thanked him for his efforts to reopen the Dunbar High School pool; for the playground that he had created, transforming an automobile junkyard; for the Summer Jobs Program; for the Stay in School fund; for the Christmas party the previous December—and "for giving them hope." Fourteen-year-old Ernest Smith thanked him for helping the Junior Stonewalls, an athletic club. Several of the children wept. They presented Ethel with a bouquet and gave Bobby a "magnificently wrapped" box of cookies for his children. Then they serenaded him. Six girls sang, "I Could Be Happy with You." The Ambassadors, a high school band, played "great tunes," including "Walk on the Wild Side," and "That's How Much I Love You Baby," inserting "Bobby" for "Baby." The stadium was full of brightly colored signs—"Bobby, Bobby, He's Our Man. If He Can't Do It No One Can," "We Shall Miss You Bobby," "God Bless You Bobby." Pointing to a sign reading "Hurry Back Bobby," he said, "I like that one." In his comments, he urged the students to stay in school and build a better life for themselves and others. He told the crowd, which included school and local officials, that Washington's children needed the help of older people and government officials to sustain their hope, adding, "if I and my brother had a role in that, that's our reward."[24]

Bobby went over the scheduled time and ran late for the rest of the day. From the high school stadium, he and Ethel went to the White House for a meeting with President Johnson. The three met for nearly an hour. After speaking in the Oval Office, they posed for photographs and chatted. Then Bobby walked to the high glass door that looked out from the president's office onto the south lawn of the White House.[25]

Watching Kennedy leave the White House, Edward Folliard of the *Washington Post* observed, "made some onlookers feel a little sad." Kennedy stopped to talk with reporters and said he had come to say good-bye to the president and to them. "The President was very kind to President Kennedy and to all of us," Bobby told the reporters. When asked whether Johnson had offered to help him in New York, he said, "Yes, he did." One reporter noted that critics said he wanted to use New York as a springboard to the White House. He laughed and said, "Somebody is already there, and I don't see any sign of him moving out." Asked about his tenure as attorney general, he said his greatest satisfaction in three and a half years was in the field of civil rights. He predicted that the biggest challenge going forward would be to improve relations between Blacks and whites. After the White House, he and Ethel attended a luncheon with fellow cabinet members before making his final visit as attorney general to the Department of Justice.[26]

The marine band struck up "When Irish Eyes Are Smiling" as Kennedy entered the courtyard, and the crowd of some two thousand cheered. Kennedy reminisced a bit and quoted a passage that had provided solace in the wake of his brother's assassination. "When I think of all the things that have happened since that snowy inauguration day in January, I like to think our role has been one that is suggested in an old Greek saying, 'To tame the savageness of man, make gentle the life of the world.'" He thanked those assembled for their loyalty and devotion to the work. "In the time of greatest need," he said, "you participated in a department that was the most important force for the domestic tranquility of the country." Phil Casey, who covered Kennedy's movements that day for the *Washington Post,* observed, "the affection and respect his associates and employees feel for him was so obvious, so pervasive, that it almost seemed tangible." Kennedy concluded his comments a few minutes before 5 p.m., the official end of the workday. Looking out over the crowd, he joked, "My wife tells me I should tell you that you can have the rest of the day off."[27]

Kennedy told reporters that he was leaving the administration "with some regret—perhaps more regret than the enthusiasm when I took over." For three and a half years, he had been at the center of one of the most remarkable transformations of a government agency since the New Deal. Historical circumstances and his close relationship to the president had offered him opportunities at this pivotal moment. But his evolving understanding of the nation's racial past and its consequences, his quality of mind and temperament, his ability to inspire others, and his dedication to teamwork were key factors contributing to what many agreed was a pathbreaking stewardship of the Department of Justice. In a profile marking this transitional moment, the *New York Times* observed that "his mind, cool, analytical, detached, weighed problems of power and pressure and seldom confused hopes with reality." This quality, combined with a capacity for empathy and compassion, and informed by a direct exposure to the lives of the poor and a commitment to "equal justice under law," shaped Kennedy's public life.[28]

Most assessments of Robert Kennedy's tenure as attorney general have identified civil rights and criminal justice reform as the major accomplishments of his tenure, placing him in a different category from his predecessors. He also chose brilliant lawyers to staff the department's top posts. "He has gotten from his top aides work of such excellence as has seldom been approached in the Justice Department," James Clayton wrote in the *Washington Post*. The loyalty and dedication of the people he hired was evidenced by the almost complete absence of turnover in the department for forty-three months. Two notable exceptions were Byron White, who was appointed to the Supreme Court, and Lee Loevinger, whom President Kennedy poached for the Federal Communications Commission. "His years as Attorney General did not fit the political stereotype of Robert Kennedy," Anthony Lewis mused late in life, "At least that is the judgment of many who are able to make a detached, professional appraisal of him as Attorney General."[29]

Civil rights, Lewis observed, "engaged Mr. Kennedy as no other problem." His actions won him many admirers—and many enemies. White southerners complained that the federal government was going too far, and civil rights leaders often criticized the Justice Department for moving too slowly or not doing enough. Lewis believed that Bobby himself would have conceded that the appointment to the federal judiciary of three southerners who turned out to be unbending segregationists was a stain on Kennedy's record. Kennedy's defining if underappreciated achievement was the leadership he provided to the administration's effort to put the forces of the federal government "on the side of the Negro's quest for equal rights." On school integration, the Justice Department, which had no power to initiate suits until 1964, sped up the process through pressure and persuasion. Kennedy's civil rights chief, Burke Marshall, filed twenty-four suits for voting violations in Mississippi alone, one in the home county of Senator James Eastland, who chaired the Senate Judiciary Committee. While Mississippi remained a bulwark of opposition, African Americans "were registering . . . without publicity" in a string of counties across the South. Kennedy also deserved a great deal of credit for the 1964 Civil Rights Act, which the *Washington Post* described as "the most important Civil Rights Act since Reconstruction."[30]

The *Post* described Kennedy as the first attorney general to have success "in harnessing the FBI," a plaudit that surely rankled J. Edgar Hoover. Both Anthony Lewis and James Clayton ranked this success as a defining achievement. While the FBI was part of the Justice Department, J. Edgar Hoover had built up such a powerful position that no other attorney general had attempted to exercise control over him. For years, the FBI had devoted its resources to hunting down communists, denying that organized crime existed, and neglecting to investigate civil rights abuses and violations. As a result of pressure from Kennedy, the FBI set up an antiracketeering division and worked with other agencies to initiate a major effort against organized crime. In the area of civil rights, Kennedy had uneven but notable success in compelling Hoover to ensure that his agents cooperate with lawyers in the field on investigations of voting rights violations and bombings. By the end of his tenure, Kennedy had succeeded in getting the FBI to infiltrate the Ku Klux Klan. He did yield to pressure by Hoover to allow a wiretap of Martin Luther King, which remained secret until the story was leaked during Kennedy's 1968 presidential run. But he did not believe King was a communist and said so in writing to US senators who raised queries. Whatever authority Kennedy had over the FBI ended on November 22, 1963. From then on, Hoover reported directly to President Johnson.[31]

During the final weeks of his tenure, Kennedy reflected that one of his main concerns had been the way poor defendants were treated in court. Other attorney generals had advocated for funds to support the legal defense of the poor but had failed to secure it. Kennedy had commissioned a report in 1961 by Francis Allen, chairman of the Attorney General's Committee on Poverty and the Administration of Federal Criminal Justice, and created legislation based on its recommendations. The Criminal Justice Act authorized the use of federal funds for poor people to pay for legal representation in federal cases and set aside funds for investigators and other services. Based on the Allen Report's findings on how the bail system penalized the poor, Kennedy directed federal prosecutors to arrange for the release of defendants before trial without bail whenever possible, and he worked with the Vera Institute of Justice to extend bail reform to local and state jurisdictions. With his attention increasingly focused on "the application of criminal law in an increasingly concentrated and complicated urban society," as one of his last official acts as attorney general he established the Office of Criminal Justice to oversee prosecutorial practices. He wanted to help ensure, he said, that "criminal law means criminal justice."[32]

———

THE DAY AFTER HIS FAREWELL VISIT to the Justice Department, Kennedy resumed his campaign. For the next two months, he would be on the stump. Ethel, now thirty-seven and pregnant with their ninth child, would often be by his side. "Ebullient, full of laughter, a dancer of the twist," the press portrayed her as a complement to her husband, who often appeared withdrawn in public. As a political operative, Kennedy was considered to be experienced beyond his years. "The 38-year-old attorney general has crammed into the dozen years since his graduation from law school political experience that many party leaders have taken a lifetime to accumulate," observed the *New York Times*." But could "this wide experience be converted into electoral appeal?"[33]

Kennedy returned to the campaign trail over Labor Day weekend. The frenzied receptions initially challenged his ability to break through as a serious contender. When he entered Grand Central station, "women screamed and girls squealed" at the sight of him, and "men and boys shoved as they tried to shake his hand." One girl shouted, "this is worse than the Beatles!" As the crowd pressed in and carried him toward the escalator, a woman fell and was almost trampled. Bobby leaped onto the banister between the escalators and shouted "Get back! Get back!" The woman was not injured. A group of policemen locked arms around him and helped him make his way to a stairway, where he briefly addressed the crowd. "If I am elected to the United States Senate, I hope you will all come to visit me in Washington," he said, "but I hope you don't all come at once." His planned one-hour visit was cut to twenty minutes because of the bedlam it created.[34]

On Sunday, Kennedy visited Long Island, where beachgoers were "almost hysterical in their enthusiasm." At Jones Beach, a crowd of ten thousand surrounded the candidate outside the West End bathhouse, all "wanting to shake his hand at once." As Kennedy was unable to move an inch, two aides hoisted him onto their shoulders and park police moved in to protect him. With his jacket off and shirt sleeves rolled up, Kennedy raised his hands and tried to quiet the shouts and cheers. "There are some little children here," he said, perspiration pouring from his face. "They are going to get crushed. Won't you please push back—please." The appeal only brought renewed cheers. With the help of the park police, he slipped back into the bathhouse and out a back door to a waiting car. Based on random interviews with those who came to see him that day, Johnny Apple found that many planned to vote for his opponent, Kenneth Keating. When asked why she came, one woman said, "Everyone wants to see someone famous. Everyone wants to see a Kennedy."[35]

The celebrity factor cut both ways, but there were more fundamental challenges. Kennedy's abrupt decision to run left little time to build a campaign organization or allow his staff time to familiarize themselves with the varied concerns of New Yorkers beyond the city. Kennedy's initial approach was to run on the record of an administration he had done so much to shape, a strategy that came across to some as running on his brother's coattails. From the start, Bobby pursued an exhausting schedule, determined to visit as many parts of the state as possible. Direct engagement with local communities helped him hone his message. Historian Richard Wade, who directed the campaign in the Buffalo-Rochester area, reflected on RFK's quick maturation, based on three visits to the region: "From the time he started as a candidate in '64 to the time he finished he went from a very ordinary campaigner to a very skilled campaigner, and much more clear in what he wanted to say. . . . And he got funny."[36]

Kennedy had a formidable opponent in Senator Kenneth Keating, a popular, sixty-four-year-old Republican from Rochester. Keating had served in Congress since 1946 and had been elected to the Senate in 1958. "A candidate straight from Central Casting," was how one journalist described him. "Standing 5 feet 9 inches with military erectness, he had a striking silver mane, beetling eye-brows, pink cheeks and stemwinder oratorical flourishes." Keating earned praise as a liberal Republican, which was notable at a time when the party had taken a hard right turn. In an editorial endorsing Keating, the *New York Times* pointed to his record of "constructive accomplishment." While allowing that the paper was not in agreement with all of his votes, his overall record distinguished him as an "enlightened, industrious liberal." Having opposed Kennedy's candidacy, the editors of the *Times* described his Senate run as "a relentless quest for greater power."[37]

A prominent group of more than one hundred liberals in New York City organized "Democrats for Keating," led by Gore Vidal and television commentator Lisa Howard, and including Paul Newman, James Baldwin, and Carey McWilliams, the editor of the *Nation*. The sources of liberal hostility and suspicions were undoubtedly varied—Gore Vidal bore a deep personal dislike of Kennedy; James Baldwin may well have still been smarting from their meeting; and many never forgave Kennedy for his association with Joe McCarthy. Part of the problem, David Halberstam suggested, was that liberals hadn't changed much since the "exhilarating days" of Adlai Stevenson's first campaign, while "Robert Kennedy carried his education on in public; his mistakes were a matter of public record; he had been the tough lightening rod of his brother's years." For many liberal intellectuals, Halberstam concluded, "it was almost an ethnic thing. He looked too Irish Catholic."[38]

"I worked tenaciously for [RFK's] campaign as senator," Harry Belafonte recalled. "I found in Bobby Kennedy a man wrestling with profound moral questions and always coming down on the right side of the answer." New York's leading Black newspaper, the *Amsterdam News,* endorsed Kennedy's candidacy in a front-page editorial, concluding, "no Attorney General in the history of America has more aggressively placed the weight of that great office behind the interests of fair play and the welfare of minority groups. He was a great Attorney General and we believe that he will make a great Senator."[39]

Kennedy was reluctant to attack Keating, who was nearly thirty years RFK's senior. Kennedy preferred to focus on the issues—an increase in the minimum wage, a national standard for unemployment insurance, racial equality, race relations, federal support for education, free college tuition for state schools—while directly engaging potential voters across the state. But as Keating continued to hold a lead in the polls, a combination of developments led Kennedy to take the offensive. Peter Edelman, a young attorney who joined the campaign mid-September after working in the Justice Department for a year, researched Keating's record and was surprised with what he found. He was the "devil who had been allowed to parade himself around as a liberal. That's what it all boiled down to for me." Edelman and John Douglas informed RFK in a memo that Keating had "voted against President Kennedy's aid to education bill, against middle income housing programs, cut the heart out of the area redevelopment administration and was a switcher on Medicare." In late September and early October, Keating issued a series of personal attacks that could not go unanswered. The most searing was the charge that Kennedy "had abandoned his post in the Department of Justice with an unfinished task before him" when "the Civil Rights Law requires zealous enforcement." Keating's comments were published in the *New York Times* on October 3. That afternoon, Kennedy would address the annual meeting of the state conference of the NAACP in Buffalo, and he decided to respond directly to the charge.[40]

Kennedy had referenced race relations in several campaign addresses—notably in Rochester, the scene of a major riot two months earlier—but his first major address devoted to civil rights was his speech at the Pilgrim Missionary Baptist Church in downtown Buffalo to a mostly Black audience of five hundred people. His comments conveyed a tone of camaraderie and joint effort. He gave a compelling account of the changes that had been achieved since 1961, followed by a pointed discussion of the challenges that lay ahead. He began by taking stock of how far the country had come over the previous three and a half years. Finally, "the full force of the government was behind equal justice and equal opportunity under law for all of our citizens." He highlighted the specific achievements of his time in government, the pinnacle of which was the Civil Rights Act of 1964, passed with bipartisan support, "an achievement of law beyond compare." But he emphasized that this effort had been carried out in concert with civil rights organizations and institutions that had done essential and foundational work—none more so than the NAACP, "who led the fight for many, many, many decades." The problem of racial injustice and discrimination had by no means disappeared, but he felt all could agree "we have really turned a corner" and shown that "the democratic process works."[41]

Midway through his comments, he segued to address Senator Keating's accusations, reported in that day's *New York Times,* and asked the audience to indulge him for a few minutes. Keating had addressed the group the previous day. In a bait-and-switch tactic, he had attacked Kennedy for running out on the civil rights movement in his prepared remarks but had neglected to make that charge in front of the NAACP. When the press had asked Keating afterward if he stood by his prepared remarks, he had said yes, and they were publicized in the *Times.* Kennedy bristled at the cheap attack that traded on an issue he and his brother had been deeply committed to.

If we did anything in the Department of Justice, he said, "we acted on the problems Negroes face in this country. We did something about them. There wasn't anything I felt stronger about or my brother, President Kennedy, felt stronger about," And then RFK vowed, "I'm going to continue that fight, whether I'm elected to the U.S. Senate or not." As he recited a litany of civil rights crisis that had unfolded over the previous years, highlighting actions taken by the Kennedy administration, he went on to ask, "Where was the Junior Senator from New York?" In an obvious swipe at Keating, Kennedy assured his listeners that if elected, he "would not be content with mere words or press releases or speeches." A voice in the crowd responded, "Tell him like it is, Bobby!" The audience laughed and cheered. In response to another comment from out in the audience, Kennedy exclaimed, "Amen!"[42]

Kennedy tacked back to the focus of his speech—the problems in New York State, particularly its urban areas. "You and I did not labor to destroy segregation of one kind without attacking a more tenacious and difficult discrimination that lies beyond that," he said. He spoke about the vast disadvantages African Americans faced across all areas of life—education, housing, employment, income, and health—and their consequences for children. If one looked at racial discrepancies in employment and income, Blacks in New York City fared more poorly than those in Atlanta. "We saw this summer in more than one place," he noted, how these conditions exploded into rioting, looting, and violence. Barry Goldwater saw these outbreaks as a police matter to be suppressed. Violence could not be condoned, Kennedy noted, but "we must speak out and attack the causes of unrest that lead to violence" and meet them head on. He had seen and felt how these conditions crushed families and robbed children of a future. "I don't think we have to accept this situation in the United States, and if I am elected Senator, I don't intend to accept it."

Education was a top priority. "The Negro in New York will not have equality until his education allows him to share fully in the opportunities of our society," he said. He promised to advocate for "federal participation to the fullest extent needed" to tackle slums, joblessness, youth dropping out of school, and racial discrimination. He advocated "Head Start free school centers for 3 to 5-year-old" children. His experiences with youth in Washington and with various federal programs initiated in communities across the country had shown what might be done—to keep young people in school, link unemployed youth with job opportunities through training programs, create recreational areas, and experiment with different approaches to teaching. Kennedy underscored the urgency of the challenge: "Just as we took action to secure freedom in the South, we must act to stimulate hope in the North. I don't believe there is any more important an issue." He had previewed what would be a primary focus of his activity as a senator.[43]

Kennedy's relationship with African American communities was demonstrated during a campaign appearance in Brooklyn's Bedford-Stuyvesant neighborhood. Thomas Jones, a New York assemblyman from the district and candidate for civil court, accompanied RFK. A crowd of people had gathered to greet them. Kennedy, Jones recalled, arrived in an automobile and "proceeded to climb through the crowd to the top of a limousine, which didn't have any kind of handholds at all." Jones and several other candidates followed along onto what was "a very slippery perch." The limo drove slowly to the corner of Nostrand Avenue and Fulton Street through "a sea of people, all of whom were highly excited and charged with enthusiasm." When they reached the intersection, the crush of people began to shake the car. The limousine "swayed like a rocking boat in a heavy storm." At one point, Jones turned to Kennedy and said, "It won't be very long before we'll all go down off the top of this car. He looked at me without a smile," Jones recalled, "and said, 'How far can you fall? The people will catch you.'" Several minutes later, Kennedy leaned over and was caught by the crowd. He looked back at Jones as if to make the point, "What are you afraid of?"[44]

The Senate race tightened up during the final weeks of October and finally tipped in Kennedy's favor. His campaign steadily gained traction, and television ads began running that featured him speaking frankly to the issues. Or, as he himself put it, "the TV spots showed that I was something more than a Beatle." While Keating had refused to endorse Goldwater, the headwinds from the presidential contest were surely a factor. In line with LBJ's historic landslide, the Democratic Party swept every county in New York state. Kennedy even beat Keating in his home county—where the Democratic Party apparatus had declined to put up a fight.

On November 3, Robert Kennedy won the race by 719,693 votes, the greatest victory for a statewide Democratic candidate since Herbert Lehman's 818,000-vote margin in 1938. At midnight, Kennedy thanked his supporters, crowded in the ballroom of the Statler Hilton Hotel. He called the victory "an overwhelming mandate to continue the policies" of John F. Kennedy. "This is what I dedicate myself to in the next six years for the State of New York." Barely a year after his brother's assassination, Bobby had set his life on a new course. He ended his comments that evening with a line from Alfred, Lord Tennyson's *Ulysses*:

Come my friends,
'Tis not too late to seek a newer world.[45]

Early the next morning, the senator-elect made a sentimental journey to the Fulton Fish Market in lower Manhattan to thank the fishmongers who had cheered him as he launched his campaign. "It smells better here than it did two months ago," he said to glad cries, as they awarded him with a halibut. Later that afternoon he flew to Glens Falls, a small town in upstate New York he had visited early in his campaign. It had been a memorable visit. He was running four hours late, but a crowd of four thousand had waited, many in pajamas, until 1 a.m. to welcome him. Surprised and grateful, Kennedy had promised to return to Glens Falls if he won. A crowd nearly as large waited for him on November 4. "I want to tell you how touched I am, again. You befriended me," he said, setting off a round of screams and cheers.[46]

CHAPTER ELEVEN

Beyond Civil Rights

║║

ROBERT KENNEDY WAS SWORN IN as the junior senator from New York on January 5, 1965. Standing at his side was his younger brother, Edward Kennedy of Massachusetts, who had joined the Senate in 1962. Bobby was thirty-nine years old. He had spent his entire professional life in government, and for nearly three years he had been one of the most powerful men in the country. Now he would assume a very different role. Concerns among close associates about his transition quickly vanished. He immersed himself in the problems, interests, and needs of New Yorkers and found a new platform through which to engage the issues that he cared about—education, poverty, youth, and criminal justice.[1]

Although he was a freshman senator, Kennedy was a national figure, and he began the next chapter of his public life on the threshold of one America's most challenging periods. In 1965, as Lyndon Johnson began to expand America's military presence in Vietnam, the long struggle for racial justice entered a critical phase. While new laws were dismantling the legally mandated separation of the races in the South, unrest in cities in the North and West exposed a systemic racism in American life and revealed its corrosive effects—in segregated and impoverished communities, in a discriminatory and often violent criminal justice system, and in the attitudes and practices of many white Americans.

Bobby and Ethel's ninth child, Maxwell, was born on January 11, 1965. Kathleen, their oldest, was fourteen. The Kennedys rented a large home in Glen Cove, on the north shore of Long Island, but the family stayed mostly at Hickory Hill, in Virginia. Bobby's weekends were reserved as much as possible for his family. A telephone call to him at Hickory Hill on a weekend would often bring the reply, "He is out playing with the children." Holidays were taken up with family outdoor adventures—skiing trips, white water rafting, or kayaking. It had been barely fourteen months since his brother's death, and grief still shadowed Bobby. Jackie and her children had moved to New York City, but Bobby and Ethel saw them often, and Bobby was a sort of surrogate father to Caroline and John. He found solace in reading the ancient Greeks, William Shakespeare, Albert Camus, and Ralph Waldo Emerson.

Physical challenges and strenuous activity had always been central to Bobby's well-being. Few of his friends were surprised when, having never climbed a mountain before, he joined an expedition in March to scale Mount Kennedy, a 13,900-foot peak in Yukon, British Columbia, renamed by the Canadian government after JFK's assassination. Mount Kennedy was "the highest unclimbed mountain in North America," according to *National Geographic*. Bobby was in one of two three-man rope teams. Jim Whittaker, the first American to climb Mount Everest, led Bobby's team. Whittaker met Kennedy for the first time at the Seattle-Tacoma International Airport at the start of the journey. The two exchanged greetings, and Whittaker asked, "What have you done to get into condition?" Kennedy said, "I've run up and down the stairs at home and practiced hollering 'help!'" Whittaker liked that answer.[2]

The climb took two days. As they approached the top of the mountain, Bobby went ahead, alone, for the last sixty feet. "He knelt down on the summit and crossed himself," Whittaker recalled. "It was a very emotional experience for all of us. I went up to him and put my arm around him and crossed myself and said a prayer." Bobby had brought with him a copy of JFK's inaugural address, three *PT-109* pins, and a Kennedy half-dollar. He carved a hole in the ice with his axe and put the tokens inside. Then he planted a flag bearing the Kennedy family crest. The group celebrated their ascent to the top, slapping one another on the back and taking photographs. When a reporter phoned Ethel at home to ask her about her husband's daring adventure, she said, "I think he wants to take his mind off the fact that he's not an astronaut."[3]

———

KENNEDY'S ABILITY TO ATTRACT AND CULTIVATE a talented and dedicated staff was by now well known. Three of the five people who formed the nucleus of his Senate staff had been associated with him for the better part of a decade. Angela Novello, his personal secretary, had worked with him since the Rackets Committee. His administrative assistant, Joe Dolan, had been assistant deputy attorney general at the Justice Department and had known Kennedy since 1956. Ed Guthman, the press secretary, was a Pulitzer Prize–winning investigative journalist whom Kennedy had pulled into public service as public information director at the Justice Department. Fresh energy came from the two young men Kennedy tapped as his legislative assistants—Peter Edelman, a twenty-eight-year-old graduate of Harvard Law School who had clerked for Supreme Court Justice Arthur Goldberg, and twenty-nine-year-old Adam Walinsky, who had clerked for a US Court of Appeals judge after graduating from Yale Law School. Both had worked in the Justice Department and on the Senate campaign. Neither had any experience on Capitol Hill. They were a study in contrasts. Walinsky, a New Yorker, could be arrogant and his political sympathies leaned left. Edelman, who grew up in Minneapolis, was more low-key. Kennedy recognized that the two men complemented each other. Working together, they created a dynamic team.[4]

Kennedy's Senate staff was run like "a taut ship in a loose kind of way," a journalist commented. There was no chain of command or artificial barriers between the people working with Kennedy, Adam Walinsky explained: "Everyone was working for what seemed like good things and working like hell." Kennedy would indicate that something needed to be done in some area, "and he expected you to grab hold and do it." If staffers wanted to do things that really interested them, they could charge ahead. What made the setup work, said Walinsky, was "the force of his personality. It wasn't the fact that he was a Senator and you worked for him. He never pulled that kind of rank." Thomas M. C. Johnston, who became head of Kennedy's New York City office, recalled how RFK was "refreshingly and astoundingly free" of the need for adulation. "People who worked with him felt that they were just helping out, whatever they did," he recalled. "He thought a lot about the people around him."[5]

Kennedy set a tone that resonated with his young staff members. He didn't want to hear complaints about people or waste time on people being disagreeable. You did the best you could, Walinsky learned, and understood that the world was full of difficult people: "That was so attractive all the time, that he didn't engage in these petty personal things but really kept going to the heart of things and kept going to the substance and kept working on it." Tom Johnston, a twenty-eight-year-old filmmaker when he volunteered for Kennedy's Senate campaign, stayed on staff after the election. Johnston felt that Kennedy had a difficult time being a politician; his "sense of humor or his sense of irony or of the ridiculous" meant Kennedy could never completely enact the traditional politician role. He was much more interested in getting "outside of his own situation . . . and to just confront things in the way one would as a student, or a citizen, or as a human being."[6]

In the immediate aftermath of the election and the early months of 1965, RFK focused on establishing himself as Senator Kennedy from New York. When asked what he enjoyed most about the campaign, he would respond that he liked getting away from Washington and getting to know upstate New York and the people who lived there. During November and December, he met with local civic leaders; discussed what federal assistance their communities needed; and held community forums on health, education, roads, and other areas of concern. Some made statements, others asked questions, and Kennedy would listen and respond. Peter Edelman, who took notes during the meetings, recalled that Kennedy always asked whether those in attendance had organized a community action agency in line with the requirements of War on Poverty programs and emphasized the importance of preparing to take advantage of these programs.[7]

In his maiden speech on the Senate floor on February 1, Kennedy proposed an amendment that would make it possible for thirteen counties in New York State to be included in a $1.1 billion aid package for Appalachia. The Senate approved the bill, along with Kennedy's amendment. Afterward, he visited the area to ensure that local leaders would follow through and make the necessary applications to receive the aid. He chided some for their inaction and complacency and allayed their fears that the stigma of poverty would impact their efforts to attract new industry. They should not ignore the fact, he advised, that in modern society "plenty and poverty live side by side." A community was not poor, he said, "because many of its citizens live in economic poverty"; a community was poor when its leaders "lacked the compassion and the capability to meet the full measure of their responsibility." Kennedy persuaded officials in the small town of Hornell that the aid could be used to widen Route 17 to four lanes, which was key to economic recovery in the area.[8]

Bobby Kennedy "didn't even tiptoe into Senate waters," wrote veteran Washington columnist Roscoe Drummond; "he dove in." Kennedy joined with members of New York City's congressional delegation to protest the closing of the Brooklyn Navy Yard and led an effort to reverse the Department of Defense's decision to close three Veterans Administration hospitals in upstate New York. After visiting each of the hospitals, he testified before a special hearing of the Committee on Veterans Affairs and succeeded in keeping two open. Early in March, Kennedy joined the senior senator from New York, Republican Jacob Javits, in cosponsoring a bill to protect the lower Hudson River by establishing a national scenic riverway between Newburgh and Yonkers.[9]

Kennedy would develop a strong working relationship with Javits, who shared his concern about harsh sentencing for drug crimes. A vocal critic of punitive approaches to the growing narcotics problem, Kennedy chided local and state officials in New York for failing to take advantage of federal funds for treatment and charged that the federal government had been "extremely derelict in not meeting this problem." In the late spring of 1965, he and Javits introduced a $75 million narcotics bill to fund a federal program "to humanize and modernize" federal narcotics law, emphasizing treatment rather than punishment. The bill would provide for the construction of treatment facilities and for job training, family counseling, and psychiatric services. That summer, Kennedy and Javits announced a $1 million grant provided by Department of Health, Education, and Welfare to shore up seven antidelinquency programs in New York City.[10]

As a senator, Kennedy demonstrated an ability to identify a problem, focus public attention on it, and encourage people to "make something happen that everybody agreed should happen." In the spring, he arranged for Stewart Udall, secretary of the interior, to visit New York City and tour parks in each of the boroughs. As a result of this visit, a special parks committee composed of federal, state, and city officials was established to develop a master plan for developing more outdoor recreation spaces in New York City. Their work was supported by a $100,000 grant from the federal government; the city pledged to add $75,000 to that amount. The plan was expected to lay out the city's future recreational needs, including neighborhood parks, new playground designs, waterfront development, and water pollution control. Kennedy commented that this was the first time the two federal funding agencies—the Interior Department's Bureau of Outdoor Recreation and the Housing and Home Finance Agency—had "worked together in response to a common responsibility."[11]

Kennedy had a personal interest in the care of people with intellectual disabilities, as his sister Rosemary had been in a private institution since the early 1940s after being incapacitated following a botched lobotomy procedure. Walinsky had read several constituent letters about conditions in Willowbrook State School on Staten Island. He dug up a series of articles on the school by Jack Mallon and gave them to Kennedy, prompting a visit. What Kennedy saw horrified him. The institution "borders on a snake pit," he said. He told Walinsky, "You better get yourself up there and take a look at that, because I've got to say something about that." The two of them also visited the Rome State Custodial Asylum, located in central New York.

Coincidentally, the Joint Legislative Committee on Mental Retardation was holding hearings in the Bronx later that week, and Kennedy testified. He described the filth and overcrowding, the neglect and cruelty. He spoke of children tranquilized and rocking aimlessly and described scenes of young children "slipping into blankness and lifelong dependence." There had been five unnatural deaths at Willowbrook in the previous year, including that of a child who had been scalded to death in a shower. Many of the rooms, Kennedy said, "were less comfortable and cheerful than the cages in which we put animals in a zoo." The institution was severely understaffed. Kennedy learned that a special investigative committee had presented a report on these conditions to the governor a year earlier—echoing the senator's own findings—and the report had been kept secret. Kennedy observed that state institutions, including the Department of Mental Hygiene, had yet to use the range of resources available to them. Walinsky described Kennedy's anger at seeing no apparent effort being made to change these conditions. It was, Walinsky recalled, "one of the moments of the greatest moral outrage I remember up to that time."[12]

The hearing was front-page news in the *New York Times*. Beyond public exposure, however, New York's junior senator had little power to influence how the Republican-led state government would respond. Kennedy made a series of recommendations in his testimony before the legislative committee. "Our shortcomings are due to no one man and no single administration," he said in closing. "The burden is ours. In the year 1965, that conditions such as those I saw should exist in this great state is a reproach to us all." He appealed directly to Governor Nelson Rockefeller, writing several letters and offering help. On January 30, 1966, the *New York Times* announced that Rockefeller had named Dr. Alan D. Miller to serve as commissioner of mental hygiene, noting that Miller had stepped into the post at a time "when the state's mental hygiene program is the subject of controversy between the Governor and Senator Robert Kennedy." Rockefeller invited Kennedy to meet with Dr. Miller, who assured the senator that the commissioner would keep Kennedy informed and seek his assistance as needed. A series of discussions followed, but nothing substantial came of them.[13]

———

KENNEDY'S ARRIVAL IN THE SENATE, *Washington Post* columnist George Lardner Jr. wrote, "means a voice not only for his own state, which keeps him busy enough, but for the District, which he doesn't intend to forget." Kennedy requested a seat on the Senate District Committee, "usually considered the bottom of the barrel of Committee assignments." Some city officials, Lardner noted, seemed "notably unenthusiastic." Kennedy's concerns included education and changing approaches to crime and criminal justice. He told Lardner that he was especially interested in seeing the development of "a program to help deprived youngsters that uses the most advanced ideas and imagination." While Kennedy was a strong advocate for home rule for Washington, DC, he believed that "a lot more can be done with what we now have." Less than a month into his term, he had already shown signs of impatience with the city's commissioners. That, Lardner noted, "may be just the tonic they require."[14]

Early in February, Lyndon Johnson introduced a bill, identical to the one John F. Kennedy had introduced in 1963, to restore self-government to the District of Columbia. Bobby Kennedy served as a cosponsor. On the opening day of the Senate District Committee's hearings on the legislation, he was the key figure. The *Washington Post* headlined its front-page story "Kennedy Raises Negro Question at First Hearing." By 1960, African Americans constituted more than 50 percent of the city's population. Kennedy asked Walter Tobriner, president of the district's Board of Commissioners, to explain the basis for opposition to home rule. Tobriner replied that the reason most frequently given for opposition was that the federal interest might not be properly represented. Then he said that, while often unexpressed, the major reason for opposition was a feeling among some that home rule "might result in a city run by Negroes." He quickly added that he did not share that fear and believed in the democratic process. If that was the issue, Kennedy said, it needed to be frankly discussed by the Senate and House District Committees and not swept under the rug. The Senate District Committee had approved previous home rule bills five times in the past, and each time the bill was killed in the House District Committee, which was dominated by southern Democrats. Alluding to the abysmal record of congressional oversight of the city, Kennedy added, "It seems to me we cannot do any worse that we have in the past."[15]

Kennedy took the opportunity to address issues facing the city. He praised the commissioners for an impressive effort "under the most difficult circumstances" but said he felt they had not been forceful enough in making use of the executive powers at their disposal to deal with discrimination, poverty, and juvenile delinquency. He specifically asked the commissioners to come up with an overall program to address crime in the city. At a time when rates of violent crime and robberies were steadily rising, fueling public demands for action against the "crime wave," Kennedy made it clear that he was talking about addressing, not simply crime itself, but its causes. Why did members of particular age groups or economic groups engage in crime? He called on district officials "to come up with an over-all program to deal with crime in the District of Columbia," perhaps outlining what needs to be done "over the next decade." The key, he told Tobriner, was to demonstrate the impact that poor homes, failing schools, "and all of the rest" had on the rising crime rate in Washington.[16]

Kennedy saw both danger and opportunity as politicians anxiously seized the platform to decry rising crime rates. Congressmen, Kennedy insisted, needed to stop making speeches about crime and do something about its causes. "If we are not going to provide adequate welfare services, adequate education, recreation for young people and employment opportunities, we aren't in any position to ask why crime is rising in this city," he said. In April, Tobriner returned to the Senate District Committee to testify on short-term crime legislation. He presented an eighteen-page report that called for gun registration, a minimum wage, more policemen, and more teams of police with dogs. In his statement to the committee, Tobriner made no reference to what groups seemed to be committing crimes. In response to Kennedy's initial question, police officials stated that 48 percent of those arrested for serious crimes in 1964 were younger than twenty-one years of age; 33 percent were under eighteen, an increase of 8 percent over the previous five years.

Kennedy grilled the officials: "How many were out of school, how many commit crimes because they have no parents, no recreation, no jobs, nothing to eat in the morning?" When told that the police did not keep such statistics, he turned to Tobriner and asked, "How can you come before this Committee with a crime program if you haven't analyzed the problem?" Visibly impatient, the boyish-looking Kennedy told the balding commissioner, "I'm not saying you're not the most conscientious worker, but we've got an emergency here." While Congress and the people of Washington were aroused by an upsurge in crime, now was the time, Kennedy insisted, "to come in here with an overall program." "That would require some work and some imagination," he allowed, but to offer a piecemeal program was "a major mistake." Kennedy saw a chance to push for many long-stymied educational and social projects the city needed, by linking them beyond question to the crime problem and presenting funding for the projects as part of an anticrime package. "Commissioner, why don't we get on with it?" he asked, with visible annoyance. The chair of the Senate Committee instructed the staff to gather the information Kennedy requested, but few expected much to come of it. "Thinking big is not one of [the committee's] strong points," one observer noted.[17]

Education remained central to Kennedy's concerns. "The best in educational opportunities, particularly for deprived children," he contended, "are absolutely essential if we are to succeed in breaking the cycle of despair that generates juvenile misbehavior." As a member of the Senate Committee on Health, Education, and Labor, he attempted to amend Lyndon Johnson's Elementary and Secondary Education Act (ESEA) to provide for federal oversight of schools receiving federal aid. The legislation, which directed aid to underprivileged schools, was a cornerstone of Johnson's Great Society program. In hearings on the bill before the Senate Education Subcommittee, Kennedy observed that educators testifying in support of the legislation routinely excused poorly performing schools by blaming the background of children who struggled. Perhaps those testifying had failed to consider, Kennedy said, that children might not be doing well because they had had "a lousy education." While Kennedy supported Johnson's initiative, the senator pressed for federal oversight to help ensure that funds were being used to develop programs and practices that worked, rather than assuming that school boards would take the necessary steps. When he raised this concern with Secretary of Health, Education, and Welfare Anthony Celebrezze, the glib response was, "That is the price of democracy, if you want to keep your education at the local level without conducting it in the Federal government." "I am not saying that," Kennedy shot back. But if complete local control with no federal oversight was the price of democracy, he went on, "we don't have to accept it."[18]

Kennedy had learned that the strongest forces for change were community-based. In mid-March he appealed directly to teachers at a conference sponsored by the Teachers Union of Washington at the Statler Hilton Hotel. "Our educational system has operated on the premise that we have not needed to change our way of doing things," he said. "When a child fails to learn, we blame the child," because the child is disruptive, comes from a deprived background, or has not had the benefit of preschool education. "But what would we think of a doctor who blames us when his treatment is inadequate?" Considering the problem of dropouts, Kennedy urged teachers to focus on adapting their practices to the needs of all students and developing new approaches that worked, rather than admitting defeat.[19]

Two weeks later, Kennedy addressed the first meeting of the DC Citizens for Better Public Education at Howard University's Rankin Chapel. He said that Washingtonians who wanted better schools had to make "the same kind of effort made in the field of civil rights." He recalled that he went to Congress in 1962 "and testified many days on a voting rights bill. There was absolutely no interest." If clergy and others had demonstrated then as they had been doing in Selma, Alabama, that month, progress on voting rights would have been made sooner. There was no substitute for organized pressure, as the successful passage of the Civil Rights Act had shown. Kennedy had the courage to say what many realized. Because Washington's population was more than 50 percent Black, "there are many people who don't want progress here. To make the schools and recreational facilities inadequate is part of their scheme." He called for "a great and intensive effort by citizens of all economic groups, colors and creeds to demand what's needed. Accept nothing less than the best educational system."[20]

———

DURING KENNEDY'S FIRST MONTHS IN OFFICE, a crisis broke out in Selma, Alabama. Kennedy had filed his first voting rights case as attorney general in Dallas County, where Selma is situated, on April 12, 1961. The case had been bogged down in delays and mired in appeals. Student Non-violent Coordinating Committee organizers had gone to Selma in February 1963 and worked with the Dallas County Voters League to register Black voters and demonstrate for voting rights, while the Justice Department continued to press its case. These efforts met the blunt, brutal force of local law enforcement, led by Sheriff Jim Clark. Justice Department officials filed a complaint against Clark, to no avail. Passage of the Civil Rights Act in July had reenergized civil rights activism in Selma, but the barrier to voting remained high. No more than three hundred African Americans were registered in Dallas County by the late fall of 1964, even though there were fifteen thousand Black citizens of voting age in the county. "The litigation method of correction has been tried here harder than anywhere else in the South," observed John Doar, yet Dallas County African Americans were still denied "the most fundamental of their constitutional rights—the right to vote."[21]

Struggles in Mississippi paved the way, but Alabama was where Black activists converged and ultimately secured meaningful federal legislation in the area of voting. At the invitation of the Dallas County Voters League, Martin Luther King Jr. and the Southern Christian Leadership Conference initiated a voting rights campaign in Selma on January 2, 1965. Meanwhile, Lyndon Johnson and the seasoned team of lawyers in the Justice Department had turned their attention to the need for voting rights legislation. Events in Selma soon gave this initiative greater urgency. Sheriff Clark and his deputies physically attacked women and men demonstrating for voting rights. Images of the standoff appeared on the front pages of newspapers across the country, turning up pressure in Washington. The murder of Jimmie Lee Jackson by police officers after a protest in Marion, Alabama, on February 18 convinced voting rights activists that they should march to Montgomery to petition Governor Wallace directly.[22]

On Sunday, March 7, six hundred men and women set out from Brown Chapel in a double column toward Edmund Pettus Bridge, led by John Lewis of SNCC and Hosea Williams of the SCLC. As the marchers reached the crest of the arched bridge spanning the Alabama River, they saw blue-helmeted Alabama state troopers, several lines deep, stretched across US 80. Behind them were a few dozen of Jim Clark's lawmen, fifteen on horseback. As the marchers moved forward, Major John Cloud stepped toward them and told them they had two minutes to turn around and go back to the church. Lewis and Williams knelt down to pray. "Advance," shouted the major. In an instant "a human wave, a blur of blue shirts and billy clubs and bull whips" charged into the crowd, Lewis recalled, creating a wedge that "moved with such force it seemed almost to pass over the waiting column instead of through it." People were pushed to the ground and pummeled by the troopers. As some retreated, they were pursued by Clark's mounted police, who flailed them with whips and nightsticks all the way back to the church. That night, footage of the assault was broadcast on national television.[23]

In the aftermath of what became known as Bloody Sunday, thousands of supporters flocked to Selma, and Justice Department lawyers, in consultation with President Johnson and key members of Congress, produced the final draft of a voting rights bill. The machinery built in the push for the 1964 Civil Rights Act moved into high gear. Nicholas Katzenbach was now attorney general, and Burke Marshall, who had left the Justice Department in December, returned to Washington to helped draft the legislation—in consultation with Republican Congressman William McCulloch and Senators Everett Dirksen and Thomas Kuchel—all working in concert with the president. On Monday, March 15, eight days after Bloody Sunday, Lyndon Johnson introduced the bill to a joint session of Congress. His powerful speech echoed the anthem of the civil rights movement when he declared that "we shall overcome . . . a crippling legacy of bigotry and injustice." Bobby Kennedy commented admiringly, "He's got some guts."[24]

Six days later, marchers set out once again on their fifty-mile walk to Montgomery. This time, three thousand people were marching under the protection of federal troops. By the time they reached Montgomery on March 25, the marchers were twenty-five thousand strong. King's address to the joyous crowd was a high-water mark of the southern civil rights movement.[25]

The voting rights legislation would remove barriers to Black voting and provide for federal registrars to counter local obstruction, promising dramatic changes in states like Mississippi, Alabama, Louisiana, Georgia, and South Carolina, where obstruction, violence, and intimidation routinely kept Black citizens from the polls. Most observers anticipated swift passage. Several key southerners who had opposed the 1964 Civil Rights Act, like William Fulbright of Arkansas and Albert Gore Sr. of Tennessee, now supported the voting rights legislation. Other southern Democrats waged a filibuster that lasted for twenty-four days but was, in the words of one reporter, "half-hearted."

That May, as the filibuster stalled the Senate vote, Robert Kennedy addressed the problem of the disenfranchisement of citizens of Puerto Rican descent in New York. All New Yorkers were required to demonstrate the ability to read and write in English in order to qualify to vote, a policy that had attracted Kennedy's attention and concern during the Senate campaign. In his speech on the Senate floor, Kennedy described the discriminatory nature of New York's policy: "You can't vote in our state unless you speak English, and we won't allow you to show your education as evidence of literacy, even though we do allow [this] to your English-speaking brother in place of taking his literacy test." Kennedy introduced an amendment, cosponsored by Jacob Javits, proposing that a person could not be denied the right to vote if he or she had an eighth-grade education; there could be no language requirement. The Senate adopted the measure by a vote of 48–19. Columnist Arthur Krock, commenting on Kennedy's action, wrote: "When an ancient constitutional grant, long judicially upheld, is swept aside—that of the states in this instance—the new broom of radicalism tends to make a clean sweep of the entire area. And directly in its path was the New York State literacy test."[26]

———

BY LATE SPRING, passage of the voting rights legislation was virtually assured, and the focus of America's racial crisis had shifted north and west, to poor, overcrowded, segregated urban communities. On June 4, 1965, Lyndon Johnson, delivering the commencement address at Howard University, took the occasion to launch what he viewed as the next phase in America's long struggle toward racial equality and justice. His speech drew from a report on the Black family by Daniel Patrick Moynihan, then assistant secretary of labor, which had arrived on Johnson's desk early in May. Moynihan, a thirty-eight-year-old New Yorker, had served in the Labor Department since the Kennedy administration. He had not been involved with civil rights issues or policy prior to 1964, but he was eager to establish himself as an expert on racial conditions in northern cities.[27]

Moynihan's report, *The Negro Family: The Case for National Action,* reflected trends among white liberals and social scientists who had turned their attention to racial inequities in northern urban areas and concluded that these were primarily a socioeconomic problem. The next stage in the civil rights struggle, these analysts offered, was to close the economic gap dividing Blacks and whites, particularly through employment programs, with the goal of helping African Americans assimilate into the mainstream of American life. Moynihan fastened on family dysfunction, widely seen as a consequence of the long history of discrimination stretching back to slavery, as a major focus of attention. This idea drew on the work of E. Franklin Frazier and Kenneth Clark, leading sociologists who were also African American. But the report, based largely on statistics and researched and written in less than three months from the confines of a government office, revealed Moynihan's cursory acquaintance with the texture and culture of African American urban life. Most significantly, the report failed to account for the contemporary forces and structures that sustained the substandard conditions and lack of opportunity that defined life for many.[28]

Moynihan's report would ultimately draw strong and conflicting reactions, in large part as the result of its inherent ambiguities, as historian Daniel Geary has pointed out, and the way in which the report appeared to "blame the victims of institutionalized racism rather than the system that victimized them." Nevertheless, when the report first appeared, Johnson saw an opportunity to set the agenda for the next stage of the civil rights movement. Speechwriter Richard Goodwin, as Geary observed, "distilled Moynihan's report into clear and graceful prose," and Johnson delivered what many consider to be one of the most powerful addresses of his presidency.[29]

Standing before Frederick Douglass Memorial Hall, the president looked out over five thousand graduates and their families and famously proclaimed, "Freedom is not enough." The "next and the more profound state of the battle for civil rights," he declared, would seek "not just freedom but opportunity . . . not just equality as a right and a theory, but equality as a fact and equality as a result." He praised the graduating class of 1965. The graduates represented "the indomitable determination of the Negro American to win his way in American life," evident in a growing middle-class minority that was narrowing the gap with their white counterparts. But, despite court orders and legislative victories, for the "great majority of Negro Americans—the poor, the unemployed, the uprooted, the dispossessed . . . the walls are rising, and the gulf is widening." The causes were complex and subtle, the president acknowledged, but he identified "two broad basic reasons." Black citizens, like many whites, were trapped in "inherited, gateless poverty," a condition that his administration was trying to tackle through a dozen or more Great Society programs. The second cause, "more difficult to explain, more deeply grounded . . . is the devastating heritage of long years of slavery; and of a century of oppression, hatred and injustice." Such conditions differentiated Black poverty, he explained, "radiating painful roots into the community, and into the family, and into the nature of the individual."[30]

Johnson observed that in 1965, 73 percent of African Americans were concentrated in cities, separate and confined, like "another nation." While considering the long arc of history, he neglected to observe the relatively recent growth of these hypersegregated urban communities, a product of local and federal government policies in response to Black migration from the South over the previous fifty years. The speech was vague and impressionistic in this regard. Neglecting to mention the sustaining power of Black culture, Johnson echoed a common view among white liberals, one Moynihan had himself emphasized, in describing the Negro cultural tradition "as twisted and battered by years of hatred and hopelessness." Johnson identified "perhaps the most important aspect of the problem—its influence radiating to every part of life"—as "the breakdown of the Negro family structure," adding that "for this, most of all, white America must accept responsibility." This breakdown flowed from the "centuries of oppression . . . of the Negro man" and from "long years of degradation and discrimination which have attacked his dignity and assaulted his ability to produce for his family." Earlier in the speech, Johnson described "the burden that a dark skin can add to the search for a productive place in our society." "Blighted hope breeds despair," he said. "Despair brings indifference to the learning which offers a way out. And despair, coupled with indifferences, is often the source of destructive rebellion against the fabric of society."[31]

Johnson's forty-minute long address was frequently interrupted with applause. He offered no specific remedies or directions to meet the vast challenges he had described. Rather, he announced plans to convene a White House conference of scholars and Black leaders in the fall, dedicated to helping "the American Negro fulfill the rights . . . he is finally about to secure." Johnson ended on a high note: "So this is the glorious opportunity for this generation to end the one huge wrong of the American Nation, and in doing so, find America for ourselves with the same immense thrill of discovery which gripped those who first began to realize that here, at last, was a home for freedom." At the conclusion of his address, the Howard University choir sang "We Shall Overcome."

The next morning, he received a telegram from Martin Luther King Jr. "Never before has a president articulated the depths and dimensions of the problem of racial injustice more eloquently or profoundly," King wrote. "The whole speech evinced an amazing sensitivity to the difficult problems the Negro Americans face in the stride to freedom. It is my hope that all Americans will capture the spirit and content of this great statement."[32]

———

THE SIGNING OF THE VOTING RIGHTS ACT on August 6, 1965, represented a monumental achievement, the culmination of several generations of struggle in the South. Bob Moses, his fellow activists, and the courageous men and women who had risked their lives and livelihoods to register to vote had educated, challenged, and inspired the team of Justice Department lawyers embedded in the field, who learned firsthand about the limits of litigation in a lawless society. The provisions of the Voting Rights Act directly emerged from those experiences. Less than a week after President Johnson signed the bill into law, however, Black rage exploded in the city of Los Angeles. After five days of fighting in the streets, thirty-four people were dead, and the Watts section of Los Angeles was in ruins. Watts marked a turning point, sparking a debate that would shape the future course of America's long struggle with race.

The Watts region of South Los Angeles had been transformed into a Black working-class community during World War II, populated largely by southern migrants drawn to California by the promise of defense industry jobs. By 1965, the twenty-square-mile district was densely populated and described as an area of "low family income, substandard housing and substandard education." The high school dropout rate was 2.2 times the rate for the city at large, and unemployment hovered around 34 percent. That summer, $22 million in antipoverty funds earmarked for Los Angeles were being held up because Mayor Samuel Yorty had failed to establish a board representing all segments of the community, as required by the US Office of Economic Opportunity. The previous November, an overwhelming majority had voted to repeal California's Fair Housing Act, meant to protect Black people from housing discrimination. Relations between majority Black neighborhoods and Los Angeles police were tense, a result of inadequate protection, harassment, and a culture of police brutality. As one local official put it, Black people in Los Angeles "generally expected the worst from the police and generally received it." It took one incident to set the riots off, but, as Al Kuettner reported in the *Washington Post*, "months and even years went into preparing for a situation of such horrendous proportions."[33]

Early on the evening of August 11, twenty-one-year-old Marquette Frye, accompanied by his brother Ronald, was driving his mother's 1955 Buick along Avalon Boulevard in South-Central Los Angeles when he was pulled over by California Highway Patrol Officer Lee Minikus. The officer had noticed that the car was weaving. A crowd of fifty gathered while Minikus gave Frye a sobriety test, which he failed. Frye bantered with Minikus and was cooperative. Ronald brought their mother, Rena Price, to the scene to retrieve her car, which the police were intending to tow. Price began berating her son for drinking and driving. Frye then began yelling at Minikus, "You're not going to take me to jail." Minikus pulled his revolver when Frye refused to get into the patrol car, and Frye shouted, "Go ahead, kill me." Several reinforcements arrived on the scene. By this time the crowd had grown to more than two hundred. When one of the officers tried to handcuff Frye, his mother jumped on the officer's back, while another swung his baton at Frye's shoulder and hit his head, drawing blood. Angry observers shouted abuse at the patrolmen. At this point, one of the officers pulled out a shotgun to hold the crowd back. Eight Los Angeles police cars arrived, instantly ratcheting up the tension on the hot sultry night. Rena Price and her two sons were taken away in handcuffs, and the police arrested a man and woman in the crowd for inciting violence. Residents later described rough treatment by the police and racial slurs. Rumors swiftly spread through the community that the police had abused Price and the second woman they had arrested. The crowd threw rocks, bricks, and bottles at the police cars, while other small groups attacked white motorists and smashed some store windows. A hundred police officers rushed to the area and until 1 a.m. battled a crowd that swelled to one thousand demonstrators. After five hours, the police sealed off an eight-block area, quelling the disturbance.[34]

The following morning, the Los Angeles County Human Relations Commission convened a public meeting at Athens Park to calm tensions. It quickly became an angry forum for the youthful audience to protest police brutality. That night, disturbances broke out in Watts and spread into neighboring communities. This time, more than seven thousand people took to the streets. They tossed Molotov cocktails at police, looted stores and then set them on fire, and reportedly stole machetes and rifles from pawnshops. Firemen attempting to douse blazing buildings were targeted by snipers and forced to seek cover. "Helmeted and shot gun carrying officers fought a virtual guerilla war during the night with mobs of frenzied Negroes," reported the Los Angeles Times, in tones of horrified disbelief.

Late the next morning, Police Chief William H. Parker told the mayor that the police force was nearing exhaustion. With Governor Pat Brown on vacation in Greece, Yorty asked Lieutenant Governor Glenn Anderson to send in the National Guard. Uncontrolled fires, sniper fire, looting, and street battles spread over a widening area encompassing 46.5 miles, with outbursts in Pasadena, Compton, and Venice and reaching close to City Hall in south Los Angeles. "A huge section of Los Angeles was virtually a city on fire as flames from stores, industrial complexes, and homes lit the sky," the Los Angeles Times reported. The first casualty was a young Black bystander, killed in a shoot-out between police and rioters. Outnumbered police sought to contain the uprising, increasingly desperate for reinforcements. The first contingents of National Guard were delayed for six hours, while the lieutenant governor pleaded with the Johnson administration for assistance with equipment and transport of troops to Los Angeles. By Saturday evening, nearly fifteen thousand National Guardsmen had poured into the city, joining all available police and sheriff deputies.[35]

During Friday night and into Saturday morning, guardsman with bayonets and tear gas swept through riot-torn areas under orders to shoot when fired on and to take whatever action necessary to restore order, "short of indiscriminate slaughter." Lieutenant Governor Anderson announced an 8 p.m. curfew on Saturday. By Sunday, August 15, the streets were quiet. Later surveys estimated that at least 30,000 people participated in the uprising. Thirty-four people were killed, more than 1,000 were injured, and almost 4,000 were arrested—the great majority of them African American. Two policemen were killed, one by friendly fire, and a fireman died when a building collapsed on him. Twenty-three of the twenty-five African Americans who died were killed by Los Angeles police or National Guardsmen. Property damage was estimated at $35 million. Watts's major business thoroughfare was "like a war-scarred shell of burned out buildings," "dotted with hulks of cars overturned and burned," with "shattered glass and rubble everywhere."[36]

The death and destruction in Los Angeles exceeded the combined impact of the urban uprising that had occurred in East Coast cities the previous summer, leaving observers reeling. Martin Luther King Jr., who was planning a campaign to challenge segregation in northern cities, flew to Los Angeles on Tuesday and was overwhelmed by what he saw and heard. Five hundred people packed the second floor of the Westminster Neighborhood Association building and overflowed down the stairs and into the street. Feelings were raw. Trying to calm emotions, King began, "All over America Negroes must join hands"—"and burn," interrupted a man standing at the edge of the crowd. King continued, "and work together creatively." He listened to a litany of grievances, many focused on Police Chief William Parker and abusive policing. "Let Parker and (Mayor) Yorty come down here and see how we're living," one woman insisted. A soft-spoken man agreed: "They're the ones who are responsible for what's going on here." There was tension, some heckling, and bursts of anger, but the crowd treated King "with respect and affection." He began speaking in an emotionally charged voice, and the crowd hushed. "I'm here because at bottom we are all brothers and sisters. . . . We'll all go up together or we all go down together. We are not free in the South and you are not free in the cities of the North."[37]

King spent several days in Los Angeles, walking through the Watts area and meeting with Black and white leaders and political officials. The day after his meeting at the neighborhood association, King met for nearly three hours with Mayor Yorty and Police Chief Parker. Both men had been quick to assign blame. Parker complained that the riots were a result of treating Negroes "with kid gloves." He said violence was to be expected "when you keep telling people they are unfairly treated and teach them disrespect for the law." The meeting between King and the city officials was frank, stormy, and "far from friendly," according to one observer. King, who was frequently interrupted, voiced his concerns about policing abuses and recommended that a civilian review board be established to investigate allegations of police brutality. Yorty called King's charges "ridiculous" and laid blame for the riots on "hardened criminals." Following the city hall session, Yorty, "flushed with anger," criticized King for "talking about lawlessness, killing, looting and burning in the same context as our police department." At a press conference afterward, King said that he had made it very clear to the mayor and the police chief "that we believe absolutely in law and order" and are just as distressed about violence "as any white citizen." But, he declared, law and order cannot be achieved "unless you have justice and human dignity in the community." Before flying back to Atlanta, King told reporters that "to treat this situation as though it were the result of some criminal element is to lead the community into a potential holocaust."[38]

Americans across the country watched on their television young Black residents of Watts battling police and looting stores as Los Angeles burned. Many observers, as one reporter commented, shared "a stunned inability to understand what it was all about." Reactions and responses to Watts revealed much about racial attitudes and the evolving politics of race. On August 19, former president Dwight Eisenhower, in Washington to attend meetings with House and Senate Republicans, assailed the "senseless violence" of the Los Angeles riots. "This riot did not occur in a vacuum," he said. "I believe the United States as a whole has been becoming atmosphered, you might say, in a policy of lawlessness." There was an imperative need, Eisenhower insisted, for "greater respect for law" and increased devotion to "moral standards" and "the national character." He predicted that "the political party that can make itself a real crusader for the restoration of these values can win a great many converts."[39]

Later that day, in what read like a direct response to Eisenhower's claim, Bobby Kennedy dismissed injunctions to "obey the law" as an inadequate response to what had happened in Watts. "There is no point in telling Negroes to obey the law," Kennedy declared in an interview. "To many Negroes the law is the enemy. In Harlem, in Bedford Stuyvesant, it has almost always been used against him." By the law, Kennedy was not referring exclusively to the police. Whites had to realize, Kennedy said in a speech the next day, that African Americans did not experience the law in the same way as whites did. The law did not protect Black citizens from unscrupulous landlords, substandard living conditions, and merchants who cheated Black consumers. He believed that few mayors of large northern cities had effective communication with their cities' Black population or an understanding of the depths of their problems and emotions. Securing voting rights or the right to public accommodations, Kennedy told the reporter, "was an easy job compared to what we face in the North."[40]

Lyndon Johnson was undone by Watts. "How was it possible after all we've accomplished?" he asked. "How could it be?" For several days during the disturbances, Joseph Califano, LBJ's principal coordinator for domestic affairs, tried unsuccessfully to reach the president at his ranch in Texas. LBJ would not return Califano's calls. Califano sought approval for the Pentagon to provide aid to California's National Guard in response to Lieutenant Governor Anderson's desperate requests. General Creighton Abrams, vice chief of staff of the US Army, called Califano, pressuring him for authorization. When Califano reached Defense Secretary Robert McNamara, on vacation in Martha's Vineyard, McNamara agreed that the army should provide whatever support the state needed. Still unable to reach the president, Califano told Abrams, "You've got the White House's approval," and sanctioned the airlift of trucks, tear gas, ammunition, and supplies to Los Angeles. When Johnson learned about the possibility of federal involvement, he finally phoned Califano on Saturday night, insisting that there be no US military presence in Los Angeles. When the president realized that orders had gone forward for the airlift of supplies, a testy LBJ reminded Califano whom he worked for.[41]

On Sunday morning, August 15, Johnson called Califano and discussed the situation in Watts and the statement the president would issue. He was still trying to make sense of what had happened and what it would mean politically. Johnson reached back to the history of the Reconstruction era, as he had learned it, and worried that "the Negroes" would make "fools of themselves" the way they had after the Civil War and "end up pissing in the aisles of the Senate." Just when the government was moving to help them, he feared, they would "once again take unwise actions out of frustration, impatience, and anger." Johnson was concerned that the riots would make it more difficult to pass Great Society legislation. He worried about political fallout in the 1966 midterm elections and was concerned that whites might conclude, as Police Chief Parker had quipped, that emphasizing the injustices Black people had suffered had contributed to racial unrest. Johnson wanted to make a statement that would "strike out against violence as a means of achieving progress in our society." He asked Califano to call King and other civil rights leaders—Roy Wilkins, A. Philip Randolph, and Whitney Young—and to urge them to do the same.[42]

In his first statement on Watts, Johnson likened "the snipers and looters in Watts" to the "night riders of the Ku Klux Klan." "A rioter with a Molotov cocktail in his hand is not fighting for civil rights any more than a klansman with a sheet on his back and a mask on his face." Speaking at a White House conference on equal employment opportunities, Johnson blamed lawbreakers and "destroyers of a free America" for the death and disaster that had exploded in Los Angeles. He warned that further disruptions and violence "may erase the accumulated goodwill of many months and many years." Blunting the stark realities exposed by the Watts uprising, Johnson said that the riots "bore no relation to the orderly struggle that en-nobled the last decade," contrasting peaceful protest against injustices with setting a great city on fire out of hatred. He thanked the members of Congress at the meeting for supporting programs "designed to give poverty-stricken areas the sense of hope and responsibility essential for human growth in a free society," and promised new, far-reaching programs.[43]

Six days later Johnson announced that he had dispatched a federal task force to Los Angeles, headed by Justice Department official Ramsey Clark, with a ten-point plan of action designed "to restore and rehabilitate the dam-aged areas of Los Angeles." The president warned that the "clock is ticking" as the possibility of similar racial uprisings in other major cities approached, and he urged those at all levels of government to avert such disturbances by ending slum conditions and other festering urban problems."[44]

———

ROBERT KENNEDY'S UNDERSTANDING OF race in America was continu-ally evolving. He began by seeing the problem of racial equality as a simple question of right and wrong, but the more exposed he was to racial condi-tions in the north, the more he understood the despair, hopelessness, and anger at injustices that permeated the fabric of daily life for many African Americans, as well as the toll these took on young people. "He actually felt it," Walter Sheridan said; "he identified with them." For Kennedy, the out-pouring of Black rage in Los Angeles was comprehensible. What alarmed him, two close associates wrote, was "the harsh and bitter white reaction." The enormous publicity given to Watts emphasized looting and mayhem without considering the reasons "and contributed to the impression among whites that Blacks rioted aimlessly and irresponsibly." Watts marked a turning point for Kennedy. He would increasingly focus his attention on the condi-tions in urban ghettos and on puncturing the prejudice, myths, and igno-rance that prevented whites from facing what he saw as the most pressing domestic crisis of the decade.[45]

On August 18, Kennedy delivered a speech before the state convention of the Independent Order of Odd Fellows in Spring Valley, New York, a mostly white gathering. His comments focused on the Watts and the vital impor-tance of mobilizing the nation's will and resources to meet a crisis that he described as "unparalleled in our history." He discussed the challenges to Black leadership and the need to help cultivate and support leadership from within ghetto communities. But Kennedy was mostly concerned with his white audience. "We have been strangely insensitive to the problems of northern Negroes," he told them. He recalled how during the Birmingham crisis in 1963, he had met with many northern leaders—businessmen, newspaper publishers, civic officials. "I told them then that they would soon face problems even more difficult in their own communities. To a man, they denied that any such problem could arise in the North." He warned that riots were waiting to happen all over the country.[46]

Kennedy asked his audience to think about what they valued in their lives and to consider the sources of their self-esteem. Surely prominent among them was "the contribution we can make to ourselves, our families and our community around us; all these things," he observed, "are built around the work we do." He asked them to imagine a community like Watts where many people were without work. Lack of work meant a lack of money—and "living in overcrowded rat-infested housing or even renting cars for a night to have a place to live, as many people do in the Watts area." Such conditions were compounded by the "blighted hopes and disappointments" of those who had left the South for what many called the "promised land." They found themselves crowded into "a dirty, stinky, uncared-for, closet size section of a great city." Their children "inherited the total lot of their parents: the disappointment, the anger," with "little hope of deliverance." He asked, "Where does one run to when he's already in the promised land?"

The struggle for justice and freedom in the North was different from the civil rights movement in the South, he explained. Northerners could not expect the kind of disciplined, nonviolent protest that characterized the southern movement. "Northern problems are the problems of everyday living." Sit-ins could not change the fact that adults were illiterate. Marches would not create jobs for Black youth. "We say to the young . . . 'Stay in school, learn and study and sacrifice, and you will be rewarded for the rest of your life.'" But a Black youth who completed high school was more likely to be unemployed or to find only a menial job than the white youth who dropped out. "One of the rioters in Watts was a biochemistry graduate. We should not be surprised," Kennedy remarked.

Kennedy contextualized the issue of law and order. Evidence suggested that some people had come to Watts with the intention of rioting, he said. They were hoodlums and "should be treated as such." But a harsh fact that everyone had to learn, he insisted, "is that just saying 'obey the law' is not going to work. . . . We have a long way to go before the law means the same to a Negro as it does to us." The laws "do not protect them from paying too much money for inferior goods, from having their furniture illegally repossessed. The law does not protect them from having to keep the lights turned on the feet of their children at night to keep them from being gnawed by rats." He urged his audience to realize that the deprivation and suffering of the ghettos were not simply a Negro problem but a problem that afflicted

American society; addressing the problem had to become part of the public agenda. Referencing the nation's pride in its revolutionary tradition, he said, "I think there is no doubt that if Washington or Jefferson or Adams were Negroes in a northern city today, they would be in the forefront of the effort to change the conditions under which Negroes live."[47]

Kennedy visited Watts early in November, during a trip to Los Angeles to deliver several speeches and attend a Democratic Party dinner. After a noontime speech on nuclear proliferation at the Town Hall, he said to Peter Edelman, "Let's go to Watts." The two men took a taxi to South Central Los Angeles and spent the afternoon in Watts. Edelman recalled walking down 103rd Street and up and down Central Avenue, seeing all the burned-out places, and talking with people in the community. "It was like seeing a war-torn area in your own country for the first time," he recalled. Standing on a street corner, the pair asked a man, "perfectly healthy looking," what the problem was. He said, "flustration." Kennedy asked, "What do you mean?" The man responded, "Well man, when you're over fifty and you is black, you can't get a job no how." Repeatedly, they heard, "Why the hell should I stay in school? There is no job for me when I get out." The pair visited various teen centers and Operation Bootstrap on South Central Avenue, a new project started in October by Robert Hall and Lou Smith, two young African Americans affiliated with the Congress of Racial Equality. When they dropped into the office of the local newspaper in the heart of Watts, they were surprised to find a big "Robert Kennedy for President" poster on the wall. "We got a kick out of that," Edelman recalled. After returning from California, Kennedy told Edelman of plans for a major speech on civil rights and asked him to work with Burke Marshall to prepare a memo.[48]

———

FOUR DAYS LATER, Kennedy was off to Latin America. The trip came at a notable moment. Scheduled to take advantage of the Senate recess during the last three weeks of November, the trip would allow the senator to mark his fortieth birthday and the second anniversary of his brother's death in Brazil. President Kennedy had been immensely popular in Latin America, where he had initiated the Alliance for Progress program. In recent months, feelings toward the United States had soured after Lyndon Johnson sent US troops into the Dominican Republic that spring to help suppress a rebellion against the military government to restore constitutional rule. Johnson justified his actions on the grounds that he was protecting American lives and preventing "another Cuba" in the Caribbean.[49]

Kennedy's trip was motivated by a personal interest in Latin America—he had only visited once before, on a brief stopover in Brazil—and his brother's attachment to the region. "My brother cared enormously about Latin America," the senator commented during the trip. "So, I came to get myself educated." Ethel and several friends, including Angela Novello, John Seigenthaler, William vanden Heuvel, and Richard Goodwin, went with him, along with aides Adam Walinsky and Tom Johnston and several reporters. The group set off on November 10 for a twenty-day long trip that took them to Peru, Chile, Argentina, Brazil, and Venezuela.[50]

Kennedy met with government officials, political leaders, leftist intellectuals, and US representatives. He immersed himself in poor communities, visited work sites, and sought out students at nearly every stop. "He wanted to meet everybody," Walinsky recalled. In Concepción, Chile, he accepted a student invitation to speak at the university, a hotbed of anti-American sentiment. Marxist students threatened a mass protest if he showed up. He went anyway, against the advice of the State Department and friends in his entourage, and was greeted by protesters throwing eggs (hitting Seigenthaler and vanden Heuvel and missing Kennedy) and shouting. Kennedy took the platform and challenged the Marxist students to a debate, but it was impossible to be heard over the pandemonium. He left to thunderous applause, with students crowding him to shake his hand.

In Brazil, he walked the sugarcane fields outside of Recife and found that cane cutters worked six days a week, earning less than a dollar a day in violation of Brazil's minimum wage law, and that they were forced to spend at least two days' salary buying necessities at the company store. Kennedy berated the company's representative for failing to pay a decent wage, warning him, "you're breeding your own destruction." The senator visited Pama de Comas, one of the largest slums in Peru, where there was no electricity and water was trucked in several times a week and sold to the residents. When he learned that it was impossible to get US aid to build a water tank because of a dispute between the International Petroleum Company and the Peruvian government, he demanded to know what aid had to do with company profits. Incredulous, he grilled a harried American official, "You mean to say we can't get a water tank for these people due to an oil dispute?"[51]

On November 22, Bobby and Ethel attended mass at São Francisco Church and Convent, an elegant two-hundred-year-old Roman Catholic church in Salvador, Brazil. They joined fifty people, mostly from the city's poorer section. After mass, the Kennedys stayed behind and prayed alone. Then Bobby headed to the *barriada,* the city's slum district, where the community center had been renamed for John Kennedy. Barefoot children gathered around him. Visibly moved, he said quietly, "President Kennedy was most fond of children. Can I ask you to do a favor for him? Stay in school, study hard, study as long as you can, and then work for your city and work for Brazil." Afterward, on the plane north to Natal on Brazil's northeastern tip, he sat by himself, head buried in his arms. In Natal, he visited a home for unwed mothers and wept when children at the center sang "God Bless America." More than one hundred thousand turned out to see him that afternoon. Energized, he leapt on a truck and shouted, "Every child an education! Every family adequate housing! Every man a job!" The next day, Walinsky was pleased to notice that the solid black tie Bobby had worn since his brother's death had been replaced by a striped one.[52]

Speculation about his political future and his relationship with Lyndon Johnson shadowed Bobby Kennedy's trip to Latin America. Martin Arnold, who traveled with the senator for the *New York Times,* said he had done "a good job for President Johnson, really, in the sense that he used [the trip] to tell these people that Lyndon Johnson had come from the soil and that he would understand their types of problems. He was very, very good that way, even though these two men obviously hated each other." Kennedy had hoped that his trip might help repair US relations with Latin America. Robert Hopkins, a businessman in Buenos Aires and son of Franklin Roosevelt's confidant Harry Hopkins, wrote that Kennedy's "desire to understand Argentine problems, his frank answer to provocative questions . . . and his youth" won people over. "By going straight to the people, he created a surge of pro-U.S. sentiment." Upon his return, Kennedy emphasized that the United States must support the trend toward progressive leadership and reforms in Latin America or "face a disaster." For Adam Walinsky, the trip reaffirmed what had attracted him to Kennedy in the first place: "The heart of him and what he really believed kept coming out."[53]

Edelman and Marshall's memo on civil rights was awaiting the senator on his return. The two had focused on southern issues, an area where Marshall's experience and legal expertise was probably unsurpassed. Based on their discussions, Edelman drafted a long memo that included a series of recommendations, such as tightening civil rights laws that still had loopholes, remedying failures of the court system, and protecting civil rights workers from official and private brutality and coercion. At the end of the memo was a brief discussion of some of the issues Kennedy had raised in his Watts speech. Kennedy read the memo and said that Edelman and Walinsky had done a great job. Then he zeroed in on the last part and said that he wanted to focus his talk on northern problems; that was where the real challenges and difficulties were.[54]

For the next six weeks, Kennedy worked closely with Edelman and Walinsky, hashing out a comprehensive approach to the racial crisis in northern cities and conditions in urban slums. Pressure points were readily identified—education, housing, employment—but such a fragmented approach failed to grasp the whole. After drafts of several speeches and hours of discussion, the men agreed that there should be a series of speeches focusing on three major areas: achieving school and residential desegregation, addressing conditions in the ghetto, and convincing whites that these issues were their concerns. Kennedy had three consecutive speaking dates on his calendar for January in New York City.[55]

A CONVERGENCE OF developments was reshaping the politics of race in America. Seasoned activists working in the South faced continuing violence as they challenged the limited reach of legislation in dismantling the social mindset underpinning Jim Crow. Black empowerment through education, institution building, job creation, voting, and control of antipoverty programs emerged as a new strategy for advancement. White resentment and fear fueled a backlash against these demands, particularly after Watts. The escalation of the Vietnam War increasingly dominated domestic politics, hastening the unraveling of a fragile civil rights coalition and threatening to sap funds from a War on Poverty that had barely begun.

The presidency of Lyndon Johnson became increasingly consumed by the war in Vietnam. Johnson had inherited a mess. During the peak years of Cold War tensions, JFK had enlarged America's role in Vietnam, increasing military assistance to the South Vietnamese government, supporting counterinsurgency operations, and sending American advisers—sixteen thousand in all by November 1963. Although Kennedy's visit to Southeast Asia in 1951 had given him a glimpse of the complexities of the struggles in that country, as a senator he had joined in enthusiastic support of Ngo Dinh Diem, the Catholic nationalist who assumed control of Vietnam south of the seventeenth parallel after France's defeat in 1954. Diem, with the support of the United States, blocked the national elections called for in 1956 by the 1954 Geneva Accords, and solidified his control over South Vietnam.[56]

The Kennedy administration found itself supporting a government that was corrupt, repressive, and unpopular, while the National Liberation Front, the communist insurgency in South Vietnam, demonstrated strength and resilience. As conditions in South Vietnam deteriorated and officials offered conflicting reports and advice, JFK attempted to steer a middle course, which only drew the United States in deeper. "If you wanted to get dissident ideas through to the White House," David Halberstam said, Robert Kennedy was "the single person open to suggestions and to accept bad news." In the fall of 1963, responding to the dramatic protest of Buddhist monks, the dysfunction of the Diem regime, and the stirrings of a possible coup, Bobby blurted out what historian George Herring called "the ultimate question": Was the South Vietnamese government capable of winning the war, and should the United States begin to extricate itself from what was becoming an impossible tangle? Most of the president's advisers remained persuaded that the United States could prevail.[57]

On November 1, 1963, Ngo Dinh Diem was ousted by South Vietnamese army officers in a coup sanctioned by the American government, and he and his brother Ngo Dinh Nhu were killed. Three weeks later, President Kennedy was assassinated in Dallas. Both events would combine, as Herring noted, to transform the course of the war and America's role in it. What direction Vietnam policy would have taken had JFK lived is impossible to know. In the wake of the Cuban missile crisis, as suggested by his American University speech, Kennedy had begun moving beyond Cold War certitudes. He had learned to be skeptical of military advisers, and relied increasingly on the counsel and judgment of his brother. President Kennedy was also firmly opposed to the commitment of US ground troops.[58]

South Vietnam was a country falling apart when Johnson assumed the presidency. Initially, he continued the approach of his predecessor, providing economic and military assistance and increasing the number of advisers to twenty-three thousand. Conditions continued to deteriorate. Diem's removal revealed how deeply fragmented the country was. His successors were corrupt and ineffectual. Meanwhile, the National Liberation Front grew in strength and numbers, with the support of North Vietnam. Johnson viewed the crisis in Vietnam, Herring observed, "as a crucial test of strength for his personal prestige, his authority as president of the United States and leader of the Free World, and indeed, his manhood." Lacking experience in foreign policy, he relied on the counsel of military and foreign affairs advisers like Secretary of State Dean Rusk, a committed cold warrior who shared Johnson's determination to prevail in Vietnam. By the summer of 1964, with chaos reigning in South Vietnam, Johnson and his advisers were prepared to alter the course of American involvement—through the initiation of a bombing campaign against North Vietnam and the introduction of ground troops.[59]

Johnson and his advisers created a framework that enabled the president to escalate the war while initially working outside the realm of congressional oversight and public knowledge. A misrepresented encounter between an

American destroyer and North Vietnamese gunboats in the summer of 1964 led Congress to overwhelming approve the administration's request for what became known as the Gulf of Tonkin Resolution, allowing the president to take "all necessary measures" to repel or prevent aggression in Southeast Asia. Retaliatory air strikes against North Vietnam soon began. In March 1965, the United States launched an intensive bombing campaign, known as Rolling Thunder, and introduced US ground troops. "A key moment had come," according to historian Fredrik Logevall, "and a line had been crossed." By the start of 1966, there were 184,000 American troops in Vietnam.[60]

Robert Kennedy was deeply troubled by Johnson's course in Vietnam. Burke Marshall recalled talking with Kennedy in 1965, after, in Marshall's words, "the United States turned that into an American war." The two men agreed that the war "was going to tear the country apart in the next two or three years." After he became a senator, Kennedy started meeting in private with Senate critics of the administration's Vietnam policy. In July 1965, he made his first public critique of that policy in a speech at the graduation ceremony of the International Police Academy in Washington, urging the United States to emphasize political rather than military solutions in responding to revolutions in emerging nations. "A government cannot make war on its own people, cannot destroy its own country," he observed. "To do so is to abandon its reason for existence." Kennedy remained restrained in his public comments on the conduct of the war, for fear that any overt criticism would be taken as a personal dispute with Johnson, but his concerns were deep and apparent.[61]

During the fall of 1965, Kennedy spoke out on issues related to America's involvement in Vietnam. He supported the right to dissent, defending the right of Professor Eugene Genovese of Rutgers to say that he did not "fear an impending Vietcong victory." In a reply to a question about whether Americans should give blood to the North Vietnamese, Kennedy replied, "I'm willing to give blood to anyone who needs it," noting that it was "in the oldest traditions of this country." Senator Barry Goldwater blasted both Kennedy and Genovese, warning that each had come close to treason. Kennedy said that he opposed college draft deferments because they discriminated against those with lower incomes. Most of all, he was concerned that the growing financial demands of the war would delay or diminish domestic antipoverty programs. At the end of 1965, administration officials indicated that domestic budgets—including the budgets of War on Poverty programs—would have to be held down as the result of an impending $10 billion boost to the defense budget. Postponing action on our domestic needs, Kennedy told a college audience in December 1965, would be a terrible mistake, one "that could split our society irretrievably."[62]

Kennedy made his first public comment on the conduct of the war at the end of January 1966, after Johnson resumed air strikes following a thirty-seven-day bombing halt. "If we regard bombing as the answer in Vietnam we are headed straight for disaster," Kennedy warned during the Senate's first real debate on Vietnam. In the weeks that followed, the Senate Foreign Relations Committee held a series of nationally televised hearings on the administration's policies in Vietnam. Senator William J. Fulbright and other members of the committee grilled key administration officials about the war and their claims of progress. Kennedy, who was not on the committee, came each day, sat in the back of the hearing room, and listened. On February 19, the last day of the hearing, he convened a press conference and publicly spoke out for a negotiated settlement of the Vietnam War, calling for the admission of the National Liberation Front, the political arm of the Vietcong, to a "share of power and responsibility." Drawing on the lessons of the Cuban missile crisis, he said, "Neither side can have complete surrender." While there was uncertainty and risk, the alternative was "widening conflict and devastation," with no certain victory in the end. He pointed to widespread dissatisfaction among noncommunists with the South Vietnamese government and rising demands for political and economic reforms. Kennedy's comments were seen as a complete break from the administration and were welcomed by those hoping to broaden the debate on Vietnam policy.

The Johnson administration "threw everything they had at us after that speech," Peter Edelman recalled. Kennedy's Senate office, for a time, became like a bunker. Vice President Hubert Humphrey led the charge, saying that including the Viet Cong in a South Vietnamese government would be like putting "a fox in the chicken coop." The *New York Times* praised Kennedy's proposal as "less a criticism of the President's policies than an invaluable contribution to the decision-making process." Johnson did not see the proposal in that light. Under his direction, the FBI had been monitoring the Senate Foreign Relations Committee hearings in February for the purpose of comparing statements made by critics of the administration's policies, particularly Senate Foreign Relations Committee chairman William Fulbright and Senator Wayne Morse, with "the Communist Party line."[63]

On March 2, 1966, Martin Luther King Jr. wrote to Kennedy, applauding his statement: "Your great brother carried us far in new directions with his concept of a world of diversity; your position advances us to the next step which requires us to reach the political maturity to recognize and relate to all elements produced by the contemporary colonial revolutions." King had been personally calling for a negotiated settlement to the widening war in Vietnam since March 1965. Resistance within the Southern Christian Leadership Conference to taking a public position on the war and the desire not to divert attention from pressing issues of poverty and racial turmoil at home initially kept him from taking a bolder stand. King resented official efforts to shame and silent opponents of America's war in Vietnam. Early in January 1966, he led 1,500 people in a march on the Georgia state capitol in Atlanta to protest the barring of Julian Bond from his seat in the legislature because of his opposition to the war in Vietnam. In King's sermon that week at Ebenezer Baptist Church, he spoke about how dissent and nonconformity were the essence of Christianity.[64]

Bob Moses saw American policy in southeast Asia as an extension of the hypocrisy and duplicity he had experienced in Mississippi. On April 17, 1965, he spoke at the first massive antiwar protest in Washington. On January 6, 1966, SNCC became the first civil rights organization to publicly oppose US involvement in Vietnam. The timing was prompted by the murder of Sammy Younge, a twenty-one-year-old student at Tuskegee Institute, active in voter registration efforts, and a veteran who had served two years in the US Navy. When attempting to desegregate a "whites only" restroom at a service station in Tuskegee, Younge was shot by the service station owner. In its statement, SNCC criticized the government for squashing liberation under the guise of preserving freedom in the world— while violence and oppression persisted in the South and the federal government failed to fully implement the recent Civil Rights Act and Voting Rights Act. The statement expressed sympathy and support for "the men in this country who are unwilling to respond to the military draft" and "contribute their lives to the United States aggression in Vietnam." Three days after this statement was released, the Georgia legislature refused to seat Julian Bond, who had been elected the previous November, because he would not distance himself from the SNCC statement.[65]

At a Southern Christian Leadership Conference meeting in Miami in April, King succeeded in winning a strong resolution calling on the government to "desist from aiding the military junta against the Buddhists, Catholics and students of Vietnam whose efforts to democratize their government are more in consonance with our traditions than the policy of a military oligarchy." The resolution warned that not only had America's foreign policy "become imprisoned in the destiny of a military oligarchy," but the "promises of the Great Society top the casualty list of the conflict." The moment was ripe "and the need urgent to reassess our position and seriously examine the wisdom of prompt withdrawal." King urged the Johnson administration to seek free elections in Vietnam. Most important, the resolution declared that the SCLC, "as an organization committed to nonviolence, must condemn this war on the grounds that war is not the way to solve social problems. Mass murder can never lead to constructive and creative govern-ment or to the creation of a democratic society."[66]

Mainstream civil rights leaders, including the NAACP's Roy Wilkins and Clarence Mitchell Jr. of the Leadership Conference on Civil Rights, opposed King's position and were keen to demonstrate their loyalty to the president. Bayard Rustin worried that opposition to the war would jeopardize the Great Society, but in fact it was the war and its growing costs that threatened the poverty programs. Prominent white allies of the civil rights movement warned King that it was "the greatest of mistakes to mix domestic civil rights and foreign policy," as Southern Regional Council director Paul Anthony put it. These sentiments were echoed by Congressman Emanuel Celler, a sponsor of the 1964 Civil Rights Act, who instructed King and other civil rights leaders to "stick to their own knitting" and refrain from "meddling with our military operations in that unhappy country." The New York Times reported that 41 percent of Harris Poll respondents said that when a civil rights group came out against the war it made them less in favor of civil rights for Negroes. Bob Moses, who had returned to Mississippi, received a notice in September 1966 to report to his draft board in New York. At thirty-one, he was five years past the mandated registration age. Unwilling to go to jail for defying the draft, Moses left for Montreal and eventually went to Tan-zania, where he would live for the next seven years.[67]

———

KING AND KENNEDY FOCUSED their attention that year on conditions in northern urban areas, testing strategies for mobilizing resources and com-munity efforts to confront the complex social realities plaguing poor, segre-gated communities. After considering several cities, King chose Chicago as the place to launch the SCLC's northern campaign. In the Senate, Kennedy would fight to maintain and expand antipoverty programs as funding for the war increasingly starved domestic priorities. He also sought more inno-vative ways to meet problems of poverty in northern cities, ultimately launching an ambitious urban redevelopment project.

On January 20, 21, and 22, Kennedy delivered a series of speeches in New York City concerning Black life in urban America. He gave these speeches at a luncheon of the Federation of Jewish Philanthropies, a community forum at the YMCA in Harlem, and a United Auto Workers dinner. The speeches emerged from weeks of discussions and reflected Kennedy's exposure to life in poor, segregated communities. He frequently walked in these neighbor-hoods and spoke with young people, deepening his awareness of, in his words, the "despair, the frustration, the futility and the alienation." The War on Poverty vastly expanded the possibilities for federal involvement, but the challenge of developing programs and approaches that worked remained. Civil disorders in Los Angeles and other cities, Kennedy said in the first speech, "were as much a revolt against official indifference, an explosion of frustration at inability to communicate and participate, as they were an uprising about inferior jobs and education and housing."[68]

Federal funding for programs was critical, but equally important was a fresh, open approach to the underpinnings of the urban crisis. Kennedy acknowledged that solutions would not be found overnight but insisted that "clearly, the present pace is unsatisfactory." He described how federal policies had contributed to the isolation of Black people in decaying neighborhoods, consigning them to "a continuing second-class citizenship." "Public housing had been a significant force in perpetuating segregation," he said. Many large urban renewal projects resulted in a ghettoized population shifting from one slum to another, and "this has not been wholly accidental." Meanwhile, federal loan and mortgage policies had encouraged white flight to the suburbs. Kennedy praised a proposal President Johnson introduced for federal aid to finance new town developments with a mandated percentage of low-cost housing outside the city and said steps had to be taken to make public housing "a truly metropolitan program," with sites throughout the city. Freedom to move and live where one chose was a fundamental right and a first step in breaking up urban slums. Kennedy advocated federal grants to private and public agencies as a stimulant to the advancement of fair housing.[69]

Breaking up the ghetto, while an ultimate goal, would take time. In the near term, Kennedy said, the focus must be on "a total effort of regeneration" that would rebuild blighted areas and transform them into "fully functioning urban communities." Kennedy cited President Johnson's recent pledge to "rebuild whole areas of our cities," which would be announced several days later as the Demonstration Cities Project (later called Model Cities), and saw his own plans as aligning with the president's new proposal. The framework Kennedy sketched out at the Harlem YMCA would guide his efforts going forward. Leaders of the community "who know what must be done better than white Americans can ever know . . . must take the lead," he said. The massive rebuilding effort would be staffed by neighborhood residents.

Kennedy had come to view employment as essential, saying that it was the key to better education. Only in a community where parents had jobs, he said, would children have the ability and desire to stay in school. Job training should be geared toward specific jobs that benefited the community—from the physical rehabilitation of the built environment to the setting up of clinics and other social services. He anticipated that, in addition to federal and state funds, support would come from business and philanthropic sources and thought that other sectors of the society, such as labor unions and universities, could also contribute in various ways. What was at stake, he said, "was not just the fate of the Negro in America, but the fate of all Americans."[70]

The day after the third speech, Kennedy told Adam Walinsky, "I want to do something about all this." The senator asked Walinsky to work with Tom Johnston, the director of Kennedy's New York City office, to see what they could put together.[71]

Two weeks later, Kennedy took a ninety-minute walking tour through the Bedford-Stuyvesant community of Brooklyn, guided by Elsie Richardson, a forty-four-year-old mother of three who worked as a school secretary and community leader. They were trailed by an assortment of city officials and reporters. Bed-Stuy, a large sprawling area of anywhere from 250,000 to 500,000 people depending on how you counted, was one of the poorest communities in New York. Roughly 80 percent of its population was African American, and on a cold, gray, winter day, Kennedy walked along crumbling sidewalks covered by wet snow, past dilapidated houses and piles of trash. Richardson took him into the apartment of a bedridden woman, who burst into tears when he entered her room. There were pictures of Jesus, Martin Luther King Jr., and John F. Kennedy on her wall. On Gates Avenue, where locals said the houses were not even worthy of the rats that infested them, Richardson rang several doorbells. Five-year-old Ricky Taggert emerged from one of the houses. When Kennedy asked him where his parents were and why he wasn't in school, the child promptly slammed the door. Richardson and Kennedy walked by boarded-up stores, empty lots strewn with litter, and crumbling tenements. Richardson also took Kennedy to the section of Bed-Stuy that housed a striving middle class, many of Caribbean descent, who had restored the Victorian brownstones that distinguished the neighborhood. She told him that these were the homes of leading community activists who were working to revitalize the neighborhood. They needed federal help.[72]

Bedford-Stuyvesant stood in the shadow of Harlem and its powerful Congressman Adam Clayton Powell Jr. Most of the federal funds and assistance going to Black advancement in New York City were channeled to Harlem. Bed-Stuy had not received any urban renewal funds in the past, and Lyndon Johnson's Demonstration Cities program stipulated that funds would go only to one community per city, making it likely that Bed-Stuy would, once again, miss out. There was great community cohesion and spirit in the neighborhood, manifested in the Central Brooklyn Coordinating Council (CBCC), a loose confederation of ninety local organizations dedicated to community improvement. But jobs continued to disappear, schools worsened, high school dropout rates were now over 50 percent, and the crime rate was rising. Two years earlier, Bed-Stuy had seen two nights of rioting after an off-duty police officer shot and killed fifteen-year-old James Powell. The promised War on Poverty had made few inroads in Bed-Stuy, and Elsie Richardson and leaders of the CBCC feared that conditions would soon spiral out of control.[73]

After the tour, Kennedy attended a meeting at the YMCA on Bedford Avenue organized by the CBCC. Bitterness and impatience poured out of those in attendance, and the frustration was directed at Kennedy. "I'm weary of study, Senator," said civil court judge David Jones. "The Negro people are angry, Senator, and judge that I am, I'm angry too. No one is helping us." The *New York Times* wrote that Kennedy sat "impassively during what were virtually harangues." Ruth Goring, the assistant Brooklyn Borough president, was "tired," she told him. "We have got to have something concrete now, not tomorrow, yesterday." When Elsie Richardson, the chair of the meeting reminded the group, "We're here to hear from our Senator and what he plans to do," Kennedy appeared to choke and utter "chee." He agreed that enough studies had been made and that there needed to be a coordinated approach to city, state, and federal agencies for money, and he said he would seek to make New York an exception in Johnson's Demonstration Cities Program.[74]

When he told Tom Johnston about what had happened, Kennedy was visibly annoyed. He said, "I could be smoking a cigar in Florida. I don't have to take that." Then he added, "We ought to really do something out there." The trouble was, he wasn't quite sure what. Johnston continued to work with the CBCC, and he and Walinsky explored ideas. Kennedy remained actively involved. The seed of the Bedford Stuyvesant Restoration Corporation had been planted.[75]

During the early months of 1966, Kennedy shared in the mix of frustration and urgency experienced by those working on the War on Poverty. It had been ten months since several million dollars in federal funds had been made available for a legal services program for the poor in New York City, and as of March not a single office had been set up. While allowing for the problems and challenges associated with setting up a new program, he felt a ten-month delay was "unforgiveable." "The time had come to ask publicly why the program has not begun," Kennedy said in a statement issued by his office. Even more "cruel and unforgivable," he charged, was the "immeasurable loss . . . for the thousands of citizens, whose lives would have been significantly improved by access to legal services and legal advice." Newly inaugurated Republican Mayor John Lindsay, who had been in office for ten weeks, agreed and assured Kennedy that his administration was close to resolving the administrative problems of the New York Legal Assistance Corporation. Kennedy said that if problems were not resolved by the end of the month, the conflict should be submitted to the Council against Poverty, the administering board of the Community Action Program, for arbitration.[76]

Of greater concern were President Johnson's proposed cuts in funding for major antipoverty programs. In a speech in Ellenville, New York, in April, Kennedy took the administration to task. Peter Edelman, who helped draft the speech, recalled how irritated—and concerned—Kennedy was. He was constantly thinking that the problems exposed by Watts required the government to do much, much more—but now the administration proposed instead to do less. Not only were major cuts proposed to federal aid to education that Congress had recently passed, specifically targeted at helping disadvantaged children, but school lunch and housing programs would also be impacted. Bobby wanted to be sure his listeners, most of whom supported the Vietnam War, did not use the war as an excuse to oppose these programs. He cited budget figures to demonstrate that the cost of the war need not stand in the way of "a responsibility to devote adequate resources and imagination to bringing the poorest fifth of our people into a position of greater participation in the wealth and politics of our country." He also reminded the upstate audience that African Americans were serving and dying in greater numbers in Vietnam.[77]

At the same time, Kennedy was beginning to broaden his focus beyond New York. As attorney general, he had become aware of the plight of migrant workers and had advocated for the establishment of a federally protected minimum wage. Now, as a member of the Migratory Labor Subcommittee of the Senate Labor Committee, Kennedy began to feel that new legislation was needed to help ensure decent working and living conditions for migrant laborers. When a representative of the American Farm Bureau came to Washington and testified against every proposal for protecting migratory workers, while admitting that his group of prosperous farmers had no program to provide decent working and living conditions for migrant laborers, Kennedy did not pull his punches. "To be opposed to a minimum wage, to be opposed to legislation that would limit the use of children," he told the witness, "to be opposed to collective bargaining . . . to oppose all without some alternative makes the rest of the arguments you have made senseless."[78]

Early in March 1966, Peter Edelman received a call from Jack Conway, assistant to Walter Reuther, the president of the United Auto Workers union. Reuther had persuaded the Migratory Labor Subcommittee to hold hearings in California, where the National Farm Workers Association (NFWA),

which later became the National Farm Workers Union (NFU), was leading
a major strike after owners had replaced migratory workers with nonunion
labor. Reuther wanted Kennedy to attend. Edelman walked into Kennedy's
office to tell him about the call and shared what he knew about Cesar Chavez,
the NFWA leader. Sure, Kennedy said, he would be glad to go. It was a hectic
time—the senator was in a major tangle with the Johnson administration
over the war, focused on getting something started in Bedford-Stuyvesant,
and busy with other matters in the Senate. On the flight out, he muttered
to Edelman, "Now why the hell am I dragging my ass all the way out to
California?"[79]

Kennedy arrived in time for the second day of hearings, on March 8. They
were held in a stifling, packed high school auditorium, and he was moved
by what he saw and heard. The testimony of the workers about their conditions, Edelman recalled, was very genuine, in contrast with the flimsy jus-
tifications of law enforcement officials for their repressive treatment and
"the blustering and not very convincing positions of the growers." Cesar
Chavez, the leader of the strike, recalled how Kennedy "immediately
asked very pointed questions of the growers; he had a way of disintegrating
their arguments by picking at the very simple questions." A high point of
the hearing came during the testimony of the local sheriff. Kennedy asked
the sheriff why he had arrested forty-four strikers who were engaged in
peaceful picketing. The sheriff responded that the strikebreakers threatened
to attack the picketers, so he had the likely cause of violence—the picketers—
removed. An incredulous Kennedy responded, "This is the most interesting concept. . . . How can you arrest somebody if they haven't violated
the law? . . . Can I suggest that the sheriff reconsider the procedures in
connection with these matters? Can I suggest during the luncheon period
the sheriff and the district attorney read the Constitution of the United
States?" The audience, filled with farmworkers and their supporters, erupted
in applause.[80]

As they stepped outside for the lunch break, Kennedy and Cesar Chavez
met in the parking lot. "It was a riveting scene," Edelman recalled. The senator and the union leader fell into a deep conversation, while surrounded by
others and followed by the press. Edelman overheard snippets as the two
discussed the conditions of the farm workers, the difficulties facing the
strikers when they could not count on the protection of the law, the nature
of nonviolence, and more. In explaining the source of Chavez's intelligence
and appeal, a biographer noted how "he read, he questioned, he listened, he
learned"—qualities that also characterized Kennedy. Both men shared a
deeply felt Catholicism that informed the moral and ethical code that guided
their public lives. Kennedy's immediate bonding with Chavez, Edelman later

commented, "was typical of the intuitive, nonlinear and even existential way in which he operated."[81]

On the second day of their trip, Kennedy and Edelman visited the headquarters of the NFWA in Delano before going to see the strikers. Once the two men returned to Washington from California, efforts to help migrant workers were added to Peter Edelman's already full agenda. Kennedy pushed harder on getting minimum wages for farm workers, worked to get collective bargaining legislation enacted, urged the Justice Department and Immigration and Naturalization Service to reform policies concerning green cards, and investigated the conditions of migrant laborers in New York State.[82]

On March 19, less than two weeks after his return from California, Bobby and Ethel were on a private plane headed to Oxford, Mississippi. He would spend the day visiting the scenes of two of the most challenging episodes of his brother's administration: the integration of the University of Mississippi and the University of Alabama. RFK had been surprised to receive an invitation from several law students at Ole Miss. "What do they say down there? Am I just going to be booed? . . . Will there be any common ground at all?," Edelman remembers Kennedy asking. He had Edelman check with several people in Mississippi, including Josh Morse, the dean of the law school. Edelman reported back that everyone said the university was changing and there were people who really wanted to see Kennedy there. He was not convinced—but there was no way to know unless he went. He finally decided to go and accepted an invitation to Alabama as well. Once it was announced that he was going to Mississippi, the FBI began receiving reports of death threats. A heavy guard of FBI agents and state police accompanied Kennedy during his time in Mississippi.[83]

More than five thousand people crowded into the Coliseum at Ole Miss to hear Kennedy, and three thousand turned out to hear him at the University of Alabama's Foster Auditorium, whose doorway George Wallace had so famously blocked three years earlier. Kennedy was greeted enthusiastically in both places, while elsewhere in the state many "seethed anew," noted *Times* reporter Roy Reed, at the presence of the man who had directed the desegregation of their flagship universities. Former governor Ross Barnett quipped that Kennedy was "a hypocritical, left-wing beatnik without a beard." Tellingly, since James Meredith had had the courage to desegregate the school nearly four years earlier, only 15 Black students, in a student body of 5,600, were enrolled at Ole Miss.

Kennedy told students in Mississippi and Alabama that he had not come there to talk about the problems of the South; he had come there to talk about the problems confronting the whole nation. "Racial injustice and poverty, ignorance and concern for world peace are to be found in the streets of

New York, Chicago and Los Angeles as well as the towns and farmlands of Mississippi," he said. He talked about a changing world that was challenging today's youth: "In such a world—such a fantastic and dangerous world—we will not find answers in the old dogmas, by repeating worn out slogans, or fighting on ancient battlegrounds after the real struggle has moved on." In the questions afterward, one of the students asked Kennedy how the Democrats would regain strength in Mississippi, given that Barry Goldwater had won 88 percent of the vote in the 1964 presidential campaign. "I think it's going to be damned tough," Kennedy replied. The students laughed. He added, "I think I made a major contribution to that difficulty."[84]

Two days after his return to Washington, Kennedy received word that his application for a visa to travel to South Africa had been approved. He and Martin Luther King Jr. had both been invited by the National Union of South African Students (NUSAS) to speak on separate occasions during the spring and summer of 1966. NUSAS, the largest nonracial group in South Africa, had long been harassed by the South African government as communistic and unpatriotic. Not surprisingly, King's application for a visa was refused; but Kennedy's was reluctantly approved.

The senator had been invited to address the organization's Day of Affirmation and Human Freedom, an annual event started in 1962 to protest new legislation restricting nonwhites from attending colleges or universities that had previously been racially mixed. His address was sure to draw international attention, but denying a visa to a sitting US senator and possible future president had potential ramifications that the South African government was not willing to risk. Shortly after Kennedy's visa was approved, the South African government denied visas to the forty American newspaper and television correspondents who had been assigned to cover the trip. In an official statement, the government explained that South Africa was "not prepared to allow the visit to turn into a publicity stunt."[85]

Robert Kennedy's visit to South Africa would be a stark introduction to a society completely structured on racial caste and test his capacity to support those struggling for justice and freedom under the most brutal circumstances.

CHAPTER TWELVE

Suppose God Is Black

||||

ROBERT AND ETHEL KENNEDY ARRIVED in Johannesburg just before midnight on June 4, 1966, accompanied by Angela Novello and Adam Walinsky. "The airport was swarming with white, black, brown Indian, every hue of skin," recalled Margaret Marshall of the National Union of South African Students, who had been sent to meet him. She had never seen anything like it. Kennedy came into the nonwhite area, where a podium had been placed for him to speak. The crowd cheered, and students hoisted signs exclaiming "We love you, Bobby!" A smaller group heckled and booed; one person waved a sign that read "Yankee go home."[1]

Bobby, smiling with Ethel at his side, told the packed crowd that he was glad to be there, adding, "I am particularly delighted that, as in my own country, there is a divergent point of view." He recognized that the race problem was more difficult in South Africa than in the United States, but he stressed the common ground: "We are facing the problem of living together regardless of our origin . . . for the benefit of all people. Both our countries face the same problem of surviving in a changing world."[2]

Ian Robertson, president of the National Union of South African Students, who had invited Kennedy to South Africa, could not come to the airport to greet him. The twenty-one-year-old law student had been "banned" for five years under the Suppression of Communism Act, which meant that he was confined to his home, limited to seeing one person at a time, and forbidden from speaking to the press. Margaret Marshall, the student group's vice president, would be Kennedy's guide for the next five days. She found him concerned and solicitous, not wanting to get anyone into trouble. Our attitude was "don't protect us," she recalled. "We wanted him to inspire us and to condemn racism and injustice."[3]

At the time of Kennedy's visit, the apartheid system was fully entrenched in South Africa, where four million whites ruled over twenty-five million people categorized as Blacks, Coloureds, and Asians. A resettlement policy had forced millions of Black South Africans and Coloured out of their homes and into designated areas. Pass laws limited and regulated their movement. For his "fight against racial discrimination" and advocacy of nonviolent methods, African National Congress (ANC) president Chief Albert Luthuli had won the Nobel Peace Prize in 1960—the first African to receive the honor. After leading the Defiance Campaign, a mixed-race movement that challenged the pass laws and voting restrictions, the Zulu chief was exiled to a remote rural area in Natal and put under house arrest. Nelson Mandela, the leader of the ANC's military arm, had advocated more direct resistance and was now in prison on Robben Island. The ANC and other political organizations had been banned, driving the anti-apartheid struggle underground. Robert Kennedy's trip marked the first visit to South Africa by anyone of stature who was known to be on the side of those under the heel of apartheid.

The prime minister, Hendrik Verwoerd, had refused to see Kennedy and would not permit other government officials to meet with him. The senator met with editors of Afrikaner newspapers and businessmen, clergy and community leaders, antiapartheid activists including the novelist Alan Paton, political leader Helen Suzman, and Chief Albert Luthuli. Kennedy spoke at four universities and visited the sprawling township of Soweto. His willingness to listen and his honesty and forthrightness were appealing, even to those who disagreed with him.[4]

Adam Walinsky marveled at how the crowds turning out to see Kennedy grew and evolved. At the beginning "his only crowds were the students. . . . But somewhere as the thing started to get across . . . there were just thousands of ordinary citizens . . . not just Englishmen but Afrikaners, coming out there into the streets to cheer and listen and to shout." Kennedy was "pressed into making countless impromptu talks," the New York Times reported, to men and women who gathered along his route or crowded around him in the street. One evening, after speaking at the University of Natal, he stopped to speak with a group of Black South Africans and led them in singing "We Shall Overcome."[5]

On June 6, his second full day in the country, Kennedy flew from Johannesburg to Cape Town, where he would deliver the "Day of Affirmation Address." As his plane banked over the city, he could see Robben Island, where Nelson Mandela was held in solitary confinement. He would later describe looking out at the "home of more than 2,000 political prisoners," Black and white, professors and farmers, "advocates of nonviolence and organizers of revolution," all "bound in the same bleak brotherhood" because "they believed in freedom [and] dared to lead the struggle against the government's official policy of apartheid." After landing in Cape Town, he visited Ian Robertson in his small apartment. Assuming the place was bugged, Kennedy suggested that Robertson turn on the record player, while Kennedy stomped on the floor to loosen any possible listening devices. Kennedy gave Robertson a copy of *Profiles in Courage,* inscribed by Jackie Kennedy.[6]

As many as fifteen thousand people were waiting when Bobby reached the University of Cape Town later that afternoon. There was an enormous buzz, recalled John Daniels of NUSAS, making the event feel like a rally. It took Kennedy half an hour to make his way through the crowd and into the hall where the program was being held. Loudspeakers brought his speech to the thousands gathered on the steps and concourse outside of the packed hall. Kennedy's address that evening has been called one of his best. He opened by describing a country that had been "settled by the Dutch in the mid-seventeenth century, then taken over by the British, and at last independent; a land in which the native inhabitants were at first subdued, but relations with whom remain a problem to this day . . . a land which was once an importer of slaves, and now must struggle to wipe out the last trace of that former bondage. I refer, of course to the United States of America."[7]

He praised the work of NUSAS and expressed regret that Ian Robertson could not be with them. An empty chair on the platform symbolized Robertson's absence. The senator spoke about the meaning of freedom and democracy, "the sacred rights of western society" and the constant difficulty of acting on these ideals. He reflected on the two-century-long struggle of "my own country . . . to overcome the self-imposed handicap of prejudice and discrimination," which was "repugnant to the theory and to the command of our Constitution." The United States had made significant progress in the previous five years, he said, noting the achievements of African Americans and Martin Luther King Jr.'s distinction as the second American of African descent to win the Nobel Peace Prize. But "much, much more remains to be done." Millions lacked access to jobs; thousands every day were "denied their full and equal rights under law; and the violence of the disinherited, the insulted and the injured looms over the streets of Harlem and of Watts and of Southside Chicago." The message, so relevant to the multitude that had gathered to hear him, was clearly stated. "The road toward equality and freedom is not easy, and great cost and danger march alongside us," he said. "Still, even in the turbulence of protest and struggle is greater hope for the future, as men learn to claim and achieve for themselves the rights formerly petitioned by others."[8]

They lived in a "revolutionary world," Kennedy said. Discrimination and injustice, "the inadequacy of human compassion," and insensitivity to suffering were manifest in different ways. "Wealth is lavished on armaments everywhere in the world. These are different evils; but they are the common works of man." New technology was continually bringing nations closer together, and "our new closeness is stripping away the false masks, the illusion of differences at the root of injustice and hate and war." The idea that one's "common humanity is enclosed in the tight circle of those who share his town or his views or the color of his skin" is a "dark and poisoning superstition." Kennedy looked to the young of the world "to strip the last remnants of that ancient, cruel belief from the civilization of man." He described youth not so much as a time of life as "a state of mind, a temper of will, a quality of imagination, a predominance of courage over timidity, of the appetite for adventure over the life of ease."

He empathized with the young people in South Africa devoted to justice and the well-being of their fellow human beings and noted how "very alone" they had to feel with "your problems and difficulties." He urged them to take heart that their struggles connected them to the struggles being waged by men and women around the world. "Few will have the greatness to bend history," he observed, " but each of us can work to change some small portion of events, and in the total of all these acts will be written the history of this generation." In the most quoted line of the speech, Kennedy said, "Each time a man stands up for an ideal, or acts to improve the lot of others, or strikes out against injustice, he sends forth a tiny ripple of hope, and crossing each other from a million different centers of energy and daring those ripples build a current that can sweep down the mightiest walls of oppression and resistance."[9]

When the speech was over, there was silence. Margaret Marshall recalled that Kennedy looked around him, "as if to say, was the speech okay?" Then the roar of applause came, and she could see that he was relieved. For Marshall, "the speech changed my life." Before she had felt "useless and isolated," but Kennedy's words had made her feel the essential role of individual action and a connectedness with other struggles for justice and human betterment. The next morning, the *Cape Times* printed the entire speech under the headline, "15,000 Acclaim Call to Youth," quickly spreading Kennedy's words to South Africans.[10]

The following day, the senator spoke at Stellenbosch University, a leading university for Afrikaner students, where all but two of South Africa's prime ministers had been educated. Everyone "expected a cool, if not hostile reception," Kennedy later wrote. "But we were greeted in the dining hall by the rolling sound of thunder—the pounding of soup spoons on tables, the students' customary applause. It was clear that although many differed with me, they were ready to exchange views." He made a brief speech and said,

"I am here in South Africa to listen as well as talk, less to lecture than to learn." His comments touched on history and growing demands for freedom and justice in their country and around the world. He appealed to the students of Stellenbosch to meet the challenges of their times "with the light of reason—with fact and logic and careful thought, unblinkered by the shades of prejudice and myth." "Pour on the holy water," one student quipped.

A lively discussion followed. Several students defended apartheid, saying that it would eventually produce two nations, one white and one Black. "Did the Black people have a choice?" Kennedy asked. "How would they live in areas whose soil was already exhausted and which had no industry?" And what of the two million "Coloured" people, neither white nor black? "Do you think you can make a worthwhile assessment of the country on such a brief visit?" one student asked. Kennedy said he wasn't going "to leave here as an expert," but he had come in good faith and insofar as possible, "in view of the government's refusal to see me, made a conscientious effort to know as much about South Africa as I can." The students appreciated the open exchange of views and gave him an ovation at the end of the discussion.[11]

At dawn on June 8, Bobby and Ethel flew by helicopter to Groutville, a remote area of Natal, where Albert Luthuli had been banished by the government. The sixty-five-year-old Zulu chief was a revered political leader who had been charged with "promoting feelings of hostility between the races." He could not be quoted, and no photographs of him could be published.[12]

Two government agents hovered close by. To speak privately, the two men walked out through the fields surrounding the home. They discussed the racial problems of their countries and the possibilities of nonviolent change. Luthuli conveyed deep hurt and despair when he spoke about conditions in South Africa. "What are they doing to my countrymen, to my country," he asked. "Can't they see that men of all races can work together—and that the alternative is terrible disaster for us all?" When they returned to the house, Kennedy gave Luthuli a portable record player and played a recording of President Kennedy's 1963 civil rights speech. They listened in silence together, along with Ethel and Luthuli's daughter. "At the end," Kennedy recalled, "Chief Luthuli, deeply moved, shook his head." He was "one of the most impressive men I have ever met," Kennedy later said. "His life was gentle, and the elements / so mix'd in him that Nature might stand up / And say to the world, 'This was a man!'" he wrote, quoting from Shakespeare's *Julius Caesar*.[13]

Later that day, Kennedy visited Soweto, South Africa's largest Black township, outside Johannesburg, where an estimated one million people lived surrounded by barbed wire. The senator was instantly exposed to the cruelty, inhumanity, and exploitation Luthuli had described. Larry Shore, then a junior high school student in Johannesburg, recalled how the visit "absolutely amazed me." White people did not go to Soweto. An antiapartheid activist might—but secretly and at night. Kennedy "went openly, he didn't ask permission, he just went, without any security." Kennedy spent several hours walking through the township, which he described as "a dreary concentration camp, with a curfew, limits on recreation, no home ownership and a long list of regulations whose violation could cause eviction." The people of Soweto gave him a joyous and enthusiastic reception. "I found myself making speeches from steps of churches, from the roof of a car and standing on a chair in the middle of a school playground."[14]

His last public event was at the University of Witwatersrand, a liberal university, where he was asked to address the charge that Black Africans were too barbarous to be entrusted with power. "It was not the black man of Africa," Kennedy responded, "who invented and used poison gas and the atomic bomb, who sent six million men and women and children to gas ovens and used their bodies for fertilizer." No race or people, white or Black, he observed, is without fault or cruelty. What must be understood and acted upon was the fact that Black and white were inescapably bound together by virtue of their common humanity. Hope lay in the "gift of reason." "Those who cut themselves off from ideas and clashing convictions . . . encourage the forces of violence and passion which are the only alternative to reason." But, asked another student, "how do you keep up dialogue with people who change the rules of debate to suit themselves, tell you what you can talk about, insist upon being the judge and referee, and ban you when you say too much for their liking?" Kennedy paused and then said, "The only alternative is to give up and admit you're beaten. I don't know about that. I have never admitted I am beaten."[15]

Kennedy and his party left Johannesburg the next morning. Over the next ten days, he would visit Tanzania, Kenya, and Ethiopia, but South Africa left the most profound mark on him. "A great shaft of daylight was let into the air-conditioned comfort and concrete corridors of the bastion that nearly everybody believed, or feared, or hoped was shut tight against such natural illumination," wrote Anthony Delius in the *Cape Times* in the wake of Kennedy's visit. Alan Paton said the senator was "like a fresh wind from a wider world." The *Rand Daily Mail* suggested, "suddenly it is possible to breathe again without feeling choked." "The Day We Will Never Forget" headlined the story by Black journalist Juby Mayet in the Sowetan newspaper, the *Golden City Post*. "He made us feel, more than ever, that it was still worthwhile, despite our great difficulties, to fight for the things we believed in," she wrote, "that justice, freedom, equality for all men are things we should strive for so our children should have a better life."[16]

Kennedy's visit stumped government officials, who had predicted it would be a publicity stunt to further his widely discussed presidential ambition. There was no more talk of that, reported the *Rand Daily Mail.* Even his most bitter critics conceded Kennedy had handled himself discreetly. While he preached brotherhood, he did not cast judgment. He kept stressing that the United States has "many long miles to go" in trying to make racial equality work. "He has stirred up ideals long in disuse. He has started conversations among us and about us."[17]

Looking back years later, Margaret Marshall recalled "how young and energetic he was." Kennedy was "easy to talk to, a great listener," and "he would talk to anybody." It struck her that he learned a huge amount during his five days in South Africa. For her and others, his visit was transforming. He reminded us, she said, "that we are not alone. . . . He put us back into the great sweep of history. He reset the moral compass, not so much by attacking apartheid but by simply talking about justice and freedom and dignity, words none of us had heard in, it seemed like, an eternity. He didn't go through the white liberals, he connected straight, standing on a car. . . . Nobody had done that. How simple it was! He was not afraid."[18]

Before leaving Johannesburg on the morning of June 9, Kennedy said he would gladly accept the invitations he had received to visit the country again the following year. Three days later, *Die Beeld,* Johannesburg's Afrikaans-language newspaper, reported that the South African government would not allow Senator Kennedy to return for another visit.[19]

At home, the *Chicago Defender* praised Kennedy for helping to "refocus attention on African issues and problems which the war in Vietnam had threatened to obscure." Despite the obstacles placed in the senator's way by the South African government, the paper noted, he made his views known to a broad segment of the population. "Since he was not an official guest of the government, Kennedy felt no compunction in airing his criticism of the country's seemingly insufferable racial policy known as apartheid." He brought hope, *the Defender* concluded, maybe not of better days presently, "but of mounting world sentiment against the discredited notion of racial inequality before the law."[20]

WHILE KENNEDY WAS IN AFRICA, the March against Fear in Mississippi, a pivotal event in the long struggle to secure the vote, was making news. Significantly, the march would be the staging ground where the call for Black Power was introduced. The year 1966 was the first election year since passage of the Voting Rights Act, which authorized the federal government to send federal observers to monitor voter registration in areas where fewer

Senator Kennedy tours Bedford Stuyvesant with Donald Benjamin on February 5, 1966. The visit led to the establishment of the Bedford Stuyvesant Restoration project at the end of the year. Kennedy poured his energies as senator into urban regeneration and tackling the roots of urban poverty and crime. Library of Congress, Prints and Photographs Division, LC-USZ62-133299

Bobby and Ethel received an enthusiastic welcome in Soweto on their five-day visit to South Africa in June 1966. "I found myself making speeches from steps of churches, from the roof of a car, and standing on a chair in the middle of a school playground," Kennedy wrote on his return. Courtesy of Peter Magubane

Willie Ricks, Bernard Lee, Martin Luther King Jr., Stokely Carmichael, Andrew Young, and Hosea Williams during the Mississippi March against Fear in June 1966. Carmichael's call for "Black Power" became the big story of the march.
Bob Fitch Photography Archives, Department of Special Collections and University Archives, Stanford University Libraries

Unita Blackwell and Fannie Lou Hamer testifying before a special Senate subcommittee hearing in Jackson, Mississippi, on April 10, 1967. They described the harassment and pressures directed against the Child Development Group of Mississippi, a pioneering Head Start program. © James Lucas Estate

Kennedy, a member of the Senate subcommittee evaluating the War on Poverty in Mississippi, listens to testimony in Jackson.
© James Lucas Estate

(left) Visiting a Head Start program in Greenville, Mississippi, following the Senate hearings on the War on Poverty. © James Lucas Estate

(below) Marian Wright took Kennedy to see the conditions in which families ▸ the Delta were living. He was shocked ▸ the hunger and poverty he witnessed and, upon returning to Washington, pressed for federal action.
AP Photo/Jack Thornell

Kennedy, with Peter Edelman and Dr. Kenneth Dean, after visiting a home in Greenville, Mississippi. © James Lucas Estate

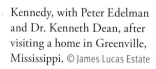

The Watts Writers Workshop sponsored a rally for Kennedy in Los Angeles on March 24, 1968, a week after he announced his candidacy for president. An estimated 5,000 people attended. AP Photo

Bobby and Ethel walked through a burnt-out neighborhood in Washington, DC, with Reverend Walter Fauntroy on April 7, 1968, three days after Martin Luther King Jr.'s assassination sparked explosive protests across the country. AP Photo/Bob Schultz

Bobby speaks to supporters in the rain outside his campaign headquarters in the Near North Side of Omaha, Nebraska, on May 13, 1968. Though not pictured here, the headquarters displayed a sign reading "Kennedy White but Alright / the one before opened the door." Bettmann Archives/Getty Image

Campaigning in Hamtramck, Michigan, a Polish-American community abutting Detroit, which had grown up around the local Dodge auto plant, then in decline. Kennedy moved easily across tight urban boundaries and was well received in white ethnic areas. Andrew Sacks/Sax Pix

Kennedy reaches out to five-year-old Sybil Turner at the intersection of 12th and Clairmount in Detroit on May 15, 1968, just blocks from the heart of the riots.
Andrew Sacks/Sax Pix

Just before midnight on June 4, 1968, Bobby addressed supporters, with Ethel at his side, after winning the California primary. Delores Huerta of the United Farm Workers is to the left, Rosey Grier stands in the back, and Jesse Unruh and Paul Schrade, who was shot with Kennedy that night, are on the right.
Julian Wasser/The LIFE Picture Collection/Getty Images

More than a million people lined the railroad tracks from New York to Washington, waiting for Robert Kennedy's funeral train.
Bettmann Archives/Getty Images

Residents of Resurrection City, the encampment of the Poor People's Campaign, joined in singing "The Battle Hymn of the Republic," as the hearse carrying Robert Kennedy's body stopped before the Lincoln Memorial. Bettmann Archives/Getty Images

than 50 percent of the nonwhite population had registered to vote. Nevertheless, very few federal observers were sent to the South. Martin Luther King Jr. and other civil rights activists insisted that the Justice Department send federal observers to rural majority Black areas where people had experienced harassment and intimidation. Attorney General Nicholas Katzenbach responded that this was a job for local organizers. Privately, Katzenbach told President Johnson that federal observers were "not going into any but the most difficult counties" and that he "was attempting to do the least I can safely do without upsetting civil rights groups."[21]

On June 5, James Meredith, who had desegregated the University of Mississippi four years earlier, initiated a "Walk against Fear" from Memphis to promote voter registration and defy racism. On the second day, he was shot and wounded by a sniper. Three civil rights organizations—SCLC, SNCC, and CORE—then continued the march through Mississippi, represented by Martin Luther King Jr., Stokely Carmichael, and Floyd McKissick, respectively. Anywhere from 30 to 250 people participated at various points in the March against Fear as it made its way through small towns and communities in rural Mississippi—Greenwood, Belzoni, Yazoo City, Canton—places familiar to Carmichael from his work during Freedom Summer.[22]

Stokely Carmichael had drawn national attention three weeks earlier when he had replaced John Lewis as chairman of the Student Nonviolent Coordinating Committee. One of the group's original members, Carmichael was born in Trinidad but grew up in the Bronx, where he attended the Bronx High School of Science. In 1960, when he was a freshman at Howard University, the sit-ins drew him into the civil rights movement. He joined the Freedom Rides the next year and served fifty-three days in the Mississippi State Penitentiary at Parchman. Carmichael continued his studies at Howard, but he started going to Mississippi every summer to work with SNCC on voter registration efforts. When the Democratic Party refused to seat the Mississippi Freedom Democratic Party at the 1964 convention, Carmichael and others rejected the integrationist approach championed by John Lewis and Martin Luther King Jr. and concluded that Blacks could achieve power only through their own political organizations."[23]

In spring 1965, as SNCC's senior field secretary in Alabama, Carmichael helped set up a new independent political party in Lowndes County. Eighty percent of the population of the county was Black, and no Black citizen had voted for nearly seventy-five years. The passage of the Voting Rights Act that summer had opened up new possibilities for building a Black political base. The Lowndes County Freedom Party chose a snarling black panther as its symbol—a fitting contrast to the Alabama Democratic Party's white rooster accompanied by the statement "white supremacy for the right." Carmichael brushed aside suggestions that he was antiwhite, explaining that "it was time for Blacks to work for themselves; to prove once and for all, that Blacks could handle Black political affairs without assistance from whites." The enthusiastic response to Carmichael's efforts raised the hope that the Lowndes County Freedom Party might be a model for organizers in other Black Belt counties and elevated Carmichael's profile as a dynamic leader within SNCC.[24]

When SNCC activists came together for a weeklong conference in Kingston Springs, Tennessee, in May 1966, the organization was at a crossroads. SNCC had steadily evolved from its beginnings as a group founded by college students at the peak of the sit-in movement in 1960. As organizers moved into rural Black communities in Mississippi, Alabama, Louisiana, Georgia, and other parts of the South, the poverty the activists witnessed, the violence and lawlessness that met their efforts, and the passion and commitment of the local people who joined their ranks transformed the movement. At the same time, "the totally unexpected rebellions in Harlem, Watts, Chicago and Philadelphia had a big impact on our thinking," SNCC activist Cleveland Sellers recalled. Many within SNCC felt that integration did not offer a solution to the problems most African Americans faced. John Lewis, who had led the organization since 1963, represented the values and beliefs that had originally inspired SNCC's creation, but for many, Stokely Carmichael spoke to current realities and offered a potent vision, more attuned to the needs of the moment. In a hotly contested election, Stokely Carmichael was elected as the new chairman on May 14.[25]

The outcome of the election drew a strong reaction from the national media. In a front-page story the *Washington Post* announced, "SNCC Dumps 2 Top Leaders, Names 'Black Panther' Chairman." In an editorial, titled "Black Supremacists," the *Post* focused on Carmichael's claim that "integration is irrelevant" and his call to "all black Americans to begin building independent political, economic and cultural institutions that they will control and use as instruments of social change in this country." The *Post* described this as "outright nihilism," countering that integration "is indispensable to social justice," a claim that, in 1966, begged for further explanation. When a *New York Times* reporter pressed Martin Luther King Jr. to comment on Carmichael's stance, King replied that, while he did not support the separatist idea, he could understand it and saw it as a reflection of "disenchantment with the whole structure of our society."[26]

Carmichael's presence on the march, in addition to King's, ensured that the march would attract national media attention. At the outset, Mississippi governor Paul Johnson, in keeping with his promise to the Johnson administration, provided twenty Highway Patrol cars to accompany the marchers. The Louisiana-based Deacons for Defense and Justice, an armed self-defense organization, provided protection for the marchers at night, guarding their campsite and monitoring possible ambush sites along the highway. John Doar, who had become assistant attorney general for civil rights, remained close by as the group made its way to Jackson. The marchers and voter registration teams faced harassment by the police. Whites, many armed, gathered along the route and outside marchers' encampments at night, shouting threats and insults. The group's notable success in registering voters in Grenada—doubling the number of Black voters literally overnight—caught the governor's attention. Charging that the march had "turned into a voter registration campaign," he cut the number of patrol cars from twenty down to four just as the group was approaching Greenwood.[27]

On June 16, the marchers reached Greenwood, site of the violent showdown over voter registration three years earlier and the center of SNCC activity in Mississippi. It was "like a homecoming," Carmichael recalled. Administrators at the Stone Street Elementary School, the local Black school, had agreed that the marchers could camp on school grounds that evening. The city council then announced that marchers would not be permitted to camp on public property. When the marchers proceeded to set up camp, local police confronted Stokely Carmichael and several others, accused them of trespassing, and demanded that they leave. When Carmichael refused, he was hauled off to jail—the twenty-seventh time he had been arrested since the summer of 1961. Bailed out in time for the late evening rally, Carmichael was angry and full of emotion: "I looked over that crowd, that valiant, embattled community of old friends and fellow strugglers. I told them what they knew, that they could only depend on themselves, their own organized collective strength." He told them to register and vote and said "the only rights they were likely to get were the ones they took for themselves. I raised the call for Black Power again."[28]

The call to Black Power had become an organizing framework for many SNCC activists and others who had long been rallying poor Black people in the Mississippi Delta. The Mississippi Freedom Democratic Party's treatment at the Democratic National Convention two years earlier had, for many, demonstrated the futility of seeking to operate within the Democratic Party. The focus had shifted to building up Black institutions and Black political organizations. SNCC's more militant turn sparked disagreement among civil rights groups and activists, as did the organization's focus on building up Black institutions and political power. But what Carmichael was saying in Greenwood did not really mark a new direction. "The only difference," he recalled, "was this time the national media were there."[29]

Arlie Schardt, who covered the march for *Time,* remembered that the call for Black Power prompted "a lot of confusion." What "Black Power" meant was never clearly explained and was open to broad interpretation. Several of the reporters following the march had come from around the country and were "new to this beat." "For some whites, for their own reasons, they wanted to take this as a signal of Black hostility and enmity," Schardt explained, "and there were others who simply didn't know how to read what was being said."[30]

Local white hostility intensified as the marchers moved on. One of the more chilling encounters occurred in Philadelphia, on the second anniversary of the murders of James Chaney, Andrew Goodman, and Michael Schwerner. After saying a prayer outside the county jail, where the three men had been held, King led several hundred marchers toward the courthouse square. Deputy Sheriff Cecil Price stepped out and blocked his path. "You're the one who had Schwerner and those fellows in jail?" King quietly asked the man responsible for their abduction and murder. The sheriff said yes, in a prideful tone. King went on to lead a prayer service in the courthouse square, where he was surrounded by a taunting mob that grew to around three hundred. He spoke about the three young men and their sacrifice. As whites heckled and shouted, he said, "I believe in my heart that the murderers are somewhere around me at this moment." King recalled later that he had "yielded to the real possibility of the inevitability of death." Later that day, a shaken King told reporters that Philadelphia was "the worst city I have ever seen. There is a complete reign of terror here."[31]

But that was before Canton, the last stop before Jackson. John Doar had been monitoring the march and now he wired President Johnson asking for federal protection. A presidential aide, brushing Doar off, told him that the state police would handle matters. Once again, the marchers had arranged to set up their tents on the grounds of the local Black school. Canton officials refused permission. After an early evening rally at the courthouse, which drew more than a thousand local Black people, Carmichael insisted that the marchers proceed to the school grounds and set up camp. By the time they had covered the fifteen blocks to the school grounds, the crowd had grown to more than three thousand. Sixty-one state troopers were lined up, waiting, as John Dittmer writes, "in full battle gear and carrying nightsticks, carbines, automatic shotguns, and pistols." Many in the crowd left, but around 2,500 remained as the marchers began setting up the camp.[32]

A state trooper issued a warning at around 8:30 p.m. stating that the marchers were not permitted to set up tents and would be removed if they did. Two minutes later, the police put on gas masks and began firing tear gas across the field. As people scattered, the troopers kept firing and chased the retreating crowd with nightsticks and guns. A journalist on the scene reported, "they came in stomping behind the gas, gun-butting and kicking the men, women and children. They were not arresting, they were pun-ishing." Dittmer described the scene in graphic detail—the violence, the beatings, the screams. After fifteen minutes, the field had been cleared and the area "resembled a zone after battle." Stokely Carmichael was near col-lapse. King told the press: "This is the very state patrol that Lyndon Johnson said today would protect us. Anyone who will use gas bombs on women and children can't and won't protect anybody." Dittmer noted, "the police riot in Canton equaled in ferocity the assault on marchers at the Selma bridge a year earlier." This time, however, the administration had little to say beyond Attorney General Katzenbach's comment that the incident was under investigation.[33]

As many as fifteen thousand people gathered outside the capitol building in Jackson to mark the end of the march. Privately, King regretted that Carmichael's call for Black Power had sparked a debate that dominated coverage of the march. For King, the larger significance and meaning of the march was clear. Over the course of ten days, the determined band of marchers and the local people they met along the way had claimed the rights long struggled for, facing down intimidation and violence. Some ten thou-sand people had joined in, and the group had helped register nearly four thousand voters. The march and rally, King told the crowd, "will go down as the greatest demonstration for freedom ever held in the state of Missis-sippi." But his focus was trained on a deep crisis facing the country, one most Americans seemed incapable of acknowledging. In a sober assessment of ra-cial conditions, he offered a variation of his earlier address in front of Lin-coln Memorial, declaring that his dream "had turned into a nightmare." Too many Black people were perishing from poverty "in a vast ocean of pros-perity," and too much injustice remained in the administration of the law. For the media, as King suspected, the big story was the ideological split in the movement defined by the call for Black Power—a controversy completely lost on the thousands who had cheered King and Carmichael in Jackson that day.[34]

King returned to Chicago to a struggle that rivaled the one he had faced in the South. Racial tensions would boil over into a riot on the city's West Side that summer. In response to endless press queries, King explained that he did not embrace a Black Power philosophy. Although they may have dis-agreed on strategy, however, King and Carmichael had strengthened their personal relationship over the course of the march. King "understood us better, more sympathetically, and was much closer to us in spirit than people think," Carmichael said. King remained concerned that the slogan of "Black Power" and the reactions it sparked would alienate sympathetic whites and distract the news media. He often answered queries about Black Power by pointing to the poverty and injustices endured by Black Americans, a situation that, he said, "demanded a militant thrust forward."[35]

———

THE FOURTH OF JULY WEEKEND, 1966, marked the start of the third successive "long hot summer" (in the media's often-used phrase) in the United States of the 1960s. Racial disturbances erupted into violence in America's heartland—Omaha, Nebraska, and Des Moines, Iowa. The trouble in Omaha started on a sweltering summer night, after two police cars pulled into the area of North Twenty-Fourth and Lake Streets, the center of the Black community. A crowd of young people had gathered there for most of the day. The police came to answer a complaint. After the officers pulled out bats and told the group to disperse, the youth attacked the officers with bottles and fireworks, demolishing the police cars. Three days of street battles followed.

Nebraska governor Frank Morrison described the Near North Side neighborhood "as an environment unfit for habitation." The mayor, A. V. Sorensen, initially thought racial conditions had nothing to do with the rioting, but he changed his mind after meeting with Black residents. The troubles, Mayor Sorenson said, lay with Black resentment "of police brutality, lack of recreation facilities, and lack of jobs" and with the failure of the federal government to provide promised aid for housing. As cities exploded, the *New York Times* worried that no federal agency had been established to deal with what had become "a regular phenomenon." Martin Luther King Jr. feared that most whites failed "to grasp the depths and dimensions of racial injustice."[36]

Press coverage of racial disturbances that summer fixated on divisions among civil rights groups and the rising militancy of various factions. The shout of "Black Power," echoing from Mississippi early in mid-June, would be associated with separatism, violence, and "antiwhite" prejudice, amplifying the tendency to shift the blame to Black people for the escalating racial crisis. For much of the mainstream media, the sensationalized coverage of Black Power and the widely reported tensions among civil rights groups drained away any interest in the underlying problems. "The battle is underway for the minds and hearts of the great mass of Negroes," the *New York Times* declared. Whites, apparently, were nervous observers.

Roy Wilkins of the NAACP was the first national figure to publicly denounce Black Power. King had anticipated this move, wryly noting, "I get the impression that the NAACP wouldn't mind a split because they think they are the only civil rights organization." In the keynote address to the NAACP's annual convention in Los Angeles on July 5, Wilkins declared,

"No matter how endlessly they try to explain it, the term 'Black power' means anti-white power." Such thinking, he said, was "a reverse Mississippi, a reverse Hitler, a reverse Ku Klux Klan." Dismissing any attempt to clarify the concept, he warned that "in the quick, uncritical and highly emotional adoption it has received from some segments of a beleaguered people [it] can mean in the end only Black death." Vice President Humphrey told the NAACP delegates that "racism is racism—and there is no room in America for racism of any color." He insisted that "we must reject calls for racism, whether they come from a throat that is white or one that is Black."[37]

Robert Kennedy had little to say about Black Power. In response to a reporter's query, the senator noted that the slogan had been interpreted in various ways and said he thought it could raise important tactical concerns. "My judgment for the future of the country is that whites and Negroes must work together. There seems to be a group amongst the Negro leaders who do not think that is necessary and that could be damaging not only to the civil rights movement, but to the country." Kennedy went on to praise the March against Fear for demonstrating that Black citizens would keep up their efforts "until they establish equality."[38]

Kennedy appeared more concerned with white attitudes and the growing backlash. "Suppose God is Black?" he asked in an article prominently featured, along with his image, on the cover of the August 23 issue of *Look* magazine. Writing about his visit to South Africa, Kennedy told of an exchange with an audience at the University of Natal in Durban. One person had told him that the church in South Africa to which most whites belonged "teaches apartheid as a moral necessity." Few Blacks could pray with whites, another said, "because God created Negroes to serve." "But suppose God is black," Kennedy replied. "What if we go to Heaven and we, all our lives, have treated the Negro as inferior, and God is there, and we look up and He is not white? What then is our response?" There was silence. In the summer of Black Power, such a question invited a different angle of vision.[39]

———

OVER A PERIOD OF NINE DAYS, from July 12 to July 21, racial disturbances broke out in Chicago, Cleveland, Brooklyn, and Troy, New York. Up until then, President Johnson had remained largely silent about conditions in urban areas. Cuts to antipoverty programs seemed to undermine the federal intervention that many believed was needed to address the root causes of urban unrest. The riots in July would compel Johnson to speak out.

In Chicago, conflict escalated when police clashed with Black youngsters who had opened a fire hydrant to cool off and play in the water. In Troy, the arrest of a seventeen-year-old girl ignited long-simmering racial tensions in the Hudson River factory town. A violent turn in a dispute between Black patrons and a white bartender was apparently at the root of racial clashes in the Hough section of Cleveland that lasted five days. It took more than two thousand National Guardsmen to restore order. Throughout the city, 240 fires burned, and 4 people were killed, 30 injured, and 300 arrested. Among the dead were a young mother, killed by police gunfire, and a fifty-four-year-old Black man, shot by white snipers. The circumstances varied, but the conditions in all three communities told similar stories—of segregated and run-down neighborhoods, poor housing and sanitation, substandard schools, no recreational facilities, jobless youth, and inadequate and often abusive policing.[40]

On July 21, Lyndon Johnson warned that "Negro riots" threatened to jeopardize civil rights gains. At a news conference, a reporter asked him to comment on whether the Black Power slogan and the disturbances in Chicago and Cleveland had "created new antagonisms among whites." Johnson responded, "We must recognize that while there's a Negro minority of 10 percent in this country, there is a majority of 90 percent that are not Negroes." He expressed confidence that most whites "have come around to the viewpoint of wanting to see equality and justice given to their fellow citizens," but "they want to see it done under law . . . in an orderly manner . . . [and] without violence." He made only the vaguest reference to the conditions in the neighborhoods in question, expressing the hope that "every citizen will obey the law . . . and do everything they can do to cooperate with the constituted authority to see that evil conditions are remedied; that equality is given, and progress is made." He added, "I shall do everything in my power to see that it's done." Three days later, Johnson briefly repeated his assessment of the riots in a speech in Indianapolis dedicated to shoring up support for the war in Vietnam. Still, the *New York Times* plucked his comments on the riots to headline its front-page story on the speech: "Johnson Asserts Riots by Negroes Impede Reforms."[41]

"A third summer of riots," wrote Thomas Foley in the *Washington Post,* "shows that the bargain basement, penny-pinching approach does not work." The disturbances, many believed, stood as an indictment of Lyndon Johnson's failure to vigorously pursue the goals and vision set out in his plans for a Great Society. The *New York Times* editorialized that "the Johnson administration talks good programs but sets its targets far too low. . . . It is not the riots in the slums, but these lame and inadequate programs that are the real disgrace of the richest nation on earth." Foley emphasized the urgency of taking constructive steps, immediately. "As the riots flare from city to city, the bitterness becomes more deep-seated, leading to a breakdown in communication between the races. Then political action becomes impossible."[42]

While urban tensions exploded that summer, LBJ's War on Poverty stalled. Multiple factors were at play. The Community Action Programs (CAPs), a cornerstone of the antipoverty campaign, called for "maximum feasible participation," which had become a major headache and political liability for Johnson. The CAPs energized community activism, with CAP-affiliated groups often challenging local officials, leading to a storm of complaints from mayors who were also vying for control of poverty funds. Urban unrest strengthened white opposition to programs viewed as aiding African Americans. But most commentators singled out Johnson's growing obsession with the war in Vietnam. The escalation of the war meant that military activities cost double their budget for the year, up to $10 billion more than the $10 billion projected. Reluctant to raise taxes, the administration cut back domestic spending to finance an ever-deepening commitment in Southeast Asia.[43]

"The worst thing about the war is not the war itself, although that is bad enough," Robert Kennedy confided to his friend Dick Goodwin in the late evening of July 25, as Goodwin recalled. The worst thing was "all the great opportunities that are going down the drain. We have a real chance to do something about poverty, to get Blacks out of the ghetto, but we're paralyzed. I don't like Johnson, but he was doing some good things. Now there's no direction." Kennedy reasoned that people were fearful. Goodwin remembered Kennedy saying, "They don't understand the war or what's going to happen. The economy's shaky. They read about hippies and the draft card burners and the riots. They feel something's happening in this country they don't understand or particularly like." Everyone puts their own families first, and individuals tend to be selfish, he said. On the other hand, people do not like to see others suffer. People "can also be compassionate and generous, and they care about their country"—but not when they feel threatened. "That's why this is such a crucial time. We can go in either direction."[44]

Three weeks later, Robert Kennedy testified at the opening session of a series of Senate hearings on "the crisis in America's cities." He was a member of the Government Operations Subcommittee sponsoring the hearings, chaired by Senator Abraham Ribicoff, Democrat of Connecticut. Ribicoff and Kennedy had collaborated on the President's Committee on Juvenile Delinquency and Youth Crime when Ribicoff was secretary of Health, Education, and Welfare. Both men believed that urban areas were being neglected "at our national peril" and that a comprehensive examination of "the nature and causes of the problems that plague our cities" was overdue. Such an examination was an essential first step toward determining how the federal government could and should mobilize the nation's will and direct its resources to meet this national emergency.[45]

Close to a hundred witnesses testified in the Senate hearings over the course of six weeks, divided between August and December. Testimony from cabinet officers, mayors, other elected officials, and government workers dominated the first set of hearings. The second set included testimony from civil rights leaders, city planners, labor leaders, housing experts, psychologists, bankers, industrial leaders, foundation officials, police officers, and clergy. Engaging a broad sweep of witnesses, Ribicoff and Kennedy aimed to probe, as Kennedy put it, "the converging forces which rip at the fabric of life in the American city" and realize the nation's capacity to face the urban crisis and begin to solve it.[46]

On August 15, the opening day of the hearings, journalists, television cameras, and spectators crowded into the Senate Caucus Room in the Russell Building. A grand and ornate space, with massive crystal chandeliers and red velvet wall hangings, the Caucus Room was mostly reserved for major public hearings. The Army-McCarthy hearings and the Rackets Committee hearings had been held there—both formative moments in Kennedy's earlier life. This was also the room where John F. Kennedy had announced his presidential candidacy nearly six years earlier. On this day, Bobby sat in the witness seat to offer testimony as a senator from New York who was deeply engaged in urban issues, including preparations for a major redevelopment project in Bedford-Stuyvesant.[47]

Kennedy opened his testimony by describing the centrality of the city in American life and what it represented to the men and women who had been drawn to cities in increasing numbers since World War II—employment, the promise of a better life, and the excitement and stimulation of urban living. He described the city as not just a political unit "but a living social and economic body" and "the nerve system of the economic life of the nation." By the 1960s a convergence of forces had created an unprecedented national crisis centered in urban areas: the overcrowding and strain caused by sheer growth; the destruction of the physical environment; the crippling of public transportation as a result of "our surrender to the automobile"; the destruction of a sense of community; and, most significantly, the concentrated poverty and racial tension in the urban ghetto.[48]

"Of all the problems most immediate and pressing is the plight of the Negro in the center city," Kennedy said. He gave a brief account of conditions where segregation is the "governing rule," a product in part of federal policies around highway construction and housing. Poverty and unemployment were "endemic"—one-third to one-half of ghetto residents lived in poverty. Unemployment rates in some cities were as high as 40 percent. The unemployment rate for Black youth nationally was 25 percent. Forty-three percent of urban Black housing was substandard. More than ten thousand children were injured or infected with rat bites each year. Education was segregated, unequal, and inadequate. The high school dropout rate was as high as 70 percent. Poor health care was reflected in an infant mortality rate in segregated Black urban neighborhoods that was two times the average for the rest of the city, and deaths from various diseases were three times as common there as elsewhere.[49]

"We will need more than poverty programs, housing programs and employment programs, though we will need all of these," to address conditions that have been one hundred years in the making, he said. "We will need an outpouring of imagination, ingenuity, discipline, and hard work." Temporary measures thus far adopted in the wake of riots would not suffice. The hearings had to point the way to solutions by getting at the underlying conditions that afflicted the cities. They would reveal, he predicted, that serious mistakes were made by addressing one aspect of the problem while ignoring broader contexts and consequence—for example, housing policies pursued without reference or relevance to underlying problems of poverty, unemployment, social disorganization, and alienation.[50]

"The web must be grabbed whole," Kennedy said. A comprehensive attack, attentive to the experiences and desires of the community, was essential. Such a framework, he suggested, would focus on four major elements: "employment, education, housing and a sense of community." He singled out unemployment as a crucial area, impacting all aspects of individual and community well-being: "We earn our living, support our family, purchase the comforts and ease of life with work." Beyond the economic effects of joblessness, which were devastating, the chronic rates of unemployment among many African Americans in urban areas "is both a measure and a cause of the extent to which the Negro lives apart." "Unemployment is having nothing to do," he said, "which means having nothing to do with the rest of us." He observed that no government program then operating gave "any substantial promise of meeting the problem of unemployment."[51]

Kennedy introduced a proposal demonstrating the approach he advocated—which, he noted, could be considered as part of the administration's Demonstration Cities Program (later called Model Cities) that the Senate would approve later that week. Kennedy's plan acknowledged "that questions of technical or surface integration are far less important now than is the building of self-sufficiency and self-determination within the Negro community." The proposal he outlined built on ideas and planning that had evolved in the wake of Kennedy's visit to Bedford-Stuyvesant in February.

Since then, Kennedy, Adam Walinsky, and Tom Johnston had been meeting regularly with leaders from Bed-Stuy and among themselves exploring what might be done for the community.[52]

The project Kennedy described featured an expansive program of urban reconstruction that would employ residents and be organized around the "the full and dominant participation of the community." The program incorporated job training directly relevant to community needs, provided for a range of employment opportunities—from unskilled to administrative positions—and interfaced with schools around work-study programs and other incentives. In addition to rehabilitating decaying structures, building projects could focus on unmet social needs, such as constructing health clinics and art and cultural facilities. A new kind of institution, the Community Development Corporation, would be established to oversee these projects. It would be run by the community and supported by federal funds initially, and arrangements involving private sources and other sectors, including labor unions, universities, and other entities. A measure of the program's ultimate success, Kennedy said, would be the extent to which it helped the Bed-Stuy become a community, with "its people acting on matters of mutual concern, with the power and resources to affect the conditions of their own lives."[53]

"One purpose which must be served by every aspect of the program I have proposed" or of any other program addressing the problems of inner cities, Kennedy argued, was to try to meet "the increasing alienation of Negro youth." Such an effort pushed up against the fear and stigma that informed how most white Americans viewed Black urban youth, reinforced by televised images of urban uprisings and a racially coded politics of law and order. The hearings provided a platform for Kennedy to try to breach the boundaries of what he described on this day as "the ghetto of our ignorance" and to compel Americans to see a social reality that they ignored at their peril.

By 1966, alienation among the young from the larger society, in the United States and around the world, was widely commented on, Kennedy observed. But for Black youth living in ghetto conditions, this alienation was of another magnitude. "We can sense in their alienation a frustration so terrible, an energy and determination so great, that it must find a constructive outlet, or it will result in unknowable danger," he said. Baldwin had described this alienation as an "absolutely inarticulate and dangerous rage inside." At a time of increasing racial polarization, Kennedy would continue to try to communicate to Americans the individual and societal crisis brought on by decades of segregation, poverty, cruelty, and a sense of "no way out.[54]

Toward the end of his lengthy statement, Kennedy identified specific questions the hearings should explore regarding the federal government. There was the financial question, "which has the most direct and fundamental relevance to the problems of the city." At a time of urgent need, federal appropriations were being cut back on existing domestic programs, leaving little room for implementation of the Demonstration Cities projects on the massive scale required. He rejected the argument that the demands of the war in Vietnam were responsible for the cutbacks. Citing relevant revenue and budget figures, Kennedy argued that the country could afford both the war and domestic programs. A more fundamental question, Kennedy said, was whether the agencies of the federal government "have the will and determination and ability to form and carry out programs that cut across organizational lines, which do not fit organizational charts, which are tailored to no administrative convenience but the overriding need to get things done? If we lack the central ability, then vast new sums will not help."[55]

"Kennedy Chides Johnson on Cities" was the *New York Times'* choice of a headline for its front-page story on the first day of the hearings; the story went on to report that Kennedy had "implied that the Johnson administration was using the war in Vietnam as an excuse for not increasing federal aid to troubled cities." Within hours after Kennedy spoke, the *Times* reported, a bill to aid an expanded urban mass transit program was rejected in the Senate, demonstrating "that it was firmly on the President's side in holding down domestic spending." Writing in the *New Yorker*, Richard Rovere singled out Kennedy's opening-day testimony for including "one of the most interesting statements made" during the three weeks of hearings. "He said of all our problems the most immediate and pressing is the plight of the Negro in the center city."[56]

Administration officials testified over the next several days and were put in the position of justifying programs that, in the words of Ribicoff and Kennedy, were "not getting the job done." President Johnson had just charged Secretary of Housing and Urban Development Robert Weaver with overseeing all agencies of the federal government working on the problems of the city. After Weaver provided a lengthy explanation of how recent urban renewal programs marked a trend toward "safe, decent, sanitary housing" for families, Ribicoff challenged the secretary with reports about the continuing negative impact of urban renewal projects on families who had been uprooted and relocated. Weaver conceded that more knowledge, research, and experimentation were needed at all levels—federal, state, and local—to meet the problems of the cities.

Senator Jacob Javits asked Weaver, "as principal government official now concerned with the cities," if he might get a commitment from the administration for a Marshall Plan approach to the urban crisis, as both Javits and Kennedy advocated. Weaver and other officials pointed to the

Demonstration Cities project as a major new departure that included many of the elements Kennedy had discussed in his testimony. Kennedy agreed that "we need the demonstration cities," but the funding was "a drop in the bucket compared to what is needed in these cities across the United States." Lyndon Johnson saw the hearings as a "prelude to a Kennedy bid for the White House," according to Robert Dallek. The following week, the president commanded a major front-page news story in the *Times* with his claim that his administration had done more for cities "than any Administration in the history of the country." And he insisted that "we can afford whatever must be done to erase slums."[57]

Mayors from urban areas across the United States testified during the second week of the hearings. Mayor Samuel Yorty of Los Angeles was defensive and defiant in response to questions about conditions in Watts a year after the neighborhood had exploded and had several testy exchanges with Ribicoff and Kennedy. Cleveland's Mayor Ralph Locher blamed professional agitators, including communists, for the turmoil in Hough. Kennedy led the mayor through a detailed review of reports documenting deteriorated and overcrowded housing, segregated schools, and high unemployment in Hough, after which Locher agreed that it would not be accurate to imply that Cleveland, or any city, could overcome its urban ills if it got rid of communists. A. V. Sorensen of Omaha declared that he was the "most frustrated Mayor in all America." He described his "desperate" efforts over a fifteen-month period to obtain assistance for federally funded housing, adding, "we have not built one single housing unit for one poor family." The exasperated mayor told the committee, "The Negro wants first-class citizenship NOW and he is tired of a lot of headline promises from Government." Sorensen warned that resentment "was, and is, enormous."[58]

During the final week of the hearings, the committee heard from writers and political figures associated with Harlem. Ralph Ellison, the acclaimed author of *Invisible Man,* had come to Harlem from Oklahoma in 1936 and spoke about his experience. "If there was one thing you could do," Kennedy asked him, "one thing you could change immediately, what would it be?" "Our way of looking at each other," Ellison responded. Kennedy asked the writer to explain. "We fail to see the Negro people as Americans who share American characteristics and American history," Ellison said. "I would like to hear less of the sociological clichés about the Negro family. They are insulting to me. They are insulting and devastating to the Negro's conception of himself. And I regard them as contemptuous of us. . . . I think this is more important than allocating funds." When Kennedy asked Ellison about Black political leadership and its role, he had no answer. "We are living in a time of chaos . . . within the total political structure, [not] just in Black neighborhoods. . . . We do not have the political structures that can contain the energies set loose by the passage of the Civil Rights bills." Kennedy said reflectively, "It is, I suppose, a problem for all of us as citizens, white or black."[59]

———

PLANS FOR A PROJECT IN BEDFORD-STUYVESANT had advanced significantly. Shortly after Kennedy's visit to the neighborhood early in February, Elsie Richardson and other members of the Central Brooklyn Coordinating Council (CBCC) had met with Ron Shiffman, head of Pratt Institute's Center for Community Development, and Adam Walinsky and Tom Johnston, who ran Kennedy's New York office. The group asked to be part of the Demonstration Cities project and presented a well-developed proposal to rehabilitate existing housing, build more housing, and provide jobs. Kennedy and his staff were ready to move forward. Tom Johnston began meeting in Bedford-Stuyvesant with CBCC leaders and people from Pratt every other week, sometimes weekly. Adam Walinsky researched the technicalities of establishing a community corporation and consulted with a wide variety of like-minded groups across the country. Walinsky and Johnston, noted journalist Jack Newfield, "picked the brains of black militants, university urbanists, federal administrators, journalists, mayors, foundation executives, and millionaires from banking and business communities." Kennedy made frequent trips to Bedford-Stuyvesant for planning meetings and agreed to help set up a community development initiative, which would be called the Bedford Stuyvesant Renewal and Rehabilitation Corporation.[60]

For Walinsky, the project connected him to a tremendous network that provided critical feedback. "You'd be in touch with people," he recalled, "you could find out, you could know what was going on and what was working and what wasn't." Walinsky worked with Kennedy to draw up legislation to secure federal funding for the type of program they envisioned. Kennedy had a good working relationship with Senator Jacob Javits, and both shared an interest in creative approaches to urban problems that would draw on private sector funds. The two ended up cosponsoring an amendment to the 1966 antipoverty bill called the Special Impact Program. The bill would fund "comprehensive" approaches to community development, with an emphasis on construction, business development, and job growth. The bill came before the Senate early in October and triggered a showdown between the administration and senators fighting cutbacks to poverty programs.[61]

Senator Joseph Clark Jr. of Pennsylvania sponsored a bill appropriating $2.5 billion for poverty programs—$750 million more than the administration had requested. Kennedy challenged efforts to pare back the appropriation, declaring that even with the full amount, "the program does not begin to meet the universe of need. In our urban ghettos alone . . . there are hundreds of thousands of young people and adults desperately in need of jobs." In the end, the administration prevailed, thanks to a bipartisan bloc led by Senator Harry Byrd of Virginia. The Senate cut the bill back to $1.75 billion. The Special Impact Program amendment remained, but funds for the program were slashed from $75 million to $25 million. Commenting on the outcome, Kennedy observed that the United States had spent more on dogs the previous year than the amount proposed in the committee's bill. To cut the bill as the Senate had done, he said, was to make the poor and the school children of America pay for the Vietnam war.[62]

The survival of the Special Impact Program marked a small but critical victory. It meant that plans for the Bedford Stuyvesant Renewal and Restoration Corporation (R&R) could go forward, and the group could apply for federal funds. Tom Johnston had suggested they enlist a group of business leaders to serve in an advisory capacity. Kennedy liked the idea, and the two went to meet with André Meyer of Lazard Frères, the French-born financier known as "the Picasso of banking." Meyer was deeply interested in the project. Meanwhile, Johnston enlisted Eli Jacobs, a former classmate at Yale, now a successful and well-connected investment banker. He helped draw up a list of possible names, which Meyer reviewed. At a third meeting, Meyer said, "I think we can do something. We have to do it; I feel very strongly." He advised, however, that the business leaders not simply act as an informal advisory board but instead create an operating organization.[63]

With the help of Meyer and Jacobs, Kennedy set up a series of meeting in October. In one day he signed up some of America's top bankers and businessmen to advise and support the Bedford Stuyvesant Renewal and Rehabilitation Corporation. They included former treasury secretary C. Douglas Dillon; IBM president Thomas Watson Jr.; CBS chairman William Paley; George Moore, president of First National City Bank; Roswell Gilpatric, partner in the Wall Street Law firm of Cravath, Swaine & Moore; and David Lilienthal, former head of the Tennessee Valley Authority. Not long afterward, Kennedy met with Benno Schmidt of J.H. Whitney & Company, and he agreed to join. Half of the men were Republicans.[64]

Kennedy's success in enlisting this group was a testimony to the persuasiveness of his presentation. Most, except for Meyer, were wary of the senator. Benno Schmidt later remarked that many saw Kennedy as "arrogant . . . unduly ambitious, vindictive," and hostile to business. The effort had the approval of Mayor John Lindsay and Jacob Javits, and that helped. But most of all, Kennedy effectively conveyed the crisis in America's cities and his innovative plan for meeting it, and these men wanted to be part of the plan. Kennedy came across as sincere, Schmidt said. Investment banker

Eli Jacobs, a Republican, had been "militantly opposed" to Kennedy in 1964 when he ran for the Senate. Jacobs later reflected on how his view changed: "Kennedy's motivations could not be narrowly political, for the chances of failure in Bedford Stuyvesant were far greater than the chances for success. I therefore saw his decision to become involved there as an act of political courage."[65]

———

IN THE WEEKS LEADING UP TO THE midterm elections, Robert Kennedy took to the campaign trail to help fellow Democrats. He traveled every weekend in October, responding to requests from candidates in all parts of the country—except for the South, from where, apparently, no invitations issued. The press entourage that trailed him, the crowds waiting at airports and lining streets to see him, and the packed venues gave his trips the feel of a national campaign. A rousing reception greeted him when he arrived in Sioux City, Iowa, at 1 a.m. Over the next eighteen hours, he campaigned for candidates in six congressional districts across the state. Crowds were everywhere, and people waved hand-printed signs reading "Kennedy in 1968," "Kennedy Minus Johnson in 1972," "Kennedy for President—Any Year." Four thousand people jammed the narrow hillside streets to hear Kennedy speak in Butte, Montana, with several waving "All the Way with RFK" signs. The Labor Temple in Portland, Oregon, was so jammed that neither Kennedy's aides nor the reporters who followed him could get in.[66]

Speculation about Kennedy's presidential ambitions spiked, but it was his performance that captivated journalists. He had developed into a terrific campaigner, wrote Tom Wicker of the *New York Times,* and seemed to enjoy it. "Senator Kennedy took the Kennedy wit, the Kennedy appeal, and the Kennedy coattails to Michigan, where the states' hard-pressed Democrats could use all three," Wicker declared. He described the senator "joking, handshaking, dazzling high school girls and spreading the Democratic gospel." During his "whirlwind tour" through the state, Kennedy "roamed in a little-noticed motorcade through Detroit, brought down the house at two university rallies [and] stopped business at a shopping center in Pontiac." Reporters following the senator found him "increasingly bold and self-confident." He told college audiences that the student deferment system under Selective Service was unfair to a young working man building his future and should be replaced by a lottery. At Seattle University, he then asked, "How many of you are in favor of doing away with student deferment?" There was a sparse showing of hands. "Well, I know I just blew this audience," he said, in his self-mocking manner. But he continued to raise the issue.[67]

"Robert Kennedy is rising and changing faster than any other political figure in the nation today," declared Pulitzer Prize–winning *Times* columnist James Reston. Kennedy was "no longer the stunned young man who walked through the political crowds in a trance two years ago and sounded uncertain and squeaky in his political talks." He was turning into an accomplished public speaker and "not only wooing the young jumpers and squealers but putting a lot of influential Democratic candidates in his debt." Even JFK at forty, Reston noted, "never created the stir or drew the crowds outside of his own state Bobby has been getting in his present tour of the west." Robert Kennedy, Reston wrote, was "turning the legend he inherited from his brother into a powerful political movement and he is coming out of the 1966 election as a winner, regardless of what happens to the Democratic or Republican Party." Tom Wicker concurred, writing that "what makes John Kennedy's brother the most remarkable figure on the political scene today . . . is the fact that he is young, open, fixed on today and tomorrow, not yesterday."[68]

On October 23, Kennedy was on a three-day swing through California, campaigning for incumbent Governor Pat Brown and several congressional candidates, when the senator briefly stepped off the campaign trail to deliver a speech at the University of California, Berkeley on the current state of the Black struggle for equality and freedom. The speech was in many ways Kennedy's most forceful statement yet on what he saw as the most pressing domestic issue facing the country. The governor, who was in an uphill race against Republican candidate Ronald Reagan, was conspicuously absent that Sunday afternoon.

For Reagan, Kennedy's visit to the university provided a high-profile opportunity to lambaste the university as well as his opponent. Reagan launched his gubernatorial campaign promising to "clean up the mess at Berkeley," a center of student activism and home to the Free Speech Movement, which had shut the campus down two years earlier. Governor Brown, Reagan claimed, was "injecting the campus again directly into politics" by allowing Kennedy to speak at the university. Reagan charged the university with a "misuse of public relations funds" in its promotion of the event. The gubernatorial candidate described Kennedy as "a Senator who comes from Massachusetts, lives in Virginia, and represents New York, has now come to California to try and get us to buy four more years of government by hack and crony, government by political payoff, government by waste and inefficiency." Reagan promised that if elected governor he would never attempt to convert the campus to his own political purposes.[69]

An overflow audience of fifteen thousand packed the campus's Greek Theatre. In his opening comments, Kennedy observed that the morning papers suggested a change in tone on the part of Ronald Reagan. "I really wanted to take this opportunity before I begin my formal speech to express my appreciation to Mr. Reagan for permitting me to come today," Kennedy said, prompting laughter and applause. He added, "it makes me feel very confident that if he is elected that he'll give me a visa and let me come back." Kennedy said he was "very pleased and highly honored" to come to one of the great educational institutions not only of the United States but of the world. "After all," he said, "you are the first college to become a political issue since George III attacked Harvard for being a center of rebellion and subversion and at that time, he was right. As for me, I am glad to be in Berkeley, for I am sympathetic with and welcome the passionate concern with the condition and future of the American nation which can be found on this campus."[70]

Kennedy began by describing qualities he saw in the students, focusing on a spirit that he called "the hope of our nation." The future, he said, would belong to those "who blend passion, reason and courage in a personal commitment to the ideals and great enterprises of American society." The future would belong to those who understand that "wisdom can only emerge for the clash of contending views." This, he said, was the "seminal spirit of American democracy." It was not enough, he said, "to allow dissent. We must demand it. For there is much to dissent from." He offered a brief litany of realities and conditions that demanded dissent and urged the students to distinguish between the right of dissent "and the way we choose to exercise it," cautioning against dramatic acts of protest that will not "assist those seriously engaged with the difficult and frustrating work of the nation."

Then Kennedy turned to the major focus of his address. "No area of national life needs this leadership more than the challenge we have gathered to consider," he said, "the revolution within our gates, the struggle of the Negro American for full equality and for full freedom." This struggle had entered a new stage, one that was more hopeful and more difficult. Important changes had taken place that held out the promise that race would no longer stand in the way of individual achievement or participation in the affairs of the country. But for many African Americans, little had changed. Although the rewards of full participation were advertised everywhere that television, radio, and newspapers reached, many remained trapped in poverty and joblessness in deteriorating neighborhoods.

It was not difficult to imagine the frustration and even fury at promises betrayed—especially, Kennedy noted to his youthful audience, among young Negroes. For the young Black man, the passage of civil rights laws counted "little against his crushing awareness that his hopes for the future are beyond his reach for reasons that have little to do with justice or his worth as a man." Kennedy insisted that the violence of the few could not be condoned, but the "terrible frustration, the feeling of hopelessness and the passion for betterment" that often lay at the root of violent outbreaks had to be acknowledged.

Persistent racial inequality could not be remedied by legislation, a lawsuit, or a single program, he said. Overcoming inequality would require "overcoming the scarred heritage of centuries of oppression, poor education, and the many obstacles to fruitful employment." Kennedy discussed the various ways in which this heritage was manifested in contemporary society, most notably in white attitudes and beliefs. Opposition to riots and violence "is a justified feeling of most Americans, white and black." But "white backlash" often masks a "hostility to complete fulfillment of equal opportunity and treatment, which contains opposition to demands for justice and freedom, which denies the need to destroy slums, provide education and eliminate poverty." "It is wrong, shameful, immoral and self-defeating," he said with evident feeling, and any leader who seeks to exploit this feeling "for momentary advantage fails his duty to the people of this country." It would be a "national disaster to permit resentment and fear to drive increasing numbers of white and black Americans into opposing camps of distrust and enmity."

Kennedy suggested that large-scale government action was necessary to crush remaining racial barriers to opportunity and "lead an accelerating national effort to give Negroes a fair chance to share in the abundance and dignity of American life." The problem would not go away on its own. There was one choice: "face our difficulties and strive to overcome them, or turn away, bringing repression, increasing human pain, and civil strife." He cautioned that even if we "act on an unprecedented scale," progress would be slow. "The problem of giving content to equality is deeply embedded in the structure of American life." But it was critical to create "steady, concrete, visible achievements" capable of justifying and sustaining the faith of Negro Americans "that their country recognizes the justice of their cause."

His address was frequently interrupted with applause. In closing, he appealed to his audience to recognize the responsibility and opportunity that was uniquely theirs. America stood at a crossroads, and they, students at UC Berkeley, were "among its most privileged citizens." Their choices would help determine how the country moved forward. Their generation, he said, was "coming of age at one of the rarest moments in history—a time when the old order of things is crumbling, and a new world society is painfully struggling to take shape." In their hands, not with presidents or leaders "is the future of your world, and the fulfillment of the best qualities of your own spirit."[71]

A lively question-and-answer session followed. Kennedy fielded a barrage of demands from the audience for comment on Vietnam, which he deflected, saying with a smile, "I'd probably agree with a slogan I've heard on campus, 'I'd rather make love than war.'" When asked about his views on Black Power, Kennedy said, "I believe in the advancement of the Negro, if that's the definition. If it means a bigger role for the Negro, I'm for that. If it means hatred and opposition to the white race, I think we'll make a major mistake." The Berkeley campus would be the site for an all-day forum on Black Power the following Saturday, featuring Stokely Carmichael among the speakers.[72]

The only time Kennedy was booed was when he said, in response to a question, that he would support President Johnson and Hubert Humphrey in 1968. Another student asked for some assurance that Kennedy would consider running for president himself. "Well," he said, "I just quite frankly don't know what the future brings. I think that one cannot plan that far in advance. I'm going to continue as long as I'm around on this globe, I'm going to continue in public life in some way."[73]

———

FOR THE REPORTERS FOLLOWING KENNEDY, the question was not whether he would run for president, but when. There was a mounting belief among politicians in both parties, reported Warren Weaver Jr. of the *New York Times*, that Kennedy was committed to seeking national office within the next six years. A spate of magazine articles concluded that the senator was out to force his way onto the 1968 Democratic ticket or, at the very least, was "carefully plotting his drive for the Presidency in 1972." "Half-amused and half irritated," Kennedy told Weaver that the senator considered reports that he might force his way into the 1968 ticket as a reflection on his political intelligence. It was obvious, he said, that it would be impossible and foolish for any Democrat, however popular, to challenge an incumbent president. Weaver reported that the senator conceded that his national exposure during the midterm campaigns put him in a position of strength if some unforeseen circumstance—"death or disability of one of the principals or some national disaster," as Weaver put it—"should suddenly alter the entire picture in the Democratic Party." But that was highly unlikely.[74]

Yes, he had thought about running for president, Kennedy responded to Weaver's insistent questioning—and that was hardly a surprise. What irked the senator was that many saw his daily activities as fitted into a 1972 timetable. "I'm not going to direct my life to where I'll be in 1972," Kennedy said. "Six years is so far away; tomorrow is far away. I don't even know if I'll be alive in six years." Kennedy argued, as Weaver reported, "that a politician who focuses too long and hard on winning a given office sacrifices his ability to act independently and tends to lose his judgment, reacts to problems in an artificial and calculating way rather than following his best instincts." Weaver remained skeptical; Kennedy's plans would remain a focus of media interest.[75]

There *was* something more than a desire to see fellow Democrats elected that moved Kennedy in 1966, wrote Richard Dougherty of the *Los Angeles Times*. But he suspected that "nobody, including quite probably Kennedy himself, knows when his bid for the White House will be brought into actual focus." Dougherty described "a detachment . . . a fatalism" stamped on what must be counted "as one of the most personalized and non-neurotic presidential efforts in the history of the Republic." For Dougherty, the real story is who Robert Kennedy had become by 1966. The journalist described the seriousness that characterized Kennedy and his aides, "but they are never solemn. Tension is rare and humor is in ample supply." While it was impossible to divorce Kennedy from his martyred brother, Dougherty believed too little account had been taken of the senator himself, "as a worker who has made infinitely more of his inherent celebrity than his brother, Senator Edward Kennedy; as a critic, albeit a loyal one of the administration's policies in Vietnam and elsewhere; as a student of history, who finds time to read and think . . . and finally as a truly professional politician who demands truly professional work of his advance men, researchers, writers and staff in general."[76]

The campaign swing took Kennedy to places he had not been to since his brother's presidential run six years earlier. Bobby was struck by how different the country was. As Peter Edelman recalled, Kennedy said: "All of these people that looked like they were having a tough time in 1960 now have cars, they can get to rallies . . . in the parking lot of a shopping center, and they're all very comfortable." He got the sense talking to them "that the major thing they're worried about is any threat to their comfort. They see the rising black aspirations as a threat to their comfort, they see inflation as a threat to their comfort." Edelman thought it all sounded rather frightening and asked Kennedy what he thought could be done. Kennedy felt if he could spend more time, really talk to people, he could turn them around. Edelman observed that this perspective was a bit messianic and somewhat egotistical, but "I think in a highly justified sense," that if Kennedy could reach people personally, and not through a television set, he could have some effect. Kennedy thought people were basically decent. He would take on a hostile audience with a "very deep sense that you could reach people personally."[77]

ON ELECTION DAY IN NEW YORK CITY, Kennedy witnessed how "a strong dose of anti-minority feeling," as the *New York Times* put it, combined with the politics of fear, could easily defeat a minor step toward improved race relations. During the fall, Kennedy had joined Senator Javits and Mayor Lindsay in a campaign to salvage a revised Civilian Complaint Review Board. Earlier that summer, Lindsay had expanded the existing Civilian Complaint Review board, consisting of three police officers, to include four civilians. The board had a modest function: to receive and review citizen complaints of police brutality or discourtesy and then make recommendations to the police commissioner that he could choose whether or not to accept. If the police commissioner found the police officer at fault, a departmental trial would be held, in which only policemen and police officials would take part. As one journalist noted, the board "will do little to help the racial minorities and will do virtually nothing to hurt the police." However, the board represented a gesture toward better relations between the community and the police, editorialized the *Times,* and aided "law enforcement by improving the climate of public confidence in which policemen work."[78]

The Police Benevolent Association, which represented 20,000 of New York's 28,000 police officers, promptly went on the attack, warning "Don't handcuff the cops," and vowing to spend its treasury of $1.5 million if necessary to dismantle the new board. The association secured the forty-five thousand signatures needed to place a referendum on the November ballot. Civil rights, religious, labor, civil liberties, and student groups organized support for the newly constituted board, along with leading politicians, who established the Federated Association for Impartial Review (FAIR), which Kennedy and Javits cochaired. The Civilian Complaint Review Board was "an important first step forward," Kennedy said, "to dispelling the argument that the police whitewashed allegations of brutality." What happened in New York City, he said, would have national significance and major implications for race relations in the city. "To snatch it away," State Senator Basil Paterson warned, "would confirm the belief of people in his district in Harlem that the city did not care about them."[79]

The Police Benevolent Association, joined by the Conservative Party and veteran groups, ran an aggressive misinformation campaign, sponsored by the Independent Citizen's Committee against Civilian Review Boards, including a series of ads that became difficult to counter in the heated racial climate of 1966. One portrayed a woman emerging from a subway station at night with the caption, "the Civilian Review Board must be Stopped! Her life . . . your life . . . might depend on it." The text explained that police might hesitate to act against criminals out of fear of unjust censure that threatened the police officer's job, pension, and reputation. The committee ran three different television ads repeatedly in the weeks leading up to the election. One showed a street scene with young men, "from the waist down, flashes of chains, tipping over ashcans, a gun for a second and a switch-blade for a second." The voice-over warned: "The addict, the criminal, the hoodlum—only the policeman stands between you and him. He must not hesitate."[80]

On November 8, New Yorkers voted overwhelmingly to abolish the Civilian Complaint Review Board by more than three to two. Manhattan was the only borough to vote to retain the board. The heaviest opposition was in Queens, but opposition was strong in Staten Island, Brooklyn, and the Bronx. Bernard Weinraub, who covered the story for the *New York Times,* reported that the Civilian Complaint Review Board died of "a massive dose of fear and prejudice and scare advertising. It was not quite four months old." The fortune spent on the campaign to defeat the board—estimated to total between $500,000 and $1 million—"appeared not so much aimed at killing the board that was, at best, a symbol, but to 'get even' finally with Negroes for being too aggressive and with the mayor for being too visionary," Weinraub wrote. An official in the police department who saw value in the board said regretfully, "the safety valve of the board has been cut off. It's obviously going to be more difficult now." Kennedy conceded that "it was a tough issue. I don't think there was a complete understanding of the board. The responsibility of the police force will be far greater than ever before."[81]

———

ON DECEMBER 10, almost one thousand people crowded into Public School 305 in Brooklyn for the third annual conference of the Central Brooklyn Coordinating Council. Standing in front of the packed auditorium, Robert Kennedy announced a new initiative for Bedford-Stuyvesant, representing eight months of intensive planning. He explained that two private, nonprofit corporations had been established. The Bedford Stuyvesant Renewal and Rehabilitation Corporation, made up of twenty civic and community leaders, would draft programs for "the physical, social and economic development of the community" and retain decision-making authority. The Bedford Stuyvesant Development and Services Corporation, composed of businessmen, was set up to provide "access to funds and managerial expertise." The purpose of the business corporation was to help translate the "talent and energy" of the local community into the "power to act." Kennedy reported that two initial grants had been received from the Ford Foundation and the Stern Foundation. In creating the first community development corporation, the initiative marked a new departure. "If our purpose is one, we can recognize many roads to the goal; but if each looks first to personal and factional advantage, we can never succeed."[82]

"Hope in Brooklyn" was how the *New York Amsterdam News* described the news. It was "the first concrete plan in urban renewal which, we think, offers sound thinking and genuine help to the community." The *New York Times* predicted that "it could be the country's most exciting endeavor to give the people in racial ghettos meaningful participation in reviving decaying neighborhoods." Elsie Richardson, who had guided Kennedy through the neighborhood on that wintry day in February, told the audience at PS 305 that "a new day has dawned in Bedford Stuyvesant."[83]

Robert Kennedy was aware of the challenges and potential pitfalls ahead. Several days before the project was publicly announced, he said, "I'm not sure this is going to work. But it's going to test some new ideas, some new ways of doing things, that are different from the government. Even if we fail, we'll have learned something. But more important than that, something has to be done. People like myself just can't go around making nice speeches all the time. We can't just keep raising expectations. We have to do some damn hard work too." At the end of a tumultuous year—with spiking racial conflict, the festering politics of white backlash, and media distracted by the specter of Black Power—the Bedford-Stuyvesant project represented a way forward for one community and a glimpse of Robert Kennedy's vision of what just might make a difference.[84]

CHAPTER THIRTEEN

Reckoning

||

ON DECEMBER 15, 1966, Martin Luther King Jr. and Robert Kennedy sat across from each other in a packed Senate Caucus Room for the final day of hearings on the crisis in America's cities. It had been nearly six years since the two had first interacted during the Freedom Rides, when King was trapped inside the First Baptist Church with a mob raging outside. Kennedy had then been in his Justice Department office, and the two men had spoken by phone just as the mob was about to overtake the church. Federal marshals arrived minutes later, warding off what could have been a horrific disaster.

Over the intervening years, both men had contributed in strikingly different ways to the dynamic, contentious, and ultimately successful movement to end legally mandated segregation in the South and secure voting rights for African Americans. The two men were not close personally and approached America's racial crisis from a different set of experiences. Nevertheless, Kennedy grew to have enormous respect for King, and King increasingly viewed the senator as one of the few white politicians who shared the minister's view that "racial injustice is still the Negro's burden and America's shame."[1]

King was the last person to testify before the subcommittee, chaired by Senator Ribicoff. Seventy witnesses had appeared over the course of the hearings, which the *New York Times* described as "a six-week Congressional seminar in the decline, fall, and possible resurrection of the American city."[2] Witnesses ran the gamut from mayors and elected officials to urban planners, civil rights leaders, ghetto residents, antipoverty workers, psychiatrists, and social scientists. For Robert Kennedy, the hearings provided a rich learning experience. The final session revealed how closely aligned King and Kennedy had become—both in their concerns about cities, Black youth, white backlash, the retreat from the War on Poverty, and the escalation of the war in Vietnam and also in their vision of what should be done in response.

King had spent much of the previous year in Chicago, where the Southern Christian Leadership Conference had joined with local organizations in a campaign to end racial discrimination in housing. The campaign had faced many challenges, including a diverse and divided African American community, a powerful and wily mayor in the person of Richard Daley, and white crowds as hostile and hateful as any King had faced in the South. He had seen firsthand the grinding poverty, exploitation, and despair that prevailed in urban neighborhoods where families were consigned to "smothering in an airtight cage of poverty in the midst of an affluent society." In a city that boasted the highest per capita income in the world, Black citizens paid a "color tax." The pattern of economic exploitation—in housing and consumer goods and by lending and banking institutions—could be defined, King said, as "our system of slavery in the twentieth century." The previous summer, Coretta and his four children had lived together in the apartment he had taken on the city's West Side, the scene of a riot in July. "As the riot raged . . . outside, I realized the crowded flat in which we lived was about to produce an emotional explosion in my own family," he said. "And I understood anew the emotional pressures which make of the ghetto an emotional pressure cooker."[3]

In his statement before the committee, King considered what had changed for Black Americans as a result of the civil rights movement. While gaining access to public accommodations may have had little impact on the material conditions of most Black people, the removal of the "caste stigma revolutionized our psychology." Personal degradation had been felt as keenly as material degradation. The shame of being Black had been lifted, but many remained "handicapped by the stigma of poverty in a society whose measure of value revolves around money." Black frustration and anger were fueled in part by the glaring fact that the promises of freedom and dignity written into the Declaration of Independence and Constitution had not been kept. He pointed to deep and persistent differences between the life experiences and opportunities of Blacks and whites. "To be born a Negro in an American city," King said, was to be "underemployed or unemployed or unpaid; to be undereducated and ill housed; to face illness and perhaps death, uncared for; to face a life of little hope, entrapped by both color and need."[4]

The plight of Black people had in fact worsened over the previous fifteen years as the distance between African Americans and the widely publicized fruits of American prosperity grew ever greater. In the face of such dire conditions, the War on Poverty, King said, is "scarcely a skirmish." He described a "grudging, parsimonious allocation of resources, measured out as if we fear overkill." Here King was echoing critiques advanced by Kennedy, Ribicoff, and others during the hearings, pointing to the need for a more comprehensive approach on the part of the federal government and a greater commitment of resources. "At no time has a total coordinated and fully adequate program been conceived," he said. Consequently, "fragmentary and spasmodic reforms have failed to reach the needs of the poor." The general attitude toward the anti-poverty effort was "impatience with its problems, indifference towards its progress and pronounced hostility towards its errors."[5]

At a time when domestic needs were so great, billions were being spent liberally on a war in which American security was not at stake, King said, questioning the wisdom of a conflict justified by "vague commitments to a reactionary regime." He noted that a recent $10 billion underestimate for the war for a single year—a sum more than five times the amount committed to the War on Poverty for that year—was promptly adjusted and the funds appropriated. "The bombs at Vietnam explode at home," King warned, destroying "the hopes and possibilities of decent Americans." Surely, he said, "the chaos of our cities, the persistence of poverty and the degeneration of our national prestige throughout the world" were compelling arguments for seeking a peace agreement.[6]

King shared his own understanding of the meaning of Black power. He emphasized that organized Black action and clear demands were necessary to convince the larger society that "no lesser alternative is possible." He acknowledged that the civil rights movement had shown that there were many white people of goodwill but warned that, for many, that goodwill "carried them only to end extremist conduct toward Negroes and introduce limited reform." More was needed from them. He emphasized that there would be no solution to the racial problem in America without creative alliances between Blacks and whites. "We must enlist consciences in the struggle," he said, "not just racial groups."[7]

Ribicoff and Kennedy engaged King in an extensive discussion after the end of his formal statement. They were the only two senators who attended this final session, which for them was clearly meant to be the capstone of six weeks of hearings. Both senators strove to make it clear that the civil rights movement had entered a different phase; many of the remaining challenges were centered in urban areas and more difficult to resolve than bringing down the legal edifice buttressing the South's racial caste system had been. "We must demand reforms that will deal with . . . basic economic issues," King conceded in response to a question from Ribicoff. "We are dealing with issues now that will call for something of a restructuring of the architecture of American society."[8]

Kennedy engaged King in a discussion of nonviolence, asking him about the development of Black leadership and the aspirations of Black youth. The senator asked King to prioritize what he would like to see done. King said he would like to see the thorough implementation of the open housing agreement that had recently been approved in Chicago. He singled out economic issues as foundational and said it was important to allow communities to organize around the effort to rebuild their neighborhoods and lead the renewal projects. King elaborated on this idea throughout his testimony, emphasizing that ghetto communities had to be involved in decisions that impacted them—and to be given a chance to shape the education, job training, and social welfare programs being set up to help these communities. The aim was not just to improve the economic well-being of the poor "but to provide the conditions for dignity and the exercise of rights." He pointed to Kennedy's Bedford-Stuyvesant project as an example, as well as a program in the Shaw neighborhood in Washington and Rev. Leon Sullivan's project in Philadelphia.[9]

Kennedy asked King whether he thought the extent of Black alienation was understood outside the ghetto. The answer was a scathing "No." "The problem of the ghetto, as you know," King said, "is that ghetto dwellers are often invisible. Thoughts unknown, words unheard, feelings unfelt." The consequences of this voicelessness were dire.

Kennedy conceded that the "lack of understanding . . . by the people who live outside of the ghetto to this very bitter condition that exists there" was deeply troubling. "I am just extremely concerned," he said, "as I think everybody should be, as to what this combination of factors is going to lead to in the United States." By this time, Kennedy had a clear vision of what might be in store. "Riots," King had warned in his testimony, "in the final analysis turn out to be the language of the unheard."[10]

———

SHRINKING FEDERAL FUNDING AND CUTBACKS in programs in the face of growing need prompted Kennedy to enlist private enterprise in a massive effort to help residents rebuild and revive their communities. His personal appeals to the men who had joined the Bedford Stuyvesant Development and Services Corporation after a third summer of urban unrest had persuaded them to commit their time and resources to the project. Kennedy was anxious to do more. He told Peter Edelman to work up some of the specific proposals floated in the Ribicoff hearings. Edward Logue, an urban planner, and several others had argued for tax incentives, and this idea interested Edelman. He had legislative fellow Myron "Mike" Curzan, a recent graduate of Columbia Law School, go through the hearings and come up with some concrete plans. Curzan concluded that tax incentives were the most promising new approach. He and Edelman discussed the idea with Kennedy. "That's fine," Edelman recalled Kennedy saying. "Do that." Curzan worked on the new legislation around the clock and six months later produced drafts of two bills to encourage private investment in housing and job creation.[11]

The Bed-Stuy project remained at the center of Robert Kennedy's attention. It had quickly progressed from its rocky start and the initially awkward relationship between the business and community boards and had become a fully functioning, community-based entity. The evolution of the project reflected Kennedy's ability to concentrate on the issue at hand, listen to varied ideas and opinions, and identify and enlist talented and dedicated individuals. He was flexible and improvisational, showed dexterity in engaging contending personalities and interests, and had an ability to learn from mistakes and move on. As Elsie Richardson later put it, in Bed-Stuy, Kennedy's innovation was figuring out how words might become action.[12]

The project began with a funding base and two separate and overlapping administrative entities—the Bedford Stuyvesant Renewal and Rehabilitation Corporation (R&R) and the business-dominated Development and Services Corporation (D&S). How they would function together was unclear. The high-powered group of businessmen and financiers who made up D&S initially assumed that they would develop renewal plans, with the help of Edward Logue, the top urban planner at the time, and "advise" the community board on what would be done and how to proceed. D&S also planned to receive and manage incoming grants. This arrangement ran counter to the idea of co-equal boards and community control of the projects, but that bone of contention was temporarily eclipsed when a major internal shake-up within the Renewal and Rehabilitation Corporation brought the whole project to the brink of collapse.[13]

Kennedy had asked Judge Thomas Jones to lead R&R. The two men had known each other since Kennedy's Senate campaign, and Jones seemed well prepared for the challenge. At fifty-five, he was a member of a pioneering generation of Black lawyers and clergymen who transformed Brooklyn politics after World War II. The *New York Times* described him as a "tireless civil rights lawyer." Jones, who'd served as a rifleman during World War II, had defended Black soldiers charged with wrongdoing in Europe—a chronic manifestation of the military's segregationist practices. In Brooklyn, he had represented victims of police brutality and targets of McCarthyism and had served as counsel to the local branch of the NAACP. In the 1950s, he, Shirley Chisholm, and a few others had come together to form the

Bedford-Stuyvesant Political League, and in 1959 they had established the Unity Democrats, which challenged the segregated clubhouses of the Democratic Party in Brooklyn. (Chisholm would go on to become the first Black woman elected to Congress.) In 1962, Jones was elected to the New York State assembly; he became a civil court judge two years later. A seasoned political operator with deep ties in the community, he was known to have a prickly personality and the limitations common to men of his generation when it came to working with strong, powerful women.[14]

Failure on the part of Kennedy and his aides to consider the broader political dynamic quickly showed its effects. The R&R board, almost exclusively middle-class, was dominated by women from the Central Brooklyn Coordinating Council (CBCC) who had played an essential role in developing the project. Elsie Richardson, one of the leading women on the board, clashed with Jones over issues of control and representation. The conflict grew into a major showdown—with tensions around gender, class, and generation. The "female clout" of the women who ran the CBCC put "men on the defensive," as historian Michael Woodsworth has noted. Jones wanted the board to expand to as many as fifty members and to be more representative of the community—drawing in members of Brooklyn CORE, unaffiliated street leaders, militant clergymen, and Puerto Ricans. His goal, in part, was to diminish the control of the "middle age matriarchy" controlling the board. Kennedy and his staff shared Jones's concern about broader representation and the dominant role of a small group of women.[15]

On March 31, Jones introduced a resolution providing for the expansion of the board, along with three other measures. When all four resolutions were voted down by the board, he resigned on the spot and stormed out of the meeting. Kennedy approved Jones's request to form a new body, the Bedford Stuyvesant Restoration Corporation. It was a bitter turn for Elsie Richardson and her colleagues on the board, who had played such an important role in conceptualizing and establishing the project. More than a thousand people turned out for a major protest rally the next week organized by Richardson and her colleagues. But the rift ended up providing a platform for other factions in the community demanding to be heard. Sonny Carson of CORE and other young militants took over the rally, denouncing Richardson and her group and saying they did not speak for everyone in Bedford-Stuyvesant. They heaped scorn on Kennedy—calling him "a colonialist"—and Jones, whom they scornfully dismissed as "a Tom."[16]

The disruption revealed deeper tensions around the fate of alternative existing programs operating in the neighborhood. A group called Youth in Action (YIA) had navigated the web of city and federal rules to set up programs supported by the War on Poverty in which thousands of local people participated. As conservatives in Congress cut funding to the antipoverty programs and angled to eliminate them altogether, the specter of Kennedy's group setting up what appeared to be a rival agency fueled tremendous resentment. Kennedy pushed everything else aside and focused his complete attention on salvaging the project, now with a fuller grasp of the dynamics within the community. He got the necessary support from Mayor Lindsay and Senator Javits for the new corporation. Most significantly, he finally succeeded in persuading Franklin Thomas to join the Restoration Corporation as executive director.[17]

One of five children of immigrants from Barbados, Franklin Thomas grew up in Bedford-Stuyvesant. His father died in 1945 when Thomas was eleven, and his mother supported the family by working as a waitress and housekeeper. Thomas excelled in school. He went to Columbia University on an academic scholarship and, at six foot four, became captain of the basketball team, leading his team through a record-breaking season. After four years in the Air Force, he returned for a law degree, after which he worked with the Federal Housing and Home Finance Agency and then as an assistant US attorney for the Southern District of New York. In 1966, he was working as New York City's deputy police commissioner in charge of legal affairs when his friend Earl Graves—who worked on Kennedy's Senate staff—suggested Thomas join the Bed-Stuy project. Graves, who had grown up with Thomas, set up a time for him and Kennedy to meet in January 1967.[18]

Their first meeting was brief. Kennedy made it clear that he was interested in having Thomas join the project as the operating head. Although the meeting was little more than "an exchange of glances and a few words," Thomas recalled, he came away with a feeling that Kennedy was "a person who was serious in his purpose" and "someone that you got the right kind of human bounce for." The following day, Jones talked with Thomas at length about the project and stressed the need for someone with his experience and ability. Next Thomas met with a committee from the board, headed by Elsie Richardson. As he walked through his old neighborhood, past "boarded up, decaying buildings," he realized that the project "could really make a difference." But his experience with the hiring committee was a deal-breaker. "What makes you think you're qualified?" asked Elsie Richardson. The question set the tone for the forty-five-minute interview. Thomas concluded that the situation would be impossible. In a follow-up meeting, Kennedy made it clear he wanted Thomas to take the position and persuaded him to wait before giving a final answer.[19]

"What made the job interesting, personally," Thomas explained, "was, one, coming back into the community that I'd grown up in and being able to bring some resources that would help improve it and, two, to be able to be exposed to and work with the senator and the businessmen on one hand, and the community on the other." What rankled him was the dual board structure, which would put a layer between him, as the operating director on the R&R side, and the senator and business board, which had its own staff. Looking back, he thought the structure basically was conceived to avoid a situation where "at the first meeting of the board, if somebody said motherfucker, the white guys wouldn't all get up and run out." He discussed his concerns at length with Kennedy and agreed to wait before giving a final answer. But at this point, he was not inclined to take the position.[20]

The rancor afflicting the Bed-Stuy project was widely publicized in the New York press. In the end, the depth of the breaches created an opportunity for a fresh start. A newly constituted board included members from the original board who chose to stay on and others who broadened the reach of the operation—including Sonny Carson of Brooklyn CORE; Albert Vann, president of the African American Teachers Association; Puerto Rican lawyer Frank Ortiaz; and two union organizers. There were now younger, more militant people involved, and the board was more decidedly male.[21]

After meeting with Kennedy and members of the D&S, and separately with Kennedy and Jones, Thomas found many of his concerns addressed. The two-board structure would remain, he was told, but he would be the "cohesive force" linking the two entities together. He would have authority over the organization—final say on projects to be undertaken, responsibility for all community meetings and battles that might take place, and complete charge of all dealings with the press. Since he was giving up a secure position to run an operation with an uncertain future, André Meyer and Benno Schmidt guaranteed that Thomas would have a safe place to land if the project imploded. Kennedy offered to be available to Thomas at any time, by phone or in person. When Kennedy was in New York, which was at least once a week, he wanted to meet with Thomas. Thomas wanted to see the Bed-Stuy project succeed, and Kennedy had made it possible to take a chance at achieving that success.[22]

Over the next several months, Thomas would focus on small-scale projects with tangible results, tailored to the needs of residents. During spring and summer 1967, he held a series of public meetings, listening to complaints, answering questions, and promising to take "whatever step are necessary" to reconcile the factions in the community. He also fought steadily to command more control in relation to D&S, hiring his own staff and demanding that funds flow directly to the Restoration Corporation. Local priorities prevailed over the grand designs of consultants. Thomas understood that the success of the project depended on the active engagement and participation of people in the community. "If you want genuine knowledge-building, knowledge-transfer to occur," he later reflected, "you have to encourage and enable people closest to the problem to participate in the process."[23]

Observing Kennedy at a meeting of the D&S board that spring, David Lilienthal recalled that the senator looked "quite handsome in spite of the fact that his tie was not fully pulled up, his suit was rumpled, and his socks were droopy." What struck Lilienthal was Kennedy's capacity to function at full throttle, holding exhaustion at bay. "He listened with an intensity that was almost painful, occasionally rubbing his eyes with fatigue, his knees drawn up to the edge of the table. . . . He never let his mind wander, nor did he relax for a second." Kennedy had just flown in from Washington for the meeting and had to return in time for an evening engagement. "I'm like a yo-yo," he commented.[24]

———

THE LOOMING SHOWDOWN between Robert Kennedy and Lyndon Johnson over Vietnam came to a head during the shaky start-up months of the Bed-Stuy project. By spring 1967, the war had vastly expanded, but only marginal gains were made. American troop levels were nearing 450,000, and the bombing campaign had assumed massive proportions, targeting industrial sites, agricultural areas, transportation networks, and cities. The CIA estimated as many as 2,800 casualties each month, heavily weighted toward civilians. Still, the North Vietnamese showed a resilience that defied American power. Vietnam, wrote LBJ biographer Robert Dallek, had become "a stalemate producing irreconcilable domestic divisions and a nightmare. . . . from which Johnson could not awake."[25]

Johnson was increasingly desperate to end the war, but "no one knew how to do it, at least on terms he believed to be acceptable." Washington and Hanoi each insisted on terms that the other rejected. As international and domestic opinion steadily turned against the United States, Hanoi hoped to stop the bombing without conceding to American demands. Johnson was committed to maintaining an independent, noncommunist Vietnam. "We have to save this country," he insisted. Early in 1967, he held on to the hope that Hanoi would bend to American might. The intensifying pressures associated with the war made Johnson even more intolerant of his opponents, Dallek observed. None rankled the president more than Robert Kennedy.[26]

An invitation to participate in an interparliamentary conference on Anglo-American affairs in London took Robert Kennedy to Europe at the end of January. He traveled from London to Paris, Bonn, and Rome, meeting with various officials, including French President Charles de Gaulle and Pope Paul VI. Vietnam was a major topic of discussion. Kennedy found no one who supported America's policy or understood its purpose. He learned from several people he spoke with, including the pope, that Hanoi was open to negotiations.[27]

In Paris, the American embassy set up a meeting with Étienne Manac'h, a former member of the French socialist president Guy Mollet's government, who was then the director of Far Eastern affairs. John Gunther Dean, the Vietnam expert at the American embassy, participated as a translator. Manac'h, a seasoned and well-respected left-leaning diplomat, was in frequent contact with Hanoi. During the conversation, Manac'h said that North Vietnamese officials might be willing to drop all previous conditions for negotiations if America would halt the bombing. Kennedy remembered that Dean got very excited and wrote it all down. As they were leaving, Dean told Kennedy he thought this was extremely important. Before Kennedy left Paris, Dean showed the senator a copy of the report Dean planned to cable to the State Department. As Kennedy later told his press secretary Frank Mankiewicz, "I had no idea whether it was an accurate account of our conversation . . . I mean if he said it, I assume it was because Manac'h spoke French. So, I said 'Sure, I suppose it was.'" He thought nothing more of it.[28]

Kennedy returned to Washington on Saturday, February 4. On Monday morning, the *New York Times* published a front-page story, "Hanoi Said to Give Kennedy Signal It's Ready to Talk." The article was based on an advanced copy of a story written by a *Newsweek* reporter who had seen Dean's cable at the State Department and concluded that Kennedy had received a "peace feeler." Kennedy was baffled by the story. He had heard from several officials during his trip that Hanoi was prepared to negotiate; this was a familiar proposal. Lyndon Johnson was furious and insisted that the source of the story be identified. When a check at the State Department failed to locate a cable (it had been misfiled), Johnson concluded that Kennedy or one of his supporters had leaked the story to *Newsweek* to embarrass the president and further undermine his Vietnam policy. Johnson was, understandably, furious.[29]

Kennedy had planned to meet with Johnson to report on the trip and decided he had better see the president as soon as possible. On Monday morning, Kennedy's secretary called the White House. Johnson said to come that afternoon. Besides Kennedy and Johnson, Walt Rostow, national security adviser, and Nicholas Katzenbach, then undersecretary of state, were the only ones present. Rostow and Katzenbach did not comment on the meeting afterward, except to say that it was very unpleasant. On returning to his

Senate office that afternoon, an incredulous Kennedy described the meeting in detail to Frank Mankiewicz.[30]

"The president started right in by getting mad at me for leaking the story," Mankiewicz recalled Kennedy saying. Kennedy said that he had not leaked the story and did not even know about a peace feeler. The leaker was probably someone in the president's State Department. Johnson shot back, "It's not my State Department, god damn it, it's your State Department," revealing his paranoia that Kennedy loyalists were everywhere. Johnson claimed that the war would be over by the summer and said, "I'll destroy you and every one of your dove friends in six months. You'll be dead politically." At some point, Kennedy asked whether Johnson wanted to hear about what the senator thought should be done. Johnson said go ahead. Kennedy laid out several steps organized around stopping the bombing as a prelude to negotiations. Johnson said, "There just isn't a chance in hell that I will do that, not the slightest chance in the world." He continued to berate Kennedy and accused him and his friends of prolonging the war and causing the death of Americans in Vietnam. Kennedy finally snapped, "Look, I don't have to take that from you," and left.[31]

After the February 6 meeting, Kennedy realized that there was no point in trying to be conciliatory or to mute his criticism of the war. A month later, he delivered his first major policy speech on Vietnam, calling for the suspension of US air raids on North Vietnam in order to open the way to peace talks. North Vietnamese president Ho Chi Minh and Soviet premier Alexei Kosygin had declared that if the bombardment of the North were halted, negotiations could begin. In contrast to previous offers to negotiate, no other conditions were set. Kennedy saw this as "a moment of promise" at a critical juncture when America could either turn toward the possibility of peace or pursue an ever-widening war. In his forty-five-minute speech, he outlined steps that would set the parameters for moving forward, involving an international presence to oversee compliance and ultimately free elections in South Vietnam. Kennedy observed that the military government in South Vietnam was not representative of the many political elements in the country. The United States, he insisted, had nothing to lose by testing the sincerity of the offer; it could resume bombing if North Vietnam failed to act in good faith. America's willingness to pursue negotiations under these conditions had the added advantage of clarifying its objectives before the international community.[32]

Kennedy's March 2 speech, editorialized the *New York Times,* came at "a crucial moment for either peace negotiations or for escalated war" and helped crystallize the debate. He added his name to a formidable list calling for an end to the bombing as a necessary prelude to peace talks—including several senators, Secretary-General U Thant of the United Nations, and the pope. Kennedy's proposal was almost instantly rejected by the Johnson administration. Secretary of State Dean Rusk said "substantially similar" proposals had been tried before and that bombing pauses were met with hostile actions. President Johnson sent a letter to Senator Henry Jackson, a leading voice on military affairs, published in the *New York Times*, which justified the expansion of the bombing campaign and described its effectiveness. Johnson pledged to "continue to use this instrument of support for our men and our allies" until "the other side" is willing to act as "part of a serious effort to end this war and bring peace to the people of Southeast Asia." The president, at this point, had public opinion firmly in his corner. A Gallup poll found that only 24 percent of Americans favored a bombing halt.[33]

Within days of Kennedy's speech, Martin Luther King Jr. and Andrew Young, SCLC's executive director, attended a fundraising dinner in New York hosted by William vanden Heuvel and Jean Stein, close friends of Kennedy. King was becoming more outspoken in his opposition to the president's Vietnam policy and disappointment in the failing War on Poverty, and the civil rights leader found agreement and support for his views among this group. The four agreed that activists and progressives like Kennedy should work more closely together. Andy Young followed up with a letter to vanden Heuvel, saying, "It seems to me that with you working from within the structure of politics and economics and us working on the outside we can move the country along much more quickly." He told vanden Heuvel to call anytime "you see a complementary role for Dr. King and / or the SCLC," adding, "there are many things that Senator Kennedy cannot say or do that present no problem for Dr. King."[34]

Early in 1967, King's opposition to the war in Vietnam had taken a qualitative turn. He was in Jamaica for a rare few weeks of quiet to work on his book, *Where Do We Go from Here: Chaos or Community* when he saw a photo essay on "The Children of Vietnam" in the January issue of *Ramparts* magazine. The preface, written by Dr. Benjamin Spock, began: "A million children have been killed or wounded or burned in the war America is carrying on in Vietnam." The photographs by William Pepper showed children burned and deformed, skeletal bodies, children crowded in squalid refugee shelters, orphans begging on the streets. The accompanying text provided an inventory of the maimed and killed and described the nature of American warfare in Vietnam—the bombing, the defoliants, the gases. In an afterword, the magazine editors wrote that "the war in Vietnam has reached its ultimate and most barbarous stage, with the massiveness of American firepower being brought to bear in rural areas occupied largely by women and children." King had spoken out against the war since 1965. When he saw the images, he committed to doing all he could to end the war.[35]

Antiwar activists had been appealing to King to take a stronger stand. He accepted an invitation to speak at a forum sponsored by the *Nation* in Los Angeles on February 25. His speech went beyond his earlier opposition, which had focused largely on the dollars the war in Vietnam drained from America's War on Poverty, and directly addressed the immorality of the war, which he described as a demonstration of "deadly western arrogance." Johnson's war policy, King charged, had put the United States in the position of supporting a dictatorial military regime in South Vietnam, leaving Americans "isolated in our false values in a world demanding social and economic justice." American forces were committing atrocities, he said, "equal to any perpetuated by the Viet Cong." King spoke of "the triple evils of racism, extreme materialism, and militarism," and called for "a vigorous reordering of our national priorities." That process might start, he said, with a halt to the bombing and the declaration of a willingness to negotiate with the Viet Cong. A month later, King participated in his first antiwar march in Chicago.[36]

On April 4, King delivered an address before three thousand people at the Riverside Church in New York City, sponsored by the Clergy and Laymen Concerned about Vietnam. "Beyond Vietnam" was one of the strongest public statements against the war made by a national figure of his stature. The speech was, he stated, "based on the mandates of conscience and the reading of history." The nearly hour-long oration was a powerful distillation of the evolution of King's own position on the war, from seeing the war as an enemy of the poor to a pointed assessment of the war's horrific impact on all parts of Vietnam. King appealed to his listeners to consider the brutalizing process experienced by US troops on the ground as they began to question the war and its purposes. "As we counsel young men concerning military service," he said, "we must clarify for them our nation's role in Vietnam and challenge them with the alternative of conscientious objection."

King talked about his experience in the ghettos of the North over the previous three summers and his efforts to convince frustrated and angry youth that meaningful social change could come through nonviolent action. Some would turn to him and ask, "What about Vietnam?" King concluded that he could not raise his voice "against the violence of the oppressed in the ghettos without having first spoken clearly to the greatest purveyor of violence in the world today: my own government." It was America's responsibility to take the initiative to end the war, he said, and he suggested five specific actions for the Johnson administration, starting with a cessation of all bombing to open the way to negotiation. The speech was a powerful appeal not only to end the war in Vietnam but also to face a "far deeper malady within the American spirit," seen in the glaring inequities and injustices in a society that continued to spend more money on military defense than on social uplift.[37]

King's speech brought immediate and widespread condemnation from the mainstream press and moderate civil rights leaders, including Roy Wilkins and Whitney Young. A. Philip Randolph and Bayard Rustin would not comment for publication. The *New York Times*, still viewing the "civil rights movement" as an entity somehow insulated from the tumult of 1967, took a patronizing tone. Now that the movement had entered an "advanced and more difficult stage" in places like Watts, Chicago, and Harlem, the *Times* instructed King that to "divert the energies of the movement . . . is both wasteful and self-defeating." The *Washington Post* charged King with doing a "grave injury to those who are his natural allies and himself. . . . He has diminished his usefulness to his cause, to his country, and to his people." "A demagogic slander that sounded like a script for Radio Hanoi," was how *Life* magazine described the speech, saying that King's proposal "amounts to abject surrender in Vietnam." With Martin Luther King Jr.'s emergence as a major critic of the war, President Johnson asked FBI liaison Cartha DeLoach how King's relationship to Stanley Levison could be publicly revealed—a move opposed by the president's new attorney general, Ramsey Clark.[38]

King conceded that the speech might have been "politically unwise," but he told Stanley Levison that it was "morally wise." "I think I have a role to play which is unpopular," King said. He felt "someone of influence has to say the United States is wrong. Everybody is afraid to say it." He continued, "I have just become so disgusted with the way the people of America are being brainwashed by . . . the administration."[39]

Liberal religious groups, progressive publications, and antiwar activists welcomed King's outspoken opposition to the war, and some urged him to consider running as a peace candidate in 1968. King was not interested in running for office. When queried by reporters late in April, he said that from a civil rights perspective he felt the two best possible presidential candidates were Robert Kennedy for the Democrats and Charles Percy, an outspoken opponent of the Vietnam War, for the Republicans.[40]

———

DURING SPRING 1967, the Senate Subcommittee on Employment, Manpower, and Poverty initiated a broadscale investigation of the poverty program. The experience further convinced Kennedy that poverty and hunger were critical national issues. As the subcommittee hearings got underway, Kennedy deflected press questions about his strained relationship with the president, saying that he looked forward to campaigning for Johnson in 1968 and reiterating the call for a bombing pause. Kennedy said without further elaboration that it was his strong feeling that "this was the course of action that must be taken."[41]

On March 15, the second day of the hearings, the senators heard from Detroit mayor Jerome Cavanagh, then serving as head of the US Conference of Mayors. Cavanaugh warned of "extremely serious problems" in the cities over the coming summer, especially if the administration failed to increase the poverty budget and refused to reconsider its announced cutbacks to existing programs. Later that day, Marian Wright, then working for the NAACP Legal Defense Fund in Jackson, Mississippi, turned the committee's attention to the utter failure of federally funded programs to even begin to address the problems of poverty in the Mississippi Delta. "After three years of the war on poverty," the twenty-seven-year-old lawyer told the committee, "Negroes in Mississippi are poorer than they were before." She testified that in most Mississippi counties not a single Negro was aided by welfare, agriculture, or employment programs financed with federal funds.[42]

Since her days as a leader of the sit-in movement in Atlanta, Wright had taken a law degree at Yale and rejoined the ranks of the movement in 1964 as an attorney with the Legal Defense Fund. She was part of the small crew on the ground providing legal advice and representation for SNCC and local activists during the Freedom Summer campaign and the Mississippi Freedom Democratic Party challenge at the Democratic convention. After completing the state's fifteen-month residency requirement, Wright became the first Black woman admitted to the bar in the state of Mississippi, at a time when there were only three Black lawyers in the state. "Practicing law in Mississippi during the extraordinary years between 1964 and 1968," Wright later recalled, "taught me about the enormously high costs of social change in violence, economic reprisals, harassment, fear, and lives lost."[43]

By the spring of 1967, there was a growing awareness among journalists and concerned policymakers of the desperate situation in rural Mississippi. A convergence of factors had created near-starvation conditions in the Delta region, where SNCC activists had fought for voting rights in the early 1960s. The white power structure remained firmly in place and was ready to reap reprisals. The mechanization of agriculture and federal application of minimum wage law to farm workers in 1966 led large plantation owners to accelerate their adoption of machinery that displaced labor. By the mid-1960s, 90 percent of the cotton crop was harvested by machines, leaving large numbers of former farm workers without income. The welfare system supported only single-parent households, so intact families had no sources of aid except food stamps or the surplus food program. By 1967, many counties had adopted the federal food stamp program, enacted in 1964. Applicants had to stand in line at the welfare office, run by local whites, to establish eligibility and secure food stamps. Qualified recipients had to pay at minimum $2.00 per person for the stamps; for a family of four, that was $8.00—putting the stamps out of reach of those who had no income at all.[44]

A major political battle emerged around a pioneering Head Start program started in the summer of 1965 by veterans of the civil rights struggle in Mississippi. The Child Development Group of Mississippi (CDGM) utilized the community-based structure that had grown up around the movement. CDGM was one of the largest and most successful Head Start programs in the country—early on serving six thousand students in eighty-four centers around the state. CDGM was constantly under attack from Mississippi's political leaders and powerful representatives in Congress, with charges of fiscal mismanagement and the use of funds for civil rights activities. Sargent Shriver, head of the Office of Economic Opportunity (OEO), finally caved in to political pressure and supported the establishment of a competing group, Mississippi Action for Progress, run by white establishment figures and middle-class African Americans. In response to pressure from CDGM's supporters, coordinated by the Citizens Crusade against Poverty, OEO renewed funding for CDGM for a scaled-down program. By spring 1967, however, CDGM was struggling to survive in the face of continued allegations and harassment.[45]

The Senate Subcommittee on Employment, Manpower, and Poverty had chosen Jackson, Mississippi, as the location for its first hearing in the field. On Monday, April 10, between eight hundred and one thousand people, mostly African American, crowded into the ballroom of the Hotel Heidelberg for a full day of testimony. At his request, Senator John Stennis testified first, using the hearings as a platform for the relentless campaign to discredit and destroy CDGM. In a long, rambling statement, Stennis repeated charges that large sums were unaccounted for and attacked the character and morality of the group's leadership. In response, Bobby Kennedy and Senator Jacob Javits both read from a recent audit, conducted by Ernst & Ernst, that found no substance to these allegations.

Dr. A. B. Britton, a Black physician based in Jackson, described the endemic poverty, hunger, and lack of medical facilities in the Mississippi Delta. Infant mortality among African Americans, he said, was double the rate for whites in the state. Testimony followed from several women and men with deep roots in the Delta, who were stalwarts of the civil rights movement in

Mississippi and now worked with CDGM and other antipoverty programs—including Fannie Lou Hamer, Unita Blackwell, and Amzie Moore. They made a deep impression on Kennedy, who immediately wanted to see what they described. He had avoided getting publicly involved in the struggles surrounding CDGM before coming to Mississippi given the prominent role of his brother-in-law, Sargent Shriver, in the conflict. Behind the scenes, however, Kennedy had supported the efforts of Richard Boone, now head of the Citizens Crusade against Poverty, which lobbied on behalf of CDGM in Washington. After the meeting—and after hearing from Hamer, Moore, Blackwell, Marian Wright, and others—Kennedy placed himself firmly on the side of CDGM, which at this point was holding on in six counties with help from the Field Foundation.[46]

Kennedy and Senator Joseph Clark, the chair of the subcommittee, toured the Delta the following day, visiting Greenville, Cleveland, and Clarksdale, guided by Marian Wright and Amzie Moore. Wright rode with Kennedy and Peter Edelman, accompanied by a federal marshal. "I was not prepared for Robert Kennedy," she recalled. "I'd formed an image of him as a tough, arrogant, politically driven man." Over the course of the day, these feelings began to dissolve. She enjoyed Kennedy on a personal level, and he clearly was intrigued by this highly educated, attractive young woman working for change in one of the poorest and most repressive areas in the country. Driving through the Delta with him, she was struck by Kennedy's "insatiable curiosity about everything." What was she reading? It happened to be William Styron's *The Confessions of Nat Turner*. He wanted to know why she had come to Mississippi. "He was quizzing her steadily," Peter Edelman recalled, and "it wasn't small talk." If she worked so hard, Kennedy asked, what did she do besides work? None of his business, she replied.[47]

A fleet of news reporters and television cameras from the three major networks followed the group. "It was terrible, shocking, eye-opening," recalled Peter Edelman. Children with "swollen bellies, and sores that wouldn't heal, and just clearly malnourished." Nick Kotz of the *Des Moines Register* described "a dark, windowless shack" that smelled "of mildew, sickness and urine." As they walked from one house to the next, Kennedy told Edelman that these were the worst conditions he'd ever seen in the United States.[48] When Kennedy would enter a home, Wright recalled, he would ask each person, "respectfully, what they had had for breakfast, lunch or dinner the night before." After asking permission, he'd open their empty cupboards and iceboxes. His way with children struck her—"he lightly touched the cheek, shoulders and hands of the children, clad in dirty, ragged clothes and tried to offer words of encouragement to their hopeless mothers." Wright and Edelman were close by when Kennedy went alone into a home where he saw a listless child around two years old sitting on a dirt floor, his stomach bloated from malnutrition. The senator hovered, talking softly and stroking the child's hair, trying in vain to get a response. No cameras were present. CBS newsman Daniel Schorr, who covered the tour, recalled, "at one point I thought he was close to tears."[49]

From their first meeting through the fourteen months she would know him, Wright said she came to associate Robert Kennedy with nonverbal communications that conveyed far more than words: a light touch on the face, a pat on the shoulder, an affectionate gentle hit on the arm or the back. "He looked straight at you and he *saw* you. His capacity for genuine outrage and compassion," she said, "was palpable." She recounted a telling incident. Toward the end of the day, as their motorcade left Cleveland, Mississippi, one of the cars ran over a dog. Kennedy got out of the car to comfort the small boy to whom the dog had belonged. Then, Wright recalled, he "angrily ordered the police escort to cut out the siren and slow down."[50]

Kennedy and Edelman flew back to Washington that night. The very next day the two of them, along with Joe Clark and his staff director Bill Smith, went to see Secretary of Agriculture Orville Freeman. Freeman, a former Minnesota governor, had been appointed by JFK and had helped create the food stamp program as part of LBJ's War on Poverty. "I just don't know, Orville," Kennedy said, "I don't know why you can't just get some food down there." Freeman would not believe conditions were as bad as Kennedy said or that there were actually people with no income. He sent two Agricultural Department officials to investigate, and Edelman took them on the same tour. The officials reported back that what Kennedy had described was true; there was widespread hunger and malnutrition in the Mississippi Delta. But Freeman was in a bind. Funding for his department depended on Mississippi congressman Jamie L. Whitten, the powerful chair of the Appropriations Committee, and Whitten and Senator James Eastland were furious at the exposure of conditions in their home state.[51]

All nine senators on the poverty subcommittee signed a letter to President Johnson describing the conditions and urging him to take emergency action. But Johnson was preoccupied with the Vietnam War and its financing and was not inclined to get embroiled in this issue or find himself on the bad side of the chair of the appropriations committee. The letter was passed along to the Office of Economic Opportunity, which issued a press release acknowledging the problem but claiming that the OEO had done more for Mississippi than other needy areas while shifting blame to Congress for cutting funding for antipoverty programs.[52]

Later in the spring, Kennedy and members of the subcommittee found further documentation of dire poverty in Mississippi in a report produced by a team of doctors, funded by the Field Foundation, who had been sent to inspect conditions in six Mississippi counties—Humphreys, Leflore, Clarke, Wayne, Neshoba, and Greene Counties. The team included Robert Coles, a child psychiatrist at Harvard and author of *Children of Crisis;* Dr. Alan Mermann, a pediatrician and assistant clinical professor at Yale School of Medicine who had made a medical survey of Lowndes County in Alabama; Dr. Joseph Brenner of the Massachusetts Institute of Technology, who had conducted medical inspections in the South and in East Africa; and Dr. Raymond Wheeler, an internist in private practice in Charlotte, North Carolina. The doctors found "literally penniless rural families" and documented thousands of men, women, and children "living outside every legal, medical and social advance our Nation has made." "Evidence of severe malnutrition" was rampant among the children in every county the team visited. "These children," the report stated, "are receiving no food from the government, they are also getting no medical attention." Commenting on the report at a news conference, Dr. Brenner said he found health conditions among the poor in the counties they visited "as bad or worse than" among the poorest Africans in Kenya and Aden. He was incredulous that "this should be so in the wealthiest nation in the world."[53]

In mid-June, following the release of the Field Foundation report, the doctors delivered a summary of their findings to the Department of Agriculture and to the Senate Subcommittee on Employment, Manpower, and Poverty and participated in a news conference. Senator Clark invited them to meet with members of the subcommittee over lunch in the new Senate Office Building. Clark, Kennedy, and Javits were the only members of the subcommittee to attend. At the end of the lunch, Kennedy said, "Well, we'll arrange for a hearing." Peter Edelman remembers getting on the phone as soon as he was back at the office, calling various subcommittee members, checking calendars, and finally setting the date for July 11.[54]

The doctors' shocking testimony, describing conditions of hunger that approached starvation, may have been the first time that the cruel conditions of the poor in Mississippi claimed a spotlight on Capitol Hill. The testimony drew a howl of protest and denial from Mississippi's two senators, whom Clark had invited to sit with the committee. The most damning testimony came from the one southern doctor on the team. Dr. Raymond Wheeler described Mississippi as "a kind of prison" for the Negro poor, "semi starving people from whom all but token support has been withdrawn." He had heard charges throughout the Delta that "those who control the state" were engaged in a campaign to "eliminate the Negro Mississippian either by driving him out or starving him to death." At first, he had found such charges hard to believe, but after reviewing "all we saw and heard it becomes more and more credible." Senator James Eastland denied the findings and accused Wheeler of libeling the state of Mississippi. Asked to respond to Eastland later in the afternoon, Wheeler said, "I reported what I saw because I love the region. . . . I invite Senator Eastland to come with me to the vast farmlands of the Delta. I will show him children with shriveled arms and swollen bellies, their hunger and their pain."[55]

Senators Eastland and John Stennis introduced Dr. A. L. Gray, director of Mississippi's Board of Public Health, as their principal witness to rebut the "out of state" doctors. Kennedy tried to get Gray to agree that he would welcome emergency medical volunteers to the state, but Gray insisted they would have to be licensed in Mississippi. "Children are dying," Kennedy exclaimed, "and you're talking about licenses?" A frustrated Kennedy held up a picture of a swollen-bellied child and said, "Look at this, doctor. This is a child." Clark and Kennedy both tried to get Eastland to agree that a federal program to bring nutritious food to Mississippi's hungry should be launched immediately. Eastland declared, "I deny there is mass malnutrition."[56]

The two days of hearings also looked beyond Mississippi. A panel of poor people from other states testified, describing conditions that were similar to the ones the doctors had found in the Delta. Dr. William Stewart, the surgeon general, was among the witnesses. In response to questions about hunger across the United States, he acknowledged, "We don't know the extent of the problem or what needs to be done." He observed that Americans knew more about the hungry in other nations than at home. Kennedy asked that the Public Health Service inquire into the number and condition of malnourished people in the United States.[57]

Throughout this period, Kennedy and Clark and sympathetic allies and organizations continued to pressure Secretary of Agriculture Orville Freeman, suggesting ways he could use his office to help aid the hungry. Freeman finally admitted to the two senators that while he had the authority to issue free food stamps and declare an emergency so that commodities could be distributed in counties where people could not afford the stamps, he could not use the power until he checked with Jamie Whitten—and, of course, Congressman Whitten said no. In the end, after the Agriculture Department's budget for 1968 was approved and the food stamp extension had passed Congress, Freeman instituted minimal reforms. In June 1967, he reduced the cost of food stamps to the poorest families from $2.00 per person a month to fifty cents, and local welfare authorities were encouraged to provide food stamp funds for the destitute. There would be no free food stamps or emergency distribution of food for those who could not afford stamps. "Orville was being subject to pressure by us," Bobby later told journalist Nick Kotz, "but he was much more worried about his own programs, for which he had to answer to Whitten, Eastland and that crowd. It boiled down to whether we could exert more pressure than the southerners—we didn't."[58]

From this point on, Kennedy took a great personal interest in the problem of hunger, Edelman recalled, and the senator would continue to do all he could to draw national attention to the issue. At Kennedy's urging, CBS News producer Don Hewitt sent young documentary maker Martin Carr to the region. "Hunger in America" would air in May 1968. Peter Edelman estimated that he devoted at least 20 percent of his time to poverty and hunger from April 1967 until the following March—researching, writing memos, working on legislative initiatives, and keeping Kennedy informed. Kennedy and Clark succeeded in getting $25 million for an emergency food program added to Office of Economic Opportunity legislation, which passed later that year, along with a provision authorizing a national nutrition survey to be carried out by the Public Health Service.[59]

Later that spring, Senator Clark's subcommittee investigated antipoverty projects in the Los Angeles area through a series of hearings and on-site visits. The hearings showed the positive impact of several programs while revealing how inadequate funding had severely limited their reach. In the area of housing for migrant farm laborers, only one-quarter to one-half of the need was being met. Kennedy, Clark, and Senator George Murphy of California toured parts of the San Joaquin Valley, where they found migrant workers living in cars and tents along a riverbank—a scene of "stark poverty," as Kennedy described it. "How do you reconcile this in a nation with a Gross National Product of $700 billion annually and the richest state in the union?" he asked.[60]

While in Los Angeles, Kennedy planned to visit the Watts Writers Workshop, screenwriter Budd Schulberg's response to the 1965 uprising. The workshop started as a small creative writing class for young residents of Watts and grew quickly to several hundred students. Schulberg supported the program by reaching out to fellow writers, including Robert Kennedy (as an author, not a senator). Kennedy sent a contribution and asked Schulberg to keep in touch about the group's progress. Schulberg sent Kennedy an anthology produced by the group, *From the Ashes: Voices of Watts,* and received a warm letter back saying Kennedy would like to visit. He asked Schulberg to arrange a private informal meeting without publicity. As Schulberg recalled, Bobby said that he did not want middle-of-the-roaders. He wanted to hear from the militants and to know "how they're really thinking."[61]

On the afternoon of May 13, after the hearings had ended, Kennedy drove with Schulberg to Douglass House at 9807 Beach Street, in the heart of Watts. For more than ninety minutes, a group of four young men and one woman unloaded on Kennedy. "What street did they bring you down? You see any change?" a fierce nineteen-year-old in a Malcolm X sweatshirt demanded. "Same old buildings," one said. "Only the spirit's changed. Watts has got to do it on its own." Another asked angrily, "Why do our brothers do all the dying in Vietnam?" As the group continued, Kennedy listened, mostly parried the questions, and occasionally said "something personal and pointed, in his quiet, diffident way," Schulberg recalled. "We look on you as the boss cat," James Thomas Jackson said as the meeting was winding down. "So we figure you should do something extra for us." "I'll try. I'll try," Kennedy responded.

Afterward, Schulberg asked one of the most vociferous young men at the meeting what he thought. "Hell, he's not as bad as some," he said. "But I'll bet he'll go back to Washington and forgets all about it."[62]

CHAPTER FOURTEEN

The Gravest Crisis since the Civil War

||

THE SUMMER OF 1967—the "summer of love" for America's youth counter-culture—was a "long hot summer" for Black urban Americans, a season of the deadliest and most widespread racial strife in US history. Racial clashes, disorders, and rebellions erupted in an estimated 164 cities in thirty-four states, bringing the nation's crisis to a boil. Incidents ranged widely from window breaking, looting, and confrontations with police to major uprisings in more than a dozen states where governors called in the National Guard.[1]

The Harvest of American Racism, a government-sponsored report based on research in twenty-three of the affected cities, concluded that the most salient feature of the disorders was a form of "generalized rebellion on the part of certain sections of the Negro community . . . against white control of Negro areas." In Newark, five days of street battles, burning, and looting approached the scale of the Watts uprising two years earlier. Less than a week after order was restored, Detroit exploded into what has been billed as "the largest civil disturbance of the twentieth century."[2]

The violence that erupted that summer intensified the country's political polarization, while exposing the failure of the Johnson administration to seriously address the desperate conditions in poor urban areas. During summer and fall 1967, Robert Kennedy and Martin Luther King Jr. felt a greater sense of urgency as each attempted to meet the challenges of the moment and formulate new strategies for healing the country's deep racial wounds while summoning America's capacity to create a more just and equitable future.

Newark, a majority Black city, mirrored conditions in large urban ghettos across the country. Unemployment was high, most residents lived in poverty, schools were substandard, there was little opportunity for job training, and racial profiling by the police was common. Feelings of power-lessness, frustration, and anger were further aggravated by the displacement of thousands of families from their homes to build a new university of medicine and dentistry. Italian-American mayor Hugh Adonnizio ran the city like an old-style Democratic Party boss. He was more responsive to his base of white blue-collar voters than to the Black people of Newark, whom local CORE president Robert Curvin described as "the most underrepresented" citizens in the country.[3]

On July 12, two white police officers arrested John Smith, a Black taxicab driver, after he signaled and passed a double-parked police car. The police pursued the cab, pulled Smith over, beat him, arrested him, and charged him with attacking the officers and making insulting comments. Residents nearby saw the driver dragged into the precinct. Rumors spread that he had been beaten to death. (Smith survived but had to be hospitalized for his injuries.) A crowd gathered outside the precinct and hurled rocks and bottles against the wall. Police waded into the crowd in hard hats with clubs. The following day a march was organized to protest police brutality. Someone smashed a window, and looting began. The National Guard and state troopers were called in to reinforce the police, but by midnight the uprising had escalated and it continued for five days.[4]

Mayor Addonizio told the police to use any means necessary to restore order. Many died in volleys of gunfire aimed at looters and suspected snipers. Six were killed when the police shot indiscriminately into crowds, including a seventy-four-year-old man who had been walking toward his car and a woman who had come out of her home to look for her children. Three women were shot on separate occasions by National Guardsmen shooting into buildings. In the end, twenty-six people were dead—mostly African Americans, as well as one white police officer and one white fireman. More than seven hundred were injured, and property damage was estimated at $10 million.[5]

Detroit offered a striking contrast to Newark in terms of city leadership, political representation, and race relations, contributing to Detroit's national reputation as a "model city." The city's growing Black population exercised electoral clout, elevating increasing numbers of African Americans to local office and to Congress. In 1965, when John Conyers Jr. was elected to Congress, he joined Charles Diggs Jr. as one of two Black congressmen representing districts within the city. Black voters helped elect insurgent candidate Jerome Cavanagh to the mayor's office in 1962. In June 1963, Cavanagh marched with Martin Luther King in the Walk to Freedom marking the twentieth anniversary of the 1943 Detroit race riot—a powerful statement in a city committed to racial progress. Cavanagh devoted time and effort to improving African American lives and race relations in Detroit. He was enormously successful in securing War on Poverty funds for the city, making Detroit second only to New York in the amount of federal funds received. Cavanagh acted to change the city's nearly all-white police department, appointing two liberal police commissioners in succession who shared the mayor's commitment to reform and made a dedicated effort to hire Black police officers.[6]

Still, the mayor's reforms and the work of groups like the NAACP and the National Urban League could not stave off a racial crisis that had been decades in the making. While a strong Black middle class had emerged in the years after World War II, Detroit remained a rigidly segregated city with overcrowded enclaves of poverty, deteriorating housing conditions, and substandard schools. The decline of the auto industry and the movement of other industrial jobs to outlying areas in the 1950s had further exacerbated high rates of unemployment. Black unemployment was around 20 percent, and many gave up on looking for work. At the time of the riot, between 25 percent and 30 percent of young Black men were unemployed. Youth alienation, as Thomas J. Sugrue has pointed out, was "most severely affected by the shrinking job market." Antipoverty programs "did not fundamentally deviate from the limited agenda that social welfare, labor and civil rights groups had set in the 1950s." Growing impatience with the glacial pace of change saw the proliferation of Black Power groups in Detroit. The voices of the tens of thousands living in the direst conditions remained largely unheard.[7]

Community-police relations were "the single most important problem of the city," in the view of an NAACP official. Despite Cavanagh's efforts, the only measurable change was in the number of Black police officers, whose representation on the force grew from 3 percent to 5 percent in a city where Blacks made up 33 percent of the population. The police were known for their brutality—both psychological and physical, reflecting the prejudices of most whites and satisfying their concerns about crime. Efforts to influence police behavior were easily undermined and were often met with work slowdowns. The overwhelmingly white force was, as Sidney Fine has stated, "poorly educated for the most part" and "poorly trained." The police "did not understand nor were they prepared to deal with the law enforcement problems stemming from the Black revolt," as events that summer would tragically reveal.[8]

Shortly before 4 a.m. on Sunday, July 23, police raided an after-hours club that was illegally serving alcohol as a neighborhood civic group hosted a welcome home party there for two soldiers just back from Vietnam. The club was over a printing shop on Twelfth Street, a bustling and densely populated area in the heart one of Detroit's largest Black neighborhoods. Police expected to find a few dozen people. There were more than eighty. It was a stifling summer night, and many were on the street, cooling off. As the police brought people outside to complete the arrests, bystanders crowded around. Some of those being arrested were well known in the community. The mood of the crowd became angry. "You wouldn't do this kind of thing in the white area," a member of the crowd charged. A young man shouted at the police and urged the group to riot. As the police car drove off, he threw a rock through the back window. Several hundred people continued to mill around after that. Someone threw a rock through the window of the Esquire Clothing Store, and several people broke into the store and came out with armfuls of hats, shirts, and shoes. Others quickly joined in, breaking store windows and looting merchandise.

The police returned but, undermanned, did nothing to stop the looting, and the crowd grew. Failure to restore order at this critical point drew wide criticism from Black leaders in Detroit, including the local NAACP. The street scenes took on a carnival-like atmosphere, with thousands of people from all parts of the community, including women, children, and some white people, joining in the fray. Late Sunday morning, an elite riot squad carrying rifles equipped with bayonets arrived, with orders to sweep the streets.[9]

Over the next four days, the confrontation rapidly escalated. Initially, the Detroit police were outmatched and unprepared in the face of a crowd of eight or nine thousand. Black youth activists aggressively challenged the police, lighting fires, setting off fire alarms, and cutting fire hoses. For a time, "looters roamed freely . . . in the embattled area, carrying clothes, lamps, golf bags and other goods from flaming shops," reported the *New York Times*. A boy of around twelve was seen racing away from a florist with an armful of gladioli, and "a stout woman strained under the weight of a mattress." Governor George Romney sent in the National Guard on Monday night, and violence escalated on both sides. An estimated eight thousand National Guardsmen joined four thousand city police. Fires raged through tenement buildings, small businesses, and individual residences. Several police and Guardsmen were wounded by sniper fire. A National Guardsman met a flash from a window with machine-gun fire, killing a four-year-old girl; the flash was the lighting of a cigarette. Early Tuesday morning, Governor Romney requested federal troops. After some delay, President Johnson sent the 89th and 101st Airborne Divisions, along with tanks, machine guns, and helicopters to subdue the rioting. Many of the troops had recently returned from Vietnam. When asked about their mood heading to Detroit, one of the soldiers replied, "they say war is war."[10]

On Tuesday and Wednesday, as Black violence decreased, police violence escalated. An investigation done for the National Advisory Commission on Civil Disorders reported that some officers and National Guardsmen acted out a desire for vengeance. Police stopped wearing badges to assure anonymity and participated in indiscriminate shooting and beatings. After responding to a report of sniper fire at the Algiers Motel, police killed three unarmed Black teenagers while they were kneeling or lying on the floor. The two white girls found with them were severely beaten. One of the officers was indicted for the murder but acquitted. There were four other reported cases of police or National Guardsmen shooting unarmed men who were not threatening them.[11]

Americans watched on the nightly news as the nation's fifth-largest city turned into a veritable war zone. "Since Sunday morning, mobs of angry Negroes have paralyzed the city," David Brinkley reported on NBC's *Huntley-Brinkley Report,* "spreading fire and destruction through large areas." When it was all over on July 27, forty-three people were dead, thirty-three of whom were African American. More than two thousand had been injured, and there had been five thousand arrests. Property damage was estimated at more than $100 million, nearly three times the damage done in the Watts uprising. More than two thousand buildings had been burned to the ground. Describing his city's charred landscape, Mayor Cavanagh said, "It looks like Berlin in 1945." While police and troops battled protesters in Detroit, uprisings erupted in neighboring cities—Flint, Pontiac, Grand Rapids, and across the Ohio state line in Toledo. Following the start of troubles in Detroit a week earlier, the *New York Times* reported on July 30, "rioting continued to spread like an infection to a total of 18 cities."[12]

Military metaphors infused television coverage and newspaper and magazine reports, describing scenes that resembled guerilla warfare. *Life* magazine reported on "troops battling snipers under the cover of night" and offered a full-color spread of burned-out buildings and armored vehicles and jeeps on patrol in residential areas. "Negroes Battle with Guardsmen in Newark" headlined a story in the *New York Times.* The liberal *Milwaukee Journal* told of "pitched battles" in Detroit, where National Guardsmen and police "battled elusive snipers" in a climate of "racial terror." *NBC Nightly News* reported that Michigan governor George Romney and Mayor Cavanagh had established command posts at police headquarters from which "they have been directing the fight to regain control of the city." The coverage reinforced the dominant white opinion of Black urban communities as dangerous, violent, and crime-infested places and helped to justify the militarization of urban policing.[13]

The uprisings set off a scramble for political advantage and scapegoats and amplified calls for law and order. In a slashing attack, Republican leaders blamed President Johnson, charging that "widespread rioting and violent disorder had grown to a national crisis since the present Administration took office." Republicans accused Johnson of failing to advance proposals "to protect our people on the street and in their homes." Senator Everett Dirksen and House Minority Leader Gerald Ford called for a joint investigation of the riots and their instigators, whether communists or other subversives. California governor Ronald Reagan, now touted as a possible Republican presidential candidate, branded the racial strife in Detroit and elsewhere as "riots of the lawbreakers and the mad dogs against the people." Former president Dwight Eisenhower accused the US Supreme Court, in recent decisions such as *Miranda v. Arizona* (1966), of "gravely" handicapping the police and endorsed a constitutional amendment "to restore the power of the police." The *Miranda* ruling held that individuals in police custody following an arrest must be informed of their constitutional right to remain silent and to have an attorney present.[14]

President Johnson had hoped to avoid direct involvement with racial troubles that summer. He had made a minor comment during the Newark disturbances, but Detroit demanded his attention. Concerned about political fallout, he dragged his feet on sending federal troops. He worried that the sight of army troops on the streets of a major city might signal the failure of his domestic agenda, and he suspected the motives of Governor George Romney, a leading Republican contender for the presidency. Romney requested troops early Monday afternoon. They were not deployed until late that evening and were sent only at the insistence of a desperate governor. At close to midnight, Johnson, flanked by Secretary of Defense Robert McNamara, FBI Director J. Edgar Hoover, and Attorney General Ramsey Clark, went on national television and announced that he was sending troops into Detroit. In his first formal comments on the racial disturbances that summer, he deplored the violence and lawlessness and appealed to people to leave the streets, repeating several times that Governor Romney had "been unable to bring the situation under control."[15]

On Thursday, July 27, Johnson gave a nationally televised address in which he explained that he had created the National Advisory Commission on Civil Disorders, chaired by Illinois governor Otto Kerner Jr., to investigate the origins of the riots and make recommendations "for measures to prevent and contain such disasters in the future." The president denounced "the looting, arson, plunder and pillage" and the "criminals who committed these acts of violence against the people." He said the FBI would continue its search for evidence of conspiracy. He stressed how important it was for law enforcement at all levels to be prepared to stop the violence quickly and permanently and announced that the Defense Department was preparing new training standards for riot control. Johnson then acknowledged that the only long-term solution was to attack "the conditions that breed despair and violence" and praised his own administration for directing "the greatest governmental effort in all of our American history at these ancient enemies." There was no commitment to escalating the War on Poverty, however. Instead, he promised to press for more laws to protect citizens from criminals. "Let us pray," he said in closing, "and let us work, for better jobs and better housing and better education that so many millions of our own fellow Americans need so much tonight."[16]

"That's it," Robert Kennedy told Frank Mankiewicz with evident exasperation. "The President is just not going to do anything more. He's through with domestic problems, with the cities. . . . He's not going to do anything, and he's the only man who can." When Mankiewicz asked Kennedy what he would do, the senator said that if he were president, he would persuade the networks to cooperate in producing a documentary depicting daily life in poor Black urban communities. "Let them show the sound, the feel, the hopelessness and what it's like to think you'll never get out," he said. "Show a Black teenager told by a radio jingle to stay in school, looking at his older brother who stayed in school and is out of a job . . . put a *Candid Camera* team in a ghetto school and watch what a rotten system of education it really is. Film a mother staying up all night to keep rats from her baby . . . Then I'd ask people to watch and experience what it means to live in the most affluent society in history—without hope." Mankiewicz later reflected about Kennedy that "the Detroit riots and the terrible feeling he had when he watched Johnson that night" had shifted the senator's thinking about running for president in 1968.[17]

Kennedy was a rare person in the upper echelons of political power and influence: one who, over a stretch of years, had personally seen and experienced the reality of life in America's poorest communities. He viewed white indifference, fear, and prejudice as the greatest obstacles to change—along with the public figures who played on those fears. Daniel Patrick Moynihan's speech to the semiannual meeting of the Americans for Democratic Action (ADA) stood as a case in point. Moynihan proposed that liberals must "overcome the curious condescension which takes the form of sticking up for and explaining away anything, howsoever outrageous, which Negroes, individually or collectively might do." He warned that "a new set of signs tell us that we must prepare for the onset of terrorism." Liberals, Moynihan concluded, must "see more clearly that their essential interest is in the stability of the social order, and that given the present threats to that stability, it is necessary to seek out and make more effective alliances with political conservatives." The audience of more than one hundred responded with a standing ovation.[18]

A few days later, Kennedy remarked to his friend Jack Newfield, a young journalist writing for the *Village Voice,* "I think the ADA should just fold up and go out of business." The group was out of touch, Newfield recalled Kennedy saying. "Most of those people are only interested in making money and having influence." He told Newfield that his generation should go out and start a new Americans for Democratic Action, one "that isn't dependent on the unions for money, and is engaged in direct action, instead of just voting and resolutions."[19]

Robert Kennedy described the racial turmoil that summer as "the gravest crisis" in domestic affairs "since the Civil War." He said that "wherever violence and mob action break out, it must be stopped," but warned that the grievance and despair of the ghetto would not be subdued by force. Speaking to Democratic legislators in San Francisco, Kennedy observed that a violent ghetto youth was not simply protesting his condition. He was "making a destructive and self-defeating attempt to assert his worth and dignity as a human being, to tell us though we may scorn his contribution, we must respect his power." People needed jobs, opportunity, and a way out, and they needed to know that their country understood and was willing to act. He proposed a public works program, building schools, roads, and clinics, to reverse an unemployment rate that in some areas exceeded Great Depression levels. He then called for an "all-out war on poverty," one that would enlist private resources to complement government programs. He underscored the urgency of action. While the season of riots may have peaked, he predicted the country was entering "a period of equal danger," marked by "deepening division between white and black America." The danger was evident in those who referred to their fellow Americans as "honkies" or "mad dogs," Kennedy said, in a not very subtle jab at California's governor.[20]

Later that summer, Kennedy and Peter Edelman had lunch with the editors at *Newsweek*'s Washington bureau. As Edelman recalled, one of the editors noted that Kennedy had made a lot of speeches about what ought to be done in the cities. Suppose you were in the White House, the editor asked; what would you really do, especially if you had trouble getting appropriations from Congress? Not an easy question to answer, Edelman thought. But it was clear that Kennedy had already given the question serious thought. He launched into a long explanation of how he would call in people from each community, city by city—business leaders, labor leaders, church leaders, civic leaders, public officials—to discuss the crisis, hear their thoughts on what could be done, and tell them that if they did not do something, the country was going to fall apart. He would not just try to convince them that they had to do something but would put it in terms of "reasoning together" and coming up with a local initiative. Then, he would "move heaven and earth" to reorient available federal money, try to get more, and work the business side as well.[21]

As the War on Poverty stalled, Kennedy focused increasingly on persuading the business community to invest money and resources in urban areas. He told his fellow senators that to neglect the contribution the business community could make was "to fight the war on poverty with a single platoon, while great armies are left to stand aside." He realized he was at a disadvantage in making the case for action because he was widely disliked among businesspeople, but he had friends who could help. E. Barrett Prettyman, Kennedy's former classmate at the University of Virginia, who had become a prominent lawyer in Washington, set up meetings with several business leaders. There was, as Prettyman describes it, a clear disconnect on the personal level. He recalled that "the business thing was a problem" for Kennedy. "He never understood them. It wasn't that Bob disliked them so much as that he felt if he were a businessman he would have focused less on profits and would have directed much more of his energies toward plans to benefit the community." Yet Kennedy made a concerted effort to enlist business support, speaking to business organizations and reaching out individually in the search for allies.[22]

On September 29, Kennedy addressed the World Trade Conference, sponsored by the Atlanta Chamber of Commerce, in the atrium of the new, ultramodern Regency Hyatt House hotel. He called on the assembled executives to apply the skills, resources, and inventiveness of private enterprise "to our most pressing domestic crisis in 100 years." He spoke about two bills he had recently introduced, which offered "a partnership between industry and community to rebuild neighborhoods—instead of destroying them through short-sighted policy or wanton chaos." Each involved tax incentives to encourage investment in low-income housing and new business construction in poor urban communities. Kennedy underscored how important it was to apply "the flexibility of our fiscal and economic tools to the great task of rebuilding our nation's shame." All Americans in leadership positions must act, he insisted, not because inaction would bring further violence, but "because we must give encouragement to those who still believe that progress is possible within our established institutions." His audience of one thousand listened passively to Kennedy's forty-five-minute address, not once interrupting with applause.[23]

Earlier that summer, Kennedy had introduced a pair of bills offering tax incentives to encourage investment in urban areas, based on the work Mike Curzan had been doing since January. One was a housing bill that provided tax credits and rapid write-offs for the construction or rehabilitation of low-cost housing. The bill called for a fund to support "management corporations" so that residents could participate in the management and maintenance of the buildings. The second, a jobs bill, provided tax credits for new construction of industrial plants in poor urban communities, with stipulations for the minimum number of jobs to be created and a requirement that two-thirds of jobs be filled by locals. The complex legislation had evolved in consultation with nearly one hundred economists, lawyers, industrialists, and administration and other government officials. The bill "involved almost a total rewriting of the tax code, and at the same time, safeguards ensuring community control," recalled Jeff Greenfield, a former Kennedy aide. Curzan produced a very thick briefing book to prepare his boss for hearings on the legislation. Edelman recalled how Kennedy, who admitted to having earned a D in an economics course at Harvard, "learned everything that was in" the briefing book. "He was a very, very intelligent human being," Edelman reflected. "I think he could understand anything he put his mind to. . . . He just had a tremendous capacity."[24]

On September 14, the bills came before the Senate Finance Committee. A front-page story in the *New York Times* reported that the Johnson administration had mounted "a concerted attack" on Kennedy's plan to build more and better low-cost housing in the slums through private enterprise. The article noted that while the legislation "had aroused widespread interest in financial, business and government circles," Housing and Urban Development Secretary Robert Weaver had criticized the plan as "superfluous." Joseph Barr, undersecretary of the treasury, opposed the use of tax incentives for what he called "narrow or specialized purposes." Kennedy was "prepared to do battle," the *Times* noted, and he effectively disputed several of Weaver's claims. Former treasury secretary C. Douglas Dillon testified in support of Kennedy's plan, challenging Barr's suggestion that the legislation was too narrow. The "crisis" in the cities, Dillon said, has created "a problem of the highest priority which has so far defied solution."[25]

Three weeks after the hearing, the Johnson administration announced its own program for involving private business in ghetto rehabilitation. Few observers missed the personal and political motivations. Conservative columnist William Buckley chided the administration's desperate move. "There's no surer way of getting upstaged," he wrote, "than unimaginatively turning down a scheme which enjoys deserved public support."[26]

Kennedy was incredulous. "How can they be so petty?" he asked Jack Newfield. "I worked on my plan for six months, and we talked to everyone in the Administration in all the relevant agencies. We accepted many of their ideas and put them in our bill. Now they came out with this thing, and the first I hear about it is on television. They didn't even try to work something out together. To them it's all just politics."[27]

———

LATE IN THE SUMMER, work of the Senate Subcommittee on Migratory Labor took Kennedy to several rural counties in New York. The senator visited migrant farmworker camps outside Rochester as part of an investigation in consideration of legislation to aid migrant workers. Kennedy and Jacob Javits were appalled to find that conditions in New York were just as bad as in other parts of the country. There were children with body sores covered with flies, and people living in shabby one-room shacks with no running water. At a fruit farm in Wayne County, Kennedy ducked into a bus that had been converted into living quarters for migrant workers. He ignored the sign saying "Anyone Entering or Trespassing without Permission Will Be Shot If Caught" and found three families living in the bus—the seats had been ripped out and replaced with filthy mattresses, and cardboard covered the windows. There was a spigot of running water outside and an outhouse. The farm owner defended his workers' accommodations. "It's like camping out," he said. "You are like something out of the nineteenth century," Kennedy shot back. "I wouldn't put an animal in those things." In Allegany County, Kennedy visited the dirt-floored shack of a tenant farmer. An image of her son, who was serving in Vietnam, hung on the wall. The photograph was a stark reminder of what the war was taking from the poor. "And," Bobby said to a friend, "there's not a damn thing I can do to stop it!"[28]

At about this time, Peter Edelman went to Hickory Hill for a meeting and brought Marian Wright along. Kennedy invited the two to stay for a swim. He asked Wright how things were going in Mississippi and wondered whether she thought anything would ever change. They had been speaking about Mississippi when Wright mentioned that she was on her way to Atlanta for a meeting with Martin Luther King Jr. She said that King did not know what to do. "You've got to get a lot of poor people who just come to Washington and say they're going to stay here until something happens and it gets really unpleasant and there are some arrests, and it's just a very nasty business and Congress gets embarrassed and they have to act," Peter Edelman recalls him saying. Wright liked the idea, and they talked about it for a while. Kennedy went on for the next ten minutes or so about what this effort would mean. Wright visited King in his SCLC office on Auburn Avenue shortly afterward. "When I told him what Robert Kennedy said, his eyes lit up," she later wrote.[29]

Martin Luther King had been devastated by the riots that summer. While he could not condone the violence, he understood the rage and despair that had fueled the uprisings and left communities destroyed—and he realized they would continue if drastic action was not taken to address the root causes. "Our real problem," he told the SCLC convention, "is that there is no disposition in the Administration nor in Congress to seek fundamental remedies beyond police measures. The tragic truth is that Congress, more than the American people, is running wild with racism." King, who at times conveyed deep pessimism, was becoming bolder and more militant. It is "impossible," he said, "to underestimate the crisis we are facing." He told a group of psychologists that it was time to "tell it like it is" to the white community. "The greater crimes of the white society" were the real cause of the uprisings, he testified to the National Advisory Commission on Civil Disorders—backlash, unemployment, racial discrimination, and the Vietnam war. At the SCLC's annual meeting in August, King declared that he and the organization "very, very definitely" would oppose Lyndon Johnson in the 1968 election unless he changed his stand on Vietnam.[30]

The immediate challenge was what to do. In preparation for the annual convention in August, King and his top strategists focused on a plan to "dislocate" northern cities with massive nonviolent demonstrations of civil disobedience. Such demonstrations would serve two critical ends—to harness Black rage "as a constructive, creative force," through such actions as school boycotts, blocking the gates of factories that refused to employ Black workers, and disrupting government operations in federal buildings; and to pressure local, state, and federal officials to respond to Black demands for jobs, improved housing, better education, and more intensive enforcement of civil right legislation. During this time, Marian Wright met with King and spoke with him at some length about Kennedy's suggestion.[31]

Two weeks after the convention, King called a retreat at Airlie House in Warrenton, Virginia, for executive staff to discuss Wright's proposal and the plans for northern cities. At the end of the meeting, he instructed everyone present to concentrate on the Washington project. On December 4, King announced plans to lead a massive campaign of civil disobedience in Washington the following April to force the administration to provide "jobs and income for all." Outlining what would become known as the Poor People's Campaign, King said demonstrators trained in nonviolent techniques would seek "massive dislocation" of the national capital "until America responds." While details remained to be worked out, King said he hoped the campaign would involve all poor people, not exclusively African Americans, and "all

Americans of good will." "These tactics have done it before," King said, "and this is all we have to go on." He warned that continued inaction by the federal government will bring "the curtain of doom" upon the nation. "America is at a crossroads of history," he said, "and it is critically important for us as a nation and a society to choose a new path and move upon it with resolution and courage."[32]

———

ROBERT KENNEDY TURNED FORTY-TWO ON NOVEMBER 20. In anticipation of the event, United Press International sent a reporter, Isabelle McCaig, to interview him. His Senate office was crowded with the largest staff on Capitol Hill, she wrote, "a mixture of intense young men and mini-skirted secretaries in patterned stockings." The phone never stopped ringing. Kennedy's private office was a bit more serene. The artwork on the wall included "a larger than life size drawing of Charlie Brown's Snoopy" by his daughter Courtney. She found Kennedy "in shirt sleeves behind his cluttered desk." He moved to a couch for the interview, and Freckles, Kennedy's black-and-white cocker spaniel, hopped up beside him. Kennedy turned aside questions about his political plans and prospects for Republican gains in 1968: "It's too early to tell. We have a whole year to go yet." He would not comment on what President Johnson might do to halt the bombing of Vietnam over Christmas. "When I have something to say, I'll make a full statement."

What he wanted to speak about was the War on Poverty. "How can a nation that spends $3 billion a year on pets do less than commit $2 billion a year for its poor?" he asked in a tone of disbelief. Kennedy dismissed rumors that he found the Senate too confining for his restless energy. It may take a good deal more time to get things done, he said, but "there is a great deal of freedom in the Senate." When asked about plans for his birthday, he said he had none—but was confident that Ethel and his ten children would surprise him.[33]

The morning of November 22 was damp and foggy when Bobby drove up to the gates of Arlington cemetery, alone, in an old Ford convertible. It was the fourth anniversary of his brother's death. He found the gate locked. It was just past 7 a.m., and the cemetery opened at 8. He vaulted over the three-and-a-half-foot wall and stood at his brother's gravesite. When he came back over the wall, several photographers were standing nearby. He asked them not to take his picture, and they agreed.[34]

———

THROUGHOUT 1967, Kennedy's thoughts and actions centered on poverty-stricken communities, their needs, and strategies for securing effective government action. While urban areas were a major concern, rural poverty was also a focus of his attention. His exposure to near-starvation conditions in the Mississippi Delta earlier that year had elevated hunger as a critical issue. During this period Kennedy also worked in various ways to expose conditions on Indian reservations, ensure access to antipoverty programs for Native Americans, and seek long-needed reforms.

Kennedy's first opportunity to address the plight of Native Americans came when he was attorney general, through the Justice Department's Land Division, then headed by Assistant Attorney General Ramsey Clark. Together, the two men had reversed the traditional policy of opposing Indian land claims and instead had settled them. Clark recalled that Kennedy had personally intervened when Senator Bob Kerr of Oklahoma objected to the size of a settlement with the Cherokee Nation. "'For God sakes,'" Clark remembered Kennedy saying, "'we owe it to the Cherokees.' He felt we'd pushed them around and he said so." Kennedy had been shocked to learn that the infant mortality rate among Native Americans was double that of any other racial group and their life expectancy twenty years less. Addressing the National Congress of Indians in Bismarck, North Dakota, in September 1963, he charged that American Indians had long been victims of social and economic oppression. Poorly housed, badly educated with few jobs and poor health status, the conditions were "nothing less than a national disgrace." He pledged that his brother's administration would work to help remedy these conditions through various forms of federal aid.[35]

In the Senate, Kennedy pursued his interest in helping Native Americans and ameliorating conditions on reservations. During the summer of 1967, as a member of the Senate Poverty subcommittee, he investigated programs at the Navajo reservations bordering Arizona and Utah, expressing special interest in a Head Start program and summer school session administered by the Office of Economic Opportunity. He reported back to the committee that he had found starvation conditions on the Navajo reservation. Kennedy made a point of visiting schools and the library when he visited a reservation. He would ask who the teachers were, and he wanted to know what the students were learning about American Indian history and culture. Scanning the library shelves on the Blackfoot reservation in Fort Hall, Idaho, he found only one book relating to Native Americans. It was called *Captives of the Delawares,* and the image on the jacket showed an Indian scalping a blond child.[36]

Kennedy persuaded Senate Majority Leader Mike Mansfield to establish a Subcommittee on Indian Education, which Kennedy chaired. During the first hearings, held in December 1967, tribal leaders described how a school system run by the federal government tried to impose an alien culture on their children. They spoke about the reservation boarding schools, started in the late nineteenth century, which separated children from their families and sent them to schools run by the Bureau of Indian Affairs—dreary places where, a clinical psychologist testified, children suffered from loneliness and depression. The result of this "middle-class white pattern" of education, studies showed, were dropout rates that were double the national average and a level of formal education half the national average. Kennedy saw these results as a failure of the American ethos. "The American vision of itself," he said, "is of a nation of citizens determining their own destiny; of cultural differences flourishing in an atmosphere of mutual respect; of diverse people shaping their lives and their children's."[37]

Describing the hearings as "salutary" and "shocking," the *Washington Post* concurred that it "was high time to begin doing what the subcommittee has set out to do." Quoting Kennedy, this was "to listen to the Indian people speak for themselves about the problems they confront and about the changes that must be made in seeking effective education for their children." The subcommittee would hold hearings on several Indian reservations in January to begin developing a program that would, in Kennedy's words, "offer Indian children a chance to take their place in contemporary American life.[38]

Indian activist Vine DeLoria Jr., in his book *Custer Died for Your Sins,* described Kennedy as a man "who could move from one world to another and never be a stranger anywhere." American Indians, DeLoria said, "saw him as a warrior, the white Crazy Horse," who "somehow validated obscure undefined feelings of Indian people which they had been unwilling to admit to themselves."[39]

While presiding over the hearings on education, Kennedy was also engaged in a fierce legislative battle around the basic provisions of welfare relief. Along with Senator Fred Harris of Oklahoma, Kennedy sought to remedy what many viewed as a major problem with welfare policy—denying relief to families with an unemployed father in the home. The two drafted an amendment to a Social Security bill requiring all states and the District of Columbia to provide welfare for families with unemployed fathers present; the bill passed the Senate by three votes. Arkansas Democrat Wilbur Mills, the powerful chair of the House Ways and Means committee, overrode the Harris-Kennedy amendment, adding a further amendment that made welfare payments more limited and restrictive. Mills's amendment would freeze the number of individuals eligible for Aid to Families with Dependent Children (AFDC), extend restrictions on unemployed fathers, and include work requirements for single mothers with children.[40]

Kennedy called the new bill "a disgrace to all Americans." The *New York Times* concurred, describing the measure as "a harsh assault on the welfare of tens of thousands of the country's poorest families . . . calculated to strip those on the relief rolls of what dignity had been left to them by existing red tape and investigative procedures." The *Washington Post* called it "deplorable, particularly at a time when the urban slums are threatened by unrest."[41]

The bill went back to the Senate for a vote. Prospects for dislodging the amendment were slim, since it was attached to a Social Security bill that provided a very generous 13 percent increase in old-age benefits. Mills insisted that the entire package be voted on, and few senators wanted to hold up a major boost in Social Security payments while heading into an election year. Kennedy and Harris tried to rally enough support to separate the Social Security part of the legislation for an immediate vote and reintroduce the welfare provision for debate after the first of the year, but they were outmaneuvered by Senator Russell Long of Louisiana and Senator Robert Byrd of Virginia (both Democrats) in an underhanded move that forced the entire bill to a vote. Disgusted, Kennedy called his colleagues out on the floor of the Senate. The way the debate had been shut down, he said, was "a reflection on those who participated not only as Senators but [on] their integrity as men."[42]

Kennedy delivered an impassioned speech to the Citizens Union dinner in New York the night before the Senate passed the bill. He said that the bill showed utter contempt for the poor and spoke about the overall failure of society to make positive and meaningful changes to address the crisis in America's cities. The man-in-the-house rule, which had forced thousands of fathers to leave their families so they might receive a welfare pittance, "is now reinforced and given a wider application." The bill was, he said, "another step toward destroying the family unit." After taking fathers from their children, "we will now take away the remaining parent by denying welfare to mothers, even those with young children, who refuse to leave them and work." While Congress whittled away meager welfare payments, "dirty, rat-infested conditions" in the slums provoked little concern. Neither federal nor local government had done enough, he charged, to build new housing, provide jobs, or improve health care for the poor. "In New York City," he told his well-heeled audience, "we know the problem, we know the magnitude and nature of the task, but the fact is, we are not doing it."[43]

—

"IF I WASN'T A SENATOR," Robert Kennedy told John Doar, "I'd rather be working in Bedford Stuyvesant than any place I know." By the end of 1967, the Bedford Stuyvesant Restoration Corporation, under the leadership of Frank Thomas, had an active presence in the community. Thomas had immediately set about establishing the Restoration Corporation as a local resource that would anticipate and respond to the needs of residents. At the start, the group printed and distributed a booklet with phone numbers and information about every available government service in the area—food stamps, legal aid, prenatal classes. The organization opened five neighborhood centers throughout Bed-Stuy, providing advice and information on welfare, tenant advocacy, and youth counseling; ran sanitation drives and clothing drives; organized baseball leagues; and even hosted a television show, *Inside Bedford Stuyvesant.*[44]

Working with the Center for Urban Education, the Bedford Stuyvesant Restoration Corporation hired and trained eighty young people in planning, organization, and survey techniques to better understand the attitudes and desires of the community. The survey revealed that decent housing was the top priority for residents, followed by jobs, better schools, and clean streets. It was clear that people were interested in targeted projects that would improve their lives now, not macro planning.[45]

During the summer of 1967, Restoration launched the Community House Improvement Program (CHIP), a signature project that focused on rehabilitating existing homes and buildings. As historian Michael Woodsworth writes, the program addressed several concerns of residents: "youth crime, unemployment, dilapidated housing, poverty, a frayed sense of community, and filthy streets." Unemployed young men were recruited to fix up the facades of homes. Working under the direction of experienced craftsmen, these young men gained skills, work experience, and the promise of referrals for permanent jobs if they stayed through the summer. Owners who participated in the project were asked to contribute. After a slow start, the project took off as the results became evident. On weekends, workers would bring their families to see their handiwork. By the end of 1967, more than seventy block associations had submitted requests for assistance. Restoration would soon take on more ambitious projects, but CHIP helped establish Restoration's presence and legitimacy.[46]

The relationship between the Restoration and D&S boards remained a serious problem. Eli Jacobs, the young investment banker who served as the acting head of D&S, viewed Restoration as a junior partner, which was not Thomas's understanding at all. Jacobs understood that by temperament and experience he was not particularly well-suited for the position and made it clear he would not object to being replaced. Early in the fall, Kennedy learned from Burke Marshall that John Doar was planning to leave the Department of Justice and had not settled on what he would do next. Kennedy reached out to Doar and asked if he would consider a position with the Bedford-Stuyvesant project.[47]

Doar, who was in Mississippi working on a case, flew up to New York for a weekend and spent Sunday by himself, walking and driving around

Bedford-Stuyvesant. On Monday he told Kennedy he was interested. Doar recalled Kennedy's approach: "We've got to get something done. We've got to make some changes." It became clear that the Bed-Stuy project was "a very, very central issue in his universe." Doar said he did not know anything about cities and thought his talents were in the area of reform rather than raising money or administering a program. Both men agreed to think about the possibility of Doar working on the project, and Doar returned to finish his work in Mississippi. The two men talked again when Doar was back in Washington. Kennedy had not found a director, and he asked Doar to go back to New York and meet with some of the D&S board members. The meeting went well, and Doar decided to take the position. Doar recalled Kennedy's response: "He wanted me to start the day before yesterday." Doar returned to Washington to finish up his work at the Justice Department and started as director of the Development and Services Corporation at the beginning of 1968.[48]

John Doar's arrival would mark a qualitative change in the functioning of the Bed-Stuy project and help set it firmly on the course Kennedy had imagined. Doar and Frank Thomas established a good partnership, though Thomas was still opposed to the dual structure. Doar acted to put the two entities on an equal footing, moving the offices of D&S from Manhattan into the same building as Restoration in Brooklyn. Disbursement of funds, which Jacobs had tightly controlled, became a shared responsibility. Under the leadership of Doar and Thomas, "the two organizations developed an amicable, effective, and productive working relationship," as historian Tom Adam Davis has written, which paved the way for Restoration to grow and ultimately become the prime mover—as Kennedy had intended. "While Restoration was becoming an increasingly powerful Black organization at the boardroom level," Adams writes, "its programs in the community were shaping into a model of institutional Black power."[49]

———

EARLY THAT FALL, Martin Luther King Jr. told close associates he thought that Robert Kennedy would be a "great president" but did not see how he could win the Democratic nomination, given LBJ's advantage as the incumbent. For most of the fall, Kennedy's electoral concerns centered on his next Senate campaign in 1970. If there was a presidential run in his future, 1972 appeared the most likely year. But circumstances were pulling the prospect of a presidential run closer. By the end of 1967, Kennedy found it difficult to imagine how the country could endure four more years of Lyndon Johnson in the White House.[50]

CHAPTER FIFTEEN

Our Country's Future

||||

BY THANKSGIVING, the Johnson presidency had assumed a bunker mentality. Johnson's increasingly obsessive pursuit of victory in Vietnam had consumed untold resources, eroded his credibility, and contributed to a major national crisis. Troop levels in Vietnam had reached nearly five hundred thousand, draft calls averaged thirty thousand per month, and there had been more than thirteen thousand American casualties, yet the United States could claim no more than a stalemate. While Johnson had come to realize that the bombing had accomplished little, he was not prepared to stop or limit it, unwilling to risk a confrontation with hawks pushing for a more aggressive strategy. The antiwar movement had grown exponentially over the course of the year and was now more broad-based. In a dramatic reversal, polls indicated that public approval of the president's handling of the war had dropped to 28 percent in October—reflecting the disapproval of both those arguing for a more aggressive strategy and those hoping to end the war.[1]

A growing number of liberal and progressive Democrats had concluded that another Johnson term would be disastrous for the country. Many looked to Kennedy as the one individual of national stature who could mount a strong challenge for the Democratic nomination. But while Kennedy aspired to serve as president someday, he held back now. The prospect of directly taking on Johnson in 1968 was fraught with difficulties. "I would have a problem if I ran first against Johnson," Kennedy told a small group that included Al Lowenstein, a leader of the "Dump Johnson" movement, early that fall. "People would say that I was splitting the party out of ambition and envy. No one would believe I was doing it because of how I felt about Vietnam and poor people," Kennedy said. In a television interview late in November, he explained to insistent queries, "If I ran it would not strengthen the dialog on the issues, but it would immediately become a personality struggle." He worried that his presence in the race would deflect attention from the critical issues needing to be addressed. "Washington is dreadful—but what to do?" he scribbled at the end of a letter to Anthony Lewis on November 29. Other factors also came into play as Kennedy consulted friends and advisers, struggling to reconcile his own instinct, which was to run, with sober political considerations.[2,3]

On November 30, Senator Eugene McCarthy of Minnesota, a strong critic of Johnson's policies in Vietnam, announced that he would challenge the president in several Democratic primaries. Anticipating McCarthy's entry into the race, Kennedy said he thought it would be "a healthy influence on the Democratic Party" and promote constructive debate on Vietnam, an assessment widely shared by the press. McCarthy's candidacy, editorialized the *New York Times,* "enables those who dissent from Administration policy in Vietnam to find political expressions for their convictions." Few thought the "relatively unknown," fifty-one-year-old McCarthy, whose Senate record was lackluster, would deny Johnson the nomination. McCarthy himself signaled that his main goal was to open the debate on Vietnam within the Democratic Party and pressure the president, with the senator indicating that he would be satisfied if his Vietnam-oriented campaign pushed Johnson to move toward a negotiated settlement.[4]

Handsome, with a dry wit, and given to quoting poets and philosophers, Eugene McCarthy had the bearing of the college professor he had once been. His eloquent speech in support of Adlai Stevenson at the 1960 Democratic convention had launched him on the lecture circuit. Elected to Congress in 1948, McCarthy "had been anything but a crusader for causes," observed *New York Times* reporter Tom Wicker. The senator had been silent during the debate on the civil rights legislation of 1964 and 1965 and had voted occasionally with special interests on drug prices and the oil depletion allowance. But he had emerged as a vocal opponent of the administration's policy in Vietnam and a strong critic of Johnson's roughshod disregard for the constitutional limits of presidential power. Friends and colleagues speculated on McCarthy's motivation for running. A sympathetic fellow senator reflected that McCarthy was not up for reelection until 1970, which made him relatively safe from reprisals. "Furthermore," this observer said, "there's hardly any risk involved when you step gently in front of an already formed army."[5]

McCarthy's "leisurely" approach and narrow appeal caused observers to question whether he was a serious contender. His first major event, in Chicago before the National Conference of Concerned Democrats, hardly suggested a party in transition. Several thousand students were bused in for his keynote speech, which was heavy on nostalgia, invoking the spirit of Adlai

Stevenson and John F. Kennedy. At plenary sessions for the five hundred delegates, a reporter counted five African Americans in the audience. McCarthy's campaign, Warren Weaver Jr. reported in the *New York Times,* "consisted largely of professional business and intellectual liberals with political feelings generally stronger than their experience, thrown together by the Vietnam issue and their opposition to LBJ." Jack Newfield, a New Left journalist who had welcomed McCarthy's entry into the race, registered dissatisfaction with the candidate in the *Village Voice:* "McCarthy's speeches were dull, vague and without poetry or balls. He is lazy and vain." McCarthy had not been planning to enter the New Hampshire primary, but he yielded under the pressure of his campaign advisers—and New Hampshire would change everything.[6]

For Robert Kennedy, McCarthy's candidacy heightened the pressure to act. McCarthy would likely attract growing support among young antiwar protesters, drawing a constituency that would be critical if Kennedy ran. More significantly, Kennedy could not support McCarthy. While the two men had never been friendly, Kennedy's opinion of McCarthy was less personal than based on his performance in the Senate. Kennedy thought, as Arthur Schlesinger reported, that McCarthy was "undependable and uninvolved, too often absent when needed for a debate or a vote, and too cozy on the Finance Committee with special interests." This impression was reinforced by their exchange when McCarthy told Kennedy that the Minnesota senator was going to run. The meeting lasted seven minutes. McCarthy did not disclose his plans or seek Kennedy's thoughts on any subject. After all, Kennedy commented later, "I've had some experience in running primaries." The meeting convinced him that McCarthy would be no more serious a candidate than he had been a senator.[7]

For the next two months, Kennedy agonized over what to do. Convinced that the country and the world could not survive four more years of Johnson, Kennedy gradually came to the conclusion that the case for running was compelling, despite the likelihood of failure. His brother Ted and trusted advisers such as Fred Dutton and Ted Sorensen counseled Bobby against the move, believing it would tear the party apart and have disastrous consequences for his political future. They had their eyes on 1972. But 1972 was less and less of a concern for Bobby. He felt in his bones that the time was now. Schlesinger and Richard Goodwin had come around to this position. Burke Marshall, one of Kennedy's closest friends and most trusted advisers, dismissed predictions. Polls, Marshall felt, were meaningless, particularly in the volatile political environment of early 1968. He felt Kennedy should trust his instincts. Ethel was pushing him to run, mostly because she thought he would never forgive himself if he did not.[8]

But there were clear indications that the campaign would be an uphill battle. Senator George McGovern had spoken to colleagues in the Senate to assess what support Kennedy might count on if he were to declare his candidacy. McGovern found that no antiwar senator would support Kennedy's run. There was "a universal reluctance to consider the possibility," McGovern reported. "The trouble is that everyone seems only interested in taking care of himself. This is the atmosphere that Johnson has created. Everyone I talked to had the attitude, 'What would this do for me?' No one was ready to stick his neck out." McGovern was surprised. He had expected a much better reaction. He advised Bobby not to run.[9]

Kennedy was sympathetic. Many of his fellow senators were up for reelection, and Johnson's capacity for retribution was well-known. There were concerns that his candidacy, by dividing the Democrats, could strengthen Republican prospects in close Senate races and possibly at the presidential level, now that Richard Nixon was emerging as the likely candidate. Beyond this, the president had a unique ability to dominate the news, especially with regard to foreign affairs. "In short," observed columnist Marquis Childs, "the shrewd Texan in the White House holds most of the high cards and against a Kennedy challenge he would never hesitate to use them."[10]

On January 31, Kennedy was invited to a weekly breakfast meeting of reporters hosted by Godfrey Sperling Jr., a journalist with the *Christian Science Monitor,* at the Carlton Hotel in Washington. When asked the inevitable question, Kennedy said he would not become a candidate for the presidency "under any conceivable circumstances." His press secretary, Frank Mankiewicz, revised the statement to read that Kennedy would become a candidate "under no foreseeable circumstances." The statement quieted rumors that he was about to get into the race. The *New York Times* found nothing surprising here. Those who expected Kennedy to lead an anti-Vietnam crusade within the Democratic Party "regardless of political cost misread their man," the *Times* editorialized. "When it comes to the crucial decisions of politics and career, he remains an old pro." Other commentators provided a more nuanced reading of the likely reasons behind his decision. Close associates who had urged Kennedy to run, the *Washington Post* reported, "held out hope yesterday that some event would still force him to change his mind."[11]

———

HOURS AFTER THE BREAKFAST MEETING, the National Liberation Front (NLF) attacked the American embassy in Saigon, pounding the building with rockets and gunfire in a siege that lasted more than six hours. The scene of enemy troops waging war in the courtyard of the US embassy shocked

Americans. The attack on the embassy was part of the Tet Offensive, a carefully coordinated assault against urban areas throughout South Vietnam by
the North Vietnamese and the NLF, striking thirty-six of forty-four pro-
vincial capitals and five of six major cities. US and South Vietnamese troops,
caught completely off guard, prevailed only after several weeks of bloody
battles. US firepower inflicted "horrendous casualties," with an estimated
forty thousand deaths. Most commentators agreed that although Tet was
ultimately a military defeat for the North Vietnamese, they had won an overwhelming psychological victory. Televised accounts of protracted fighting
in Saigon and other cities further undermined the Johnson administration's
optimistic claims about the war. "What the hell is going on?" exclaimed
trusted CBS newscaster Walter Cronkite. "I thought we were winning the
war!" The Tet Offensive had opened up the administration's handling of the
war to more intensive scrutiny and left Washington in a state of "troubled
confusion and uncertainty."[12]

Tet was a breaking point for Robert Kennedy. On February 8, he delivered "the most sweeping and detailed indictment of the war and of the
Administration's policy yet heard from any leading figure in either party,"
according to the *New York Times*. The luncheon speech, delivered at the
Ambassador East hotel in Chicago, was not meant to signal Kennedy's entry
into the campaign, but rather "reflected the feeling that refusal to run had
freed him to speak his mind." "It is time for the truth," Kennedy declared.
The Viet Cong offensive had "finally shattered the mask of official illusion"
about the war because it demonstrated that "no part or person of South
Vietnam was secure from attack." He continued, "Half a million American
soldiers with 700,000 Vietnamese allies, with total command of the air, total
command of the sea, backed by huge resources and the most modern weapons
are unable to secure even a single city from the attacks of an enemy whose
total strength is 250,000."

The time had come to take a new look at the war in Vietnam, "not by
cursing the past but using it to illuminate the future," Kennedy advised. He
went beyond criticism of the war to challenge the fundamental reasons the
Johnson and Kennedy administrations had given for waging it. He himself,
Bobby said, had participated in policymaking and optimistic predictions
during his brother's administration. But we can "no longer pretend" that we
are fighting to end the threat of Communism in Asia, Bobby said. "The outcome in each country depends and will depend on the intrinsic strength of
the government, the particular circumstances, and the particular character
of the insurgent movement." Furthermore, it was not in the national interest
to wage a war so destructive and cruel that "our best and closest friends ask,
more in sorrow than in anger, what has happened to America."

It was the people of Vietnam, "the people we are seeking to defend, who are the greatest losers." For them, "the last three years have meant little but horror. Their tiny land has been devastated by a weight of bombs and shells greater than the Nazis knew in the second World War." More than two million Vietnamese were now homeless refugees. Kennedy pointed to the "enormous corruption which pervades every level of South Vietnamese official life," and charged that the government of President Nguyen Van Thieu was a "government without supporters." The people of South Vietnam, Kennedy said, "will not fight to line the pockets of generals or swell the bank accounts of the wealthy." Our nation, he insisted, "must be told the truth about this war, in all its terrible reality, because it is right and because only in this way can any administration rally the public confidence and unity for the shadowy days that lie ahead."[13]

Less than a week after this speech, Kennedy was in eastern Kentucky to chair field hearings by the Senate Subcommittee on Employment, Manpower, and Poverty examining the state of antipoverty programs in the region, with a focus on hunger. Twenty of the country's thirty poorest counties were concentrated in this part of the state, the heart of Appalachia. The area, once a center of well-paying if dangerous coal-mining jobs, had been transformed by automation and the advent of strip-mining into a ravaged landscape surrounded by "a vast ghetto of unemployables," as Homer Bigart put it in the *New York Times* in fall 1963. That year, the publication of Henry Caudill's *Night Comes to the Cumberland: A Biography of a Depressed Area* had brought national attention to the desperation of the region, prompting President Kennedy to appoint a commission to investigate conditions. JFK had been planning to visit in December 1963.

Lyndon Johnson made Appalachia a keystone of the War on Poverty, taking two widely publicized tours through the region in the spring of 1964 after introducing the Equal Opportunity Act. In addition to "arousing nationwide support" for his "anti-poverty crusade," Johnson, as Robert Dallek wrote, aimed "to encourage the belief that an attack on poverty would do as much or more to help whites as blacks."[14]

Peter Edelman and Tom Johnston had organized a packed two-day itinerary for the field hearings, covering more than two hundred miles, with a band of reporters tagging along. The first day started with a hearing in a one-room schoolhouse in Vortex, Kentucky. Later that day Kennedy visited another one-room school in Barwick, where he found eight young students and a teacher. William Greider, then with Louisville's *Courier-Journal*, recalled how startled the class was when Senator Kennedy and his entourage walked in. Greider remembered that the students were "hunkered down at their desks" when Kennedy entered the room. "He went around, one by one, kneeling by their desks. He didn't say very much. Nodded at them, talked to them in whispers, held their hands. It was such a human response. This was a side of the politician you don't often see."[15]

On the move through "the hard core of Appalachian poverty," Kennedy stopped in many small towns, walking the streets, shaking hands, going door-to-door. Television footage offered a glimpse of his stop in Hazard, where he visited Liberty Street, an African American neighborhood. "He was cheered everywhere," the *New York Times* reported, and received "carnation boutonnieres, boxes of homemade candy . . . amid cries of 'Please run for President.'" In several counties, Kennedy met with men who had participated in the Work-Experience and Training program and had recently been cut off as the program's funding was reduced. His attempt to tour a strip-mining facility was blocked by the foreman, but Kennedy got close enough to witness firsthand the physical and environmental destruction of the shredded landscape. At hearings the next day, he described what he had seen: a land "ravished by the extraction of rich resources, creeks polluted with trash, and acid waste that seeps down from scarred hills." He ended his day at Alice Lloyd College in Pippa Passes with Congressman Carl D. Perkins, an alumnus who had represented the area in Congress since 1949.[16]

The next day, Kennedy spoke on the steps of the Letcher County Court-house to an enthusiastic audience of several hundred high school students who braved ten-degree temperatures to see him. For the rest of the day, he and Congressman Perkins presided over formal hearings in the gym of the local high school. A crowd of locals, including students from two neigh-boring high schools, filled the folding chairs set up for the occasion.[17]

Henry Caudill, whose family had lived in the area for several generations, was the first to testify. "Today the poorest people and the most prosperous corporations in the United States are found right here in eastern Kentucky," he told the legislators. He pointed to some of the manifestations of this dichotomy—nearly 24 percent of white adults over twenty-four years old were functionally illiterate; in some counties, 25 percent of the population depended on public assistance; seventy thousand men who had worked in the coalfields were totally disabled. He spoke of tens of thousands who could never find a job. "They lack the education modern industry demands. They are sick. Their lungs are choked with coal dust and sandstone. They have been crippled in mining accidents." The rate of unemployment in the area, Caudill said, was higher than anywhere else in the country.[18]

Twenty-three witnesses appeared in all. Most addressed the impact of antipoverty programs on employment and hunger. Edwin Stafford, the Community Action Program director for four counties, spoke in withering terms about the Work, Experience and Training (WE&T) and Manpower programs—which in most cases trained men for nonexistent jobs. Those who participated received a monthly check and short-term work, but the work rarely lasted. Several men testified about their experiences, and it quickly became clear that for most of those who went through the program, it did not result in a permanent job. Federal budget cuts at the start of 1968 had triggered a massive reduction in staffing, and many of those who had been enrolled in the programs were sent home. Stafford emphasized the need for an approach specifically geared toward rural areas that would generate jobs, paid for by the federal government if necessary, that could lead "to the creation of new public assets, such as public buildings, housing, roads, bridges, parks, and schools." Kennedy agreed. He and Perkins had pushed for a program modeled on the New Deal's Works Progress Administration.[19]

Frank Collins told the committee that he had worked on a WE&T program for two years before being transferred to the Manpower Development School. When his wife was paralyzed, he had to quit. If he had stayed, he said, there would have been no job for him anyway. Kennedy asked about Collins's training. Collins responded that he had done some carpentry work, electrical work, plumbing, and painting. "So much needs to be done in this area," Kennedy said with evident frustration, "where you can use these skills. . . . Housing needs to be constructed, and plumbing facilities—all these things need to be done desperately in Eastern Kentucky. We have the manpower and we have the resources in the United States, it seems we should bring them all together and get the job done."[20]

Severe malnutrition was not evident in eastern Kentucky—but hunger and poor nutrition were prevalent. Grants for prenatal care and federal programs like Medicaid and food stamps had made a qualitative difference—as one witness put it, they had "made the state of poverty more livable." Children were smaller than average, and roughly 50 percent had intestinal parasites, Harlan County pediatrician Dr. Doane Fischer testified. Lynn Frazier, a public health nurse, said that the low-protein diet of the poor impacted their development in their formative years, leaving them dull and listless, with reduced learning ability and memory, and behavioral problems. "I gather from what you're saying," Kennedy offered, that "the food situation is really not satisfactory." "It is not satisfactory," Frazier responded, "and that is the biggest problem I see in public health."[21]

The cost of food stamps and their method of allocation meant that families routinely ran out of stamps a week or more before the end of the month. Pat Gish, who worked with the Community Action council serving four counties, drily commented that the USDA "apparently believes the poorer you are, the less you are entitled to eat." Several men and women testified about the limited reach of the food stamps they received and how hard it was to obtain even their meager monthly allotments. Gussie Davis, who lived far from public transportation, described how she often had to pay five dollars for a ride to the distribution center to purchase her monthly allocation of food stamps.[22]

Cliston "Clickbird" Johnson, from Partridge, Kentucky, was the most dynamic witness. He had been in the WE&T program six months before he was cut off. Politicians had "sold them down the river," Johnson charged. He was convinced that most of the antipoverty money was spent before it reached those most in need. He explained that he supported his family of fifteen children on a welfare check of $60 a month, $26 of which went to purchase $112 in food stamps. The food stamps lasted about two weeks. "From then on beans and bread," he quipped, "and the next week bread and beans"—prompting laughter. He added, "We change it around that way and get better meals."

"Did you ever see fifteen kids in three beds?" he asked the senator and congressman. "I'm moving in that direction," Kennedy, a father of ten, offered. Johnson closed with a final tip on "how we manage this: The more children you've got, you just add a little more water to the gravy." Later that spring, Johnson would be named to the national coordinating committee for the SCLC's Poor People's Campaign and asked to bring a group from Harlan and Letcher County to Washington.[23]

David Zegeer, the division manager of Bethlehem Steel, asked for an opportunity to testify in response to Harry Caudill's claims. Zegeer began by dismissing the charge of "absentee ownership"—"whatever that means." Bethlehem Steel, he said, had eight hundred shareholders in Kentucky. Kennedy asked him how many shareholders Bethlehem Steel had in total. "I would say 50 or 75,000, I really don't know," Zegeer answered. "You would hardly say that was a Kentucky-owned company," Kennedy shot back. Zegeer rattled off figures to show what Bethlehem Steel had contributed to Kentucky—listing, for example, the Mine Workers Welfare and Retirement Fund, a $50,000 donation to regional hospitals, and upward of $500,000 in taxes paid. It was "only proper for you to know this," Zegeer told Kennedy, "so you can have the benefit of what is going on from the standpoint of free enterprise in our area."

Kennedy acknowledged that there was a real need for more industry in Appalachia, but looking over the history, he suggested, "you would have to reach the conclusion . . . the outsiders have come in and taken the great wealth that existed in Eastern Kentucky, and destroyed some of the natural resources, which have not been utilized to the benefit of the people of Eastern Kentucky and have created tremendous profits for people elsewhere in the United States." While, admittedly, he was not from Kentucky, Kennedy said,

"I can certainly see what has happened here, and I have read the history of Kentucky, and I know that's part of it." He asked Zegeer, "Would you agree with that?" "No," Zegeer answered flatly. But then he corrected himself. "In part, some of your statement is correct," he said, "but also great wealth has been left here and not taken out."

"As I go around, as I did and have, I recognized the great wealth that existed in this state; I recognized the great wealth that has gone out of this state," Kennedy rejoined, "to all parts of this country, and . . . all around the world, and I see people by the thousands with not enough to eat, and obviously, there has not been a proper distribution of that wealth to the people of eastern Kentucky." Zegeer had nothing to say in response. He tried to end the discussion by thanking Kennedy for "the opportunity to let me give you at least our side." But Kennedy was not prepared to let the dialogue end there and pressed for a response to the specifics of Harry Caudill's testimony. Kennedy raised a battery of questions relating to the cost of the newest plant, the assessed value of the company's property, profit margins, and the company's tax rate. Zegeer did not have answers but assured the legislators he would find out and provide the information for the record. When Kennedy finally thanked Zegeer for his testimony, Zegeer said, "I do want to say when I came here, I knew I was walking into the lion's den. But I thank you anyway."[24]

The hearings showcased Kennedy's approach to the problem of poverty, both in its localized and national dimensions. "We need an opportunity . . . to hear from people who know this firsthand," he had said at the opening, "who have suffered poverty and know the condition." He wanted to hear "your complaints, and ideas and thoughts about what needs to be done," he said, and he focused his line of inquiry on documenting conditions, getting to the root of the problems, and fleshing out ideas for improvement. While he felt the federal government could and must help, he believed the local community had to play a critical role in defining the problem and formulating and implementing solutions.[25]

By the end of the daylong hearing, specific inadequacies with the food stamp and school lunch programs had been identified, some of which Kennedy and Perkins said they thought they could remedy fairly easily in Washington. Other issues could be acted on at once. Lynn Frazier, the public health nurse, had suggested that schools and local antipoverty workers could teach better nutritional practices, even within the limits of the food stamp program. Kennedy and Perkins saw no reason why stamps could not be mailed to recipients and promised to try to amend the distribution policy. Kennedy had his aides take the names of the men who had been cut off from the WE&T and promised to investigate the program further. "There can be no mistake after his public statements, his astute comments, and his private comments," local antipoverty activist Anne Caudill commented, "that he understands that we have a real American problem and that he is on our side."[26]

Addressing reporters in Neon after the hearing, Kennedy spoke bluntly about the failure of the Johnson Administration's welfare and antipoverty programs in the Appalachian Mountains and in the nation's urban areas. It was essential, Kennedy said, that some of the billions being spent on the war in Vietnam be used instead to provide jobs rather than training programs "for jobs that are nonexistent." "The struggle in Vietnam is taking a great deal of money—$30 billion a year," he said. "Some of that should be coming down here to help the people of this area and to help the unemployed of the ghetto." He endorsed a federal job plan proposed in 1967 by Senator Joseph Clark and again in the current Congress by Congressman Perkins. The legislation was floundering and failed to garner the support of the administration.[27]

At the end of the day, Harry Caudill drove Kennedy to a little airstrip nearby for a flight to Louisville, where he would have dinner with the Barry Bingham Sr., editor of the *Courier-Journal*. Kennedy said goodbye and began walking toward the plane. Then he turned around, came back to the car, and took Caudill's hand. "Mr. Caudill," Kennedy said, "we're going to do something about this."[28]

Back in Washington, Kennedy and Senator John Sherman Cooper of Kentucky went to see Agriculture Secretary Orville Freeman. Kennedy asked Freeman about a fund dedicated to surplus commodities. "You have several million dollars there," Kennedy said. "Why don't you use it? Why can't you use it? Why haven't you used it?" Cooper recalled that when Freeman said that Congress had to grant authority for appropriating the funds, Kennedy "got very angry." He told Freeman "that he *could* do something if he tried to do it and if he would take some initiative himself and not just wait until the Congress did something." It would be several months, but funds were eventually used to provide more powdered milk, surplus cheese, cornmeal, and canned meats to the region.[29]

———

AS HE BECAME MORE OUTSPOKEN in his criticism of the war in Vietnam, Kennedy did not slacken his pace. He traveled to the West and Southwest as chair of the Senate Subcommittee on Indian Education, holding hearings and visiting reservations. Four days after his visit to Kentucky he was in Oklahoma meeting with students at the Seneca Indian School in Wyandotte. Later, in San Francisco, Rupert Costo, founder of the American Indian Historical Society, testified about the slanderous treatment of American Indians in nearly all school textbooks. Kennedy and his subcommittee staff spent nearly a week in California, where he visited the Sherman Institute, a sixty-seven-year-old boarding school serving eight hundred Native American students. He found that eight of the buildings had been closed because they did not meet the state's tightened earthquake code. The curriculum focused on silversmithing, home economics, and typing—not exactly a suitable education for contemporary life. Kennedy spoke scathingly about the nation's betrayal "of our Indian people," saying, "we've broken our promises many times."[30]

Back in New York State, Kennedy met with the New York Press Association and the Rochester Chamber of Commerce and visited colleges. At a meeting with faculty and students from the State University of New York (SUNY) at Buffalo School of Law, Kennedy outlined his thoughts on crime control, which included an emphasis on community-based policing. He felt that alcohol and drug addiction should be considered medical problems and distanced from the criminal justice system. During the question-and-answer session, he stressed the importance of understanding the despair of people who have "lost all hope." He asked SUNY students to try to imagine the perspective of a father whose children were hungry and malnourished and to consider "if he questions what allegiance he owes to the laws of a system that permits that to happen."[31]

Kennedy frequently polled his audiences on America's policy in Vietnam. In mid-January he administered an impromptu poll in Rochester, asking his listeners whether they would back an end to the bombing and the start of negotiations to end the war. Most of the seven hundred gathered raised their hand, by far the largest support for ending the war he had found, and surprising among such a conservative audience. College students frequently asked why Kennedy hadn't entered the presidential race, accusing him of political opportunism. He was met by pickets outside Brooklyn College. Some students pressed him to support McCarthy. "I'll do what I think is right," Kennedy said, "and in the best interest of the country."[32]

At the end of January, he introduced legislation together with Senator Fred Harris to repeal the restrictive welfare provision written into the Social Security Act of 1967, contending that the provisions were punitive and would cut off federal aid to nearly half a million children. The Kennedy-Harris bill would eliminate the "freezing" provision, which had indiscriminately cut off tens of thousands of children. The bill also required all states to provide Aid to Families with Dependent Children payments to families headed by an unemployed father—only twenty-two states did so at the time—and eliminated the work requirement for mothers with preschool- and school-age children.[33]

Speculation about a possible candidacy hardly abated after his statement at the end of January that he would not run barring "unforeseeable circumstances." On the popular *Tonight Show,* when guest host Harry Belafonte asked Kennedy directly if he would run for president, Kennedy flashed a smile and ducked the question, saying he was just hoping for a happy ending. He grew serious when the host asked Kennedy about his recent visit to Appalachia. "I've seen children who are starving in the United States," he said. "I mean, not 'I read about children who are starving in the United States,' but I've seen children who are starving. . . . And as reports have said, they will never recover mentally after the age of four."[34]

Late in February, it was widely reported that if he tossed his hat in the ring, Kennedy could not count on support from at least one major group—businesspeople. News sources reported on a forthcoming *Forbes* article stating that not since Franklin Roosevelt in the 1930s had a potential presidential candidate aroused such intense opposition in the business community. A nationwide survey of business leaders found that "mention of the name Kennedy produced an almost unanimous chorus of condemnation." Some speculated that RFK's upbringing, with exposure to his father's career as a financier, had "left him with a distorted view of how business operates." Whatever the case, *Forbes* concluded, Kennedy "seems to have little grasp of the business point of view."[35]

———

HENRY "SMITTY" SMITH, an eighteen-year-old sophomore at South Carolina State University, said his life goals were "happiness and success." Smitty came from a small country town where he and his three siblings were raised by his mother and grandmother, "He wanted to make things better for Black people," his sister recalled. Eighteen-year-old Samuel Hammond Jr., a freshman at SC State, was an outstanding athlete—a halfback on the football team and star sprinter on his high school track team—who aspired to be a teacher. Delano Middleton was a high school senior whose only real interests "were sports and church," according to his mother, who worked as a maid at the college. On the night of February 8, 1968, all three young men were shot and killed on campus in an assault by state police that left twenty-seven others wounded and hospitalized.[36]

The Orangeburg Massacre, as it came to be known, was a tragic result of a racial climate of hostility and fear, political opportunism, and reckless policing. A small town forty miles from the state capital, Orangeburg was home to two historically Black colleges—Claflin University and South Carolina State University. The town had been an important center of sit-ins in 1960 and of community-wide efforts to desegregate schools in the wake of

Brown v. Board of Education, giving rise to a strong chapter of the White Citizens' Council—an organization mostly made up of businessmen and public officials dedicated to enforcing segregation. Despite the passage of the Civil Rights Act, several facilities would not serve Black students. Harry Floyd, owner of the bowling alley, had hastily replaced his "Whites Only" sign with a "Privately Owned" sign, after which he claimed his establishment was not in violation of the law. It was a sore point for the local Black community: bowling was a popular recreational activity, and the next closest bowling alley was an hour away.[37]

The series of encounters that culminated with the shooting on February 8 began four days earlier, when John Stroman, a student who "loved to bowl," had organized a few dozen students to sit in at the bowling alley after several South Carolina State students had tried unsuccessfully to bowl the previous week. Anticipating trouble, the alley was closed early under police orders. The next night, Governor Robert McNair Sr. (having been contacted by the owner) sent Chief Pete Strom, head of the South Carolina Law Enforcement Division, to Orangeburg. When Stroman went back to the bowling alley with another group of students, they were met by Strom and twenty state and local police, armed with riot clubs. Strom warned the students that they would be arrested if they entered the bowling alley, and Floyd charged them with trespassing. The students went in anyway, and the fifteen students who refused to leave were arrested.[38]

When word of the arrests reached campus, several hundred students came to the bowling alley to protest. Strom sent for reinforcements. College officials intervened, and the students were preparing to head back to campus when a fire truck arrived, suggesting a plan to use fire hoses on the students. The police met student outrage by wading into the group in riot gear and beating them indiscriminately. Two young women were severely beaten, and seven students had to be hospitalized. Angered by the assault, a few students hurled bricks through the windows of white-owned businesses as they walked back to campus.[39]

Governor McNair called up 250 National Guardsmen and instructed them to report to a nearby armory. The forty-four-year-old governor, a liberal Democrat who had been elected with the support of Black voters, had a relatively strong record on civil rights, particularly with regard to school desegregation. But his response to the trouble in Orangeburg suggests that he was more attuned to white fears, amplified by the specter of the urban uprisings that summer, than he was interested in the exact nature of the crisis brewing in the college town.

The day after the confrontation outside the bowling alley, students requested a permit to hold a march to protest what had happened. The city turned them down. Maceo Nance, the president of South Carolina State University, called for a boycott of white-owned businesses, and faculty worked with students to draw up a list of grievances. The list, which was submitted to city officials, included demands for an end to police brutality, the desegregation of the bowling alley and other public facilities, enforcement of the 1964 Civil Rights Act, and the disciplining of an officer who had fired into the university grounds. With no outlet for their anger, students tossed rocks at cars driving past campus and taunted the growing number of law enforcement officials ringing the campus.[40]

As tensions rose, Governor McNair ignored appeals by NAACP state leader Isaiah DeQuincey Newman to intervene personally. Instead, the governor activated several hundred National Guard troops and more Highway Patrol officers until Orangeburg was "bristling with armed men." McNair manipulated public perceptions of what was happening, charging that the protests were the work of "outside agitators." Chief Strom later testified that the authorities "knew" the plan of "the Black Power people" was to attack public utilities, and the governor wanted to be sure those sites were protected. But there was no evidence that the Black Power movement had a strong constituency in Orangeburg or that there was any plan to attack the utilities. The governor fastened on the presence at the protests of Cleveland Sellers, a SNCC field representative who was a native of South Carolina.[41]

Sellers had grown up in nearby Denmark, South Carolina, where as a high school student he had participated in the sit-in movement. He continued his activism at Howard University, working with fellow student Stokely Carmichael. The two became close friends. Sellers was a field organizer in Mississippi during Freedom Summer, and he joined the group that went to the Democratic National Convention. Now an advocate of Black Power, he had established a Black Awareness Coordinating Committee on campus, but the group had attracted fewer than two dozen students. Sellers had moved beyond integration as a goal and did not lend support to the bowling alley campaign.[42]

As the police presence on the outskirts of campus increased, students tossed rocks and other objects at patrolmen and taunted them with epithets. On the night of February 8, with temperatures now below freezing, several students made a bonfire on the embankment at the edge of campus. They ripped out banisters and wood from an abandoned house to feed the fire. Around two hundred students gathered around and began singing "We Shall Overcome, "We Shall Not be Moved," and other songs of the civil rights movement. "Everyone was enjoying the fire," one remembered, "gleeful, cracking jokes." He recalled that they never thought they'd be arrested or anything. The bonfire was a way to let out their frustrations. Students threw burning objects toward the abandoned house, and a few objects set patches of dry grass on fire. At 10:30 p.m., Strom and others decided it was time to put the fire out before it spread further. The fire department was called in, and patrolmen were instructed to move toward the campus to protect the fire truck.[43]

The patrolmen arrived in a state of high tension and confusion. Lieutenant D. W. Shealey was hit with a flying banister post tossed from the crowd, bloodying his head; rumors soon spread among the police that he had been shot. Some students retreated to their dormitories, and the fire was doused. Around one hundred fifty students remained, spread across one hundred square yards of the campus. Resentful of the police presence on campus, the students threw things and shouted at the police. The students were shadowy silhouettes against the night on a campus that was dimly lit by two utility-pole lights, a streetlight, and police car headlights. Students were probably not aware that they were surrounded by law enforcement on the left and right—the combined number of National Guard, state police, and local police officers roughly equaled the number of students. A carbine fired, then several shots were released in the air, as a patrolman's intended warning. Students turned to run, and some dropped to the ground. There was no general order to fire. A lieutenant later said that he shouted "now," and his squad began shooting. Patrolmen opened fire from different directions into the crowd of students for eight to ten seconds, leaving wounded and bloodied bodies scattered across the field.[44]

Harry Smith was shot five times. As he lay on the ground, police prodded him with riot sticks and, according to several witnesses, an officer struck Smith with a gun butt. High school senior Delano Middleton, who had been drawn to the excitement on campus, lay nearby. He had been hit in the spine, thigh, wrist, and forearm. The police dragged both men by their hands and feet to a nearby rescue truck, which sped off to Orangeburg Regional Hospital, a racially segregated medical facility. Efforts to save the two men failed. Samuel Hammond, who had one gunshot wound in the upper back, walked off the field and then collapsed. He died as a physician tried to save his life. At least twenty-seven more students had been shot, all but two in the back or side. The police had used buckshot, which is generally used to kill deer and other big game. Television reporters listening to their police-band radio heard a patrolman telling others headed to Orangeburg, "You should have been there ol' buddy; got a couple of 'em tonight."[45]

At a press conference the next day, Governor McNair appeared to be most concerned about the public relations aspect of the tragedy. Describing it as "one of the saddest days in the history of South Carolina," he said that his greatest regret was that the "state's reputation for racial harmony has been blemished." There was no mention of the dead students. It was "apparent" McNair said, spinning what would remain his version of events, that "the incident last night was sparked by black power advocates." A week later, he compared what had happened in Orangeburg to the "riotous conditions that plagued major cities last summer." The militants are "continually crying 'burn baby burn' and shouting blood is going to flow," McNair observed. "You have to take them at their word." He suggested that this rationale more than justified the militarization of the college town. Cleveland Sellers became the governor's fall guy—McNair charged Sellers with instigating the trouble. Sellers, who had not been involved in the protests, had been shot while observing events. He was put under arrest while being treated for his wounds and booked on multiple charges including arson, inciting to riot, assault with intent to kill, and damaging property.[46]

The initial press coverage described an exchange of gunfire between armed students and the police. The white media, for the most part, accepted the official version of events and failed to do their own investigating. The *Washington Post*'s early reporting of a "collision between authority and mobs" bolstered Governor McNair's claims. Ten days after the shootings, drawing from his own exhaustive reporting, Jack Nelson wrote in the *Los Angeles Times* that there was "no material evidence that any Negro students were armed with firearms." A federal investigation would result in charges against nine Highway Patrol officers. All were later acquitted. Cleveland Sellers was ultimately convicted of inciting a riot and served seven months in prison. It wasn't until 1993, when he was forty-nine, that the South Carolina state government finally pardoned him.[47]

In the immediate aftermath of the Orangeburg Massacre, Black activists, journalists, and educational leaders vigorously protested the police assault and pointed to its broader implications. Civil rights leaders in Orangeburg organized a highly effective boycott against white-owned businesses. Sympathy marches were held at Black colleges in the Carolinas and Virginia, where students carried coffins in memory of the three who had been killed. There were protests at Howard University and a demonstration outside Madison Square Garden in New York; the Black Student Alliance at the University of Chicago held a memorial service for the three slain men. The presidents of five Black colleges in Atlanta published an appeal addressed to public officials and private citizens. "We urge you to remove from service all armed, untrained law enforcement officers who are prejudiced, brutal and impulsive," the appeal stated, before warning "that a Congress which gives a thunderous ovation to plans for the use of destructive police power and only polite applause to presidential promises for constructive social action creates an atmosphere within which a democratic society cannot long exist."[48]

"The Carolina Slaughter" was how the *Chicago Defender* described the event. The editorial blasted McNair for failing to commiserate with the community on the death of three young men while rushing to pin the blame on Black Power advocates without producing a shred of evidence. "It was a wild, irresponsible accusation which was intended to discredit the whole black power movement," the *Defender* fumed before recounting how "the real trouble began when the white owner of a bowling alley refused to admit Negroes." (By the end of February, a Justice Department lawsuit had compelled Harry Floyd to admit Black patrons to his bowling alley.) The "injection of the black power movement" into a dispute that ended with the death of three teenage students, the *Defender* warned, is "a doleful forerunner of the pattern of excuse that will precede police brutality in future racial disturbances Such scapegoating, however, cannot destroy the black power movement. It is here to stay."[49]

A fifth summer of urban uprisings in the United States was widely anticipated. The unemployment rate for Black residents of major cities was four times higher than that of whites, federal antipoverty programs were being cut, and half a million children were due to be cut off welfare in July. Community organizer Saul Alinsky described Chicago's slums as "one mass ulcer of discontent" and predicted that unless public officials acted swiftly to address the poverty and distress, the city would explode. Early in February, Martin Luther King Jr. was in Washington for an antiwar meeting and to make plans for the poor peoples' march later that spring. While in Washington, King met with Stokely Carmichael and others. The protest, King explained, aimed to pressure Congress to enact legislation that would guarantee employment and a decent income to those unable to work. While that was the long-term plan, his hope was for immediate federal aid to the poor to provide a "constructive channel" for the anger and frustration that had erupted in cities. King warned that the nation was facing its last chance for nonviolent change.[50]

What happened in Orangeburg, which is not widely known to this day, shows how a growing obsession with Black militancy and urban disorder both fueled and was used to justify increasingly repressive police action. Late in February, the NAACP sponsored a two-day conference with twenty leading African Americans representing a spectrum of opinion, including historian John Hope Franklin, then a professor at the University of Chicago; Howard University law professor Patricia Harris; and John Wheeler, president of the Mechanics and Farmers Bank of Durham, North Carolina. Fear of "massive repression of Negroes" in the event of urban disturbances was the dominant theme of the discussions. "Our people are angry," Alvin Prejean, assistant director of the Chicago Urban League, told *Wash-*

ington Post reporter William Chapman. Prejean continued, "They just feel that the police are going to sit on them all summer long." Recalling the violence in Detroit the previous summer, NAACP leader Robert Tindal told Chapman, "We saw the use of machine guns and carbines in this town, you know. One girl was shot lying on the floor when a machine gun bullet ripped through the floor."[51]

The last week of February, the *Washington Post* published a series of articles by Chapman on the "Garrison City." He described how Philadelphia, Cleveland, Detroit, and other cities were stockpiling weapons, purchasing armored cars and armed helicopters, and developing advanced surveillance and infiltration techniques. A "burgeoning riot control industry" was actively marketing the latest military-style vehicles and equipment. One of the most prized items, the .50-caliber machine gun, the *Post* noted warily, was used "when wholesale slaughter is required, not to flush out a sniper or individual troublemakers." For the first time, the federal government was working directly with cities and states to control and repress civil disturbances. The army, with a dedicated operations center in the Pentagon, designated fifteen thousand men in the field "to be ready for duty this summer," prepared to respond where needed.[52]

———

ON MARCH 1, 1968, the President's National Advisory Commission on Civil Disorders, appointed in the wake of the Detroit uprising, officially released its report—dramatically altering the public conversation on the root causes of urban unrest. The report was a "stinging indictment of white society," said the *New York Times,* "filled with findings to bear out" this charge. "White racism," the report concluded, was chiefly to blame for the explosive conditions that had ignited urban unrest over the last four summers. "What white Americans have never fully understood," the report stated, "but the Negro cannot forget—is that white society is deeply implicated in the ghetto. White institutions created it, white institutions maintain it, and white society condones it." The 1,400-page report stated that "discrimination and segregation have long permeated American life" and warned that "they now threaten the future of every American." The report called for nothing less than a complete reordering of national priorities. Unless drastic and costly remedies were undertaken at once, there would be "a continuing polarization of the American community and, ultimately, the destruction of basic democratic values."[53]

The Kerner Commission report, as it is commonly known, echoed many of the observations, facts, warnings, and recommendations presented during the Ribicoff hearings. It reflected what Robert Kennedy, Martin Luther

King Jr., and many others understood, but its highly publicized release, its bold warning, and its expansive recommendations commanded attention as no other statement on race in America in the 1960s had. A 708-page version of the report, published by Bantam Books, became an instant best seller, with nearly one million copies sold in the first two weeks after its publication.[54]

The searing report was the work of an unlikely group—an eleven-member commission dominated by white men. It included representatives from business, organized labor, and law enforcement, as well as elected officials from both parties. The commission included two African Americans—NAACP head Roy Wilkins and Senator Edward Brooke, Republican of Massachusetts, both men considered to be moderates—and one woman, Katherine Graham Peden, commissioner of commerce in Kentucky. Governor Otto Kerner of Illinois chaired the group, and New York Mayor John Lindsay served as vice chairman.[55]

Few of those who served on the commission could have predicted the outcome of their assignment. But over a six-week period in the late summer and early fall of 1967, the commissioners visited Newark, Detroit, and other cities that had experienced riots. The commissioners went separately or in pairs, with no advance warning or media attention. They walked through impoverished and blighted areas, talking with residents, community groups, Black militants, and city officials. The level of segregation shocked the commissioners. The gap between official explanations and reality was glaring. Fred Harris remembered the smells, the garbage in the streets, the shoddy and overcrowded housing. The major issues people spoke about were the same: police brutality, lack of jobs, inadequate and poorly resourced schools, substandard housing. Men and women communicated a cumulative sense of powerlessness, which fostered bitterness, anger, and despair. Activists had marched and organized, a young man told Harris, and they finally realized "that you white people ain't going to give the Black man nothing; we've got to take it from you." Reflecting on the impact of the tours and the attendant hearings, Otto Kerner described the riots as starting with "a dry-grass situation in a congested area full of frustration and broken promises."[56]

The commissioners' on-site visits were supplemented by the work of forty field investigators who fanned out in teams of six to twenty-six cities, amassing the information that would undergird the report's startling revelations and conclusions. In addition to the issues of jobs, housing. and schools, Black people reported feeling exploited but lacking the power to stop exploitation by landlords, businessmen, and city officials. Many areas were untouched by federal antipoverty programs. In other places, like Milwaukee, the programs were "deplorably uncoordinated." Field investigators noted that younger Blacks would not tolerate the police the way an older generation had and would fight back. Individuals who had experienced or witnessed police brutality, they found, were most likely to riot. Investigations in Cambridge, Maryland, revealed that overreaction by the police was more responsible for the uprising in that city than anything else, contradicting media reports. For the young field investigators, their work was a radicalizing experience. "I came to see an America I've never known before," one said.[57]

The most revelatory report was done by a team of social scientists led by social psychologist Robert Shellow. They were charged with investigating why the riots had occurred—a nearly impossible task in the few months that the group had. But their conclusions were pointed and hard-hitting. While shocking to some, these conclusions would have been familiar to Robert Kennedy and others who had investigated conditions in poor, segregated urban communities and heard firsthand from residents. The report found that young Black men played a significant role in the uprisings. Facing oppressive conditions and lacking access to traditional levers of power, the actions of these young men, the report concluded, were a rebellion against the white establishment—and were "rational" and "political." The report's section on the police concluded that police had in most instances either incited violence or overreacted once it occurred. Based on an extensive review of data, the report noted that "some 75 percent of the police departments in the country" showed "evidence of strong racist attitudes." A draft of the report, titled *The Harvest of American Racism: The Political Meaning of Violence in 1967*, was rejected wholesale by the commission's senior staff. David Ginsburg, the executive director, described it as "unusable," partly due to the complicated politics of the commission. It was clear, in any case, that the senior staff did not agree with *Harvest's* conclusions about the riots and their causes. Ginsburg ordered all copies of the report destroyed. One copy survived, however, and would be resurrected and published in 2018, the fiftieth anniversary of the release of the Kerner Commission report.[58]

The Kerner Commission's stark conclusions and bold recommendations emphasized that the country could not afford to continue on its present course without disastrous consequences. Costs were not considered in presenting specific recommendations. The report called for immediate action to create twelve million new jobs; a long-range approach to providing for a guaranteed minimum income; and bringing six million new and existing dwellings within the reach of low- and moderate-income families. The report also called for revamping the welfare system, with the federal government assuming a much higher percentage of the costs, and changing the distribution of benefits so as to help hold families together rather than tear them apart; decentralizing city governments to make them more responsive to neighborhoods; creating an institute that would train and educate journalists on urban affairs; and bringing more African Americans into journalism. The report condemned "the equipment of police departments with mass destruction weapons such as automatic rifles, machine guns and tanks. Weapons which are designed to destroy, not control, have no place in densely populated urban areas."[59]

Lyndon Johnson was undone by his commission's report. He disagreed with its conclusions and felt betrayed by those who wrote it. Johnson refused "to accept a diagnosis of deep racism," he later told biographer Merle Miller, and the president was critical of the report for failing to acknowledge what he had achieved: "I can't ignore the progress we have made in a decade to write equality on our books of law." Some of the report's findings were published in the *Los Angeles Times* the week prior to its release, and a full copy was leaked to the *Washington Post* a day before the official release date, further infuriating Johnson. He canceled a planned White House reception for the commissioners and refused to accept the bound presidential copy of the report. Despite the pleas of close advisers, Johnson would not issue a public statement about the Kerner Commission report. On March 1, he left Washington for a hastily organized trip to his Texas ranch.[60]

Coming in the wake of the Tet Offensive, the Kerner Commission report was a powerful indictment of a war that drained resources desperately needed at home. Johnson's refusal to even acknowledge the report deeply rankled Kennedy. On March 3, he and Burke Marshall had lunch with Walter Cronkite in Washington. Cronkite urged Kennedy to run for president, and in the wake of the Tet Offensive, Kennedy began to seriously consider the idea again. Several days earlier, Cronkite, who had recently returned from Vietnam, had disputed claims that the United States was moving closer to victory on his widely watched CBS evening news program. That "we are mired in a stalemate," he told millions of viewers, was the "only reasonable, yet unsatisfactory conclusion." Still, under pressure from military advisers, Johnson was considering sending fifty thousand to two hundred thousand more troops to Vietnam. Kennedy, working with Senators Mike Mansfield and William Fulbright, coordinated a strong Senate offensive against any escalation of the war.[61]

On March 7, Senator Fulbright took to the Senate floor and "touched off a rare extemporaneous debate," wrote John Finney of the *New York Times*. "His speech provoked an outpouring of protest against President Johnson's policy exceeding any previously heard" in the Congress. It went on for three hours. Most of the administration's supporters sat silent, as Mansfield and Kennedy delivered extended comments, as did Senators Jacob Javits and Frank Church. A few senators rose to defend Johnson; most were Republican. Senator Mansfield, his "voice ringing to an emotional pitch," said, "we are in the wrong place and fighting the wrong kind of war." He warned, "We are facing the most troublesome days in the entire history of the Republic." Fulbright agreed. Focusing the debate on the constitutional issues, Fulbright emphasized the Senate's right to advise on and consent to foreign policy. He renounced the Tonkin Gulf Resolution, charging that it was obtained on the basis of misinformation and declaring it "null and void."[62]

Kennedy warned that it would be a mistake for the president to take a step toward escalation "without the support and understanding of the Senate and the American public." Kennedy emphasized the importance of a full and open debate and said that the Senate had to be consulted, and its approval obtained, before any troop increases could be allowed. He spoke at length about the failure of a policy that met every difficulty with escalation, forever promising that victory lay just ahead. "The fact is that victory is not just ahead of us. It was not in 1961 or 1962, when I was one of those who predicted light at the end of the tunnel. It was not in 1963 or 1964, or 1965 or 1966 or 1967. And it is not now." He went on, "if we have learned anything over the past seven years, it is that sending more troops and increasing the bombing is not the answer in Vietnam." Beyond the military disappointments, he concluded, "there is a question of our moral responsibility."[63]

As Ethel Kennedy and Burke Marshall watched the debate from the Senate gallery, Ethel leaned over and said, "What do you think he'll decide to do?"[64]

———

ON SUNDAY, MARCH 10, Bobby Kennedy left Des Moines, Iowa, and flew to California to be with Cesar Chavez when he broke his twenty-five-day fast, a sacrifice for nonviolence. John Seigenthaler had joined Kennedy and Peter Edelman in Des Moines for the trip west, and Ed Guthman met up with them in Los Angeles for the flight to Delano. Sitting with two of his closest friends and his long-time aide, Kennedy said, "I'm going to get in, I'm going to run."[65]

The Tet Offensive, Johnson's response to the racial uprisings and the devastation in Detroit, and the president's failure to accept the Kerner Commission report were all pushing Kennedy to enter the race. There was also the growing strength of McCarthy's campaign. McCarthy's candidacy had caught fire with college students, tapping the growing vein of antiwar sentiment in the wake of the Tet Offensive and the end of most draft deferments for graduate students. Hundreds of college students flocked to New Hampshire over the two weekends leading up to the March 12 primary. The students fanned out across the state, trudging through mud and ice to knock on doors and talk to Democratic voters in the largely conservative state. Reporters marveled at how the candidate's small, inexperienced staff organized the influx of young people into an effective campaign operation. "Clean for Gene" was their byword. Young men wore sports jackets and slacks, their hair trimmed. "Girls can be mini-skirted, but not too audaciously," according to campaign standards. The *New York Times* credited McCarthy with generating "a political renaissance among the young."[66]

Kennedy decided to wait until after the primary to declare but, through Richard Goodwin, then serving as an advisor to the McCarthy campaign, Kennedy relayed his intentions to McCarthy. McCarthy's strong showing in New Hampshire, where he took 42.2 percent of the vote against a write-in campaign for Lyndon Johnson, gave McCarthy's campaign an enormous boost. When Kennedy called to congratulate the candidate, Kennedy said he was reappraising his own situation and suggested they might work together in some coordinated way—an awkward proposition. Their conversation was brief. McCarthy told Kennedy he could do what he wanted and that he, McCarthy, would do what he wanted. A confident McCarthy told reporters in the wake of his stunning victory, "I always thought I could go all the way."[67]

On March 13, Kennedy participated in a hearing of the Senate subcommittee on Labor and Public Welfare on a bill to provide 2.4 million jobs for the unemployed over the next four years. Job creation had been one of the major recommendations of the Kerner commission. Kennedy took the lead in a bipartisan attack on the Johnson administration for failing to endorse the Kerner Commission report or make any attempt to translate its recommendations into action. Senators Joseph Clark and Jacob Javits described Johnson's silence as "fantastic" and "disturbing."[68]

Otto Kerner, John Lindsay, and Fred Harris, all of whom had served on the commission, were the main witnesses at the hearing. Each one praised the jobs bill. Lindsay said it presented "the nation and the Congress with the opportunity to reverse the present trend." But the witnesses would not be drawn into a criticism of the president. A frustrated Kennedy said, "I would like to see the executive branch of Government—the president, members of the Cabinet"—say that this jobs program is a valid plan of action. "We are now in March," Kennedy said; summer was not far off, "and there has been no word from the executive." Later that day, Kennedy told reporters that Lyndon Johnson's silence on the Kerner Commission report was a key reason why the senator was "actively considering" whether to challenge Johnson for the presidential nomination.[69]

That afternoon, Walter Cronkite conducted an interview with Kennedy that would air on the *CBS Evening News*. Having publicly acknowledged that he was reassessing the possibility of running for president, Kennedy spent much of the interview discussing the factors that had brought him to this point. The divisions in the country were so deep, Kennedy said—between the races, between age groups, on the war—he worried that "very difficult days were ahead of us unless something is done." He spoke specifically about the war and the Kerner report and pointed out that neither the president nor any member of his Cabinet had approved the report's findings or its recommendations. Kennedy further noted that Richard Nixon's victory in New Hampshire made it very likely that he would be the Republican nominee, "and it is quite clear from the statements that he made that there will be no difference in attitude, either in domestic or foreign relations, if he is President of the United States."[70]

When asked whether Kennedy thought it was realistic to assume that anybody "could unseat an incumbent president," the senator said confidently, "If I decided to run against the President, it would be on the basis that I could win." Kennedy added, "I understand the difficulties, I understand the problems." But "what's facing the country is so difficult, and I think we just have to move in a different direction than we have. It seems to me that that's quite clear." What concerned him most, he said, was that "what we do now and the policies we put into operation, the programs we effectuate—they're going to have tremendous bearing on the next generation of Americans and the young children who can neither vote nor participate in political life, so we have a responsibility to them—and I feel that strongly. . . . I am distressed at the direction we are moving in, both at home and around the rest of the world, and I think that we have to do something about it."[71]

Two days later, as Robert Kennedy prepared his statement, Ted Kennedy traveled to Green Bay, Wisconsin, to meet with Eugene McCarthy with a proposal for a joint effort to defeat Johnson. The idea was Richard Goodwin's. Goodwin, who had been working with the McCarthy campaign, reasoned that together, the two challengers could amass more anti-Johnson delegates than McCarthy could on his own. Blair Clark, McCarthy's campaign manager, thought the idea worth pursuing and arranged for Ted Kennedy to meet with Clark's boss that night. But McCarthy got cold feet and went to bed instead. His wife, Abigail, was unhappy with the proposal and mistrustful of Goodwin and Clark. Clark insisted McCarthy get out of bed to meet with Kennedy. When he finally appeared, McCarthy told Kennedy that the candidate did not want any help in Wisconsin—the location of the next primary—and would not let Ted share the plan for a coordinated campaign. After forty-five minutes, Ted Kennedy left with no agreement. He returned to DC that night and made it back to his brother's home in McLean just before dawn on the morning of March 16.[72]

On the evening of March 15, while Ted was on his mission to Wisconsin, Robert Kennedy asked Burke Marshall to call Martin Luther King Jr. and tell him he was entering the race and would announce his candidacy the next day. King was in California, preparing to speak to the California Democratic Council. According to Marshall, it was believed that King was planning to endorse McCarthy because of his stance on the Vietnam War. As Marshall recalled, "I called Dr. King and told him that Senator Kennedy was going to announce. I didn't ask him to endorse Senator Kennedy, but I asked him not to endorse Senator McCarthy. He said that he agreed with that, he was glad Senator Kennedy was entering the race, and that he would handle the speech in that way."[73]

—

JUST AFTER 10 A.M. ON SATURDAY, MARCH 16, Robert Kennedy said, "I am today announcing my candidacy for the Presidency of the United States." He was forty-two, the same age his brother had been in 1960. Ethel and two of the couple's children, Matthew, then three, and Christopher, four, sat to Bobby's right; his seven older children had front-row seats in the Caucus Room in the Old Senate Office Building, which was packed with reporters, television cameras, and members of Kennedy's Senate staff.[74]

"I run," he said, "because I am convinced that this country is on a perilous course, and because I have such strong feelings about what must be done, and I feel that I am obliged to do all that I can." He continued, "I run to seek new policies to end the bloodshed in Vietnam and in our cities." And he went on, "I run because it is now unmistakably clear that we can change these disastrous, divisive policies only by changing the men who are now making them."[75]

In his brief statement, Kennedy acknowledged the challenges ahead, as well as "the extraordinary demands of the presidency," which, he said, no one could be certain any mortal could adequately meet. But service in his brother's administration "taught me something about the uses and limitations of military power." As a cabinet member and then a US senator, Robert Kennedy had seen the "inexcusable and ugly deprivation" that caused children to starve in Mississippi, "black citizens to riot in Watts," young American Indians to commit suicide because they "lacked all hope and saw no future," and "proud, able-bodied families . . . wait out their lives in empty idleness in eastern Kentucky." And, in his travels around the nation, he had "listened to young people and felt their anger about the war they are sent to fight." His decision to run for the presidency reflected "no personal animosity or disrespect toward President Johnson." The issue "is our profound differences over where we are heading and what we want to accomplish." While Kennedy did not discount the dangers and difficulties of challenging an incumbent president, the senator offered in conclusion that "these are not ordinary times, and this is not an ordinary election."

In the question-and-answer session that followed, Kennedy responded to charges of opportunism in the wake of McCarthy's success in New Hampshire. The two campaigners had different strengths, Kennedy observed. His entry into the race would only broaden the discussion. He emphasized the value of the primary system in this regard. "I'm going to present my case and what I believe has to be done for the country as soon as possible," he said. "I'm going into the primaries. I'm going to present my case to the American people. I'm going to go all across the country."

One sentence in his formal statement conveyed the essential point: "I cannot stand aside from the contest that will decide our nation's future and our children's future."[76]

CHAPTER SIXTEEN

A Time of Danger and Questioning

||||

AS ROBERT KENNEDY EMBARKED ON A campaign for president, Martin Luther King Jr. was organizing national support for the Poor People's Campaign. Kennedy and King each offered a unique kind of leadership, forged in the tumult of the 1960s and shaped by experiences during peak years of the civil rights movement. During the early 1960s, activists in communities across the South mounted a powerful challenge to the region's segregation system and showed the capacity of government to remedy stark injustices. Broader challenges quickly loomed as the pervasive consequences of racism in American life became manifest. But the civil rights movement had fostered a shift in American political culture, loosening the grip of Cold War politics and reigniting the belief that government should serve the common good and that civic engagement was worth the attention of a younger generation.

By early 1968, if there was one point of agreement in a deeply divided nation, it was that the country had reached a breaking point. The Johnson administration appeared paralyzed after the Tet offensive exposed the failure of American policy in Vietnam. The Kerner Commission report boldly documented the poverty, joblessness, police brutality, and alienation that fueled Black rebellions in America's cities. In this environment, King was preparing to bring thousands of poor people to Washington to protest economic and racial injustice and compel government action. As a presidential candidate, Robert Kennedy sought to capture the dedication and faith that had stirred citizens to work for racial and social justice and to protest the war in Vietnam in an effort to build a political movement capable of moving the country in a new direction.

The obstacles facing both men in their quests may have been insurmountable. But the power of their leadership at this moment was consequential in ways that are not easily measured. In 1968 King was, as Black Panther Party historians Waldo Martin and Joshua Bloom wrote, "the living symbol of the insurgent civil rights movement." He was arguably the only Black leader, on a national scale, who kept open the possibility of bridging an ever-deepening racial divide. Robert Kennedy, more than any national white political figure, had earned the trust of many African Americans and had demonstrated a capacity to reach large numbers of white Americans, whom he told unequivocally that the resolution of America's racial crisis rested with them. Taking the measure of Kennedy at this time, Muhammad Ali observed: "black and white youth are all for Robert Kennedy. He tells the truth about race, religion and the war."[1]

———

IN MARCH 1968, former SNCC chairman John Lewis was working with the Southern Organization Project in Jackson, Mississippi, helping to set up cooperatives and credit unions, when he saw a group of people gathered around a small television set and wondered what had so captivated their attention. As he drew closer, he heard Robert Kennedy announce that he was entering the presidential race. "The America Bobby Kennedy envisioned," Lewis recalled thinking, "sounded much like the Beloved Community I believed in." Lewis had helped draft SNCC's statement on the Vietnam War, but he was most drawn by Kennedy's "concern for America's 'invisible poor' . . . and his commitment to confront and close the racial rifts that were turning the streets of the nation's largest cities into battlefields."

"I immediately sent him a telegram offering my support," Lewis recalled. "I told him I wanted to help in any way I could." On returning to Atlanta, he received a call from Kennedy aide Earl Graves, who led in organizing Black support for the candidate, saying that Kennedy would very much like for Lewis to work on the campaign. Lewis arranged to take time off from his job and, at the end of March, flew to Indiana, where Kennedy would face his first primary.[2]

While African Americans would provide a critical base support for RFK's campaign, Kennedy's main challenge was to prove to the Democratic Party establishment and delegates to the convention that he had a broad appeal to voters, for delegates and party leaders at the convention would ultimately elect the nominee. Most states selected delegates through a system of party caucuses and a state Democratic Party convention dominated by party officials. In states like Illinois, party bosses like Mayor Richard Daley would decide how the Illinois delegation voted. Only fourteen states and the District of Columbia held primaries, open to all registered voters. The results offered a significant measure of a candidate's appeal but never enough to sway the convention. Kennedy's challenges in the primaries were clear. How would he fare among white suburbanites and blue-collar voters in the primary states of Indiana, Oregon, and California? Or among rural whites in Nebraska and South Dakota? For older campaign advisers, who had worked on JFK's campaign, these were major concerns. Younger aides pushed back against any shading of Kennedy's positions. The candidate himself was guided by his own vision and instincts as he moved through the heartland, the South, and along the West Coast, confident that many Americans shared his desire to set the country on a fresh and more promising course.

Before concentrating on the primary races, Kennedy barnstormed through sixteen states over a fifteen-day period to demonstrate his ability to reach voters across race, class, and geography. He launched the campaign in Kansas, where he had two long-standing speaking engagements at Kansas State University and the University of Kansas. Kennedy connected to college students, with his youthful style and appeal to public service. But the reception at Kansas State on March 18 exceeded all expectations. Hanging from the rafters, crowding the stairwells, and even sitting under the press table at the Ahearn Field House were 14,500 students: girls in long skirts who wore no makeup and short-haired boys with neckties. Bobby studied the students in the first rows as he made final edits to his speech. He had decided to make an aggressive attack on Johnson's policy in Vietnam and to put forward proposals he had advanced for peace in Vietnam. "We are in a time of unprecedented turbulence, of danger and questioning," he began, before acknowledging his own role in shaping Vietnam policy during his brother's administration. But "past error is no excuse for its own perpetuation." RFK came, he said, "to ask for your help; not for me, but for your country and for the people of Vietnam. . . . You are the people, as President Kennedy said, 'who have the least ties to the present and the greatest stake in the future.'"[3]

The speech was repeatedly interrupted by thunderous applause. The lively question-and-answer session that followed turned playful. "Put yourself in President Johnson's place," one student suggested. "That's what I'm trying to do," Bobby joked. Hays Corey of *Time* said the electricity in the room was "real and rare." "Our country is in danger," Kennedy concluded, "not just from foreign enemies but above all from our own misguided policies. . . . In these next eight months we are going to decide what this country will stand for." Then he raised his fist in the air. The audience erupted in cheers and foot stomping. As he left the stage, students rushed the platform. *Look* magazine's Stanley Tretick, photographing the scene, cried out, "This is Kansas, *fucking* Kansas! He's going all the way!"[4]

The seventeen thousand packed into the Allen Field House at the University of Kansas, his next stop that day, were even more enthusiastic. "Students stamped and clapped in rhythm as he entered," Jules Witcover reported. Kennedy began talking about Vietnam, repeating some of the points he had made earlier. Then he moved deftly "from troubles abroad to troubles at home, and the crowd was with him." He talked about the "other Americans"—starving children in the Mississippi Delta, "their bodies crippled by hunger . . . here in the United States with a gross national product of 800 billion dollars." Yet, he said, "we haven't developed a policy so that they can get enough food so they can live and so that their lives are not destroyed." He described seeing families in urban areas "listening to ever greater promises of equality and justice, as they sit in the same decaying school and huddle in the same filthy rooms, without heat, warding off the cold and warding off the rats." He said he'd seen "proud men in the hills of Appalachia, who wish only to work in dignity, but they cannot for the mines have closed and their jobs are gone and no one—neither industry, labor nor government—has cared enough to help." "If we believe that we, as Americans, are bound together by a common concern for each other," he said, "then an urgent priority is upon us. We must begin to end the disgrace of the other America."[5]

Kennedy went on to critique a society that enjoyed unprecedented prosperity but had "surrendered community excellence and community values in the mere accumulation of material things." Referring again to America's gross national product (GNP), he asked whether that metric should be the benchmark of the nation's worth. He went on to list some of the GNP's constituent parts and their costs: "air pollution and cigarette advertising . . . special locks for our doors and jail for those who break them . . . the loss of our natural wonder in chaotic sprawl. It counts napalm and the cost of a nuclear warhead, and armored cars for police who fight riots in our streets. . . . It counts television programs which glorify violence in order to sell toys to our children." He asked his audience to consider what the GNP did not take into account—"the health of our children, the quality of their education, or the joy of their play. It does not include the beauty of our poetry, or the strength of our marriages, the intelligence of our public debate or the integrity of our public officials. It measures neither our wit nor our courage . . . neither compassion nor our devotion to our country." In short, he said, the GNP measured everything "except that which makes life worthwhile. And it can tell us everything about America except why we are proud that we are Americans."[6]

The speech was interrupted many times by wild applause. At the end, it was nearly impossible for Kennedy to leave the field house as the throng of enthusiastic students surrounded him. Jim Tolan, a campaign advance man, recalled: "Those kids were out of control. He could have got hurt, they liked him so much."[7]

Kansas was a spectacular kickoff. On the plane back to Washington that night, a reporter asked Kennedy how he felt now that he was running. "I feel good," Bobby said. "All those things I was saying [about supporting Johnson]—that wasn't me. The others, those who didn't want me to run, they never got out into the country and saw the crowds. I saw them in 1966. They didn't know what I knew. I felt it in my gut. I had to go."[8]

On March 21, he campaigned in Alabama, Tennessee, and Georgia, delivering major speeches at the University of Alabama and Vanderbilt University in Nashville. Johnson's failed leadership and its consequences were a major theme, as Kennedy attempted to broaden the way people viewed the challenges facing the country. He began developing his approach to more conservative whites. He started from a point of agreement—violence and looting could not be tolerated—but then asked his audience to think about the deeper causes of this urban unrest. "The gulf between our people will not be bridged by those who preach violence . . . or those who meet legitimate grievances with the heavy hand of repression," he told eleven thousand students gathered at Vanderbilt. "I run for President because I want to do something about violence in the streets. I run also because I want citizens to have an equal chance for jobs and equal housing."[9]

Kennedy spoke about the growing divisions between Blacks and whites and suggested that these were fueled in part by Johnson's response to four years of explosive urban unrest. "The President tells us that we can look forward to summer after summer of riot and repression," Kennedy said. He spoke of other divisions, equally serious, that were tearing the nation apart. "Young people—the best educated in our history—turn from the Peace Corps and public commitments of a few years ago to lives of disengagement and despair, turning on with drugs and turning off America." He asked who was dividing America. "It is not those who call for change, it is those who make present policy, who bear the responsibility for our present course." Those calling for an end to dissent "would appear not to comprehend what this country is all about. For dissent and debate are the very heart of the American process."[10]

Ten thousand students at the University of Alabama, many of whom had waited for nearly two hours in the Coliseum, greeted him with a standing ovation. Kennedy stood near the place where, five years earlier, Governor George Wallace had stood in the doorway to block the admission of Vivian Malone and James Hood. On this day, Lyndon Johnson was Bobby's main focus as he called for the reconciliation of a deeply divided country. Americans were divided, Kennedy said, "by our age, our beliefs, by the color of our skin." He sought to join with the students in building a better country. "Free talk and free dissent," he emphasized, are the basis of "a politics of challenge and change aimed at creating a national consensus and the mobilizing of citizen involvement in redirecting the country."[11]

Kennedy was determined to bring this politics of challenge and change to Washington. "The election will mean nothing if it leaves us, after it is all over, as divided as we were when it began," he said. Those seeking high of-fice "must go before all Americans. Not just those who agree with them, but also those who disagree; recognizing that it is not just our supporters, not just those who vote for us, but all Americans, who we must lead in the dif-ficult years ahead." There will be many issues on which we disagree, he told his audience, and "we can confront them with candor and truth." There was no need to "paper over our differences on specific issues—if we can, as we must, remember always our common burden and our common hopes as Americans."[12]

—

ON MARCH 23, Kennedy headed west for a campaign swing through eight states. Frank Mankiewicz called it the "Free at Last Tour." After months of indecision and conflicting advice, Kennedy had taken the plunge and felt an immediate release. He was talking directly to people across the country, listening to them, and sometimes debating with them in the lengthy question-and-answer sessions that followed his talks. Adam Walinsky and Jeff Greenfield, Kennedy's primary speechwriters, worked on the fly, often pro-ducing talking points on note cards. There was no entourage of advisers, poll-sters, and media analysts traveling with Bobby. He was spontaneous and impulsive, and he made important decisions himself. Most significantly, as veteran correspondent Jules Witcover observed, all at once Kennedy "was freed of a long self-discipline against open criticism of Johnson." During these early days of the campaign, as Witcover saw it, Kennedy "became a force on the stump seldom seen in American national politics."[13]

California, the most important primary state, was Kennedy's first stop. Jesse Unruh, the powerful speaker of the State Assembly, who served as Ken-nedy's campaign manager in California, remarked at the start of a three-day campaign swing through the state, "We can't just sit down at a table and expect to bargain for delegates. We've got to produce a groundswell in this country." *Los Angeles Times* reporter Robert Donovan agreed, writing that Kennedy had to "stir up such tremendous excitement . . . that the shockwaves will jar loose Democratic delegates aligned with the President." After intensive campaigning across California, there was no question that the process was well underway.[14]

From the time his plane touched down in San Francisco on March 23, Kennedy was greeted by enthusiastic crowds, which some described as "frenzied." There was "a fervor that has not been seen in many years." Eight thousand people jammed the courthouse plaza in Stockton, in the Central Valley farmlands. The audience, with a large contingent of Chicanos, reminded the *New Yorker's* Jim Stephenson of the crowd that had mobbed the Beatles at Carnegie Hall. In Sacramento later that day, some four thousand middle-class whites packed the Florin Shopping Center and "simply went wild about Kennedy," reported the *Los Angeles Times*. In San Jose that evening, fifteen thousand people filled a downtown park. There was "an unmistakable gladness in the air at his noisy reception," in San Jose, one reporter noted. The next morning, Kennedy attended mass at Our Lady of Guadalupe Church in a predominantly Mexican American neighborhood. Fifteen hundred people crowded into the nine-hundred-seat chapel and spilled out onto the sidewalk.[15]

In the first appearances that were not primarily at universities, Kennedy appealed to a shared vision and sought to establish common ground. Upon arrival at the San Francisco airport, he told the thousand people who greeted him, "I think we can build a new America so that every man has the right to obtain a job and we don't have the deep divisions between black and white." There was no easy answer on Vietnam, he told the crowd in Sacramento, "but I say we can do better—I think we can meet the issues with candor and truth." In Sacramento, Kennedy underscored the strategic underpinnings of his campaign when he told the cheering crowd, "the people themselves should have a say in who should be their nominee." The reaction of the crowds, Robert Donovan reported, "was an indication that the Kennedy candidacy offered them some vague, new hope."[16]

Kennedy arrived in Los Angeles to what Witcover described as a "frightening reception." Thousands pursued Kennedy as he made his way through the tunnel to the street, chanting "We Want Bobby!" That evening he spoke in the Greek Theatre, an amphitheater cut out of a hill. Eight thousand packed the venue, and three thousand more spilled into the adjoining hillside park. Kennedy spoke about the Vietnam War and about the crippling divisions plaguing the country. "For almost the first time," he observed, "the national leadership is calling upon the darker impulses of the American spirit—perhaps not deliberately, but through the actions and examples it sets—an example where integrity, truth, honor and all the rest seem like words to fill out speeches rather than guide our belief." Members of the national press corps thought these comments went too far, bordering on the demagogic, particularly in the context of a wildly enthusiastic crowds. But time would suggest that Kennedy had his finger on the pulse of a definite turn in national political culture.[17]

An estimated five thousand greeted Kennedy at a rally held by the Watts Writers Workshop. As his motorcade drove through the streets, people crowded his car, stood on car roofs, and perched in the branches of live oak trees. Kennedy made several stops for street corner addresses. He spoke about the Kerner Commission report, which "has told us what we should have known long ago: that racial injustice, racial deprivation, racial exploitation is a national issue. It infects our great metropolitan areas as much as it does the South." And he cautioned that "the gulf between our people will not be bridged by those who preach violence, or by those who burn or loot." A man in the crowd told reporter David Wise that the man was voting for Kennedy, "not just for Watts. I'm not just pullin' for Watts. I'm pullin' for the whole country. I'd like somebody to pull the country out."[18]

"If the spectacle of the first nine days suggests anything," wrote Robert Donovan in the *Los Angeles Times*, "it is that the candidacy has touched a live nerve." By the end of Kennedy's campaign across California, he had won the endorsement of City Councilman Billy Mills, the influential chairman of the Los Angeles County Democratic Party. Mills, a leading Black political figure, had pledged to support LBJ's slate at the Democratic National Convention, and state law prevented Mills from switching to another slate. When this problem was pointed out to him, Mills said that he would "do everything within my power to support Senator Kennedy and the concept and attitude of hope he offers for the solution to urban problems." An aide summed it up this way: "As of this morning, we are going on the Kennedy team. Our whole operation will go for Kennedy." Carmen Warschaw, former women's chair for the Democratic Party of Southern California, "told all who would listen" that if it were legally possible, she would give her allegiance to Kennedy, but she was already pledged to run on the Johnson slate. She said at least twenty pledged delegates felt the same way.[19]

While Kennedy was campaigning in California, Lyndon Johnson addressed the Annual Legislative Conference of the AFL-CIO's Building and Construction Trades Department, which represented 3.5 million members. LBJ sounded more like a candidate than at any time since 1964, reported the *Washington Post,* seeming to draw the battle lines for the fight ahead.

Johnson pledged to "build a better America in a climate of law and order" while meeting the nation's commitment to Vietnam, prompting cheers and repeated applause from his labor audience. He renewed his commitment to the administration's policy in Vietnam. "Now the America we are building would be a threatened nation if we let freedom and liberty die in Vietnam," Johnson declared. "We will do what must be done—we will do it at home, and we will do it wherever our brave men are called to stand." He described his legislative achievements as "a program of social justice that never has been written into law by any Administration at any time in all the history of America." AFL-CIO president George Meany effusively praised the "commander and chief" and accused the "peace candidates" of offering honorable surrender on the installment plan. "We should make it clear that the Communists are not going to win victory at the ballot box," Meany insisted, "which they can't win on the battlefield."[20]

——

FROM CALIFORNIA, Kennedy headed north for a day of campaigning in Washington and Oregon, followed by stops in Idaho, Utah, Colorado, Nebraska, New Mexico, and Arizona. The crowds were large and enthusiastic, if not as frenzied as in California. While a handful of McCarthy supporters occasionally turned up—with signs that might read, "Where were you in New Hampshire?"—Kennedy's late entry did not noticeably impact his appeal among college students. College venues were packed to overflowing, and Kennedy engaged students with banter during question-and-answer segments. Nearly twenty thousand turned out at the University of Utah. At the University of Arizona, a contingent of booing students unrolled a huge picture of Barry Goldwater, the state's first presidential candidate. Kennedy paused, took it in, and then said, "I was wondering whatever happened to him." When a low-flying jet drowned out a student asking a question, Kennedy interrupted and said, "Would you wait until Barry is finished?" The crowd roared with delight.[21]

Kennedy's tour made it clear that he had a strong base of support among African Americans and Mexican Americans. A crayoned sign in the window of the newly opened campaign office in a predominantly African American area of Omaha, Nebraska, read, "Kennedy White but Alright / the one before opened the door." His challenge was to broaden his appeal beyond these constituencies, and by every indication he was making headway. He explained his proposed Vietnam policy in a way that engaged his audiences and struck a chord with a nation weary of the war. People appreciated how he took "a share of the blame" for the policies of his brother's administration. Bobby's call for an end to deferments, and his insistence that the burden of the war be borne by rich and poor alike so long as the fighting continued, resonated with many. At Brigham Young University, Kennedy advanced a plan for alternative service that could be put into effect during peacetime, allowing draft-age youth to do community action work rather than serve in the armed forces. "America should be a nation where a man can serve his country without putting on a uniform," he said.[22]

Through his speeches and interactions with the tens of thousands who turned out to hear him, Kennedy outlined domestic policies designed to meet the challenges of contemporary society. The solutions to national problems advanced by the New Deal and JFK's New Frontier, Bobby said, were no longer adequate. He advocated a community-based approach, putting federal funds directly into communities rather than "flowing through an inefficient, overstructured, often tyrannical bureaucracy which is immobilized by sheer size to act swiftly and directly." That approach would mean, he explained, "establishing new kinds of organizations, small in size and scale, working in neighborhoods, able to establish that sense of personal concern and cooperation we have lost all too often with the growth of government." Kennedy opposed welfare as a solution to poverty, a position that might appeal to "anti-welfare" sentiment. But his position was clearly linked to the need for an ambitious effort on the part the federal government and private enterprise to invest in a massive jobs-creation program, which he estimated would cost eight billion dollars.[23]

"Participatory democracy" was a major theme running through Kennedy's speeches. The concept was critical to the kind of campaign he was waging. The *Washington Post*'s Richard Harwood described the idea as "the strategy of revolution, of a popular uprising of such intensity and scale that the 2,622 men and women who will choose the Democratic nominee in August will dare not pass Kennedy by." Kennedy viewed the Democratic Party as too beholden to interest groups that had become insular and power-driven, largely irresponsive to the political energies that had been unleashed over the course of the previous decade—among youth, African Americans, the poor, and those suburbanites who wanted action on social problems. Kennedy constantly urged people to register and vote and to organize their communities. At San Fernando Valley State College, he told his audience "as tens of thousands of young men and women are doing all over this land, organize yourselves to register and vote, to go to your precincts, your districts, to talk with your parents and friends and work to restore the spirit of youth—to win back the moral leadership of our Nation, of our world, of our own people."[24]

On March 27, Kennedy interrupted his tour and flew to Indianapolis to meet the filing deadline for the Indiana primary. Recent polling suggested he would have a fighting chance in this conservative state, and Indiana would be a major proving ground of his viability as a candidate. Many predicted an uphill battle. While Kennedy was edging out Eugene McCarthy in the most recent poll, Bobby would face Roger Branigin, the amiable and popular governor of the state, a stand-in for Lyndon Johnson, who had the backing of the strongest Democratic state organization in the country. Indiana was, as Jules Witcover noted, "the center of old line Americanism," with Indianapolis serving as the national headquarters for the American Legion. Observers saw considerable risk in making such a state the critical first test of Kennedy's candidacy. Kennedy could count on Black support in urban areas, but Black people made up only 9 percent of the total population of the state. George Wallace had scored his strongest primary victory in Indiana in 1964, taking 30 percent of the vote. When warned that Indiana was a gamble, Kennedy responded that the "whole campaign is a gamble."[25]

Bobby returned to the campaign trail with final stops in Arizona and New Mexico. Suffering a bad case of laryngitis, he told a crowd in Phoenix, "the trip has convinced me that the American people want to move toward policies of reconciliation here at home."

———

OVER THE COURSE OF FIFTEEN DAYS, the campaign had moved at an exhausting pace, spanning the South, the West Coast, the Midwest, and the mountain states. "It was hard in those first dizzy two weeks," Jules Witcover wrote, "to recall when one day ended and the next began." Kennedy visited sixteen states with nearly 800 of the 1,312 delegates needed for the nomination. He addressed more than a quarter of a million people and was seen on the nightly news by hundreds of thousands of more. By the end of the tour, he was convinced he understood the temper of the times and that the campaign was hitting its stride. He was persuaded that the Democratic nomination could be wrested from Lyndon Johnson.[26]

On Sunday, March 31, Kennedy and his entourage returned from their two-week campaign swing. At John F. Kennedy International Airport in Queens, New York State Democratic Party chair John Burns pushed his way onto the American Airlines plane to deliver the news: "Johnson isn't running." Lyndon Johnson had just stated on national television that he would not seek reelection, following a prepared speech announcing a bombing halt in Vietnam and plans to pursue a negotiated peace settlement. Kennedy sat quietly in his seat while other passengers brushed past him and fought their way through the crowd of young admirers waiting on the ramp. "I don't know quite what to say," he told reporters who had flown with him from Phoenix.[27]

Johnson's announcement came as a surprise even to his closest advisers. LBJ had not convinced himself to forgo the presidential race until shortly before he delivered the speech that evening, though his biographer Robert Dallek tells us that Johnson had been considering the possibility of staying out of the race for more than a year. A number of factors weighed in the balance: poll numbers, broadening opposition to his policy in Vietnam, health concerns, and mounting exhaustion. Pressures increased during the early months of 1968. By March, Johnson's approval rating had sunk to 36 percent, and support for his Vietnam policy had bottomed out at 26 percent. Robert Kennedy's announcement was the crowning blow. Johnson told Clark Clifford his "worst nightmare had come true."[28]

In his speech to the country, Johnson said that "no other question so occupies our people" as peace in Vietnam. He extended an offer to Hanoi to stop the bombardment of North Vietnam and stated that the United States was "prepared to move immediately toward peace through negotiations." He declared that there had been "progress in building a durable government during the last three years," saying that "a peaceful Asia is far nearer a reality because of what America has done in Vietnam." Johnson spoke about the divisiveness tearing the country apart and said he would not allow the presidency to be involved in the partisan divisions of the election year while America's sons fought abroad. With world peace "hanging in the balance," he said he felt he should not devote one hour of the day "to any duties other than the awesome duty of my office—the presidency of your country. Accordingly, I shall not seek, nor will I accept, the nomination of my party for another term as your President."[29]

In the wake of his announcement, Johnson's approval rating spiked up to 56 percent. Editorials across the country praised his courage and wisdom, and the stock market soared. Newspaper headlines claimed that "Withdrawal Opens the Race for Humphrey" and "Administration Supporters Now Looking to Humphrey." Calls by Kennedy's top aides and the candidate himself to key Democrats around the country seeking their support yielded little. Johnson's supporters remained noncommittal; no governor or congressman was ready to back Kennedy.[30]

After a strong start, Kennedy now faced a different political landscape. In an instant, a main point of reference in his campaign—opposition to Lyndon Johnson's presidency—had been eliminated; and the impact of another point of Kennedy's campaign, his Vietnam policy, had been diminished. At a press conference the next day, Kennedy read the telegram he had sent to Johnson the previous evening expressing hope that his new efforts in Vietnam would be successful and calling his decision "truly magnanimous." When asked if Kennedy would now set aside the issue of Vietnam, the senator said the conduct of the war in Vietnam would continue to be a crucial question for the American people "until peace comes to that land." A day later, in Philadelphia, Kennedy declared that a reduction in bombing, the singular action advanced by Johnson, should be just one part of a "coordinated plan" for peace. America's entire position, Kennedy insisted, should be reexamined. His comments were cheered by thousands at a street corner rally, and by ten thousand students at the University of Pennsylvania.[31]

"As we move toward a political resolution of the agonies of Vietnam," he told the crowd, "we can start to redirect our national energies and resources toward the vital problems in our own national community." Kennedy turned his full attention to what had been and would remain a major focus of his campaign. "The crisis of our cities, the tensions among our races, the complexities of a society at once so rich and so deprived—all these call urgently for the best efforts of all Americans all across this country. We must," he continued, "reach across the false barriers that divide us from brothers and from countrymen to seek and find peace abroad, reconciliation at home and the participation in the life of our country. That," he claimed, "is the deepest desire of the American people and the truest expression of our national goals. In this spirit," he concluded, "I will continue my campaign for the Presidency of the United States."[32]

———

WHILE KENNEDY NAVIGATED the early weeks of his campaign, Martin Luther King Jr. was crisscrossing the country recruiting volunteers. The Poor People's Campaign, King said in a March 25 speech, would bring the full range of domestic issues "out in the open enough so that congressmen, who are in no mood at the present time to do anything about this problem, will be forced to do something about it." He hoped to confront America's domestic crisis and make everyone "face the fact that America is a racist country." When asked several days later whether any circumstances might compel him to call the campaign off, he said the only possibility was if President Johnson quickly implemented the recommendations of the Commission on Civil Disorders—a highly unlikely prospect. The following week, John Lindsay, a commission member, charged the president and the Congress with ignoring the commission's recommendations and warned that this attitude could lead to worse racial violence than the riots of the previous summer.[33]

The Poor People's Campaign was slated to begin on April 22 with King and a small delegation conducting a "lobby-in" on Capitol Hill. At the same time, caravans of poor people would begin moving toward Washington from nine cities and from rural areas in Mississippi, Louisiana, Georgia, North and South Carolina, and Virginia. Several demonstrations were planned in Washington during the month of May, while participants lobbied Congress to address their demands for action on jobs, housing, welfare, and chronic poverty. If Congress responded favorably, the SCLC would stage an early June event on the model of the 1963 March on Washington. If Congress failed to act, the SCLC would pursue a campaign of civil disobedience, stage protests at the political conventions that summer and possibly call for a national economic boycott.[34]

King traveled extensively all of March in an effort to recruit volunteers and raise financial support. He visited Los Angeles, Detroit, Chicago, Washington, and numerous towns in Alabama, Mississippi, and Georgia. His efforts fell far short of enlisting the anticipated number of volunteers. SCLC was in bad shape financially, spending more than it was taking in and unable to meet the minimal expenses of field staff. In several cities, undercover FBI operatives worked to disrupt local efforts to build support for the campaign, stirring up dissension.[35]

A profound state of emotional and physical exhaustion had settled over King. His schedule was unrelenting, but he pushed himself on. His close friend Dorothy Cotton felt it was "just weariness of the struggle, that he had done all he could do." He had come face-to-face with the racism and moral rot that plagued the nation. "There aren't enough white people in our country," he told one audience, "who are willing to cherish our democratic principles over privilege." True integration remained elusive. "Integration is more than something to be dealt with in aesthetic or romantic terms," he told an audience in upstate New York. "What is necessary now is to see" real movement toward "that ultimate goal, which is a truly integrated society where there *is* shared power." He was trying to discover some method, he told the group, "as attention getting as a riot" to make the nation deal with its problems. "I've been searching for that answer," he said, "for over the last eighteen months."[36]

Early in March, Rev. James Lawson, who was the pastor of Centenary Methodist Church in Memphis and had been a mentor to the nonviolent movement in Nashville, asked King to come to Memphis to support the strike of 1,300 Black sanitation workers protesting unfair working conditions. They had asked for a fifteen-cent increase to their $1.70 hourly wage and recognition of their union, Local 1733 of the American Federation of State, County and Municipal Employees (AFSCME), as well as a host of changes to workplace regulations. Mayor Henry Loeb III offered to raise salaries by eight cents but refused to recognize the union or consider other grievances and the city council declined to act on the strikers' demands. The dismissive attitude of the city government triggered a release of pent-up resentment over low wages and the underemployment of Black people in local government. The first march in support of the striking workers led to a violent encounter with the police. King agreed to go to Memphis following his visit to Mississippi.[37]

On March 19, King addressed fifteen thousand people crowded into the Mason Temple in Memphis, the central headquarters of the Church of God in Christ. His spirits were lifted by the size and enthusiasm of the crowd. He intermixed his comments on the situation in Memphis with a preview of plans for the Poor People's Campaign, telling his audience how he planned to take dilapidated shacks from Mississippi to DC on flatbed trucks to show the nation the conditions under which thousands of people were forced to live. King said they would stay in DC until something was done. He conceded that he sometimes felt discouraged, "having to live under the threat of death . . . having to take so much abuse and criticism, sometimes from my own people." But eventually, he said, the Holy Spirit would revive his soul. The crowd erupted in applause. King suggested that Memphis should stage a one-day general work stoppage to strengthen the power of the strike, an idea that appealed to Lawson and the union leadership. When King finished, thunderous applause filed the cavernous space. "I've never seen a community as together as Memphis," he said. He agreed to return to take part in a march at the end of the week.[38]

King spent several days in New York and New Jersey delivering speeches, meeting with various groups, and participating in church rallies in Paterson, Orange, and Newark. While in Newark on March 27, he met with Amiri Baraka, the playwright, poet, and essayist, along with other members of the Committee for Unified Newark, a leading Black Power organization founded in the wake of the 1967 uprising. On the first night of the 1967 disturbances, Baraka had been driving through the city with some friends when he was stopped by the police, dragged from his car, beaten, and pistol-whipped. Then he was arrested and jailed on charges of carrying an illegal weapon and resisting arrest. What happened in Newark that summer, Baraka said, was a rebellion by Blacks enraged by racism and exploitation. Brutal police repression helped fuel the rise of a Black liberation movement in Newark, which embraced community control and armed self-defense. Baraka told King that he, Baraka, had no use for nonviolence—those days were over. He vowed to tear Newark down if necessary.[39]

Later that evening, Harry Belafonte hosted a fundraiser for the Poor People's Campaign at his New York apartment—a revealing evening that Belafonte described at some length in his memoir. After the press and paying guests had left, King slipped off his shoes, loosened his collar, poured himself his customary Bristol Cream sherry, and relaxed. Stanley Levison, Andrew

Young, and Clarence Jones sat on either side of him at the oak bar, which
Belafonte tended, and Bernard Lee lay stretched out on the floor.

"What bothers you, Martin?" Belafonte asked. "Newark," King answered,
and he went on to describe the meeting with Baraka. King was disturbed,
he said, by what he was hearing—"this idea that the solution resides in violence." What he couldn't seem "to get across to these young people is that I
totally embrace what they feel! It's just the tactics we can't agree on." Belafonte was all ears. "I have more in common with these young people than
with anybody else in the movement," he recalled King saying. "I feel their
rage. I feel their pain. I feel their frustration. It's the system that is the
problem, and it's choking the breath out of our lives."[40]

The next day, King flew to Memphis. The march had been rescheduled
because of weather conditions and King's plane was late, delaying the start
by an hour, to 11 a.m. In the interim, some of the estimated six thousand
waiting at Clayborn Temple AME Church grew restless, angered by rumors
that a high school student had been injured and perhaps killed as police tried
to prevent young people from joining the march. Shortly after the march
began and the line of demonstrators turned onto Beale Street, trouble broke
out at the rear of the march when several teenagers smashed sticks through
the windows of two shops. The disruption spread, more store windows were
shattered, and some people began looting goods from the damaged store-
fronts. James Lawson grabbed a bull horn and urged the marchers to head
back to the church. By this time police reinforcements had arrived with
orders to disperse the crowd, leading to an indiscriminate assault on the
demonstrators.[41]

The city, state, and police response to the disturbance reflected the siege
mentality that infused law enforcement practices in urban areas—escalating
the violence and exacerbating the situation. Within two minutes of the
smashing of the first window, Mayor Loeb later boasted, he had called Governor Buford Ellington, who promptly dispatched four thousand National
Guard troops and 250 riot-trained state troopers. Meanwhile, police stormed
into the area and began clubbing anyone within reach. Leading citizens of
the Black community, including banker and march participant James Ward,
charged that the police were out of control, launching a full-scale offensive
instead of moving in and arresting the estimated thirty to seventy teenagers
involved in the looting.[42]

"As marchers retreated back along Main Street onto Beale . . . and toward
the Clayborne Church officers followed, raining blows upon them," the
Washington Post reported. "Men, women and youth stumbled beneath the
police clubs. . . . Police piled on a middle-aged man and struck him at least
twenty times and cursed him." A young girl in a pink dress who could not

keep up with the fleeing marchers was jabbed in the back by police night-sticks. One officer yelled, "Black bitch, get out of here." Two others pulled a fellow policeman off a man he was pummeling. He gasped, saying, "I would have killed that son-of-a-bitch if you hadn't pulled me back."[43]

Older demonstrators who retreated into Clayborne Church were subject to a barrage of tear gas as police lobbed canisters into the church sanctuary. A deep voice from the church loudspeaker system directed at the police officers outside pleaded: "Don't gas us anymore. We're going to leave. . . . Don't shoot. Don't you know this is the house of the Lord?" Baxton Bryant, head of the Tennessee Council on Human Relations, observed: "What the police did today has encouraged plenty of disciples of violence."[44]

The youth fought back, hurling rocks and bottles at the police. "Street warfare raged for several hours," the Washington Post reported, confined to a few blocks where the trouble had started. Police wielded clubs and fired tear gas and Mace. Young people engaged in hit-and-run raids, looting pawn shops, liquor stores, and other businesses. Sixteen-year-old Larry Payne was shot and killed by a police officer who caught him looting a store. The officer later claimed that Payne had charged at the officer with a knife. More than sixty people were injured, and more than one hundred arrests had been made by day's end. The city bristled with a military presence. "People stood and stared as armored personnel carriers ground over the streets mounted with machine guns," Walter Rugaber of the New York Times reported. "National Guardsmen, holding rifles with bayonets attached, stared back."[45]

As soon as the trouble broke out, aides promptly got King out of the area and to his room at the Holiday Inn Rivermont. He was shaken and upset, trying to make sense of how a peaceful march had dissolved into violence. Lawson and others believed the window breaking had been instigated by the Invaders, a group of militants who were high school and college age and whom Lawson had excluded from playing a role in the planning of the march. King privately speculated that there was more to the violence than that. On the phone with Harry Belafonte that day, King said he felt strongly that the FBI fomented the violence to undermine him and discredit the Poor People's Campaign. "There are forces of evil at work here, Harry. I feel it," he said. Years later, after revelations about COINTELPRO (the FBI's counterintelligence program), Belafonte felt it was hardly far-fetched to conclude that the FBI may indeed have tipped the scales toward chaos.[46]

King knew that critics of the Poor People's Campaign would point to Memphis and charge that King could not ensure that the thousands he planned to bring to Washington would remain peaceful. The New York Times incorrectly claimed that King had organized the Memphis march, which, the paper speculated, only served to "solidify white sentiment against the strikers." The editorial went on to warn, "his descent on Washington is likely to prove even more unproductive." Several papers repeated the charge that King was responsible for the march in Memphis. King decided the best way to counter these charges was for the SCLC to organize a second march in Memphis to demonstrate its ability to organize and conduct a nonviolent protest. In preparation, he invited members of the Invaders to meet with him. A date was tentatively set for April 5.[47]

On Sunday, March 31, King delivered a sermon at the National Cathedral in Washington to a mostly white, overflow audience of four thousand. He addressed the evils of racism, poverty, and the war in Vietnam—which he portrayed as at once distinct and interrelated. He described the war as "one of the most unjust wars in the history of humankind" and one that "wreaked havoc with our domestic destinies." He charged that America's war in Vietnam had violated an international agreement, strengthened the military-industrial complex and the forces of reaction in the United States, and put the United States in alliance with a corrupt government and in opposition to the self-determination of the majority of the Vietnamese people.

There was nothing more urgent in King's estimation "than for America to work passionately and unrelentingly to get rid of the disease of racism." It was an unhappy truth, he said, "that racism is a way of life for the vast majority of white Americans, spoken and unspoken, acknowledged and denied, subtle and sometimes not so subtle—the disease of racism permeates and poisons a whole body politic." King highlighted a history that revealed the deep, cruel, and twisted roots of America's racial crisis. He challenged the myth that time would resolve the problem of racial injustice. "Human progress never rolls on the wheels of inevitability," he warned. "It comes through tireless efforts and the persistent work of dedicated individuals. And without this hard work, time itself becomes an ally of . . . social stagnation." He called on all Americans and all sectors of public and private life to look into their hearts with honesty. "We must come to see that the roots of racism are very deep in our country and there must be something positive and massive in order to get rid of racism and the tragedies of racial injustice."

King confirmed that the Poor People's Campaign would be coming to Washington in a few weeks to demand that the government address the problem of poverty. He cited the founding principles laid out in the Declaration of Independence—"We hold these truths to be self-evident, that all men are created equal and endowed by their Creator with certain inalienable Rights, among these are Life, Liberty and the pursuit of Happiness"—and then observed that "if a man doesn't have a job or an income, he has neither life nor liberty nor the possibility for the pursuit of happiness. He merely exists." The poor were coming to Washington "to engage in a dramatic non-violent action, to call attention to the gulf between the promise and the fulfillment; to make the invisible visible." For those who asked, "Why do it this way?" King offered: "Because it is our experience that the nation doesn't move around questions of genuine equality for the poor and for black people until it is confronted massively, dramatically in terms of direct action."[48]

He then added a warning that was reported in the *Washington Post* but not included in the transcript of his speech. "I don't like to predict violence," he said, "but if nothing is done between now and June to raise hope in the ghettos, I feel this summer will not only be as bad, but worse than last year." In the press conference that followed, he said that he did not think rioting in Memphis damaged chances for the success of the Poor People's Campaign. "The opposition was already here," he said. He lambasted Congress as dominated by "rural Southern conservatives and reactionaries who are unconcerned about the plight of the poor." He warned that if Congress adjourned without acting there would be "a real awakening in Chicago" when the Democrats would meet in August to select the party's presidential candidate.[49] Later that evening, President Johnson's surprise announcement that he would not seek reelection boosted King's spirits.[50]

On the morning of April 3, King went from Atlanta to Memphis with Ralph Abernathy to begin plans for the second march, now scheduled for April 8. A bomb scare delayed the departure of their flight. After checking in at the Lorraine Motel, his usual lodgings in Memphis, King attended a meeting of Black clergy at James Lawson's church. King learned that, in response to the city's request for a ban on a second march, District Judge Bailey Brown had granted a temporary restraining order, prohibiting the SCLC from staging a mass protest within the next ten days. Movement lawyers rallied to help King fight the ban. During a meeting with attorneys later that afternoon, he indicated that he intended to go ahead with the march on Monday, whether or not the judge's order was rescinded. He agreed to the lawyers' suggestion that they seek a modification of the order, allowing for a limited march.[51]

That evening, a meeting was scheduled at Mason Temple. It was a stormy night and the turnout would likely be modest. Ralph Abernathy went to address the gathering, giving King a chance to rest. When Abernathy arrived, he found barely two thousand people in the cavernous space, where seven times as many had greeted King two weeks earlier. Abernathy quickly realized the crowd was disappointed that King had not come. He phoned King and told him to come to the church.[52]

"We're going to march on, we've got to march again," King told the gathering, "for when people get caught up with that which is right and are willing to sacrifice for it, there is no stopping point short of victory." He spoke about the importance of anchoring direct action with the power of economic boycotts. "We've got to give ourselves to the struggle until the end." "The nation is sick," he said, but he assured them, "God is working in this period of the twentieth century . . . something is happening in the world . . . the masses are rising up." Whether in Johannesburg, Nairobi, Accra, New York, Atlanta, Jackson, or Memphis, the cry was always the same: "We want to be free."

Toward the end of his speech, as the storm rattled the church windows, King recalled his brush with death ten years earlier when a deranged woman had stabbed him at a Harlem bookstore. The tip of the blade reached the edge of his aorta, and doctors told King that if he had sneezed, he would have died. King segued into a litany of all that had been achieved over the past decade, highlighting some of what he would have missed "if I had sneezed." The sit-ins in 1960, when students "were really standing up for the best of the American dream and taking the whole nation to those great wells of democracy which were dug deep by the Founding Fathers in the Declaration of Independence and the Constitution." There was the Albany movement in 1962, "when Negroes decided to straighten their backs up. . . . And when men and women straighten their backs up, they are going somewhere." There was Birmingham, in 1963, "when the black people . . . aroused the conscience of this nation and brought into being the Civil Rights Bill." If he had sneezed, "I would not have had a chance . . . to try and tell America about the dream I had had," nor "been down there in Selma" in 1965, "to see the great movement there." And he would have missed being in Memphis, "to see a community rallying around those brothers and sisters who are suffering."

"Well, I don't know what will happen now," he intoned at the soaring conclusion of his speech. "We've got some difficult days ahead. But it doesn't matter with me now. Because I've been to the mountaintop. And I don't mind. Like anybody," he said, "I would like to live a long life. Longevity has its place. But I'm not concerned about that now. I just want to do God's will. And He's allowed me to go up to the mountain. And I've looked over. And I've seen the promise land." Then, invoking the powerful imagery of a Baptist preacher, he declared, "I may not get there with you. But I want you to know tonight, that we, as a people will get to the promised land. And I'm happy tonight. I'm not worried about anything. I'm not fearing any man." Sweat streaming from his brow, King proclaimed, "Mine eyes have seen the glory of the coming of the Lord."[53]

ON APRIL 4, John Lewis spent the day preparing for Robert Kennedy's arrival in Indianapolis. Kennedy was scheduled to speak that evening at Seventeenth and Broadway, the center of the city's Black community. He kicked off his first full day of campaigning in Indiana with speeches at Notre Dame and Ball State University. While he was en route to South Bend, Indianapolis mayor Richard Lugar summoned Kennedy's local campaign chief, Mike Riley, and demanded that the rally that evening be canceled. Lugar said the neighborhood was too dangerous for police to guarantee Kennedy's safety. Riley refused. Lugar threatened to order the fire department to lay hoses across the street to block cars from entering the area. "Then we'll tell the people to walk," Riley said curtly.[54]

On both campuses that day, Kennedy spoke about the challenges and responsibilities that awaited the students on graduation. At Notre Dame, he appealed to a central tenet of Catholic teaching, the call for active works of mercy, in a speech entitled "Feeding the Hungry." He developed the theme of national redemption through good works, suggesting that the students might heal the wounds of Vietnam by working to end hunger and poverty. He contrasted their affluence with the starvation and poverty of others. "We cannot—you cannot escape your own responsibility to correct these conditions," he told five thousand students. "They exist because of our indifference—yours and mine. Because you know we can do something about it. And we have a moral obligation."[55]

At Ball State, he implored students to "decide what obligations we have to other people" across the globe and to examine "how we can help the millions of our fellow citizens who lead lives of hopelessness and poverty where, as Sophocles said, 'day follows day, with death the only goal.'" Kennedy spoke about the experiences of young people not much younger than they were, living in poverty in the ghettos of America's cities, where only three out of ten students graduated from high school. "No jobs. No employment. So what would you do? What should they do?" Seventeen thousand children were bitten by rats every year. "What would you do?" he reprised. Only 40 percent of the men living in these communities earned more than $65 a week. "How can you support a family on that?[56]

During the question-and-answer period that followed, a young Black man, one of roughly twenty in the audience, said, "Mr. Kennedy, I agree with the programs and proposals you are making. But in order to make them work, you're placing a great deal of faith in white America." Then he asked, "Is that faith justified?" Kennedy responded yes, he believed it was, adding that he was also placing his faith in Black America. While there were extremists on both sides, he believed "most people want to do the decent thing."[57]

———

FIVE HUNDRED MILES AWAY IN MEMPHIS, plans for the march were progressing. After a daylong hearing, Andrew Young reported to King that Judge Brown had approved a tightly disciplined march on Monday. King began teasing Young for not checking in during the day as they all had waited anxiously for news. King threw a pillow at Young, and "I threw it back," Young recalled. "We ended up with five or six of us in a pillow fight." As the dinner hour approached, King reminded his friends that it was time to get ready, Rev. Billy Kyles would soon be there to take them to a soul food dinner. Kyles arrived just before 6 p.m., and while they waited for the others, King stepped out onto the balcony of his room. He greeted friends gathered in the parking lot below.

A rifle shot rang out. Kyles, Young, and Abernathy rushed to King. He had a gaping wound in his right jaw. An ambulance soon arrived and took him to St. Joseph's Hospital, where Martin Luther King Jr. was pronounced dead.[58]

Kennedy was boarding a plane in Muncie when he heard the news that King had been shot. King's condition, Kennedy was told, was critical. On his arrival in Indianapolis, *Washington Post* reporter Richard Harwood boarded the plane and told Kennedy that King was dead. Kennedy covered his face and said, "Oh God, when is the violence going to end." Campaign aide Jim Tolan found Kennedy "shook, really shook"—more disturbed than Tolan had ever seen the senator. Kennedy asked about his schedule, and Tolan told Kennedy about the rally at Seventeenth and Broadway, "in the middle of the worst part of the black ghetto." Tolan suggested Kennedy might cancel the event and send someone to read a statement. "I'm going there and that's it," Kennedy said, "and I don't want any police going with me."[59]

There were tears in Kennedy's eyes when he emerged from the plane. He made a brief statement in a voice close to breaking: "Dr. King dedicated himself to justice and love between fellow human beings. He gave his life for that principle and I think it is up to those of us who are here to end the divisions that exist so deeply in our country." Police Chief Winston L. Churchill approached Kennedy and urged him to cancel the rally at Seventeenth and Broadway. Riots were certain, the chief warned. It would not be safe. "I could take my wife and family and we could sleep at the middle of Seventeenth and Broadway and there would be no problem," Kennedy replied. "If you can't do that, it's your problem." He asked campaign volunteer Bill Gigerich to take Ethel to the hotel and stay with her until Kennedy returned. As he was driven to the rally, he starred silently out the window and scribbled some notes on a yellow piece of paper.[60]

By early evening, a large crowd had gathered at the rally site; nearly a thousand people waited. The weather was brisk and overcast. The crowd, John Lewis recalled, was upbeat, eager, and excited. Kennedy was due to arrive at 7:30 p.m. At around 6:30, a visibly upset Walter Sheridan, Kennedy's longtime aide, came rushing up to Lewis, pulled him aside and told him that King had been shot. Lewis recalled that he was "frozen"—"stunned stockstill, inside and out." The crowd waiting for Kennedy had not yet heard the news. "No one knew a thing. Kennedy was coming. That's all they knew," Lewis recalled. Sheridan, Lewis, Earl Graves, and several local African Americans involved in planning the event huddled in a circle. They agreed that the rally had to go on and that Kennedy should be the one to break the news to the men, women, and children who waited as darkness set in.[61]

It was close to 9 p.m. by the time Kennedy arrived at the rally site, a large open lot surrounded by several tall, run-down buildings. The area was lit by a single spotlight and two floodlights mounted on polls. A group of Black musicians were playing on the flatbed truck, which served as the stage, and some people were dancing in the front. It was cold and windy, with temperatures in the upper thirties. A light drizzle was falling. By now, people who had poured into the streets after hearing the news of King's death had gathered at the outer edges of the crowd. Anger and tension boiled up among those who had heard, and several began taunting the whites, who made up around 25 percent of the gathering. But the news had not yet filtered through the crowd, "packed in like sardines," as one participant recalled. At the front, people were laughing, cheering, and waving signs as Kennedy emerged from a black sedan, wearing a black trench coat. He climbed onto the flatbed truck.[62]

Before he began speaking, Kennedy asked the local dignitaries sitting on the platform, "Do they know about Martin Luther King?" "To some extent," one responded. "We've left that up to you." He looked out to the crowd, shadowed in darkness. "I am only going to speak to you for a minute or so this evening because I have some very sad news for all of you." He asked them to lower their signs and continued, his voice trembling. "I have some very sad news for all of you and I think some sad news for all of our fellow citizens and people who love peace all over the world. And that is that Martin Luther King was shot and killed tonight in Memphis, Tennessee."[63]

A gasp rose from the audience, punctuated by screams: "No!" People broke down weeping, and some dropped to their knees. Toward the back of the crowd, there were bursts of cheering and applause, as some had not heard him clearly. But soon what he said and "the sobriety of his tone," John Lewis recalled, "moved through the crowd like a wave." Kennedy's voice was close to breaking. "He had no notes," Lewis recalled. "He spoke simply and honestly . . . completely extemporaneously . . . and the crowd hung on every word."[64]

"Martin Luther King dedicated his life to love and to justice between fellow human beings. He died in the cause of that effort," Kennedy said, as silence fell over the crowd. "In this difficult day, in this difficult time for the United States, it's perhaps well to ask what kind of nation we are and what direction we want to move in." The country could move toward "greater polarization—black people amongst blacks, and white people amongst white, filled with hatred toward one another. Or we can make an effort, as Martin Luther King did, . . . to comprehend, and replace that violence, that stain of bloodshed that has spread across our land, with an effort to understand, compassion, and love."

"For those of you who are black and are tempted to be filled with hatred and mistrust of the injustice of such an act, against all white people, I would only say that I can also feel in my own heart that same kind of feeling. I had a member of my family killed, but he was killed by a white man." Reflecting on the deep sorrow he had endured, he quoted the ancient Greek playwright Aeschylus, "who once wrote: 'Even in our sleep, pain which cannot forget / falls drop by drop upon the heart / until, in our own despair, / against our will, / comes wisdom / through the awful grace of God.'"

"What we need in the United States is not division," he said, "what we need in the United States is not hatred; what we need in the United States is not violence and lawlessness, but is love and wisdom and compassion toward one another, and a feeling of justice toward those who suffer within our country, whether they be white or whether they be black. So I ask you tonight to return home, to say a prayer for the family of Martin Luther King—yeah, it's true," he said, responding to a cry of disbelief from the crowd—and continued, "but more importantly to say a prayer for our country, which all of us love—a prayer for understanding and that compassion of which I spoke."

Kennedy went on, "We can do well in this country. We will have difficult times. We've had difficult times in the past. And we will have difficult times in the future. It is not the end of violence; it is not the end of lawlessness; and it is not the end of disorder. But," he continued, reaching for hope in a dark and despairing moment, "the vast majority of white people and the vast majority of black people in this country want to live together, want to improve the quality of our life, and want justice for all human beings who abide in our land."

Again, returning to words that had brought him solace in the wake of his brother's death, he closed, "Let us dedicate ourselves to what the Greeks wrote so many years ago: to tame the savageness of man and make gentle the life of this world. Let us dedicate ourselves to that and say a prayer for our country and a prayer for our people.[65]

John Lewis was stunned to hear Kennedy reference his brother's assassination. Bobby had never spoken about the murder of his brother in public before. "To do it that night was an incredibly powerful and connective and emotionally honest gesture. He stripped himself down. He made it personal. He made it real."[66]

Kennedy returned to the Marriot Hotel, where Ethel was waiting, and he phoned Coretta Scott King. After talking with her, he asked what he could do. She told him she was planning to go to Memphis in the morning to bring her husband's body back to Atlanta. Kennedy offered to charter a plane. He called Burke Marshall, who was in New York, and asked him to fly down to Memphis and accompany Mrs. King and Dr. King's body back to Atlanta. Kennedy offered to hook up more phone lines in her house, to handle all the calls that would be coming in. She said she had not thought about that. "I'll get that done tonight," he said. The telephone men arrived and installed the lines soon thereafter.[67]

That night and over the next several days racial unrest exploded in more than one hundred cities and towns across the United States. Forty-six were reported dead, and hundreds more were injured. Indianapolis was spared. By Friday afternoon, several neighborhoods in Washington, DC, were in flames—mostly along Fourteenth and Seventh Streets NW and H Street NE. Flying into the city on Friday night, Justice Department official Roger Wilkins described seeing "a great big orange ball. . . . It looked like the city had been bombed from the air." More than 1,200 fires had been lit that night, and property damage was estimated at $24 million dollars, putting the unrest in the nation's capital on a par with the uprisings in Watts in 1965 and in Detroit and Newark in 1967. President Johnson federalized the National Guard and called out four thousand federal troops to restore order. For the first time since the Civil War, federal troops were guarding the Capitol.[68]

—

ROBERT KENNEDY CANCELED ALL CAMPAIGN EVENTS, except for one, until after King's funeral. On April 5, Kennedy went to the City Club of Cleveland, where twenty-two hundred civic leaders had gathered. He spoke quietly and movingly about the tragedy of King's death and the violence that pervaded American life. "This is a time of shame and sorrow," Kennedy began. "It is not a day for politics. I have saved this one opportunity to speak briefly to you about the mindless menace of violence in America which once again stains our land and every one of our lives."[69]

"Violence is not the concern of any one race," he said. "The victims are black and white, rich and poor, young and old, famous and unknown." Reflecting on the moment, he declared, "no martyr's cause has ever been stilled by an assassin's bullet. No wrongs have ever been righted by riots and civil disorders."

In his short speech, Kennedy highlighted the pervasiveness of violence in American society and culture—violence in the name of the law and in defiance of the law, and violence in the daily routines of life. "We calmly accept newspaper reports of civilian slaughter in far off lands. We glorify killing on movie and television screens and call it entertainment," he said. "We make it easy for men of all shades of sanity to acquire the weapons and ammunition they desire. Too often we honor swagger and bluster and the wielders of force."

"There is another kind of violence," he continued, "slower but just as deadly, destructive as the shot or the bomb in the night. That is the violence of institutions, indifference and inaction and slow decay. This is the violence that afflicts the poor," he said, "that poisons relations between men because their skin has different colors. This is a slow destruction of a child by hunger, and schools without books and homes without heat in the winter. This is the breaking of a man's spirit by denying him the chance to stand as a father and as a man among other men."

The question, he said, was "whether we can find in our own midst and in our own hearts that leadership of human purpose that will recognize the terrible truths of our existence. We must admit," he implored, "the vanity of our false distinctions among men and learn to find our advancement in the search for the advancement of all. We must admit to ourselves that our own children's future cannot be built on the misfortune of others. . . . Our lives on this planet are too short and the work too great to let this spirit flourish any longer."

There were no easy answers, he acknowledged, no resolution or program capable of redressing this pervasive malady. But perhaps Americans could "remember . . . that those who live with us are our brothers, that they share with us the same short movement of life and they seek—as we do—nothing more but the chance to live out their lives in purpose and happiness, winning what satisfaction and fulfillment they can. Surely this bond of common faith, this bond of common goal, can begin to teach us something."

King's death marked a turning point in Robert Kennedy's presidential campaign. He had long held the views he expressed in the Cleveland speech, and they had been a major force behind his domestic positions. However, "from this point forward," Witcover recalled, "Kennedy's campaign took on the theme of racial justice and reconciliation to a degree that made Vietnam almost a subordinate issue."[70]

Bobby and Ethel flew back to Washington that night, as thousands of federal troops poured into the city. The next day, the couple attended Palm Sunday services with Peter Edelman and Marian Wright at New Bethel Baptist Church on Ninth Street NW, pastored by Rev. Walter Fauntroy, city councilman and SCLC board member. The church was just a few blocks from the battle-scarred area of the city. Kennedy spoke briefly to the congregation and said he had come to join them in paying respects to Dr. King. Afterward, he and Ethel walked with Fauntroy down Seventh Street, then north past scores of burned-out buildings. "The stench of burning wood and broken glass was all over the place," Fauntroy recalled. As the group approached the intersection of Fourteenth and U Streets, more and more people gathered around Kennedy. Several soldiers fixed their bayonets on their rifles and began putting on their gas masks when they saw the crowd. But when they recognized Kennedy they took off the masks and let the crowd through. Children tugged at Kennedy's sleeve. One woman said, "Is that you?" He nodded and she grabbed his hand. "I knew you would be the first to come here, darling," she said. "Kennedy blushed," the *Washington Post* reported.[71]

On Monday, Bobby and Ethel flew to Atlanta. King's funeral would be the following day. Upon landing the Kennedys went directly to the home of Coretta Scott King. After meeting privately with her, they went to Ebenezer Baptist Church, where King's body lay in an open casket. They returned to the Hyatt Regency Hotel, where Kennedy spent most of the night in a series of private, unpublicized meetings with Black leaders and entertainment figures. Someone, Burke Marshall could not recall who, suggested that this was a rare opportunity, with many of the country's leading Black figures all in one place. John Seigenthaler organized the gatherings into three groups—political leaders, entertainment figures, and King's friends and associates from the SCLC.[72]

Kennedy said he was there to listen and learn what could be done to help carry King's work forward. There is no record of the meetings. Julian Bond, then a state legislator, turned up at the wrong meeting, joining the entertainers. He said it was "very strange," with several celebrities boasting about what they were doing for the movement. Bill Cosby finally said, "this is a lot of shit," and left. As the meeting broke up, Bond recalled, "Kennedy said to me, 'Julian, I bet you've been to a lot of meetings like this before, haven't you.' And I said, 'yes.' And he said, 'I bet you don't want to go to anymore.' And I said, 'No.'"[73]

It was after 2 a.m. when the meetings ended. Bobby wanted to return to Ebenezer. John Lewis accompanied him and Ethel to the church. "It was three in the morning," Lewis remembered. "The inside of the church was pitch dark and empty. . . . There was a faint glow as we stepped into the sanctuary, the flicker of candles throwing shadows against the wall. Flowers were everywhere." King lay there, in a black suit, white shirt and black tie, and a handkerchief in the breast pocket. "The body looked as if it was sleeping," Lewis wrote. There were some honor guard and security people standing quietly by the doors. "Bobby and Ethel . . . made the sign of the cross, knelt and prayed and spent several long minutes in silence." Then Lewis went forward to say his final farewell to his friend. "It felt unreal," Lewis said.[74]

Later that morning, white governors, congressmen and presidential candidates, Black civil rights leaders and activists, leading Black entertainers, sports figures, and diplomats packed Ebenezer Baptist Church, with its 750-seat capacity. Following the service, a mule-drawn farm wagon carried King's casket in a four-mile-long procession to Morehouse College, King's alma mater. Blacks and whites walked arm in arm, singing "We Shall Overcome," "Keep Your Eyes on the Prize," and other anthems of the civil rights movement. Kennedy walked the entire way, marching through a southern city for the first time, with thousands of African Americans. Hands reached out to touch him, and he was continually cheered and applauded.

Dogwoods and azaleas dotted Morehouse's historic campus. From the platform holding Black dignitaries, including Morehouse president emeritus Benjamin Mays, Ralph Abernathy announced over the microphone, "I see Senator Robert F. Kennedy out there. Will you please make way for him to come to the platform?" The crowd cheered as Kennedy, the only white person on the platform, joined Coretta Scott King, Rosa Parks, Andrew Young, and others. This invitation caused a temporary ruckus as allies and aides of other political figures insisted that they also be recognized. Abernathy amended his announcement and summoned Nelson Rockefeller, Hubert Humphrey, Eugene McCarthy, Richard Nixon, and others—many of whom had already left.

In a powerful and at times militant eulogy, Benjamin Mays charged, "Make no mistake, the American people are in part responsible for Martin Luther King's death. The assassin"—at this point still unknown—"heard enough condemnation of King and Negroes to feel he had public support." He continued, "Let us see to it that we do not dishonor his name by trying to solve our problems by rioting in the streets . . . but let us see that the conditions that cause riots are promptly removed." Mays concluded by linking King and John F. Kennedy. "And to paraphrase the words of the immortal John Fitzgerald Kennedy, permit me to say that Martin Luther King Jr.'s work on earth must truly be our own." As Mays concluded, Bobby Kennedy and others on the platform joined hands and sang "We Shall Overcome," looking out over the mostly Black gathering of more than ten thousand people, weeping and swaying in unison, lifting their voices in song.[75]

After King's funeral, Burke Marshall and John Doar flew with Bobby and Ethel from Atlanta to Washington. Marshall and Doar continued on to New York, where Doar had recently taken the position of director of the Bedford Stuyvesant Development and Services Corporation. John Lewis returned to the campaign in Indiana. "Dr. King's death made it all the more important for me to put everything I had into Kennedy's campaign," Lewis recalled. "I saw this as the final extension of the movement. I transferred all the loyalty I had left from Dr. King to Bobby Kennedy."[76]

CHAPTER SEVENTEEN

The Last of the Great Believables

|||

ON APRIL 10, Robert Kennedy returned to the campaign trail. Three and a half weeks into his presidential run, Lyndon Johnson was out of the race, Martin Luther King Jr. had been killed, and American cities had once again gone up in flames. In less than a month, Kennedy would face the first of six primary contests that would determine the fate of his candidacy. He had a crack team of aides, advisers, and strategists working with him, including Steve Smith, Fred Dutton, Kenny O'Donnell, and Ted Sorensen—all seasoned operatives who had worked on JFK's campaign. That month, Richard Goodwin left McCarthy's campaign to join RFK, and Lawrence O'Brien resigned as US postmaster general and joined the campaign. Dick Tuck, a brilliant campaign strategist and prankster, was also in the mix, along with Senate aides Adam Walinsky and Peter Edelman, and Jeff Greenfield, who had worked on Kennedy's Senate staff.[1]

David Hackett and Richard Boone led in organizing through VISTA, Head Start, and other poverty programs to recruit volunteers for voter registration work. The campaign reached out to African Americans, Latinos, and Native Americans, as well as to local labor organizations and peace activists, working toward a massive effort to register voters and get them to the polls on election day. Each primary race tested Kennedy's ability to build from these varied constituencies a winning coalition, capable of not only swaying the Democratic Party establishment but also fundamentally changing the trajectory of the party.

Hubert Humphrey waited until April 27 to officially enter the race, conveniently missing the deadlines for all state primaries. As LBJ's candidate, he had the administration behind him and the backing of much of the Democratic Party establishment. Humphrey avoided engaging Kennedy and McCarthy and devoted his efforts to courting delegates and lining up endorsements from labor leaders and other party stalwarts instead. Many decided to withhold their endorsements until they had had a chance to see how the candidates fared at the polls.[2]

———

KENNEDY'S FIRST APPEARANCE after King's funeral was at the Scottish Rite Cathedral in Fort Wayne, Indiana. He began by explaining to the largely white, middle-class audience that he was not going to talk about issues that concerned only Indiana. Hinting at what was to come, he said he saw very few Black faces in the audience and that he realized there were only a small number of Black people in the state. Nevertheless, he told his audience that the country was facing "what is rapidly becoming the most terrible and urgent domestic crisis since the Civil War." King's death, he said, was "one of those huge events that signaled a turning point in our country's history." Americans faced a choice. The country could strive to become "one nation of all people, equal in justice and equal in opportunity," or America could enter a prolonged period of civil strife that would turn our cities into "armed camps." Concerns about law and order should not obscure the fact that white Americans bore a responsibility for the racial unrest in urban areas. King's promise that nonviolent action would bring justice and opportunity had not been realized. "Frustrated hope and loss of faith breeds desperation," Kennedy said—and desperation leads to violence. Repression was not the answer, he insisted: "there is no way to suppress men filled with anger, who feel they have nothing to lose." White America should fulfill the "simple claims" for decent jobs for Black Americans, Kennedy said, and provide a sense "that they are part of this country." Otherwise white Americans could expect more riots that would threaten their comfort and safety and continue to "diminish the idea of America." He concluded by saying that laws and government programs could not guarantee racial peace. It was the responsibility of every American to "make one nation out of two."[3]

Kennedy spent a full day campaigning in Indiana. Starting the following morning, he began a ten-day swing through Nebraska, Oregon, South Dakota, and California—all primary states—and visited several nonprimary states—Colorado, North Dakota, and Michigan—before fully plunging into the race in Indiana. King's assassination did not convince Kennedy to adjust his behavior so far as safety was concerned. He was in his hotel suite in Lansing, preparing to leave for the airport, when Fred Dutton was told that police had spotted a man with a rifle on a rooftop nearby. Dutton casually walked into the bedroom and pulled the curtain. Kennedy, who was putting on a fresh shirt, looked up and said, "Don't close them. If they're going to shoot, they'll shoot." As they were leaving the hotel, Dutton directed the elevator past the lobby floor to the basement garage, where the car was waiting. "What's the car doing down here?" Kennedy asked. "We have a report; it may be serious," Dutton tried to explain. Kennedy, showing a touch of annoyance, instructed his closest campaign aide, "Don't ever do that. We always get into the car in public. We're not going to start ducking now."[4]

On April 16, Kennedy briefly stepped away from the campaign to preside over a previously scheduled field hearing of the Senate Subcommittee on Indian Education at the Pine Ridge Reservation in South Dakota, exposing his entourage of reporters to the conditions on the reservation. It was part of Kennedy's "education agenda," said Father Jim Fitzgerald of Holy Rosary Mission, who had helped arrange the visit. Pine Ridge had a 75 percent unemployment rate. The landscape was littered with junked cars and shacks. Only half the homes had electricity, and even fewer had running water. Kennedy met ten-year-old Christopher Pretty Boy, whose parents had been killed in a car accident the previous week. Christopher then accompanied Kennedy for the rest of the day, often holding his hand.[5]

Kennedy spoke to the students of the Red Cloud Indian School, telling them that their "tremendous culture has been unequaled by any group in the United States." They were poor, he said, "because the white man has not kept his word." Later that afternoon, close to one thousand people crowded into Billy Mills Hall to attend the subcommittee hearings. As they were about to begin, Kennedy noticed tribal elders standing along the wall. He stopped the proceedings and asked that chairs be found for them and set up in the front. Leona Winters, a tribal councilwoman, described the dire conditions on the reservation. There was no employment in her community, she testified. What do you eat? Kennedy asked. Cornmeal, she said. When he asked her about health care, she said a medical clinic was open once a week in her community; the nearest hospital was one hundred miles away. When she finished testifying, Kennedy said that, considering that America was spending $30 million annually in Vietnam, "it seems [America] could spend some in the United States to alleviate the poverty here."

Senator George McGovern of South Dakota, who had joined the hearings, mentioned that the monument at Wounded Knee was the most important site for Great Plains Indians. By the time the hearing ended, Kennedy was late for a campaign event in Rapid City. He insisted that McGovern take him to Wounded Knee, where more than 250 Lakota men, women and children were slaughtered by the US Army in 1890. He stood at the site with Christopher Pretty Boy and read the inscription memorializing those lives. "I should have brought flowers," he said quietly.[6]

On April 22, Kennedy hunkered down in Indiana, preparing for his first primary contest. "Indiana is the ball game," Kennedy said. "This is my West Virginia," he continued, comparing his campaign to John F. Kennedy's uphill yet ultimately triumphant battle in that state. Indiana had been a stronghold of the Ku Klux Klan in the 1920s. The southern part, close to Kentucky and Tennessee, was steeped in southern culture, while the blue-collar workers concentrated outside cities in the northwestern part of the state were responsible for George Wallace's impressive showing in the 1964 Democratic primary. Early surveys showed that Kennedy was losing support among Indiana voters because many whites, especially in the southern part of the state, identified him as a champion of Black people, "wild" youth, and the "far-out" critics of the Vietnam War.[7]

After a late start, Kennedy created a tight, well-organized campaign with three major components: heavy spending on television, an extensive professional and volunteer operation, and strenuous use of personal appearances by the candidate to generate enthusiasm. When Gerard Doherty, former chair of the Massachusetts Democratic Party, arrived in Indianapolis at the end of March to head up the Indiana campaign, his only local allies were Mike Riley, head of the Young Democrats, and a man who had worked for JFK in 1960. There was constant traffic of Kennedy people back and forth from Washington, New York, and Massachusetts, the *Washington Post* reported: "they all work very late at night, and every waking hour they are either on the telephone or darting from one place to another." About fifty professionals managed the statewide operation. Between 1,500 and 2,000 students were canvassing the state for Kennedy, matching McCarthy's "children's crusade." Two thousand volunteers, including rank-and-file unionists, community organizers, and peace activists, worked out of a dozen offices in the larger communities.[8]

Kennedy's main challenge was to break through to the state's white, conservative voters. His more senior aides insisted that he needed to mute his talk on civil rights and urban problems and emphasize issues that concerned rural and working-class whites. His younger advisers pushed back. This was a tough needle to thread, given Kennedy's strong feelings on the subject of racial justice, but he understood that finding a way to reach whites was essential not just to win in Indiana but to begin repairing the country's deep racial divisions. "We're going to talk about what people will listen to," he told Jules Witcover. "The rural whites don't want to listen to what blacks need. You have to get them listening by talking about what they're interested in before you can start trying to persuade them about other matters."[9]

Ethel, with three of the couple's children—David, 12; Courtney, 11; and Michael, 10—and their dog, Freckles, accompanied Bobby on a swing through the southwestern part of the state. Bobby did his best to connect to voters. The family visited monuments and memorials to local leaders, and Kennedy demonstrated his knowledge of local history. He delivered speeches in several towns that emphasized conservative themes. He promoted the role of private enterprise through tax incentives and said he supported job creation over "welfare handouts." The task of the next administration, he said, would be to develop fiscal, monetary, and foreign policies that could bring the cost of living under control, while cutting unnecessary government spending. When asked a question about law and order, he reminded his audience that he'd been the chief law enforcement official of the country during his brother's administration. "The law has been my life," he said, and he emphasized that violence would not be tolerated.[10]

The people attending his campaign events were friendly, their applause "polite," but the crowds were "not overly large or overly demonstrative," wrote David Broder. One woman commented, "He's got oomph. . . . We loved his brother. But this is different. We're for Nixon." Kennedy knew he was not getting through to these transplanted Kentuckians and Tennesseans. "Sometimes you can feel them hate straight at you," David Halberstam recalled Kennedy saying.[11] The northwestern part of the state was more promising, with its concentration of urban Blacks and working class white ethnics. Kennedy and his strategists would work to bridge the racial divide and build a coalition of the "have-nots."[12]

Personal campaigning was Kennedy's great strength. He barnstormed through the state, being seen and heard by as many people as possible, and listening as well. He took a whistle-stop tour through north central Indiana, talking with crowds at depot stops from the back of the train—emphasizing the message of building a new and better America. He traveled by motorcade through Lake County, a center of steel mills, refineries, and factories, going from blue-collar white neighborhoods to the predominantly Black city of Gary. Discounting the advice of senior advisers to keep Richard Hatcher, Gary's first Black mayor, at arm's length, Kennedy met Hatcher at the city line along with the mayors of adjoining majority-white communities—John Nicosia of East Chicago, Joseph Klen of Hammond, and Frank Harangody of Whiting—and the five rode together in a convertible through downtown Gary. They ended up at the Gary Memorial Auditorium, where a largely Black audience of five thousand greeted them with chants of "We want Bobby!"[13]

Kennedy was often at his best when sparring with a hostile audience, believing that he could not change minds unless he engaged his opponent. Such an audience was exactly what he found at Indiana University School of Medicine in Indianapolis, where eight hundred students had turned out for his talk. As he entered the auditorium, a Black janitor shouted from the balcony, "We want Bobby!" "No, we don't!" a group of medical students responded in unison. One of the most vocal students held a blue balloon with

"Reagan" scrawled on it. Kennedy talked about his plan for restructuring medical care and his views on society's responsibility to the poor. The students questioned several aspects of the senator's plan. They argued that the higher costs of medical care could be handled by private insurance; another suggested that the poor in urban ghettos were not making use of the medical facilities that were available to them. When one finally asked, "Where are you going to get all the money for these federally subsidized programs you're talking about?" Kennedy answered: "From you!"[14]

Leaning toward the students, he began, "Let me say something about the tone of these questions. I look around this room, and I don't see many Black faces. You don't see many people coming out of the ghettos or off the Indian reservations to attend medical school," he told them. "You are the privileged ones here." There were boos and hisses. It was easy, he said, to sit back and blame the federal government, "but it's our responsibility too. It's our society that spends twice as much on pets as the poverty program. It's the poor who carry the major burden of the struggle in Vietnam. You sit here as white medical students, while Black people carry the burden in Vietnam."[15]

He mused that now he understood why his aides were having such trouble "forming a doctor's committee for me in Indiana." A few students began to laugh. One stood up and said, "A lot of us agree with what you are saying." There were cheers and applause from the crowd as Kennedy prepared to leave. It had been a lively exchange, the kind he liked. But it was also an example of his inability to keep his feelings in check when the strategy called for wooing conservative voters. "Well, we'll get lots of votes here," he said sarcastically under his breath to Adam Walinsky as they left the auditorium.[16]

"You know, the Negroes and the poor—they aren't very numerous," Kennedy told Hays Gorey of *Time*. "But their situation is what's wrong with our country." Kennedy could not resist the opportunity to talk about his deepest concerns, and a pivotal moment presented itself during a speech at Purdue University on May 1. He delivered a prepared speech to a conservative, unresponsive audience of several thousand people. Then someone asked a question about poverty, and Kennedy launched into what was, in effect, a second speech, speaking passionately about what it was like to grow up in a ghetto—rats, dilapidated housing, failed schools, no jobs, the feeling there was no way out—and decrying "the almost impassable barrier between the poor and the rest of the country." The reaction in the room was palpable. "The sincerity and compassion wrapped around every word reached out and pulled that audience to its feet," John Bartlow Martin recalled, for a "roaring, whistling, cheering standing ovation." The audience knew "that this was not just a politician, but a man who cared and truly believed that we could do better." James Reston of the *New York Times* said he always felt that John Kennedy never educated people about the country but told his fellow reporters that, in Bobby's speech, "you've just seen as good as an example as you'll see in American politics."[17]

Kennedy's last event on the day before the primary was a massive get-out-the-vote effort, concentrated in a marathon motorcade through the northwest corner of Indiana. The day started with a rally in La Porte, and the candidate continued on through Porter and Lake County. Seemingly endless stretches of people lined the streets, "from suburban road through tree shaded residential section into downtown commercial street and out again," Jules Witcover reported in his lively account of Kennedy's travels that day. "He moved from Negro neighborhoods to blue collar ethnic back to Negro, over and over." Standing in the back of a convertible, Kennedy shook thousands of hands. Sometimes, when the crowd was thick, he "simply put his arm out, letting it run through the outstretched hands like Tom Sawyer scraping a stick along a picket fence." Children often ran or rode their bikes alongside the candidate's car. "A young boy with a basketball ran for blocks playing catch."[18]

Described "as the longest continuous motorcade in American history," it stretched over 175 miles and took nine hours, slowed by the immensity of the crowds. Kennedy reached Whiting, the final stop, at 10 p.m., five hours later than scheduled, passing a car with a mattress on the roof and several children dressed in pajamas and bundled in blankets. Kennedy stopped and walked back to the car. "We tried to keep them awake," the children's mother said, "but they fell asleep waiting for you." The kids woke up with all of the commotion, and there were handshakes all around. Bobby and Ethel held the two smaller ones, drinking coffee brought out by neighbors.[19]

When it was all over, several exhausted reporters stopped for a nightcap in the bar at the Holiday Inn Airport hotel at Chicago's O'Hare airport, just across the state line in Illinois. Kennedy and his party were also staying the night and flying back to Indianapolis in the morning. It was well after midnight when Bobby wandered in, "weary but obviously still keyed up over the incredible Lake County turnout." He stopped and stood by a table where Witcover sat with another reporter. "Well, I've done all I can do," Kennedy said. "Maybe it's just not my time. But I've learned something from Indiana. The country is changing." The old Democratic coalition was not the answer anymore, he said. Somehow Blacks and whites in the cities had to be pulled together. More people in Washington "should get around the country and see how worked up people are."[20]

The next day, Kennedy won a comfortable victory in the Indiana primary, and also had a strong win in the primary in Washington, DC. He took

42 percent of the vote in Indiana, Roger Branigin (a stand-in for Humphrey) won 31 percent, and Eugene McCarthy trailed with 27 percent in a primary race that saw record-breaking voter turnout. Kennedy's victory, wrote David Broder of the *Washington Post*, "was more impressive than it looked," particularly considering that the candidate had started late and was vehemently opposed by the state's leading newspapers, which had given scant coverage to his campaign. Kennedy carried nine of Indiana's eleven congressional districts, practically assuring him all of the state's sixty-three delegates at the convention. He ran strongest in Black precincts. "Everything that moves is voting," said the Lake County Democratic Party chair of the Black sections of the city. But Kennedy also came in well ahead of his opponents in white working-class areas. The coalition of "have-nots" had prevailed. The only places where he trailed his opponents were "the partly suburban, partly small-town, upper income white Protestant counties" outside major cities.[21]

Indiana was a boost, but there was no time to rest. The Nebraska primary loomed on May 14, followed by Oregon on May 28, and South Dakota and California on June 4. While the campaign concentrated its efforts in the primary states, the candidate made side visits to nonprimary states as well. The continuing challenge was to leverage demonstrations of popular support to persuade Democratic Party officials and noncommitted delegates in nonprimary states to support Kennedy—or at least remain neutral.

In Nebraska, a mostly rural state, Kennedy seemed to unwind. Pat Lucey managed the campaign, building an operation, as Joseph Palermo has written, that "reached every Democratic voter in the state at least four times with literature and telephone calls." Kennedy toured a countryside of cornfields and cattle herds. After watching him campaign among farmers, Peter Edelman found that Kennedy seemed more like himself, quieter and more playful. Among the whistle-stop crowds, he demonstrated "the most spontaneously witty political style of any presidential candidate in the twentieth century," wrote Ward Just of the *Washington Post*. Reporters and aides remarked on how quickly Kennedy won over these hardworking farmers. He was no agricultural expert and did not pretend to be. Farmers appreciated the senator's concern with the problems they faced and his honest and unpolished manner.[22]

Two days before the primary, Kennedy spoke at a large noontime rally on the quadrangle of Creighton University, a Jesuit institution in Omaha. It was a hot, sunny day, and Kennedy peeled off his jacket as he approached the microphones. The students lounged on the grass and perched on the ledges of adjoining buildings. Kennedy drew on what had long been a major message to college students, urging them to realize that "a college education gives them a responsibility and an opportunity" to involve themselves and

their talents in facing the poverty and injustices that tore at the society.
During the question-and-answer period, the subject turned to the draft.
Kennedy criticized the inequity of student deferments while African Americans and other poor and working-class people were drafted. There were some
boos, and then one student asked, "But isn't the army one way of getting
young people out of the ghettos . . . and solving the ghetto problem?"

Kennedy was stunned. "Here at a Catholic university," he asked, "how
can you say that we can deal with the problems of the poor by sending them
to Vietnam?" How many of you favored student deferments? he asked. A
majority of hands shot up. "How can you possibly say that?" he exclaimed.
"How many Black faces do you see here? How many Mexican Americans?"
He instructed them, "the fact is if you look at any regiment of paratroopers
in Vietnam, forty-five percent of them are Black. How can you accept this?"
Visibly agitated, he continued, "What I don't understand is you don't even
debate these things among yourselves. You are the most exclusive minority
in the world. Are you going to sit on your duffs and do nothing? Or just
carry signs and protest?" By the time he had finished, one reporter noted,
he had shamed the students "into red-faced silence." Another observed that
Kennedy could understand selfish indifference among older, uneducated citizens, but "when he found it among supposedly aroused, activist youth, he
was appalled."[23]

From Creighton, Kennedy's motorcade drove to his campaign headquarters in Omaha's Near North Side, a predominantly Black section of the city,
to give a final speech there. The day was now overcast, and the street was
packed. As he spoke, the rain began to pour down. Most people stayed, and
Kennedy continued talking, his head tucked under his raincoat. Finally, it
got so bad that he shouted, spoofing his fondness for quoting great thinkers,
"As George Bernard Shaw once said . . . run for the buses!"[24]

On May 14, Kennedy won the Nebraska primary, taking 52 percent of
the vote. McCarthy, who had devoted little time to campaigning in the state,
took 31 percent of the vote. He had moved on to Oregon, the next major
primary race, to prepare for a decisive contest.

———

ON THE NIGHT OF MAY 14, Kennedy flew to Columbus, Ohio, to meet
with the state's 115 delegates, who were strongly leaning toward Hubert Humphrey, so that Kennedy could ask them to remain uncommitted until the end
of the primaries. Humphrey had delivered a rousing address to the state
Democratic Party's Jefferson-Jackson Day dinner ten days earlier. Veteran
Kennedy adviser Kenny O'Donnell, who had organized the meeting in Columbus, urged Bobby, notorious for running behind schedule, to be on time.[25]

His plane landed with time to spare, but as his car made its way through the east side of the city, a predominantly African American area, "wall to wall people" packed the streets, making them nearly impassable. "Veteran crowd watchers here," the *New York Times* reported from Columbus, "could not recall a more exuberant demonstration on behalf of a political candidate in the city's history." Kennedy arrived nearly three hours late for the meeting at the Neil House Hotel. The delegates, "a hard bitten, tough crowd of guys," O'Donnell recalled, were "so mad, almost sullen."

Kennedy went on to make "the best damn speech I ever heard," said O'Donnell. The senator was low-key, asking the delegates to remain neutral until he was able to show his popularity in the primaries. He told them that he was going to the people for a verdict, and if he failed he did not expect the delegates to support him. But he made it clear that that he fully expected their support if the primaries established him as the leading vote getter. Kennedy's "soft-sell" manner and the unprecedented crowd that turned out to greet him in the Black districts persuaded the delegates. The Cuyahoga County Democratic Party chair had ridden in with Kennedy from the airport and experienced the crush of the crowd. Eighty of the 115 delegates shifted back into the uncommitted column.[26]

———

KENNEDY'S WINNING STREAK ABRUPTLY ended in Oregon on May 28. Eugene McCarthy carried the state by six points in what the *New York Times* called "a stunning upset." The loss weakened Kennedy's case with Democratic Party power brokers and raised the stakes in California one week later. Kennedy had hoped that McCarthy would fold, allowing him to concentrate on the Johnson-Humphrey record in California, the most critical and delegate-rich primary state. In Oregon, however, supporters of McCarthy and Humphrey found common cause in their joint desire to drive Kennedy out of the race—a convergence of McCarthy's intense personal dislike for RFK and Humphrey's fear that if Bobby were not eliminated in the primaries, he would present a formidable challenge at the Democratic National Convention.[27]

McCarthy ran a strong campaign in a state whose demographics favored him. Oregon was mostly white, with a large middle class that was economically comfortable and relatively well educated. Antiwar sentiment was strong, and that issue alone ensured many voters' deep affinity for McCarthy, who had emerged as the anti-war candidate nearly six months earlier. The campaign cultivated strong support on university and college campuses. McCarthy had pretty much bypassed Nebraska and concentrated his efforts in Oregon, running a well-organized, energetic campaign.[28]

McCarthy had also ramped up his attacks on Kennedy, charging that "he's not brought anything new to politics in 1968" and was just using the old technique of "adding up a consensus or composite of minorities who have special problems." McCarthy ridiculed Kennedy's supporters as "the less intelligent and less well-educated voters of the country." Thomas Finney, a former law partner of Secretary of Defense Clark Clifford, came on as McCarthy's new campaign director. Finney was personally close to Humphrey, and during the final week of the campaign, McCarthy indicated in an interview that he would support Humphrey for the nomination if he modified his position on the war. The statement alarmed many of McCarthy's volunteers, and he quickly backed away from it, saying that he was "absolutely neutral" regarding Kennedy and Humphrey. Nevertheless, a number of resignations followed the statement, by those who felt that McCarthy's desire to defeat Kennedy had eclipsed the idealism that had drawn them to McCarthy's campaign. Several joined the Kennedy campaign.[29]

Kennedy had maintained a slight lead in the polls, but he had problems in Oregon. Congresswoman Edith Green headed up his campaign in the state, and while she was a strong and effective politician, she proved to be an inept campaign manager. A mid-April report described the situation as "a disaster—nothing going on—no headquarters—far behind." The demographics were not in his favor either, with African Americans making up only 1 percent of the population of the state and few Hispanics in Oregon. Exhausted after weeks of intense campaigning, Kennedy had a hard time shifting gears to reach a different kind of constituency. Oregonians, Tom Wicker reported, listened to him talk about race and poverty, "with no particular interest or engagement." Oregon, Kennedy commented, "is like one giant suburb."[30]

At a campaign event in Roseburg, deep in hunting country, he seemed more focused on changing minds than winning votes. Signs reading "Protect Your Right to Keep and Bear Arms" were scattered through the crowd of 1,500. Standing on the steps of the Douglas County Courthouse, Kennedy said, "I see signs about guns. I'm wondering if any of you would like to come and explain?" A heavyset man in a lumberjacket stepped forward. "I'm Bud Stone," he said, as he took the microphone. He said the signs referred to a Senate bill (recently passed) that he charged was a "backdoor bill for the registration of guns." Kennedy, who had voted for the bill, which McCarthy had voted against, said he understood that gun legislation was a big deal in this lumber town, but "if we're going to talk about legislation, let's talk about it honestly and not say that it does something that it does not do."[31]

He explained that all the legislation did was "keep guns from criminals and the demented and those too young. With all the violence and murder and killing we've had in the United States, I think you will agree that we must keep firearms from people who have no business with guns or rifles." The men, women, and children carrying the signs did not seem impressed. A man in a cowboy hat booed loudly and shouted, "They'll get them anyway." Others protested, "Nazi Germany started with the registration of guns." Kennedy pointed out that the registration of automobiles and drug prescriptions had not destroyed democracy and suggested that the John Birch Society was spreading disinformation about the Senate bill. He probably changed few minds that day—a survey of the county revealed that the gun issue was a big factor against Kennedy in people's minds.[32]

On May 28, primary day, Robert Kennedy became the first person in his family to lose an election. At a gathering with campaign workers that evening, he took responsibility for the loss, blaming his inability to communicate with the voters of Oregon. Hayes Gorey of *Time* asked him if he would change his strategy in California. "No," Kennedy said. "I have a program I believe in, and I'm going to press forward with it. I may have misjudged the mood of America, but I don't think so." But he knew that failing to win in Oregon would make it much more difficult for him to win over unpledged delegates at the convention. When a reporter asked the candidate if he thought the Oregon defeat had hurt him, the ridiculousness of the question made Kennedy laugh. "It certainly wasn't the most helpful development of the day."[33]

As the Oregon primary wound down, Drew Pearson of the *New York Times* published a column revealing that Robert Kennedy had authorized a wiretap on Martin Luther King Jr., a story leaked by the FBI. Pearson had recently held a fundraiser for Humphrey. The story, picked up by newspapers across the country, was obviously designed to dent Kennedy's support among Black voters in the upcoming California primary. Burke Marshall discussed the matter with Kennedy. "He wasn't going to lie about it," Marshall explained. They both agreed that it was not a good idea "to try and explain the whole business about the wiretaps and the Bureau" in the middle of the California campaign. The candidate's response, through Pierre Salinger, was that Kennedy did not discuss individual cases. When Peter Edelman brought the matter up, Kennedy brushed it aside. "I'm on the cover of *Time* magazine"; that was the main event that day, he told Edelman. "If Luce knew this, he'd be turning in his grave." (Henry Luce, the publisher of *Time* and a lifelong Republican, had died the previous year.) The wiretap story quickly faded from the headlines.[34]

—

ON MAY 29, Bobby flew directly to Los Angeles. His motorcade toured Latino and Black neighborhoods and the business district of downtown. It was early afternoon, and the turnout was extraordinary. Streets were packed, hands reached out, and people tried to climb into the car. The motorcade stopped every half block or so, and Kennedy would speak briefly. "I need your help!" "Will you give me a hand on June 4?" "Yes! Yes!" people shouted. "Sock it to 'em, Bobby!" Kennedy beamed. "These are my people," he said.

As the motorcade made its way through the business area, office workers showered the candidate with confetti and shredded newspapers. He stood on the back seat of the convertible, his shirt drenched with perspiration, punching his fist in the air. "I need your help!" "You've got it! You've got it," they called back. As the motorcade left the downtown area, Kennedy exclaimed, "Los Angeles is my Resurrection City!"[35]

Kennedy had lunch with campaign workers at the Beverly Hilton, a swank hotel on Wilshire Boulevard. He talked about his visit a year before to Watts, which was around twenty miles from Beverly Hills, and recalled how a young man in the Watts Writers Workshop had accused Kennedy of seeing only the wide, clean streets. The young man had described how garbage was piled high in his mother's backyard because the city did not offer the same services to poor Black people as it did to middle-class whites. Kennedy told his team how he had tried to explain that this was a municipal problem and not something he could solve in the Senate. But he recognized the depth of the anger and felt it was symbolic of the problems all Americans had to work to resolve—or "sacrifice our claims on greatness with liberty and justice to all," as Budd Schulberg recalled the senator saying. "He had a remarkable memory," Schulberg said, "as well as a unique capacity for indignation."[36]

After lunch, Kennedy continued with an eight-hour motorcade through heavily populated middle-class and working-class parts of Southern California—El Monte, Fontana, San Bernardino, Riverside. He opened a campaign office and spoke at street rallies and a high school auditorium. It was after midnight when he returned to his hotel, weary but in high spirits.[37]

—

THERE WERE ONLY SIX DAYS until the primary on Tuesday, June 4, and the stakes could not be higher. California was the largest, most populous state in the country, and the most ethnically and racially diverse. At stake in the winner-takes-all primary were 174 delegates. Robert Kennedy had spent ten days in California since late March, and his campaign and local supporters had created a strong infrastructure, with a flexibility that enabled it to function at full capacity.

Jesse Unruh, the most powerful Democrat in the state, was the campaign manager for California, but his strengths lay more in courting party stalwarts than in conducting ambitious grassroots voter engagement efforts. Steve Smith, the national campaign manager based in New York, moved his operation out to California, where he was joined by Kenneth O'Donnell, who had worked closely with JFK. John Seigenthaler worked with the Northern California office, and Frank Mankiewicz, who had taken a leave from his post as press secretary, returned to his home state to help with tactics and organizing. Collectively, these four men helped create in effect a parallel campaign organization, complementing Unruh's effort.[38]

The key to California, so far as Kennedy and his aides were concerned, was a massive voter registration and turnout drive in the communities where the candidate had strong support: Los Angeles, the San Francisco Bay Area, and other cities. Local supporters often took the initiative. Cesar Chavez suspended the United Farm Workers strike and boycott activities and provided a "small army" of canvassers and organizers. By the first week of April, the national campaign headquarters received reports that thousands of Latino farmworkers had been added to the voter rolls in the San Joaquin Valley. Bert Corona, the powerful head of the Mexican American Political Association and former labor leader for the CIO, was one of several prominent Latino leaders to join the campaign, providing four of its top organizers and ground troops. John Lewis worked with Latino leaders in the Los Angeles area, mobilizing young Latinos and African Americans to galvanize support and register voters. Mankiewicz, who had headed up Latin American affairs in the Peace Corps, set up Community Action for Kennedy, which enlisted the active support of former Peace Corps and VISTA volunteers across the state.[39]

As in other states, Kennedy's labor support in California did not come from the top. The leadership of the AFL-CIO was firmly in Hubert Humphrey's corner and supported the Vietnam War. Kennedy, who had a topnotch labor record in the Senate, was supported by a small but active contingent of unionists who embraced his vision and policies. In addition to Chavez and Corona, Kennedy had the strong backing of Paul Schrade, the western regional director of a ninety-thousand member union, the United Automobile, Aerospace and Agricultural Implement Workers of America (UAW); Schrade put all of its muscle behind Kennedy's campaign.[40]

Frank Mankiewicz and Pierre Salinger created state-level committees of clergy, professors, students, and law enforcement officials and secured some prominent endorsements. Rafer Johnson, the 1960 Olympic gold medal winner in the decathlon, headed up Athletes for Kennedy. One of the events he organized was a tennis clinic in Oakland featuring twenty-four-year-old tennis star Arthur Ashe. The Hollywood for Kennedy Committee attracted a range of entertainers, reflecting Kennedy's deep family ties in Hollywood as well as his appeal to African American artists like Sidney Poitier, Mahalia Jackson, as well as others who shared Kennedy's views on the war and on race relations. Dianne Feinstein, future mayor of San Francisco and US senator, chaired Northern California Women for Kennedy.[41] Kennedy's breakneck schedule of public appearances during the final days of the primary campaign provided the essential and ultimate push to ensure that all the work that had been done would translate into a large voter turnout on June 4.

———

ON MAY 30, Memorial Day, Kennedy campaigned from the caboose of the San Joaquin Daylight Special. The crowds grew as the train carried him through the farmlands in California's richest agricultural area. The candidate mixed humor with serious discussion of issues. To the three thousand who gathered at Turlock, in the heart of California's Central Valley, he emphasized the contributions his large family made to the agricultural economy. "Do Gene McCarthy and Hubert Humphrey eat Turlock turkeys and Turlock grapes?" he asked. "No!" the crowd responded in unison. "My family does," he said with a wide grin. Over and over, at each stop, according to the *Los Angeles Times,* "he hammered at his Democratic presidential campaign theme that the Johnson-Humphrey approach to problems is inadequate." "I don't think we have to accept the gap that exists between races and age groups," he told the crowd in Fresno. Kennedy continued to refrain from attacking McCarthy, "and concentrated his fire on Vice-President Hubert Humphrey." The Humphrey-Johnson slate was represented on the ballot by California attorney general Thomas Lynch. But Humphrey was counting on a McCarthy win to sink Kennedy.[42]

Later that night, Kennedy attended an unscheduled and unannounced meeting at the Taylor Memorial United Methodist Church in West Oakland with representatives of the area's "Black Caucus." The group included members of the Black Panther Party, which was based in Oakland, as well as attorneys, teachers, government workers, and local NAACP officials. John Seigenthaler and California state assemblyman Willie Brown had organized the gathering; Brown would moderate the discussion. As they drove to the church, Kennedy prepared friends who came along—including Rafer Johnson and former astronaut John Glenn—for what to expect. It would not be pleasant, he warned them. There was much hostility toward whites among this group, and with good reason. The point was to listen and respond as thoughtfully as he could.[43]

Kennedy did not exaggerate. The meeting, which went on for more than two hours, was a collective unloading of grievances and charges. As usual, Kennedy was running late, and arrived an hour after the 10 p.m. scheduled start. He walked down the aisle and stood against the altar rail facing the group. The charges ranged from a general attack on whites who came into Black neighborhoods only when they wanted something, to accusations that the government was building concentration camps for Blacks. Kennedy denied their existence. "We don't believe you," he was told. Another charged that the only thing he and other whites did was "talk, talk, talk." That was followed by an attack on the Kennedy family. At one time Rafer Johnson said, "I've had enough," and moved to intervene. Kennedy said, "No. This is between them and me."[44]

Curtis Lee Baker, Bay area Black Power advocate affiliated with the Black Panther Party, demanded that Kennedy and his family open and fund a bank in West Oakland. Kennedy tried to respond, but Baker quickly interrupted, saying, "I don't want to hear none of your shit. What the goddamned hell are you going to do boy . . . you want this vote? Put up a black bank." When Kennedy found an opening, he described the Bedford-Stuyvesant project and said that a similar type of organization might work in Oakland, but he would not make any promises.[45]

Willie Brown finally brought the meeting to a close. "Well," Seigenthaler commented afterward, "I think you had all the votes you were going to have when you went in there." Willie Brown disagreed. "We're going to do very well over there. Everybody who was there tonight will help out." And he was right. The next day, many who had been at the church called Thomas Berkley, a Kennedy supporter and the leading Black newspaper publisher in the Bay Area, offering to work for the campaign. Back at the Fairmont Hotel at the end of an eighteen-hour day, Kennedy had a hankering for ice cream. A hotel worker reopened the café, and Bobby sat with John Glenn, Seigenthaler, and Fred Dutton, eating chocolate ice cream and recapping the day. Kennedy said how glad he was that he had gone to West Oakland.[46]

The next day, Kennedy was scheduled to speak in Long Beach and San Jose. He canceled those meetings to return to Oakland. Rosey Grier, a long-time friend and former defensive tackle with the Los Angeles Rams, joined the candidate. The motorcade made frequent stops at street corners, small parks, and in front of public buildings. Kennedy gave short speeches and accompanied Grier in singing "There is a Rose in Spanish Harlem," Grier's signature song. They ended with a huge, enthusiastic rally in De Fremery

Park. "How many are registered? Up with hands!" Kennedy called out. Shame on you! he said to those whose hands did not shoot up. Register, vote, he urged them—get your spouses and neighbors to vote. At the end of the rally, Curtis Baker took the lead in clearing a path for Kennedy to make his way through the crowd. Herbert Lopez, a local activist, commented on how he and other African Americans felt about Kennedy. He was not "the last of the great liberals," Lopez said, but Kennedy was "the last of the great believables."[47]

———

KENNEDY SPENT JUNE 1 preparing for the debate with McCarthy scheduled for that evening. Kennedy had previously refused to debate without Hubert Humphrey present, but after Oregon, he agreed to go one-on-one with McCarthy. Kennedy had two sessions with close advisers during the day, reviewing facts, going over major issues, and preparing the points he wanted to emphasize—establishing his experience, demonstrating his grasp of the issues, and dispelling his ruthless image. Burke Marshall flew in from New York to help with the debate preparation.[48]

Eugene McCarthy was a latecomer to the racial crisis roiling America. As a senator, he was not associated with any of the major proposals or debates relating to poverty and urban conditions. As a candidate, he did not issue a statement on race and civil rights until April 11, nearly five months into his presidential campaign. According to press reports, McCarthy's aides had been rattled by the enthusiastic reception Kennedy received in Watts during his first campaign swing through California at the end of March. They persuaded McCarthy to deliver an address on civil rights and the need for "reconciliation" between the races.[49]

As the Minnesota senator turned his sights on California, with the hope of delivering a final blow to Kennedy's candidacy, McCarthy began attacking Kennedy's racial record, seeking to cut into his base of support with Black voters. The first signal came after Oregon, when in a speech delivered at the University of California, Davis, McCarthy described Kennedy's plan for rehabilitating the ghetto as a form of "apartheid" and a "retreat from the ideal of integration." He advocated bringing Black workers from the central cities to the fringe suburbs where the jobs were.[50]

Two days later, on May 30, McCarthy's campaign hosted a barbecue in Will Rogers Memorial Park in Watts. The candidate spoke to what the *Times* described as "a rather small and inattentive crowd," offering a "qualified endorsement" of the Black Power movement, comparing it to "Irish power and Italian power," and adding "there has never been a group in America who had more reason to organize themselves to get their rights." One man commented to a reporter, "I'm eating the ribs, but I'm voting for Kennedy." Others around him nodded and laughed.[51]

In one of the McCarthy campaign's more desperate moves, aides excerpted the speech King had delivered to the California Democratic Council on March 16, using a segment in which King had praised McCarthy to imply that the civil rights leader had endorsed the senator's candidacy, which King had not. The excerpt was put on a record that was sent around to Black radio stations. Kennedy "wasn't going to lose the Black vote anyway," Burke Marshall said, "but we had to do something about it," and "that was my job." Marshall spoke with Coretta Scott King, who issued a statement saying that her husband had not supported Senator McCarthy. Marshall called the Black radio stations directly to make sure they got the message.[52]

The hour-long debate, televised nationally on Saturday evening, was a polite, low-key affair. The three journalists and the candidates were seated around a coffee table. Both candidates appeared more intent on making their case to California voters than on debating each other. Kennedy did take a swipe at Hubert Humphrey, questioning his optimistic forecasts on the war. McCarthy "spoke quietly and easily," the *Los Angeles Times* reported. Kennedy's manner was "studiously aimed at eradicating the notion that he is arrogant."[53]

The only real flash point that evening was on the subject of the Bedford-Stuyvesant approach to rebuilding urban neighborhoods. "We have to work in the suburbs. We shouldn't perpetuate the ghetto," McCarthy said, touting his half-baked idea of relocating African Americans to the suburbs, "or we're drafting a sort of apartheid." "You mean to say you're going to take 10,000 black people and move them into Orange County?" Kennedy asked, in a clear dig at McCarthy's prized suburban base. Kennedy went on to outline just how disruptive it would be for people without jobs or resources to find themselves uprooted and moved to a place where they could not afford housing, where their children would struggle to keep up in school, and where there was little chance for employment. The whole idea behind a plan like Bedford-Stuyvesant was to help residents develop the skills and resources to move into other areas of the city or the suburbs. In the meantime, Americans had to face the facts about residents of inner cities: "the conditions that they are living under at the present time" were intolerable. After the debate, one of McCarthy's aides admitted, "the whole business of the ghetto stuff . . . was bad for us."[54]

The next day, the McCarthy campaign attempted to spin the episode to the candidate's advantage. During a campaign stop in Bakersfield, McCarthy accused Kennedy of "scare tactics" that could "increase suspicion and mistrust among the races." Kennedy dismissed this charge as a sign of desperation. "My comments were an accurate and fair reflection of McCarthy's plan to move Negroes to the suburbs," Kennedy said. "If he thought I was not being precise, he had ample time to respond when we were face to face," rather than "waiting until he was 500 miles away before he starts attacking me." He reiterated that his goal was to help ghetto residents develop the resources and skills they needed to move into other neighborhoods, as they chose; to link his campaign to racism, he said, was "self-evidently absurd."[55]

———

ROBERT KENNEDY'S FINAL DAY OF campaigning took him across California. From San Francisco he flew to Los Angeles and Long Beach. John Lewis accompanied the candidate through the Black and Latino parts of Los Angeles where Lewis had been working. "The outpouring of emotion as we passed through those streets was much more than support for Kennedy," Lewis recalled. "It was love. It was adoration. People, especially young people, just mobbed us, climbing over the cars, trying to get close to Kennedy." The candidate concluded the day in San Diego with a motorcade through the predominantly Black section of Logan Heights and a rally at the El Cortez hotel, feeling ill and completely exhausted.[56]

Late that night, Bobby went to the Malibu home of his friend, film director John Frankenheimer. He and Ethel, pregnant with their eleventh child, along with six of the couple's children, would spend the night there and most of primary day. It was the family's first free day together in a while. Bobby slept until 11 a.m. The day was chilly and overcast, but after lunch he spent the afternoon on the beach and in the surf with his children. At one point his son David, who was twelve, was pulled out by a strong undertow; Bobby swiftly dove into the surf and rescued his son. That afternoon, Ted Kennedy and Dick Goodwin arrived. The early returns looked good.[57]

At 6:30 p.m., Bobby was dressed and ready to head to the Ambassador Hotel. Ethel was not ready yet, so he persuaded Frankenheimer to drive him in; Ethel would follow later. The Royal Suite, location of Kennedy's on-site operations, was packed with reporters, campaign aides, and assorted Democratic Party functionaries. Shortly after their arrival, South Dakota campaign manager Bill Dougherty called to say partial returns showed Kennedy winning more than 50 percent of the vote in the election, which recorded the largest number of ballots ever cast in the South Dakota primary. The final tally would be Kennedy, 49.7 percent; Johnson-Humphrey, 29.7 percent; and McCarthy, 20.4 percent. The scale of the victory was unexpected; this was Humphrey's native state, and his supporters had waged a strong campaign. Kennedy ribbed aides who had chided him about spending too much precious time on Indian reservations. Have you heard about the Indian vote? he asked. In one county with 858 votes, he told them, 856 went for Kennedy, 2 for Humphrey, and 0 for McCarthy.[58]

Polls in California closed at 8 p.m. By 10:30, with more than 50 percent of the returns in, CBS declared Kennedy the winner. Black and Hispanic voters had turned out in record numbers. In Oakland, the turnout was close to 100 percent, with Kennedy taking 90 percent of the vote. The final tally showed Kennedy taking 95 percent of the vote in most Hispanic precincts, winning one precinct with 100 percent turnout. The mood in the Royal Suite reached a high pitch, with aides and reporters helping themselves to drinks. A reporter asked Kennedy how he planned to celebrate. "Have a drink," he said. "Maybe three." He invited most of the press corps to a celebration later that night at The Factory, a trendy Los Angeles discotheque.[59]

Bobby paced the rooms, watching the televised returns, taking phone calls, and talking with friends. He sought out Budd Schulberg and spoke with him briefly about the Watts Writers Workshop and the Douglass House theater, as Kennedy thought about all that needed to be done. He compared the Watts projects to the Federal Theatre Project and Federal Writers' Project of the New Deal. "We have to encourage not just mechanical skills and find jobs in those areas, but creative talent—I saw it in Watts—at the Douglass House—so much talent to be channeled, strong self-expression," Schulberg remembered Kennedy saying. "I'd like to see it on a national scale with Federal help," he said.[60]

With victory in sight, he took Fred Dutton and Dick Goodwin aside to a private space in the bathroom to talk strategy. New York was up next on June 18, but Kennedy needed to go to nonprimary states to talk to delegates. Now that the race had clearly come down to him and Humphrey, Kennedy said, "My only chance is to chase Hubert's ass all over the country." Bobby spoke to Goodwin about reaching out to McCarthy and seeing whether he wanted to join forces. Next, Kennedy called his old friend Kenny O'Donnell, whom he had known since their days on the Harvard football team. O'Donnell congratulated the senator and said it looked like he was on his way to taking the nomination. "I think I may," Bobby said. And then added, "I feel now for the first time, I've shaken off the shadow of my brother. I feel I made it on my own."[61]

As Bobby prepared to leave the suite and head to the Embassy Ballroom to declare victory, he stuck his head into the room where John Lewis and others were crowded in. "John," Kennedy teased, shaking Lewis's hand, "you let me down today. More Mexican Americans voted for me than Negroes." Everyone laughed. Then Kennedy said, "Wait for me. I'll be back in fifteen or twenty minutes." Remembering that moment, Lewis said, "He looked as if he could have floated out of the room. He was in such wonderful spirits."[62]

Shortly before midnight, Bobby and Ethel, accompanied by Rafer Johnson and Rosey Grier, took the freight elevator down to the area outside the hotel kitchen on their way to the ballroom. Bobby wore a dark blue suit and blue-and-white striped tie; Ethel brightened the pair in her sleeveless orange-and-white mini-dress and white stockings. Kennedy shook hands with hotel workers and supporters lining the corridor that led to the ballroom. He spoke briefly with Jules Witcover and *Boston Globe* reporter Bob Healy and invited them to the party at The Factory. "He was as elated as either of us had seen him during the entire campaign," Witcover recalled. Witcover teased Kennedy about a television interview he did earlier in the evening with Roger Mudd, telling him he had been "very ruthful," a play on the ruthless tag long attached to RFK. Bobby "laughed heartily," and after walking a few steps further, turned and said with a broad smile, "I'm getting better all the time."[63]

Supporters erupted in cheers, shouts, and whistling as Bobby and Ethel entered the ballroom. ABC newsman Bob Clark, reporting from the floor, described the "pandemonium" as Kennedy made his way through the crush of campaign workers to the platform. The crowd resembled the coalition that had brought this pivotal win—white, Black, and Hispanic supporters—waving hats and arms, signaling for peace and victory. Bobby and Ethel stepped up onto the small, crowded podium. As the news feed widened for a full view of the ballroom, a dark haired young man jumped up to get his face on the camera for a moment. Kennedy brushed his hair from his forehead with his hand and looked out on the gathering. A "People for Kennedy" balloon floated past his face as the crowd chanted, "We Want Kennedy." "Anyone who could work their way into this hall is very happy," Clark could be heard saying on the live broadcast.[64]

There was momentary frustration with the two microphones: "Can you hear this? Can you hear that? Can we get something that works?" Kennedy asked. The technical problem was quickly resolved, and he began his brief set of remarks. Bobby congratulated Don Drysdale of the Los Angeles Dodgers for pitching his sixth straight shut out that night, adding, "May we have such good fortune in our campaign." His speech was a litany of thanks, including to Jesse Unruh, brother-in-law Steve Smith, and his dog, Freckles, "who has been maligned" by his opponent. "As FDR said," Kennedy quipped, "I don't care what they say about me, but when they start to attack my dog. . . ." Continuing in a humorous tone: "I am not doing this in the order of importance, but I also want to thank my wife, Ethel," who was standing to his right. He put his arm around her, and as voices in the crowd shouted, "Come forward" and "Say something, Ethel," he gently tugged her toward the microphone. She acknowledged them, though what she said could barely be heard. "Her patience during this whole effort has been fantastic," Kennedy added as they looked at each other, both smiling and laughing. "Fantastic," she repeated.[65]

Kennedy called out the names of specific individuals: Cesar Chavez, Delores Huerta, Bert Corona, Paul Schrade, Rosey Grier, and Rafer Johnson. He acknowledged the intersecting communities and groups that were responsible for this victory: "my friends in the Black community who made such a major effort . . . with such a high percentage of voting today"; members of labor organizations and the labor movement; students who had canvassed; voters in the agricultural area of the state and in the cities and suburbs. They represented the hope that countered what Kennedy described as "the division, the violence, the disenchantment" that had taken hold of the country over the past three years, "whether it's between black and white, between the poor and the more affluent or between age groups or over the war in Vietnam." What he had seen and experienced over the previous ten weeks, culminating with wins in California and South Dakota on the same day, renewed his faith that "we can start to work together."

The packed room under the bright television lights became sweltering. "Everybody must be dying of the heat," Kennedy said, promising "just to take a moment more of your time." He emphasized that "change can only come if they—the delegates in Chicago—recognize the importance of what has happened." He hoped now that the California primary was over that "we can concentrate on having a dialogue or debate between the vice-president and, perhaps, myself on what direction we want to go in the United States." He believed that the primaries and party caucuses had indicated that the "country wanted to move in a different direction. We want to deal with problems in our own country, and we want peace in Vietnam."

It was approaching 12:15 a.m. when Kennedy came to the end of his short speech. He again thanked everyone "who made all this possible . . . all of the people whose names I haven't mentioned" who worked "at the precinct level, who got out the vote, who did all of the efforts that [are] required. I was a campaign manager eight years ago. I know what kind of a difference that kind of effort and commitment can make. . . . So, my thanks to all of you, and on to Chicago, and let's win there!"[66]

The crowd let loose with cheers and applause, and supporters pushed toward the stage. Kennedy reached down to shake hands and touch outstretched fingers before stepping down into the crowd. He told Bill Barry, the former FBI agent who served as his sole bodyguard, to help Ethel, who was three months pregnant. When Barry tried to assist Ethel down from the stage, she said, "I'm all right. Stay with the senator." As Barry pushed through the crowd to catch up, assistant maître d' Karl Uecker guided Kennedy toward the shortest route to the waiting press conference, back through the pantry and kitchen area. Reporters trailed along.[67]

Walking alongside the candidate, Andrew West, who was taping for Mutual radio, asked Kennedy how he was going to counter Humphrey's delegate strength. Kennedy replied, "It just goes back to the struggle—" Gunshots and screams interrupted his reply. "Senator Kennedy has been shot—Senator Kennedy has been shot," West exclaimed. "Is that possible? . . . Oh my God—Senator Kennedy and another man. . . ." In the chaos, Uecker grabbed the arm holding the gun and pushed it down. Bill Barry, Rosey Grier, and Rafer Johnson subdued twenty-four-year-old Sirhan Bishara Sirhan, pushing him onto a steam table. Sirhan kept firing until the gun was finally wrestled from his hand. Within minutes, five others, in addition to Kennedy, had been shot and wounded.[68]

Bobby Kennedy lay on the concrete floor, bleeding from a head wound. Juan Romero, a busboy who had shaken Kennedy's hand seconds earlier, wrapped a rosary around the senator's left hand. Kennedy asked, "Is everybody all right?" Dr. Ross Miller, an African American surgeon and Kennedy delegate from Compton, and Dr. Stanley Abo of Los Angeles responded to pleas in the ballroom for a doctor and tended to Kennedy until an ambulance arrived. Ethel, who had been pulled back to safety, came to her husband, knelt beside him, and held his hand. As photographers crowded in, she rose briefly and pleaded, "Please go. Please go. Give him room to breathe." Aware of her presence, Bobby said softly, "Ethel, oh Ethel." Two medical attendants arrived with a low hospital stretcher. As they moved to lift Kennedy, Ethel said, "gently, gently." Aide Dick Tuck lifted his legs. "Oh no, no," Kennedy said in pain. After he was strapped on the stretcher, he lost consciousness.[69]

Robert Kennedy had suffered fatal brain injuries. Twenty-six hours after he had been shot, Frank Mankiewicz announced his death to reporters waiting in the makeshift pressroom at the Good Samaritan Hospital: "Senator Robert Francis Kennedy died at 1:44 a.m. today, June 6, 1968. With Senator Kennedy at the time of his death were his wife, Ethel; his sisters, Mrs. Stephen Smith, Mrs. Patricia Lawford; his brother-in-law Mr. Stephen Smith; and his sister-in-law Mrs. John F. Kennedy. He was forty-two years old."[70]

Epilogue

ON JUNE 8, Edward "Ted" Kennedy, the youngest Kennedy of that generation and the last surviving brother, looked out over his brother's flag-draped
coffin as he prepared to address the 2,100 mourners who filled New York's
St. Patrick's Cathedral. He began his unannounced eulogy by speaking for
the family about what Bobby meant to them "as a brother, and as a father,
and as a son." "Love is not an easy feeling to put into words," Ted said. "Nor
is loyalty or trust or joy. But he was all of these. He loved life completely
and he lived it intensely." In a tribute "full of pride and sorrow, grief and
promise," as the *Post* reported, he then turned his attention to Robert Kennedy the man and the public figure. "What he leaves to us is what he said,
what he did, and what he stood for."

Ted drew on his brother's words, reading from Bobby's speech to the
young people fighting apartheid in South Africa to show how he understood
the nature and power of human effort in a world where discrimination, poverty, slaughter, greed, and repression—the common works of humankind—
were manifest. The capacity to fight such conditions and advance justice
took moral courage—"a rarer commodity than bravery in battle or great
intelligence"—a recognition of the fleeting nature of time, and faith in the
transformative capacities of individual action. "Each time a man stands up
for an ideal or acts to improve the lot of his fellow or strikes out against injustice he sends forth a tiny ripple of hope," Ted said, quoting from his brother's
speech at the University of Cape Town. "And crossing each other from a million different centers of energy and daring, those ripples build a current that
can sweep down the mightiest walls of opposition and resistance."

Ted Kennedy choked up as he concluded his remarks: "My brother need
not be idealized, or enlarged in death beyond what he was in life to be remembered simply as a good and decent man, who saw wrong and tried to

right it, saw suffering and tried to heal it, saw war and tried to stop it. Those of us who loved him and take him to his rest today, pray that what he was to us and what he wished for others will someday come to pass for all the world."[1]

Family members, President and Mrs. Johnson, government officials, foreign dignitaries, reporters who had covered the campaign, civil rights and peace activists, artists, and the multitude of people with whom Bobby had worked in his public life were among the congregants. Coretta Scott King, who had flown to Los Angeles and returned to New York with the Kennedy family, had a prominent place. The requiem funeral mass was less solemn than President Kennedy's service had been, according to Rev. Thomas Connellan. He remembered Ethel, sturdied by her faith, saying "I want this Mass to be as joyous as it possibly can be." Andrew Young, King's closest aide, compared the service to a Black funeral, a big social event bringing together all of those who played a part in the person's life. "You had that feeling in St. Patrick's," Young recalled.[2]

After the service, the large funeral entourage went by train from New York to Washington for the burial at Arlington National Cemetery. More than one thousand people boarded a twenty-one-car train. Robert Kennedy's casket was propped up in the last car on two red velvet chairs. The train emerged from the Holland Tunnel into New Jersey, where crowds of mourners had gathered along the tracks. The line would stretch for 225 miles. Those who were gathered looked like the people "who mobbed him and cheered him in Gary Indiana, in San Francisco's Chinatown, in East Chicago, Harlem and Watts," observed Richard Harwood in the *Washington Post*. There were "huge numbers" of people, cab drivers and factory hands, nuns, multitudes of children, and old women with their hands clasped in prayer as the train made its way past fields, industrial sights, junkyards, and urban centers.[3]

"It was a sort of Saturday afternoon America," said Russell Baker. There were men in undershirts and coveralls and "women with their hair up in curlers." Percy Sutton, Manhattan Borough president, was captivated by faces of people "in silent vigil," people of "all sizes, colors, shapes and descriptions." Among the most memorable sights for Sutton was that of "five little black boys, clean and proud, standing near the train in Baltimore and holding forth their outstretched arms each with a single rose" pointed toward the train and holding a sign saying "God Bless the Kennedy Family." For Steve Northrup of the *Washington Post*, "it felt like we were riding a train to the end of an era."[4]

Ivanhoe Donaldson, a former SNCC field secretary in Mississippi who had been befriended by Kennedy when Donaldson moved to Washington to work for the Institute for Policy Studies, looked out from the train feeling sadness and awe. He noticed that every so often, the train would go under a trestle, "and there, standing all by himself would be a cop . . . quietly standing and saluting the train. . . . I remember seeing cops holding young children in their arms so that they could see the train—oftentimes black kids. I just thought, people can be so damn human sometimes, and so destructive at other times. I couldn't understand. I was trying to place the image of the cop . . . obviously moved, some of them crying, some of them holding children, some of them quietly by themselves a hundred yards from anyone else, saluting the train in the ultimate privacy . . . and yet the image *I* have of cops, you know, well I couldn't correlate the two. . . . That was the train ride for me. . . . It was trying to bridge the gap between the dream and the reality. There was the dream, all along the train tracks," he said. But "in the last car, in that caboose, that was the reality."[5]

It was estimated that between one and two million people lined the route. The train moved at a slow pace and was further delayed when a man and woman, accidentally pushed from the platform, were killed by an oncoming train. The funeral train arrived in Washington at 9:08 p.m., more than four hours behind schedule. With the hearse leading the way, a caravan of limousines started down First Street, past Kennedy's office in the Senate Office Building, past the Capitol and down Constitution Avenue. The procession paused briefly as it went by the Department of Justice. The caravan moved along, through silent lines of people and past Resurrection City, the encampment of the Poor People's Campaign since mid-May, toward the circle around the Lincoln Memorial. For most of the long, hot day, crowds had gathered all along the route from Union Station to Arlington National Cemetery.[6]

The hearse bearing Kennedy's body stopped directly in front of the Lincoln Memorial. Residents of Resurrection City were among the thousands gathered around the reflecting pool. Tom Wicker described people "dressed in denims, T-shirts, bandanas and Levi jackets." One wore a white T-shirt reading, "Black Power—Sock it to me baby." A brilliant moon illuminated the scene as a choir led the assembled crowd in singing "The Battle Hymn of the Republic." Then the hearse moved on, across Arlington Memorial Bridge, toward the eternal flame at John Kennedy's grave, shining against the night.

It was after 10:30 p.m. when the procession arrived at the grave site. The Harvard University band played "God Bless America" in the glow of floodlights, and Robert Kennedy's younger children lit candles. A short prayer service followed. Ethel Kennedy, her oldest son, Joseph Kennedy III, and Ted Kennedy knelt by the coffin, prayed briefly, then leaned forward and kissed the mahogany surface. Other family members followed. After the simple ceremony, Robert Kennedy was laid to rest on the hillside not far from his brother's grave.

———

SIRHAN BASKIRA SIRHAN, a twenty-four-year-old Palestinian immigrant, was apprehended at the scene of the assassination, tried, and convicted of Robert Kennedy's murder. Speculation has long surrounded the assassination, prompted by a combination of factors: a rushed investigation by the Los Angeles Police Department, the destruction of potential physical evidence, recollections of people who were there, and evidence that there may have been more than one gunman. Five people in addition to Robert Kennedy were shot that night; he was the only fatality. Paul Schrade was struck by the first bullet Sirhan fired. Schrade is one of many who has concluded that the bullet that killed Robert Kennedy was not fired by Sirhan. He and others have called for a new investigation. In 2018, Robert Kennedy Jr. publicly called for a reinvestigation of the crime. The unresolved questions surrounding the assassination are compelling, but beyond the scope of this work. What remains central is that Robert Kennedy's life was tragically cut short at a pivotal moment.[7]

"It seems they only kill somebody that's trying to help," an eighteen-year-old from Marks, Mississippi, encamped at Resurrection City reflected. For many Black Americans, the assassinations of King and Kennedy folded into the violence that too often met those fighting for racial equality and justice. "Something is dramatically sick about so many assassinations of so many men of humanistic and idealistic philosophy," offered Josephine Baker, the acclaimed entertainer. "He helped me to return to the USA when he did not have to," she recalled about Kennedy. "I shall never forget him, and I shall never let my children forget him." Coming at the end of a decade when struggle and triumph had yielded to violence and repression, the twin assassinations of King and Kennedy in two short months stood for many as a coda of the era.[8]

"I am really scared to death about where we are right now," Andrew Young said shortly after Kennedy's funeral. There are "so many parallels to the period right after the assassination of Lincoln." He remembered how, during the short window of Reconstruction, "liberated blacks wrote the most progressive and enlightened legislation in the history of the republic" providing for free public education and other reforms. But then, with "the return of the slaveocracy . . . racism regained its grip on our throat." Thinking of the national leaders who had engaged and supported the forces of social justice in the 1960s, Young reflected, "a country can't afford to lose, you know, three men like Robert Kennedy and John F. Kennedy and Martin King. It takes too long to build people like that."[9]

"I think things might be very different in this country if we had not had so many assassinations," James Baldwin told Jean Stein. He talked about

John and Robert Kennedy, as well as his close friends Medgar Evers, Malcolm X, Martin Luther King Jr.—all killed within a five year period. Baldwin regretted that he and Bobby had not spoken again after the May 1963 meeting. They saw each other one more time, across a distance, at Martin Luther King's funeral. Now that Bobby was gone, Baldwin reflected on what had been lost. "He was somebody in the twentieth century with enough passion and energy and patience." Speaking of Bobby and his brother, Baldwin commented that they "both had minds that could be reached." Bobby may have been "exasperated with those people" at the infamous 1963 meeting, "being hit against the wall [and] described as naïve," but "at least there's some contact, some connection, there's dialogue, there's something happening that makes things possible." He continued, "You know, black people had a very different feeling toward government when Bobby and JFK were alive than we've had since. I can't repeat it too often . . . that is one of the most sinister facts of present day American life. That atmosphere no longer exists."[10]

Bayard Rustin, the longtime activist who orchestrated the March on Washington, offered a scorching assessment of America in the immediate wake of the assassinations of King and Kennedy. "The tragic removal of these two men at this time from the American scene reveals the problems and crisis that plague our society," he wrote. "Both men were committed to the elimination of poverty in a land of such plenty. Both men were dedicated to peace and to the restrained and moral exercise of American power abroad . . . both stood for and supported the absolute necessity for the total freedom of black Americans. Both were in touch with the alienation of American youth, black and white, and their demand to be involved in the shaping of a new and more just society." Finally, "both were fully aware of the risks they ran and the penalties they faced for trying to work against the current American moral grain." Yet they "accepted the risk" and paid the ultimate price "for trying to make a difference in their times and for striving to show mankind that it can be better than it is."

"We are creating a no-man's land," Rustin warned, "which the armies of extreme reaction and extreme despair may well rush to fill." Reflecting on the toll of the decade, he suggested that "with each assassination, the bill for moral and social change in America mounts higher and higher."[11]

———

THE DEMOCRATIC NATIONAL CONVENTION met in the last week of August and dissolved into chaos. Antiwar activists from across the country converged on Chicago to challenge the Democratic Party establishment and protest the nomination of the establishment's candidate, Hubert Humphrey.

While delegates engaged in shouting matches within the convention hall, the Chicago police waged war on protesters outside. In scenes that replicated the battles that had raged in America's cities for several summers, police officers "took off their badges and waded into chanting crowds of protesters to club them to the ground," *Washington Post* reporter Haynes Johnson recounted. "I can still recall the choking feeling from the tear gas hurled by police amid the protesters gathered in parks and hotel lobbies." The convention laid bare the deep hostility between the Democrat Party's political establishment and those pushing to remake the political system—destroying the faith of many in the country and its institutions.[12]

Ralph Bunche was deeply impacted by the assassinations of King and Kennedy. Robert Kennedy's death "hung like a shroud over the 1968 election," as Bunche's biographer writes. When Bunche was asked how he would vote, he said he had never seen such bad alternatives. "Hubert has lost irretrievably his liberal image. He is now a shadow image of LBJ. He made a grave mistake in accepting the role of vice-president. He became something akin to a court jester in King Lyndon's court. Nixon, in my view, is an utter hypocrite, without conviction or principle. He is a small, ambitious, dangerous man. Thus, in November, I shall close my eyes, hold my nose and vote for Hubert only because to do otherwise would be to help Nixon. Anything but that."[13]

Richard Nixon won the election, taking 43.4 percent of the popular vote, with Humphrey close behind at 42.7 percent and American Independent Party candidate George Wallace securing 13.5 percent of the vote. In the face of a greatly weakened and fractured Democratic Party, what had been a losing strategy for Barry Goldwater four years earlier triumphed in 1968. Nixon and Wallace had both run on a strong law-and-order platform, competing for the white southern vote.

Cynical and opportunistic, Nixon harvested the resentments, fears, and racial prejudices of the so-called silent majority and built a criminal justice apparatus targeting poor Black urban areas. Although the Johnson Administration's "war on crime" had begun to overshadow its War on Poverty, the Nixon administration institutionalized criminal justice policies that amplified and solidified this shift in priorities—further militarizing policing, deploying undercover squads in urban areas, and incentivizing prison construction. Nixon's "war on drugs" used growing public concern about drugs as a cover for aggressive crime control polices in poor urban communities. "As implemented and augmented by opportunistic Congresses," writes biographer John Farrell, "governors like Nelson Rockefeller, and Nixon's successors, notably Ronald Reagan and Bill Clinton—the 'war' on drugs and the battle for 'law and order' would metastasize, yielding punitive measures like mandatory sentences, no-knock raids and other relaxations of defendants' rights." Starting in the late 1960s, America's prison population skyrocketed, with a move to mass incarceration that disproportionately impacted Black Americans. As Elizabeth Hinon pointed out in her study of the transition from the War on Poverty to the War on Crime, "African Americans born after 1965 and lacking a high school diploma are more likely to eventually go to prison than not."[14]

The criminal justice policies and law enforcement practices that became normalized in the 1970s and 1980s have culminated with a racial reckoning today on a scale not seen since the civil rights era. The crisis runs much deeper than the criminal behavior of some law enforcement officers, which colleagues, supervisors, and politicians long tolerated and even condoned. In 1968, the Kerner Commission issued a warning and a set of recommendations that were dismissed or ignored at the highest levels of power. Racial inequities and injustices were left to fester, politics became more polarized and dysfunctional, and law enforcement was enlisted on an even larger scale to enforce "order," while African Americans and their allies demanded that the deep structures of racial inequality be confronted and rooted out.

"Like it or not," Robert Kennedy said in 1966, "we live in times of danger and uncertainty." That year, he suggested that "no area of national life" was more pressing than "the revolution within our gates," the struggle of Black Americans "for full equality and full freedom." While acknowledging the gains that had been made, Kennedy pointed out that the struggle had entered a "new stage, one that was more hopeful and more difficult." It had become clear that persistent inequality could not be remedied by a lawsuit, by legislation, or by protest alone. Ending inequality would require nothing less than overcoming "the scarred heritage of centuries of oppression" manifested throughout America life, most notably in white attitudes and beliefs. Kennedy warned that "it would be a national disaster to permit resentment and fear to drive increasing numbers of white and black Americans into opposing camps of distrust and enmity." There was but one choice, he said: "to face our difficulties and strive to overcome them, or turn away, bringing repression, increasing human pain, and civil strife."[15]

More than fifty years later, the most relevant legacy of the 1960s may be the hopes and the lives of those who, during a brief time of promise and intense civic engagement, faced the pervasive effects of America's racial past and struggled, at all levels of society, to pave a new way forward.

NOTES

PREFACE

1. M. S. Handler, "Malcolm X Scores Kennedy on Racial Policy," *New York Times,* May 17, 1962, 14.

2. James Baldwin, *The Fire Next Time* (New York: Vintage International, 1993), 68, 105.

3. James Baldwin, interview by Jean Stein, February 2, 1970, Jean Stein Personal Papers, box 1, John F. Kennedy Presidential Library and Museum, Boston (hereafter cited as "JFKL").

4. James Baldwin, "Lorraine Hansberry at the Summit, No. 4, 1979," in Esther Cooper Jackson, ed., *Freedomways Reader: Prophets in Their Own Time* (Boulder: Westview, 2000), 79.

5. Kenneth Clark, interview by Jean Stein, January 30, 1970, Jean Stein Personal Papers, box 1, JFKL.

6. Jerome Smith, "Louisiana Story," *Freedomways* 4, no. 2 (1964), 242–251.

7. Accounts of the meeting are based on Clark interview, January 30, 1970; Reminiscences of Kenneth Clark (1967), War on Poverty project, Oral History Archives at Columbia, Rare Book and Manuscript Library, Columbia University, New York; Baldwin interview, February 2, 1970; Baldwin, "Lorraine Hansberry at the Summit," 77–81; Harry Belafonte, interview by Vicki Daitch, May 20, 2005, John F. Kennedy Oral History Collection, John F. Kennedy Presidential Library and Museum, Boston (hereafter cited as JFKOH); Clarence Jones to the editor, *New York Times,* June 11, 1963, 22; James Gavin, *Stormy Weather: The Life of Lena Horne* (New York: Atria Books, 2009), 310–311; Henry Morgenthau, interview by author, May 10, 2013.

8. Clark interview, January 30, 1970; Baldwin, "Lorraine Hansberry at the Summit," 269–273.

9. John Doar, interview by Anthony Lewis, November 13, 1964, JFKOH.

10. Address by Robert F. Kennedy, Attorney General of the United States, at Kentucky's Centennial of the Emancipation Proclamation, Freedom Hall, March 18, 1963, Speeches of Attorney General Robert Kennedy, U.S. Department of Justice, https://www.justice.gov/ag/speeches-25.

11. Gertrude Samuels, "Even More Crucial Than the South: A Report on the Forms the Negro Revolution is Taking against Discrimination, Economic and Social, in the North," *New York Times Magazine,* June 30, 1963, 143; Edwin Guthman, *We Band of Brothers* (New York: Harper & Row, 1971), 220–221; James Wechsler, "RFK and Baldwin," *New York Post,* May 28, 1963, 30.

12. Thurgood Marshall, interview by Berl Bernhard, April 7, 1964, JFKOH.

13. President John F. Kennedy, "Televised Address to the Nation on Civil Rights," June 11, 1963, JFKL, https://www.jfklibrary.org/learn/about-jfk/historic-speeches/televised-address-to-the-nation-on-civil-rights.

14. Clark interview, January 30, 1970; editorial, *Chicago Defender,* June 13, 1963.

15. David S. Broder, "Yorty and Shriver Disagree on Riots," *New York Times,* August 18, 1965, 20.

16. Statement by Martin Luther King Jr., "The Federal Role in Urban Affairs," Hearings before the Subcommittee on Executive Reorganization of the Committee on Government Operations, United States Senate, 89th Congress, second session, December 14 and 15, 1966, Part 14 (Washington, DC: US Government Printing Office, 1967), 2981, 2990–2994.

17. Statement by Martin Luther King Jr., "The Federal Role in Urban Affairs," 2970; "Kennedy Notes a Peril," *New York Times,* June 30, 1966, 18; Statement of Hon. Robert F. Kennedy, US Senator from the State of New York, "Federal Role in Urban Affairs," Hearings before the Subcommittee on Executive Reorganization of the Committee on Government Operations, US Senate, 89th Congress, second session, August 15–16, 1966, Part I (Washington DC: Government Printing Office, 1967), 34; Senator Robert F. Kennedy, "Suppose God is Black," *Look,* August 23, 1966.

18. "Senator Robert Kennedy in Berkeley," Pacifica Radio Archives, American Archive of Public Broadcasting (WGBH and the Library of Congress), Boston and Washington DC, http://americanarchive.org/catalog/c-b-aacip-28-pc2t43jg47.

19. Thurston Clarke, *The Last Campaign* (New York: Henry Holt, 2008), 95.

1 · MISFIT

1. "Bunche Warns of USA Isolation in Cabel Address," *Virginia Law Weekly,* April 5, 1951, 1.

2. David Nasaw, *The Patriarch: The Remarkable Life and Turbulent Times of Joseph P. Kennedy* (New York: Penguin Press, 2012), 3–23, 28–31, 105–106, 204–205, 272–277, 485–504.

3. Murray Kempton to Mr. Murphy, August 18, 1958, box 43, Papers of Robert F. Kennedy, Pre-administration Papers, JFKL.

4. Nasaw, *Patriarch,* 619; Arthur Schlesinger Jr., *Robert Kennedy and His Times* (Boston: Houghton Mifflin Company, 1978), 21.

5. Schlesinger, *Robert Kennedy,* 22–23.

6. Jack Newfield, *RFK: A Memoir* (New York: Thunder's Mouth Press / Nation Books, 1969), 41–42; Nasaw, *Patriarch,* 547.

7. Jean Stein and George Plimpton, ed., *American Journey: The Times of Robert Kennedy* (New York: Harcourt Brace Jovanovich, 1970), 37; Mary Bailey "Paidi" Gimbel, interview by Arthur Schlesinger, February 19, 1975, box 500, Arthur M. Schlesinger Jr. Papers, Manuscripts and Archives Division, New York Public Library, New York (hereafter cited as "Schlesinger Papers"); teachers' reports, English, French, Math, Milton Academy, November 1942, box 31, Joseph P. Kennedy Personal Papers, JFKL (hereafter cited as "JPKPP"); David Hackett, interview by John Douglas, July 22, 1970, Robert F. Kennedy Oral History Collection, JFKL (hereafter cited as "RFKOH").

8. Emma Brown, "David L. Hackett, Kennedy Administration Youth Advocate, Dies at 84," *Washington Post,* May 3, 2011; Hackett interview, July 22, 1970; RFK to Joseph P. and Rose Kennedy, n.d., box 2, JPKPP.

9. Hackett interview, July 22, 1970; David Hackett, interview by Arthur Schlesinger, January 27, 1975, box 495, Schlesinger Papers.

10. Schlesinger, *Robert Kennedy,* 51–52; Nasaw, *Patriarch,* 548–49, 555–557; Joseph P. Kennedy to Commander E. S. Brewer, July 14, 1943, box 32, JPKPP.

11. J. B. Lynch to Joseph P. Kennedy, February 9, 1944, box 32, JPKPP.

12. Schlesinger, *Robert Kennedy,* 51–53; Nasaw, *Patriarch,* 548–549.

13. Nasaw, *Patriarch,* 564–567.

14. Joseph P. Kennedy Jr. to Joseph P. and Rose Kennedy, June 23 and July 26, 1944, box 3, JPKPP.

15. Joseph P. Kennedy Jr. to Joseph P. and Rose Kennedy, August 4, 1944; Joseph P. Kennedy to Joseph P. Kennedy Jr., August 9, 1944, box 3, JPKPP; Nasaw, *Patriarch,* 570–572.

16. Schlesinger, *Robert Kennedy,* 58; RFK to David Hackett, March 13, 1945, copy provided by Judith Hackett; RFK to David Hackett, Schlesinger Papers, n.d., box 495.

17. RFK to Joseph and Rose Kennedy, February 8, February 28, and March 5, 1946, box 3, JPKPP.

18. Schlesinger, *Robert Kennedy,* 56.

19. Schlesinger, *Robert Kennedy,* 63.

20. Edwin O. Guthman and Jeffrey Shulman, eds., *Robert Kennedy in His Own Words: The Unpublished Recollections of the Kennedy Years* (New York: Bantam, 1988), 431–436; Ralph E. Martin and Ed Plaut, *Front Runner, Dark Horse* (New York: Doubleday & Co., 1960), 140–141, 145–146; Schlesinger, *Robert Kennedy,* 63–65.

21. Schlesinger, *Robert Kennedy,* 65–68.

22. Schlesinger, *Robert Kennedy,* 65–66; Stein, *American Journey,* 38–39.

23. Robert Kennedy, "Communism Not to Get a Foothold," *Boston Post,* June 6, 1948.

24. RFK to Joseph and Rose Kennedy, April 6, 1948, box 3, JPKPP.

25. RFK to Joseph and Rose Kennedy, April 6, 1948, box 3, JPKPP; RFK, "1949 [sic] Trip Diary with George Terrien: Italy, Palestine, etc.," typed ms., box 32, JPKPP; Robert Kennedy, "British Hatred by Both Sides," *Boston Post,* June 3, 1948; Robert Kennedy, "Jews Have Fine Fighting Force," *Boston Post,* June 4, 1948; Robert Kennedy, "British Position Hit in Palestine," *Boston Post,* June 5, 1946; Robert Kennedy, "Communism Not to Get a Foothold," *Boston Post,* June 6, 1948.

26. RFK, "Trip Diary."

27. Nasaw, *Patriarch,* 620–621.

28. RFK, "Trip Diary"; RFK to Joseph and Rose Kennedy, June 30, 1948, box 3, JPKPP; Schlesinger, *Robert Kennedy,* 78.

29. RFK to Joseph and Rose Kennedy, June 30, 1948, box 3, JPKPP.

30. RFK, "Trip Diary"; RFK to Joseph and Rose Kennedy, June 30, 1948, box 3, JPKPP.

31. Schlesinger, *Robert Kennedy,* 77–81.

32. Mortimer Caplin, interview by author, December 5, 2012.

33. Schlesinger, *Robert Kennedy,* 88–89; Evan Thomas, *Robert Kennedy: His Life* (New York: Simon & Schuster, 2000), 56–58.

34. Eric Williamson, "The Long Walk," *UVA Law,* Spring 2018.

35. Margaret Laing, *The Next Kennedy* (New York: Coward-McCann, 1968), 120.

36. Laing, *Next Kennedy,* 120; RFK to Colgate Darden, March 7, 1951, box 5, Presidential Papers, Special Collections, University of Virginia Library.

37. "Bunche Warns of USA Isolation in Cabell Address," *Virginia Law Weekly,* April 5, 1951, 1; Schlesinger, *Robert Kennedy,* 87; author interview with Ethel Kennedy, October 2014.

38. Ethel Kennedy interview; Brian Urquhart, *Ralph Bunche: An American Life* (New York: W. W. Norton, 1993), 421.

39. Robert F. Kennedy, "Parley on Jap Treaty to Open Soon," *Boston Post,* September 4, 1951; Schlesinger, *Robert Kennedy,* 90; Robert Dallek, *An Unfinished Life: John F. Kennedy, 1917–1963* (Boston: Back Bay Books, 2003), 165.

40. Dallek, *An Unfinished Life,* 165–66; Frederick Logevall, *Embers of War: The Fall of an Empire and the Making of America's Vietnam* (New York: Random House, 2012), xi.

41. RFK, October 23, 1951, "1951 Travel Diary," box 24, RFK Papers, Pre-administration Papers, JFKL.

42. RFK, "1951 Travel Diary," box 24, Papers of Robert Kennedy, Pre-administration Papers, JFKL; RFK to Joseph Kennedy, October 19, 1951, box 4, JPKPP.

43. Logevall, *Embers of War,* xiii–xiv; RFK, "1951 Travel Diary," ca. October 22, 1951; RFK to Joseph Kennedy, October 19, 1951, box 1950, JPKPP.

44. Logevall, *Embers of War,* xii–xiii; RFK, "1951 Travel Diary," October 23, 1951.

45. RFK, "1951 Travel Diary," October 23, 1951.

46. Logevall, *Embers of War,* xiv; RFK, "1951 Travel Diary," October 23, 1951.

2 · ALONG THE COLOR LINE: THE 1950S

1. "Not the Last Word," editorial, *New York Times,* March 18, 1949, 24.

2. James Baldwin, *Notes of a Native Son* (Boston: Beacon Press, 1955), 111; Khalil Muhammad, *The Condemnation of Blackness: Race, Crime and the Making of Modern America* (Cambridge, MA: Harvard University Press, 2010)

3. John A. Stokes with Lois Wolfe, *Students on Strike: Jim Crow, Civil Rights and Me,* (Washington, DC: National Geographic, 2008), 44–51.

4. David Nasaw, *The Patriarch: The Remarkable Life and Turbulent Times of Joseph P. Kennedy* (New York: Penguin Press, 2012), 661–664; Anthony Lewis, "What Drives Bobby Kennedy: An Appraisal of the Qualities That Have Put Him, at 37, at the Center of Power," *New York Times,* April, 7, 1963, SM34; Jean Stein and George Plimpton, ed., *American Journey: The Times of Robert Kennedy* (New York: Harcourt Brace Jovanovich, 1970), 40–41.

5. Edwin O. Guthman and Jeffrey Shulman, eds., *Robert Kennedy In His Own Words: the Unpublished Recollections of the Kennedy Years* (New York: Bantam Books, 1988), 441–443; Ralph G. Martin and Ed Plaut, *Front Runner, Dark Horse* (New York: Doubleday, 1960), 164–165; JFK quoted in Peter Maas, "Robert Kennedy Speaks Out . . . ," *Look,* March 28, 1961, 23.

6. Martin and Plout, *Front Runner,* 164–165.

7. Helen Keyes in Stein and Plimpton, *American Journey,* 42, 43; Kenneth P. O'Donnell and David F. Powers, *Johnny, We Hardly Knew Ye: Memories of John Fitzgerald Kennedy* (Boston: Little, Brown, 1972), 85; Ruth Batson, interview by Sheldon Stern, January 24, 1979, JFKOH.

8. Martin and Plaut, *Front Runner,* 165; O'Donnell and Powers, *Johnny, We Hardly Knew Ye,* 86; Stein and Plimpton, *American Journey,* 42–43; Guthman and Shulman, *Robert Kennedy in His Own Word,* 446–447.

9. Martin and Plaut, *Front Runner,* 164, 182.

10. Arthur Schlesinger Jr., *Robert Kennedy and His Times* (Boston: Houghton Mifflin Company, 1978), 100–102; Evan Thomas references Schlesinger as his source in claiming Joe Kennedy was responsible for getting RFK a job on McCarthy's committee, *Robert Kennedy,* 64; Edwin Guthman, *We Band of Brothers* (New York: Harper and Row, 1971), 16–18; Ruth Young Watt, oral history interview, July 19 to November 9, 1979, Senate Oral History Project, Senate Historical Office, Washington, DC, p. 113. Kennedy wrote that when he joined the committee, "I went to work for Francis Flanagan." Robert Kennedy, *The Enemy Within* (New York: De Capo Press, 1994), 176.

11. Kennedy, *Enemy Within,* 176; Edwin Guthman, *We Band of Brothers* (New York: Harper & Row, 1964), 17; Schlesinger, *Robert Kennedy,* 100; Nasaw, *Patriarch,* 667; Patricia and Eunice Kennedy, interview by Arthur Schlesinger, June 23, 1975, box 499, Schlesinger Papers; Ethel Kennedy, interview by author, October 2014.

12. RFK, 1951 trip diary, 103; Schlesinger, *Robert Kennedy,* 104; Doris Fleeson, *Washington Star,* August 25, 1954, box 499, Schlesinger Papers.

13. Kennedy, *Enemy Within,* 176; Peter Maas, "Robert Kennedy Speaks Out," *Look,* March 19, 1961, 27; Guthman, *We Band of Brothers,* 19; Schlesinger, *Robert Kennedy,* 105–106; Ruth Young Watt interview, 112–113; Roy Cohn, interview by James Oesterle, March 24, 1971, RFKOH.

14. Earl Browder, interview by Mike Wallace, June 2, 1957, https://hrc.contentdm.oclc.org/digital /collection/p15878coll90/id/12/.

15. RFK to Earl Browder, March 16, 1954; Joseph Starobin to Arthur Schlesinger, n.d., box 499, Schlesinger Papers.

16. Schlesinger, *Robert Kennedy*, 110–112.

17. David M. Oshinsky, *A Conspiracy So Immense: The Word of Joe McCarthy* (New York: Oxford University Press, 2005), 403–406.

18. W. H. Lawrence, "Cohn Threatens to 'Get' Senator for Jibe at Schine," *New York Times*, June 12, 1954, 1; "Cohn, Kennedy Near Blows in 'Hate' Clash," *New York Daily News*, June 12, 1954; Guthman, *Band of Brothers*, 21–22; Schlesinger, *Robert Kennedy*, 112–113.

19. Guthman, *Band of Brothers*, 23.

20. RFK, handwritten notes, May 4, 1957, box 490, Schlesinger Papers.

21. *New York Daily News*, May 7, 1957; Nasaw, *Patriarch*, 685.

22. Peter Mass interview, Jean Stein Personal Papers, box 3, JFKL.

23. Pauli Murray to Caroline Ware, May 18, 1954, MC 412, box 101, file 1819, Papers of Pauli Murray, Schlesinger Library, Radcliffe Institute, Harvard University, Cambridge, MA; *Atlanta Daily World*, May 18, 1954, 1, 3; *Pittsburgh Courier*, May 22, 1954, 9; *Los Angeles Sentinel*, May 20, 1954, A1.

24. Manning Marable, *Malcolm X: A Life of Reinvention* (New York: Viking, 2011), 107–110.

25. Avon Kirkland, comments at *Brown v. Board of Education* Fiftieth Anniversary Symposium, University of South Carolina, April 23, 2003.

26. Patricia Sullivan, *Lift Every Voice: The NAACP and the Making of the Civil Rights Movement* (New York: New Press, 2009), 421–426.

27. Jeanne Theoharis, *The Rebellious Life of Rosa Parks* (Boston: Beacon, 2013), 35–42.

28. Schlesinger, *Robert Kennedy*, 117–121; *Boston Globe*, May 18, 1956; Stein and Plimpton, *American Journey*, 54.

29. Robert F. Kennedy, "A Look Behind the Russian Smiles," *U.S. News and World Report*, October 21, 1955, 146; William O. Douglas, interview by Roberta Greene, November 13, 1969, RFKOH.

30. Carol Polsgrove, *Divided Minds: Intellectuals and the Civil Rights Movement* (New York: W.W. Norton, 2001), 6–9.

31. Theodore White, "The Negro Voter: Can He Elect a President?" *Collier's*, August 1956, 19.

32. Theoharis, *Rebellious Life of Rosa Parks*, 110–115; Sullivan, *Lift Every Voice*, 423.

33. David A. Nichols, *A Matter of Justice: Eisenhower and the Beginning of the Civil Rights Revolution* (New York: Simon & Schuster, 2007), 34–42, 111–125.

34. Newman Bartley, *The Rise of Massive Resistance: Race and Politics in the South during the 1950s* (Baton Rouge: Louisiana State University Press, 1999), 62–63; Steven Gillon, *Politics and Vision: The ADA and American Liberalism, 1947–1985* (New York: Oxford University Press, 1988), 84, 94, 97, 101.

35. Robert Dallek, *An Unfinished Life: John F. Kennedy, 1917–1963* (Boston: Back Bay Books, 2003), 204–207; Schlesinger, *Robert Kennedy*, 132.

36. Nick Bryant, *The Bystander: John F. Kennedy and the Struggle for Black Equality* (New York: Basic Books, 2006), 57–59; Dallek, *Unfinished Life*, 207–208; RFK to Charles Bloch, September 5, 1956, box 19, Papers of Robert F. Kennedy, Pre-administration Papers, JFKL.

37. Belford Lawson, interview by Ronald J. Grele, January 11, 1966, JFKOH

38. Belford Lawson interview; Marjorie McKenzie Lawson, interview with Ronald J. Grele, October 25, 1965, JFKOH.

39. RFK to Charles J. Bloch, Sept 5, 1956, Box 19, Papers of Robert F. Kennedy, Pre-administration Papers, JFKL.

40. William Blair, interview by Jean Stein, Schlesinger Papers, box 499; Newt Minow, interview by Arthur Schlesinger, August 30, 1974, box 499, Schlesinger Papers; Schlesinger, *Robert Kennedy*, 134; White, *Making of a President*, 246.

41. Stein and Plimpton, *American Journey*, 65–67; Schlesinger, *Robert Kennedy*, 135–136.

42. Robert F. Kennedy, *The Enemy Within* (New York: Da Capo Press, 1994), 3–16; Schlesinger, *Robert Kennedy*, 137–142.

43. Dallek, *Unfinished Life*, 218–219.

44. Murray Kempton, "The Uncommitted," *Progressive*, September 1960, 17.

45. *Time*, January 17, 1955.

46. Schlesinger, *Robert Kennedy*, 137–138.

47. Stein and Plimpton, *American Journey*, 52.

48. Ruth Young Watt interview; Stein and Plimpton, *American Journey*, 56.

49. Schlesinger, *Robert Kennedy*, 150, 169; Stein and Plimpton, *American Journey*, 53; Kempton, "The Uncommitted," 17.

50. Thomas, *Robert Kennedy*, 85–86.

51. Jack Conway, interview by Larry J. Hackman, April 10, 1972, RFKOH.

52. Conway interview, April 10, 1972; Robert F. Kennedy, *The Enemy Within* (New York: DeCapo Press, 1994), 274–276.

53. Nichols, *A Matter of Justice*, 141.

54. Bryant, *Bystander*, 61–63.

55. Nichols, *A Matter of Justice*, 118–119.

56. Nichols, *A Matter of Justice*, 147–149.

57. Bryant, *Bystander*, 66.

58. Bryant, *Bystander*, 68–69; Nichols, *A Matter of Justice*, 155–156.

59. Bryant, *Bystander*, 73–74.

60. Nichols, *A Matter of Justice*, 161–162; "Civil Rights-Reactions to Jury Trial Amendment and the Key Vote," *New York Times*, August 4, 1957, E1; Bryant, *Bystander*, 76–77.

61. Nichols, *A Matter of Justice*, 162–166.

62. Nichols, *A Matter of Justice*, 167–168.

63. Robert J. Norrell, *Reaping the Whirlwind: The Civil Rights Movement in Tuskegee* (Chapel Hill: University of North Carolina Press, 1998), 112–116.

64. James Baldwin, "The Harlem Ghetto" (1948), *Notes of a Native Son*, in *James Baldwin, Collected Essays* (New York: Library of America, 1998), 42.

65. David Leeming, *James Baldwin: A Biography* (New York: Random House, 1994),100–101.

66. Leeming, *James Baldwin*, 133; James Baldwin, *No Name in the Street*, in Baldwin, *Collected Essays* (New York: Vintage, 2007), 383.

67. James Baldwin, "A Letter from the South: Nobody Knows My Name," *Partisan Review*, Winter 1959, 72–73; Leeming, *James Baldwin*, 139.

68. James Baldwin, "The Hard Kind of Courage," *Harper's Magazine*, October 1958, 162–164; Lemming, *James Baldwin*, 139–140.

69. Baldwin, "Hard Kind of Courage," 63–63; Baldwin, "A Letter from the South," 75.

70. Baldwin, "A Letter from the South," 75–76.

71. Lemming, *James Baldwin*, 141–144; Baldwin, "A Letter from the South," 81.

72. Johanna Miller Lewis, "Implementing *Brown* in Little Rock," in Brian Daugherity and Charles C. Bolton, *With All Deliberate Speed: Implementing Brown v. Board* (Fayetteville: University of Arkansas Press, 2008), 12–13.

73. Bob Smith, *They Closed Their Schools* (Chapel Hill: University of North Carolina Press), 151–152.

74. Kennedy, *Enemy Within*, 240.

75. Kennedy, *Enemy Within*, 318–320.

76. Kennedy, *Enemy Within*, 345.

3 · FAITH, HOPE, AND POLITICS

1. Fentress, February 4, 1960, dispatches from *Time* magazine correspondents: second series, 1956–1968, Ms Am 2090.1, Houghton Library, Harvard University.

2. Claude Sitton, "Negro Sit-Downs Stir Fears of Wider Unrest in the South," *New York Times*, February 15, 1960, 1.

3. Miller, May 20, 1960, dispatches from *Time* magazine correspondents.

4. Marian Wright, interview by Dudley Doust (Atlanta), May 23, 1960, dispatches from *Time* magazine correspondents.

5. Mehrtens, "Sympathy Demonstrations," April 1, 1960, 397; Cotton, "Undergraduate Attitudes," May 20, 1960, 408; Segal, "Campus Intellectual Climate," May 20, 1960, 408; "Sympathy Protests in Northern Schools," May 20, 1960; dispatches from *Time* magazine correspondents.

6. "Truman Reiterates His View on Sitdowns," *New York Times*, March 25, 1960, 12; "Truman Repeats Charges on Sit-Ins," *New York Times*, June 13, 1960, 20.

7. Theodore White, *The Making of the President, 1960* (New York: Harper Perennial Political Classics, 2009), 133; Kole, "Kole, Negro Population in Milwaukee," May 26, 1960, dispatches from *Time* magazine correspondents.

8. White, *Making of the President*, 49–53; Marjorie Lawson, interview by Ronald Grele, November 14, 1964, JFKOH.

9. White, *Making of the President*, 55–58; Robert Kennedy, "Meeting at Hyannisport," memo, October 28, 1960, box 39, Papers of Robert Kennedy, Pre-administration Papers, JFKL; Marjorie Lawson interview, November 24, 1964.

10. RFK, memo of Georgia and Virginia, November 16, 1960, box 39, Papers of Robert Kennedy, Pre-administration Papers, JFKL.

11. "Washington Story Suggestions," February 16, 1960, dispatches from *Time* magazine correspondents 389; Arthur Krock, "Southerners Face Bleak Future . . . Johnson Shifts His Role," *New York Times*, February 14, 1960, E3.

12. "The Civil Rights Debate," editorial, *New York Times*, February 26, 1960, 26; John D. Morris, "Senate Deletes School Provision from Rights Bill," *New York Times*, March 12, 1960, 1.

13. MacNeil, "Civil Rights II," February 19, 1960, dispatches from *Time* magazine correspondents, 390; "Both Parties Seek Civil Rights Credit," *New York Times*, February 20, 1960, E3; Russell Baker, "Rights Bloc Split on Move for Vote to End Filibuster," *New York Times*, March 8, 1960, 1; Russell Baker, "Civil Rights Bill Passes House, Gains in Senate," *New York Times*, March 25, 1960, 1.

14. Russell Baker, "Final House Vote Set for Next Week for Civil Rights," *New York Times,* April 12, 1960, 1.

15. Chamberlin, "Civil Rights II," April 9, 1960 dispatches from *Time* magazine correspondents; Baker, "Final House Vote Is Set for Next Week for Civil Rights"; Anthony Lewis, "Long Fight Ends: House Backs Senate Version 288–95," *New York Times,* April 22, 1960, 1.

16. Chamberlin, "Civil Rights II;" *New York Times,* August 2, 1959, E8; Krock, "Southern Democrats Face a Bleak Future"; Claude Sitton, "Johnson Holding Support in the South," March 6, 1960, 1; Baker, "Final House Vote Set"; Arthur Krock, "Johnson's Leadership," April 10, 1964, E11; Anthony Lewis, "Long Fight Ends."

17. Claude Sitton, "Negroes' Protest Spreads in the South," *New York Times,* February 13, 1960, 1; Claude Sitton, "Negro Dissatisfaction with Slow Pace of Action on Rights Brings Sit-ins and White Resistance," *New York Times,* March 6, 1960, E3.

18. Claude Sitton, "Integration Pace Slows in the South," *New York Times,* May 22, 1960, E7.

19. Doust to Johnston, May 30, 1960, dispatches from *Time* magazine correspondents; Sitton, "Negro Dissatisfaction with Slow Pace of Action on Rights Brings Sit-ins and White Resistance."

20. Davidson, "Mood of the Nation," February 18, 1960, dispatches from *Time* magazine correspondents, 390.

21. Doust to Johnston, "Sit Down and Be Counted (Take Two)," May 24, 1960, dispatches from *Time* magazine correspondents.

22. Marian Wright Edelman, *Lanterns: A Memoir of Mentors* (New York: Harpers Perennial, 2000), 65; Doust to Johnston, "Sit Down and Be Counted (Take One)," May 23, 1960, dispatches from *Time* magazine correspondents.

23. Doust to Johnston, "Sit Down and Be Counted (Take One)."

24. Barbara Ransby, *Ella Baker and the Black Freedom Movement: A Radical Democratic Vision* (Chapel Hill: University of North Carolina Press, 2005), 166–169, 238–247.

25. Harrison Salisbury, "Fear and Hatred Grip Birmingham," *New York Times,* April 12, 1960, 1.

26. Virginia Durr to Clark Foreman, April 7, 1960, in *Freedom Writer: Virginia Foster Durr, Letters from the Civil Rights Years,* ed. Patricia Sullivan (New York: Routledge, 2003), 205.

27. James Reston, "Stop Kennedy Drive Fails; Nixon Loses Edge in Polls," March 7, 1960, 1.

28. Robert Dallek, *An Unfinished Life: John F. Kennedy, 1917–1963* (Boston: Back Bay Books, 2003), 249–252.

29. Marjorie McKenzie Lawson, interview by Ronald Grele, October 25, 1965, JFKOH.

30. Lawson interview, October 25, 1965; Meyers, Charleston, West Virginia, April 29, 1960, dispatches from *Time* magazine correspondents.

31. Richard Goodwin, *Remembering America: A Voice from the Sixties* (Boston: Little, Brown and Company, 1988), 84–90; Evan Thomas, *Robert Kennedy: His Life* (New York: Simon & Schuster, 2000), 93–96; White, *Making of the President,* 104–114.

32. Goodwin, *Remembering America,* 89–90.

33. White, *Making of the President,* 219–222.

34. George Belknap, "Political Behavior Report: The Northern Negro Vote," May 1960, box 39, Papers of Robert Kennedy, Pre-administration Papers, JFKL; Murray Kempton, "The Uncommitted," *Progressive,* September 1960.

35. Harris Wofford, *Of Kennedys and Kings: Making Sense of the Sixties* (New York: Farrar, Straus, Giroux, 1980), 47.

36. Lawson interview, October 25, 1964; "Alabama OK of Kennedy Gets Blast," *Chicago Defender,* May 31, 1960, 19; "Jackie Robinson Raps Kennedy," *Chicago Defender,* April 9, 1960, 1.

37. Thurgood Marshall, interview by Berl Bernhard, April 7, 1964, JFKOH.

38. Lawson interview, October 25, 1964; Alex Poinsett, *Walking with Presidents: Louis Martin and the Rise of Black Political Power* (New York: Madison Books, 1997), 65; Wofford, *Of Kennedys and Kings,* 109–113, 115–118.

39. Wofford, *Of Kennedys and Kings,* 47; Anthony Lewis, "Kennedy Pledges to Stand Firm in Support of Negro Rights," *New York Times,* July 2, 1960, 6; Anthony Lewis, "Kennedy Salutes Negro Sit-Ins," *New York Times,* June 25, 1960, 13; Belford V. Lawson, interview by Ronald J. Greele, June 11, 1966, JFKOH; Geoffrey Pond, "Powell May Back Johnson in Race," *New York Times,* June 26, 1960, 45.

40. Martin Luther King Jr. to Marjorie Lawson, September 17, 1959, MLK Papers Project; Martin Luther King Jr., interview by Berl Bernhard, March 6, 1964, JFKOH; Lewis, "Kennedy Salutes Negro Sit-Ins"; Chester Bowles to JFK, June 29, 1960, box 490, Schlesinger Papers.

41. Lewis, "Kennedy Salutes Negroes Sit-Ins"; "Truman Repeats Charges on Sit-Ins."

42. Leo Egan, "Kennedy Assures Liberals He Seeks No Help in the South," *New York Times,* June 24, 1960, 1; "Kennedy's Remarks on South Weighed," *New York Times,* June 25, 1960, 18; Arthur Schlesinger Jr., *Robert Kennedy and His Times* (Boston: Houghton Mifflin, 1978), 215.

43. Cleveland Sellers, *River of No Return: The Autobiography of a Black Militant and the Life and Death of SNCC* (Jackson: University Press of Mississippi, 1990), 40–41.

44. White, *Making of the President*, 154–156.

45. Anthony Lewis, "The Civil Rights Plank," *New York Times,* July 20, 1960, 20.

46. Irving Bernstein, *Promises Kept: John F. Kennedy's New Frontier* (New York: Oxford University Press, 1991), 26–27.

47. William Blair, "Southern Democrats Will Fight Any 'Sting' in Civil Rights Plank," *New York Times,* July 7, 1960, 16; William Blair, "South Asks Curb on Civil Rights Plank," *New York Times,* July 8, 1960, 1; "Demand Demos Oust Bigots; Ten Point Rights Plank Also Asked," *Chicago Defender,* July 16, 1960, 1. Sellers, *River of No Return,* 40–41.

48. Blair, "South Asks Curb on Civil Rights Plank."

49. Wofford, *Of Kennedys and Kings,* 51–52.

50. Wofford, *Of Kennedys and Kings,* 52; Schlesinger, *Robert Kennedy,* 205, 215–216; Anthony Lewis, "The Civil Rights Plank: Tougher Line Signals Major Shift in the Democratic Party," *New York Times,* July 20, 1960, 20.

51. Lewis, "The Civil Rights Plank."

52. Claude Sitton, "10 Southern States Wage Bitter Fight," *New York Times,* July 13, 1960, 1; "Analysis of 1960 Democratic platform by Strom Thurmond," box 204, Howard Worth Smith Papers, University of Virginia; W. H. Lawrence, "South—the Loser," *New York Times,* July 13, 1960, 1; Clayton Knowles, "Wilkins Defends Plank on Rights," *New York Times,* July 18, 1960, 11; "Hails Demos Plank," *Chicago Defender,* July 23, 1960, 1; Louis Martin, "Dope and Data," *Chicago Defender,* July 23, 1960, 10.

53. Russell Baker, "Rivals Smashed Trying to Resist: Favorite Sons Impotent," *New York Times,* July 15, 1960, 9; White, *Making of the President,* 155–158.

54. Schlesinger *Robert Kennedy,* 206–211.

55. Claude Sitton, "Johnson Choice Hailed by the South," *New York Times,* July 15, 1960, 8; James Reston, "Johnson—Key to Unity," *New York Times,* July 16, 1960, 2; Arthur Krock, "The Kennedy Machine," *New York Times,* July 17, 1960, 141; W. H. Lawrence, "Kennedy Takes Control," *New York Times,* July 18, 1960, 12; William Nunn, "Driver Seat Belongs to Negro," *Pittsburgh Courier,* July 23, 1960, 8; "Democratic Party Is Rejuvenated," *Chicago Defender,* July 23, 1960, 10.

4 · BLACK VOTES

1. Theodore White, *The Making of the President, 1960* (New York: Harper Perennial Political Classics, 2009), 203–204.

2. "Statement of Senator John F. Kennedy on Civil Rights Section," Hyannis, MA, August 2, 1960; Gerald Peters and John T. Woolley, *The American Presidency Project,* https://www.presidency.ucsb.edu/documents/statement-senator-john-f-kennedy-civil-rights-section-hyannis-ma.

3. Joseph A. Loftus, "Nominees Appeal for Negro Votes," *New York Times,* July 16, 1960, 1; "Re Civil Rights Section," memo to RFK, n.d.

4. "Statement of Senator John F. Kennedy on Civil Rights Section"; Marjorie McKenzie Lawson, interview by Ronald J. Grele, November 14, 1965, JFKOH.

5. Oliver W. Hill, interview by Larry J. Hackman, February 29, 1968, JFKOH; Alex Poinsett, *Walking with Presidents: Louis Martin and the Rise of Black Political Power* (New York: Madison Books, 1997), 62–65, 68; *Amsterdam News,* November 19, 1960, 11.

6. Poinsett, *Walking with Presidents,* 65.

7. Louis Martin, interview by Ronald Grele, March 14, 1966, JFKOH.

8. Martin interview; Robert Kennedy, interview by Anthony Lewis, in *Robert Kennedy in His Own Words: The Unpublished Recollections of the Kennedy Years,* ed. Edwin O. Guthman and Jeffrey Shulman (New York: Bantam, 1988), 72.

9. "Dixie Ready to Bolt Democrats," *Chicago Defender,* July 19, 1960, 3; Harry Truman to Howard W. Smith, October 5, 1960, Howard Worth Smith Papers, MSS 8731, box 204 (hereafter cited as "HWS Papers"), Special Collections, The University of Virginia Library, Charlottesville, VA; Tom Wicker, "Southern Group Greets Kennedy," *New York Times,* August 20, 1960, 9; "Kennedy Gains Support," *New York Times,* August 14, 1960, 50; Claude Sitton, "Dems Block Bolt in Louisiana," *New York Times* August 12, 1960, 1; Claude Sitton, "SC in Kennedy Shift," *New York Times,* August 15, 1960, 14; "Kennedy Backed in Alabama," *New York Times,* August 13, 1960, 12.

10. "The Barry Show," WMCA, New York, August 24, 1960, transcript, box 256, Harry F. Byrd Papers, Special Collections, University of Virginia Library; RFK to Howard Worth Smith, September 1, 1960, MS 8731, box 204, HWS Papers.

11. Howard W. Smith to RFK, September 9, 1960, MS 8731, box 204, HWS Papers.

12. Howard W. Smith to "Dear Colleague," September 26, 1960; Harry Dent for Strom Thurmond to Howard Smith, September 30, 1960; William Tuck to Howard Smith, n.d.; Lewis Powell to Clifford Miller, September 19, 1950; *Florida News and Sun Sentinel,* September 4, 1960, box 204, HWS Papers.

13. Scott I. Peek, oral history interview, January 13, 1992, Senate Historical Office, Washington, DC; *Savannah Morning News Index,* 1960.

14. Laura Visser-Maessen, *Robert Parris Moses: A Life in Civil Rights Leadership at the Grassroots* (Chapel Hill: University of North Carolina Press, 2016), 10–33.

15. Visser-Maessen, *Robert Parris Moses,* 33–48; Robert Moses, interview by author, July 25, 2016.

16. Visser-Maessen, *Robert Parris Moses,* 48–59.

17. John Doar, interview by author, September 5, 2008; John Doar, interview by Brian Lamb, January 25, 2009, C-SPAN, uncorrected transcript, 9–10.

18. Doar interview, January 25, 2009; John Doar, "The Work of the Civil Rights Division in Enforcing Voting Rights under the Civil Rights Acts of 1957 and 1960," *Florida State University Law Review* (Fall 1997), 1–2.

19. Sullivan, *Lift Every Voice,* 237–242; Doar interview, September 4, 2008.

20. Doar interview, September 4, 2008; Doar interview, January 25, 2009, 8; "Negro Evictions Stayed by Courts," *New York Times,* December 31, 1960, 1.

21. Martin Luther King Jr., interview by Berl Bernhard, March 9, 1964, JFKOH.

22. Harris Wofford, *Of Kennedys and Kings: Making Sense of the Sixties* (New York: Farrar, Straus, Giroux, 1980), 62.

23. Martin interview, March 14, 1966; "Select Judges on Merit," *Chicago Defender,* September 24, 1960, 1; *Chicago Defender,* October 29, 1960, 3.

24. Transcript of JFK's speech, Howard University, October 7, 1960, Senate speech file, Prepresidential papers, JFKL; *Washington Post,* October 8, 1960, A2; *Chicago Defender,* October 10, 1960, A5; *New York Times,* October 8, 1960, 12.

25. Wofford, *Of Kennedy and Kings,* 63–64; Martin interview, March 14, 1966; *New York Times,* October 13, 1960, 23.

26. Editorial, *Amsterdam News,* October 15, 1960, 10; James Booker, "Kennedy Promises Rights Bill," *Amsterdam News,* October 15, 1960, 1; Martin interview, March 14, 1966.

27. *Chicago Defender,* October 11, 1960, 1; Louis Martin, "Baptist Leader Taylor Backs Kennedy Ticket," *Chicago Defender,* October 20, 1960, 4. "Taylor Backs Kennedy," *Amsterdam News,* October 22, 1960, 1.

28. Taylor Branch, *Parting the Waters: America in the King Years, 1954–63* (New York: Simon & Schuster, 1989), 344–359; Martin Luther King Jr. interview, March 9, 1964.

29. Clifford M. Kuhn, "'There's a Footnote to History!' Memory and the History of Martin Luther King's October Arrest and Its Aftermath," *Journal of American History* 84, no. 2 (September 1997), 583–595.

30. Wofford, *Of Kennedys and Kings,* 11–19; Ernest Vandiver, interview by John F. Stewart, May 22, 1967, JFKOH.

31. Louis E. Martin, interview by Ronald J. Grele, April 7, 1966, 49–51; Wofford, *Of Kennedy and Kings,* 19–20.

32. Vandiver interview.

33. Wofford, *Of Kennedy and Kings,* 21; Martin interview, April 7, 1966, 51; RFK, interview by Anthony Lewis, December 4, 1964, JFKOH.

34. Wofford, *Of Kennedy and Kings,* 22; Martin Luther King Jr., interview by Berl Bernhard, March 9, 1964, JFKOH.

35. Richard Nixon, Columbia, SC, November 3, 1964, transcript; Thurgood Marshall, interview by Berl Bernhard, April 7, 1964, JFKOH.

36. Wofford, *Of Kennedys and Kings,* 23.

37. Wofford, *Of Kennedys and Kings,* 24–25; Martin interview, April 7, 1966, 52–53.

38. Thomas Oliphant and Curtis Wilkie, *The Road to Camelot: Inside JFK's Five Year Campaign* (New York: Simon and Schuster, 2017), 361–362; White, *Making of the President, 1960,* 354; "Admit Negro Vote for Jack Whipped Nixon," *Chicago Defender,* November 10, 1960, 1, 3; Paul von Hippel, "Here's a Voter Fraud Myth: Richard Daley 'Stole' Illinois for John Kennedy in the 1960 Election," *Washington Post,* August 8, 2017.

39. *Amsterdam News,* November 19, 1960, 11.

5 · SIMPLE JUSTICE

1. John Doar, comments on the Fiftieth Anniversary of the Installation of Robert Kennedy as Attorney General, C-SPAN, January 20, 2011; "U.S. Accuses 11 in Louisiana of Coercing a Negro Witness," *New York Times,* January 20, 1961; "U.S. Files Voter Suit in Louisiana," *Washington Post,* April 29, 1961, A4. The case was *U.S. v. Deal.*

2. John Doar, interview by Brian Lamb, January 25, 2009, C-SPAN, transcript, 17; "Rights Action Won by Louisiana Negro," *New York Times,* February 4, 1961, 9; "Bob Kennedy Serves Notice," *Baltimore Afro American,* February 14, 1961.

3. Robert Cohen, "'Two, Four, Six, Eight We Don't Want to Integrate': White Student Attitudes toward the University of Georgia's Desegregation," *Georgia Historical Quarterly* (Fall 1996), 616–618; Claude Sitton, "U.S. Judge Weighs Georgia U. Action," *New York Times,* January 13, 1961, 1.

4. Harris Wofford, *Of Kennedys and Kings: Making Sense of the Sixties* (New York: Farrar, Strause, Giroux, 1980), 136; Simeon Booker, *Shocking the Conscience: A Reporter's Account of the Civil Rights Movement* (Oxford: University of Mississippi Press, 2013), 182.

5. John Seigenthaler, interview by Ronald J. Grele, , February 22, 1966, 320–326, JFKOH.

6. Nicholas Katzenback, *Some of It Was Fun: Working with RFK and LBJ* (New York: W. W. Norton, 2008), 22; Arthur Schlesinger Jr., *Robert Kennedy and His Times* (Boston: Houghton Mifflin Company, 1978), 233–236; Alexander M. Bickel, "Robert F. Kennedy: The Case against Him for Attorney General," *New Republic,* January 9, 1961, 15–19; JFK quoted in Peter Maas, "Robert Kennedy Speaks Out," *Look,* March 28, 1961, 23.

7. Schlesinger, *Robert Kennedy,* 338–339; John Seigenthaler interview, by Ronald J. Grele, February 23, 1966.

8. Meyer to Parker, "Patterson Cover-Kennedy I," May 25, 1961, dispatches from *Time* magazine correspondents, second series, 1956–1968, Ms Am 2090.1, Houghton Library, Harvard University; Katzenbach, *Some of It Was Fun,* 28–32.

9. Maas, "Robert Kennedy Speaks Out," 24.

10. Maas, "Robert Kennedy Speaks Out," 24; Katzenbach, *Some of It Was Fun,* 28.

11. Richard Goodwin, *Remembering America: A Voice from the Sixties* (Boston: Little, Brown, 1988), 4–5.

12. Robert Manning, "'Someone the President Can Talk To': Brother Bob the Attorney General Makes the Loneliest Job Far Less Lonely," *New York Times,* May 28, 1961, SM22.

13. Seigenthaler interview, February 23, 1966, 490–491, JFKOH; *New York Times,* May 28, 1961; Wofford, *Of Kennedys and Kings,* 141; Robert Kennedy to Dean Edward Hirsch Levi, May 4, 1961, University of Chicago Library; copies of 131 letters to law school deans, written May 2–8, 1961, box 24, Papers of Robert Kennedy, Attorney General Papers, JFKL.

14. Wofford, *Of Kennedys and Kings,* 141–142; Peter Braestrup, "U.S. Opens Drive to Hire Negroes," *New York Times,* March 13, 1961, 11.

15. Carroll Kirkpatrick, "President to End Job Color Bar," *Washington Post,* March 7, 1961, A1; Roscoe Drummond, "A Tough Job for LBJ," *Washington Post,* March 12, 1961, E5; "Opportunity by Order," *Washington Post,* March 8, 1961, A14; Wofford, *Of Kennedys and Kings,* 141–142.

16. "Senate Confirms Choice of Weaver," *New York Times,* February 10, 1961, 14; "Negro is Chosen as U.S. Attorney," *New York Times,* April 16, 1961, 68; Wofford, *Of Kennedys and Kings,* 144; Chamberlin to Parker, "Discrimination in Washington, III," April 13, 1961, dispatches from *Time* magazine correspondents.

17. Alvin Shuster, "Civil War Centennial Rebuffs Kennedy's Desegregation Plea," *New York Times,* March 22, 1961, 1; "President Tells Civil War Unit Not to Hold Segregated Meeting," *New York Times,* March 24, 1961, 1; "Civil War Parley Bows to Kennedy," *New York Times,* March 26, 1961, 1; Wofford, *Of Kennedys and Kings,* 148–149.

18. Wofford, *Of Kennedys and Kings,* 144–145.

19. Wofford, *Of Kennedys and Kings,* 145–148.

20. Elizabeth Singer More, *Report of the President's Commission on the Status of Women: Background, Content, Significance,* https://www.radcliffe.harvard.edu/sites/default/files/documents/report_of_the_presidents _commission_on_the_status_of_women_background_content_significance.pdf.

21. Wofford, *Of Kennedy and Kings,* 93–94; "Marshall Is New to Civil Rights Field," *Washington Post,* February 3, 1961, A5; "Burke Marshall, a Key Strategist of Civil Rights Policy, Dies," *New York Times,* June 3, 2003.

22. Owen Fiss, *Pillars of Justice: Lawyers and the Liberal Tradition* (Cambridge, MA: Harvard University Press, 2017), 65; Burke Marshall to Mrs. Sidney Barnett, April 20, 1961, Chronological Files, 1961–1965, Burke Marshall Papers, JFKL; Victor Navasky, *Kennedy Justice* (New York: Atheneum, 1971), 98.

23. Katzenbach, *Some of It Was Fun,* 40.

24. Marshall to Richard Goodwin, February 15, 1961, Burke Marshall Papers.

25. "Justice Aides Meet on Rights Problems," *New York Times,* February 14, 1961, 33; Burke Marshall, interview by Anthony Lewis, June 13, 1964, JFKOH; Marshall memo to attorney general, February 13, 1961; press release, February 13, 1961, Burke Marshall Papers; Meyer to Jones, "Louisiana Integration, based on an interview with Attorney General Bob Kennedy, February 23, 1961, dispatches from *Time* magazine correspondents; James E. Clayton, "The School Crisis," *Washington Post,* February 18, 1961.

26. Meyer to Jones, "Louisiana Integration"; Brian Lee, "A Matter of National Concern: The Kennedy Administration and Prince Edward County" (PhD diss., Virginia Commonwealth University, 2009), 72, 79; Marshall to attorney general, February 28, 1961, box 1, Burke Marshall Papers; *Time,* April 24, 1961; *Time,* August 31, 1961; *Washington Post,* April 28, 1961, A1. Later that summer, a three-judge federal court declared the closure of public schools in St. Helena Parish unconstitutional.

27. Marshall to attorney general, February 28, 1961; Anthony Lewis, "President Hails Louisiana Drive for Integration," February 26, 1961, 1; "Text of Rights Telegram," *New York Times,* February 26, 1961, 43; *Washington Post,* April 28, 1961, 1.

28. Marshall to Albertis Harris, April 19, 1961; Lee, "A Matter of National Concern," 85–86; Anthony Lewis, "U.S. Sues to Force Virginia County to Open Schools," April 27, 1961, 1.

29. Lee, "A Matter of National Concern," 85–90.

30. "Hopeful Prince Edward County Children Visit D.C.," *Washington Post,* April 29, 1961, A4; editorial, *New York Times,* April 30, 1961, 30; Lee, "A Matter of National Concern," 87.

31. Jean White, "Almond Sets Meeting on School Suit: Sen. Byrd Blasts Kennedy Move on Prince Edward," *Washington Post,* April 28, 1961, 1; Carole Bowie and Jean White, "School Compromise Hinted by Almond," *Washington Post,* April 29, 1961, 1; Elsie Carper, "Stiffer Resistance to School Opening Predicted in Prince Edward County Today, *Washington Post,* May 2, 1961, B1; Elsie Carper, "Edward School Issue Free of Politics; Almond Decries U.S. Intervention," May 4, 1961, B1.

32. Elsie Carper, "New Edward School Battle Opens in Court: Government, State and County Present Arguments in Richmond," *Washington Post,* May 9, 1961, B1; James E. Clayton, "Edward School Case Intervention is Denied," *Washington Post,* June 15, 1961, A1; address by Honorable Robert F. Kennedy . . . to the University of South Carolina Chapter of the American Association of University Professors, Columbia, SC, April 25, 1963.

33. Lyles Glenn, interview with the author, May 9, 2012; Ernest Finney, interview with the author, May 6, 2014.

34. Marshall interview, June 13, 1964; Seigenthaler interview, February 22, 1966; Marshall, memo to Byron White, June 30, 1961, BM Papers; Reed Barrett to Burke Marshall, August 11, 1961, Desegregation, General 1961, Burke Marshall Papers; Calvin Trillin, "Desegregation Process," September 12, 1961, dispatches from *Time* magazine correspondents.

35. Drew Pearson, "Bob Kennedy's Quiet Revolution," *Washington Post,* March 23, 1961, B17; "In Pursuit of Justice," editorial, *Washington Post,* April 23, 1961, E4; Anthony Lewis, "Action on Civil Rights," *New York Times,* April 30, 1961, E7; Trillin, "Desegregation Process."

36. Atlanta Bureau to Norris, "The Hard Rule of Law," March 29, 1961; Fentress to Norris, "Education," March 29, 1961; dispatches from *Time* magazine correspondents.

37. Dispatches from *Time* magazine correspondents, March 28–30, 1961, submitted by Latimer, McDonald, Whitt, Brown, Fentress, Gibson, Trillin, Rutherford.

38. "Robert Kennedy Sees U.S. in Back of New Civil Rights Bill," *Washington Post,* April 4, 1963, A2; John Doar, "Introduction," in Robert F. Kennedy Jr., *Frank M. Johnson: A Biography* (New York: Putnam, 1978), 12–13; Robert J. Norrell, *Reaping the Whirlwind: The Civil Rights Movement in Tuskegee* (New York: Knopf, 1985), 118–124.

39. Doar, "Introduction," 13–14; Norrell, *Reaping the Whirlwind,* 124–125.

40. Norrell, *Reaping the Whirlwind,* 125–126; John Doar, "The Work of the Civil Rights Division in Enforcing Voting Rights under the Civil Rights Acts of 1957 and 1960," *Florida State University Law Review* (Fall 1997), 2–3; Anthony Lewis, "US Wins Round on Negro Vote," *New York Times,* April 2, 1961, E6.

41. Doar, "The Work of the Civil Rights Division," 3–4; Meyers, February 9, 1962, dispatches from *Time* magazine correspondents.

42. Doar, "The Work of the Civil Rights Division," 4. Thurgood Marshall, interview by Berl Bernhard, April 7, 1964, JFKOH.

43. John Doar and Dorothy Landsberg, "The Performance of the FBI in Investigation Violations of Federal Laws Protecting the Right to Vote, 1960–67" (unpublished article, 1971), 7–8; "U.S. Sues Alabama over Negro Votes," *New York Times,* April 14, 1961, 21; "U.S. Files Voter Suit in Louisiana," *Washington Post,* April 29, 1961, A4; Doar, "The Work of the Civil Rights Division," 4.

44. John Seigenthaler, comments on Fiftieth Anniversary of the Installation of Robert F. Kennedy as Attorney General, January 20, 2011, C-SPAN.

45. Seigenthaler comments, January 20, 2011; James E. Clayton, "U.S. Vows Firm Fight on Rights," May 7, 1961, A1; Charlayne Hunter Gault, *In My Place* (New York: Farrar Straus Giroux, 1992), 208–209.

46. Reg Murphy, "Robert Kennedy Was Nice but Firm in His Athens Speech," *Atlanta Constitution,* May 8, 1961, 5; Douglas Kiker, "Bob Kennedy Vows Speed in School Edict, *Atlanta Constitution,* May 7, 1961, p. 1; Hunter Gault, *In My Place,* 209; Robert Kennedy, Law Day address, University of Georgia Law School, Athens, GA, May 6, 1961.

47. Robert Kennedy, Law Day address.

48. Hunter Gault, *In My Place,* 211.

49. Booker, *Shocking the Conscience,* 182, 184.

50. Raymond Arsenault, *Freedom Riders: 1961 and the Struggle for Racial Justice* (New York: Oxford University Press, 2006), 121–122; Booker, *Shocking the Conscience,* 188–89.

51. Wofford, *Of Kennedys and Kings,* 152.

52. Booker, *Shocking the Conscience,* 198.

53. Meyers to Parker, Bob Kennedy II, May 18, 1961, dispatches from *Time* magazine correspondents; Robert Kennedy and Burke Marshall, interview by Anthony Lewis, December 6, 1964, JFKOH; Seigenthaler interview, February 22, 1966, JFKOH; Booker, *Shocking the Conscience*, 198.

54. Burke Marshall interview, June 13, 1964; Seigenthaler interview, February 22, 1966; Arsenault, *Freedom Riders*, 181.

55. Katzenbach, *Some of It Was Fun*, 44; Arsenault, *Freedom Riders*, 189–190; Louis Oberdorfer, interviewed by Charles T. Morrissey, December 18, 1964, JFKOH.

56. Burke Marshall, interview by Louis Oberdorfer, May 29, 1964, JFKOH.

57. Marshall interview, May 29, 1964.

58. Seigenthaler interview, February 22, 1966; Marshall interview, May 29, 1964,

59. Arsenault, *Freedom Riders*, 209–215.

60. Aresenault, *Freedom Riders*, 215; Seigenthaler interview, February 22, 1966.

61. Arsenault, *Freedom Riders*, 220–227.

62. Arsenault, *Freedom Riders*, 232–235.

63. Aresenault, *Freedom Riders*, 233–236.

64. Aresenault, *Freedom Riders*, 239–242; Kennedy/Marshall interview, December 6, 1964

65. John Doar, interview by Anthony Lewis, November 13, 1964, JFKOH; Arsenault, *Freedom Riders*, 246–247.

66. Edwin O. Guthman and Jeffrey Shulman, eds., *Robert Kennedy In His Own Words: The Unpublished Recollections of the Kennedy Year*, (New York: Bantam, 1988), 96–98; Arsenault, Freedom Riders, 254–257.

67. Calvin Trillin, "Freedom Riders Take II," May 25, 1961, dispatches from *Time* magazine correspondents; Burke Marshall, *Federalism and Civil Rights* (New York: Columbia University, 1964), 68–71.

68. "Robert Kennedy Asks ICC to End Bus Discrimination," *New York Times*, May 30, 1961, 1; "Excerpts from Bus Petition to ICC," *New York Times*, May 30, 1961, 7; Robert McNamara to RFK, June 21, 1961, General Records of the Department of Justice: Civil Rights Division, Subject Files of Assistant AG Burke Marshall, National Archives, box 76; Burke Marshall interview with Anthony Lewis, June 13, 1964; Joseph A. Loftus, "ICC Orders End of Racial Curbs on Bus Travelers," *New York Times*, September 23, 1961, 1; "Integration on Buses," editorial, *New York Times*, September 24, 1961, E10.

69. Meyers to Parker, "Patterson Cover—Kennedy—I," May 25, 1961, dispatches from *Time* magazine correspondents.

70. James Carroll, *Crusade: Chronicles of an Unjust War* (New York: Metropolitan Books, 2004), 49.

71. James Baldwin, interview by Studs Terkel, July 15, 1961; Carroll, *Crusade*, 49.

6 · THE CHALLENGE OF A DECADE

1. Edwin Guthman, *We Band of Brothers* (New York: Harper & Row, 1964), 226–217; Arthur Schlesinger Jr., *Robert Kennedy and His Times* (Boston: Houghton Mifflin Company, 1978), 409–410; *Washington Post*, March 9, 1961, A1.

2. Eve Edstrom, "Guidance Centers Sought for Juvenile Offenders: Counseling Planned," *Washington Post*, March 7, 1961, A2.

3. Peter Edelman, *Searching for America's Heart: RFK and the Renewal of Hope* (Washington, DC: Georgetown University Press, 2003), 34; Richard Boone, interview by Robert Korstad, Southern Rural Poverty Collection, DeWitt Center for Media and Democracy, Duke University, Durham, NC; Michael L. Gillette, *Launching the War on Poverty: An Oral History* (New York: Twayne Publishers, 1996), 18.

4. Peter Maas, "Robert Kennedy Speaks Out . . . ," *Look*, March 28, 1961, 24; Edelman, *Searching for America's Heart*, 34; "Kennedy and Ribicoff Letters on Youth Problems," *Washington Post*, May 10, 1961, A 4; address by Honorable Robert F. Kennedy, Attorney General of the United States, prepared for delivery at the National Committee for Children and Youth Conference of the Unemployed, Out of School Youth in Urban Areas, Washington, DC, May 24, 1961.

5. Schlesinger, *Robert Kennedy*, 409–412.

6. Richard Boone, interview by Robert Korstad, 1992, Southern Rural Poverty Collection, DeWitt Wallace Center for Media and Democracy, Duke University, Durham, NC, 4; Michael L. Gillette, *Launching the War on Poverty: An Oral History* (New York: Twayne Publishers, 1996), 18.

7. Eve Edstrom, "Delinquency Plan Sent to Congress," *Washington Post*, May 12, 1962, A1; Marjorie Hunter, "Congress Passes Delinquency Bill," *New York Times*, September 13, 1961, 30; "Federal Experiment Aims to Aid Juveniles," *Washington Post*, September 17, 1961, A5.

8. Edelman, *Searching for America's Heart*, 34.

9. David Hackett, interview by John W. Douglas, October 21, 1970, RFKOH. Schlesinger, *Robert Kennedy*, 411. Pilot programs were established in New York (Harlem); Cleveland; Minneapolis; Philadelphia; Chicago; St. Louis; Charleston, WV; Syracuse; Houston; Detroit; Providence; Los Angeles; Washington, DC; Lane County, Oregon; and Boston. See "Counter-Attack on Delinquency: The Program of

the Federal Government to Stimulate Communities to Develop National Answers to a Growing Crisis," prepared by the President's Committee on Juvenile Delinquency and Youth Crime, August 8, 1963, box 95, Papers of Robert F. Kennedy, Attorney General Papers, JFKL.

10. David Garrow, *Bearing the Cross: Martin Luther King Jr., and the Southern Christian Leadership Conference* (New York: William Morrow and Company, Inc., 1986), 173–180.

11. Garrow, *Bearing the Cross,* 180–187.

12. Robert Shelton, "Songs as a Weapon in Rights Battle," *New York Times,* August 20, 1962, 1; Garrow, *Bearing the Cross,* 183.

13. Garrow, *Bearing the Cross,* 209; "Determined Police Chief: Laurie Pritchett," *New York Times,* July 23, 1962, 13; Claude Sitton, "President Chided Over Albany, GA," *New York Times,* November 15, 1962, 1.

14. Burke Marshall, interview by Anthony Lewis, June 13, 1964, JFKOH.

15. Marshall interview, June 13, 1964; John W. Finney, "Kennedy Accepts Monitoring by Each Nation," *New York Times,* August 2, 1962, 1; "Transcript of President's News Conference," *Washington Post,* August 2, 1962, A2.

16. Garrow, *Bearing the Cross,* 205–207; Claude Sitton, "Dr. King Denounces U.S. Judge for Ban on GA Protest," *New York Times,* July 23, 1962, 1; "Negro Leaders Discuss Protests in Georgia with Robert Kennedy," *New York Times,* August 4, 1962, 11.

17. Hedrick Smith, "U.S. Intervenes on Negroes' Side in GA Case," *New York Times,* August 9, 1962, 1.

18. Garrow, *Bearing the Cross,* 215–219.

19. Martin Luther King Jr., "A Bold Design for a New South," *Nation,* March 30, 1963; Garrow, *Bearing the Cross,* 271; Burke Marshall, interview with Anthony Lewis, June 14, 1964, JFKOH, 69; Burke Marshall, interview with Larry J. Hackman, June 17–19, 1970, 45, RFKOH.

20. Garrow, *Bearing the Cross,* 217; Robert Kennedy, interview by Anthony Lewis, December 4, 1964, 394–395.

21. Kennedy interview, December 4, 1964.

22. Robert E. Gilbert, "John F. Kennedy and Civil Rights for Black Americans, *Presidential Studies Quarterly* (Summer 1982), 390; David A. Nichols, *A Matter of Justice: Eisenhower and the Beginning of the Civil Rights Revolution* (New York: Simon & Schuster, 2007), 83; Marshall interview, June 4, 1964, 86–88. The other three segregationist judges were Elmer Gordon West of Louisiana, Griffin B. Bell of Georgia, and Walter P. Gerwin to the Fifth Circuit.

23. "Eloquent Federal Judge: James Robert Elliott," *New York Times,* July 31, 1962, 17; Marshall interview, June 14, 1964, 91–93.

24. Marshall interview, June 14, 1964, 88–90.

25. Kennedy interview, December 4, 1964, 402, 406.

26. Kennedy interview, December 4, 1964, 406.

27. John Doar, "Burke Marshall Memorial," *Yale Law Journal* (January 2004), 791–795; John Doar, "The Work of the Civil Rights Division in Enforcing Voting Rights under the Civil Rights Acts of 1957 and 1960," *Florida State University Law Review* (Fall 1997): 3–4.

28. Robert P. Moses, interview with author, December 7, 2008; David Garrow, *Protest at Selma: Martin Luther King and the Voting Rights Act of 1965* (New Haven, CT: Yale University Press, 1978), 9–10; Burke Marshall, *Federalism and Civil Rights* (New York: Columbia University Press), 17.

29. Mark Lowry III, "Population and Race in Mississippi, 1940–1960," *Annals of the Association of American Geographers* 61, no. 3 (September 1971), 576–577; Burke Marshall to director, FBI, April 4, 1961, University of Mississippi file, Burke Marshall papers; Burke Marshall to attorney general, May 13, 1961; John Doar to Andrew Oehmann, August 1, 1961, box 8, John Doar Papers, Mudd Manuscript Library, Princeton University, Princeton, NJ.

30. Moses interview, December 7, 2008; Laura Visser-Maessen, *Robert Parris Moses: A Life in Civil Rights Leadership at the Grassroots* (Chapel Hill: University of North Carolina Press, 2016), 67; John Dittmer, *Local People: The Struggle for Civil Rights in Mississippi* (Urbana: University of Illinois Press, 1995), 104–105.

31. Dittmer, *Local People,* 104–106; Visser-Maessen, *Robert Parris Moses,* 64, 70–72; John Doar and Dorothy Landsberg, "The Performance of the FBI in Investigation Violations of Federal Laws Protecting the Right to Vote, 1960–67" (unpublished article, 1971), 35.

32. *United States of America, Appellant, v. John Q. Wood, et. al., Appellees,* 295 F.2d 772 (5th Cir. 1961); Doar and Landsberg, "The Performance of the FBI," 37

33. Doar and Landsberg, "The Performance of the FBI," 34–37; Visser-Maessen, *Robert Parris Moses,* 75–76.

34. Taylor Branch, *Parting the Waters: America in the King Years, 1954–1963* (New York: Simon & Schuster, 1988), 508–509.

35. Robert Moses notebook, box 24, John Doar Papers; Dittmer, *Local People,* 106–110; Visser-Maessen, *Robert Parris Moses,* 74–80.

36. Burke Marshall to Robert Kennedy, May 13, 1961, box 8, John Doar Papers; Doar, "Burke Marshall Memorial."

37. Dittmer, *Local People*, 109, 215. Burke Marshall to FBI director re. Lewis Allen, August 22, 1962; Gordon Martin to John Doar, October 2, 1962; Burke Marshall to FBI director, October 9, 1962, box 24, John Doar Papers.

38. Thelton Henderson, interview by author, December 2, 2014. As the only Black attorney working for the Justice Department in the South, Thelton Henderson soon became what he described as a kind of "free-lance" lawyer, with Burke Marshall assigning him to movement trouble spots. Consequently, he became well-acquainted with Martin Luther King Jr., Medgar Evers, and various SNCC leaders, making it increasingly difficult for him to maintain a professional distance from the movement. He ultimately left his position in the fall of 1963.

39. John Doar to Harry Golden, November 6, 1963, NB 2, box 87, John Doar Papers; Marshall, *Federalism and Civil Rights*, 32–34; David Garrow, *Protest at Selma: Martin Luther King Jr. and the Voting Rights Act of 1965*, (New Haven, CT: Yale University Press), 31.

40. Marshall, *Federalism and Civil Rights*, 27–28; "A Report on the Progress in the Field of Civil Rights by Attorney General Robert F. Kennedy to the President," January 24, 1963, https://www.justice.gov/sites/default/files/ag/legacy/2011/01/20/01-24-1963.pdf.

41. Irving Spiegel, "Robert Kennedy Asks Vote Equity," *New York Times*, May 6, 1962, 75; Marshall interview, June 13, 1964.

42. Anthony Lewis, "Robert Kennedy Warns on Rights," *New York Times*, March 16, 1962, 1; "The Literacy Bill," *New York Times*, March 22, 1962, 34.

43. Anthony Lewis, "Robert Kennedy Debates Ervin on Literacy Tests," *New York Times*, April 11, 1962.

44. Lewis, "Robert Kennedy Debates Ervin"; James Clayton, "Rights Program Literacy Test is Argued at Hearing," *Washington Post*, April 11, 1962, A2; "Senate Factions Turn Up Heat on CR Fight," *Chicago Defender*, May 8, 1962, 19; Robert Albright, "Senate Fails in Second Move for Cloture," *Washington Post*, May 15, 1962, A1; Miller, "Exit 87th Congress," dispatches from *Time* magazine correspondents, October 5, 1962.

45. Lewis, "Robert Kennedy Debates Ervin."

46. Clayton, "Rights Program Literacy Test Is Argued at Hearing."

47. Irving Spiegel, "Robert Kennedy Asks Vote Equity," *New York Times*, May 6, 1962, 75; Marshall interview, June 13, 1964.

48. Anthony Lewis, "Civil Right Fight Opens in Senate," *New York Times*, April 26, 1962, 1; Robert Albright, "Literacy Fight Ends First Week in the Senate," *Washington Post*, April 28, 1962, A2.

49. James E. Clayton, "Robert Kennedy Prods Virginians," *Washington Post*, May 3, 1962, D1; address by Attorney General Robert F. Kennedy at the Law Day Ceremonies of the Virginia State Bar, May 1, 1962.

50. Clayton, "Robert Kennedy Prods Virginians"; Spiegel, "Robert Kennedy Asks Vote Equity."

51. Wallace Terry, "Clergy Cited for Inaction in Bias Fight," *Washington Post*, May 20, 1962, A1; Peter Braestrup, "Clergy's Stand on Bias Deplored," *New York Times*, May 20, 2019, 58; "JFK Action on Civil Rights Lacking, says MLK," *Washington Post*, April 10, 1962, A13.

52. "The Right to Vote," *Chicago Defender*, May 7, 1962, 11; "The Right to Vote," editorial, *Washington Post*, May 7, 1962, A18; "Hit Segregated Voting Machines," *Chicago Defender*, May 17, 1962, 3; "Judge Orders Integration of Georgia Voting Places," *Chicago Defender*, June 5, 1962, 18.

53. Burke Marshall, memorandum for the attorney general, December 21, 1961, John Doar Papers; Garrow, *Protest at Selma*, 27–28; Marshall, *Federalism and Civil Rights*, 25–28, 32; Claude Sitton, "Sheriff Harasses Negroes at Voting Rally in Georgia," *New York Times*, July 27, 1962, 1; Gene Roberts and Hank Klibernoff, *The Race Beat: The Press, the Civil Rights Struggle and the Awakening of a Nation* (New York: Vintage, 2007), 265–266.

54. "Chronology of Events, May 1961–October 1962," Burke Marshall Papers, https://www.jfklibrary.org/asset-viewer/archives/BMPP/019/BMPP-019-004?image_identifier=BMPP-019-004-p0001; "Defiant Dixie Governor: Ross Robert Barnett," *New York Times*, September 20, 1962, 27; Claude Sitton, "Barnett Defiant," *New York Times*, September 25, 1962, 1; Marshall interview, June 14, 1964, 71–72.

55. Edwin O. Guthman and Jeffrey Shulman, eds., *Robert Kennedy in His Own Words: The Unpublished Recollections of the Kennedy Years* (New York: Bantam, 1988), 161; Claude Sitton, "200 Policemen with Clubs Ring Campus to Bar Negro," *New York Times*, September 28, 1961, 1; Marshall interview, June 14, 1964, 72–76.

56. "Telephone conversation between Attorney General Robert Kennedy and Governor Ross Barnett ," September 30, 1962, American Radio Works, American Public Media. http://americanradioworks.publicradio.org/features/prestapes/rfk_tw_bm_093062.html; Nicholas Katzenbach, *Some of It Was Fun: Working with RFK and LBJ* (New York: W. W. Norton, 2008), 74–75.

57. John F. Kennedy, "Radio and Television Address on the Situation at the University of Mississippi," September 30, 1962, White House Audio Collection, JFKWHA-132-002, JFKL.

58. Katzenbach, *Some of It Was Fun*, 75–76; Claude Sitton, "Negro at Mississippi U as Barnet Yields," *New York Times*, October 1, 1962, 1.

59. Katzenbach, *Some of It Was Fun*, 75–79; Sitton, "Negro at Mississippi U as Barnett Yields"; Claude Sitton, "Shots Quell Mob," *New York Times*, October 2, 1962, 1; Marshall interview, June 14, 1964, 79; Kathleen Wickham, *We Believed We Were Immortal: Twelve Reporters Who Covered the 1962 Integration Crisis at Ole Miss* (Oxford, MS: Yoknaptawpha Press, 2017), excerpt, chap. 1.

60. Marshall interview, June 14, 1964, 79–81; Katzenback, *Some of It Was Fun*, 77–80; Guthman and Shulman, *Robert Kennedy in His Own Words*, 166–168.

61. Sitton, "Shots Quell Mob"; Sitton, "Meredith Plans to Leave Campus," *New York Times*, October 4, 1962, 1; Claude Sitton, "Mississippi: The Mood of the Deep South," *New York Times*, October 7, 1962, E10.

62. Claude Sitton, "Violence in Mississippi Has Roots in Slavery Furor of the 1830s; Racial Views Are Probably Unshaken," *New York Times*, October 3, 1962, 28.

63. Guthman and Shulman, *Robert Kennedy in His Own Words*, 160–161.

64. Guthman and Shulman, *Robert Kennedy in His Own Words*, 160–166; Robert Kennedy, "On the Duty of Lawyers," in *RFK: Collected Speeches*, ed. Edwin O. Guthman and C. Richard Allen (New York: Viking, 1993), 89–90.

65. Evan Thomas, *Robert Kennedy: His Life* (New York: Simon & Schuster, 2000), 209–214; Matthew A. Hayes, "Robert Kennedy and the Cuban Missile Crisis: A Reassertion of Robert Kennedy's Role as the President's 'Indispensable Partner' in the Successful Resolution of the Crisis," *History: The Journal of the Historical Association* 104, no. 361 (May 7, 2019): 474–503; quote on 487.

66. Thomas, *Robert Kennedy*, 224–230; Hayes, "Robert Kennedy and the Cuban Missile Crisis," 502–503.

67. Peter Braestrup, "Ban on Color Line in Housing Due," *New York Times*, September 28, 1961, 1; Marshall interview, June 13, 1964; Fentress to Parker, November 23, 1962; dispatches from *Time* magazine correspondents.

68. Peter Braestrup, "Weaver Is Sworn in as Housing Chief," *New York Times*, February 12, 1961, 1; Patricia Sullivan, *Days of Hope: Race and Democracy in the New Deal Era* (Chapel Hill: University of North Carolina Press, 1996), 46–56; James Banon, "Robert C. Weaver, 89, First Black Cabinet Member Dies," *New York Times*, July 9, 1997; Morroe Berger, "The Problem of Negro Housing," *New York Times*, August 8, 1948, BR11.

69. "Kennedy Backs Weaver as Dixiecrats Balk," *Chicago Defender*, February 8, 1961, 1; Jack Eisen, "Nomination of Weaver Hits Snag in Senate Committee," *Washington Post*, February 8, 1961, 1; Robert G. Spivack, "Watch on the Potomac," *Chicago Defender*, February 13, 1961, 10; "Dramatic Note at Hearing," February 9, 1961, 3; Jack Eisen, "Weaver's Approval Seen Sure," *Washington Post*, February 9, 1961, A1; Jack Eisen, "Weaver Is Confirmed as Director of Housing," *Washington Post*, February 10, 1962, A1.

70. Sidey to Parker, "Prex Week—the matter of Congress," January 18, 1962; Miller to Parker, "Congress Week—Urban Affairs Bill (Nation)," January 25, 1962; MacNeil to Parker, "Congress Week—I," February 2, 1962, "Congress Week I and Take 2," February 22, 1962; dispatches from *Time* magazine correspondents, second series, 1956–1968, Ms Am 2090.1, Houghton Library, Harvard University; Tom Wicker, "Kennedy Faces Stiff Challenges," *New York Times*, February 25, 1962, E7; Sidey to Parker, January 18, 1962: "CR—partisan issue; Dirksen block Kennedy from getting CR victory in urban affairs," dispatches from *Time* magazine correspondents.

71. John D. Morris, "Order Forbids Any Racial or Religious Discrimination—Pledge Is Fulfilled," *New York Times*, November 21, 1962, 1. Marshall interview, June 13, 1964; Fentress to Parker, November 23, 1962.

72. "Transcript of President's Press Conference on Foreign and Domestic Affairs," *New York Times*, November 21, 1963, 10; Richard E. Mooney, "Officials Hopeful on Housing Order; South is Critical," *New York Times*, November 22, 1962, 1; "Dr. King Hails Housing Order; Stennis Charges Power Move," *New York Times*, November 21, 1962, 19; "Acclaim JFK Housing Order," *Chicago Defender*, November 24, 1962, 1.

73. Calvin Trillin, "Back on the Bus: Remembering the Freedom Rides," *New Yorker*, July 25, 2013, 36–37; Martin Luther King Jr., "A Bold Design for the New South," *The Nation*, March 30, 1963.

74. King, "A Bold Design for the New South."

75. JFK to the Congress of the United States, "Special Message on Civil Rights," February 28, 1963; Theodore C. Sorenson, *Kennedy* (New York: Harper & Row, 1965), 494; Roscoe Drummond, "Civil Rights . . . Legislation Likely in 1963," *Washington Post*, March 7, 1963, A25.

76. Marshall interview, June 13, 1964; Nicholas Katzenbach interview, September 18, 1965, SUNY-Civil Rights Act; William Geoghegan, August 30, 1965, David B. Filvaroff and Raymond E. Wolfinger, Civil Rights Acts Papers, University Archives, University Libraries, University at Buffalo, the State University of New York (hereafter cited as FWCRP).

77. Dittmer, *Local People*, 143–147; Visser-Maessen, *Robert Parris Moses*, 133–137.

78. Dittmer, *Local People*, 147–152; Visser-Maessen, *Robert Parris Moses*, 137–140.

79. Dittmer, *Local People*, 153–154; John Doar, interview by Anthony Lewis, November 13, 1964, John Doar Papers.

80. Dittmer, *Local People*, 154–156; Visser-Maessen, *Robert Parris Moses*, 141–142.

81. Dittmer, *Local People*, 156.

82. "Attorney General at News Conference Asks Action on Rights," *Washington Post*, April 3, 1963, A7; address by Hon. Robert F. Kennedy, Attorney General of the United States, at the meeting of the University of South Carolina chapter of American Association of University Professors, Columbia, SC, April 25, 1963.

83. Attorney General Robert Kennedy to the Speaker, House of Representatives, April 2, 1963, FWCRP; "Attorney General at News Conference Asks Action on Rights," *Washington Post*, April 3, 1963, A7; "R. Kennedy Sees U.S. in Back of Rights Bill," *Washington Post*, April 4, 1963, A2.

84. Address by RFK, April 25, 1963.

85. Address by Honorable Robert F. Kennedy at Kentucky's Centennial of the Emancipation Proclamation, Louisville, KY, March 18, 1963.

<h2 style="text-align:center">7 · FREEDOM NOW</h2>

1. Edwin O. Guthman and Jeffrey Shulman, eds., *Robert Kennedy in His Own Words: The Unpublished Recollections of the Kennedy Years* (New York: Bantam, 1988), 189–190; Simmons Fentress, "Bobby in Dixie II (Nation)," April 26, 1963, dispatches from *Time* magazine correspondents, second series, 1956–1968, Ms Am 2090.1, Houghton Library, Harvard University.

2. David Garrow, *Bearing the Cross: Martin Luther King, Jr., and the Southern Christian Leadership Conference* (New York: William Morrow and Company, 1986), 225–229.

3. Garrow, *Bearing the Cross*, 236–241.

4. Garrow, *Bearing the Cross*, 236–237, 239–243.

5. Garrow, *Bearing the Cross*, 242–246.

6. RFK telegram to George Wallace, April 17, 1963; Wallace to RFK, April 20, 1963, box 24, Papers of Robert Kennedy, Attorney General Papers; Simmons Fentress, "Bobby Down South," April 26, 1963, Dispatches from *Time* magazine correspondents.

7. Fentress, "Bobby in Dixie."

8. Transcript of conversation between Robert F. Kennedy and Governor George Wallace, April 25, 1963, Montgomery, AL, Ms., Stuart A. Rose Manuscript, Archives and Rare Book Library, Emory University, Atlanta, GA; Guthman and Shulman, *Robert Kennedy in His Own Words*, 186.

9. Guthman and Shulman, *Robert Kennedy in His Own Words*, 185–186; Simmons Fentress, "Bobby Down South," "Bobby in Dixie," "Bobby in South, Take III," April 26, 1963, dispatches from *Time* magazine correspondents.

10. Garrow, *Bearing the Cross*, 246–249.

11. Garrow, *Bearing the Cross*, 249–250; Burke Marshall, interview by Anthony Lewis, June 20, 1964, JFKOH.

12. Marshall interview, June 20, 1964; Joe Dolan, interview by David Wolfinger, August 2, 1965, file 22.9, FWCRP.

13. Marshall interview, June 20, 1964; Foster Hailey, "The Birmingham Story: Segregation Is Teetering under Fire," *New York Times*, May 26, 1963, 58.

14. Claude Sitton, "Rioting Negroes Routed by Police in Birmingham," *New York Times*, May 8, 1963, 1.

15. Marshall interview, June 20, 1964; Burke Marshall, interview by David Wolfinger, September 24, 1964, box 22.9, FWCRP; Dolan interview, August 2, 1965; Burke Marshall, transcript, White House meeting, May 12, 1963, 14, FWCRP.

16. Garrow, *Bearing the Cross*, 255–259; Hailey, "The Birmingham Story," 58.

17. Claude Sitton, "Fifty Hurt in Negro Rioting after Birmingham Blast," *New York Times*, May 13, 1963, 1; Anthony Lewis, "US Sends Troops to Alabama after Riots Sweep Birmingham," *New York Times*, May 13, 1963, 1; Burke Marshall, transcript, White House Meeting, May 12, 1963, 13–14; Dan T. Carter, *The Politics of Rage: George Wallace, the origins of the new conservatism and the transformation of American Politics* (New York: Simon & Schuster, 1995), 125.

18. Anthony Lewis, "U.S. Troops into Alabama after Riots Sweep Birmingham," *New York Times*, May 13, 1963, 1; Fentriss to Parker, May 17, 1963, dispatches from *Time* magazine correspondents.

19. Marshall interview, June 20, 1964.

20. "John F. Kennedy, Nicholas 'Nick' Katzenbach, Robert F. 'Bobby' Kennedy, Burke Marshall, Robert S. McNamara, Pierre E. G. Salinger, Theodore C. 'Ted' Sorenson, and Earl G. 'Bus' Wheeler on 12 May 1963," JFK Meeting Tape 86.2 (PRDE Excerpt A), *Presidential Recordings Digital Edition* [Kennedy and Civil Rights, ed. Kent B. Germany with Kieran K. Matthews and Marc J. Selverstone] (Charlottesville: University of Virginia Press, 2014–), http://prde.upress.virginia.edu/conversations/4006291.

21. "Kennedy Statement," *New York Times*, May 13, 1963, 25.

22. Fentress to Parker, May 16, 1963, dispatches from *Time* magazine correspondents.

23. Fentress to Parker, May 17, 1963; Ray Larsen to Parker, May 17, 1963; dispatches from *Time* magazine correspondents; Garrow, *Bearing the Cross*, 262–263; Arthur Schlesinger Jr., *Robert Kennedy and His Times* (Boston: Houghton Mifflin Company, 1978); 330.

24. "The Long March," *Time*, June 21, 1963; "Segregation: Is the Dam Breaking in Dixie North?" *Chicago Defender*, June 8, 1963, 9; "NAACP Opens a Drive in North," *New York Times*, May 19, 1963, 1; Charles and Barbara Whelan, *The Longest Debate: A Legislative History of the 1964 Civil Rights Act* (Washington, DC: Seven Locks Press, 1985), 19; Adam Fairclough, *Better Day Coming: Blacks and Equality, 1890–2000* (New York: Viking, 2001), 274.

25. Guthman and Shulman, *Robert Kennedy in His Own Words*, 173; Marshall interview, June 20, 1964; Louis Oberdorfer, interview by David Wolfinger, November 14, 1966, box 22.9, FWCRP.

26. Marshall interview, June 20, 1964; Norbert Schlei, interview with David Wolfinger, August 27, 1965, box 22.9, FWCRP; Norbert Schlei, interview by John Stewart, February 20–21, 1968, JFKOH.

27. Cabell Phillips, "Special Team Met Racial Crisis," *New York Times*, June 21, 1963, 12.

28. Roland Evans and Robert Novak, "Civil Rights and Congress," *Washington Post*, June 11, 1963, A4; Anthony Lewis, "Kennedy Weighs New Rights Law," June 2, 1963, 164; Victor Navasky, *Kennedy Justice* (New York: Atheneum, 1971), 99; Guthman and Shulman, *Robert Kennedy in His Own Words*, 177.

29. Fentress to Parker, "Civil Rights (Nation)," June 6, 1963, dispatches from *Time* magazine correspondents; Anthony Lewis, "Campaign for Integration: Major Battle Looming in Congress," *New York Times*, June 9, 1963, 169.

30. Hugh Sidey to Parker, May 31, 1963, dispatches from *Time* magazine correspondents; James Clayton, "Race Crisis Action put up to JFK," *Washington Post*, May 30, 1963, A1.

31. US Congress, House, Education and Labor, Hearings of the Select Committee on Labor of the Committee on Labor and Education, 1965, vol. 5, 228; David A. Harmon, *Beneath the Image of the Civil Rights Movement and Race Relations in Atlanta, 1946–1981* (New York: Routledge, 2019); Claude Sitton, "U.S. Prodding South on Hiring Negroes," *New York Times*, March 1, 1963, 1; JFK memo to Vice President Lyndon Johnson, February 21, 1963, box 33, Burke Marshall Papers, JFKL; Burke Marshall, interview by Anthony Lewis, June 13, 1964, JFKOH.

32. Nicholas Katzenbach, interview by Larry J. Hackman, October 8, 1969, RFKOH; John Seigenthaler, interview by Larry J. Hackman, June 5, 1970, RFKOH; Ramsey Clark, interview by Larry J. Hackman, July 7, 1970, RFKOH; Guthman and Shulman, *Robert Kennedy in His Own Words*, 151–152; John Macy, interview by Fred Holborn, May 29, 1964, JFKOH; LBJ to RFK, May 23, 1963, box 33, Burke Marshall Personal Papers, JFKL.

33. Clay Risen, *The Bill of the Century: The Epic Battle for the Civil Rights Act* (New York: Bloomsbury Press, 2014), 52–53; Jack Conway, interview with Larry J. Hackman, April 11, 1972, RFKOH.

34. Guthman and Shulman, *Robert Kennedy in His Own Words*, 152; Ralph Horton to RFK, June 4, 1963, box 33, Burke Marshall Personal Papers, JFKL.

35. Risen, *The Bill of the Century*, 53–54; "Johnson Urges Nation Strike Chains of Bias," *Chicago Defender*, January 7, 1963, 5; "Johnson Says Nation Will Not be Free Until All Are Blind to Color," *Washington Post*, May 31, 1963, A1; "A Voice from the South," *Washington Post*, editorial, June 1, 1963, A10; Roscoe Drummond, "Where's Johnson? Role in Racial Crisis," *Washington Post*, June 8, 1963, A13; Marquis Child, "Johnson Pitches In on Racial Crisis," *Washington Post*, July 26, 1963.

36. Zim to Parker, May 30, 1963, dispatches from *Time* magazine correspondents; Oberdorfer interview, November 14, 1966; Marshall interview, September 24, 1964. The majority opinion in *Peterson v. City of Greenville, SC* drew on the argument made in the federal government's amicus curiae brief. Anthony Lewis, "Supreme Court Legalizes Sit-Ins in Cities Enforcing Segregation," *New York Times*, May 21, 1963, 1.

37. Robert Kennedy and Burke Marshall, interview by Anthony Lewis, December 6, 1964, JFKOH; Edwin Guthman, *We Band of Brothers* (New York: Harper & Row, 1964), 219–220.

38. Kennedy/Marshall interview, December 6, 1964; James Baldwin, interview by Jean Stein, February 2, 1970, Jean Stein Personal Papers, JFKL; Kenneth Clark, interview by Jean Stein, January 30, 1970, Jean Stein Personal Papers, JFKL.

39. "Louisiana Story: Jerome Smith," in *Freedomways Reader: Prophets in their Own Country*, ed. Esther Cooper Jackson with Constance Pohl (Boulder: Westview Press, 2000), 247.

40. James Baldwin, "Lorraine Hansberry at the Summit, No. 4, 1979," in *Freedomways Reader*, 79–80; Guthman, *We Band of Brothers*, 22; Baldwin interview, February 2, 1970; Clark interview, January 30, 1970.

41. "Louisiana Story: Jerome Smith," 247; Clark interview, January 30, 1970; Kennedy/Marshall interview, December 4, 1964.

42. Harry Belafonte with Michael Shnayerson, *My Song: A Memoir* (New York: Knopf, 2011), 269.

43. Kennedy/Marshall interview, December 4, 1964.

44. Kennedy/Marshall interview, December 4, 1964; Guthman, *We Band of Brothers*, 221.

45. Fentress to Parker, "Civil Rights I," June 6, 1963, dispatches from *Time* magazine correspondents.

46. Douglas Martin, "Vivian Malone Jones, 63, Dies: First Black Graduate of the University of Alabama," *New York Times,* October 14, 2005; Richard Goldstein, "James A. Hood, Student Who Challenged Segregation, Dies at 70," *New York Times,* January 20, 2013.

47. Fentress to Glasgow, May 24, 1963, dispatches from *Time* magazine correspondents; Claude Sitton, "US Seeks to Bar Alabama U Crisis of Integration," *New York Times,* May 25, 1963, 1; Hedrick Smith, "Wallace Ordered Not to Bar Negroes," *New York Times,* June 6, 1963, 1; Guthman and Shulman, *Robert Kennedy in His Own Words,* 191.

48. Tom Wicker, "President Bids Governors Lead Rights Campaign," *New York Times,* May 30, 1963, 1; Hugh Sidey to Parker, May 31, 1963, dispatches from *Time* magazine correspondents; "Businessmen Tell the President of Progress in Integration," June 5, 1963, *New York Times,* 23.

49. Tom Wicker, "President Says Racial Barriers Imperil Schools," *New York Times,* June 7, 1963, 1; "JFK Flying to Hawaii to Address Mayors," *Washington Post,* June 6, 1963, A2; Kenny O'Donnell, interview by David Wolfinger, April 11, 1967, box 22, folder 8, FWCRP.

50. John F. Kennedy, "Address in Honolulu Before the United States Conference of Mayors," June 9, 1963, *The American Presidency Project;* UC Santa Barbara https://www.presidency.ucsb.edu/documents/address-honolulu-before-the-united-states-conference-mayors; Tom Wicker, "Kennedy Appeals for Local Action on Race Problem," *New York Times,* June 10, 1963, 1; Lawrence E. Davies, "US Mayors of North and South Back Kennedy's Integration Aims," *New York Times,* June 11, 1963, 19; Edward T. Folliard, "Kennedy Tells Mayors Cities Must Aid Rights, *New York Times,* June 10, 1963, A1; *Chicago Defender,* June 1, 1963; "Jackson Police Jail 600 Negro Children," *New York Times,* June 1, 1963, 1.

51. JFK, "Address in Honolulu," June 9, 1963.

52. JFK, "Address in Honolulu," June 9, 1963.

53. Andrew Cohen, *Two Days in June: John F. Kennedy and the Two Days That Made History* (New York: McClelland & Stewart, 2014), 29–30.

54. John F. Kennedy, "Commencement Address at American University, June 10, 1963," C-SPAN audiovisual recording (there is minor variation with the printed text in word choice); transcript of speech printed in the *New York Times,* June 11, 1963, 16.

55. *New York Times,* June 10, 1963, 1.

56. Guthman and Shulman, *Robert Kennedy in His Own Words,* 187–192; Nicolas Katzenbach, *Some of It Was Fun: Working with RFK and LBJ* (New York: W. W. Norton, 2008), 110; "Ol' Miss Profs Leave; 30 Percent Student Drop Noted since Riot," *Chicago Defender,* June 15, 1963, 7.

57. James Clayton, "U.S. Made Moves at Alabama U. All Felt Out as Action Unfolded: No Talks with Wallace," *Washington Post,* June 14, 1963, A5; *Crisis: Behind a Presidential Commitment,* 1963 documentary directed by Robert Drew; Kennedy / Marshall interview, December 4, 1964; Marshall interview, June 20, 1964; Katzenbach, *Some of It Was Fun,* 110–112; Claude Sitton, "State Seals Off Alabama Campus," *New York Times,* June 9, 1963, 1.

58. Drew, *Crisis*; Marshall interview, June 20, 1964.

59. "U.S. Made Moves at Alabama U . . . ," *Washington Post,* June 14, 1964; Drew, *Crisis;* Katzenbach, *Some of It Was Fun,* 111–112.

60. Drew, *Crisis;* Claude Sitton, "Governor Leaves, but Fulfills His Promise to Stand in Door and Avoid Violence," *New York Times,* June 12, 1963, 1; Katzenbach, *Some of It Was Fun,* 113–114.

61. "The Long March," *Time,* June 21, 1963.

62. Sitton, "Governor Leaves"; Katzenbach, *Some of It Was Fun,* 114–115; *Newsweek,* June 24, 1963, 31.

63. Cohen, *Two Days in June,* 178–181; Charles E. Flinner, "Hoses Used on Negroes in Danville," *Washington Post,* June 11, 1963, 1.

64. Hugh Sidey to Parker, "Crisis at Home," Robert Kennedy Cover II (Nation), June 12, 1963, dispatches from *Time* magazine correspondents.

65. Sidey, "Crisis at Home"; Kennedy / Marshall interview, December 4, 1964.

66. Sidey, "Crisis at Home"; Kennedy / Marshall interview, December 4, 1964.

67. Sidey, "Crisis at Home"; Kennedy / Marshall interview, December 4, 1964; Marshall interview, June 20, 1964.

8 · "A GREAT CHANGE IS AT HAND"

1. "The Presidential Address," editorial, *Chicago Defender,* June 13, 1963, 14.

2. John F. Kennedy, Televised address to the nation on civil rights, June 11, 1963, JFKL, https://www.jfklibrary.org/learn/about-jfk/historic-speeches/televised-address-to-the-nation-on-civil-rights.

3. Martin Luther King Jr. telegram to JFK, June 11, 1963 (Atlanta, GA, 8:15 p.m.), JFKL, https://www.jfklibrary.org/asset-viewer/june-11-1963-telegram; Kenneth Clark, interview by Jean Stein, January 30, 1970, Stein Papers; *Chicago Defender,* editorial, June 13, 1963.

4. *New York Post,* June 13, 1963.

5. *The Open Mind*, PBS, transcript, June 12, 1963, November 13, 1993. James Farmer and Wyatt Tee Walker reconvened with Heffner thirty years later to assess what had transpired in the intervening decades. Farmer conceded that while Jim Crow had been knocked out, racism remained. Walker acknowledged that they were more optimistic about the possibilities of change in American society than they should have been and that "Malcolm's assessment on where America was at on race was more accurate at the time." The two also noted how Malcolm's views had evolved in the time before his death—and they remarked on the convergence of forces in the wake of 1963, as the civil rights movement increasingly incorporated and emphasized Black identity and racial pride.

6. Tom Wicker, "Presidential Plea: Asks Help of Citizens to Assure Equality of Rights to All," *New York Times*, June 12, 1963, p. 1; *Times-Picayune* (New Orleans), June 12, 1963; Thomas O'Neill, "Testing Time," *Baltimore Sun*, June 14, 1963; "We Face a Moral Crisis," editorial, *Milwaukee Journal*, June 12, 1963; Carroll Kilpatrick, "President Calls Others to Talks on Racial Crisis," *Washington Post*, June 13, 1963.

7. Jack Anderson "Race Kettle Declared Boiling," *Washington Post*, June 14, 1963, D13; RFK quoted in Ann Garity Connell, *The Lawyers Committee for Civil Rights Under Law: The Making of a Public Interest Law Group* (Chicago: ABA Publishing, 2003), 83.

8. Gertrude Samuels, "Even More Crucial than the South: A Report on the Forms the Negro Revolution Is Taking against Discrimination, Economic and Social, in the North," *New York Times*, June 30, 1963, 13–14, 24, 27, 30.

9. "JFK Huddles with 100 Businessmen on Rights," *Chicago Defender*, June 5, 1963, 3; "Businessmen Act on Integration after White House Conferences," *New York Times*, June 15, 1963, 8; Burke Marshall, interview by Anthony Lewis, June 20, 1964, JFKOH; Ralph A. Duncan, memorandum for the president, June 14, 1963, Papers of John F. Kennedy, Presidential Papers, President's Office Files, Subject: Civil rights, meeting with religious leaders, June 17, 1963. Clay Risen, *The Bill of the Century: The Epic Battle for the Civil Rights Act* (New York: Bloomsbury Press, 2014), 62–63, 72, 96–97.

10. Marie Smith, "Georgia Woman Fired JFK's Call," *Washington Post*, July 11, 1963, B3; Dorothy McCardle, "JFK Organizes Womanpower in Fight for Civil Rights," *Washington Post*, June 11, 1963, B1; Maria Smith, "Committee Formed to Speed JFK's Rights Program," *Washington Post*, July 12, 1963, C1.

11. Connell, *Lawyers Committee for Civil Rights*, 74–81.

12. Connell, *Lawyers Committee for Civil Rights* 81–84.

13. Margaret Hunter, "Lawyers Promise Kennedy Aid in Easing Race Unrest," *New York Times*, June 22, 1963, 1; Connell, *Lawyers Committee for Civil Rights*, 84–86.

14. Marshall interview, June 20, 1964; Edwin O. Guthman and Jeffrey Shulman, eds., *Robert Kennedy in His Own Words: The Unpublished Recollections of the Kennedy Years* (New York: Bantam, 1988), 202–211; Robert C. Albright, "GOP Offers Rights Collaboration: Hopes for Bill," *Washington Post*, June 18, 1963, A1.

15. "Text of the President's Message to Congress Calling for Civil Rights Legislation," *New York Times*, June 20, 1963, 16; Charles Whelan and Barbara Whelan, *The Longest Debate: A Legislative History of the 1964 Civil Rights Act* (Washington DC: Seven Locks Press, 1985), 1–2.

16. "Kennedy Warns Rights Group on Demonstrations," *Washington Post*, June 23, 1963, A1; John Lewis, *Walking with the Wind: A Memoir of the Movement* (New York: Simon & Schuster, 1998), 206–207.

17. "Negroes Inform Kennedy of Plans for New Protest," *New York Times*, June 23, 1963; Risen, *Bill of the Century*, 81–84.

18. David Garrow, *The FBI and Martin Luther King, Jr.: From "Solo" to Memphis* (New York: W.W. Norton & Co., 1981), 44–60. The newspapers were the *Augusta* (Georgia) *Chronicle*, the *Birmingham News*, the *St. Louis Globe-Democrat*, the *Times-Picayune* (New Orleans), and the *Long Island Star-Journal*.

19. Garrow, *FBI and Martin Luther King, Jr.*, 62–63; Stanley Levison, interview by Arthur Schlesinger, August 9, 1974, Schlesinger Papers, box 494.

20. E. W. Kenworthy, "Robert Kennedy Offers to Modify Civil Rights Bill," *New York Times*, June 27, 1963, 1; "Excerpts from Attorney General's Statement on Civil Rights Legislation," *New York Times*, June 27, 1963, 18.

21. "Opening Gun," editorial, *Washington Post*, June 27, 1963, A20; Chalmers Roberts, "First Rights Skirmish," *Washington Post*, June 27, 1963, A21.

22. Burke Marshall interview, April 5 and 7, 1967, FWCRP; E. W. Kenworthy, "One Rights Plea Expected to Fail," *New York Times*, June 20, 1963, 1; E. W. Kenworthy, "Rights Bill: The Arguments in Congress," *New York Times*, August 4, 1963, 138; "Rights Plan Hit by Southern Bloc," *New York Times*, June 20, 1963, 18; E. W. Kenworthy, "South Seeks to Water Down Civil Rights Bill," *New York Times*, July 21, 1963, 113; E. W. Kenworthy, "Wallace Asserts Air Force Offers Aid to Race Riots," *New York Times*, July 16, 1963, 1. Excerpt from George Wallace's testimony, *New York Times*, July 16, 1963, 16; RFK to Senator A. S. Mike Mahoney, July 22, 1963, 13.10, FWCRP.

23. Louis Harris, "JFK's Popularity Registers 59 Percent," *Washington Post*, July 1, 1963, p. 1; "Rights Plan Hit by Southern Bloc," *New York Times*, June 20, 1963, 18; Anthony Lewis, "Issue in Rights Debate," *New York Times*, July 14, 1963, 112; E. W. Kenworthy, "Kennedy to Offer Civil Rights Plan with Job Training," *New York Times*, June 19, 1963, 1; Whelan and Whelan, *Longest Debate*, 1–28.

24. Nicholas Katzenbach to RFK, June 29, 1963; 8.1, FWCRP; Burke Marshall to Nicholas Katzenbach, July 22, 1963, 13.10, FWCRP; Whelan and Whelan, *Longest Debate*, 9–13; Nicholas Katzenbach, *Some of It Was Fun: Working with RFK and LBJ* (New York: Norton, 2008), 120–124.

25. Joe Dolan to Katzenbach, July 8 1963, FWCRP; Chuck Daly, memo to RFK, July 16, 1963, FWCRP; Joe Dolan to RFK, July 17, 1963, FWCRP; William Geoghegan to Katzenbach, July 23, 1963, July 29, 1963, August 6, 1963, FWCRP; Joe Dolan's notebooks, box 8, FWCRP; Joe Dolan to RFK, July 23, 1963, FWCRP; William Geoghegan, July 23, 1963, FWCRP; interview with William Geoghegan, August 30, 1965, box 22.9, FWCRP.

26. "President Moves," *New York Times*, June 16, 1963, 139; Gertrude Samuels, "Even More Crucial Than the South," *New York Times*, June 30, 1963, 24.

27. Peter Levy, *Civil War on Race Street: The Civil Rights Movement in Cambridge, Maryland*, (Gainesville: University Press of Florida, 2003), 55–57, 75–90; "Warns of Civil War," *New York Times*, July 22, 1963, 10.

28. Jean White, "Robert Kennedy Meets Key Cambridge Figures," *Washington Post*, July 23, 1963, A1; John Lewis, *Walking with the Wind*, 214–215; Gloria Richardson Dandridge, "The Energy Passing through Me," in *Hands on the Freedom Plow*. ed. Faith Holsaert et al. (Urbana: University of Illinois Press, 2010), 279–280.

29. William Chapman, "Peace Pact Signed in Cambridge," *Washington Post*, July 24, 1963, A1; Levy, *Civil War on Race Street*, 86–88; Dandridge, "Energy Passing through Me," 281–282.

30. Burke Marshall, interview by Anthony Lewis, June 13, 1964; Sue Conk, "Funds Urged for Dropouts Urged by Kennedy," *Washington Post*, June 20, 1963, F2.

31. Summer Job Programs—Organizational Procedure, May 13, 1963; Rodney Clurman to Mr. E. Barrett Prettyman, May 13, 1963; E. Barrett Prettyman Jr., memorandum to the attorney general, August 1, 1963, box 31, Papers of Robert Kennedy, Attorney General Papers; Eve Edstrom, "Two Agencies Seek to Run Youth Jobs," *Washington Post*, June 23, 1963, B1; "R. Kennedy Writes Jobs Project Youths," *Washington Post*, June 26, 1963, B12.

32. Walter Tobriner to RFK, April 9, 1963; E. Barrett Prettyman Jr. to RFK, July 8, 1963, box 31, Papers of Robert Kennedy, Attorney General Papers; Eve Edstrom, "Donated Cash Opens School Pool," *Washington Post*, July 10, 1963, D1.

33. Dorothy Gilliam, "R. Kennedy Cheered by Students as Dunbar High Pool Is Reopened," *Washington Post*, September 12, 1963, A26.

34. Brian Lee, "A Matter of National Concern: The Kennedy Administration and Prince Edward County, Virginia" (Ph.D. diss., Virginia Commonwealth University, 2009), 143.

35. This discussion of the Prince Edward County case is informed by chapter 3 of Lee, "A Matter of National Concern"; William J. vanden Heuvel, "Closing Doors, Opening Doors: Fifty Years after the School-Closing in Prince Edward County, Virginia," keynote address, symposium at Hamden-Sydney College, Prince Edward County, Virginia (copy provided by William vanden Heuvel).

36. Lee, "A Matter of National Concern," 165–177; vanden Heuvel, "Closing Doors, Opening Doors."

37. Vanden Heuvel, "Closing Doors, Opening Doors"; Neil Sullivan, *Bound for Freedom: An Educator's Adventures in Prince Edward County* (Boston: Little, Brown, 1965), 1–47.

38. Chalmers Roberts, "August 28 'March' Could Prove Negroes' Vindication," *Washington Post*, July 21, 1963, E1.

39. Louis Martin, memo to the attorney general, RE: the March on Washington Movement, etc., May 13, 1963, box 494, Schlesinger Papers; Burke Marshall and RFK interview with Anthony Lewis, in *Robert Kennedy in His Own Words*, ed. Guthman and Shulman, 27; John W. Douglas, interview by Larry Hackman, June 16, 1969, RFKOH.

40. "Randolph Counsels against Disorder," *New York Times*, July 24, 1963, 20; John Lewis, *Walking with the Wind*, 208–216.

41. John W. Douglas, interview by Larry J. Hackman, May 5, 1970, RFKOH,; Alfred E. Lewis, "Murry Discusses Big Rally with Key Negro Leaders Here," July 10, 1963, A7.

42. Douglas interview, May 5, 1970.

43. Douglas interview, May 5, 1970.

44. Douglas interview, May 5, 1970; Lewis, *Walking with the Wind*, 218–228.

45. Marquis Childs, "Triumphal March Silences Scoffers," *Washington Post*, August 30, 1963.

46. Robert Baker, "Echoes of Rights Rally Awaited," *Washington Post*, August 30, 1963, A1; "Dream Songs: The Music of the March on Washington," *New Yorker*, August 28, 2013.

47. "The News of the Week in Review: For Rights: The March-and After," *New York Times*, September 1, 1963, E1; James Reston, "'I Have a Dream,'" *New York Times*, August 29, 1963, 1.

48. Laura Visser-Maessen, *Robert Parris Moses : A Life in Civil Rights and Leadership at the Grass Roots* (Chapel Hill: University of North Carolina Press, 2016), 154.

49. "Scoreboard on Dixie School Desegregation," *Chicago Defender*, August 31, 1963, 9; "Desegregation Fronts," *Amsterdam News*, August 31, 1963, 35; "Charleston Schools Desegregate Calmly," *Washington Post*, August 31, 1963, A2; "Danville Starts Integration Plan," *New York Times*, August 27, 1963, 23; "Virginia is Slow to Desegregate," September 1, 1963, 44; M. S. Handler, "Savannah is Calm Over Integration,"

September 2, 1963, 6; Claude Sitton, "Status of Integration: The Progress So Far Is Characterized as Mainly Tokenism," *New York Times,* September 1, 1963, E3.

50. Claude Sitton, "Alabama Tension on Schools Rising," *New York Times,* September 1, 1963, 40; Marjorie Hunter, "U.S. Ready to Use Troops if Necessary if Needed in Alabama Crisis," *New York Times,* September 4, 1963, 1; "Battle of Birmingham," *Chicago Defender,* September 7, 1963, 9; "Seven Have Died in Rights Fight," *Chicago Defender,* September 7, 1963, 19.

51. Tom Wicker, "Kennedy Decries Racial Violence; Impugns Wallace," *New York Times,* September 17, 1963, 1; "'Alabama Church Bombing Barbaric:' Dr. King," *Chicago Defender,* September 16, 1963, A3; "Bombing Causes Shock, Horror All Over the World," *Chicago Defender,* September 17, 1963, 20; "White Youths Charged in Birmingham Murder," *Chicago Defender,* September 19, 1963, 2.

52. David J. Garrow, *Bearing the Cross: Martin Luther King, Jr., and the Southern Christian Leadership Conference* (New York: William Morrow, 1986), 291–292; Guthman and Shulman, *Robert Kennedy in His Own Words,* 229–230; Burke Marshall interview, April 6–7, 1967, FWCRP.

53. Jay Caspian Kang, "What the World Got Wrong about Kareem Abdul Jabbar," *New York Times Magazine,* September 17, 2015; Tom Maxwell, "A History of American Protest Music: When Nina Simone Sang What Everyone was Thinking," *Longreads,* April 2017, https://longreads.com/2017/04/20/a-history-of -american-protest-music-when-nina-simone-sang-what-everyone-was-thinking/; M. S. Handler, "Negro Passivity is Held Out of Date," *New York Times,* September 21, 1963, 8.

54. Mary McGrory, "Was the Melting Pot an American Myth?," *Washington Star,* September 22, 1963, 26.

55. Garrow, *The FBI and Martin Luther King, Jr.,* 68.

56. Navasky, *Kennedy Justice,* 135–155; Evan Thomas, *Robert Kennedy: His Life* (New York: Simon and Schuster, 2000), 165–170; Peter Edelman, interview by author, March 12, 2020.

57. Garrow, *The FBI and Martin Luther King, Jr.,* 72–76.

58. Katzenbach, *Some of It Was Fun,* 121.

59. Whelan and Whelan, *Longest Debate,* 29–38.

60. Whelan and Whelan, *Longest Debate,* 38–39.

61. Interview with Burke Marshall, September 24, 1964, FWCRP; interview with Robert Kennedy, September 24, 1965, FWCR; Whelan and Whelan, *Longest Debate,* 42–44.

62. Whelan and Whelan, *Longest Debate,* 43–47.

63. Whelan and Whelan, *Longest Debate,* 45–46.

64. Katzenbach, *Some of It Was Fun,* 121, 124; Whelan and Whelan, *Longest Debate,* 53.

65. Whelan and Whelan, *Longest Debate,* 49.

66. Whelan and Whelan, *Longest Debate,* 49–52; first interview with Charles Halleck, September 21, 1965, FWCRP.

67. Whelan and Whelan, *Longest Debate,* 54–62; interview with Nicholas Katzenbach, September 25, 1965, FWCRP.

68. Whelan and Whelan, *Longest Debate,* 62–63.

69. Whelan and Whelan, *Longest Debate,* 51–66; "House Unit Votes Bipartisan Plan for Civil Rights," *New York Times,* October 30, 1963, 1.

70. Anthony Lewis, "Two Parties Soften Civil Rights Bill; Key Test Today," *New York Times,* October 29, 1963, 1; "Forward Step on Civil Rights," *New York Times,* October 30, 1963, 38; interview with Charles Halleck, September 23, 1965, FWCRP.

71. Anthony Lewis, "Civil Rights Bill Is Sent to Rules Committee," *New York Times,* November 21, 1963, 34; Richard Lyons, "House Unit Asks Rights Bill Action," *Washington Post,* November 22, 1963, 14.

72. Interview with Robert Kennedy, September 24, 1965, FWCRP.

73. John Douglas, interview by Larry J. Hackman, June 16, 1969, RFKOH.

74. Arthur Schlesinger Jr., *Robert Kennedy and His Times* (Boston: Houghton Mifflin Company, 1978), 606–607.

9 · ON HIS OWN

1. Arthur Schlesinger, *Robert Kennedy and His Times* (Boston: Houghton Mifflin, 1978), 607–608; Burke Marshall, interview by Larry J. Hackman, January 19–20, 1970; Anthony Lewis, "Robert Kennedy May Keep Cabinet Post as Attorney General under Johnson," *New York Times,* November 23, 1963, 12; John Seigenthaler, interview by Larry J. Hackman, December 1, 1970, RFKOH; William vanden Heuvel, interview by author, November 2011; William vanden Heuvel and Milton Gwirtzman, *On His Own: RFK 1964–1968* (New York: Doubleday & Co., 1970), 2.

2. Walter Sheridan, interview by Roberta W. Greene, June 12, 1970, RFKOH; David Hackett, interview by John W. Douglas, July 22, 1970, RFKOH; Marshall interview, January 19–20, 1970; Thomas Johnston, interview by Larry J. Hackman, February 9, 1970, RFKOH; Mortimer Caplan, interview by author, December 5, 2012.

3. Ted Coleman, "Kennedy, Like Lincoln, Killed; A Dear, Dear Friend,is Dead. Southsiders Shocked. Feel Loss Deeply," *Chicago Defender,* November 23, 1963, 1; "Sad Harlem Faithful Pay Tribute to 'Our Man,'" *New York Amsterdam News,* November 25, 1963, 8; "Hatred Bears Bitter Fruit," *Pittsburgh Courier,* November 30, 1963, 12. Based on review of three leading Black newspapers: *New York Amsterdam News, Chicago Defender, Pittsburgh Courier,* November 23–December 15, 1963.

4. George E. Barbour, "JFK Kept Promises He Made to Negroes," *Pittsburgh Courier,* November 30, 1963, 1.

5. Thurgood Marshall, interview by Berl Bernhard, April 7, 1964, JFKOH; "We've Lost a Friend," editorial, *Chicago Defender,* November 25, 1963, 15; "Measure of a Man," editorial, *Pittsburgh Courier,* November 30, 1963, 12; Benjamin Mays, "My View: The Late President John F. Kennedy," *Pittsburgh,* December 14, 1963, 10.

6. Transcript, Lyndon B. Johnson, Address to Joint Session of Congress, November 27, 1963, *New York Times,* November 28, 1963, 20; Tom Wicker, "Johnson Bids Congress Enact Civil Rights Bill with Speed; Asks End of Hate and Violence," *New York Times,* November 28, 1963, 1.

7. Nicholas Katzenbach, interview by Larry J. Hackman, October 8, 1969, RFKOH.

8. Vanden Heuvel and Gwirtzman, *On His Own,* 6; Schlesinger, *Robert Kennedy and His Times,* 609–610, 631.

9. Edwin O. Guthman and Jeffrey Shulman, eds., *Robert Kennedy in His Own Words: The Unpublished Recollections of the Kennedy Years* (New York: Bantam, 1988), 211–212; Charles Whelan and Barbara Whelan, *The Longest Debate: A Legislative History of the 1964 Civil Rights Act* (Washington DC: Seven Locks Press, 1985), 125–130; Robert Kennedy, interview by Raymond Wolfinger, September 24, 1965; Nicholas Katzenbach, interview by Raymond Wolfinger, September 25, 1965, FWCRP; Francis R. Valeo, interview by Don Ritchie, July 3, 1985 to March 11, 1986, Senate Oral History Project, Senate Historical Office, Washington, D.C., 319, 330–331; Clay Risen, *The Bill of the Century: The Epic Battle for the Civil Rights Act* (New York: Bloomsbury Press, 2014), 144, 163-64.

10. E. W. Kenworthy, "Civil Rights Bill Passed in House by 290–130 Vote; Hard Senate Fight Seen," *New York Times,* February 11, 1964, 1; Richard L. Lyons, "Strong Rights Bill Passed by House," *Washington Post,* February 11, 1964, 1; "Milestone," *Washington Post,* February 12, 1964, 16; Whelan and Whelan, *Longest Debate,* 121; Risen, *Bill of the Century,* 160–161.

11. Patricia Sullivan, *Lift Every Voice: The NAACP and the Making of the Civil Rights Movement* (New York: New Press, 2009), 105–109.

12. Whelan and Whelan, *Longest Debate,* 163.

13. Joe Dolan to Harold Reis, February 17, 1964, folder 8.1; Jack to Ed, "Notes on informal civil rights briefings with the Deputy Attorney General," March 12, 1964, folder 14.2; David Filvaroff to Nicholas Katzenbach et al., March 11, 1964; Katzenbach interviews, September 24 and 25, 1965; Burke Marshall interview, September 24, 1964, FWCRP.

14. Risen, *The Bill of the Century,* 98–99, 145–46; William Buckley, *National Review,* April 16, 1964, 346, cited in Risen, *Bill of the Century,* 197–198.

15. Claude Sitton, "Wallace Presses Wisconsin Drive," *New York Times,* March 22, 1964, 52; Austin Wehrwein, "Wallace's Vote Exceeds 200,000 in Wisconsin Test," *New York Times,* 1; Claude Sitton, "Wisconsin Vote Hailed in South by Rights Foes," *New York Times,* April 9, 1964, 1.

16. Whelan and Whelan, *Longest Debate,* 145–146; Homer Bigart, "Kennedy Makes Four Speeches in Metro Area," *New York Times,* May 21, 1964, 36.

17. "Rights Pressures," *New York Times,* April 19, 1964, E1; Fred Powledge, "In North Negroes Seek to Widen the Scope of Demonstrations as Both Sides Gird for Summer of Increased Protest in the South," April 19, 1964, E3; Junius Griffin, "Stall-in Leaders Defy Plea," *New York Times,* April 21, 1964, 1; "Drivers Take up Positions to Block Road at 7 a.m.," *New York Times,* April 22, 1964, 1; "Stall-in Leaders Erred on Backing," *New York Times,* April 23, 1964, 1.

18. Anthony Lewis, "Civil Rights Campaign: The Moderates vs. the Extremists," *New York Times,* April 19, 1964, E3; "Rights Pressures," *New York Times,* April 19, 1964, E1; "Homer Bigart, Kennedy Makes Four Speeches in Metro Area," *New York Times,* May 21, 1964, 36.

19. "New Plea to Youth Urged by Kennedy," *New York Times,* April 15, 1964, 14; address by Attorney General Robert Kennedy, University of Chicago Law School, Law Day, May 1, 1964; Anthony Lewis, "Robert Kennedy Bids Bar Join Fight against Social Ills," *New York Times,* May 2, 1964, 22; address by Attorney General Robert F. Kennedy before the U.S. Conference of Mayors, New York Hilton Hotel, May 25, 1964; address by Attorney General Robert F. Kennedy, commencement exercises, Marquette University, Milwaukee, WI, June 7, 1964, Speeches of Attorney General Robert Kennedy, US Department of Justice, https://www.justice.gov/ag/speeches-25.

20. Excerpts from remarks by Attorney General Robert F Kennedy at a panel discussion, "After the Civil Rights Act, What?," American Society of Newspaper Editors 1964 Convention, Washington, DC, April 16, 1964, Speeches of Attorney General Robert Kennedy.

21. Guian McKee, *Lyndon B. Johnson and the War on Poverty: Introduction to the Digital Edition* (Charlottesville: University of Virginia Press, 2010), 8–9. https://rotunda.upress.virginia.edu/pdf/american-cent/WarOnPoverty-introduction-USletter.pdf

22. Dwight McDonald, "Our Invisible Poor," *New Yorker,* January 12, 1963; Peter Edelman, *Searching for America's Heart: RFK and the Renewal of Hope* (Washington: Georgetown University Press, 2003), 36–37; Michael L. Gillette, *Launching the War on Poverty: An Oral History* (New York: Twayne Publishers, 1996), 17.

23. McKee, *Lyndon B. Johnson and the War on Poverty,* 5–6, 13.

24. McKee, *Lyndon B. Johnson and the War on Poverty,* 1, 10–1.

25. McKee, *Lyndon B. Johnson and the War on Poverty,* 11, 13–14.

26. Marjorie Hunger, "Kennedy Defends Antipoverty bill," *New York Times,* April 8, 1964, 26.

27. Jack Landau, "Kennedy Details Plan for Bail Reforms," *Washington Post,* May 30, 1964, A5; Anthony Lewis, "Kennedy Scores Bail Injustice," *New York Times,* May 30, 1964, 41; Laurie Johnson, "Louis J. Schweitzer Dead; Founder of Vera Institute," *New York Times,* September 21, 1971, 40.

28. Address by Attorney General Robert Kennedy, University of Chicago Law School, Law Day.

29. Address by Attorney General Robert Kennedy, University of Chicago Law School, Law Day; Lewis, "Robert Kennedy Bids Bar Join Fight against Social Ills"; "Kennedy in West Virginia," April 29, 1964, 22; address by Attorney General Robert F. Kennedy before the U.S. Conference of Mayors, New York Hilton Hotel, New York, May 25, 1964.

30. "Kennedy in West Virginia," April 29, 1964, 22; address by Attorney General Robert F. Kennedy before the U.S. Conference of Mayors.

31. Samuel Kaplan, "U.S. Will Assist Youth of Harlem," *New York Times,* May 7, 1964, 1.

32. Jean White, "Farmville Children Thank RFK," *Washington Post,* May 12, 1964, B1; "Kennedy Draws Virginia Cheers," *New York Times,* May 12, 1964, 12.

33. "Farmville Children Thank RFK"; "Kennedy Draws Virginia Cheers."

34. Address by Attorney General Robert Kennedy at Manhattan College commencement exercises, June 12, 1962.

35. Address by Attorney General Robert Kennedy, commencement exercises, Marquette University, June 7, 1964; Kennedy also delivered addresses at the University of Chicago Law School (May 1, 1964); Hampden-Sydney College (May 11, 1964); a joint meeting of Rutgers University and Seton Hall University law students (May 19, 1964); Fairleigh Dickinson University (May 19, 1964); and the University of West Georgia in Carrollton, Georgia (May 26, 1964).

36. Homer Bigart, "Kennedy Makes 4 Speeches in Metropolitan Area," *New York Times,* May 21, 1964, 36; John Herbers, "Georgia Campus Cheers Kennedy," *New York Times,* May 27, 1964, 40; Remarks by Attorney General Robert F. Kennedy at the dedication of the John F. Kennedy Interfaith Chapel, West Georgia College, Rome, GA, May 26, 1964.

37. "Georgia Campus Cheers Kennedy."

38. Laura Visser-Maessen, *Robert Parris Moses: A Life in Civil Rights Leadership at the Grassroots* (Chapel Hill: University of North Carolina Press, 2016), 155–177; John Dittmer, *Local People: The Struggle for Civil Rights in Mississippi* (Urbana: University of Illinois Press, 1996), 198–207.

39. Claude Sitton, "Negro Queue in Mississippi Is Symbol of Frustration in Voter Registration Drive," *New York Times,* March 2, 1964, 20.

40. John Doar and Dorothy Landsberg, "The Performance of the FBI in Investigating Violations of Federal Laws Protecting the Right to Vote, 1960–1967" (unpublished ms., 1971); Sitton, "Negro Queue in Mississippi"; Claude Sitton, "Mississippi Is Gripped by Fear of Violence in Civil Rights Drive," *New York Times,* May 30, 1964, 1; Walter Sheridan, interview by Roberta Greene, May 1, 1970, 8–13, RKOHC.

41. "Rights Pressure: How Much Militancy?" *New York Times,* April 19, 1964, E1; E. W. Kenworth, "Civil Rights: Politics," *New York Times,* April 26, 1964, E6; Austin C. Wehrwein, "Midwest Weighs Wallace Impact," *New York Times,* May 10, 1964, 69; Claude Sitton, "Goldwater Finds North Is Uneasy," *New York Times,* May 2, 1964, 22.

42. James Reston, "The Outlook for Civil Rights in the Senate," *New York Times,* April 3, 1964, 32; Whelan and Whelan, *Longest Debate,* 164–165.

43. Whelan and Whelan, *Longest Debate,* 164–185; E. W. Kenworthy, "Civil Rights Bloc Reaches Accord on Amendments," *New York Times,* May 14, 1964, 1.

44. Risen, *Bill of the Century,* 223–236; Whelan and Whelan, *Longest Debate,* 201–226; Nicholas Katzenbach, interview with Raymond Wolfinger, September 18, 1965, FWCRP; Robert Kennedy interview, September 24, 1965, FWCRP.

45. Dittmer, *Local People,* 237–228; Doar and Landsberg, "Performance of the FBI"; Walter Sheridan, interview by Roberta W. Greene, May 1, 1970, RFKOH; Kenneth O'Reilly, *Racial Matters: The FBI's Secret File on Black America* (New York: Free Press, 1989), 162.

46. Sheridan interview, May 1, 1970; Dittmer, *Local People,* 238.

47. Claude Sitton, "Students Briefed on Peril in South," *New York Times,* June 17, 1964, 18; "Students Warned on Southern Law," *New York Times,* June 19, 1964, 16; "U.S. Official Warns Mississippi Bound Students," *New York Times,* June 20, 1964, 12; "Rights Campaigners Off for Mississippi," *New York Times,* June 20, 1964; Visser-Maessen, *Robert Parris Moses,* 196–202,

48. Claude Sitton, "Three in Rights Drive Reported Missing," *New York Times,* June 23, 1964, 1.

49. Visser-Maessen, *Robert Parris Moses,* 202–206.

50. Anthony Lewis, "Robert Kennedy Rules Out Race for Senate Seat," *New York Times*, June 24, 1964, 1.

51. Doar and Landsberg, "Performance of the FBI"; Claude Sitton, "President Acts; Sends CIA to South after Seeing Parents of Youths," *New York Times*, June 23, 1964, 1; M. S. Handler, "FBI Augments Mississippi Force; but Kennedy Tells NAACP He Cannot Order Police Action," *New York Times*, June 25, 1964, 1; Visser-Maessen, *Robert Parris Moses*, 207; O'Reilly, *Racial Matters*, 168.

52. M. S. Handler, "FBI Augments Mississippi Force."

53. Risen, *Bill of the Century*, 240–244.

54. Robert C. Albright, "White 'Backlash' Scares Democrats," *Washington Post*, August 30, 1964, E1; Robert David Johnson, *All the Way with LBJ: The 1964 Presidential Election* (Cambridge: Cambridge University Press, 2009), 129–134.

10 · TRANSITIONS

1. Michael Flamm, *In the Heat of the Summer: The New York Riots of 1964 and the War on Crime* (Philadelphia: University of Pennsylvania Press, 2017), 80–100.

2. "Lyndon Johnson, J. Edgar Hoover, and Lee White on 21 July 1964," Conversation WH6407-11-4295, *Presidential Recordings Digital Edition* [Lyndon B. Johnson: Civil Rights, Vietnam, and the War on Poverty, ed. David G. Coleman, Kent B. Germany, Guian A. McKee, and Marc J. Selverstone] (Charlottesville: University of Virginia Press, 2014–), http://prde.upress.virginia.edu/conversations/4000564.

3. "Lyndon Johnson and Robert F. Kennedy on 21 July 1964," Conversation WH6407-12-4299, *Presidential Recordings Digital Edition* [Lyndon B. Johnson: Civil Rights, Vietnam, and the War on Poverty], http://prde.upress.virginia.edu/conversations/4000565.

4. "Lyndon Johnson and Robert F. Kennedy on 21 July 1964," Conversation WH6407-12-4299.

5. Memorandum for the president, from the attorney general, "Racial Violence in Urban Centers," August 5, 1964, delivered by hand, 8:30 p.m.

6. Robert David Johnson, *All the Way with LBJ: The 1964 Presidential Election* (Cambridge: Cambridge University Press, 2009), 145–150; "Lyndon Johnson and Richard Daley on 25 July 1964," Conversation WH6407-14-4336, *Presidential Recordings: Digital Edition* [Lyndon B. Johnson: Civil Rights, Vietnam and the War on Poverty], http://prde.upress.virginia.edu/conversations/4000671; "Lyndon Johnson and Clark Clifford on 29 July 1964," Conversation WH6407-18-4392, 4393, *Presidential Recordings Digital Edition* [Lyndon B. Johnson: Civil Rights, Vietnam, and the War on Poverty], http://prde.upress.virginia.edu/conversations/4002758.

7. "Lyndon Johnson and George Reedy on 4 July 1964," Tape WH6407.04, Citation #4155, *Presidential Recordings Digital Edition* [Mississippi Burning and the Passage of the Civil Rights Act, vol. 8, ed. Kent B. Germany and David C. Carter] (Charlottesville: University of Virginia Press, 2014–), http://prde.upress.virginia.edu/conversations/9080147.

8. "Lyndon Johnson and Hubert Humphrey on 20 August 1964," Conversation WH6408-29-5045, 5046, *Presidential Recordings Digital Edition* [Lyndon B. Johnson: Civil Rights, Vietnam, and the War on Poverty], http://prde.upress.virginia.edu/conversations/4002794; "Lyndon Johnson and Walter Reuther on 14 August 1964," Conversation WH6408-20-4926, *Presidential Recordings Digital Edition* [Lyndon B. Johnson: Civil Rights, Vietnam, and the War on Poverty], http://prde.upress.virginia.edu/conversations/4002774.

9. David Garrow, *The FBI and Martin Luther King, Jr.: From "Solo" to Memphis* (New York: W.W. Norton & Co., 1981), 106–107.

10. Garrow, *The FBI and Martin Luther King Jr.*, 101–109, 127; Marshall interview, January 17–19, 1970; Katzenbach, *Some of It Was Fun: Working with RFK and LBJ* (New York: W. W. Norton & Company, 2008), 153–155.

11. "Lyndon Johnson and John Connally on 23 July 1964," Conversation WH6407-13-4320, 4321, 4322, 4323, http://prde.upress.virginia.edu/conversations/4000666; "Lyndon Johnson and George Smathers on 18 August 1964," Conversation WH6408-28-5020, https://prde-upress-virginia-edu.pallas2 .tcl.sc.edu/conversations/4002782/notes_open; *Presidential Recordings Digital Edition* [Lyndon B. Johnson: Civil Rights, Vietnam, and the War on Poverty].

12. "Lyndon Johnson and Hubert Humphrey on 14 August 1964," Conversation WH6408-19-4917, 4918, http://prde.upress.virginia.edu/conversations/4002772; "Lyndon Johnson and Hubert Humphrey on 20 August 1964," Conversation WH6408-29-5045, 5046, https://prde-upress-virginia-edu.pallas2.tcl.sc.edu /conversations/4002794/notes_open; "Lyndon Johnson and Walter Jenkins on 21 August 1964," Conversation WH6408-32-5107, https://prde-upress-virginia-edu.pallas2.tcl.sc.edu/conversations/4002812/notes_open; *Presidential Recordings Digital Edition* [Lyndon B. Johnson: Civil Rights, Vietnam, and the War on Poverty].

13. Laura Visser-Maessen, *Robert Parris Moses: A Life in Civil Rights Leadership at the Grassroots* (Chapel Hill: University of North Carolina Press, 2016), 221; Bob Moses, interview with author, March 7, 2019; Martin Luther King, telegram to Attorney General Robert Kennedy, August 22, 1964, box 8, Burke Marshall Papers.

14. Burke Marshall to MLK, August 25, 1964, box 8, Burke Marshall Papers.

15. "Lyndon Johnson and Hubert Humphrey on 20 August 1964," Conversation WH6408-29-5045, 5046, *Presidential Recordings Digital Edition;* Johnson, *All the Way,* 183–184; John Dittmer, *Local People: The Struggle for Civil Rights in Mississippi* (Urbana: University of Illinois Press), 291–302.

16. Dittmer, *Local People,* 302; Cleveland Sellers, *The River of No Return: The Autobiography of a Black Militant and the Life and Death of SNCC* (Oxford: University of Mississippi Press, 1999), 111.

17. Johnson, *All the Way,* 160, 189; R. W. Apple, "Kennedy Gets an Ovation; Recalls Ideals of his Brother," *New York Times,* August 28, 1964, 1.

18. John Seigenthaler, interview by Larry J. Hackman, July 1, 1970, RFKOH.

19. Seigenthaler interview, July 1, 1970; Apple, "Kennedy Gets an Ovation."

20. Apple, "Kennedy Gets an Ovation."

21. Johnson, *All the Way,* 196; Seigenthaler interview, July 1, 1970.

22. Layhmond Robinson, "Nomination Seen as Bid for Unity," *New York Times,* September 2, 1964, 25; "Kennedy Enters Race for Senate," *New York Times,* August 26, 1964, 1; "Kennedy's Statement on His Candidacy," *New York Times,* August 26, 1964, 30; "Mr. Kennedy Declares," (editorial), *New York Times,* August 26, 1964, 38.

23. R.W. Apple, "Kennedy Opens His Campaign at Fulton Fish Market," *New York Times,* September 3, 1964, 1.

24. Phil Casey, "Students Steal Show as Kennedy Resigns," *Washington Post,* September 4, 1964, A4; Don Bacon, "RFK: A Force in the Federal Community," October 10, 1964, in press file, box 3, Ken J. Lupino Papers, JFKL.

25. Robert E. Thompson, "Bob Kennedy Resigns to Enter Senate Race," *Los Angeles Times,* September 4, 1964, 2.

26. R. W. Apple, "Kennedy Quits Post in Cabinet to Wage Campaign in State," *New York Times,* September 4, 1964, 1; Edward Folliard, "Attorney General Quits to Campaign," *Washington Post,* September 4, 1964, A4.

27. Apple, "Kennedy Quits Post"; Casey, "Students Steal Show."

28. Folliard, "Attorney General Quits to Campaign"; "Lighting His Own Way: Robert Francis Kennedy," *New York Times,* September 2, 1964, 25.

29. James Clayton, "Kennedy Top Rated as Justice Boss," *Washington Post,* August 23, 1964, E1; Anthony Lewis, "Kennedy's Role as Attorney General," *New York Times,* September 4, 1964, 14.

30. Clayton, "Kennedy Top Rated as Justice Boss"; Lewis, "Kennedy's Role as Attorney General."

31. Clayton, "Kennedy Top Rated as Justice Boss"; Lewis, "Kennedy's Role as Attorney General"; "Mr. Kennedy's Record" (editorial), *Washington Post,* September 5, 1964, A8; John Doar and Dorothy Landsberg, "The Performance of the FBI in Investigating Violations of Federal Laws Protecting the Right to Vote, 1960–1967" (unpublished ms., 1971).

32. Address of Attorney General Robert F. Kennedy to the Criminal Law Section of the American Bar Association, American Hotel, New York, August 10, 1964; Lewis, "Kennedy's Role as Attorney General"; Clayton, "Kennedy Top Rated Justice Boss."

33. "Kennedy Enters Race for Senate," 1; "Lighting His Own Way."

34. Martin Arnold, "Kennedy Mobbed in Grand Central," *New York Times,* September 5, 1964, 8.

35. R. W. Apple, "Throngs Mob Kennedy at the Beach," *New York Times,* September 7, 1964, 1.

36. William vanden Heuvel and Milton Gwirtzman, *On His Own: RFK 1964–1968* (New York: Doubleday & Co., 1970), 40–41; Richard Wade, interview by Roberta Greene, December 13, 1973, RFKOH.

37. Alder Whitman, "Keating Dies at 74; Envoy, Ex-Senator," *New York Times,* May 6, 1975, 1; "Keating v. Kennedy," *New York Times,* October 18, 1964, E10

38. Layhmond Robinson, "Democrats Form a Keating Group," *New York Times,* September 29, 1964, 1; David Halberstam, "Travels with Bobby," *Harper's Magazine,* July 1968, 55.

39. Harry Belafonte, interview by Vicki Daitch, May 20, 2005, RFKOH; "For Robert Kennedy: An Editorial," *Amsterdam News,* October 10, 1964, 1.

40. Vanden Heuvel and Gwirtzman, *On His Own,* 45–46; Peter Edelman, interview by Larry Hackman, December 12, 1969, RFKOH; Peter Edelman, interview by author, March 13, 2020; Layhmond Robinson, "Keating Speaks at Negro Session," *New York Times,* October 3, 1964, 15.

41. Speech to the NAACP by Robert F. Kennedy, Buffalo, New York, October 3, 1964, box 1, Ken J. Lupino Papers.

42. Speech to the NAACP by Robert F. Kennedy, Buffalo; Martin Arnold, "Kennedy Asserts Foe Incites Bias," *New York Times,* October 4, 1964, 82.

43. Speech to the NAACP by Robert F. Kennedy, Buffalo; Ken Lupino, notes on the scene in the church, box 1, Ken J. Lupino Papers; Arnold, "Kennedy Asserts Foe Incites Bias."

44. Thomas R. Jones, interview by Roberta W. Greene, November 26, 1971, RFKOH.

45. Vanden Heuvel and Gwirtzman, *On His Own,* 54.

46. Homer Bigart, "Kennedy Fulfills Some Campaign Pledges," *New York Times,* November 5, 1964, 31.

11 · BEYOND CIVIL RIGHTS

1. Warren Weaver Jr., "Kennedy Gets a Back Seat," *New York Times,* January 5, 1965, 18; Warren Weaver Jr., "Senator Kennedy (D., N.Y.) Settles in New Job," *New York Times,* February 21, 1965, E1.

2. Warren Weaver Jr., "Kennedy Will Join Mt. Kennedy Climb," *New York Times,* March 19, 1966, 1; James Whittaker, interview by Roberta Greene, April 25, 1969, RKOHC.

3. Whittaker interview, April 25, 1969; Martin Arnold, "Kennedy Arrives at Yukon Mountain Base," *New York Times,* March 23, 1966, 19.

4. Warren Weaver Jr., "Old Hands to Run Kennedy's Office," *New York Times,* January 10, 1965, 51; Peter Edelman, interview by author, March 12, 2020.

5. Adam Walinsky, interview by Thomas Johnston, November 29, 1969, RFKOH; Thomas M. C. Johnston, interview by Larry J. Hackman, February 9, 1970, RFKOH.

6. Warren Weaver Jr., "Senator Kennedy Settles in New Job"; Walinsky interview, November 29, 1969; Thomas Johnston, interview by Larry J. Hackman, October 27, 1969, RFKOH; Johnston interview, February 9, 1970; Edelman interview, March 12, 2020.

7. "Kennedy Discusses Campaign Tactics," *New York Times,* November 5, 1964, 31; Peter Edelman, interview by Larry Hackman, December 12, 1969, RFKOH.

8. Marjorie Hunter, "Senate Approves $1.1 Billion in Aid for Appalachia," *New York Times,* February 2, 1965, 1; Homer Bigart, "Upstate Apathy Annoys Kennedy," *New York Times,* March 30, 1965, 74.

9. Roscoe Drummond, "RFK Moves In . . . Acts at Home in the Senate," *Washington Post,* February 8, 1965, A19; William vanden Heuvel and Milton Gwirtzman, *On His Own: RFK 1964–1968* (New York: Doubleday & Co., 1970), 118–119; Homer Bigart, "Upstate Apathy Annoys Kennedy," *New York Times,* March 30, 1965, 74; "Senate Gets Bill on Scenic Hudson," *New York Times,* March 5, 1965, 35

10. ; Edith Evans Asbury, "Lag on Narcotics Seen by Kennedy," *New York Times,* April 25, 1965, 68; Eve Edstrom, "Kennedy, Javits Introduce $75-Million Narcotics Bill," *Washington Post,* June 10, 1965, A2; "$1 Million Grant to Help Youth Here," *New York Times,* August 14, 1965, 13.

11. Walinsky interview, November 30, 1969; Phillip Benjamin, "Kennedy Inspects Hudson's Blight," *New York Times,* May 3, 1965, 39; "Recreation Plan for City Pressed," *New York Times,* July 26, 1965, 17; Samuel Kaplan, "U.S. Funds to Aid Recreation Here," *New York Times,* July 27, 1965, 1.

12. John Sibley, "Kennedy Charges Neglect in State Care of Retarded," *New York Times,* September 10, 1965, 1; "Excerpts from Statement by Kennedy," *New York Times,* September 10, 1965, 21; John Sibley, "Kennedy Backed by Secret Report on Mental Homes," *New York Times,* September 11, 1965, 1; Walinsky interview, November 30, 1969.

13. Richard Madden, "Rockefeller Names New Mental Aide," *New York Times,* January 30, 1966, 41; Walinsky interview, November 30, 1969. In 1972 the New York Civil Liberties Union and the Legal Aid Society filed class action lawsuits over the conditions at Willowbrook, leading to a landmark 1975 court settlement in which the state said it would protect Willowbrook residents from harm. According to a recent *New York Times* investigative story, conditions remained deplorable. Benjamin Weiser, "Beatings, Burns and Betrayals: The Willowbrook Scandal's Legacy," *New York Times,* February 21, 2020.

14. George Lardner Jr., "Robt. Kennedy Is Seen as D.C. Gadfly," *Washington Post,* February 18, 1965, A22.

15. Elsie Carper, "Race Issue Linked to Home Rule; Kennedy Raises Negro Question at First Hearing," *Washington Post,* March 10, 1965, A1.

16. Carper, "Race Issue Linked to Home Rule"; George Lardner Jr, "Kennedy Broadside on Crime Came as No Surprise," *Washington Post,* May 3, 1965, A18.

17. Elsie Carper, "Justice Dept. Urges Delay on Crime Bill, Plans New Proposals," *Washington Post,* April 28, 1965, C1; Elsie Carper, "Tobriner Bears Attack At Crime Bill Hearing," *Washington Post,* April 29, 1965, G1; Lardner, "Kennedy Broadside on Crime Came as No Surprise."

18. "R. Kennedy Disputes Brother-in-Law at Hearing on School Aid for Poor," *Washington Post,* February 5, 1965; A6; "D.C. Tax Bill Offered, Half That Asked by Johnson," *Washington Post,* April 8, 1965, G2; Evans and Novak, "Robert Kennedy and the School Bill," *Washington Post,* February 23, 1965, A 17; Walinsky interview, November 30, 1969; Robert Dallek, *Flawed Giant: Lyndon Johnson and His Times, 1961–1973* (New York: Oxford University Press, 1998) , 195–201.

19. Maureen Hoffman, "Kennedy Charges Schools Are Blind to Own Failures," *Washington Post,* March 14, 1965, A4.

20. "Bob Kennedy Spurs Better-Schools Rally," *Washington Post,* March 29, 1965, D1.

21. "U.S. Sues Alabama Over Negro Voters," *New York Times,* April 14, 1961, 21; David Garrow, *Protest at Selma: Martin Luther King and the Voting Rights Act of 1965* (New Haven, CT: Yale University Press, 1978), 31–34.

22. Garrow, *Protest at Selma,* 61–66.

23. Garrow, *Protest at Selma,* 72–80.

24. Arthur Schlesinger Jr., *Robert Kennedy and His Times* (Boston: Houghton Mifflin Company, 1978), 779.

25. Garrow, *Protest at Selma,* chap. 2; Edelman interview, January 3, 1970; Schlesinger, *Robert Kennedy,* 779.

26. E. W. Kenworth, "Senate Approves Voting Rights Bill in 77–19 Ballot," *New York Times,* May 27, 1955, 1; Arthur Krock, "In the Nation: Broadening of the Voting Rights Ban," *New York Times,* May 30, 1965; Edelman interview, January 3, 1970.

27. Dallek, *Flawed Giant,* 221–222.

28. Daniel Geary, *Beyond Civil Rights: The Moynihan Report and Its Legacy* (Philadelphia: University of Pennsylvania Press, 2015), 52–64; Daryl Michael Scott, *Contempt and Pity: Social Policy and the Image of the Damaged Black Psyche, 1880–1996* (Chapel Hill: University of North Carolina Press, 1997), 150–151.

29. Geary, *Beyond Civil Rights,* 72–79; Richard Goodwin, *Remembering America: A Voice from the Sixties* (Boston: Little, Brown, 1988), 342–345.

30. Tom Wicker, "Johnson Pledges To Help Negroes to Full Equality," *New York Times,* June 5, 1965, 1; Lyndon B. Johnson, "To Fulfill These Rights," commencement address at Howard University, June 4, 1965, Teaching American History website, https://teachingamericanhistory.org/library/document /commencement-address-at-howard-university-to-fulfill-these-rights/.

31. LBJ, "To Fulfill These Rights."

32. Wicker, "Johnson Pledges to Help Negroes"; LBJ, "To Fulfill These Rights," 348.

33. "Illiteracy Rate High in Riot Area," *Washington Post,* August 15, 1965, A15; James Queally, "Watts Riots: Traffic Stop Was Spark That Ignited Days of Destruction in L.A.," *Los Angeles Times,* July 29, 2015; David S. Broder, "Yorty and Shriver Disagree on Riots," *New York Times,* August 18, 1965, 20; Robert Fogelson, "White on Black: A Critique of the McCone Commission Report on the Los Angeles Riots," *Political Science Quarterly* (September 1967), 348; Al Kuettner, "Bloody Rioting in L.A. Is Called War against Society," *Washington Post,* August 16, 1965, A1.

34. "1000 Riot in L.A.," *Los Angeles Times,* August 12, 1965, 1; Queally, "Watts Riots"; Burt A. Folkart, "Marquette Frye, Whose Arrest Ignited the Watts Riots in 1965, Dies at Age 42," *Los Angeles Times,* December 25, 1965, VI; "Rena Price Dies at 97; Her and Sons' Arrest Sparked Watts Riots," *Los Angeles Times,* June 23, 2013; Jack McCurdy and Art Berman, "New Rioting," *Los Angeles Times,* August 13, 1965, 1.

35. Fogelson, "White on Black," 327; Queally, "Watts Riots"; Art Berman, "Eight Men Slain, Guard Moves In," *Los Angeles Times,* August 14, 1965, 1; Kuettner, "Bloody Rioting in Los Angeles"; Joseph Califano, *The Triumph and Tragedy of Lyndon Johnson: The White House Years* (New York: Simon & Schuster), 59–61.

36. Queally, "Watts Riots"; Fogelson, "White on Black," 358–359; Kuettner, "Bloody Rioting in L.A."; Charles Davis, "Anatomy of a Riot: Minor Incident Ignited Violence," *Los Angeles Times,* August 15, 1965, A; Richard West, "Inquest on Riot Dead to Begin on Tuesday," *Los Angeles Times,* September 12, 1965, B; Fogelson, "White on Black," 245.

37. Dick West and Paul Weeks, "Dr. King Hears Watts Protests over Heckling," *Los Angeles Times,* August 19, 1965, 3.

38. West and Weeks, "Dr. King Hears Watts Protests"; Erwin Baker and Bob Jackson, "King Assailed by Yorty after Stormy Meeting," *Los Angeles Times,* August 20, 1965, 1.

39. David S. Broder, "Yorty and Shriver Disagree on Riots," *New York Times,* August 18, 1965, 20.

40. Broder, "Yorty and Shriver"; vanden Heuvel and Gwirtzman, *On His Own,* 83.

41. Dallek, *Flawed Giant,* 223; Califano, *Triumph and Tragedy,* 59–62.

42. Califano, *Triumph and Tragedy,* 62.

43. Robert E. Thompson, "Johnson Compares L.A. Rioters to Klan Riders," *Los Angeles Times,* August 21, 1965, 1.

44. Robert Thompson, "President Warns Other Cities of Riot Dangers," *Los Angeles Times,* August 27, 1965, 1.

45. Sheridan interview, June 12, 1970; vanden Heuvel and Gwirtzman, *On His Own,* 80.

46. "Reflections on the 1965 Watts Riots: State Convention, Independent Order of Odd Fellows, Spring Valley, New York, August 18, 1965," in *RFK: Collected Speeches,* ed. Edwin O. Guthman and C. Richard Allen (New York: Viking, 1993), 160–161; David Kraslow, "North Needs Negro Leaders, Kennedy Says," *Los Angeles Times,* August 19, 1965, 3.

47. "Reflections on the 1965 Watts Riots," 159–163.

48. Edelman interview, January 3, 1970; Edelman interview, March 12, 2020; Russ Ellis, "Operation Bootstrap: Beginnings," http://www.russellis.net/writings/OperationBootstrap.pdf.

49. Schlesinger, *Robert Kennedy,* 699; Dallek, *Flawed Giant,* 262–266.

50. Schlesinger, *Robert Kennedy,* 699; Martin Arnold, "Kennedy to the Latins: 'I Have Come to Learn,'" *New York Times,* November 28, 1965, E3.

51. Walinsky interview, November 29, 1969; Arnold, "Kennedy to the Latins"; Martin Arnold, "Robert Kennedy Ends Peru Tour," *New York Times,* November 14, 1965, 36; Schlesinger, *Robert Kennedy,* 696.

52. "Brother Prays in Brazil," November 23, 1965, 32; Schlesinger, *Robert Kennedy,* 697; Walinksy interview, November 29, 1969.

53. Schlesinger, *Robert Kennedy*, 696–697, 699; Walinksy interview, November 29, 1969; "Kennedy, Back Home, Warns U.S.," *New York Times*, December 2, 1965, 35.

54. Peter Edelman, interview by Larry Hackman, January 3, 1970, RFKOH.

55. Edelman interview, January 3, 1970; vanden Heuvel and Gwirtzman, *On His Own*, 85.

56. Fredrik Logevall, *Embers of War: The Fall of an Empire and the Making of America's Vietnam* (New York: Random House, 2014), xiv–xv.

57. George Herring, *America's Longest War: America in Vietnam, 1950–1975*, 5th ed. (New York: Mc-Graw Hill, 2013), 91–92, 114–125; David Halberstam, "Travels with Bobby Kennedy," *Harper's Magazine*, July 1968, 56–57.

58. Herring, *America's Longest War*, 92.

59. Herring, *America's Longest War*, 137–146.

60. William C. Gibbons, "The 1965 Decision to Send U.S. Ground Forces to Vietnam," paper delivered at the annual meeting of the International Studies Association, April 16, 1987, Washington, DC; Fredrik Logeval, *Choosing War: The Last Chance for Peace and the Escalation of the War in Vietnam* (Berkeley: University of California Press, 1999), 375.

61. Burke Marshall, interview by Larry J. Hackman, January 17–19, 1970, RFKOH; "Kennedy Urges Political Stance; Decries Military Solutions to Revolutions Abroad," *New York Times*, July 10, 1965, 1; David S. Broder, "Kennedy Vietnam Pleas Spur Popularity on Democratic Left," *New York Times*, February 21, 1966, 1.

62. Richard Eder, "Kennedy Asks Talks on G.I. Buildup," *New York Times*, December 6, 1965, 8; Ronald Sullivan, "Kennedy Defends Academic Liberty," *New York Times*, October 15, 1965, 33; "Kennedy Voices Concern," *New York Times*, November 6, 1965, 2; Lawrence E. Davies, "Goldwater Attacks Kennedy on Vietnam," *New York Times*, November 7, 1965, 1; "Kennedy Attacks Draft as Unfair," *New York Times*, February 12, 1966, 12; "Kennedy Opposes Curbing Effort on Home Front to Pay for War," *New York Times*, December 17, 1965, 25; Robert E. Baker, "Dr. King to Lead against Fund Rollback," *Washington Post*, December 17, 1965, A1.

63. E. W. Kenworthy, "Senators Reluctantly Back President on Air Strikes," *New York Times*, February 1, 1966, 1; E. W. Kenworthy, "Kennedy Bids U.S. Offer Vietcong Role in Saigon," *New York Times*, February 21, 1966, 1; David S. Broder, "Kennedy's Vietnam Plea Spurs Popularity on Democratic Left," *New York Times*, February 21, 1966, 1; Tom Wicker, "Humphrey Scores Kennedy Plan for Vietcong Role," *New York Times*, February 21, 1966, 1; Peter Edelman, interview by Larry Hackman, July 15, 1969, RKFOH; "Coalition in Vietnam," editorial, *New York Times*, February 22, 1966, 20; William C. Gibbons, *The U.S. Government and the Vietnam War: Executive and Legislative Roles, Part IV; July 1965–January 1968* (Princeton, NJ: Princeton University Press, 2014), 228–229.

64. Martin Luther King Jr. to Robert Kennedy, March 2, 1966, Morehouse College, Martin Luther King Jr. Collection, Atlanta University Center, Robert W. Woodruff Library Archives and Special Collections, Atlanta, GA; David Garrow, *Bearing the Cross: Martin Luther King, Jr., and the Southern Christian Leadership Conference* (New York: William Morrow, 1986), 394, 422, 428–430, 436, 437–438, 458–459.

65. Laura Visser-Maessen, *Robert Parris Moses: A Life in Civil Rights and Leadership at the Grassroots* (Chapel Hill: University of North Carolina Press, 2016), 282–283; "Student Nonviolent Coordinating Committee Statement on Vietnam, January 6, 1966," Civil Rights Movement Archive, https://www.crmvet.org/docs/snccviet.htm; Roy Reed, "Georgia House Bars War Critic, a Negro," *New York Times*, January 11, 1966, 1.

66. Roy Reed, "Dr. King's Group Scores Ky Junta," *New York Times*, April 14, 1966, 1; Garrow, *Bearing the Cross*, 469–470.

67. Visser-Maessen, *Robert Parris Moses*, 283, 292–294; Reed, "Dr. King Scores Ky Junta"; "Cellers Bids Rights Leaders Restrain from Vietnam Criticism," *New York Times*, April 15, 1966, 60.

68. "Kennedy Raps Northern Housing," *Chicago Defender*, January 22, 1966, 2; address by Attorney General Robert Kennedy, University of Chicago Law School, Law Day, May 1, 1964.

69. "Kennedy Raps Northern Housing"; Richard J. H. Johnston, "Kennedy Warns on Negro Revolt," *New York Times*, January 21, 1966, 51; Edward R. Schmidt, *President of the Other America: Robert Kennedy and the Politics of Poverty* (Amherst: University of Massachusetts Press, 2010), 124–125.

70. Steven V. Roberts, "More Jobs Urged to Relieve Ghettos," *New York Times*, January 22, 1966, 11; Schmidt, *President of the Other America*, 125.

71. Jack Newfield, "Robert Kennedy's Bedford-Stuyvesant Legacy," *New York Magazine*, December 16, 1968, 28.

72. Michael Woodsworth, *Battle for Bed-Stuy: The Long War on Poverty in New York City* (Cambridge, MA: Harvard University Press, 2016), 1–7; Ralph Blumenthal, "Brooklyn Negroes Harass Kennedy," *New York Times*, February 5, 1966, 17.

73. Woodsworth, *Battle for Bed-Stuy*, 4; Keith Williams, "Bed-Stuy: A Very Brief History," *Weekly Nabe*, posted June 23, 2012, Brooklyn, NY.

74. Blumenthal, "Brooklyn Negroes Harass Kennedy."

75. Thomas Johnston, interview by Larry J. Hackman, January 21, 1970, RFKOH.

76. Douglas Robinson, "Kennedy Assails Legal Aid Delay," *New York Times,* March 20, 1966, 46.

77. Peter Edelman, interview by Larry Hackman, February 21, 1970, RFKOH; Warren Weaver Jr., "Kennedy Assails Johnson's Plans for Budget Cuts," *New York Times,* April 20, 1966, 1.

78. Margaret Hunter, "Kennedy Defends Anti-Poverty Bill," *New York Times,* April 8, 1964, 26; Schlesinger, *Robert Kennedy,* 790.

79. Edelman interview, July 15, 1969; Peter Edelman, *Searching for America's Heart: RFK and the Renewal of Hope* (Washington, DC: Georgetown University Press, 2003), 43–44.

80. Edelman interview, July 15, 1969; Chavez quoted in Schlesinger, *Robert Kennedy,* 791.

81. Peter Edelman, *Searching for America's Heart: RFK and the Renewal of Hope* (Washington: Georgetown University Press, 2003), 45, 47; Frank Bardacke, *Trampling Out the Vintage: Cesar Chavez and the Two Souls of the United Farm Workers* (London: Verso, 2011), 43–66.

82. Edelman interview, July 15, 1969.

83. Edelman interview, February 21, 1970

84. Roy Reed, "Kennedy Cheered in Ole Miss Talk by Crowd of 5,500," *New York Times,* March 19, 1966, 1; Robert E. Baker, "Bobby Charms Ole Miss Despite '62," *Washington Post,* March 19, 1966, A2; "The New South," editorial, *Washington Post,* March 20, 1966, E6; "Barnett Raps Statements by Kennedy," *Washington Post,* March 20, 1966, A2.

85. "King Accepts African Student's Speaking Bid," *Chicago Defender,* November 13, 1965, 4; "South Africa Denies King Visa," *New York Times,* March 25, 1966, 4; "Robert Kennedy Gets Visa to Visit South Africa," *New York Times,* March 23, 1966, 7; Arthur Schlesinger, *Robert Kennedy,* 743; vanden Heuvel and Gwirtzman, *On His Own,* 146–148.

12 · SUPPOSE GOD IS BLACK

1. "Students Cheer Bob Kennedy at S. Africa Airport," *Los Angeles Times,* June 5, 1966, 1; *RFK in the Land of Apartheid: A Ripple of Hope* (Shoreline Productions, 2009), DVD.

2. "Students Cheer Bob Kennedy at S. Africa Airport"; Arthur Schlesinger Jr., *Robert Kennedy and His Times* (Boston: Houghton Mifflin Company, 1978), 744.

3. "South African Ban Angers Students," *New York Times,* May 13, 1966, 12; ; Margaret Marshall, interview by author, August 25, 2020.

4. Marshall interview, August 25, 2020.

5. Schlesinger, *Robert Kennedy,* 744–747; "Kennedy Warns on Racial Issue," *New York Times,* June 10, 1966, 18.

6. Robert Kennedy, "Suppose God Is Black," *Look,* August 23, 1966; Schlesinger, *Robert Kennedy,* 745.

7. Schlesinger, *Robert Kennedy,* 745; *RFK in the Land of Apartheid;* Robert F. Kennedy, "Day of Affirmation Address," University of Cape Town, South Africa, June 6, 1966, JFKL, https://www.jfklibrary.org /learn/about-jfk/the-kennedy-family/robert-f-kennedy/robert-f-kennedy-speeches/day-of-affirmation -address-university-of-capetown-capetown-south-africa-june-6-1966.

8. Kennedy, "Day of Affirmation Address."

9. Kennedy, "Day of Affirmation Address."

10. Marshall interview, August 25, 2020; William vanden Heuvel and Milton Gwirtzman, *On His Own: RFK 1964–68* (New York: Doubleday, 1970), 155.

11. Kennedy, "Suppose God Is Black"; Robert Kennedy, Stellenbosch University, South Africa, June 7, 1966, http://www.rfksafilm.org/html/speeches/unistell.php; vanden Heuvel and Gwirtzman, *On His Own,* 157–158.

12. Schlesinger, *Robert Kennedy,* 747; Marshall interview, August 25, 2020; Shore interview, April 3, 2010; "Albert Luthuli Killed by Train; Zulu Won '60 Nobel Peace Prize," *New York Times,* July 22, 1967, 1.

13. Schlesinger, *Robert Kennedy,* 747; Marshall interview, August 25, 2020; Shore interview, April 3, 2010; "Albert Luthuli Killed by Train; Zulu Won '60 Nobel Peace Prize," *New York Times,* July 22, 1967, 1; Kennedy, "Suppose God Is Black"; Schlesinger, *Robert Kennedy,* 747; vanden Heuvel and Gwirtzman, *On His Own,* 159.

14. Larry Shore, interview by author, September 10, 2020; Kennedy, "Suppose God Is Black"; vanden Heuvel and Gwirtzman, *On His Own,* 160.

15. Schlesinger, *Robert Kennedy,* 747; vanden Heuvel and Gwirtzman, *On His Own,* 160.

16. Schlesinger, *Robert Kennedy,* 748–749; Larry Shore, "Background," *RFK in the Land of Apartheid* website, http://rfksafilm.org/.

17. Schlesinger, *Robert Kennedy,* 748–749; "Kennedy Warns on Racial Issue," *New York Times,* June 10, 1966, 18.

18. Marshall interview, August 25, 2020; Thomas, *Robert Kennedy,* 323.

19. "Kennedy Warns on Racial Issue"; "South Africa Won't Admit Kennedy Again, Paper Says," *New York Times,* June 13, 1966, 8.

20. "Kennedy's Trip," *Chicago Defender,* July 2, 1966, 10.

21. Robert E. Baker, "Katzenbach for Voter Education Drive," *Washington Post,* March 1, 1966, A5; David J. Garrow, *Bearing the Cross: Martin Luther King, Jr., and the Southern Christian Leadership Conference* (New York: William Morrow, 1986), 471; John Dittmer, *Local People: The Struggle for Civil Rights in Mississippi* (Urbana: University of Illinois Press, 1995), 394.

22. Garrow, *Bearing the Cross,* 473–476; Stokely Carmichael, *Ready for Revolution: The Life and Struggles of Stokely Carmichael (Kwame Ture)* (New York: Scribner, 2003), 501–503.

23. Stokely Carmichael, SNCC Gateway Project, Duke University; Jack Nelson, "SNCC Dumps 2 Top Leaders, Names 'Black Panther' Chairman," *Washington Post,* May 17, 1966, 1.

24. Hassan Kwame Jeffries, *Bloody Lowndes: Civil Rights and Black Power in Alabama's Black Belt* (New York: New York University Press, 2010), 1–2, 58–62, 146–147, 161–163, 171–172.

25. Cleveland Sellers, *The River of No Return: The Autobiography of a Black Militant and the Life and Death of SNCC* (Jackson: University Press of Mississippi, 1990), 146–158; Lewis, *Walking with the Wind,* 381–385; Cynthia Griggs Flemming, *Soon We Will Not Cry: The Liberation of Ruby Doris Smith Robinson* (Lanham, MD: Rowan & Littlefield Publishers, 1998), 149–150, 159–162; *Bloody Lowndes,* 180–182.

26. Nelson, "SNCC Dumps 2 Top Leaders"; "Black Supremacists," editorial, *Washington Post,* May 29, 1966, E6; Austin C. Wehrwein, "Dr. King Disputes Negro Separatist," *New York Times,* May 28, 1966, 1.

27. Dittmer, *Local People,* 394–396.

28. Garrow, *Bearing the Cross,* 481; Carmichael, *Ready for Revolution,* 507.

29. Carmichael, *Ready for Revolution,* 505–508.

30. Quoted in Carmichael, *Ready for Revolution,* 509.

31. Garrow, *Bearing the Cross,* 482–483.

32. Garrow, *Bearing the Cross,* 485; Dittmer, *Local People,* 398–399.

33. Dittmer, *Local People,* 399–401.

34. Garrow, *Bearing the Cross,* 487–488; Dittmer, *Local People,* 402; Gene Roberts, "12,000 End Rights March to Jackson," *New York Times,* June 27, 1966, 1.

35. Carmichael, *Ready for Revolution,* 512–514; Garrow, *Bearing the Cross,* 488–489; Gene Roberts, "Dr. King on the Middle Ground," *New York Times,* July 17, 1966, 145.

36. "'Black Power:' Negro Leaders Split over Policy," *New York Times,* July 10, 1966, 143; "Trouble in the Streets: Scene Changes, Pattern Doesn't," *New York Times,* July 24, 1966, 128; Eve Edstrom, "Reds Behind Riots, Ohio Mayor Insists: Nebraskan Testifies," *Washington Post,* August 27, 1966, A2; "Statement of Martin Luther King," Federal Role in Urban Affairs: Hearings before the Subcommittee on Executive Reorganization on the Committee on Government Operations, US Senate, 89th Congress, second session, part 8, December 15, 1966 (Washington D.C., Government Printing Office, 1967), 2970.

37. "Black Power," *New York Times,* July 10, 1966, 143; Garrow, *Bearing the Cross,* 490; Jack Jones and Ray Rogers, "NAACP Director Condemns Moves for 'Black Power,'" *Los Angeles Times,* July 6, 1966, 3; Jack Jones and Ray Rogers, "Humphrey Assails All Racist Beliefs," *Los Angeles Times,* July 7, 1966, 3.

38. "Kennedy Notes a Peril," *New York Times,* June 30, 1966, 18.

39. Kennedy, "Suppose God Is Black."

40. Paul Hofmann, "Unrest in Brooklyn: The Causes," *New York Times,* July 23, 1966, 1; Paul L. Montgomery, "East New York Peaceful, But Police Stay on Alert," *New York Times,* July 25, 1966, 1; Walter Rugaber, "Cleveland Police Wound Negro Mother, 3 Children," *New York Times,* July 22, 1966, 1; Walter Rugaber, "Troops Relax, Too, as a Sunday Calm Returns to Cleveland's Riot Area," *New York Times,* July 25, 1966, 1; Walter Rugaber, "Cleveland Negro Slain by Gunfire," *New York Times,* July 23, 1966, 9; Jonathan Randal, "Racial Troubles a Shock to Troy," *New York Times,* July 25, 1966, 17; "Trouble in the Streets: Scene Changes, Pattern Doesn't, High Hopes and Frustration," *New York Times,* July 24, 1966, 128.

41. John Pomfret, "President Warns Negroes of Peril to Their Advance," *New York Times,* July 21, 1966, 1; Transcript of President's News Conference on Foreign and Domestic Policy, *New York Times,* July 21, 1966, 14; John D. Pomfret, "Johnson Asserts Riots by Negroes Impede Reforms," *New York Times,* July 24, 1966, 1.

42. Thomas J. Foley, "Riots Prove All-Out Slum Fight Must be Made: Public Hearings," *Washington Post,* August 7, 1966, K2; "Again the Riots," editorial, *New York Times,* July 23, 1966, 17.

43. Robert Dallek, *Flawed Giant: Lyndon Johnson and His Times* (New York: Oxford University Press, 1998), 329–334; Foley, "Riots Prove All Out Slum Fight Must be Made;" William C. Gibbons, *The U.S. Government and the Vietnam War: Executive and Legislative Roles and Relationships,* part IV: July 1965–January 1968 (Princeton: Princeton University Press, 1965), 424–426.

44. Richard Goodwin, *Remembering America: A Voice from the Sixties* (Boston: Little, Brown, 1988), 464.

45. Robert B. Semple Jr, "Urban 'Crisis' Will be Studied at Hearings Called by Ribicoff," *New York Times,* August 2, 1966, 48.

46. Statement of Hon. Robert F. Kennedy, US Senator from the State of New York, August 15, 1966, *Federal Role in Urban Affairs, Hearings before the Subcommittee on Executive Reorganization of the Committee on Government Operations*, US Senate, 89th Congress, second session, August 15–16, 1966, part I (Washington, DC: Government Printing Office, 1967), 26.

47. Marjorie Hunter, "Kennedy Chides Johnson on Cities," *New York Times*, August 16, 1966, 1.

48. Kennedy statement, *Federal Role in Urban Affairs* hearings, 25–28.

49. Kennedy statement, *Federal Role in Urban Affairs* hearings, 27–28.

50. Kennedy statement, *Federal Role in Urban Affairs* hearings, 26, 29, 30.

51. Kennedy statement, *Federal Role in Urban Affairs* hearings, 31–34.

52. Kennedy statement, *Federal Role in Urban Affairs* hearings, 34.

53. Kennedy statement, *Federal Role in Urban Affairs* hearings, 34–38.

54. Kennedy statement, *Federal Role in Urban Affairs* hearings, 39; James Baldwin, "A Talk to Teachers," *Saturday Review*, December 21, 1963, reprinted in *Selected Articles from The Price of the Ticket: Selected Non Fiction, 1948–1985* (New York: St. Martin's Marek, 1985), 84.

55. Kennedy statement, *Federal Role in Urban Affairs* hearings, 40.

56. Hunter, "Kennedy Chides Johnson"; Richard Rovere, *New Yorker*, September 10, 1966, 108;

57. Statement of Hon. Robert C. Weaver, Secretary of Housing and Urban Development, August 16, 1966, *Federal Role in Urban Affairs* hearings, 99, 144–146, 155–157, 184; statement of Hon. Nicholas deB. Katzenbach, Attorney General of the United States, August 17, 1966, *Federal Role in Urban Affairs* hearings, part 2, August 17–19, 1966, 286; Dallek, *Flawed Giant*, 321; Marjorie Hunter, "Johnson Defends Urban Aid Record as Best in History," *New York Times*, August 25, 1966, 1.

58. Statement of Ralph S. Locher, Mayor, City of Cleveland, August 26, 1966, *Federal Role in Urban Affairs* hearings, August 24–26, part 4, 987–1036; Eve Edstrom, "Reds Behind Riots, Ohio Mayor Insists; Nebraskan Testifies," *Washington Post*, August 27, 1966, A2.

59. Statement of Ralph Ellison, Author, August 30, 1966, *Federal Role in Urban Affairs* hearings, August 29–30, part 5, 1147–1150, 1162–1166.

60. Michael Woodsworth, *Battle for Bed-Stuy: The Long War on Poverty in New York City* (Cambridge, MA: Harvard University Press, 2016), 229–230; Thomas Johnston, interview by Larry J. Hackman, January 21, 1970, RFKOH; Jack Newfield, *RFK: A Memoir* (New York: Thunder's Mouth Press, 2003), 95.

61. Adam Walinsky, interview by Thomas Johnston, November 30, 1969, RFKOH; Woodsworth, *Battle for Bed-Stuy*, 232–233.

62. Robert Albright, "Bill Voted as Congress Speeds Up," *Washington Post*, October 5, 1966, 1; Joseph A. Loftus, "Senate Approves Antipoverty Bill; $746 Million Cut," *New York Times*, October 5, 1966, 1.

63. Johnston interview, January 21, 1970.

64. Johnston interview, January 21, 1970; Woodsworth, *Battle for Bed-Stuy*, 240.

65. Woodsworth, *Battle for Bed-Stuy*, 240–241.

66. Richard Dougherty, "California Arena Next on Bob Kennedy Route," *Los Angeles Times*, October 19, 1966, 29; Warren Weaver Jr., "Kennedy in Iowa: Eighteen Hour Triumph," *New York Times*, October 10, 1966, 1; James Reston, "Portland, Ore.: Kennedy's Western Invasion," *New York Times*, October 26, 1966, 46; Warren Weaver Jr., "All the Way with RFK," *New York Times*, October 30, 1966, E3.

67. Tom Wicker, "Kennedy Lends a Hand to Michigan Dems," *New York Times*, October 30, 1966, 83; Reston, "Portland, Ore.: Kennedy's Western Invasion"; "Bob Kennedy Favors Lottery for Draft," *Los Angeles Times*, October 25, 1966, 6.

68. Reston, "Portland, Ore.: Kennedy's Western Invasion"; Tom Wicker, "In the Nation: After Nineteen-Sixty, What?" *New York Times*, November 1, 1966, 40.

69. Richard Bergholz, "Reagan Criticizes UC for Permitting Bob Kennedy Talk," *Los Angeles Times*, October 21, 1966, 3.

70. Daryl E. Lembke, "Robert Kennedy Warmly Applauded at UC Berkeley," *Los Angeles Times*, October 24, 1966, 3; "Senator Robert Kennedy in Berkeley," October 23, 1966, Pacifica Radio Archives, American Archive of Public Broadcasting (WGBH and the Library of Congress), Boston, MA, and Washington, DC, accessed May 25, 2020, http://americanarchive.org/catalog/c-b-aacip-28-pc2t43jg47.

71. "Senator Robert Kennedy in Berkeley."

72. Lembke, "Robert Kennedy Warmly Applauded at UC Berkeley."

73. Warren Weaver Jr., "Kennedy Deplores Racism of a 'Few' Negro Leaders," *New York Times*, October 24, 1966, 1.

74. Warren Weaver Jr., "Kennedy Derides Idea He Is Concentrating Now on the Presidency in 1972," *New York Times*, October 19, 1972, 34.

75. Weaver, "Kennedy Derides Idea He Is Concentrating Now on the Presidency in 1972."

76. Dougherty, "California Arena Next on Bob Kennedy Route."

77. Peter Edelman interview by Larry Hackman, December 12, 1969; Peter Edelman, author interview, March 12, 2020.

78. Sidney E. Zion, "Civilian Review Board: Now a Nasty Campaign," *New York Times*, July 3, 1966, 94; Bernard Weinraub, "City Police Board Called U.S. Issue," *New York Times*, October 13, 1966, 1; Ber-

nard Weinraub, "Kennedy Joins Lindsay in Drive to Retain Police Review Board," *New York Times*, October 20, 1966, 59; "The Real Review Board," editorial, *New York Times*, September 28, 1966, 46.

79. Zion, "Civilian Review Board: Now a Nasty Campaign"; "The Real Review Board"; Weinraub, "City Police Board Called U.S. Issue."

80. Zion, "Civilian Review Board: Now a Nasty Campaign"; "The Real Review Board"; Bernard Weinraub, "Kennedy Sees Peril to Civilian Control of Police," *New York Times*, November 4, 1966, 29; Philip H. Dougherty, "Advertising: Civilian Review Board Fight," *New York Times*, October 18, 1966, 58.

81. Bernard Weinraub, "Police Review Board Killed by Large Majority in City," *New York Times*, November 9, 1966, 1; Bernard Weinraub, "Now a Police Board to Police the Police," *New York Times*, November 13, 1966, 217.

82. Steven V. Roberts, "Redevelopment Plan Set for Bedford Stuyvesant," *New York Times*, December 11, 1966, 1; Sheppard Daphne, "New Look Coming to Bedford-Stuy," *New York Amsterdam News*, December 17, 1966, 27.

83. "Hope in Brooklyn," *New York Amsterdam News*, December 17, 1966, 18; "Remaking Brooklyn's Slums," editorial, *New York Times*, December 12, 1966, 46; Woodsworth, *Battle for Bed-Stuy*, 235.

84. Newfield, *RFK*, 97.

13 · RECKONING

1. Statement of Martin Luther King Jr., *Federal Role in Urban Affairs: Hearings before the Subcommittee on Executive Reorganization of the Committee on Government Operations*, US Senate, 89th Congress, second session, part 8, December 15, 1966 (Washington, DC: Government Printing Office, 1967), 2978.

2. Robert B. Semple Jr., "Prescriptions for the Slums," *New York Times*, December 19, 1966.

3. King statement, *Federal Role in Urban Affairs* hearings, 2976.

4. King statement, *Federal Role in Urban Affairs* hearings, 2968, 2975.

5. King statement, *Federal Role in Urban Affairs* hearings, 2970, 2972.

6. King statement, *Federal Role in Urban Affairs* hearings, 2970.

7. King statement, *Federal Role in Urban Affairs* hearings, 2978, 2982.

8. King statement, *Federal Role in Urban Affairs* hearings, 2980–2981.

9. King statement, *Federal Role in Urban Affairs* hearings, 2974, 2987–2990.

10. King statement, *Federal Role in Urban Affairs* hearings, 2981, 2990–2994.

11. Peter Edelman, interview with Larry Hackman, July 15, 1969, RFKOH; Jack Newfield, "Robert Kennedy's Bedford-Stuyvesant Legacy," *New York Magazine*, December 16, 1968, 33.

12. Michael Woodsworth, *Battle for Bed-Stuy: The Long War on Poverty in New York City* (Cambridge, MA: Harvard University Press, 2016), 239.

13. Woodsworth, *Battle for Bed-Stuy*, 238–239, 243–244.

14. Sewell Chan, "Thomas R. Jones, 93, a Judge Who Agitated for Urban Reform," *New York Times*, November 1, 2006; Woodsworth, *Battle for Bed-Stuy*, 102–104.

15. Woodsworth, *Battle for Bed-Stuy*, 248, 251–252.

16. Woodsworth, *Battle for Bed-Stuy*, 251–252, 256–259; Newfield, "Robert Kennedy's Bedford-Stuyvesant Legacy," 32.

17. Woodsworth, *Battle for Bed-Stuy*, 140–144, 258–260.

18. Woodsworth, *Battle for Bed-Stuy*, 229, 268; Franklin A. Thomas interview by Roberta Greene, March 23, 1972, RFKOH.

19. Thomas interview, March 23, 1972.

20. Thomas interview, March 23, 1972.

21. Newfield, "Robert Kennedy's Bedford-Stuyvesant Legacy," 33.

22. Thomas interview, March 23, 1972

23. Thomas interview, March 23, 1972; Woodsworth, *Battle for Bed-Stuy*, 265–66, 269–70/

24. Arthur Schlesinger Jr., *Robert Kennedy and His Times* (Boston: Houghton Mifflin Company, 1978), 788.

25. George Herring, *America's Longest War: The United States and Vietnam, 1950–1975*, 5th ed. (New York: McGraw-Hill Education, 2013), 210–211; Robert Dallek, *Flawed Giant: Lyndon Johnson and His Times, 1961–1973* (New York: Oxford University Press, 1998), 443–444.

26. Dallek, *Flawed Giant*, 446.

27. William vanden Heuvel and Milton Gwirtzman, *On His Own: RFK 1964–1968* (New York: Doubleday & Co., 1970), 227–237; Frank Mankiewicz interview by Larry Hogan, August 12, 1969, RFKOH.

28. Mankiewicz interview, August 29, 1969.

29. "Hanoi Said to Give Kennedy a Signal It's Ready to Talk," *New York Times*, February 6, 1967, 1; Mankiewicz interview, August 12, 1969; Dallek, *Flawed Giant*, 447; Schlesinger, *Robert Kennedy*, 767–768.

30. Mankiewicz interview, August 12, 1969; Schlesinger, *Robert Kennedy*, 768.

31. Schlesinger, *Robert Kennedy,* 768–69; Mankiewicz interview, August 12, 1969.

32. Mankiewicz interview, August 12, 1969; "Excerpts from Kennedy Speech and Texts of Rusk Statement and Johnson Letter," *New York Times,* March 3, 1967, 10; Hedrick Smith, "Kennedy Asks Suspension of U.S. Air Raids on North; Administration Unmoved," *New York Times,* March 3, 1967, 1.

33. "The Vietnam Debate," editorial, *New York Times,* March 3, 1967, 34; "Excerpts from Kennedy Speech and Texts of Rusk Statement and Johnson Letter," 10; Schlesinger, *Robert Kennedy,* 771.

34. David Garrow, *Bearing the Cross: Martin Luther King, Jr., and the Southern Christian Leadership Conference* (New York: William Morrow, 1986), 547.

35. Garrow, *Bearing the Cross,* 543; *Ramparts* Extra, "The Children of Vietnam," reprint from *Ramparts,* January 1967.

36. Garrow, *Bearing the Cross,* 545–546, 549–550.

37. Martin Luther King Jr. "Beyond Vietnam," April 4, 1967, New York, NY, https://kinginstitute .stanford.edu/king-papers/documents/beyond-vietnam; Douglas Robinson, "Dr. King Proposes a Boycott of the War," *New York Times,* April 5, 1967, 1.

38. "Dr. King's Error," editorial, *New York Times,* April 7, 1967, 36; Garrow, *Bearing the Cross,* 553–554. 570.

39. Garrow, *Bearing the Cross,* 554.

40. Garrow, *Bearing the Cross,* 559.

41. Richard Reeves, "Kennedy Will Aid Johnson in 1968," *New York Times,* March 18, 1967, 15; Peter Edelman, interview by Larry Hackman, March 13, 1974, RFKOH.

42. Joseph A. Loftus, "Antipoverty Fund Held Inadequate," *New York Times,* March 16, 1967, 27; "RFK Says $2 Billion Johnson Asks Is 'Inadequate' for Poverty War," *Washington Post,* March 16, 1967, A4.

43. Jean White, "Senators Hear Experts on Poverty," *Washington Post,* March 14, 1967, A2; Marian Wright Edelman, *Lanterns: A Memoir of Mentors* (Boston: Beacon Press, 1999), 69–70, 73–79.

44. Edelman interview, March 13, 1974; John Dittmer, *Local People: The Struggle for Civil Rights in Mississippi* (Urbana: University of Illinois, 1995), 364–365.

45. Crystal R. Sanders, *A Chance for Change: Head Start and Mississippi's Black Freedom Struggle* (Chapel Hill: University of North Carolina Press, 2016), 147–177; Dittmer, *Local People,* 367–380.

46. Joseph A. Loftus, "Poverty Hearing Set in Mississippi," *New York Times,* April 10, 1967, 13; Joseph Loftus, "Inquiry Told of 'Relatively Minor" Spending Gap in Mississippi Head Start," *New York Times,* April 11, 1967, 18; Richard W. Boone, oral history interview, North Carolina, 1992, with Robert Korstad, Southern Rural Poverty Collection, DeWitt Wallace Center for Media and Democracy, Duke University, 32–33; Edelman interview, March 13, 1974; Dittmer, *Local People,* 376–382.

47. Edelman, *Lanterns,* 107; Edelman interview, March 23, 1974.

48. Joseph A. Loftus, "Clark and Kennedy Visit the Poor of Mississippi," *New York Times,* April 12, 1967, 29; Edelman interview, March 13, 1974.

49. Edelman, *Lanterns,* 107; Edelman interview, March 23, 1974; Edwin Schmitt, *President of the Other America: Robert Kennedy and the Politics of Poverty* (Amherst: University of Massachusetts Press, 2011), 179.

50. Edelman, *Lanterns,* 107.

51. Nick Kotz, *Let Them Eat Promises: The Politics of Hunger in America* (Garden City, New York: Doubleday & Company, 1971), 62–63; Edelman interview, March 23, 1974; Nan Robertson, "Stennis and Eastland Reject 'Libel' on Mississippi," *New York Times,* July 12, 1967, 22.

52. Kotz, *Let Them Eat Promises,* 62; Edelman interview, March 23, 1974; Schlesinger, *Robert Kennedy,* 795.

53. Nan Robertson, "Severe Hunger Found in Mississippi," *New York Times,* June 17, 1967, 14.

54. Robertson, "Severe Hunger Found in Mississippi"; Edelman interview, March 23, 1974.

55. Kotz, *Let Them Eat Promises,* 69; Robertson, "Stennis and Eastland Reject 'Libel.'"

56. Eve Edstrom, "Visit Starving, Miss. Senators Told," *Washington Post,* July 12, 1964, 12.

57. Edstrom, "Visit Starving, Miss. Senators Told"; Nan Robertson, "Javits and Freeman Trade Shouts at Hunger Inquiry," *New York Times,* July 13, 1967, 1; Kotz, *Let Them Eat Promises,* 78.

58. Kotz, *Let Them Eat Promises,* 66.

59. Edelman interview, March 23, 1974; Edelman, *Lanterns,* 108.

60. Daryl Lembke, "Senators Find Migrants Living in Cars, Tents," *Los Angeles Times,* May 12, 1967, 28.

61. Budd Schulberg, "RFK: Harbinger of Hope," *Playboy,* January 1969, 250–251; Paul Weeks, "Watts Writers Pour Out Woes to Kennedy," *Los Angeles Times,* May 14, 1968, G7.

62. Schulberg, "RFK: Harbinger of Hope," 251.

14 • THE GRAVEST CRISIS SINCE THE CIVIL WAR

1. Malcolm McLaughlin, *The Long Hot Summer of 1967: Urban Rebellion in America* (New York: Palgrave Macmillan, 2014), 7; Robert Shellow, ed., *The Harvest of American Racism: The Political Meaning of Violence in 1967* (Ann Arbor: University of Michigan Press, 2018), 1.

2. Shellow, *Harvest of American Racism*, 21; "Uprising of 1967," *Encyclopedia of Detroit*, Detroit Historical Society, https://detroithistorical.org/learn/encyclopedia-of-detroit/uprising-1967.

3. McLaughlin, *Long Hot Summer*, 16, 48.

4. McLaughlin, *Long Hot Summer*, 86; "The Newark Tragedy: A Week-Long Inquiry," *Washington Post*, July 24, 1967, A1.

5. "The Newark Tragedy: A Week-Long Inquiry"; Albert Bergesen, "Race Riots of 1967: An Analysis of Police Violence in Detroit and Newark," *Journal of Black Studies* 12, no. 3 (March 1982), 265–266.

6. Sidney Fine, *Violence in the Motor City: The Cavanagh Administration, Race Relations, and the Detroit Riot of 1967* (East Lansing: Michigan State University, 2007), 32–33, 103–113; Thomas Sugrue, *The Origins of the Urban Crisis: Race and Inequality in Postwar Detroit* (Princeton, NJ: Princeton University Press, 2014), 263–264.

7. Sugrue, *Origins of the Urban Crisis*, 12, 260–262, 264; Fine, *Violence in the Motor City*, 24–25.

8. Fine, *Violence in the Motor City*, 95–113.

9. Shellow, *Harvest of American Racism*, 23–24; "Black Challenge: The Violence Spreads," *New York Times*, July 30, 1968, 133.

10. Shellow, *Harvest of American Racism*, 24–25; Jerry M. Flint, "Detroit Negroes Call Police Slow," *New York Times*, July 26, 1967, 1; "Detroit Is Swept by Rioting and Fires; Romney Calls in Guards; 700 Arrested," *New York Times*, July 24, 1967, 1; Gene Roberts, "U.S. Troops Sent into Detroit; 19 Dead; Johnson Decries Riots," *New York Times*, July 25, 1967, 1; McLaughlin, *Long Hot Summer*, 6.

11. Shellow, *Harvest of American Racism*, 25–27; Bergesen, "Race Riots of 1967," 266.

12. Roberts, "U.S. Troops Sent to Detroit"; Steven M. Gillon, *Separate and Unequal: The Kerner Commission Report and the Unraveling of American Liberalism* (New York: Basic Books, 2018), 4–5; Shellow, *Harvest of American Racism*, 27; "Black Challenge: The Violence Spreads."

13. Elizabeth Hinton, *From the War on Poverty to the War on Crime: The Making of Mass Incarceration* (Cambridge, MA: Harvard University Press, 2016); McLaughlin, *Long Hot Summer*, 101–104.

14. Chalmers Roberts, "Looting and Arson Spread in Detroit; GOP Blames Johnson for Race Riots," *Washington Post*, July 25, 1967, A1; Rowland Evans and Robert Novak, "Fiddling while Detroit Burns," *Washington Post*, July 27, 1967, A17; Lawrence E. Davies, "Reagan Brands Those Who Riot 'Mad Dogs against the People,'" *New York Times*, July 26, 1967, 19.

15. Max Frankel, "President Calls on Nation to Combat Lawlessness," *New York Times*, July 25, 1967; Gillon, *Separate and Unequal*, 25; Evans and Novak, "Fiddling while Detroit Burns."

16. Lyndon Johnson, "Speech to the Nation on Civil Disorders," July 27, 1967, Presidential Speeches, Miller Center, University of Virginia, https://millercenter.org/the-presidency/presidential-speeches/july-27-1967-speech-nation-civil-disorders.

17. Frank Mankiewicz, interview by Larry Hackman, November 6, 1969, RKOHC; Frank Mankiewicz, interview by author, May 17, 2014; Thurston Clarke, *The Last Campaign: Robert Kennedy and 82 Days that Inspired America* (New York: Henry Holt & Company, 2008), 110–111.

18. Joseph A. Loftus, "Moynihan Calls on ADA to Seek Ties with Conservatives," *New York Times*, September 24, 1967, 1.

19. Jack Newfield, *RFK: A Memoir* (New York: Thunder's Mouth Press, 2003), 63.

20. Chalmers M. Roberts, "Bills Offered for Probe of Urban Riots," *Washington Post*, July 26, 1967, A1; "Kennedy Urges Jobs, Not Whip for Ghettos," *Washington Post*, August 5, 1967, A4.

21. Peter Edelman, interview by Larry Hackman, December 12, 1969.

22. Edwin Schmitt, *President of the Other America: Robert Kennedy and the Politics of Poverty* (Amherst: University of Massachusetts Press, 2011), 187; E. Barrett Prettyman, interview by Larry Hackman, June 5, 1969, RKOH.

23. "Business Asked by RFK to Aid Nation's Cities," *Washington Post*, September 30, 1967, A5; Newfield, *RFK*, 98–99.

24. Edelman interview, July 15, 1969; Newfield, *RFK*, 104–105; Jack Newfield, "Robert Kennedy's Bedford-Stuyvesant Legacy," *New York Magazine*, December 16, 1968, 33.

25. Robert B. Semple Jr., "Kennedy's Plan on Slums Scored," *New York Times*, September 15, 1967, 1; "Kennedy Plan on Slum Housing Defended by Dillon and Caplan," *New York Times*, September 16, 1967, 17.

26. Schmitt, *President of the Other America*, 190.

27. Newfield, *RFK*, 106.

28. Peter Milliones, "Kennedy and Javits Are Shocked by Housing of Migrants Upstate," *New York Times*, September 9, 1967, 25; Schmitt, *President of the Other America*, 190.

29. Peter Edelman, interview by Larry Hackman, August 5, 1969; Edelman, *Lanterns*, 109.

30. Gene Roberts, "Dr. King Planning Protest to 'Dislocate' Large Cities," *New York Times*, August 16, 1967, 1; Willard Clopton Jr., "Psychologists Hear Dr. King Explain Riots," *Washington Post*, September 2, 1967, D12; David Garrow, *Bearing the Cross: Martin Luther King, Jr. and the Southern Christian Leadership Conference* (New York: William Morrow, 1986), 579; Gene Roberts, "Dr. King to Back Peace Candidate," *New York Times*, August 18, 1967, 14.

31. Roberts, "Dr. King Planning Protest to 'Dislocate' Large Cities"; Garrow, *Bearing the Cross,* 576.

32. Garrow, *Bearing the Cross,* 577–578; Walter Rugaber, "Dr. King Planning to Disrupt Capitol in Drive for Jobs," *New York Times,* December 5, 1967, 1.

33. Isabelle McCaig, "RFK Has Birthday on Monday," *Washington Post,* November 19, 1967, E3.

34. Phil Casey, "Quiet Rites Recall the Death of a President," *Washington Post,* November 23, 1967, 23.

35. Arthur Schlesinger Jr., *Robert Kennedy and His Times* (Boston: Houghton Mifflin Company, 1978); 408–409; "Indians Victims, R.F. Kennedy Says," *New York Times,* September 14, 1963, 11.

36. "Kennedy Visits Navajos on Arizona Reservation," *New York Times,* July 5, 1967, 23; Schlesinger, *Robert Kennedy,* 793; Schmitt, *President of the Other America,* 193.

37. Homer Bigart, "Senate Panel Hears Why Indians Don't Riot," *New York Times,* December 16, 1967, 22; Schlesinger, *Robert Kennedy,* 793.

38. "Indian Education," editorial, *Washington Post,* January 5, 1968, A12.

39. Schlesinger, *Robert Kennedy,* 793.

40. Peter Julius, "Social Security Bill Jolts Welfare Plan," *Washington Post,* December 10, 1967; "Social Insecurity Bill," editorial, *New York Times,* December 9, 1967, 46; "House Votes Rise in Social Security; Fight Looms on Welfare," *New York Times,* December 14, 1967, 36.

41. "House Votes Rise in Social Security; Fight Looms on Welfare"; "Social Insecurity Bill," 46; "Social Security Package," editorial, *Washington Post,* December 15, 1967, A28.

42. "Senate Liberals Seek to Defer Welfare Cuts," *Washington Post,* December 13, 1967, A2; Robert C. Albright, "Social Security Bill Slated to Be Passed Today; Kennedy Critical Sneak Play Charged," *Washington Post,* December 15, 1967, A9; John W. Finney, "Senate Liberals Caught Napping," *New York Times,* December 15, 1967, 1.

43. "Bill on Aid to Aged Scored by Kennedy," *New York Times,* December 15, 1967, 12.

44. John Doar interview, July 31, 1968, Jean Stein Papers, JFKL; Michael Woodsworth, *Battle for Bed-Stuy: The Long War on Poverty in New York City* (Cambridge, MA: Harvard University Press, 2016), 276–277.

45. Woodsworth, *Battle for Bed-Stuy,* 277–278.

46. Woodsworth, *Battle for Bed-Stuy,* 278–282.

47. Tom Adam Davis, "Black Power in Action: The Bedford Stuyvesant Restoration Corporation, Robert F. Kennedy, and the Politics of the Urban Crisis," *Journal of American History* 100, no. 3 (December 2013), 750; Doar interview, July 31, 1968.

48. Doar interview, July 31, 1968.

49. Davis, "Black Power in Action," 751–752.

50. Garrow, *Bearing the Cross,* 576; Mankiewicz interview, November 6, 1969; Joseph Alsop, "1972—and the Loneliness of the Long-Distance Candidate," *Washington Post,* December 1, 1967, A21.

15 · OUR COUNTRY'S FUTURE

1. George Herring, *America's Longest War: The United States and Vietnam, 1950–1975,* 5th ed. (New York: McGraw-Hill Education, 2013), 197, 214, 220, 226; William C. Gibbons, *U.S. Government and the Vietnam War: Executive and Legislative Roles and Relationships* (Princeton: Princeton University Press, 1995), iv, 426–429.

2. Arthur Schlesinger Jr., *Robert Kennedy and His Times* (Boston: Houghton Mifflin Company, 1978), 832.

3. Jack Newfield, *RFK: A Memoir* (New York: Thunder's Mouth Press, 2003), 186; Schlesinger, *Robert Kennedy,* 832; *Face the Nation,* November 26, 1967, YouTube video, https://www.youtube.com/watch?v=jkbW5yJanzc.

4. John Herbers, "McCarthy Buoys Kennedy Backers," *New York Times,* November 30, 1967, 26; "McCarthy Statement on Entering the 1968 Primaries," *New York Times,* December 1, 1967, 40; "The McCarthy Challenge," editorial, *New York Times,* December 1, 1967, 46.

5. Walter Pincus, "McCarthy Is a 1-Man Show," *Washington Post,* December 3, 1967, B1; Tom Wicker, "In the Nation: McCarthy Enters the Game," *New York Times,* December 3, 1967, 267; George Rising, *Clean for Gene: Eugene McCarthy's 1968 Presidential Campaign* (Westport, CT: Praeger), 55–58; William H. Honan, "A Would be Candidate for this Season," *New York Times,* December 10, 1967, 295.

6. Warren Weaver Jr., "McCarthy Denies Kennedy Plot," *New York Times,* December 3, 1967, 42; Warren Weaver Jr., "A Statesman Who . . . ," *New York Times,* December 4, 1967, 41; David Halberstam, "McCarthy and the Divided Left," *Harper's Magazine,* March 1968, 34, 40, 41.

7. Schlesinger, *Robert Kennedy,* 831–833.

8. Schlesinger, *Robert Kennedy,* 832–835; Burke Marshall interview by Larry Hackman, January 19–20, 1970, RFKOH.

9. Schlesinger, *Robert Kennedy,* 837.

10. Schlesinger, *Robert Kennedy,* 837; Marquis Childs, "A Kennedy Move against Johnson," *Washington Post,* January 24, 1968, A20.

11. William vanden Heuvel and Milton Gwirtzman, *On His Own: RFK 1964–1968* (New York: Doubleday & Co., 1970), 203–204; E. W. Kenworthy, "Kennedy Repeats: No Johnson Fight," *New York Times,* January 31, 1968, 19; "Kennedy Backs Off," editorial, *New York Times,* February 1 1968, 1; David S. Broder, "RFK Won't Oppose LBJ Renomination," *Washington Post,* January 31, 1968, A1.

12. Herring, *America's Longest War,* 233–241; Joel Achenbach, "Did the News Media, Led by Walter Cronkite, Lose the War in Vietnam?," *Washington Post,* May 25, 2018.

13. Tom Wicker, "Kennedy Asserts U.S. Cannot Win," *New York Times,* February 9, 1968, 1; "Excerpts from Text of Kennedy Speech," *New York Times,* February 9, 1968, 12; Marshall interview, January 19–20, 1970.

14. Homer Bigart, "Kentucky Miners: A Grim Winter," *New York Times,* October 20, 1963, 1; Edwin Schmitt, *President of the Other America: Robert Kennedy and the Politics of Poverty* (Amherst: University of Massachusetts Press, 2011), 196–197; Robert Kennedy's opening address, *Field Hearings, Eastern Kentucky,* Subcommittee on Employment, Manpower, and Poverty, US Senate, 90th Congress, second session, February 14, 1968 https://rfkineky.org/docs/Neon_transcript.pdf; Tom Wicker, "President Johnson Spurs Drive on Poverty in Six-State Tour," *New York Times,* May 8, 1964, 1; Robert Dallek, *Flawed Giant: Lyndon Johnson and His Times, 1961–1973* (New York: Oxford University Press, 1998), 107.

15. Paul Schwartzman, "They Were Kentucky's Poorest, Most Desperate People. And He Was a Kennedy with an Entourage," *Washington Post,* February 21, 2018.

16. Peter Edelman telephone interview with the author, July 8, 2020; Robert F. Kennedy Performance Project, *RFK in EKY,* https://rfkineky.org/; Schwartzman, "They Were Kentucky's Poorest, Most Desperate People"; "Kennedy Blocked on Strip-Mining Tour," *New York Times,* February 14, 1968, 56; *Field Hearings: Eastern Kentucky,* 3–4; Ben A. Franklin, "Kennedy Calls Antipoverty Program a Failure," *New York Times,* February 15, 1968, 26.

17. Franklin, "Kennedy Calls Poverty Program a Failure."

18. *Field Hearings: Eastern Kentucky,* 11–12.

19. *Field Hearings: Eastern Kentucky,* 36–44.

20. *Field Hearings: Eastern Kentucky,* 61–62.

21. *Field Hearings: Eastern Kentucky,* 44–50.

22. *Field Hearings: Eastern Kentucky,* 19–20, 52–55.

23. *Field Hearings: Eastern Kentucky,* 64–69.

24. *Field Hearings: Eastern Kentucky,* 69–75.

25. *Field Hearings: Eastern Kentucky,* 25–26.

26. *Field Hearings: Eastern Kentucky,* 55–58; Schmitt, *President of the Other America,* 198.

27. *Field Hearings: Eastern Kentucky,* 40; Franklin, "Kennedy Calls Antipoverty Program a Failure."

28. Anne Caudill interviewed in *Harry Caudill: A Man of Courage,* KET Documentaries, Kentucky Educational Television / PBS, https://www.ket.org/program/ket-documentaries/harry-caudill-a-man-of-courage-33660/.

29. Schmitt, *President of the Other America,* 199.

30. Lawrence E. Davies, "Kennedy Expects to Back Johnson Despite Differences on the War," *New York Times,* January 5, 1968, 5; "Kennedy Deplores Nation's 'Betrayal' of Indian Education," *New York Times,* January 6, 1968, 18; "Kennedy Visits Indians," *New York Times,* February 19, 1968, 30.

31. Richard Witkins, "Pressures on Kennedy," *New York Times,* January 22, 1968, 28; "Improved Planning Urged by Kennedy," *New York Times,* February 10, 1968, 18; J. Anthony Lukas, "Kennedy Makes Plea Upstate for Help to End Bias," *New York Times,* January 17, 1968, 21.

32. J. Anthony Lukas, "Kennedy Polls 700 in Rochester; Most Urge an End to Bombing," *New York Times,* January 16, 1968, 2; Witkins, "Pressures on Kennedy."

33. "Senators Decry Welfare Curbs," *New York Times,* February 1, 1968, 18.

34. Jack Gould, "TV: Belafonte Reinvigorates the Late Night Scene," *New York Times,* February 7, 1968, 95; Harry Belafonte with Michael Shnayerson, *Harry Belafonte: My Song; A Memoir* (New York: Albert A. Knopf, 2011), 323–324.

35. "Business Reported Hostile to Kennedy," *New York Times,* February 26, 1968, 2.

36. Jack Bass and Jack Nelson, *The Orangeburg Massacre* (Macon, GA: Mercer University Press, 1996), 99–121.

37. Bass and Nelson, *Orangeburg Massacre,* 15–22; Patricia Sullivan, *Lift Every Voice: The NAACP and the Making of the Civil Rights Movement* (New York: New Press, 2009), 423.

38. Bass and Nelson, *Orangeburg Massacre,* 15–16, 23–28.

39. Bass and Nelson, *Orangeburg Massacre,* 23–32.

40. Bass and Nelson, *Orangeburg Massacre,* 37–45.

41. Bass and Nelson, *Orangeburg Massacre,* 33–36, 49–54.

42. Bass and Nelson, *Orangeburg Massacre,* 50–52; Cleveland Sellers with Robert Terrell, *The River of No Return: The Autobiography of a Black Militant and the Life and Death of SNCC* (Jackson: University Press of Mississippi, 1990).

43. Bass and Nelson, *Orangeburg Massacre,* 55–60.

44. Bass and Nelson, *Orangeburg Massacre,* 61–66.

45. Bass and Nelson, *Orangeburg Massacre*, 66–77.

46. Bass and Nelson, *Orangeburg Massacre*, 80–81; Douglas Robinson, "South Carolina Governor Says Black Militants Caused Rioting," *New York Times*, February 18, 1968, 58.

47. Bass and Nelson, *Orangeburg Massacre*, 79–80, 82–83; "Curfew Imposed by Governor in Orangeburg, SC," *New York Times*, February 10, 1968, 23; "Curfew Stills College Town," *Washington Post*, February 10, 1968, A1; "Tragedy at Orangeburg," editorial, *Washington Post*, February 13, 1968, A12; Jack Nelson, "Orangeburg Students Unarmed, Study Shows," *Los Angeles Times*, February 18, 1968, A3.

48. Bass and Nelson, *Orangeburg Massacre*, 87, 92; "Effective Boycott Follows Massacre," *Chicago Defender*, February 27, 1968, 19; "Violence Erupts during Durham, NC Protest," *New York Times*, February 16, 1968, 16; William Clopton Jr., "Flag Furled in Howard Protest," *Washington Post*, February 17, 1968, A1; "S.C. Violence Protested at Virginia St.," *Washington Post*, February 17, 1968, B6; "Memorial for S.C. Students Set," *Chicago Defender*, February 15, 1968, 3.

49. "The Carolina Slaughter," *Chicago Defender*, February 13, 1968, 13; William R. Cotterell, "Segregated Bowling Alley Opens up for S.C. Students," *Chicago Defender*, February 28, 1968, 8.

50. Hobart Rowen, "LBJ Melts Some Butter to Provide More Guns," *Washington Post*, January 30, 1968 A1; Donald Janson, "Alinsky, 'Professional Agitator,' Warns of Summer Riots," *New York Times*, 16; "Negro Jobless Rate Called 4 Times White in Big Cities," *New York Times*, 34; Walter Rugaber, "Civil Rights: Strong Challenge by King," *New York Times*, February 11, 1968, E4.

51. C. Gerald Fraser, "Negroes Discuss Repression Fears," *New York Times*, February 25, 1968, 46; William Chapman, "Police Arms Spawn Alarming Rumors: Negroes Fear One-Sided Arms Race," *Washington Post*, February 26, 1968, A1.

52. William Chapman, "U.S. Police Arm for Summer," *Washington Post*, February 25, 1968, A1; Chapman, "Police Arms Spawn Alarming Rumors"; "The Garrison City," editorial, *Washington Post*, February 28, 1968, A14; Chapman, "Vigorous, Unprecedented Preparations Made to Control Riots," *Washington Post*, March 1, 1968, A11.

53. John Herbers, "Panel on Civil Disorders Calls for Drastic Action to Avoid 2-Society Nation," *New York Times*, March 1, 1968, 1; "Text of Summary of Report by National Advisory Commission on Civil Disorders," *New York Times*, March 1, 1968, 20.

54. Steven M. Gillon, *Separate and Unequal: The Kerner Commission Report and the Unraveling of American Liberalism* (New York: Basic Books, 2018), 269.

55. Gillon, *Separate and Unequal*, 45–54.

56. Gillon, *Separate and Unequal*, 92–103.

57. Gillon, *Separate and Unequal*, 111–131.

58. Gillon, *Separate and Unequal*, 251–261. The team of social scientists who contributed to *The Harvest of American Racism* included David Boesel, Louis Goldberg, Gary T. Marx, David O. Sears, and director Robert Shellow. The report, archived at the Lyndon Baines Johnson archive, was published by the University of Michigan Press in 2018.

59. Herbers, "Panel on Civil Disorders."

60. Gillon, *Separate and Unequal*, 249–256.

61. Burke Marshall interview, January 19–20, 1970; Herring, *America's Longest War*, 249.

62. John W. Finney, "Criticism of War Widens in Senate Build-up Issue," *New York Times*, March 8, 1968, 1; "Excerpts from Debate over the Administration's Policy in Vietnam," *New York Times*, March 8, 1968, 8.

63. "Excerpts from Debate in Senate over the Administration's Policy in Vietnam."

64. Burke Marshall interview, January 19–20, 1970.

65. Peter Edelman, interview by Larry Hacknab, July 15, 1969; Edwin Guthman, *We Band of Brothers* (New York: Harper & Row, 1964), 326.

66. Neil Sheehan, "Most Draft Deferments to End for Graduate Students," February 17, 1968, 1; E. W. Kenworthy, "College Students Drum Up Votes for McCarthy," *New York Times*, March 4, 1968, 16; "McCarthy Rides Student Power," *New York Times*, March 10, 1968, E1; "McCarthy's Appeal to Youth," editorial, *New York Times*, March 14, 1968, 42; "Clean for Gene," *New York Times*, March 10, 1968, E1; Lawrence Van Gelder, "Survey Shows College Students Back McCarthy over Kennedy," *New York Times*, March 17, 1968, 1.

67. Schlesinger, *Robert Kennedy*, 847–849; E. W. Kenworthy, "McCarthy Says, 'I Think I Can Get the Nomination,'" *New York Times*, March 14, 1968, 1; "Survey Shows College Students Back McCarthy over Kennedy."

68. Oswald Johnston, "Riot Study Hush Angers Senators," *Baltimore Sun*, March 14, 1968, A1.

69. "Riot Study Hush Angers Senators"; Richard Madden, "Three in Senate Charge Johnson with Inaction on Riots," *New York Times*, March 14, 1968, 37.

70. "Transcript of Interview with Kennedy," *New York Times*, March 14, 1968, 30; "Transcript of Television Interview with McCarthy," *New York Times*, March 15, 1968, 25.

71. "Transcript of Interview with Kennedy."

72. Schlesinger, *Robert Kennedy*, 856–857.

73. Marshall interview, January 19–20, 1970.

74. David S. Broder, "Senator Enters Presidency Race," *Washington Post,* March 17, 1968, A1; "Kennedy's Statement and Excerpts from News Conference," *New York Times,* March 17, 1968, 68.

75. "Kennedy's Statement and Excerpts from News Conference."

76. "Kennedy's Statement and Excerpts from News Conference."

16 · A TIME OF DANGER AND QUESTIONING

1. Joshua Bloom and Waldo E. Martin, Jr., *Black against Empire: The History and Politics of the Black Panther Party* (Berkeley: University of California Press, 2011), 116–118; "Muhammad Ali at Fairleigh Dickinson," *New York Amsterdam News,* April 20, 1968, 32.

2. John Lewis with Michael D'Orso, *Walking with the Wind: A Memoir of the Movement* (New York: Simon & Schuster, 1998), 403.

3. Jules Witcover, *85 Days: The Last Campaign of Robert Kennedy* (New York: G.P. Putnam's Sons, 1968), 101–104; Thurston Clarke, *The Last Campaign: Robert F. Kennedy and 82 Days that Inspired America* (New York: Henry Holt and Company, 2008), 43.

4. Witcover, *85 Days,* 105; Clarke, *Last Campaign,* 46–47.

5. Witcover, *85 Days,* 107; Clarke, *Last Campaign,* 48.

6. Robert Kennedy, "Recapturing America's Moral Vision," March 18, 1968, University of Kansas, in *RFK: Collected Speeches,* ed. Edwin O. Guthman and C. Richard Allen (New York: Viking, 1993), 328–330.

7. Guthman and Allen, *RFK,* 230.

8. Witcover, *85 Days,* 107–108.

9. Richard Harwood, "RFK Says Johnson Divides the Nation," *Washington Post,* March 22, 1968, A1.

10. Harwood, "RFK Says Johnson Divides"; John Herbers, "Kennedy Charges Johnson is Divisive," *New York Times,* March 22, 1968, 1.

11. "Kennedy in Alabama," *New York Times,* March 22, 1968, 37; Guthman and Allen, *RFK,* 334.

12. Guthman and Allen, *RFK,* 333–334.

13. Clarke, *Last Campaign,* 51; Witcover, *85 Days,* 110.

14. Witcover, *85 Days,* 118; Guthman and Allen, *RFK,* 350.

15. Carl Greenberg, "Kennedy Given Warm Welcome in N. California," *Los Angeles Times,* March 24, 1968, E1; Clarke, *Last Campaign,* 56–57; Guthman and Allen, *RFK,* 355; "RFK Is Booed by Some of 5000 at L.A. Airport," *Washington Post,* March 25, 1968, A2.

16. Greenberg, "Kennedy Given Warm Welcome"; Donovan quoted in Guthman and Allen, *RFK,* 335–336.

17. Witcover, *85 Days,* 115; Clarke, *Last Campaign,* 59–60.

18. Richard Harwood, "5000 Greet Kennedy in Watts Area," *Washington Post,* March 26, 1968, A1; Clarke, *Last Campaign,* 58.

19. Donovan quoted in Guthman and Allen, *RFK,* 335–36; Harwood, "5000 Greet Kennedy in Watts Area"; Richard Harwood, "Crowd Madness and the Kennedy Strategy," *Washington Post,* March 28, 1968, A29.

20. Frank C. Porter, "LBJ Ties Viet War to Freedom in the U.S.," *Washington Post,* March 26, 1968, A1.

21. Richard Harwood, "Kennedy to Run in Indiana; Clark's Talk Hissed," *Washington Post,* March 28, 1968, A1; Witcover, *85 Days,* 122.

22. Clarke, *Last Campaign,* 65; Richard Harwood, "RFK Kids Self, Tells Stories to Cheering Crowds in West," May 27, 1968, A2; Harwood, "Kennedy to Run in Indiana."

23. Harwood, "Kennedy to Run in Indiana."

24. Harwood, "Kennedy to Run in Indiana"; Harwood, "Crowd Madness and Kennedy Strategy" ; David S. Broder, "Unruh's Turnabout on Liberals Reflects His New Look at RFK," *Washington Post,* January 16, 1968, A15.

25. Harwood, "Kennedy to Run in Indiana"; Witcover, *85 Days,* 122–125.

26. Witcover, *85 Days,* 125; Guthman and Allen, *RFK,* 344; Harwood, "Kennedy to Run in Indiana."

27. Homer Bigart, "Kennedy, Told News on Plane, Sits in Silence among Hubbub," *New York Times,* April 1, 1968, 27; Clarke, *Last Campaign,* 70–71.

28. Robert Dallek, *Flawed Giant: Lyndon Johnson and His Times* (New York: Oxford University Press, 1998), 519–530; William C. Gibbons, *The U.S. Government and the Vietnam War: Executive and Legislative Roles and Relationships, Part V,* (unpublished ms.), 185.

29. Lyndon B. Johnson, "Remarks on Decision Not to Seek Re-election," March 31, 1965, Presidential Speeches, Miller Center, University of Virginia.

30. Clarke, *Last Campaign,* 74.

31. "Excerpts from the Transcript of Senator Kennedy's News Conference," *New York Times,* April 2, 1968, 28; John Herbers, "Kennedy Resumes Criticism of War," *New York Times,* April 3, 1968, 29.

32. "Excerpts from the Transcript of Senator Kennedy's News Conference."

33. David Garrow, *Bearing the Cross; Martin Luther King, Jr., and the Southern Christian Leadership Conference* (New York: William Morrow, 1986), 609, 618; Richard Reeves, "Mayor, in Denver, Warns of Rioting," *New York Times,* March 31, 1968, 44.

34. William Clopton Jr. and Robert Maynard, "King Aide Says Mistakes Won't Recur; Memphis Strikers March Peacefully," *Washington Post,* March 30, 1968, A1; Garrow, *Bearing the Cross,* 600.

35. Garrow, *Bearing the Cross,* 600–601, 607–608, 617.

36. Garrow, *Bearing the Cross,* 602, 604, 608.

37. Garrow, *Bearing the Cross,* 604–605; Walter Rugaber, "A Negro Is Killed in the Memphis March," *New York Times,* March 29, 1968, 1.

38. Garrow, *Bearing the Cross,* 605–606.

39. Garrow, *Bearing the Cross,* 609; Komozi Woodard, "It's Nation Time in NewArk: Amiri Baraka and the Black Power Experiment in Newark, New Jersey," in Jeanne F. Theoharis and Komozi Woodard, *Freedom North: Black Freedom Struggles Outside the South, 1940–1980* (New York: Palgrave Macmillan, 2003), 287–288, 290–297; Malcolm McLaughlin, *The Long Hot Summer of 1967: Urban Rebellion in America* (New York: Palgrave Macmillan, 2014), 85.

40. Harry Belafonte, *My Song: A Memoir* (New York: Alfred A Knopf, 2011), 327–28.

41. Garrow, *Bearing the Cross,* 610–611; Nicholas C. Chriss, "King's Memphis March Explodes into Violence," *Washington Post,* March 29, 1968, A1.

42. Chriss, "King's Memphis March Explodes into Violence"; Walter Rugaber, "A Negro Is Killed in the Memphis March," *New York Times,* March 29, 1968, 1; Walter Rubaber, "Race Relations: A Hot Spring Begins in Memphis," *New York Times,* March 31, 1968, E2.

43. Chriss, "King's Memphis March Explodes into Violence."

44. "Rioting: Violence Shakes Memphis," *Los Angeles Times,* March 31, 1968, K4; Chriss, "King's Memphis March Explodes into Violence."

45. Rugaber, "Race Relations: A Hot Spring Begins in Memphis."

46. Garrow, *Bearing the Cross,* 611; Belafonte, *My Song,* 329.

47. "Mini-Riot in Memphis," editorial, *New York Times,* March 30, 1968, 32; Chriss, "King's Memphis March Explodes in Violence"; Garrow, *Bearing the Cross,* 612–613, 614–615.

48. Martin Luther King Jr., "Remaining Awake through a Great Revolution," delivered at the National Cathedral, Washington, DC, March 31, 1968, Martin Luther King Papers Project, Martin Luther King Jr. Research and Education Institute, Stanford University.

49. Bernadette Carey, "4000 Hear Dr. King at National Cathedral," *Washington Post,* April 1, 1968, A1.

50. Garrow, *Bearing the Cross,* 618.

51. Garrow, *Bearing the Cross,* 619–620.

52. Garrow, *Bearing the Cross,* 620.

53. Martin Luther King Jr., "I've Been to the Mountaintop Address," April 4, 1968, delivered at Bishop Charles Mason Temple, in *The Landmark Speeches of Martin Luther King Jr.* ed. Clayborn Carson (New York: IPM / Warner Books, 2001).

54. Lewis, *Walking with the Wind,* 395, 404; Clarke, *Last Campaign,* 60, 84.

55. Leroy F. Aarons, "Kennedy Launches Indiana Campaign," *Washington Post,* April 5, 1968, A2; Witcover, *85 Days,* 139; Clarke, *Last Campaign,* 84–85

56. Clarke, *The Last Campaign,* 85–88

57. Clarke, *Last Campaign,* 84–86; Witcover, *85 Days,* 139.

58. Garrow, *Bearing the Cross,* 622–24.

59. Clarke, *Last Campaign,* 88–90.

60. Clarke, *Last Campaign,* 89–90

61. Lewis, *Walking with the Wind,* 405.

62. Lewis, *Walking with the Wind,* 404–405; Karl W. Anatol and John R. Bittner, "Kennedy on King: The Rhetoric of Control," *Today's Speech* 16, no. 3, March 21, 2009, 31, https://www.tandfonline.com/doi/abs/10.1080/01463376809385493.

63. Clarke, *Last Campaign,* 94.

64. Lewis, *Walking with the Wind,* 406.

65. Clarke, *Last Campaign,* 95–96.

66. Lewis, *Walking with the Wind,* 407.

67. Witcover, *85 Days,* 142; Burke Marshall, interview by Larry Hackman, January 19–20, 1974; Clay Risen, *A Nation on Fire: America in the Wake of the King Assassination* (New York: John Wiley & Sons, 2009), 51.

68. Jules Witcover, *The Year the Dream Died: Revisiting 1968 America* (New York: Warner Books, 1997); Risen, *A Nation on Fire,* 133–136.

69. Robert F. Kennedy, Remarks to the Cleveland City Club, April 5, 1968, speech files, Robert F. Kennedy Senate Papers, JFKL.

70. Witcover, *85 Days*, 145.

71. Bernadette Carey, "Sen. Kennedy Tours Areas Torn by Riots," *Washington Post*, April 8, 1968, B1; Stein, *American Journey*, 261.

72. Marshall interview, January 19–20, 1970.

73. Witcover, *85 Days*, 145–146; Clarke, *Last Campaign*, 124–125; Jean Stein and George Plimpton, ed., *American Journey: The Times of Robert Kennedy* (New York: Harcourt Brace Jovanovich, 1970), 260–261.

74. Lewis, *Walking with the Wind*, 410–411; Clarke, *Last Campaign*, 124.

75. Clarke, *Last Campaign*, 129–135.

76. Lewis, *Walking with the Wind*, 413.

17 · THE LAST OF THE GREAT BELIEVABLES

1. Jules Witcover, *85 Days: The Last Campaign of Robert Kennedy* (New York: G.P. Putnam's Sons, 1968), 130–131, 137–138; Joseph A. Palermo, *In His Own Right: The Political Odyssey of Robert Kennedy* (New York: Columbia University Press, 2001), 201–202.

2. Palermo, *In His Own Right*, 190–191.

3. Thurston Clarke, *Last Campaign: Robert F. Kennedy and 82 Days that Inspired America* (New York: Henry Holt and Company, 2008), 142–144.

4. Witcover, *85 Days*, 147.

5. Ryan Winn, "Robert Kennedy's Indian Commitment," *Tribal College: Journal of American Indian Higher Education*, June 1, 2018; Fitzgerald quoted in Clarke, *Last Campaign*, 157.

6. Clarke, *Last Campaign*, 158–161; Winn, "Robert Kennedy's Indian Commitment."

7. David S. Broder, "RFK Tours Small-Town Indiana," *Washington Post*, April 23, 1968, A2; Clarke, *Last Campaign*, 141.

8. David S. Broder, "Kennedy Indiana Feat Raises Doubt that McCarthy Can Rally," *Washington Post*, May 9, 1968, A1; John Herbers, "Kennedy Outspends Rivals as Staff and Students Step Up Drive for Crucial Votes in Indiana," *New York Times*, April 26, 1968, 28; Palermo, *In His Own Right*, 201.

9. Witcover, *85 Days*, 153–154; Clarke, *Last Campaign*, 157–162.

10. Witcover, *85 Days*, 154–155.

11. Broder, "RFK Tours Small Town Indiana"; David Halberstam, "Travels with Bobby Kennedy," *Harper's Magazine*, July 1968, 55.

12. Witcover, *85 Days*, 160; Clarke, *Last Campaign*, 148.

13. Clarke, *Last Campaign*, 147–151.

14. Maurice Carroll, "Kennedy Chides Future Doctors," *New York Times*, April 27, 1968; Witcover, *85 Days*, 165.

15. Witcover, *85 Days*, 165; Carroll, "Kennedy Chides Future Doctors."

16. Witcover, 85; Clarke, *Last Campaign*, 189.

17. Clarke, *Last Campaign*, 181; Halberstam, "Travels with Bobby Kennedy," 66.

18. Witcover, *85 Days*, 175.

19. Witcover, *85 Days*, 175–176.

20. Witcover, *85 Days*, 177.

21. Broder, "Kennedy Indiana Feat Raises Doubts McCarthy Can Rally."

22. Palermo, *In His Own Right*, 207; Clarke, *Last Campaign*, 199–201; Ward Just, "For Another Kennedy: Triumph and Tragedy," *Washington Post*, June 7, 1968, A12.

23. Witcover, *85 Days*, 193–194.

24. Witcover, *85 Days*, 194.

25. "Kennedy Scores in Ohio; Delegates Shift to Uncommitted," *Washington Post*, May 15, 1968, 4; Helen O'Donnell, *A Common Good: The Friendship of Robert F. Kennedy and Kenneth P. O'Donnell* (New York: William Morrow and Company, 1998), 409–410.

26. "Kennedy Scores in Ohio"; O'Donnell, *A Common Good*, 410.

27. Warren Weaver, "McCarthy Beats Kennedy in Oregon Primary Upset," *New York Times*, May 29, 1968, 1; "Why Oregon," editorial, *New York Times*, May 29, 1968.

28. Witcover, *85 Days*, 203; Clarke, *Last Campaign*, 228.

29. Witcover, *85 Days*, 208–209; Palermo, *In His Own Right*, 212, 215–216, 241–242.

30. Clarke, *Last Campaign*, 227–229; Witcover, *85 Days*, 202; Palermo, *In His Own Right*, 210.

31. John Herbers, "Kennedy Heckled in Oregon over Gun Controls," *New York Times*, May 28, 1968, 10.

32. Herbers, "Kennedy Heckled in Oregon."

33. Palermo, *In His Own Right*, 217; Clarke, *Last Campaign*, 237; Witcover, *85 Days*, 221, 224.

34. Fred P. Graham, "Drew Pearson Says Robert Kennedy ordered Wiretap on Phone of Dr. King," *New York Times*, May 25, 1968, 17; Witcover, *85 Days*, 212; Palermo, *In His Own Right*, 233; Peter Edelman, interview by author, June 30, 2020.

35. Witcover, *85 Days*, 233–235.

36. Witcover, *85 Days*, 235; Budd Schulberg, "RFK: Harbinger of Hope," *Playboy*, February 1969, 252.

37. Witcover, *85 Days*, 235.

38. Palermo, *In His Own Right*, 228–229; Witcover, *85 Days*, 230–231.

39. Palermo, *In His Own Right*, 224–228, 236; Lewis, *Walking with the Wind*, 414.

40. Palermo, *In His Own Right*, 195–199, 231.

41. Palermo, *In His Own Right*, 236–237.

42. Daryl E. Lembke, "Kennedy Campaigns on Caboose through San Joaquin Valley," *Los Angeles Times*, May 31, 1968, 1.

43. Witcover, *85 Days*, 237–238; Clarke, *Last Campaign*, 253–254.

44. Clarke, *Last Campaign*, 253.

45. Joshua Bloom and Waldo E. Martin Jr., *Black against Empire: The History and Politics of the Black Panther Party* (Berkeley: University of California Press, 2011), 34; Clarke, *Last Campaign*, 253–254.

46. Clarke, *Last Campaign*, 254.

47. Clarke, *Last Campaign*, 256.

48. Burke Marshall, interview by Larry Hackman, January 19–20, 1970.

49. Ward Just, "McCarthy Offers Civil Rights Program," *Washington Post*, April 12, 1968, A1.

50. E. W. Kenworthy, "Assails Kennedy Slum Program," *New York Times*, May 29, 1968, 18.

51. E. W. Kenworthy, "McCarthy Backs Black Power Bid," *New York Times*, May 31, 1968, 17; Witcover, *85 Days*, 237.

52. "Rev. Martin Luther King Luncheon Address at California Democratic Council," March 16, 1968, broadcast May 19, 1968, Pacifica Radio Archives, American Archive of Public Broadcasting (WGBH and the Library of Congress), Boston, MA, and Washington, DC, accessed May 25, 2020, http://americanarchive.org/catalog/c-b-aacip-28-pc2t43jg47; Marshall interview, January 19–20, 1970.

53. Robert Donovan, "Clashes Minor in Polite TV Debate," *Los Angeles Times*, June 2, 1968, D12A.

54. Donovan, "Clashes Minor in Polite Debate"; Palermo, *In His Own Right*, 240.

55. Ken Reich, "McCarthy Accuses Kennedy of Scare Tactics," *New York Times*, June 3, 1968, 1; Daryl E. Lembke, "Kennedy Sees Desperation in McCarthy Talk," *Los Angeles Times*, June 4, 1963, 3.

56. Lembke, "Kennedy Sees Desperation in McCarthy Talk"; Lewis, *Walking with the Wind*, 414.

57. Witcover, *85 Days*, 253–254.

58. Clarke, *Last Campaign*, 266–267.

59. Clarke, *Last Campaign*, 267–268.

60. Schulberg, "RFK: Harbinger of Hope," 152.

61. Clarke, *Last Campaign*, 269

62. John Lewis with Michael D'Orso, *Walking with the Wind: A Memoir of the Movement* (New York: Simon & Schuster, 1998), 414–415.

63. Witcover, *85 Days*, 261; ABC-LA Network Feed, RFK 1968 California primary victory speech, ambassador hotel, https://www.youtube.com/watch?v=AhDQhlvwGgw.

64. ABC-LA Network Feed, RFK 1968 California primary victory speech.

65. ABC-LA Network Feed, RFK 1968 California primary victory speech.

66. ABC-LA Network Feed, RFK 1968 California primary victory speech; transcript of Kennedy primary victory speech, *New York Times*, June 6, 1968.

67. Witcover, *85 Days*, 264–265; William Klaber and Philip Melanson, *Shadow Play: The Unsolved Murder of Robert F. Kennedy* (New York: St. Martin's Press, 1997), 4,

68. Witcover, *85 Days*, 266, 268–269; Klaber and Melanson, *Shadow Play*, 6; "Black Men Who Helped RFK," *Jet*, June 20, 1968.

69. Witcover, *85 Days*, 270–273; Klaber and Melanson, *Shadow Play*, 7.

70. Witcover, *85 Days*, 290.

EPILOGUE

1. "Text of Edward Kennedy's Tribute to His Brother in Cathedral," *Washington Post*, June 9, 1968, 56.

2. Jean Stein and George Plimpton, ed., *American Journey: The Times of Robert Kennedy* (New York: Harcourt Brace Jovanovich, 1970), 23, 29.

3. Robert G. Kaiser and J. Y. Smith, "Post Reporter, Editor, Ombudsman Richard Harwood Dead at 75," *Washington Post*, March 20, 2001.

4. Stein and Plimpton, *American Journey*, 32; "Sutton's Memories of the Funeral Train," *New York Amsterdam News*, June 15, 1968, 54; Northrup quoted in Nick Kirkpatrick and Katie Mettler, "Reflecting on RFK's 200 Mile Funeral Train," *Washington Post*, June 1, 2018.

5. Stein and Plimpton, *American Journey*, 107.

6. Jack Eisen, "Last Trip Stalked by Tragedy," *Washington Post*, June 9, 1968, A1.

7. Paul Schrade, interview by author, March 10, 2018; Diane S. Nixon, "Providing Access to Controversial Public Records: The Case of the Robert F. Kennedy Assassination Files," *Public Historian* (Summer 1989), 30–34, 37; Tom Jackman, "Who Killed Bobby Kennedy? His Son RFK Jr. Doesn't Believe It Was Sirhan Sirhan," *Washington Post,* June 5, 2018.

8. Eighteen-year-old quoted in Jesse Lewis, "Poor Voice Anger and Dismay over Kennedy Assassination," *Washington Post,* June 7, 1968, A19; Loften Mitchell, "Where Is It Going to End?" *New York Amsterdam News,* June 8, 1968, 1; Inquiring Photographer, *Chicago Defender,* June 10, 1968, 13; "America's Illness," *New York Amsterdam News,* June 15, 1968, 14; Baker quoted in "Community Reacts to Another Killing," *New York Amsterdam News,* June 15, 1968, 1.

9. Stein and Plimpton, *American Journey,* 341–342.

10. James Baldwin, interview by Jean Stein, February 2, 1970, Jean Stein Personal Papers.

11. Bayard Rustin, "Now Kennedy: The Bill Mounts Higher," *New York Amsterdam News,* June 15, 1968, 15.

12. Haynes Johnson, "1968 Democratic Convention: The Bosses Strike Back," *Smithsonian Magazine,* August 2008.

13. Brian Urquhart, *Ralph Bunche: An American Odyssey* (New York: W. W. Norton & Company), 421.

14. John A. Farrell, *Richard Nixon: A Life* (New York: Random House, 2017), 378–379; Elizabeth Hinton, *From the War on Poverty to the War on Crime: The Making of Mass Incarceration in America* (Cambridge: Harvard University Press, 2016), 2–4.

15. "Senator Robert Kennedy in Berkeley," recorded October 23, 1966, Pacifica Radio Archives, American Archive of Public Broadcasting (WGBH and the Library of Congress), Boston, MA, and Washington, DC, accessed May 25, 2020, http://americanarchive.org/catalog/c-b-aacip-28-pc2t43jg47.

ACKNOWLEDGMENTS

The questions that inform this book began to take shape when I traveled to the South as a graduate student to research Paul Robeson's tours for his biographer Andrew Bunie. I met southerners, Black and white, who had confronted and fought against the racial system that grew up in the wake of Reconstruction. They became the subject of my first book on the New Deal and World War II era. I then researched and wrote a history of the early decades of the NAACP. For nearly twenty years, Waldo Martin and I codirected a series of National Endowment for the Humanities summer institutes exploring complex struggles for freedom, civil rights, and racial justice across several generations after the Civil War. I want to express my gratitude to all who, along the way, have taught me and deepened my understanding of this history and its significance.

When I embarked on this book, I wanted to take a fresh look at the 1960s. My literary agent Ellen Geiger read my proposal and said, "You mention Robert Kennedy twice; write a book about him." At the time, the idea of writing a book about Robert Kennedy was the furthest thing from my mind. But as I read more and talked with colleagues and friends who had been active in the movement, I realized that a focus on Kennedy would allow me to explore the 1960s from a perspective that would yield new insights into the racial dynamics of this era, as well as Robert Kennedy.

I am deeply grateful to Ellen Geiger for setting me on this course. Ellen secured a contract with Joyce Seltzer at Harvard University Press. I am indebted to Joyce for seeing the promise early on and for her support and patience as the book grew to be more than I had anticipated.

Joy de Menil became my editor after Joyce retired, as the chapters started flowing. Joy sharpened my focus, challenged me to think more deeply about critical points, and helped me to say what I wanted to say clearly and directly. Even with the disruptions caused by the pandemic, we kept going at an intense pace. Joy is a brilliant editor and a pleasure to work with. She has my enduring gratitude. I am also grateful to her assistant, Joy Deng; to Simon Waxman, who guided the book through the editing process; and to the terrific team at Harvard University Press. Copyeditor Catherine Cambron gave the manuscript the most careful and thorough review, and production editor Mary Ribesky guided the project through the final stages. My thanks to you both.

The W. E. B Du Bois Research Institute at the Hutchins Center for African and African American Research at Harvard University provided me with a residential fellowship and excellent research support. The William A. Elwood Fellowship, awarded by the University of Virginia's Mary and David Harrison Institute for American History, Literature, and Culture, offered me support and a perfect place to work. A fellowship from the Virginia Foundation for the Humanities provided a generous stipend and a collegial environment.

The University of South Carolina has supported this project from start to finish—through a provost grant, two sabbaticals, help with research, and excellent library services. I am especially grateful to Dean Lacy Ford, to my colleagues Jessica Elfenbein, Kent Germany, Lawrence Glickman, Lauren Sklaroff, and Mark Smith, and to Lori Carey, for her help on many fronts.

The John F. Kennedy Presidential Library was the major base for my research. In addition to the rich archival collections, the library's vast and substantial JFK and RFK Oral History Collections have been invaluable. I am deeply grateful to the library staff, who were always enormously helpful and accommodating. The David B. Filvaroff and Raymond E. Wolfinger Civil Rights Acts Papers at University Archives, State University of New York at Buffalo, was also a major archival source. My thanks to the archivists and reading room staff for their generous assistance. Jonathan Eaker and his associates in the Prints and Photographs Division of the Library of Congress have my gratitude for their help at a critical moment.

Meeting with Ethel Kennedy was a high point in my research. Her recollections of individuals and events, including the trip to South Africa in 1966, were enormously helpful, as was her enthusiastic, open, and outgoing spirit. A proposed sailing excursion was nixed because of high winds; instead, we toured Hyannis Port in a golf cart.

Robert Kennedy's friends, aides, and associates shared recollections and answered queries. Anthony Lewis, Frank Mankiewicz, Paul Schrade, John Seigenthaler, and William vanden Heuvel each contributed a great deal to my understanding of Robert Kennedy, along with sharing specific recollections. Judith Hackett, widow of David Hackett, offered memories of her husband's friendship with Bobby and shared the correspondence between "Dave and Bob" as young men. Peter Edelman worked with Robert Kennedy from 1963 to 1968. In addition to extensive oral history interviews, Peter has been available to answer questions all along the way, and he read and commented on several chapters. Peter has been an wonderful supporter and a generous friend.

Robert L. Carter, as general counsel of the NAACP, collaborated with Robert Kennedy's Justice Department on the Prince Edward County school case and was preparing to join RFK's campaign when Kennedy was assassinated. Bob helped me realize early on that Bobby Kennedy was a rare figure on the national political scene. Thelton Henderson, the first African American attorney to work for the Department of Justice in the South, shared recollections of his experiences. John Lewis and Marian Wright Edelman provided personal accounts of the civil rights struggle and their interactions with Kennedy. Bob Moses helped me better understand the relationship between movement activists in Mississippi and the Kennedy Justice Department, as well as the Johnson administration. Cleveland Sellers encouraged me from the start of this project and has deepened my knowledge of the movement and the tragedy of the Orangeburg Massacre. SNCC activist and historian Martha Prescod Norman Noonan contributed much to my understanding of this era. Margaret Marshall, RFK's student guide during his visit to South Africa, and Larry Shore, who shared his recollections as a twelve-year-old living in Johannesburg and produced a wonderful film, *RFK in the Land of Apartheid,* have been tremendously helpful.

It is my good fortune to have a close circle of friends who are deeply engaged with the study of American history and ever mindful of the complex ways in which past struggles for racial and economic justice speak to our current moment. Waldo Martin is a brilliant scholar of African American history and culture and a teacher beyond compare. Our collaborations over the years, along with many discussions about this project, count more that I can measure. Conversations with John Simon about the tangled history of race, politics, left-wing movements, and government repression from the 1930s through the 1960s have been guiding me since I began work on my first book. His insights and comments on sections of the manuscript have been formative. John's recollection of his unexpected trip with Bobby Kennedy from Washington back to New York on a summer day in 1966 is a gem. Eric Bargeron, with his expanse of historical knowledge, keen understanding of politics, and excellent editorial skills, has helped in countless ways. He read chapters, discussed key points, made critical suggestions regarding organization, and kept me up to date on late-breaking historical news relevant to this book. I'm delighted to finally thank him in print.

Daniel Geary and Kenneth Mack read the manuscript and provided insightful critiques and suggestions, as did a third anonymous reader for Harvard University Press. They have my deep gratitude. Other scholars and friends have contributed through their own work, ongoing conversations, research leads, and comments on chapters. I am especially grateful to Fred Aman, the late Raymond Gavins, Carol Greenhouse, Blair Kelley, Peter Lau, Leon Litwack, Ron Rapoport, Julius Scott, Lara Smith, Valerie Smith, Marie Tyler McGraw, and Howard Wachtel

This project has benefited from my long friendship with Patricia McAdams Gibbons and her late husband, William C. Gibbons. Bill worked for Lyndon Johnson in the early 1960s and provided insights on the personalities and politics of that period. Bill's four-volume study of the US government and the Vietnam war, which Pat carries forward, has deepened my understanding of the war and its impact. Pat has read the entire manuscript, has been a cogent critic, and provided a wonderful retreat at High Peak Farm.

Lucy Caplan was there at the start during my fellowship term at Harvard, a fantastic research assistant who mined the collection of dispatches from *Time* magazine correspondents at Harvard's Houghton Library and created an invaluable index to the material. Jeff Williams, a doctoral student at the University of South Carolina, helped with research during the later stages and provided terrific assistance tracking down photographs and obtaining releases.

Sheldon Hackney and Lucy Durr Hackney have long been an inspiration to me and to my work as a historian. Their friendship drew me to Martha's Vineyard, a perfect place to write a book and to celebrate book publications on the Hackneys' lawn. Their memory is a blessing. Missy Daniel and I have been talking about "the RFK book" all along the way; she listened, offered suggestions, and was always passing along relevant leads and articles. Ideas that helped to shape the book percolated during summer-morning walks with Martha Mae Jones. Virginia "V V" Harrison and Marilyn Melkonian have been unflagging supporters of this project. Our discussions over many dinners in Washington and on the Vineyard have been a wonderful part of the journey. V V, who volunteered for Bobby Kennedy's Senate campaign when she was around twenty, gave me rare insight into those days. Marilyn initiated a trip to Ireland that turned up surprising sources early on. Michael and Ann Marie Plunkett welcomed me into their home and helped tremendously with my research efforts in Charlottesville. Rose Styron has shared recollections of the Kennedy administration, including the White House reception where James Baldwin first met Bobby Kennedy, and helped me make valuable research connections. At the midpoint of the project, Liza Coogan hosted a pre-book publication event at The Wharf on Martha's Vineyard—a boost that moved me toward the finish line. Marge Harris has read along as I completed chapters and cheered me on. James Lyon, Elizabeth Hackney McBride, and Declan McBride, fellow committee members of the Clifford and Virginia Durr Lecture Series, have been great allies in creating public forums for bringing this history forward and engaging its contemporary relevance.

I am grateful to many others who have helped in various ways, including Donna Bohanan, Anne Burke, Lewis Burke, Jane Chandler, Christie Coon, Allen Green, Jane Hearn, Lisa Jones, Gil Kerlikowske, Anna Laszlo, Suellen Lazarus, Rhoda Litwack, Catherine Macklin, David Meyer-Gollan, Susan Rappaport, Kitty Steel, Lewis Steel, and Grace Kennan Warnecke.

Love and thanks always to my sisters and brother—Kathleen Basil, Mary Sullivan-Lester, Eileen Sullivan, and Tom Sullivan—and their families for their love and support. To my wonderful nephews and nieces who nudged me along: "Done yet?" Yes—read on! A special note to Aidan Sullivan and Elena Shostak, who started college this year: there is a message here for you.

Justice Rising is dedicated to my mother and to the memory of my father, who passed while I was writing the book. Tom and Doris Sullivan exemplify the good life—love, compassion, devotion to family, generosity of spirit, and the Irish way of embracing life's joys and weathering its tragedies. I am ever grateful for their love, encouragement, and example, which remain the light of our family.

INDEX